2nd EDITION

Entrepreneur. MAGAZINE'S

JUN 8

ULTIMATE

1500 GREAT BUSINESS

START-UP

DIRECTORY

JAMES STEPHENSON
with
Rich Mintzer

EP
Entrepreneur. Press

Managing editor: Jere Calmes
Cover design: Beth Hansen-Winter
Composition and production: MillerWorks

This publication is designed to provide accurate and authoritative information in regard to the subject
matter covered. It is sold with the understanding that the publisher is not engaged in rendering legal,
accounting, or other professional services. If legal advice or other expert assistance is required, the
services of a competent professional person should be sought.

Library of Congress Cataloging-in-Publication Data

Stephenson, James, 1966-
   Ultimate start-up directory : 1500 Great Business Start-Up Ideas by James Stephenson with Rich
   Mintzer. — 2nd ed by James Stephenson with Rich Mintzer. p. cm.
   Rev. ed. of: Entrepreneur's Ultimate Start-Up Directory / James Stephenson. c2001.
   ISBN 978-1-932531-98-5
   ISBN 1-932531-98-X (alk. paper)
   1. New business enterprises—United States—Directories. 2. Small business—United States—
   Directories. 3. Entrepreneurship—United States—Directories. 4. New business enterprises—
   Canada—Directories. 5. Small business—Canada—Directories. 6. Entrepreneurship—
   Canada—Directories. I. Mintzer, Richard. II. Stephenson, James, 1966- Entrepreneur's ultimate
   start-up directory. III. Entrepreneur Press. IV. Title. V. Title: Start-up directory. VI. Title: 1500
   great business start-up ideas. VII. Title: Fifteen hundred great business start-up ideas.

HD62.5.S742 2007
658.1'141—dc22   2006035595

Printed in Canada

CONTENTS

49 CHILD-RELATED
Businesses You Can Start

38 CLOTHING
Businesses You Can Start

23 COMPUTER TECHNOLOGY AND HOME OFFICE SUPPORT

Businesses You Can Start

33 CRAFT

Businesses You Can Start

64 FOOD-RELATED
Businesses You Can Start

29 FURNITURE

Businesses You Can Start

37 HEALTH

Businesses You Can Start

60 HOME IMPROVEMENT
Businesses You Can Start

37 HOME REPAIR
Businesses You Can Start

30 HOME SERVICE
Businesses You Can Start

33 IMPORT/EXPORT AND MAIL-ORDER
Businesses You Can Start

54 INSTRUCTION
Businesses You Can Start

62 MANUFACTURING
Businesses You Can Start

48 OUTDOOR SERVICE

Businesses You Can Start

43 PET-RELATED
Businesses You Can Start

39 PHOTOGRAPHY
Businesses You Can Start

49 RENTAL
Businesses You Can Start

72 RETAIL
Businesses You Can Start

30 SECURITY
Businesses You Can Start

95 SPECIAL SERVICE
Businesses You Can Start

39 SPORT AND FITNESS
Businesses You Can Start

53 TRANSPORTATION
Businesses You Can Start

32 TRAVEL
Businesses You Can Start

21 WEB-BASED FUN AND ENTERTAINMENT
Businesses You Can Start

38 WEB-BASED RETAIL
Businesses You Can Start

93 WEB DIRECTORIES, EDUCATIONAL AND SERVICE

Businesses You Can Start

8 WEB-BASED EBAY
Businesses You Can Start

35 WRITING
Businesses You Can Start

INTRODUCTION

"What is easy to do is easier not to do.
And most people will take the path of least resistance!"

—Brian Tracy

Millions of people want to start their own business, and yes, it is easy to start a business. However, it is easier not to start a business. And the majority of people considering business ownership will take the path of least resistance and simply choose to do nothing about fulfilling a lifelong dream of becoming a successful entrepreneur.

Why? The fear of the unknown, a feeling of being overwhelmed, the loss of security a job or career seemingly provides, and not knowing what business is the right business to start.

That is... until now.

Entrepreneur's *Ultimate Start-Up Directory* has been specifically developed to help you unlock the mystery of what type of businesses can be started and operated for success. Each business is presented in a straightforward manner with useful information that you can use as a starting point to managing and marketing your new business, regardless of your experience or skills.

GETTING STARTED

Every citizen of the United States of America and Canada can start their own business. This is one of the greatest privileges of living in a democratic and free enterprise society. The only way that most people living in North America will ever become financially secure and build wealth in less than a lifetime of working a job is to become self-employed by operating their own business.

There are exceptions to the rule. You could win the lottery, inherit a million dollars, or hit the jackpot in the stock market. For the most part, however, wealth and financial stability do not happen by chance or luck; they are the result of careful planning and hard work. Setting personal and business goals and working hard to realize these goals is the only sure way to financial stability. Successful entrepreneurs are no different from you, aside from the fact that they all decided that working for someone else was not going to enable them to reach their goals in life.

The business ventures and the information featured in this directory were compiled over a decade-long period, born from the author's keen interest in the multitude of business and self-employment opportunities that are available to people from every walk of life to start and operate for success. Sources of information included business experiences; personal interviews with many small business owners, government agencies, and small business associations; and thousands of hours of research devoted to identifying sound business start-ups.

This brand-new, updated version has been compiled by a different author with new businesses, additional web resources, and a new section that reflects the numerous internet business opportunities today. The latest version delves further into some of the original listings and has replaced some that are no longer relevant or practical in our ever-changing world.

The objective was to create a business start-up directory listing hundreds of businesses and self-employment opportunities representing a wide cross-section of industries. The data and information featured for each business start-up is brief in nature and is meant to give the reader a "snapshot" or short overview of the opportunity. The theme of this directory is not "how to start and operate a business," but rather a collection of business start-up ideas. These ideas will provide a catalyst to get you thinking about the various types of businesses that can be started, and ultimately help you decide on one that is right for you to start.

ICON SYSTEM

As you read through each business you will notice a line of icons directly beneath the business title. These icons rate each business according to the ease of start-up, the cost to start-up, and whether it can be a homebased business, has potential legal issues, part-time possibilities, and franchise or licensing potential. This system is not to recommend any one business over another, but to give the reader an idea of which might be easier or simpler to start than another.

★ Stars

Every business start-up featured in the directory is rated on a scale of one to four stars, with four stars being the highest recommendation. The purpose of the rating system is not to predetermine the potential for business success or failure; the ratings system is based purely on logic or common sense to assist you in identifying what might be the right business start-up for you.

The star system is based on the following criteria:

- Start-up costs

- Market demand and the potential for growth
- Competition in the marketplace
- Special skill and legal requirements
- Operating overhead costs
- Potential for profitability
- Stability and uniqueness

A business that requires less than a $10,000 investment to start and has the potential to generate income or profits in excess of $50,000 per year receives a high rating. However, if the same business start-up also requires a high degree of specialized skills to operate or is in an extremely competitive industry with declining consumer demand, the rating is reduced.

$ Start-Up Cost

The majority of business start-ups featured in the directory include an approximate financial investment that will be needed to start the business. Once again, this is generalized information and should only be used as a relative measure to determine business start-up costs. In most cases, the investment indicated will be in the middle of the high-low range, but will vary due to factors such as equipment and transportation purchases, licenses and permits, training requirements, operating location, working capital, initial marketing, and advertising budgets. Remember, a successful entrepreneur is one who carefully researches and plans every aspect of a new business venture, including the financial investment needed to start a business and the working capital required to achieve positive cash flow.

Start-Up Cost Symbols

$	Less than $1,000
$$	$1,000–$10,000
$$$	$10,000–$25,000
$$$$	Greater than $25,000

Profit or Income Potential

Profit is not a dirty word. Business owners work hard—in fact many entrepreneurs work in excess of 50 hours per week. Where indicated, income or profit potential is considered industry average. Thus the amount of income or profit that can be realized by running a particular business may indeed be greater or substantially lower than indicated in the directory. Factors such as sales volumes, operating overheads, profit margins, management fees, and wages will all have an effect on a business's potential profitability.

Homebased

Do you want to work from the comfort of home, cut your commuting time down to a few seconds, and increase interaction time with your family? If so, you have come to the right place. In the directory, you will find hundreds of business start-ups that are ideal candidates to be operated or managed from a homebased location. These homebased business ventures have been specifically identified in the directory with a small house symbol.

Running a business from home has many advantages including low operating overhead, less time spent commuting, flexible work hours, a comfortable and familiar work environment, and the ability to create a more balanced schedule in terms of family needs and commitments. However, running a business from home still requires the same amount of planning and research, as any new business venture will. Laws governing the operation of a business from home vary greatly across North America, but some municipalities require no more than the purchase of a simple business license to make the homebased business legitimate. Of course, a lot will depend on the nature of the business and in some cases, municipalities require fire and safety inspections of the home prior to issuing the business license.

There is no "across the board" set of standard rules and regulations in terms of operating a business from home. It is the responsibility of every entrepreneur considering a homebased business venture to become acquainted with, and conform to, the rules and regulations governing homebased business enterprises as set forth by local governments.

Part-Time Opportunity

Not too sure if you are ready to jump ship from working for someone else and tackle business ownership on a full-time basis? Would you like to test the waters and see if you have what it takes to start and succeed in business? Are you perhaps just looking for a way to earn an extra few hundred dollars each month to grow the college education fund? Regardless of your reason, you will find hundreds of business start-ups in the directory that can be operated on a part-time basis indefinitely or that can be started on a part-time basis and expanded to a full-time business from the profits that the business earns. Almost any business can be operated part time; however, business start-ups in the directory featuring the clock symbol are outstanding business venture options for part-time entrepreneurs.

Legal Issues

The scales of justice symbol indicates that there are special permits or certificates of training required to start and operate the business featured. Remember, all new business ventures require that you apply for and receive a business license or permit, as well as registering or incorporating your business at the local or federal level. A major component of starting a business is to research all the legal elements and aspects of the business venture. This includes, but is not limited to, licenses and permits, liability insurance, zoning and building-use codes, fire and health regulations, employee regulations, and certificates of training.

Franchise or License Potential

For entrepreneurs looking for big business and market opportunities, we have taken the guesswork out of determining what is a good business, product, or service to expand nationally on a franchise or license-to-operate basis. Look for business start-ups in the directory featuring the globe symbol. These business start-ups have been selected as potentially prime franchise or license opportunities and are purposely included in the directory to appeal to the entrepreneur that is seeking a real business challenge.

Green Businesses

The little plant symbol indicates a "green" or environmentally friendly business. The concern about protecting the environment continues to grow after too many years of neglect. Running a business that is not only profitable but also benefits the environment can be satisfying, and profitable, on multiple levels.

RESOURCES

Web

Throughout the directory you will find hundreds of handy web resources. The purpose of these listings is not to promote or endorse any one association, program, or business; they are there to give you a research tool in terms of "how can I find out more?" You will find that the web resources featured in the directory will enable you to quickly locate and compile further information about a particular business opportunity of interest to you. In many instances the resources are associations and organizations that can guide your search for additional information about your possible new business venture.

Marketing

Every business needs paying customers in order to survive, succeed, and grow. Marketing is the single largest business challenge facing entrepreneurs and often the source of the most start-up funding. Nearly all of the listings provide some thoughts on marketing the product or service and how to reach and secure that market. In some cases, specific marketing tips and ideas are included to help you reach your demographic market. Of course, there is no one right answer to marketing; for that reason, various options are discussed and you are encouraged to seek out all cost-efficient marketing methods for your business from using print and broadcast media to the increasingly popular word-of-mouth marketing.

BUSINESS START-UP PREVIEW

The Business Start-Up Preview has been specifically developed to assist you in determining what might be the right new business enterprise for you to start and operate. The purpose of the information and questions featured in this section is not to predetermine your ability to start and run a business, but rather a collection of data and information that can be used as a helpful resource in identifying the right new business start-up for you.

What Is the Right Business Start-Up for You?

There is only one person that can answer this question: You. The process of starting a business is comprised of many elements: What is the right business? When is the best time to start this business? Where is the best place to start? Who will my customers be? How will this business generate income and profits?

Remember, anyone in the United States and Canada can start a business. The fact remains, however, that many new business ventures fail within the first five years of operation. Businesses fail for a number of reasons, but invariably failure can usually be traced back to lack of planning and research or an unsuitable match between the business owner and the type of enterprise they are operating.

Once again, the theme of this directory is not how to start and operate a business, but rather a collection of business start-up ideas that can be used as a catalyst to get you thinking about the various types of businesses that can be started and, ultimately, one that is right for you to start. The function of the preview is to help you identify the right business start-up that will match your needs, motives, and ambitions.

Personal and Family Situation

Before you decide to start or purchase a business it is important to carefully analyze your reasons for this decision, as well as the effect it will have on you and your family. While an increasing number of businesses today can be one-person operations (thanks largely to the internet), family still factors into the equation—you need to consider how your business will affect those around you. You should, therefore, consider your reasoning and motivations. Ask yourself, "Why do I want to operate my own business?" and fill out the table on the next page.

Remember, the purpose of your answers and thoughts is to help you determine your motives and find the right business venture. If you rank wanting to spend more time with your family as very important, then a homebased business might be an excellent choice. Conversely, if you are looking for a business to start after taking an early retirement, you may decide that you want a business that gets you out of the house every day. Your business should fit your family's lifestyle. Remember, when you start a business, you are very often making decisions for more than yourself, so it is important to include family members in the decision-making process. Additionally, never assume that family members will have the same excitement as you about starting or working in the business.

Reasons to Operate My Own Business	IMPORTANCE		
	Low	Medium	High
1. I am dissatisfied with my current job or career.			
2. I want to spend more time with my family.			
3. I want to earn additional income for myself and my family.			
4. I have career potential that I want to utilize to the fullest.			
5. I am retired (or retiring soon) and want to remain active and productive.			
6.			
7.			
8.			
9.			
10.			
11.			
12.			

Special Skills

What are the special skills that you currently possess, and how can these skills be applied to the new business venture that you would like to start? While you certainly do not have to possess all the skills necessary for running a business, identifying your strengths and weaknesses prior to starting a business just makes good sense. It can help you determine which business opportunity is a good match. Look at the checklist on the next page, and analyze your strengths and weaknesses.

Keep in mind that the skills shown to be the weakest are not necessarily reason for concern, they simply just have to be improved. Successful entrepreneurs are people that never stop learning or seeking ways to improve their business skills. They know where they excel and where they should seek out help in the form of advisors, consultants, or employees. You need not know everything about a specific business to run that business—many people with a great head for business hire people to handle the areas in which they are not experts.

Income

If your ambition is to earn a six-figure income, then perhaps starting a part-time lawn-care service is not the right venture. However, if you aspire to earn an extra $10,000 per year to supplement your family income, a part-time lawn-care service would be a wise choice. The key to successfully establishing a required or desired business income is to be completely realistic in your expectations. Yes, a lawn care service can generate a six-figure income for the owner of the business, providing the business employs many people, has a substantial customer base, and is expanded geographically. However, it is unrealistic to assume that a part-time lawn care service will generate a six-figure income.

If your single largest motivation for starting a business is to get rich, I will guarantee you that you are going to be

My Special Skills	Excellent	Good	Needs Work
Sales and negotiation skills			
Record and bookkeeping skills			
Organizational skills			
Computer and software skills			
Technical troubleshooting skills			
Ability to listen and seek expert advice			
Problem-solving skills			
Ability to handle stress			
Ability to stay motivated and committed			
Planning and research skills			
Ability to budget and manage money			
Ability to speak in public			
Decision-making abilities			
Ability to manage and motivate others			
Ability to multitask			
Strong communications skills			
Ability to self-start and work independently			
Creative skills, such as computer graphics, PR writing, etc.			

sadly disappointed. However, if one of the many motivations for starting a business is to build and maintain a long-term, comfortable income level, then I will also guarantee that this can be accomplished by using sound business judgment.

Income desired per year: $ _____

Income required per year: $ _____

Short- and Long-Term Goals

The only way to know if a business venture has the potential to meet or exceed your short-term and long-term personal and financial goals is to know exactly what your goals are. The best way to identify them is to compile a list of your goals and expectations for yourself and for your family. Keep the list close so that you can reflect back to it in times of business, personal, and financial decisions. If the end result of your decision will mean sacrificing a short-term or long-term goal, then it is safe to assume this would not be a wise decision to make.

Business Location

Where will your new business be located or operated from, and how will this affect your and your life and that of your family? Business location is a very important aspect of finding the right business to start. If you have always dreamed about working from home, then you have already narrowed your choices in terms of a suitable business match. Don't fret, however, as more and more businesses today can be run from the home. If, however, you feel your current living accommodations are not suitable for a homebased business, then this is also a factor to consider in finding the right business enterprise.

I want to be able to operate a business from home.
❏ Yes ❏ No

If yes, why? _____

_____

My home is suitable for a homebased business.
❏ Yes ❏ No

If the business is not suitable to be operated from home, is there a suitable location available in the community?
❏ Yes ❏ No

I would be comfortable working within:
❏ 1 to 10 miles from home
❏ 10 to 15 miles from home
❏ 15 to 30 miles from home
❏ More than 30 miles from home

I am prepared to move to a new community to pursue a business opportunity.
❏ Yes ❏ No
If yes, how will this decision affect my family and myself?

_____

_____

What are the special requirements for the type of business I am considering?

Space: _____

Budget: _____

Fire/Zoning/Safety Codes: _____

Personal Appeal

Almost everyone dreams of owning some type of business, whether or not they ever take the plunge and actually start the business. For some people it is an opportunity to utilize a skill they cannot use on their current jobs; for others it is a means of following in the footsteps of someone they admire, whether it is a family member or even a celebrity. Perhaps it is an adjunct to a profession, like the writer who opens a small bookstore or the dentist who starts his own dental supply business. The possibility of turning a dream into a business venture is usually within the grasp of an individual if he or she takes the necessary steps toward following that dream.

What type of business is most appealing to you?
❏ Retail sales
❏ B2B sales
❏ Internet sales
❏ Other means of sales
❏ Manufacturing
❏ Something in the arts, such as writing or designing
❏ A job that involves using your hands, such as a crafts business or repair
❏ Providing a service to individuals
❏ Providing a service to other businesses
❏ Consulting
❏ Opening a restaurant
❏ Other: _____

_____

_____

_____

Finding A Good Match

A particular interest in a business or industry is not the same as being a well-suited person to start that particular business, or a good match with the business opportunity. You may have a great understanding and interest in a particular business, but that certainly does not ensure that the business is a good match for you. Ask yourself the following questions to ensure a good business match:

• Am I physically and mentally healthy enough to handle the potential physical and mental strains of starting and running this business?

- Does this business opportunity match my personality type?
- Can I see myself still excited about this business five years from now?
- Does this business opportunity have the potential to help me reach my personal and financial goals?
- Can I commit to this business and am I prepared to work hard to ensure success?
- Is this the type of business that I initially envisioned as a self-employment venture that would be suitable and a good match for me?

The key is to do some soul searching and determine what business fits you best. For example, someone who is very introverted may like the idea of being a public speaker, but it may not be the ideal business choice for that individual. However, people can, and have, found ways to work in their fields of interest without fulfilling their initial dreams. The person who enjoys the idea of being a public speaker could run a speakers' bureau in which he or she books speakers for all sorts of situations. Many sports coaches, for example, never made first string when playing, but learned how to teach the game to others and remained in the field that interested them. Be open to a variety of options within your areas of interest.

Existing Resources

What existing resources do you have or have access to that can be utilized in the business? You would be very surprised by what you may have sitting around the house that can be used in starting and running a business—and even more surprised by the amount of money you can save in business start-up and operation costs by utilizing existing resources.

	Yes	No
Do you have computer equipment and software?	❏	❏
Do you have hi-tech tools that allow you to be mobile? (i.e. laptop or notebook computer, cell phone, organizer or planner, etc.)	❏	❏
Do you have a good contact base of people within the community?	❏	❏
Do you have a substantial e-mail or mailing list?	❏	❏

	Yes	No
Do you have suitable transportation for a new business?	❏	❏
Do you possess general office equipment and fixtures that can be used in the business?	❏	❏
Do you have access to a resource library for research and planning purposes?	❏	❏
Are there business clubs, associations, and networking opportunities in your community?	❏	❏
Do you know any professionals or current business owners that can assist you with business decisions?	❏	❏

These are only a few examples of existing resources you may have or have access to. Carefully consider what information, equipment, and research needs to be included to start the business. Compile a list of what is needed and write any existing resources you may have beside the needed item or information. Also consider human resources. Are there other people around you who are willing and available to help you in your business endeavor? Do you have an attorney, accountant, consultant, or other advisor(s) who are familiar with the type of business that interests you? Human resources are a valuable commodity in business. However, choose wisely. Your brother-in-law, the divorce attorney, may be very well meaning, but may not be the right person to answer your legal questions about starting up an online cosmetics business.

Start-Up Investment and Working Capital

Do you have, or have access to, the investment money necessary to start the business you are considering? If so, do you also have or have access to further money to be used as working capital for the day-to-day operations of the business? Beyond start-up capital, working capital is needed to achieve positive cash flow. What this means is that you need a steady stream of money—or cash flow—to keep a business operational. I have yet to come across a business opportunity that can be started today and generate a profit tomorrow. Every new business venture requires financing beyond the initial start-up costs in order to achieve positive cash flow, and believe me, a lot of time can pass before a business shows a profit or even breaks even.

One of the most common errors entrepreneurs make when starting a business is not calculating the true start-up investment needed to reach positive cash flow. As a rule of thumb use the 75/25 ratio rule, meaning that 75 percent of the total available capital will be used for the hard costs associated with establishing the business, such as equipment purchases, initial advertising campaigns, inventory, permits, and transportation. The remaining 25 percent of available capital will be held in reserve to be used for working capital in the business. An example of the 75/25 rule would be a business start-up that is calculated to require an initial investment of $60,000 to open for business. A further $15,000 should be held in reserve as working capital for the business, bringing the total start-up costs for the business to $75,000. For anyone considering the purchase of an existing business or franchise this 75/25 rule still applies regardless of financial statements or immediate cash flow projections.

Show Me the Money

The process of finding the money is one of the most difficult aspects of starting a business and one reason why there are numerous businesses included that can be started up for under $10,000. Business loans are not easy to get unless you have collateral or a track record in business that impresses lenders. For this reason, the Small Business Administration is one place to contact to discuss financing options. The trick for many entrepreneurs is to start small and continue to feed the money they earn back into the business over the first few years. The problem, of course, is what money can you use for yourself and your family? For this reason, you need to work on a means of procuring enough money to start the business through loans, investors, or additional income from another source, while not touching that which you need for living expenses. Often starting a business means tightening your belt and looking for places where you can save money, such as dining out less often, keeping the old car for another two or three years, or taking a less glamorous vacation—if you even find the time for one. One caution is that starting a web-based business often seems much less expensive, since you can run it from home and setting up (and maintaining) a web site are relatively inexpensive. Don't be fooled. Unless you put a lot of money into marketing and advertising the site, you will not see a profit from it.

While seeking out backers or places from which to borrow money it has long been advised—and still is—to be careful when borrowing from friends and family. Make sure everything is spelled out in advance and understood. Do they expect interest? When are they expecting you to repay the loan? Do they understand that every business comes with a risk factor? Are they a silent partner or backer, or does the person expect to be involved in the planning process and the running of the business? Even the closest of friends and family members have had great friction and resentment arise because of money/business situations. Proceed with caution.

If you are seeking outside backers, show them a good business plan, a winning formula and a very practical, realistic reason why this business will make money. Also, show them that you are putting in some money yourself, so you are not expecting other people to take a risk that you won't take. Your primary avenues of funding are:

- Small Business Administration (they don't actually make loans but can secure them)
- Banks and various lending institutions
- Venture capitalist firms (usually looking for large businesses)
- Angel and private investors (people with money looking to invest some of it)
- Family and friends
- Your own savings—and investment portfolio—beyond that which you need for living expenses

Research and Planning

Research and planning is vital to the success of every business venture. Once you have decided, or narrowed down, the list to the business opportunities that you would be most interested in pursuing, you will need to do your homework, so to speak, or research the field more closely. Research means looking at the business, industry, products, services, and competition on a local and national level. The goal is to find a comfort zone in which you are confident that such a business can be profitable in a given market. Sometimes a certain market is overcrowded or an industry is struggling. You will want to know this before proceeding full steam ahead. In other instances, you may be entering a crowded industry with a marvelous new twist on an existing business idea, one that can give you the competitive edge.

Planning is typically the result of doing solid research and having determined that the information you have discovered indicates that you can make this a successful business venture. You will need:

- Action plans
- Financial plans
- Marketing plans
- Long-and short-term business goals and objectives.

While this directory does not include detailed information specific to the research and planning aspects of starting a business, a new section, on the importance of a business plan, has been added as an incentive that will help you think through your prospective business opportunity.

The Business Plan

There are books, articles, web sites, and software packages designed to guide you through the steps of putting together a business plan, complete with templates to follow. The inclusion of some business plan basics here is to start you thinking about possibilities. Once you have decided which business is right for you, the many pieces that go into the jigsaw puzzle that comes with starting a business will all be part of your business plan.

Whether you are opening a small part-time pet sitting business, or launching a limousine rental company complete with twenty limos and a host of drivers and employees, a business plan is worthwhile for several reasons.

First, a business plan is a way of organizing, on paper, all of the pieces of the pie, from your equipment needs to the weekly schedule of hours you will be open for business. It allows you to have a "blueprint" so that no stone is left unturned. A business plan is also a way of showing other people, from friends and family to investors (who may be friends and family), that you have crossed all the "t's" and dotted all the "i's." A well thought out business plan tells the

story of a business and details your vision in such a way that can help you generate the necessary funding. Finally, it is a living, breathing document that can not only serve as a benchmark, but also be altered and expanded as the business grows and changes over the years.

A typical business plan includes the following:

1. *Executive Summary.* This is a short, broad, yet enticing, summary of the business. What is it all about and why are you excited about it? Although it usually appears first, this part is often written last, after you've put all the pieces in place.

2. *Business Description.* How does the business work? Can you describe what this business will be doing? Give the basics of what you are selling or manufacturing and the service you are providing.

3. *Products and/or Services.* Here you can include specific items that you will sell, or services you will perform. Include products and services you expect to offer down the road. Explain their value and why your customers will seek them out.

4. *Industry analysis.* Here you will paint a picture of the overall industry in which your business will be a player. From your research, talk about the "big picture."

5. *Competitive analysis.* This is a biggie. Do your research carefully and know who you are up against. Be realistic and list the strengths and weaknesses of the most direct competitors. Then, see if you can provide something—a product, a service, customer service—that your competitors do not provide. This can be your competitive edge.

6. *Marketing and Sales.* Now that you have plenty of details regarding what the business does and the products or services offered, you need to explain how you will let the world know that you are in business. In this section, you discuss your plans for marketing and promoting your business as well as how you will sell your products and services. Are you selling strictly over the internet? Through a retail outlet? By mail order? Catalog? All of the above?

7. *Management and Organization.* Another very important section—this is where you will let readers know who is running the business. Potential financial backers will be particularly interested in this section,

since they want to know to whom they are lending their money. Include all of the key people involved in making this business happen.

8. *Operations.* From hours of operation to who oversees which aspect of the business, this explains how the business will be run on a day-to-day basis.

9. *Financial Pages or Forms.* The goal here is to make realistic projections based on researching similar businesses, with help from your accountant or financial planner. You want to show when you see the business turning a profit and how much you believe the business can make in three or five years. Include a cash and balance sheet for a year to show a cash flow. Hint: Be conservative in your financial estimates.

10. *Financial Requirement.* This is a very important step, if you are seeking funding; it is where you include the amount of financing needed, based on the previous sections, to reach your goals. Be realistic, research costs carefully, and indicate how much money you anticipate putting into the business venture. Hint: You stand a much greater chance of getting investors interested, or bankers to approve a loan, if you have invested your own money into a business.

Add to this supporting documentation, which will include various financial reports, and you will have a business plan. Do not try to dazzle prospective readers with hype, just provide the real story of the business so that it is clear on paper how it will operate and make money.

Of course, this is just a very basic outline. Before you sit down and start writing, you will need to do research and look at other business plans in books or online to see the phrasing and style of such a business plan. If nothing else, thinking about each aspect of the plan will force you to start thinking about all of the many details that go into starting up a business. That's when it gets exciting, and a little scary, as you see all of the pieces come together.

◆ ◆ ◆

Entrepreneurs and small businesses drive the economies of the United States and Canada. Joining the estimated 30 million business owners may be easier than you think. You have already taken the first step toward becoming an entrepreneur by investing in the most authoritative business start-up directory available. The next step is to harness the power of this book and put it to work for you to find and start the right new business.

39
ADVERTISING
Businesses You Can Start

OUTDOOR BICYCLE RACKS
★★ $$ 🏠 🕐 ⚖️ 🌐

Are you searching for a unique advertising business opportunity that can be managed from a homebased office and has the potential to generate a six-figure annual income? If so, consider starting a bicycle rack advertising service. The business concept is very straightforward. Simply design, build, or purchase bicycle lock-up stands that can accommodate four to six bicycles each and can be securely fastened to the ground in outdoor locations. The bicycle stands serve two purposes: First, they introduce a terrific advertising medium by creating an advertising space on the top of the stand that can be rented to local merchants and service providers for advertising purposes, though you may need to install such ad space yourself if you have purchased the racks. The second purpose of the stand is to provide a secure location for cyclists to lock up their bikes while shopping at community retailers. Check local ordinances carefully before placing bike racks and always include a sign that you are not responsible for the bicycles, since you are only providing the bike rack and not the locks that bicyclists should already have.

WEB RESOURCE: www.bikeparking.com
Manufacturers of outdoor bicycle lock-up stands.

CAMPUS COUPON BOOKS
★★ $$ 🏠 🕐 🌐

Starting a business that creates and markets campus coupon books directly to university and college students is a fantastic new business venture to put into action. Securing local merchants to be featured in the campus coupon books should not prove difficult, as there is no cost to participate—only a requirement to provide honest and generous discounts on products or services that their companies sell. Furthermore, you can enlist students to sell the discount coupon books to other students right on campus on a revenue split basis. The key to success in this unique advertising business is to ensure that the coupon books contain genuine discounts on products and services that students would regularly use and purchase. You also want to have a book with eye-catching appeal to college students. Modern desktop publishing programs and places like FedEx Kinko's or Staples make printing such coupon books easier than ever.

WEB RESOURCE: www.couponpros.org
Association of Coupon Professionals

LITTER CANS
★ $ 🏠 🕐

Purchasing 200 commercial-grade litter cans and securing high-traffic indoor and outdoor locations for the litter cans to be installed can potentially generate advertising revenues of $6,000 per month. In order for this very unique advertising business to succeed, the following two aspects must be considered. First, secure highly visible locations to install the litter cans, such as in front of retail stores, inside malls, and inside community and recreation centers. Additionally, the property or business owners must agree, not only to allow you to place the litter cans, but also to maintain them in exchange for a portion of the advertising revenues generated. Next, aggressively market the advertising service to local companies who want to participate in a highly effective advertising campaign that costs only $30 per month.

WEB RESOURCE: www.victorstanley.com
Manufacturers of commercial-grade outdoor litter receptacles.

DOOR HANGER SERVICE
★★★ $ 🏠 🕐

Thousands of renovation and home service companies are missing out on a very effective and extremely low-cost advertising method for their business. And you can capitalize financially by introducing them to this advertising medium by starting your own door hanger design and delivery service. Door hangers are simply a type of marketing brochure that has been designed to fit on an entrance door handle. What makes door hangers such an effective advertising medium is the fact that door hangers are noticed as people enter their homes. Additionally, door hangers can also act as a discount coupon with a company advertising message printed on the front and a coupon or special promotion printed on the back. Current delivery rates are in the range of 25 to 30 cents per door hanger delivered, plus design and printing costs.

WEB RESOURCE: www.laserblanks.com
Suppliers of blank door hangers.

INFLATABLE ADVERTISING
★★ $$ 🏠 🕐 ⚖️ 🌐

Twenty-foot-high inflatable gorillas, blimps, and cartoon caricatures get noticed by traffic, especially when these large inflatables are sitting on a retailer's rooftop with a "sale in progress" sign emblazoned across them.

Starting a business that rents inflatable advertising objects is a fantastic new business venture to set in motion. The business can be operated on a full- or part-time basis right from home, and clients can include just about any retail business in your community that regularly conducts special sales or promotions. Currently, new inflatables are retailing for approximately $3,000 to $5,000. But as a method to reduce the start-up investment needed to get the business rolling, secondhand inflatables can be purchased for about half the cost of a new one. Rental rates are in the range of $75 to $150 per day including delivery.

WEB RESOURCE: www.windship.com
Manufacturers of hot and cold air advertising inflatables.

COMMUNITY DIRECTORY BOARDS
★★ $$ 🏠 🕐 🌐

Do you live in a busy tourist area of the country? If so, perhaps you should consider starting a business that installs, markets, and maintains community directory boards. Community directory boards are simply an outdoor board, covered in protective glass or plastic, featuring information about the local community that they serve. Information featured can include a map of the area, tourist attractions and where they are located, a list of community services, the location of sports complexes and playing fields, and additional information about the community in general. Revenues are earned by selling highly visible advertising spaces on the community directory boards to local merchants wishing to advertise their products and services.

WEB RESOURCE: www.visiontron.com
Sales of outdoor directory/bulletin boards

FLIER DISTRIBUTION SERVICE
★ $ 🏠 🕐

Not only is a flier delivery service a very easy business to start, it also has the potential to generate a fantastic annual income. Companies have utilized promotional fliers for decades as a low-cost highly effective advertising method. Starting a flier delivery service requires no more than a telephone and a good pair of walking shoes. Currently, flier delivery services are charging delivery rates in the range of 7 to 15 cents per hand-delivered flier.

As a method to increase your delivery workforce, consider hiring retirees and students to deliver fliers during busy times. Make sure fliers are given out in areas that are zoned for such handouts. Fliers can also be put into local newspapers or placed in shopping bags at local stores for an additional fee to your client, some of which is passed on to the retailers or newspaper publishers for handling such placement. The printing of the actual fliers themselves can be the responsibility of the business owner who hands you a finished product to distribute. However, you can also bring in additional revenue by using desktop publishing software, such as Print Shop or MSPublisher to design and print the fliers.

SPORTS COMPLEX ADVERTISING
★ $$ 🏠 🕐

A very successful advertising business can be built by securing contracts with privately and publicly owned sports complexes to manage and operate their advertising programs. Most sports complexes, like arenas, recreation centers, and baseball fields, feature some form of interior or exterior advertising space that is rented by local companies to promote their products and services. Generally the owners or operators of the sports complex do not market the advertising spaces for rent. This task is left to an outside contractor who has successfully bid in a tender process for the right to market and manage the advertising program. Be forewarned that this is a very competitive segment of the advertising industry that will require careful research and planning prior to establishing a business that specializes in this type of advertising sales. However, the profit potential is outstanding for the determined entrepreneurs that are awarded these types of advertising contracts.

BENCH ADVERTISING
★ $$ 🏠 🕐

The very first step in doing such advertising is to gain permission from the property owners or the town/municipality to place the benches. This may require sharing a percentage of your profits. Nonetheless, once you get the okay to place the benches, you can then generate gross sales of $60,000 per year from a part-time business that rents advertising space on park or seating benches. You then need to design, construct, or purchase 50 outdoor seating benches that feature a large and highly visible advertising space on the back or front of the bench (depending on bench placement). Typically, this is either in a frame, where the ad is slipped between two pieces of metal, or a large wooden frame to which the ads are glued or attached with self-adhesive material. Finally, you can then rent the advertising spaces to local merchants wishing to advertise and promote their products and services, and charge a monthly rate for each advertising space. Depending on the traffic in the area where the bench is placed, you can charge accordingly. You might start at $100 per month in low traffic areas and $500+ per month in busier urban locations. Providing that all of the above can be accomplished, the end result will be an advertising business that can be operated from home, and generates yearly revenues of $60,000. In addition to outside benches, indoor advertising benches can also be located in buildings such as recreation centers, public markets, and malls.

WEB RESOURCE: www.victorstanley.com
Manufacturers of outdoor park benches.

PROMOTIONAL PRODUCTS
★★★ $$ 🏠

Billions of dollars are spent annually in North America on promotional items such as T-shirts, pens, hats, and calendars by companies that give these promotional items away to existing and potential clients of their business. Securing just a small portion of this very lucrative market can make you rich. The key to success in the promotional products marketing industry is not to manufacture and print the promotional items yourself, but to simply market these items and enlist the services of existing manufacturers and printers to fulfill the orders. This is a business that requires excellent sales and marketing abilities, and this business opportunity is not suitable for an individual who is scared to go out and ask for business. Aim to achieve yearly sales of $300,000 while maintaining a 50 percent markup on all products sold, and the end result will be a homebased advertising business that generates a pretax and expense earnings of $100,000.

WEB RESOURCE: www.motivators.com
Promotional products and custom promotional items.

TAXI CAB PUBLICATION
★ $$ 🏠 🕐 🌐

Starting a taxi cab publication will take some clever negotiations skills to accomplish, but like any new business venture the effort is generally rewarded financially for the determined entrepreneurs that take the initiative. A taxi cab publication is simply a daily or weekly two-page paper that is distributed free of charge for taxi customers to enjoy during their ride. The paper can feature information about the local community, as well as trivia and games. Revenues are earned by selling display-advertising space in the paper to local business owners and professionals. Ideally, the business could be formed as a joint venture with an established printer who can produce the newspaper, while you concentrate on the marketing and sales aspects of the business. Once established and proven successful, the business could easily be expanded by a franchise or licensed-to-operate basis nationally.

TRANSIT ADVERTISING
★ $$$$

Like many advertising service contracts, operating and marketing a transit advertising program is generally awarded by the transit commission or agency that operates the transit service on a tendered basis. Typically, the tenders renew every few years and the decision to award the contract to one particular service provider is made on the basis of reliability, revenue generation, and performance record. This type of advertising service contract can be extremely difficult to acquire. However, for the successful bidding contractor the financial rewards can be outstanding as transit advertising is some of the most sought after advertising media by companies, agencies, and merchants. Your best bet is to be proactive and find out if any new bus lines will be starting in your community or a new cab service is starting up. Look for businesses that have recently expanded or been granted contracts by the local government.

WEB RESOURCE: www.oaaa.org/outdoor/councils/transit.asp The Outdoor Advertising Association of America has a section of their web site dedicated to transit advertising.

HOARDING ADVERTISING SERVICE
★★ $$ 🏠 🕐

For anyone who is not familiar with the term hoarding, it is the temporary plywood fencing that is erected around the perimeter of a construction site. Typically, hoarding is used for construction sites in densely populated urban areas to prevent foot traffic from being potentially injured as a result of coming into contact with falling debris or construction equipment. While many people illegally post advertising posters and notices on hoarding fences, a very successful advertising business can be built by legally acquiring permission to post advertising on the fencing. Marketing this type of advertising is very easy as most hoarding is erected in highly visible areas and that is exactly the kind of exposure advertisers are seeking. Additionally, be sure to negotiate a revenue split arrangement with the contractors or property developers of the site, as this will definitely remove any potential objections. The advertisers should supply their own printed matter, or you can work out a deal with a printer to introduce your clients to their services for preferred customer service, such as fast turnaround time.

ELEVATOR ADVERTISING
★★ $$ 🏠 🕐

Elevator advertising is probably the most effective advertising available in terms of consumer awareness, simply because occupants of elevators are a captive audience surrounded by few distractions. The key to successfully operating an advertising service that specializes in marketing elevator advertising spaces is to secure the busiest elevators in the community for the service. Ideally, you should concentrate on securing elevators in commercial buildings such as malls, office towers, and hospitals. The higher the elevator foot traffic, the easier it will be to secure advertisers to purchase the advertising spaces. Furthermore, to secure the best elevator locations for the business, consider a revenue split arrangement with the owner of the building or property manager of the building and develop interesting ways to display the advertisements. The latest in elevator advertising are flat panel television screens posting hi-tech ads. While selling this advertising space can be highly lucrative in high-traffic locations, such as major hotels, there is a significantly higher cost outlay, plus maintaining the equipment means having some technical expertise or hiring someone who does.

CHARITY EVENTS
★ $$ 🏠 🕐

Do you want to start an advertising business that helps local charities raise much needed funding, while building a profitable business for yourself? If so, perhaps you should consider starting a business that organizes community charity events like golf tournaments and craft sales. The charities would receive all event admission fees while you would retain advertising revenues generated by selling advertising spaces in the event's program as well as promotional items such as event hats and T-shirts. The key to success is to build alliances with well-recognized charities in the community, as well as ensuring the events are well promoted and fun for all in attendance. You need to have strong organizational and planning abilities for this type of business.

JOURNAL COORDINATOR
★★★ $ 🏠 🕐

Each year, numerous charities, associations, organizations, schools, and even hospitals have fundraising dinners in which they put together journals. The journals are great means of advertising for local businesses or even for individuals to place personal ads in support of the organization, charity, or institution. While many such journals are the end result of volunteer labor, many generate far less revenue than they could or never even get completed in time for the big dinner or gala event. This is where you come in. By coordinating journals, for a small percentage of the ad revenue, you can boost the money raised from $1,000 to $10,000 for the organization or institution. Therefore, if your cut is 10%, or $1,000, this leaves $9,000 for a good cause. Meanwhile, if you can put together 50 journals a year, you can earn $50,000 with virtually no overhead from a business you can do from the comfort of your own home. The key abilities necessary for success include good sales skills, being able to communicate effectively with many potential advertisers, and great

organizational skills so that you can be working on two or three journals at one time. If you possess layout skills or know someone who does, you can also make additional money laying out the journal and getting it printer ready.

COMMUNITY BULLETIN BOARDS
★★ $$ 🏠 🕐 🌐

High quality four- by eight-foot wall-mounted bulletin boards can be built for about $250 each, and spending $10,000 to construct 40 bulletin boards has the potential to return advertising revenues in excess of $20,000 each month. How? Easy. Simply secure permission to install community bulletin boards in 40 high traffic locations such as food markets, malls, and recreation centers. Then, secure ten advertisers for each bulletin board and provide the advertisers with an 8-inch by 10-inch advertisement on the community bulletin board in exchange for $50 per month. The advertisements can be located around the outside of the bulletin board and be protected by tamper proof glass or plastic, while the inside of the bulletin board is cork and used by people in the community to post notices. To attract advertisers, the bulletin boards must be located in high-traffic community gathering places. To secure the best locations for the boards consider a revenue split arrangement with the owner of the building or business where the community bulletin boards are installed.

WINDOW DISPLAYS
★ $ 🏠 🕐

Retailers often must rely on an elaborate window and in-store displays to attract the attention of passing consumers. Starting a business that specializes in creating effective window displays for retail merchants is the focus of this business opportunity. Marketing a window display service can be as easy as approaching local retailers and initially providing your services for free until the owner of the business starts to realize the benefits and increased sales that a well-designed window display can garner. Additionally, the "free" display that you create can also be used as a powerful marketing tool to present to other shop owners. Placing a sign by the display that explains your service and gives contact information will help in getting the word out. Furthermore, be sure to build an inventory of interesting props so that you can provide clients with an "all-inclusive" display service.

SITE SIGN INSTALLATION SERVICE
★★ $ 🏠 🕐

Here is a terrific business to start and operate in conjunction with a door hanger service. Company site signs are temporally installed in front of a customer's home telling people in the neighborhood who the company is that is performing work, as well as what business they are in and how to contact the company. Most construction, renovation, and home service companies realize the value of installing site signs. However, time restrictions usually mean the sign never gets installed. Thus, the free advertising benefits never get realized. This is a wise choice for a new business venture especially when combined with a door hanger service, as clients will get a double whammy for their advertising buck.

WEB RESOURCE: www.victorystore.com
Online resource for creating business signs.

ADVERTISING CLIPPING AND CHECKING SERVICE
★ $ 🏠 🕐

Did you know that companies that compete within the same industry regularly retain the services of an advertising clipping service to keep them up-to-date on how, why, and where the competition is advertising? In addition, advertisers need to know that their own advertisements were properly run in newspapers or on other mediums, especially co-op advertising, in which a manufacturer is supposed to receive x amount of space while sharing an ad with a retailer. Here is your opportunity to capitalize financially by starting an advertising clipping and checking service. The key to success in this business is not to overcharge clients, but to work in volume. Charging clients a monthly rate, or a low fee based on number of ads checked, will guarantee that you retain existing clients and attract new clients to the service very easily. To check ads successfully, you will need to collect advertisements from newspapers, directories, magazines, and now the internet, as well as monitor and record radio or television advertising, charting the time at which the ads were run.

If they are concerned about whether or not their ads were run properly, or run at the designated times, you can charge to review the ads for mistakes or misplacement. Securing and maintaining 50 to 100 regular clients can generate a good annual income.

AERIAL ADVERTISING
★ $$ 🏠 🕐 ⚖

If you are looking for a unique and inexpensive advertising business to start, look no further than starting an aerial advertising service. The best way to initiate this business is to form a joint partnership with a pilot who has, or has access to, an airplane as the pilot can concentrate on the aerial aspect of the business while you can concentrate on marketing the business and selling the advertising service. Typically, this is a business that works best over large, unobstructed outdoor areas in which people gather, such as beach resort areas or popular outdoor tourists locations. Make sure you have permission to fly over such areas prior to starting the business. Demand for the service is not likely to be large enough to operate the business on a full-time basis. However, an aerial advertising service even operated on a part-time basis, in the right location, can still generate revenues in excess of $50,000 per year, prior to taxes and operating overhead.

WEB RESOURCE: www.flysigns.com
A national supplier of aerial signs.

RESTAURANT MENUS
★★ $$ 🏠 🕐

How do you provide business owners in your community with highly effective low-cost advertising options, while also providing restaurant owners with high quality menus printed free of charge every month and make a profit for yourself? Easy! Start a restaurant menu advertising program in your community. The business concept is very basic. Secure agreements with busy restaurants in your local community that would be prepared to allow advertising to be printed on the front and back covers of their menus in exchange for receiving new and updated menus free of charge each month. Once this has been accomplished, you can set out to market the advertising spaces on the menu covers to local merchants and service providers. The business will take patience to establish, but a terrific annual income could be eventually realized.

WEB RESOURCE: www.restaurantmenus.com
A portal for menu printers and designers.

COMMUNITY BUSINESS MAPS
★ $$ 🏠 🕒 🌐

Community business maps are simply maps featuring information about local attractions and points of interest within a community, as well as highlighting the participating businesses that sponsor or advertise on the maps. Typically, business advertisers will receive a display-size advertisement on the back of the map, and the advertiser's business location will be featured on the front of the map. The maps are given away free of charge to tourists visiting the community, of course with the intention that the tourists will take notice of the advertisers on the maps and purchase their products or services. The maps are generally published once per year, and expanding the business is as easy as introducing the map advertising strategy to new communities.

BILLBOARDS
★ $$$$

Billboards are one of the most competitive segments of the advertising industry, and starting a business that installs billboards and markets billboard advertising will take a lot of research and clever planning. However, with that said, the profit potential for a business that markets billboard advertising is outstanding. The billboard advertising industry works like this. A site to install a billboard is selected based on excellent street visibility and high traffic count. If zoning and local ordinances permit placement of a billboard, the owner of the building or land where the billboard is installed will then receive a yearly fee; the amount of money paid to the landowner is based on a percentage of the projected advertising revenues that the billboard will generate. Advertisers wishing to advertise on the billboard pay a one-time art fee to create the ad and a fee for the amount of time the ads are featured on the billboard. One billboard can generate upwards of $10,000 or more each year.

WEB RESOURCE: www.outdoorbillboard.com
Supplier of outdoor billboards.

ADVERTISING BROKER
★ $$$ 🏠

Why pay retail prices to advertise your business? That is the question that you will be asking potential clients if your intentions are to become an independent advertising broker. Purchasing various advertising mediums in advance and in bulk can cut the cost by as much as 50 percent or more. To reinforce this statement, contact your local radio station and ask for the rate for ten 30-second advertising spots versus three hundred 30-second advertising spots. The cost difference will amaze you. Once you have successfully negotiated and secured various advertising mediums in bulk, you can set about reselling the radio advertising spots, display newspaper ads and more to local businesses in your community at a cost saving to them of 25 percent off the regular advertising rates. Providing clients with a 25 percent discount will still leave you with a 25 percent markup or more on the advertising spots and spaces you have sold.

PIZZA BOXES
★★ $$ 🏠 🕒

Did you know that pizza boxes are not recyclable due to the grease from the pizza that gets into the cardboard? While this may seem like a useless bit of trivia, it is not, as it can become your greatest and most powerful marketing tool for persuading pizza shop owners and local merchants to partake in a pizza box advertising and recycling program. Here is how it works: Owners of the pizza shop get their pizza boxes for 50 percent of the regular cost for allowing local non-competing merchants to advertise on the pizza box. This can potentially save them thousands of dollars each year. Local merchants that advertise on the pizza boxes receive low-cost highly effective advertising and the advertisement can be in the form of a cutout coupon featuring a discount for the merchant's products and services. Consumers still receive a great-tasting pizza, plus valuable discount coupons that can be redeemed at local stores. Last, but not least, the pizza box is partially recycled into coupons and gets a renewed lease on life, which in turn helps us all.

WEB RESOURCE: www.modelboxco.com
Manufacturers of pizza boxes.

HOSPITALITY KIOSKS
★★ $$$$

Free computer terminals, known as hospitality kiosks, contain specific information about the location in which they are placed, such as about a museum, hotel, or a shopping mall. Due to the fact that the kiosks provide information, they are frequently used and advertising space on the kiosks can be sold to local companies to generate sales and profits for the business. Once you secure permission to set up a hospitality kiosk in a specific destination, you can sell ads to accompany the information and provide a percentage of the revenue to the owner of the location in which you have placed the kiosk.

WEB RESOURCE: www.thekioskfactory.com
Sellers of numerous types of kiosks.

RESTAURANT PLACEMATS
★★ $$ 🏠 🕐

Like restaurant menus, many restaurant owners are more than happy to have community businesses featured on their table placemats in exchange for receiving the placemats for free. Here is how the business works. Assume that a busy 50-seat restaurant would use 200 paper placemats each day or approximately 6,000 per month, and the cost to print 6,000 black and white placemats on color paper would be around 10 cents each, or a total of $600. Furthermore, the placemats would feature 16 business card-sized display advertisements around the outside of the placemat, while the inside of the placemat would feature trivia questions or games. Charging local merchants a mere 1.5 cents per advertisement, per placemat would generate total sales of $1,440 per restaurant each month, or a gross profit of $840. Now times that by ten restaurants, and you would have a great little advertising business generating sales in excess of $100,000 per year.

ADS-THAT-WORK BOOK
★ $$$ 🏠 🕐

Calling all advertising and marketing specialists! The time has never been better than now to write and distribute a book in print (and electronic format), that teaches business owners and managers how to create effective advertisements that work for their businesses, in terms of creating consumer demand for a product or service and increasing sales. Ideally, the book or guide will be broken into sections relating to various advertising mediums such as how to create winning classified ads, how to create effective display advertisements, and information about advertising on the web. Once the advertising book or guide has been completed, it can be sold on a wholesale basis to book retailers or distributors or directly to business owners via the internet. Other avenues for sales are seminars, direct mail campaigns, and business association networking meetings. The key is to provide very well researched, solid information that is up-to-date. Interviewing people in the advertising field will help you enhance the credibility of the book.

HUMAN BILLBOARDS
★★★ $$ 🏠 🕐 🌐

Here is a terrific homebased business start-up for entrepreneurs with good marketing skills, but limited investment capital. Human billboards advertise everything from new home developments to car dealerships and are starting to catch on as a highly effective cost-efficient method of advertising and promoting their products and services. Human billboards are simply people that hold, or wear, signs or carry banners emblazoned with promotional and advertising messages in high-traffic areas of the community; usually outside, in front, or in close proximity to the business they are promoting. The objective of a human billboard is twofold. First, get the attention of passing motorists and pedestrians, and once you have their attention, get them to take action. This simply means you want these people to go to the business that is being promoted. There are really two aspects to operating this type of business: marketing and the people who will be the actual human billboards. In terms of the people who will work as the human billboards, seek to hire homemakers, students, actors, musicians, and retirees, basically anyone that is available to work on a part-time, as-needed basis. Additionally, you will want to develop a short training program. Vital to the success of the business will be the ability of the human billboards to get the desired response, which of course is to be noticed. The training program can focus on body language and vocal phrasing, both of which, if used correctly, can be highly effective. Marketing the service can be as easy as setting appointments with local business owners to explain and promote the benefits of your service. Joining community business associations and networking clubs are also good ways to promote the service. Rates for human billboards vary based on factors such as the number of people (billboards), the length of the promotion, and other items like signage and if the people (billboards) require special costumes. Ideally, you will want to develop a few packages. As an example, a basic package could include one person for four hours with two large promotional signs such as "sale today" or "stop here for a great deal" and a dozen helium-filled balloons attached to the signs. The cost of this basic program could be in the range of $75 to $100 and you could have optional upgrade packages. People enlisted to work as the billboards could be paid on a subcontract hourly basis or on a percentage of the value of the contract.

INDOOR AND OUTDOOR SPECIALTY ADVERTISING
★★ $$ 🏚 🕒

Mentioned in this directory are numerous indoor and outdoor advertising businesses that can be started and operated for profit and success. However, in the spirit of being unique, also consider these additional types of indoor and outdoor advertising opportunities that perhaps might be the right new venture for you to specialize in.

Window Billboards

Vacant storefronts and professional offices that do not utilize window space for display purposes are two highly visible and potentially profitable places to display window billboards. Window billboards are two-foot by three-foot color poster advertisements that are laminated in plastic. The mini-billboards can be installed in commercial window spaces using small and transparent suction cups. Strike deals with retailers, property owners, and professional offices to join your window billboard advertising program. In exchange for allowing the window billboards to be displayed, participants would receive 40 percent of the monthly revenues the window billboards generate. Solicit local merchants and service providers to rent the

advertising spaces at $50 per month plus the cost to create the poster.

Golf Driving Ranges

If your local golf driving range does not have an advertising program in place then you should seriously consider approaching the management of such a facility to initiate one. There are two fantastic locations for highly visible advertising at most golf driving ranges: tee box dividers and distance targets. The golf driving range provides the space for the advertisements and you market the program to local businesses that want this type of advertising exposure. Split the revenues with the golf range and all win.

Washrooms

Who would want to advertise their business in a washroom? Lots of businesses. Why? A captive audience. Washroom advertising has become extremely popular in the last few years, and many media companies are feverishly working to secure the rights to the busiest washrooms in the country. However, this does not mean that an opportunity does not exist for the small operator to start this type of unique advertising service as there are millions of good locations, and it will take years before the market is saturated. Washroom ads are generally 12-inches wide and 18-inches high, full color, and sealed in an aluminum frame with a plastic covering face. The ads are typically installed beside vanity mirrors, above urinals, and on the back of stall doors. Good washroom locations include airports, restaurants, bars, roadside rest stops, community markets, sports complexes, and arenas.

Planters

Purchase commercial grade, highly attractive rectangular box planters and supply the planters for both indoor and outdoor use complete with plants to retailers, professionals, and restaurants free of charge. Of course in exchange for providing the planters the host location must agree to water and allow a small advertising place card (12" x 12") featuring a non-competing business ad to be installed on the planter. Solicit local merchants and service providers to rent these highly visible advertising spaces for $25 per month or more.

Delivery Vehicles

In every community across North America there are delivery vehicles of all sizes that make fantastic mobile billboards. Strike up a partnership with a courier company, moving company, or basically any company that operates a fleet of service or delivery vehicles to initiate an advertising program. The delivery company allows their vehicles to have advertisements installed on them, and you promote and sell the advertising spaces and split the ad revenues with the delivery company

WEB RESOURCE: www.oaaa.org

The Outdoor Advertising Association provides a wealth of information on outdoor advertising possibilities.

PROMOTIONAL BUTTONS
★★ $$ 🏠 🕐

Making promotional buttons is a great homebased business opportunity for the entrepreneur that is looking for a way to generate extra part-time income. The business is easy to start, requires little in the way of experience, equipment, or investment capital, and has the potential to earn you $25 per hour. Promotional buttons have been used by businesses, charities, and organizations for decades as an highly effective, low-cost marketing tool to get a message out about a product, service, or event. Creating promotional buttons could not be easier, especially when you consider that the customer can supply the design or message featured on the button in digital format. It can also be easily created on a computer and then simply transferred via software to a printing stamp or pad to create the finished product. In addition to a computer and software, you will also need a button press, a pad printing press, and a few supplies to get started—all of which add up to an initial investment of less than a few thousand dollars. Market the buttons to businesses, charity organizations, schools, and just about any other business, club, or group that is seeking a way to create a low-cost promotional campaign. Join business and social clubs to network for clients and be sure to hand out a lot of buttons promoting your promotional button business. Much more memorable than handing out a business card, wouldn't you agree?

WEB RESOURCE: www.badgeaminit.com

Manufacturers and distributors of badge-making equipment and supplies.

VEHICLE ADVERTISING
★★ $$ 🏠 🕐

Ever see a truck or van driving around with an advertisement on it? You could be the party responsible for getting that ad on that vehicle, provided, of course, the vehicle slows down just long enough for you to place the ad. Seriously, there is money to be made in almost any sure fire means of putting a product before the public and this is no exception. You serve as the middle person, finding interested advertisers and suitable vehicles. Unlike busses, which are run by municipalities, trucks and vans are privately owned and you only need the permission of the owners, who would be glad to take a split of the ad revenue. There are also trucks that drive around exclusively for the purposes of carrying a large billboard ad. This can be a bit more costly, as you would need to own or lease the trucks. With the price of gas today (and the backlash from people who say you are contributing to pollution only to advertise a product) you may not wish to go this route unless you can justify the cost and perhaps use alternative fuels for the environment.

PRODUCT PLACEMENT
★★★★ $$ 🏠 🕐

Here's a billion dollar industry, growing rapidly, and most people do not even know it exists. Product placement is just as it sounds: placing name products before the public. It is done routinely in television, film, and even now to a degree in theater performances. When someone on a popular television show reaches for a can of soda, you can be sure Coke or Pepsi has paid good money to make sure it is their brand of soda. Likewise, when your favorite movie star jumps into his or her automobile and drives off, it is very likely that Ford, Jaguar, or some other car company made sure that it was their vehicle in which the star made their getaway. In short, if you can align with companies, at any level, and production companies (starting with small local TV and film companies) to get products onto production, you can make a lot of money. Manufacturers will pay for this service and pay well depending on the size of the potential demographic market. According to the Nielsen Company, the leading source of television ratings, there were over 110,000 product placements on prime time television in 2005, up 41% from the previous year.

To get in on this exciting and growing industry, you will need to do some research to learn about product placement and determine how much you can charge in your region to make such connections. Also, if you are intrigued by the prospect, watch episodic television shows (not news) and films more closely and you will see (much to your surprise) how many placements are actually out there and how immense the possibilities are for success in this advertising career.

WEB RESOURCE: www.marketingpower.com/content24146.php
The American Marketing Association's web information on product placement

CALENDARS
★★★ $$ 🏠 🕐

Each year, thousands of businesses give out promotional calendars to clients and vendors. An excellent low-cost start up businesses is putting together calendars specifically for clients. Photos can be included from the client, from local photographers or even from outside sources with the permission of the photographer. Other forms of art and electronic graphics can also be an option. You bill the client for putting together the calendar and handling layout and printing.

You can also make money by selling advertising space to various businesses to advertise for a calendar and supply you with the graphics or artwork. The advertisers pay to be included in the calendar and you then distribute the calendars for free. The only cost you will need to cover is that of the print run or the software if you can find and learn to use a good calendar making program.

NEWSPAPER BOXES
★★ $$ 🏠 🕐 ⚖

As long as people still read newspapers, there will still be newspaper boxes from which to deposit money and take a copy (or two). It is on these newspaper boxes that mounted frames can house advertisements for just about any company. Selling this advertising space can be lucrative, with a single box generating anywhere from $50 to $500 per month in advertising revenue, depending on the traffic volume in a given location. Of course, you will either need to work with newspaper publishers to sell advertising on their boxes (which may mean adding the mounted frame for advertising purposes) and giving the publisher a cut, or placing the boxes for the newspaper publishers.

Make sure you have permission from business owners, or the municipality in which you are planning to do business, to place the boxes. Also, make sure to secure them.

WEB RESOURCE: www.shorack.com
Manufacturers and distributors of newspaper boxes.

ADVERTISING AGENCY
★★★ $$$$ 🏠

Even the giants on Madison Avenue in New York had to start somewhere, and you too can start an advertising agency. All it requires, is creativity, chutzpah (a.k.a., nerve), and some marketing of services. Advertising agencies create the ads, images, and the right "look and feel" that will help their clients sell their products and services to the public. Copywriters and graphic artists are two key elements that make an agency work and if you have one of those key skills it is a great starting point. Of course, you will then need to find someone with the other skill to serve as the yin to your yang. Ad executives, the men and women in the suits, interact with the clients to let them know how your creativity will give them the competitive edge. A good media planner will decide which are the right promotional venues for each client, and how they can effectively position themselves. And finally, you will need someone to run the business aspect of the agency by paying the bills, ordering the supplies, invoicing clients, and balancing your budget. Whether you serve as a one person, creative, production, and financial whiz, or find a few key people to help launch the business from your basement or attic, an advertising agency can start off with just a handful of local clients and build into an empire. Read everything you can get your hands on about advertising first.

ADVERTISING SALES REP
★★★ $$ 🏠 🕐

Unlike a broker, you do not sell in bulk as an Advertising Sales Representative, but instead you sell advertising space in all magazines to the advertisers who need it. Good contacts throughout the magazine industry are essential for making this type of independent business work. For less than $1,500, you can startup your business by repping for local community newspapers, newsletters, or local magazines. In time, you can work your way up to larger periodicals and even major web sites (since smaller ones do not have much advertising or much revenue). Commonly reps charge a flat fee for your services, a commission based on the advertising sold, or a split where you receive some of each. As an independent, you can work for numerous publications at one time, although you typically won't represent competing publications in the same subject area.

Your only start-up expenses should be for basic office equipment that you don't already own, plus envelopes, letterhead stationary, some reference guides to magazine personnel and of course business cards. Advertising reps for major publications make in excess of $100,000 per year.

MEDIA BUYING/PLANNING AGENCY
★★★ $$$ 🏠

TV? Radio? Internet? Signage? What is the best means of advertising for a particular client and at what cost? These are the concerns of a media buyer, who works with advertising agencies and sales reps at media companies in order to purchase the most appropriate advertising space within a range of media including digital, radio, press, television, and the internet. Some companies focus primarily on buying the ads, but to bring in more income, you can also serve as a media planner, helping the business owners and managers determine the best advertising plan of attack by studying the industry and the product and looking for a perfect match.

Some advertising experience and a thorough knowledge of the media are very valuable assets when getting this business started. Contacts in the industry are also essential as is an understanding of advertising budgets, media strategies and how to build and create a media campaign.

If you have the knowledge and above credentials, this is a marvelous business opportunity. Although not an easy business, as the media is constantly changing, you can build from a small market company to work with larger businesses on major multi-million dollar advertising accounts. As a result, in time, this can be a very lucrative business.

NOTES:

_____

_____

_____

_____

_____

_____

_____

_____

_____

_____

_____

_____

_____

_____

KEY

RATINGS ★

START-UP COST $$

HOMEBASED
BUSINESS

PART-TIME
OPPORTUNITY

LEGAL ISSUES

FRANCHISE OR
LICENSE POTENTIAL

GREEN
BUSINESSES

32
ART
Businesses You Can Start

ART SUPPLIES
★★ $$$$

Millions of people enjoy creating art as a hobby. It is a great way to be creative and reduce stress. All of these people require art supplies to be able to enjoy their hobbies, and this fact creates a terrific opportunity to open a start-up art supplies retail store. The store does not have to be large, just well stocked with all the popular art supplies. You can also conduct painting and sculpting classes at night to earn extra income. The investment required to start an art supply store will be in the range of $35,000. However, the profit potential is very good as art supplies are often marked up 100 percent or more. Furthermore, you may also want to occasionally take the business mobile and deliver art supplies to elderly homes and care facilities, as it can often be difficult for these people to get out and pick up supplies for their art projects.

WEB RESOURCE: www.namta.org
National Art Materials Trade Association.

HOTEL ART SUPPLY
★★ $$ 🏠 🕐

Look closely and you will notice that hotels are virtually art galleries. You will find paintings, prints, and sculptures in almost every room, hallway, lounge, and lobby. Assume that one hotel has 150 rooms, one lobby, two banquet rooms, one lounge, and ten hallways. The hotel's art requirements could be as many as 200 paintings or prints alone. Simply supplying one hotel with a complete art decor package can make you thousands of dollars in profits. To activate this business you will want to establish a relationship with at least 15 to 20 different artists who work in various art mediums. You can place photos of artwork on CD-ROMs or have a virtual gallery online to show hotel owners. The key to starting off such a business is having access to a wide variety of prints, and even some originals from young, unknown artists, that can be copied and made into prints if the hotel owner is interested. Of course, the big profit opportunities are landing art supply contracts with hotels that are being constructed or undergoing total interior renovations.

WEB RESOURCE: www.ahma.com
American Hotel and Lodging Association.

WEB RESOURCE: www.artlot.com
Suppliers of low cost prints.

JUNKYARD SCULPTURES
★ $ 🏠 🕐

There are two ways to make money in a junkyard sculpture business. The first: create and sell art sculptures made from junkyard items. The second: supply art schools and artists with interesting junkyard items. In both instances a little bit of innovation can make you a lot of money. When my wife and I were first married, as with most newlyweds, our money was tight. Out of 50 percent inspiration and 50 percent desperation my wife decided to try and remedy the situation by creating a part-time income to supplement our family income. Her inspiration was to go to auto recycling yards and purchase old car springs for about 25 cents apiece. Once home, she sanded and painted the springs lively colors and placed silk flower arrangements inside. The recycled car springs became known as "Spring's Springs." She sold "Spring's Springs" to gift shops, garden centers, and interior designers on a wholesale basis, and it didn't take long until it became a full-time and very profitable venture. There are a great deal of business opportunities available; sometimes it just requires us to open our minds to imaginative ideas.

WEB RESOURCE: www.rengaarts.com/index.html
Unique ideas, listings of artists, and areas to promote work.

PAINTER
★ $ 🏠 🕒

Painting fine works of art definitely requires a great degree of talent, and if you possess this talent it is a wonderful way to make a living. As an artist you can paint commissioned and noncommissioned pieces. Commissioned paintings for corporations can be a very good way to stabilize your income. There are also many art galleries that will accept and display your artwork for a commission on the sale of the artwork. Either way, there is nothing like being self-employed in a business or profession that you enjoy and at which you can earn money, whether it is a good living or a part time income.

WEB RESOURCE: www.pearlpaint.com
Major supplier of art supplies.

PRINTS DEALER
★★ $$$

Whether you are the artist or someone else has created the original art, there is big money in prints. Art prints are relatively inexpensive to have produced and can retail for as much as $1,000 for a popular piece. Once you have chosen the works that will be reproduced, you can begin to sell the art prints. Set up a sales booth at a mall on a busy weekend at high-traffic flea market. You can also market the art prints to business professionals for office decorations or to interior designers for home decorations. I talked to one gentleman who operated an art print shop in an airport location. He told me that he was selling between 75 and 100 prints per week to business travelers who were taking the prints home as gifts. Assuming he only cleared an average $15 on each print after all expenses and taxes, he would still be earning more than $60,000 annually.

WEB RESOURCE: www.artlot.com
Suppliers of low cost prints

ART AUCTIONS
★★ $$ 🏠 🕒

Every home in North America features some sort of art as decoration. The market for art is enormous and continues to grow as our population expands. Starting an art auction and liquidation sales service is a great way to become your own boss. There are thousands of artists who have works that they cannot, or do not have the ability, to sell. Why not sell it for them? You can advertise the art auctions and liquidation sales in local newspapers, via e-mail, or fax broadcasts, and start making money right away. Start by visiting art schools and associations so you can begin to market your services to artists who want to sell their works. Once you have a few hundred works of art committed, you can hold the first art auction or sale. You will need to rent a temporary location for your "one-day art sale;" good locations include hotel ballrooms or banquet facilities. Room rental may not even cost any money providing you can convince the hotel manager potential food and drink concession sales will be sufficient for rent payment. The rest is straightforward; hold the first art auction or sale. You do not need to be an auctioneer to start and operate this type of business, just wear formal clothes for a professional appearance. Once you have perfected the business locally, you can duplicate the process and hold art auctions and sales across the country. Silent auctions can be very lucrative if you are not comfortable in the role of "auctioneer."

REQUIREMENTS: A computer, printer, scanner and digital camera will be advantageous when you start to catalog the art for listing purposes.

START-UP COSTS: The only cost associated with starting an art auction service is time and an initial advertising budget. Once you have established the approximate value of the items to be sold, you will be able to set an advertising budget. I would suggest about 5 to 10 percent of the estimated total sale value of the items to be sold at the art auction or sale. Total start-up costs are $5,000 to $10,000.

PROFIT POTENTIAL: You should be able to use a very basic formula for establishing a billing rate. Charge a 50 percent commission on all sales (no reserve pricing in effect), and allow half of the commission to cover the total overhead associated with the sale. Providing each sale averages $10,000 in gross revenues, and one show per month is conducted, the business would net $30,000 per year. Auctioneering is not always as easy as it looks, and a professional auctioneer can help you raise the bidding. Of course, this will add to your expenses, so you will need to weigh the potential advantage vs. cost factor.

WEB RESOURCE: www.auctioneers.org
The National Auctioneers Association will help you find an auctioneer in any part of the country.

MATTING AND FRAMING SHOP
★★ $$$

There is a lot of competition in the art framing and matting industry, and it can only mean one of two things. No one is making any money. Or, the second and more logical reasons is that this is big business and there is plenty of work, and profits, to go around. Framing stores are relatively inexpensive to start and operate and, like a lot of retail products and services sold, there are gigantic markup percentages placed on the wholesale costs of art and picture framing goods. A large markup allows most retail operations the ability to survive and continue to offer valuable products and services to consumers. Begin with researching your local market to determine if there is a demand for this service or room for an additional framing store. The business requires some special skills, in terms of making custom frames and cutting glass. However, both of these skills can be mastered in a short period of time, and you can generally find instruction classes offered on these subjects in your local community.

WEB RESOURCE: www.framingsupplies.com
Distributors of matting and framing supplies and equipment.

WALL MURALS
★ $$ 🏠 🕐 ⚖️

Many building and business owners are now having wall murals painted on large areas of their buildings (interior and exterior) for promotional purposes and as a method to deter graffiti. If you have the ability, or can form a group of people with the ability, to produce attractive wall murals, then you can make a lot of money operating your own custom wall mural painting service. Paint your first wall mural for free (with permission of course) and use the finished product as your presentation. I will guarantee you that no one else has a presentation portfolio like it. Approach businesses with photographs of your work, or email them samples of your work straight from your digital camera. Additionally, have a few suggestions and rough drafts of the wall mural you are proposing for their location with you to show during the presentation. It may take a few stops and presentations, but soon your art services will be in high demand. While searching for artists to help you paint, you can approach art students in nearby schools.

WEB RESOURCE: www.pearlpaint.com
A major supplier of art supplies.

CUSTOM AIRBRUSHING
★★★ $$ 🏠 🕐

Airbrush painting is very popular and has many uses including customizing cars, creating wall murals, decorating clothing, and creating one-of-a-kind paint finishes on almost any product. The equipment necessary for this business is inexpensive and can be ordered through art supply or paint supply stores. I contacted two businesses that offered custom airbrushing services; one was in the yellow pages, and the second was referred to me by an automotive body shop. In both instances, the charge to create custom airbrushed images was $60 per hour (plus material) with no guarantees on how long it would take to finish the job. Working a mere 25 hours a week providing airbrushing services can earn you as much as $70,000 per year.

WEB RESOURCE: www.airheadairbrush.com
Suppliers of airbrushing equipment and supplies.

NATIVE AMERICAN ART
★ $$ 🏚 🕐

Native peoples of the United States and Canada create some of the most beautiful art available and these artworks are in high demand, especially in overseas markets such as Japan, Germany, and the United Kingdom. The demand for native art creates a great business opportunity for you, if you have a good contact base in foreign countries. This business allows you to work as a highly compensated broker by representing native artists locally and using your international contacts to set up distribution channels in foreign countries. The business can also work in reverse. You can set up distribution channels in North America representing artists from foreign countries. The business does require a lot of research and set up time, but the potential rewards can justify the effort.

WEB RESOURCE: www.iaca.com
Indian Arts and Crafts Association.

MOBILE ART GALLERY
★★★ $$ 🏚 🕐

Once again, art is big business, and starting a mobile art gallery can put you on the road to riches. Take a traditional art gallery, place wheels on it, and you have this business opportunity in a nutshell. Maybe it is not that simple, but pretty close. In this enterprise you will want to work with perhaps a hundred artists or more. This is a volume-based operation. Once you have selected the artists, begin to establish locations where the artworks will be featured. Good locations include doctor office waiting rooms, office lobbies, restaurants, shopping malls, hospitals, and all other high-traffic gathering places. The art can be displayed in these locations with a small place card on each piece, which reads, "This art is for sale, for further information call (your business name and a toll-free number)." When a potential customer calls to inquire about a particular piece of art for sale, you would simply sell the art over the phone and arrange delivery to the purchaser. If a piece sells for $100 then you would give the artist $50, the host location $10 and keep $40 for yourself. As you can see, on a volume basis there is enormous potential for profit. Imagine if you had only 100 locations selling just two pieces of art per month at an average sale price of $150—you would stand to make more than $10,000 every month.

REQUIREMENTS: Operating a mobile art gallery business requires excellent cold calling, presentation, organization, and negotiation skills. You will also need reliable transportation and a computer to track and maintain customer files and inventory lists.

START-UP COSTS: The investment to set this business enterprise in motion is minimal, in the range of $8,000 to $10,000 will be sufficient to purchase any required equipment and leave enough working capital to operate on for a few months while the business is being established.

PROFIT POTENTIAL: Charging a flat commission of 40 percent for you, and generating gross sales of $250,000 per year will generate business revenues of $100,000. Once again, I stress that you must secure as many art installation locations or "silent salespeople" as you possibly can.

HAND-PAINTED CALENDARS
★★ $ 🏚 🕐

Small business and large corporations alike give away millions of calendars every year in hopes that they will be posted in a visible area and remind customers of their products and services. Starting a business that produces hand-painted calendars enables you to fill the growing market demand for calendars while making excellent profits for yourself. Hand-painted calendars make wonderful gifts for business owners to give to special customers and clients. Using watercolor paints to depict landscapes or pictorial themes, you can create the calendars quickly and inexpensively. Marketing the calendars can also be inexpensive. All that is required are a few samples of your work and some time to stop into businesses and present your talents. Or in other words, simply go out and ask for the business.

REQUIREMENTS: Watercolor painting techniques can be learned very easily, and there are many instruction classes available in almost every community to assist you in learning this painting technique. You will also need calendars to practice with, as well as providing you with an initial inventory. Of course if you find that your particular talents are better suited to the marketing side of the business, you can always enlist the services of hungry art students to produce the calendars.

START-UP COSTS: Even if you factor in the cost of art classes and materials to get started, the initial investment into this new venture will still be less than $500. If you choose the route of having others create the calendars for you, the start-up costs could be cut in half, unfortunately so will the profits.

PROFIT POTENTIAL: Hand-painted calendars retail in the price range of $60 to $100 each, and can go even higher if the theme is very elaborate. If you are painting the calendars yourself, you can keep your costs down to around $2 or $3 per calendar, including all materials. In terms of time to paint the 12 pictures required for the calendar, I am told by an artist friend that it would take about three to four hours in total to complete. Based on these figures you would expect to earn about $25 per hour, which is excellent for a business that can be started for less than $500.

HAND-PAINTED GREETING CARDS
★★ $ 📷 🕐

Like hand-painted calendars, there is large market demand for hand-painted greeting cards and postcards. Once again, if you have the ability to produce the finished product yourself, that's great. If not, there are many artists who will be glad to assist you for a fee. The greeting and postcards can be wholesaled to retailers or sold directly to companies to give as corporate gifts to clients. If you plan to specialize in hand-painted postcards, you will want to sell them in high-traffic tourist areas like airports, tourist attractions, and beaches. Whichever you decide, this business can be both fun and profitable, and best of all, it can be started for peanuts. Using some digital photographs of your work, you can easily market greeting cards, of calendars for that matter, on web sites, whether it is your own site or on the sites of other online businesses. While they may take a percentage of the profits, they also provide great exposure.

WEB RESOURCE: http://dmoz.org/Shopping/Gifts/Stationery
This large portal of mostly hand-made greeting cards is an excellent place in which to link your site for greater exposure.

PORTRAIT ARTIST OR ARTIST REPRESENTATIVE
★ $$ 📷 🕐

Once again, artistic talent does not need to be on your side for this new business enterprise. Person, pet, or object, many people wish to have something immortalized on canvas for a myriad of reasons. The first step will be to establish a working relationship with a few professional portrait artists or art students seeking income opportunities. Next, you will want to acquire some samples of their artwork and start to market your new business. Simply put, start asking around for businesses, professionals, pet shops, animal breeders, sports celebrities, and anyone else who may be interested in a painted portrait of themselves or of a loved one. The only requirement to get started is a good camera so that once you have secured a paying client you can take a picture of the subject for the artist to work from. This can also be accomplished by using a digital camera and emailing the photos to the artist. Revenues for your business will be by way of a 30 to 40 percent commission of the total selling price of the completed artwork.

ARTIST AGENT
★ $$ 📷 🕐

An artist agent is the same as any other industry agent. You represent and market the talents or skills of one artist or several. Remuneration is by way of a commission charged on work sold; generally the commission rate is between 10 and 20 percent of the total selling value of the art. Why would an artist seek to be represented by an agent? For greater exposure and recognition, negotiation experience, privacy, marketing abilities, contacts, and various other resources that may not be available to the artists themselves. If you are considering becoming an artists' agent, you will definitely need the aforementioned skills and have to be prepared to research the art industry in great depth. This type of business does have a very steep learning curve. With proper preparation, working as an artist agent can be a very rewarding profession, both financially and personally. However, you must have connections, or establish them, in galleries and any places in which buyers gather. Additionally, you need to be a very good judge of what might sell commercially. It will take some time to establish yourself in this field and gain a reputation.

FRAMED MOVIE POSTERS
★★ $$ 🏠 🕐

Movie posters can often be purchased for less than $1 each from video stores and movie theaters. Once framed, these valuable pieces of art can be resold at flea markets, mall kiosks, and to interior designers for terrific profits. Older movie posters are also in high demand as collector items, and this side of the business is best suited for internet sales. You can develop your own web site for a small investment and start marketing collectible movie posters. There are guides available that list the value of collectable movie posters depending on condition. These guides will be an invaluable source of information if you intend to offer collectible movie posters for sale. In addition, theater posters are also valuable collectibles, particularly from shows that have been on Broadway.

WEB RESOURCE: www.filmsite.org/posters.html
A comprehensive movie poster dealer, this can give you an idea of the cost of movie posters prior to your adding the frame.

CHARCOAL PORTRAITS
★ $ 🕐

Can you produce attractive charcoal portraits of people in a very short time frame? If not, you may want to take some courses so you can, as people portraits created from charcoal drawings is one of the greatest all time "cash" art business that can be started. We have all seen street artists who produce quick charcoal portraits of people. These portraits usually cost $20 and the artist receives cash, sometimes for as many as five an hour on a busy day. Your math skills do not have to be good to know that adds up to $100 an hour for about $2 or $3 worth of art supplies. Perhaps traveling to foreign destinations is your dream. If so, this is the perfect business opportunity for you. With little more than a passport, suitcase, and a few art supplies, you could easily work your way around the world producing charcoal portraits in every tourist Mecca. Just check to make sure you are not breaking any laws—in many cities you will need a permit to work, and sell, on the streets.

WEB RESOURCE: www.misterart.com
Put in the word "charcoal" in the search box and you will find more than 150 charcoal products to choose from.

CARICATURES
★ $ 🏠 🕐

Big, easily recognizable heads and faces with small bodies is funny stuff, especially if the caricature is of a person we know and do business with. If you do not have the skills to draw caricatures yourself (and most people do not), then hire, and represent, a caricature artist who is prepared to work on a piecework basis and market caricature drawings to local business owners and for parties. You will be amazed at the interest you will receive right out of the blocks. Restaurants will purchase caricatures of their staff to adorn the front of menus, professionals will purchase a caricature of themselves to send to clients in the form of a thank-you card, and retail businesses will purchase caricatures of valued regular customers to hang above the cash register. People love having caricatures drawn of their friends or themselves at parties and celebrity caricatures are always a hit. This is a great business enterprise to put into action as it only requires a little bit of creativity to ignite, about $2,000 to do some marketing and launch a web site, and, of course, a talented caricaturist. While this is not typically a way of getting rich, it is a fun means of making some extra income.

MIRROR ART
★ $ 🏠 🕐

Mirror art is simply small pieces of mirror in varying colors and shapes that have been assembled together to resemble a picture, landscape or even abstract design. Mirror art is becoming very trendy for use as home decorations. In most cases a trip to your local glass shop will result in all the mirror you will need for this new venture, and usually at no cost. Why? Most glass shops dispose of mirror cutoff pieces that are too small to sell, but these same pieces of mirror are perfectly sized to create mirror art. The equipment needed to create the art is inexpensive and includes a few hand tools and a glass grinder. Also, patterns are available to make the mirror art or you can create your own. Once completed, the art can be sold via flea market booths, on a web site or to interior decorators and designers.

WEB RESOURCE: www.mirrorart.com
Inexpensive mirrors can be found at this large portal.

STENCILING
★★ $ 🏠 🕐

Specializing in custom stenciling is a fantastic low-investment business you can start and manage right from a homebased office. In the past few years stenciling has once again become a popular interior decorating art medium. The uses vary from decorative wall borders to creating beautiful patterns on cabinet doors. To get started all you have to do is practice. There are many how-to books and videos available that will teach you specific secrets and methods about creative paint stenciling. Basic materials that will be required include paint, paintbrushes, additional paint applicators, and pre-designed stenciling templates. Of course if you have creative flair, you can design your own custom stenciling templates. A paint stenciling service is best marketed by way of referral or word-of-mouth advertising. It may take a little longer to establish a client base this way, however, the extra time will enable you to gain valuable stenciling practice and experience for your new service.

WEB RESOURCE: www.misterart.com
Enter the word "stencil" into the search box and you will find plenty of stenciling materials.

SCULPTOR
★★ $$ 🏠 🕐

While becoming a sculptor may or may not make you rich, it is certainly one of the oldest professions, with early sculptures dating back about 32,000 years. Obviously, a passion for "making things" and a bit of talent are two prerequisites for success as a sculptor. However, the field is open for great interpretive and creative experimentation.

You can work with clay, metal, wood, marble, or a combination of household junk that is carved, cast, welded, or shaped in any of a variety of manners. Along with trying to get your work into galleries, you can take your work straight to architects, designers, building planners, and anyone who buys art for hotels, corporate offices, restaurants, or any public gathering place. Sculptors are also hired to create props for movies and theater and some create busts or sculptures for individuals being honored by associations, hospitals, corporations, etc. Whether or not you choose to seek out commercial work or commissioned assignments is up to you. However, a career in sculpting can be very gratifying as well as financially rewarding if your work is good.

WEB RESOURCE: www.sculpturetools.com
Tools of the trade.

CARTOONIST
★★ $ 🏠 🕐

Funny, poignant, silly, off-color... there are numerous ways to describe the cartoons we see in magazines, books, newspapers, advertisements, and on web sites. Political cartoons, in particular, always seem to be in vogue. If you have a knack for drawing, you can serve as a commercial cartoonist for any type of publishing or advertising. To market your skills, you'll need to put together a portfolio of your best work and set up appointments to meet editorial directors, publishers, editors, writers, and/or art directors, any of whom may need your services. Some cartoonists work on their own, meaning you will create the message behind the cartoon yourself, while others team with someone else who comes up with the concept, the captions, or both. Good cartoonists, working for major newspapers can make upwards of $70,000 annually, while freelancers can do well if they establish a niche (i.e., political cartoons) and work regularly for several clients.

WEB RESOURCE: www.reuben.org
National Cartoonists Society.

BOOK ILLUSTRATOR
★★★ $ 🏠 🕐

If you love to draw and have ability, here's a great way to make some nice profits doing what you enjoy. To start, put together a portfolio of book covers and illustrations for non-existent books, or even your visions for existing books. These will serve as samples for you to show clients, who will include book publishers, book packagers, agents, and authors—any of whom can hire you to illustrate forthcoming books. You may want to specialize in a particular area such as children's books. Royalties for illustrating a children's book are typically a 50/50 split with the author as is also the case with the advance. However, an illustrator who is hired to do x number of drawings for a fiction or non-fiction book may be paid per illustration, which will be determined by the market for the type of book, the size of the publishing house, and other factors.

WEB RESOURCE: www.picturebookartists.org
Picture Book Artists Association.

FASHION ILLUSTRATOR
★★ $ 🏠 🕐

Specializing in an industry can make it easier to get work because you will have mastered specific skills. In some cases, depending on the specialty, there is less competition. In the case of fashion illustration, however, you will face some steep competition. Fortunately there are many possible avenues from which to seek work. If you have the technical and drawing skills, plus proficiency on the computer, and a good eye for detail, you can draw fashions and their many accessories (hats, handbags, etc.) for periodicals, advertising agencies, department stores, retailers, catalogues, galleries, and designers, just to name a few of the possibilities. As is typically the case with a career in the visual arts, you will need to have a portfolio of your work, which today means the actual large portfolio book, the CD-Rom version, and a web site that you can direct people to for samples. Most often, you can run your career as a fashion illustrator from your home office/studio. Start-up costs are minimal and, if you are good, there is a tremendous upside to this business, depending on how well you market yourself.

SKETCH ARTIST
★★ $ 🏠 🕐

"Could you give us a description of the criminal?" asks the prosecutor or police detective, at which time someone whips out a sketch pad and begins drawing based on the account of the witness. That someone could be you, if you have the ability to draw quickly and accurately based on what is being described. A specialized skill indeed, but one that can get you a lot of work in the law enforcement industry and your local court system. You can get your feet wet in the field by drawing for local newspapers and for special events while taking some time to learn and research law enforcement and how such sketches are used to track down criminals. Unlike some of the more creative aspects of art, this field requires you to draw as realistically

as possible. Market yourself to law enforcement agencies, county clerks offices, and the media that cover court trials.

MEDICAL ILLUSTRATOR
★★ $ 🏠 🕐

A specialized profession, medical illustrators can earn anywhere from $40,000 to over $100,000 with good skills and steady clients. Along with the ability to draw well, a medical illustrator needs to be proficient and knowledgeable when it comes to human anatomy. Much of the work for a medical illustrator comes from textbook publishers, medical journals, and drug companies that need to illustrate how a medication works on the human body. Market your skills to medical publishers, medical web sites, pharmaceutical companies, and hospitals, since they also produce a great deal of literature, much of which needs illustrations. Networking and marketing skills will help you significantly when looking for clients since this is a specialized market.

WEB RESOURCE: www.mcg.edu/medart
Department of Medical Illustration, Medical College of Georgia.

ANIMATION
★★★★ $$ 🏠 🕐

Whether you are a freelance animator or intent upon opening your own animation studio, there is a lot of work for good animators who know how to use computer software to enhance their creative visions. Commercially, you can market animation skills to film and production companies as well as advertising agencies, architectural design houses, interior designers, and the makers of video games, DVDs, and CD-ROMS. Familiarize yourself with software tools and packages such as PhotoShop, SoftImage, Alias/Wavefront, Maya, and others. If you are working on your own, create a portfolio that provides 2D and 3D examples of your abilities, since the basic 2D line drawing is still at the center of this craft.

START-UP COSTS: $2,000-$3,000 for computer software and for marketing yourself. If you elect to open a studio, obviously there will be higher overhead costs as you will be paying for the space. A good freelance animator can make upwards of $50,000 with regular clients. If, however, you secure the rights to original characters and they are utilized for books, films, or other mediums, you can make a lot more money through royalty agreements. Have a lawyer on hand, so you do not lose out on great sums of money if you create the next animated star. Too many stories of the artist signing away all rights have been told over the years including that of the original creator of Superman.

WEB RESOURCE: www.animationguild.org

STORYBOARD ARTIST
★★ $$ 🏠 🕐

Storyboard artists help draw the basic concepts from the pages of a script for television shows, films, cartoons, commercials, and videos. You could use your drawing skills to work with directors and producers in such a capacity. Be forewarned that this is a very competitive industry, with many film storyboard artists holding high-level degrees in the field. It is to your advantage to take courses in computer animation, which is a growing aspect of the film industry. Computer and art schools now offer specialized degrees for students who are looking for a way to get into the animation field, so you may choose this route prior to starting in the field.

Once you have honed your skills, look for work from production companies, advertising agencies, and independent producers and directors. New, up-and-coming directors and producers may not have a lot of money to afford the well-established storyboard artists, allowing you to get in the door with your first storyboard clients by charging less. Once you establish yourself as a storyboard artist, $65,000 is the average salary, with much higher possibilities, and there is very little in the way of overhead.

GRAPHIC DESIGNER
★★★★ $$ 🏠 🕐

Graphic art is big business today and college courses and programs are very competitive as more and more people head into the field. Fortunately, there is a tremendous need for graphic art, from product packaging to marketing to signage and so on. It is your job, in most cases, to work with designers and printers to communicate the message of the manufacturer or retailer. This is a multi-step process, as you will need to create and recreate depending on the needs and wishes of your clients and the practical and logistical design aspects of the work. If you are good at creating an overall image for a company and designing the product packaging, marketing, print ads, and so forth to present that image, you can generate a lot more business. Additionally, the better you are at solving visual, image, design, and marketing problems, the easier it will be to wow new clients. As a graphic designer, you can start as a homebased business and seek to share studio space once you have outgrown your home office. Most graphic designers charge by the project, which will require you to stay on top of the going rates in your area. Graphic design for architectural and engineering firms generates higher rates. Either way, you can make upwards of $60,000 with little overhead as a graphic designer. Should you open your own graphic design firm, while you will have far greater overhead with employees and equipment, in time you can pull in six figures.

WEB RESOURCE: www.aiga.org
American Institute of Graphic Arts

SAND ART
★ $ 🏠 🕐

All you need is colorful sand, uniquely shaped bottles, and/or a terrarium and you are all set. Millions of people love sand art and it is both inexpensive and decorative. In fact, for a few hundred dollars you can launch a home-based business whereby you can use your creative skills to make a profit. In addition to selling the finished products, you can also purchase sand art kits for wholesale and sell them at a 100% mark up. A booth at a local fair or mall can be an excellent place to kick off this part time business. You can also sell through local retailers.

RESTORATION SERVICE
★★ $$ 🏠 🕐

Over the course of time, paintings begin to lose their color or turn yellow, paint begins to crack and bronze statues begin to tarnish. If you have the skills to carefully and patiently restore artwork, you can start a successful business. Other than the tools to work on the art, there are few start-up costs involved.

You may specialize, working on canvas and paper restoration or on bronze sculpture, marble, antiques, and tapestries. An eye for detail is essential and studying restoration techniques with master restorers can help you build your reputation. You may opt to work on pieces of lesser value to get your feet wet in this business endeavor.

CHAINSAW ART
★★ $$ 🏚 🕐

Who said you needed a delicate touch to be an artist? If you've got a chainsaw, protective gear, and an imagination, you can take the plunge into one of the latest art forms to catch on. Chainsaw art is basically sculpture that is created from large pieces of wood, including cedar, oak, palm, and deadwood. It usually features animals, especially bears, of different sizes and shapes; some pieces are painted and others not. Works typically sell for anywhere from $50 to $1,500 depending on the size and complexity of the work. You can set up your own gallery, use a web site to display your work and reach a larger audience and/ or sell to local art shops, as well as gift shops. Chainsaw art is growing in popularity, but it is not easy to do—you need to practice and by all means be careful!

WEB RESOURCE: www.chainsaws.com

NOTES:

_____

_____

_____

_____

_____

_____

_____

_____

_____

_____

_____

_____

_____

_____

_____

_____

49
CHILD-RELATED
Businesses You Can Start

CLOTH DIAPER SERVICE
★★★ $$ 🏠 🕐 🌐 ⚖️ 🍃

The not-so-sweet smells of success! Disposable diapers are not environmentally friendly and can often irritate a baby's skin. The solution? Environmentally-friendly cloth diapers made of natural fibers. A baby can go through as many as 4,000 diapers before being fully toilet-trained, and this fact of life creates an outstanding business opportunity. Depending on your business start-up budget, there are two methods of pursuing this venture. In the first, you offer a complete service, meaning you supply, deliver, and pick up the cloth diapers, and you also clean the diapers. The second start-up method is to simply supply delivery and pickup of the diapers and have an established commercial laundry clean them. If start-up capital is not a problem, the first option will definitely leave more profits for you. To market a cloth diaper service, try to obtain a list of new baby births from local hospitals. If these lists are not available, start to scan newspapers for birth announcements. Once you have compiled a list of potential clients, simply drop off or mail a marketing presentation to parents outlining the benefits of your service and how they can contact you. Once you have a number of regular clients you can also buy cloth diapers in bulk and sell them along with baby powder.

WEB RESOURCE: www.littlesproutsdiapers.com
One of several online sources for purchasing diapers.

BICYCLE SAFETY COURSES
★★ $ 🏠 🕐 🌐

Thousands of children are seriously injured each year as a result of bicycling accidents. Many of these accidents and injuries could have been avoided had the children and parents attended a cycling safety instruction course. Here is your opportunity to not only start your own business, but also provide a service that can help prevent needless cycling accidents involving children. A bicycle safety instruction service can be initiated on a shoestring budget and operated on a year-round basis using all of the latest bicycling safety methods and equipment. The total investment cost to get you going will be under $1,000, including marketing and promotional materials and bicycle safety equipment. In terms of an operating location, a roped-off section of a parking lot would be ideal in the summer and an indoor school gymnasium or a recreation center would be great for wintertime classes. In both cases you will be required to get permission and possibly pay a small amount of rent. Incorporate bicycle repairs and maintenance tips into your cycling safety course as they can be used as terrific marketing tools. Selling safety equipment can bring in additional income. Before starting out on this venture, read up on the latest in preventative measures and know the bike laws in your community.

WEB RESOURCE: www.bicyclinginfo.org/
Pedestrian and bicycle information center.

BRONZE BABY SHOES
★★ $$ 🔒 🕐

For preserving baby shoes, toys, or keepsakes, a bronzing service is a surefire winner. Low investment, low overhead, and little competition means big profits for you. To get started in a bronzing service you will need to invest a small amount of money into bronzing equipment and samples, and you should launch a basic web site. Start by simply producing samples of your bronzing work and locate the sample items in every baby or child-related store in your community. Provide the retailers with order forms, bags, and nametags for the items to be bronzed. Also post some photos of your work on your web site. Customers can then either drop off the items they want bronzed and pick them up from the same retailer a week later or have items delivered to you at a postal box or at your home address. Then have them pay the additional fee for shipping the items back to them. If you work in conjunction with retailers, they should receive a percentage of the cost. You should also provide the retailer with a sales price list. There should be no problem in getting retailers on board, as they are not required to buy or warehouse any inventory for you.

PARTY ENTERTAINMENT SERVICE
★★ $ 🔒 🕐

There are a couple of options available in terms of starting a party entertaining service. You can work as an agency representing entertainers for children's parties, or, you can be an entertainer yourself, if you have the required skills. The different types of entertainers for children's parties include clowns, magicians, trained pet shows, singers, and skit plays. This is a relatively low-investment business to start and operate, and the profit potential is very good. I contacted four different agencies and found the average rate for party entertainers to be $50 per hour with a minimum charge for one and a half hours including travel. Make sure all of the acts are suitable for children and any costumes worn are not scary. It is also very important that you work with entertainers who are reliable, so check references carefully. It is very disappointing to a child when an entertainer does not show up for his or her party, and it can also destroy your reputation since

this is very much a word of mouth business. Representing entertainers for parties, or being an entertainer yourself, is a good homebased business that allows for flexible hours, good income potential, and loads of fun.

WEB RESOURCE: www.costumecraze.com
Costumes ranging from clowns to TV personalities.

DAY-CARE CENTER
★★ $$ 🌐 ⚖️

The rising cost of living has made child day care a booming industry simply due to the fact that most families today require two full-time incomes just to survive financially. There are various types of day-care centers, such as homebased, storefront locations, mall and business locations, and mobile day care, and all have their benefits and drawbacks. Once you have determined the operating location and type of day care, the next step will be to get parents to bring their children. This can be accomplished in many ways, and a good starting point is a strong marketing presentation. Parents today want to know their children will be safe, happy, well cared for, and mentally stimulated. I recently visited a day-care center that was very successful, and the key to their success was the fact they installed video cameras in every part of their day-care facility. The digital video cameras gave the day-care center the ability to broadcast over the internet via their web site. What a great idea. Parents at work were able to check on and watch their children anytime they wanted to simply by logging onto the day-care web site.

REQUIREMENTS: In almost all areas of North America, day-care centers and staff require certification. It is very important that you meet all requirements and in most cases you strive to exceed these legal requirements. You will also be required to carry liability insurance and have on-site safety equipment such as first-aid kits, fire safety equipment, and well-thought out emergency action plans. You will also need to determine how many children you can accommodate. Typically the ratio of adults to children needs to be a small one (such as three to one for infants and toddlers, or five to one for preschoolers) to gain the trust of the parents (and possibly for licensing requirements). This means you may need to hire some reliable people, preferably with a background in childcare or early childhood education. College or graduate students, majoring in education, or simply good with kids, may be a good fit. Screen all applicants carefully. If your approach is professional and very well planned, you will have no difficulty in charging a premium over other competing day-care services in your community.

START-UP COSTS: Homebased day-care facilities can cost as little as $5,000 to establish, while full-scale day-care centers operating from an independent business location can cost as much as $100,000 to start. Of course, zoning laws may force you to put the brakes on a homebased day-care business.

PROFIT POTENTIAL: Once you have established the type of day care you will be operating, the next step will be to factor in all overheads and establish a cost per child to provide your service. You will then add a markup or profit margin onto this cost to establish a retail price. Regardless of the size or type of service you provide, you can expect a healthy return on investment. You should have no difficulties earning in excess of $40,000 per year.

WEB RESOURCE: www.nccanet.org
National Child Care Association.

CHILDREN'S PARTY SERVICE
★★ $$ 🏠 🕒

Every day thousands of children have birthdays, graduate to the next grade, or just deserve some fun, and all of these events are a very good reason to celebrate and have a party. The main consideration for starting this type of party service is whether the business will be operated from a fixed location or on a mobile basis. Once you have established the base of operations, you can begin to market the party service. A great starting point will be a well-designed and colorful marketing brochure describing your service. Set up a web site with prices and various party theme possibilities. Tap into what today's kids are interested in and then create themes for different age groups. Offer a variety of well-planned two-hour party packages and make the party service a one-stop shopping experience, which includes a choice of party favors, cakes, and other food as well. It's not a bad idea to include some educational value too, if you can make the kids think it's fun. If you do set up a fixed location from which to hold the parties, you will need to look into liability insurance before opening your doors. Then set up the space to be completely child-friendly. See if you can find a location with plenty of space, good lighting, few stairs, and ample parking before opening a party zone, so to speak.

WEB RESOURCES: www.partypalooza.com and
www.birthdayexpress.com
Great places to find supplies and get party theme ideas.

EDUCATIONAL TOYS
★ $$ 🏠 🕒

Traditional educational toys and games for children will always be popular and in demand. You can design and develop the toys and games yourself or act as an agent for manufacturers. Both methods can be a very profitable way to earn an income and be self-employed. There are various approaches to marketing educational toys and games including the internet, mail order, home parties, flea markets, and sales to specialty retailers on a wholesale basis. A unique marketing method may be to hold free seminars for parents with a central theme—perhaps "improve your child's reading skills." The seminar would state all the facts and benefits that improved reading comprehension has for their children. Of course, during the free seminar you would promote the products you want the parents to purchase at the conclusion. If you choose this route, be sure to establish alliances with experts in the field of child education to speak at the seminars on the subject of the benefits of educational children's toys and games.

WEB RESOURCE: www.globalsources.com/manufacturers/
Educational-Toy.html
Educational toys from a variety of toy manufacturers.

PIÑATA SALES
★★ $ 🏠 🕒

This is one of my favorite business start-up enterprises of all the opportunities featured in the children's chapter of the directory. What a great business and concept—homebased, unique, low overhead, minimal start-up costs, virtually no competition, and no limitations on business growth and expansion. Thousands of children's parties take place every day, and tapping into this very lucrative market is easy. Simply develop samples of your products, create (and distribute) brochures, and set up a web site. I will guarantee that you will find little resistance to your product, and chances are the biggest business challenge you will face is trying to keep up with the demand for the piñatas. I suggest that you strictly focus on the wholesale market and establish accounts with retail children's stores, party planners, and online retailers of children's products. Try to get your product into as many mail-order catalogs as possible.

REQUIREMENTS: The largest is creativity, in both manufacturing the piñatas and how you will market them. Of course there are always the safety concerns, so be sure to place prizes inside that cannot harm, spoil, or create potential liability for you.

START-UP COSTS: It should cost you less than $200 to develop your samples and possibly another $500 to begin marketing your products. This is the ultimate quick return on investment business.

PROFIT POTENTIAL: I purchased a piñata that retailed for $80 and was based on a birthday sports theme. Upon returning home and careful examination, I determined that it would require about an hour to make the piñata using $5 worth of materials. Inside this particular piñata I found hard candy and a toy prize, maybe another $2-3 worth. Even at $25 per hour, the total cost to manufacture this product would be in the $30 range. This still allows for a 30 percent markup on your material costs and labor, while the retailer can maintain a 100 percent markup. Now you see why there will be no problem in establishing wholesale accounts with retailers, especially if you can come up with some colorful, unique looking piñatas.

WEB RESOURCES: www.bry-backmanor.org/holidayfun/pinata.html and www.coolest-kid-birthday-parties.com/make-pinata.html
Piñata making instructions.

PERSONALIZED STORY TIME BOOKS
★★★ $$$ 🚗 🕐 🌐

The market for personalized story time books for children is enormous. Every child in the world loves to hear stories, and the best aspect of this new venture is the fact that this business enables you to create books that include children in the story. This is a business that once you have established a relationship with a client you will want to keep that relationship strong as the product has the ability to almost be classified as a consumable. This means that once you form the relationship with the client, it is a given that the relationship will continue to generate revenues for the business, providing the quality of service and product remains excellent. The average child can easily have five or six favorite books, and these books change on a year-by-year basis. This can add up to 20 to 30 different story time books that can be sold to the same client, and that number can multiply by the number of children the client has. There are software applications available including the reprint rights for creating this type of book, or of course you can use the customer's and your imagination to create original stories. A marketing technique that can help get you started is to pick relatives and friends with children and customize books using their children's names. Once you have the books produced, simply show the story time books to your friends and relatives. It will be nearly impossible for them to say no once they see the finished product and how much work you put into creating the book.

REQUIREMENTS: You will need a good computer system and printer if you plan to produce the books yourself. It can be very costly to have a print shop run a single copy of one item. Additional requirements will include software that legally allows you to reprint the books or good writing skills to create your own stories. The latter is more fun, and you can base the stories on your local community and community events.

START-UP COSTS: The business can be started on a modest budget of less than $10,000, which will include all the necessary computer equipment, software programs, and an initial supplies inventory.

PROFIT POTENTIAL: Once you have established a solid client base, this business venture has the ability to return excellent profits on a part- or full-time effort. As with any business, be sure to use a bottom up approach to product pricing. Factor in all costs, including materials, labor, and overheads, and multiply by the desired markup. The end result of this formula will give you your retail selling price.

WEB RESOURCE: www.hefty.com
Distributors of create-a-book software and printing equipment.

COLORING BOOKS
★★ $$$ 🚗 🕐 🌐

The main focus of this business enterprise is to personalize children's coloring books. The equipment requirements and approach to marketing are very similar to that of the story time book venture. However, an additional marketing technique that can be employed is to design a retail sales kiosk, and locate the kiosk in a busy community mall on weekends. This kind of retail location will enable you to personalize and sell the coloring books right on site. Remember, do not limit your ability to generate revenue. With the right software, you can also produce children's "u-color-it posters," restaurant placemats, and even specialty greeting cards, all of which can also be sold via the sales kiosk, as well as at flea markets and fairs, to increase revenues and profits.

CHILDREN'S BOOKS AND SOFTWARE STORE
★★ $$$$

The name says it all. In terms of a specialty retail business, this is one of the best. On the book side, try to stock hard-to-find titles covering a wide range of topics revolving around children's interaction and involvement. On the software side of the business, try to include software applications for children and for parents to do with children. Good topics include games, education, how to, instruction, music, sports, and family relationships. You will not need a lot of floor space for the store as all of the items that are stocked are very compact. Of course, you can't forget "location, location, location." Be sure the store is located in a high-traffic and visible area of the community. Furthermore, you may even want to consider being a "retail store within a retail store." Excellent matches for this type of retailing arrangement include large children's clothing retailers, toy stores, and family entertainment centers. To compete with the mega-stores, you can maximize your success by having various in-store promotional

activities, such as inviting children's authors to come and read from their books. You can also have a story-telling room where an adult can read to children after school, and even various children's reading clubs for all ages. A web site and/or newsletter (e-mail or printed) can feature your upcoming in-store activities as well as your latest arrivals.

WEB RESOURCE: www.abfc.com
Association of Booksellers for Children

CHILDREN'S BOOKS BY CHILDREN
★★ $$$ 🚗 🕐

Starting a publishing business that specializes in publishing children's books written by children is a very unique and interesting business enterprise to set in motion. In addition to the books being available in print, they can also be on CD-ROM as well as in an e-book format sold via the internet. The books can be on numerous topics and subjects such as puzzles and games, short stories, and comics. Marketing the books can be by way of establishing wholesale accounts with retailers as well as establishing alliances with children's charity groups, schools, after school and community centers.

NURSERY DESIGNER
★★★ $$ 🚗 🕐 🚗

I recently visited a designer who works from her home and exclusively designs baby nurseries for expecting parents. During this meeting, I gained great insights into this business and how to market this service. First lesson is to throw away everything you know about marketing and promote your service solely on "goo goo ga ga" (as the designer puts it). What she means is that most of the decisions expecting parents make in terms of a baby nursery defy logic and are made on an emotional basis. Her secret to business success is to promote her design talents using elaborate displays at any trade show that is even closely associated with babies and children. This method of marketing enabled her to build a solid client and referral base, with very little (if any) competition at these trade shows. Of course, there are additional marketing options that are open to you in terms of promoting the design service, including working with architects, interior designers, retail children's stores, web sites geared to parents, and custom homebuilders. If you can afford to purchase special design software, do it. This will give you an advantage when you present your ideas and concepts to potential clients. Most of this software allows you to build a 3D virtual tour model of the new room on your computer; just make sure that your notebook computer will support these programs so you have the ability to make your presentations mobile.

REQUIREMENTS: Like any design business, you will need a flair for the dramatic plus solid design skills. You don't need formal training in most areas of the country as you are not generally changing the structure of the building. However, any certification credentials that you have will definitely be a great marketing tool to use in the business. There are numerous schools offering interior design and/or decorating courses that can get you started.

START-UP COSTS: Providing you already have a computer, the investment capital required to get a nursery design service up and rolling will be less than $10,000.

PROFIT POTENTIAL: Excellent. The above-mentioned nursery designer is netting in excess of $80,000 per year after expenses.

WEB RESOURCE: www.baby-place.com/furniture.php
A portal with links to numerous suppliers of baby furniture and hand made accessories for a nursery.

CARDBOARD PLAYHOUSES
★★★ $$ 🏠 🕐 🍃

Have you ever purchased a new refrigerator, only to find that your children play with the empty box for weeks instead of playing with their expensive toys? Now is your chance to capitalize on this strange phenomenon. Custom cardboard playhouses are great for kids. They are mobile and can be packed up easily and moved to the beach, Grandma's house, or outside in the summer. To get mobilized in this business, simply design your own playhouse and visit a box manufacturer for an estimate to produce the cardboard playhouses in volume. The playhouses can be sold via retail accounts, mail order, the internet, craft shows, and flea markets. Using recycled materials can make this a very environmentally friendly endeavor. Design tip: Be sure the cardboard playhouses

will be interesting to children, and make sure there are a lot of colorful images and themes printed on them.

WEB RESOURCE: www.argrov.com
Manufacturer and distributor of made-to-order cardboard boxes.

SANDBOX MANUFACTURING
★★★ $$$ 🏠 🕐

Custom sandboxes are the new hot product in the children's play equipment industry. These are not the normal 5-foot by 5-foot poorly crafted wood boxes, but new mega-sandboxes based on a theme, such as outer space, cowboys, or racecars. One manufacturer, whom I recently spoke to, expanded his operation of six full-time employees to more than ten, just to keep up with the demand of building and installing his custom "Sand Play Centers" as he refers to them. This may be a great opportunity for you to introduce custom sandboxes into your area, given the number of children and backyards in this country. Even if there is competition, there should still be enough business to go around. The first step will be to design and develop your own products or to find an existing manufacturer and promote their products, preferably under your own company and brand name. Selling the sandboxes should not be difficult. Basically, once you have a sample, simply start to establish alliances with other companies in your community that also specialize in children's products. Likewise, displaying and marketing your products at home and garden trade shows can also be an excellent forum to introduce and promote your new products.

REQUIREMENTS: If you plan to design and manufacture your own custom sandboxes, you will probably be required to register the product to safety standards. You may also need specialized manufacturing equipment and skilled staff. Research various kinds of manufacturing material to find out what will best suit your particular application, and make your product safe, durable, and easy to maintain.

START-UP COSTS: Beware. This type of new business venture has a way of costing two or even three times as much as anticipated to start. The reason is that when you are dealing with an item that is custom designed the process of building a prototype can be very long and include many changes throughout the design process; all of this starts to add up in terms of development costs. However, with careful planning and keeping a tight control on budgets, a business that manufactures and installs custom sandboxes can be successfully initiated for $25,000.

KITE BUILDING AND SALES
★★★ $$ 🏠 🕐

Starting part-time from your home you can manufacture one-of-a-kind kites and sell them locally through retail accounts, kiosks, mail order, and the internet. The investment needed to put this business in action is less than $500, and the operating overheads are virtually nonexistent. On a recent vacation to Cannon Beach, Oregon, I was amazed to find a retail store that specialized only in kites. For the hour or so that I was there browsing around at least 15 to 20 people walked through the door and many left with a purchase. To get started you can buy some sample kites to find out what material is used to manufacture the kites and how they are constructed. The store I visited even had "how to build kites" books, videos, and kits. A great promotional idea for the business may be to have a "try before you buy" kite sale. Simply advertise the event in local newspapers, and let potential customers try out the kites before they purchase one. You can hold this event in a local park or at the beach. One thing is for sure: It will not take long before a crowd assembles to see what is going on.

WEB RESOURCE: www.aka.kite.org
American Kite Fliers Association.

DOLL MAKING
★★ $ 🏠 🕐

It may not seem like it, but doll making and repairs is a giant segment of the craft and toy industry. To research this, simply visit an antique shop that specializes in antique dolls or a retailer of new, custom, one-of-a-kind dolls, and you will soon see that the prices are out of this world. Like kite building, doll making can be started from home on a part-time basis. Once again, the dolls you make can be sold through retail accounts, mail order, craft shows, and the internet. This is an enterprise that requires very little in the way of start-up investment, and the ongoing monthly overhead adds up to what it costs to

buy a bag of groceries. Once you have sharpened your skills in doll making, you can proceed to antique doll repairs. Some of the antique dolls that I came across were selling for as much as $500 for the "real thing" and $300 for replicas of the original version. To get started in this aspect of the business, find out if doll-making classes are available in your local community. If you find that these types of classes are not available in your community, then once you have mastered the art of doll making and repairs you can begin to hold your own "how-to" classes on nights and weekends to earn additional income. Do not forget that in the doll world all of these creations need accessories such as houses, cars, clothes, kitchens, and other doll friends, thus a further opportunity exists.

WEB RESOURCE: www.thedollnet.com
Portal with links to suppliers and industry information.

SPECIALTY CAMPS FOR CHILDREN
★★ $$$$ 🕐

Every year, millions of parents shuffle their children off to various types of camps for a myriad of reasons. Typically these camps run for one- to three-week sessions during the summer and you can plan for two or three sessions if you can secure the location and the staff to do so. You can also run this camp during different times of the year. Try to make your camp all-inclusive. For example, in the case of an acting camp, this would include a child's acting resume, headshot, and on-air tape or a final on-stage theater production to which the campers invite family and friends to watch them perform. There are numerous themes for camps, including dance camps, art camps, photography camps, and even heritage camps for children adopted from other nations where they learn about their heritage and meet children of their same ethnic background. To run a camp, you will typically need some type of certification for working with children, a great rapport with kids, skills in the area you are featuring, liability insurance, a staff (typically older teens), and a location that adheres to safety requirements and also meets your needs. The beauty of such specialty camps is that you do not typically need the vast acreage of sleep-away camps or traditional day camps. Marketing will require a savvy campaign, including brochures, free information seminars, a web site, and possibly even a noted professional spokesperson in the profession of the camp you are hosting.

CHILDREN'S PERSONAL SAFETY COURSES
★★ $$ 🚗 🕒

Generally speaking we live in a relatively safe society. However, crime still affects all of our lives at some point. Of course, we always hope that our children will never be victims of criminal acts. Criminal acts can be in the form of personal attacks on our children or in the form of having children involved in a criminal act. Another leading concern today is the safety of internet use by kids and teens. This scenario can be the basis of your new business. You can hold courses and/or seminars for parents and children on how to prevent, react to, and understand criminal behavior. The courses can be conducted in a group environment, such as at a school or community center or in an in-home "one on one" basis. A great method for marketing these services can be to "tag on" to similar children's courses in your community. For example, if a business, association, or group is holding neighborhood watch meetings, you can attend as a guest speaker with the focus of your presentation aimed at promoting your service. Additional methods to market this service include utilizing press releases about the business to gain interest and establishing alliances with police services and home alarm companies. Also, you will want to design a complete child personal safety guide that can be included in the cost of the course or consulting visit. The guide can become an invaluable marketing tool for promoting your business. Promote the guide as "professional" and "exclusive" to your business. A police, security, or psychology background, along with being internet savvy, would be recommended for this business.

WEB RESOURCE: www.safekidsusa.com
Current safety information.

CHILDREN'S USED CLOTHING SALES
★★ $$ 🕒

Children's clothes are expensive. While all parents want the best clothes for their children, many families are more than happy to buy some good quality hand-me-downs. After all, kids outgrow clothes very quickly. To generate such a business, you can open a store or rent booths at local flea markets and at fairs and sell secondhand children's clothing. In both cases, you can purchase good quality secondhand children's clothing at bargain basement prices and resell the clothing for a profit. Accepting consignment clothing is one way to reduce business start-up costs.

REQUIREMENTS: Selling secondhand clothing will require a retail store location or booth at a busy weekend flea market, or a fair. Additionally, all the clothing will need to be washed prior to offering the garments for sale. Be sure you have catalogs or know the web addresses of leading retailers so that you can properly estimate the value of the clothing you will be purchasing for resale purposes.

START-UP COSTS: If you decide to operate from a fixed retail store location you will need about $25,000 to purchase equipment, and start, stock, and operate the business. If you choose the route of the weekend flea market booth, the business start-up costs will be greatly reduced and you could get started for less than a $3,000 initial investment.

PROFIT POTENTIAL: To be profitable in this type of retail business venture, always attempt to maintain a 100 percent markup on clothing items you purchase for resale, and charge a 40 to 50 percent commission for any consignments you accept and sell. If you can maintain yearly gross sales of $100,000 you should have no problem netting $30,000 per year after expenses. If the business is operating from a fixed location, you can add additional revenues from renting children's costumes. There will be a one-time expense to purchase the costumes, however, with good care, the costumes will last a long time and generate sizable rental revenues for a great number of years.

WEB RESOURCE: www.smallbizbooks.com
Business-specific start-up guides and books.

CUSTOM PLAY SETS
★★ $$$+ 🚗 🕒

The demand for custom designed and constructed children's play sets started to boom a few years ago, and these play sets still continue to be a hot seller today. In order to compete for market share in this industry, you will need some very elaborate play set designs and very ingenious marketing strategies. The higher-end multi-station play centers seem to be the most popular, thus commanding the largest retail dollar. This may indeed create your niche. You can design and manufacture a smaller, more compact, and affordable version of the large play sets to promote and market. Home and garden trade shows are probably the best bet, in terms of marketing the play sets. Displaying unique and interesting products at trade shows can generate substantial sales leads and interest in the products.

REQUIREMENTS: The main requirements to launching this type of business endeavor are as follows: design abilities, manufacturing equipment, skilled staff, and adequate transportation. Likewise, you will also have to commit a large amount of time into researching the market and consumer buying habits and trends prior to starting the business. You will also have to make sure to meet child safety requirements.

START-UP COSTS: The start-up investment required for this type of business can greatly vary. However, on a smaller scale the business can be successfully established for less than $25,000. A full-scale operation that includes a fully equipped manufacturing facility could easily cost in excess of $100,000 to establish.

PROFIT POTENTIAL: This type of specialized manufacturing business can generate profits greater than $100,000 per year, providing the business and market have been properly researched and established.

CHILDREN'S TOYS
★★ $$ 🏭 🕐

A few years ago, I spent five days at a home and garden show promoting my home renovation service and generating sales leads. Beside my booth was a gentleman selling windup flying toy helicopters that he had imported from China. Not exactly the type of product you would expect to see at a home improvement trade show. I remember asking him at the beginning of the show how long he had been doing this; he replied that he had been traveling the home show circuit to various cities around the country for two years selling only the windup toy helicopters. At that time I couldn't understand how he could make a living selling $10 toys at trade shows when the booth rent

alone was more than $150 per day, not including the additional cost to travel from show to show. By the end of the first day I learned a valuable lesson from this innovative entrepreneur in terms of marketing and promotion, for he sold more than 500 toy helicopters. He told me the cost to purchase the toy helicopters was $2.25 each and the cost to be at the show for the day including travel and accommodations was an additional $300 dollars, bringing his total cost to $2.85 for each helicopter. In one day by himself he had netted more than $3,500 after expenses. By the end of the five-day show, he sold more than 2,000 windup flying toy helicopters. The secret to his success? Simple. He had a unique and uncomplicated product in an environment that had no competition for his product and was surrounded by items that retailed for 100 times more than his did. More important was his ability to demonstrate his product and grab the attention of the show's audience. Imagine being two or three aisles away and seeing flying helicopters overhead. Human nature says you have no choice but to see what all the commotion is about.

WEB RESOURCE: www.nahpco.com
Directory service listing toy manufacturers, distributors, and links to toy industry information.

USED BABY EQUIPMENT
★ $$$

Similar to children's clothing, baby equipment such as strollers, car seats, and cribs are very expensive and often out of the financial reach of many parents. So why not start your own business that specializes in clean, good-quality secondhand equipment for babies? The business can be started for less than $15,000 and can be operated from a small retail store location, or as part of an established location. You can purchase items from parents and mark them up by at least 100 percent for resale purposes, depending on the item. Likewise, you can also take in items on a consignment basis to reduce business start-up costs. This business is ideally suited for a person who has a good number of contacts with parents within the community. Additional income and profits can also be earned by adding a cloth diaper delivery service, which is also covered in this chapter of the directory.

MARKETING TIP: If your business specializes in used products, always refer to your merchandise as refurbished or renewed. This will give your business a more professional appearance and even allow you to charge a premium for your used, I mean refurbished, merchandise.

COMPUTER TRAINING CLASSES
★★ $$$ 🕐 🌐

Starting computer training classes, or even a computer camp, for children is a terrific new business venture to set in motion. In spite of the fact that many children now receive computer training in school, attending computer camps ensures parents and children a better and more complete understanding of the course material. Typically these classes or camps are offered for three to five days and are available for various training needs from beginner to advanced. Once again, this is the kind of children's business that can be operated as an independent business venture or operated in conjunction with a community program or community center. Obviously, you will need to be up on the latest in software programs and computer technology and be good at talking to children in a manner that they will understand. You will need to purchase several computers and make sure that wherever you set up this camp, the location has the electrical capacity to handle the equipment. Hint: You don't need the latest models of computers. If you call Dell or Apple and purchase the previous top-of-the-line computers in bulk (5 to 10) you can get typically a good price on them. Also, use the software that is being used in the neighborhood schools so the middle to advanced kids are somewhat familiar with what is in front of them.

WEB RESOURCE: www.dell.com or www.apple.com
Places to research the purchase of computers.

WOODEN TOY MANUFACTURING AND SALES
★★★ $$ 🏠 🕐

Wooden toys not only appeal to children for play, but also to adults for home and office decorations. Manufacturing wooden toys is a wonderful homebased business opportunity that can be activated for peanuts and has the potential to return big profits. Marketing the toys can be accomplished by way of wholesale sales to merchants, the internet, mail-order catalogs, craft shows, mall kiosks, and home shopping parties. Traditionally, wooden toys that have been popular include trains, jigsaw puzzles, cars, numbered building blocks, and wooden soldiers. But that's just the tip of the iceberg. The only limitation to the different kinds of wooden toys that can be designed and manufactured is your own imagination. Additionally, approach local building and home improvement centers to see if they will let you set up a mini-manufacturing facility right in their store. If this can be accomplished, it would be a great marketing tool to be able to build the toys in front of a live audience.

REQUIREMENTS: The requirements for this type of woodworking business enterprise are relatively basic, and include woodworking skills and a well-equipped woodworking shop. Design and building plans are available for various types of wooden toys, or you can design your own toys as your skills improve. In the age of being politically correct, it is not a bad idea if you were to use only recycled wood to make your toys. Not only would you be helping the environment and saving money on material costs, but it can also be a useful and powerful marketing tool. Recyclable wood material includes beach driftwood, used building materials, cedar rail fencing, pallets, packing crates, and fallen forest brush, and most, if not all, of these waste wood materials can be acquired for free.

START-UP COSTS: If you already have the woodworking equipment that is required for this manufacturing business, you can get going for less than $500 in total investment. If you have to purchase equipment, the start-up costs will be substantially higher, in the range of $1,500 to $2,000.

PROFIT POTENTIAL: There are very little raw material costs involved to produce wooden toys. This type of business is mostly time-based and you will have to assess your own requirements when it comes to establishing an hourly rate. However, you still have to add a mark-up percentage onto the finished product costs to cover overheads, equipment repairs, and replacements. In terms of establishing an hourly rate, I would suggest at least $25 per hour, thus you could easily generate an income of $20,000+ per year, and best of all, have a whole lot of fun in the wooden toy manufacturing business.

WEB RESOURCE: www.woodentoyplans.com

Wooden toy construction plans and links to information about the wooden toy building industry.

PARTY BALLOON SERVICE
★★ $ 🚗 🕐 🌐

Less than $500 will set you up in your own Party Balloon Service, featuring balloons to fit all occasions. The demand for this service is endless and certainly not limited to only children's birthday parties. Marketing a party balloon service is best achieved by creating a colorful presentation to be distributed to all local event planners, children stores, daycare centers, catering companies, wedding planners, and banquet halls. Likewise, attending local networking clubs or chamber of commerce meetings is also a fantastic way to get the message out about your new service. A small amount of research into your local market will assist you in product pricing as well as determining demand and competition. Should you encounter a great deal of competition in your local community, you may want to add additional services to your enterprise to create a competitive advantage, such as party clean up and, or event planning. This is a business that can be successfully operated from home; however, you will require adequate transportation as the balloons should be filled with helium the day of the event and not prior to. Make sure helium tanks are stored in a safe location, and do not leave them unattended at the parties.

WEB RESOURCE: www.balloonbasics.com
Wholesale distributor of balloons and related supplies and equipment including helium.

VIDEO ARCADE
★★ $$$$

Gone are the days of 25-cent video and pinball games. Today's high-tech games can often cost as much as $2 or $3, and the children (and adults) are still lined up to play. A video arcade is a high-investment business to properly establish; nevertheless, the potential profit returns are also extremely high. Like any business that requires a large volume of people to be successful, you will want your video arcade to be located in a high-traffic, highly visible location. Malls and tourist attractions make fantastic operating locations for video arcades. The largest and most successful video arcades also include food concession

stands, retail product sales such as theme T-shirts, and family pass options, all of which you will want to consider implementing. Prior to starting a video arcade, complete a full and in-depth market survey into its viability. The investment into this business warrants the expense of such a market study. Also, before you select a location, carefully review the zoning ordinances. A number of towns and cities only allow video arcades in specific retail-zoned areas or within malls. A less expensive possibility is to buy a few video arcade games and rent them out for parties and special occasions. For this, you will need to lease or buy a van or truck rental and add that into your costs. Using brochures and a web site, you can let your customers select the games they would like to rent.

WEB RESOURCE: www.arcade-equipment.com
Directory service listing manufacturers and distributors of video arcade equipment.

DOLLHOUSE MANUFACTURING AND SALES
★ $ 🚗 🕐

Manufacturing custom-designed dollhouses is a great part-time homebased business venture to set in motion. The dollhouses you build can be sold through retail accounts, flea markets, craft shows, mail order, the internet, and booths at malls. The only requirement for this business to succeed is your ability to manufacture a good, high-quality dollhouse. Design plans are available at any hobby shop for dollhouse construction, or you can create your own custom designs. Business start-up cost is less than $500, and the monthly operating overheads are extremely low. The potential profits this business enterprise can produce are varied. However, a well-established dollhouse manufacturing business should have no difficulty generating annual sales in excess of $50,000 per year.

WEB RESOURCE: www.thedollnet.com
Portal listing manufacturers and suppliers of products and equipment for the doll industry.

PUPPET SHOWS
★ $$ 🚗 🕐

Jim Henson's puppet creations made him millions, so why can't yours? Starting a children's puppet show service is a fantastic way to own and operate your own business. Children cannot help but be fascinated by puppets.

Spending a few dollars to purchase or make your own puppets and a portable stage can be the beginning of a rewarding and moneymaking business venture for you. To get business, simply design some fliers and distribute them to local children's stores and daycare centers. Also market yourself to party planners, local schools, after-school centers, hospitals, libraries, and any place where children are likely to be found. Plan and rehearse five or six different twenty-minute shows that will work for different age groups. Try to stay with current and popular children themes for your puppets and puppet shows, such as space creatures and dinosaurs. If using established shows, remember to secure the rights to use such shows.

WEB RESOURCE: http://home.earthlink.net/~lbrodie/extra/supplies.html
This is a homespun puppet resource page with catalogues and names and phone numbers of places to buy materials for making puppets.

NATURAL CHILDBIRTH CLASSES
★ $+ 🌐 ⚖️

Natural childbirth is and will always be a hot topic. This business has limitless possibilities and avenues including natural childbirth classes, seminars, products, and services. This business opportunity will have to be of particular interest to you and will require training and a great amount of research. However, well-accepted professionals who specialize in a field generally are well paid and always in demand. This business may be of particular interest to nurses, childcare givers, and early childhood education teachers. Be sure to do your homework so that your new business will comply with all rules and regulations of your particular community.

WEB RESOURCE: www.naturalchildbirth.org
This site includes a discussion forum, business directory, and library of articles on the subject of natural childbirth.

PLAY CENTERS
★★ $$$$ 🌐 ⚖️

Play centers are indoor fun locations designed to entertain children, often found in shopping malls in and around major cities. If you choose a mall location, the kids can play in the play center while the parents go off and shop. Starting a play center can be a successful and profitable venture, which is exactly what you want to hear if starting this type of business is a consideration for you. Establishing a children's play center will take careful planning, especially for legal and liability issues. You will need to be insured and certified to take care of children. All of the equipment, which can include a sandbox, climbing toys, blocks, games and other popular items, will need to meet safety criteria. If you are in a mall, some of your toys may be provided for free by toy stores, in exchange for some advertising on your walls. Although it will take some due diligence to start such a business, there is great potential to generate excellent income for the owner-operator of this business enterprise. Many children's parties also take place in play centers, so by default, you will practically be dragged into the party planning business as well. Make the location as safe, cheery, and fun as possible and you will generate business via word of mouth.

TALENT AGENT FOR CHILDREN
★ $$ 🚗 🕐

Are you searching for a low investment homebased business opportunity that has the potential to be a lot of fun and potentially very profitable? If so, perhaps you should consider starting a talent agency for child actors. This type of business enterprise is very easy to activate and there will certainly be no shortage of potential clients, as many children dream about hamming it up for the camera. Currently, agents for child actors are charging a commission rate of between 10 and 20 percent of their client's earnings. Many agents also represent children in the modeling profession as well as those involved in voice-over work for radio and TV. To gain exposure to producers and directors for the business, you can start an e-mail newsletter to local production companies and theater groups, and personal visit campaign promoting your talent agency, clients, and services. Note: Talent agencies for children have come under fire because many operate solely to collect money from unsuspecting parents for providing acting lessons and photo portfolios while the children never get a legitimate chance at an audition. Be sure to operate your agency in an ethical manner, and only refer parents to other businesses if they inquire about acting lessons or photograph portfolios.

Fair warning: The reality of being a successful agent in any field is based 90% on your connections. Therefore, if you have a background in which you have built up numerous contacts that employ young actors and models (such as having worked in advertising or at a television station) you have a much better chance of succeeding in this field. Also, make sure you are well versed in child labor laws.

WEB RESOURCE: www.agentassociation.com
The Association of Talent Agents has been around for 70 years, providing information on the industry.

MINI-TRAIN RIDES
★ $$$$

Be prepared to invest more than $250,000 to start a mini-train ride business. But also be prepared to generate daily business sales that can easily exceed $1,500. Starting a mini-train ride business for children takes a lot of careful planning, research, and business expertise, and there are numerous considerations including the most important, which is where the business will be located. Good locations include parks, amusement centers, indoor malls, and zoos. Additionally, depending on the business location, sales of products such as hats, T-shirts, and food items can also be added to boost sales and profits. This business has the potential to become a real going concern. Joint venture opportunities with existing businesses that can provide a good operating location for the business should not be overlooked.

EDUCATIONAL DAY CAMPS
★★ $$+ 🕑 🌐 🏫

Mathematics, grammar, computer training, and arts and crafts can all be included into the curriculum of an educational day camp for kids. The camps can be held in a daylong format on weekends during school months and throughout the week in summers. The main focus on this type of specialized kids' day camp business is to provide parents with an alternate choice for additional education as opposed to educational tutoring. The day camps can be run as an independent business or in conjunction with a community program or community center. Start-up costs for this kind of business will vary as to the operating format and size of the business and will range from a low of $5,000 to a high of $25,000. Be sure to seek legal advice in terms of regulations and certifications that may be required to operate a business specializing in educational day camps for kids in your community prior to establishing the business.

PONY RIDES
★ $$$$ 🕑

An old favorite, this is a business with a time-tested formula. Being a mobile business will enable you to travel to where the demand is greatest for the service. Logical locations include high-traffic community gathering places such as malls, fairs, festivals, flea markets, and community parades. You will also want to establish a working relationship with other similarly related businesses that can help support your business, such as carnival companies, kids' party services, property managers, clubs, and associations. Additionally, be sure to associate yourself with all the charity events in your area as your service is unique, which can help generate interest for the charity event and profits for you. Furthermore, to gain additional revenue, add a photograph or video service. What parent can resist purchasing a picture of their child on a pony?

REQUIREMENTS: Transportation, boarding space, liability insurance, and of course the ponies are among the requirements. Additionally, you will want to be familiar with ponies and their needs and requirements. The business will take careful planning to put together, but the rewards can be both financially and personally rewarding.

START-UP COSTS: The costs associated with starting a pony ride business will vary depending on the number of ponies and if you will be boarding them or housing them in your own stables. You will also have to take into account the cost and method of transportation. I talked to a person who has been in the business for more than 15 years. He informed me that to start and operate this business properly would take about $25,000 in start-up capital and a fixed monthly operating budget of $2,000 to $3,000.

PROFIT POTENTIAL: The same person I talked to about the business start-up and operating costs told me that he has generally cleared $5,000 per month after expenses. Of course, the profit potential will vary to each operation, but overall this business appears to be fun and rewarding as well.

WEB RESOURCE: www.ponyclub.org
Directory listing pony clubs in the United States.

HOUSE SAFETY OR CHILDPROOFING SERVICE
★★ $$ 🏠 🕒

Statistically, the greatest numbers of injury-causing accidents involving children happen at home. This creates a fantastic opportunity to remedy this very real situation as well as start your own business as a professional house safety consultant. Your service can focus on all the household items that can potentially harm children and you can provide the service of showing parents how to secure these household items so accidents don't happen. Establishing the service will require a fair amount of research to educate yourself about harmful household chemicals, cabinet safety latches, and overall proper procedures to making a home a safe and child-friendly environment. Begin to market your consulting services by designing and distributing brochures, building alliances with related businesses for referrals, and most important, offer your service for free. Wait, what do you mean free? Exactly that—provide no-charge in-home consultations to potential clients. Once in the client's home, it will be your opportunity to blow them away with your knowledge (the old fear sale) on how to make their homes a child-friendly environment. By the time your "free" consulting visit is over, the chances are good that clients will have committed to hundreds of dollars worth of installed safety products and information manuals, all of which you can provide.

WEB RESOURCE: www.iafcs.com
International Association for Child Safety

CHILDREN'S THEATER COMPANY
★★★ $$$ 🕒

Whether you have your own theater space or travel from location to location, staging theatrical productions for children can be both profitable and emotionally fulfilling. There are numerous plays designed for children, including classics that have been re-written in abbreviated form specifically for young audiences. Make sure to pay for licensed works unless you have an original playwright on hand, or can pen suitable shows yourself (which is not as easy as you think).

You then need a few talented performers, some fun scripts, and a lot of promotion to make this work. Posters, handouts, and ads in local papers can help you sell out your performances. Start-up costs include props, makeup, (possibly) puppets, and printing up programs and tickets. Most of these can be offset by ads in the program for child-friendly businesses, such as a local ice cream parlor or toy store. You can also tap benefactors who pledge money to support children's theater and get some of the items you need—including costumes and sets—by bartering. "Provide us with some costumes and we'll advertise your party store in our program for free." Also, try staging and promoting Halloween and Christmas/holiday season shows to really bring in some additional income.

WEB RESOURCE: www.mtimusicalworlds.com
A great selection of shows for children.

KIDS COSTUME SALES AND RENTAL
★★★ $$ 🏠 🕒

From school plays to dance recitals to parties to the ultimate night for costumers renting and retailing—Halloween—there is money to be made from renting and/or selling costumes and accessories. A small retail location, a good web site, and some imaginative marketing can draw a regular customer base. The long lines in some costume shops as Halloween approaches and the sounds of cash registers working overtime is definitely encouraging for those who have the entrepreneurial spirit, especially if you can find a good location with minimal competition. You can also work in conjunction with a party store or even a toy store to save on overhead. Spread the word to all places in your area where children are frequently found, including after school and community centers. Magic tricks and costumes for adults can help increase your profits. Make sure to always take deposits in the event the renter never returns the costume, and be sure your inventory is kept clean and in good condition.

CHILDREN'S FITNESS CLASSES
★★ $$$ 🕒

There is an increasing concern about childhood obesity in the United States, largely because video games do not provide much exercise other than for the thumb on the controller. If you can make fitness fun, you may be able to entice concerned parents to sign their kids up to work out. You can either schedule classes to be taught from various locations or seek out a good location for a dedicated fitness center. You want the environment to be colorful, trendy, and fun, with popular music and a kid-friendly décor. One kids/teens-only fitness club has a large screen television taking up literally an entire wall, playing videos while kids work out on treadmills and other exercise machines. Supervisors are always on hand to help, encourage and teach kids the right way to exercise.

REQUIREMENTS: To do this right, you should be either a certified fitness instructor or have a background as a nutritionist or dietitian. Of course, to run such a program without such accreditation, you can always hire the experts and work on the business administration end, scheduling and promoting classes, as well as special programs to teach kids to eat in a healthier manner. Start-up costs depend largely on the type of fitness classes offered and who is doing the teaching. Boxing, aerobic classes, or other activities that do not require specific machines will be less expensive than a room full of trampolines, stationary bikes, and other equipment. However, the more equipment you have the more you can charge. You will also need liability insurance and supplies on hand, including mats, towels, a first-aid kit or two, and beverages, along with some healthy snacks.

WEB RESOURCE: www.afpafitness.com
American Fitness Professionals and Associates

BABY CARE WORKSHOPS
★★★ $ 🏠 🕒

If you have a background in childcare or nursing, you can start your own baby care workshops for new moms—and dads too. There's a lot to learn, and in the excitement of bringing home a baby, it's hard to figure out exactly what to do next. Sure, parents have been raising babies on their own for a very long time, but classes can certainly help make it much easier in today's busy world. Feeding, nutrition, diapering, home safety, bathing, dealing with rashes, and how to maneuver the latest in high-tech car seats are just a few of the areas you can cover in a two-hour course.

REQUIREMENTS: You need to rent a space, schedule convenient times, and market your services to OBGYN offices, hospitals, baby clothing and furniture shops, adoption agencies and attorneys as well as any place new (or soon to be) parents are typically found. Charging $30 per couple (or single) and having 12 paying attendees per class can bring in $360, less approximately $60 for a room rental at a health facility or community center, will leave you with a $300 profit per class. Two classes weekly for 40 weeks a year can bring in $24,000 for a few hours of work per week.

FACE PAINTING
★★ $ 🕒

Kids love face painting and typically line up whenever it is offered. No, this is not likely to become a full time career, but as a part-time means of generating some additional income, this can be a winner. Market your talents for parties and social activities such as picnics, fairs, and school gatherings and you can make a few hundred dollars a week. Make sure to use paints that are safe for the skin and, if possible, make your own since theatrical stage makeup can be costly. Have a few specialties that you have practiced drawing many times before, such as a cat. Also, hone your child-friendliest manner, so that you can bring a smile to any young face, even those who are a little jittery or scared when you are painting. You might also have a few balloon animal tricks up your sleeve.

WEB RESOURCE: http://painting.about.com/od/faceandbody painting/a/FacePaintCindy.htm
Top ten safety tips for face painting.

ARTS AND CRAFTS BUSINESSES
★★★★ $$$$

Build-A-Bear, Little Shop of Plaster, and Abrakadoodle are the names of successful business that offer children the opportunity to use their creative skills to make art, toys, or even decorative items to display. From a storefront, or a mobile location, you need only to have a creative building concept and good marketing skills to get this off the ground. Most children love working with clay, paints, paper maché, and other such materials, and all you need to do is to provide the materials in a safe, supportive setting with plenty of room and a little guidance. Even t-shirt designing is very popular with kids of all ages! In an era of mass technology, parents love finding new places to take young children on a Saturday afternoon to get them away from the television or the computer screens. If you can sell accessories or have work framed, shellacked, or finished in any other manner, you can make some extra money. You can also sell take home arts-and-crafts items ranging from finger paints to clay. Have liability insurance, take all safety precautions and set up a place for parents to sit and read, talk, and buy some snack foods. With some first rate marketing, which should include sending out numerous press releases to local family-friendly magazines, a business such as this can be very lucrative.

CHILDREN'S MUSEUM
★★ $$$$ 🕒

No, it's not as hard as it sounds to open a children's museum. Unlike traditional museums, you are not dealing with art and artifacts from centuries ago. Most children's museums are places with educational, hands-on exhibits that are constructed so that children can climb through or jump on something, while pressing levers, pulling handles, and enjoying an interactive experience. Popular exhibits include topics such as how the body works and making your own TV show. Another favorite teaches children how machines work with displays that encompass gear wheels and other movable parts. Exhibits that focus on animals and insects are also crowd pleasers. Exhibits need to be educational, safe, and durable, since kids will wear them down over time.

Financing such an endeavor is the first major hurdle. This typically means preparing a solid business plan detailing how the space will be utilized, the educational benefits of each exhibit (work with teachers or educators to make them grade appropriate) and the layout of the facility. The building of the exhibits will need to be detailed as well. You will need to locate a safe, roomy location with parking nearby. Finally, once you have the entire concept thought out, you can seek out benefactors and corporations that are looking to donate to such a worthwhile endeavor. A children's museum that is well planned and in a good location can be very well received by the community.

This type of endeavor will take time and great planning to launch. Once it gets rolling, however, you will feel a tremendous sense of accomplishment and have a career as a museum director.

WEB RESOURCE: www.familytravelguides.com/articles/museums/kidmuse.html
A listing of children's museums around the country.

GOODY BAGS
★★ $ 🏠 🕒

No, this business probably won't make you rich, unless you are buying goody bags for a billionaire's kids. However, you can make some steady money being a one-stop goody bag distributor. Parents know how the many minor details of a kid's party can build and build, making party planning quite time consuming, particularly for a two-working parent household. Typically, one of the last pieces of the party planning puzzle is the gift bag, or goody bag, which requires running around and getting the items, along with keeping up with the Joneses—after all, if they gave every kid a t-shirt, you need to at least match that.

Market your business to party shops, party planners, parents associations, and any place you will find parents of young children. Buying some basics in bulk, like small toys and candy, will cut your costs to assemble the bags so that you can make a profit. You can have four or five pre-arranged bags to promote, and feature them on fliers and on your web site, at different price points, with different levels of giveaways, including at least one without candy for the health-minded parent. You can also offer the custom goody bag, where the parents or kids pick each of five or six items. In addition, you can market your business for special occasions, such as Sweet Sixteen parties and Bar Mitzvahs where the giveaways are of a higher caliber, and include sweat pants, blankets, or other such items. This is a fun business that you can easily run from the comfort of your own home.

MOMMY (OR DADDY) AND ME CLASSES
★★★ $ 🕒

Singing songs, making things, and interacting with mommy, daddy, and other children are all fun activities for most young children. This makes a well-marketed mommy/daddy and me class a great little business to start. There is little overhead to starting such classes, other than rental of a location, which can be a room in a school, community center, or religious institution. As long as you find a "cheery" location, or decorate it as such, and can accommodate a dozen moms or dads and their youngsters, you are all set. You then need a theme. One class for example, met once a week for eight weeks and featured a young singer/guitar player, who led parents and youngsters in fun-filled songs for the 40-minute class. The "teacher" also led them in some dance steps and, for the last song, she handed out instruments so they could all play along. Very simple, but a great bonding experience for parents and their youngsters.

You can charge from $50 to $100 for six or eight weeks depending on the market. You can have one or several different classes a day for ages two through four or five. As a side business, three days a week, with a total of six classes and ten parent/kid combos per class (at $100 for two months) you could make $3,000 per month, which, in 10 months a year (skipping the summer) would be $30,000, less perhaps $5,000 for rental, marketing and insurance. $25,000 a year from a part-time business is not bad.

MOBILES
★★ $ 🏠 🕒

You'll find them on almost every crib, entertaining babies with bright colors and music. Whether you manufacturer mobiles yourself or buy them wholesale for resale purposes, children's mobiles have long been and continue to be a best selling item, making them a great choice for a part-time business venture. You can start a business in mobiles from a home base, marketing your product to baby furniture and clothing stores as well as at malls, fairs, and mommy and me classes. A web site should feature your products as well. If you are purchasing mobiles, you'll find a wide variety of colors and styles which you can usually markup significantly, since

the more elaborate, unique mobiles can sell for as much as $90 or $100. If you are manufacturing mobiles yourself, you should look at as many styles as possible and then decide what sizes, shapes, materials, and types of mobiles you want to create. Make sure you keep safety in mind at all times, have a string length that is short and test out all products to make sure they are in working order.

CHILD I.D.S
★★ $ 🏠 🕒

The fear that your child will be lost when in the responsibility of others is one that parents try not to think about. However, there is a very real concern and one that you can lessen by starting a business that sells child ID wristbands along with shoe and backpack tags. The name and identity of a child is important information so that an adult can immediately contact a parent regarding a child that is lost, injured, or waiting to be picked up. Velcro fasteners, wristbands, and other such products can be bought in bulk and sold for $7 to $10 to all parents of young children. Not only will you be starting a business that requires little start-up funding, but you will also feel very good about providing a valuable service to parents.

STROLLERS
★★★ $$$$

Lightweight, classic, jogging, even double and triple strollers can be part of your inventory if you open a stroller store and accompanying web site. Strollers are priced from $50 to $500 depending on the style, features, and size. The markup can be very good if you research manufacturers and find one that can provide you with good prices. While you can save some overhead by going into business with someone else, such as a children's clothing store, you can do well on your own by establishing a good location where you will catch the eye of soon-to-be parents. Along with traditional marketing to expectant parents in local newspaper ads and on web sites, send fliers to OBGYNs.

WEB RESOURCE: www.twinslist.org/strollerlinks.html
Online stroller manufacturer listings.

TEEN TRAVEL CAMP
★★ $$ 🏷️

Not nearly as complicated as planning full-fledged tours to other parts of the world, teen travel camps are a fairly recent, innovative concept. You set up an itinerary with three to six weeks of daily camp trips within a 90-minute radius. Then, three to five days a week (however many you choose to run the camp), the teens (usually ages 11-15) travel to a different location. One camp that operates from a location one hour north of New York City, for example, visits the Bronx Zoo and the Empire State Building, takes a boat tour around Manhattan, and goes to local amusement and water parks, as well as a day at a shopping mall, a trip to a Yankees game, and a day of bowling. The idea is to plan a fun day trip for each camp day. Parents are provided with an itinerary and are told which days to pack a lunch and on which days lunch will be provided.

COSTS: If the bus and activities come to an average of $600 per day for 40 kids, and you run the camp for six weeks in the summer at four days a week, your cost would be $14,400, plus paying for counselors, paperwork, insurance and advertising. In all, you should be ready to spend $25,000 to run the camp. If each child were paying only $1,000 to attend, or $167 per week, you would be making $40,000 or a $15,000 profit for a six-week business endeavor. Not bad for part-time work.

NOTES:

38
CLOTHING
Businesses You Can Start

SENIOR CITIZEN CLOTHING
★★★ $$

Are you searching for a unique clothing retail business that can be operated on a mobile basis and managed from a homebased office? If so, consider starting a business that retails clothing to residents of in retirement and senior living facilities. Simply build alliances with clothing manufacturers and make arrangements with operators of retirement homes to put on a monthly fashion show for the residents. Additionally, models for the fashion shows can be the residents of the homes, and at the end of the show you can take orders for clothing purchases with delivery to follow within a few days. This could prove to be not only a profitable business to operate, but also a very fun business that provides clients with the convenience of easy shopping as well as a little bit of entertainment at the same time.

WEB RESOURCE: www.wardrobewagon.com
A supplier of traditional adult clothing.

DRIVE-THROUGH LAUNDROMAT
★★ $$$$

There are drive-through banks, restaurants, and photo finishing stores, so why not drive-through laundromats? A drive-through laundromat is not a new business concept; they have been around for a few years. However, recently they have become more popular, and a few companies have even begun to franchise their drive-through laundromat businesses. Starting a drive-through laundromat does not require a great deal of business experience or knowledge. It does, however, require a good location and a fairly substantial capital investment to establish the business. In terms of a business location, ideally the drive-through laundromat should be established on a busy road, but not so congested with traffic that entering and exiting for customers is a problem or potentially dangerous. Additional location considerations will also include proximity to potential clients most likely to utilize the service such as universities, police stations, hospitals, and industrial business areas. Street visibility, accessibility for walk-in customers, parking, and overall building condition and appearance are also important. In addition to providing customers with a drive-through service, also provide a walk-in and laundry drop-off service as well as a free pickup and delivery service. The profit potential for this type of business venture is excellent and can easily exceed $75,000 per year, providing the correct steps have been taken to select the right location as well as promoting the service to its full potential.

WEB RESOURCE: www.speedqueen.com
Manufacturers and distributors of commercial laundromat equipment.

T-SHIRTS IN A CAN
★★ $$ 🚗 🕐

Designing novelty T-shirts, and the can in which the shirt will be sold, is a very interesting business opportunity to get rolling. The T-shirts can feature jokes, images, or messages based on a variety of themes from political humor to children's cartoon caricatures. Once the silk-screening is completed, the T-shirts can be packaged in tin cans that have a slot in the top to serve a second function of a piggy bank. T-shirts in a Can make a terrific novelty gift, or party gift, and can be sold to retailers on a wholesale basis or directly to consumers at flea markets, fairs, local outdoor events or through your own web site or those of other online retailers. Furthermore, to keep initial start-up costs to a minimum, the silk-screening aspect of the business can be contracted to a local silk-screener as opposed to purchasing the equipment. In addition to selling T-shirts in a Can, larger sweatshirts can also be printed with humorous messages and packaged in larger one-gallon paint cans.

WEB RESOURCE: www.interchangecorp.com
Distributors of new and used silk-screening equipment.

COLLECTIBLE CLOTHING
★★ $$$$

The value and popularity of collectible clothing has been on a steady increase for the past decade, and the demand for collectible clothing from the 1940s to the 1970s (also now known as "vintage" and "retro") show no signs of diminishing. Starting a business that sells collectible clothing from a retail storefront location is a good business venture to set in motion. Start-up costs, including business setup costs, banking, legal, initial inventory, office equipment and supplies, initial advertising and marketing budget, and working capital, could run anywhere between $30,000 and $70,000.

PROFIT POTENTIAL: Like most businesses, the profit potential for a retailer of collectible clothing will vary based on factors such as operating overheads, volume of sales, etc. However, a markup of around 100 percent should be maintained, and a higher markup on rarer collectible clothing items is certainly not out of line. Maintaining annual sales of $200,000 will create a pretax and expenses profit of $100,000 with good marketing. To test the waters, since internet collectible sites are providing significant competition, you might start such a business as part of another retail location or as a part time business, selling at fairs, flea markets or from a booth at a mall.

WEB RESOURCE: www.rustyzipper.com
Online vintage clothing and a good place to get an idea of pricing.

WORK UNIFORMS
★★ $$$$ 🌐

There are a few options available when starting a business that retails work uniforms and work clothing. The first option is to establish a retail storefront location to stock and sell work uniforms, and the second option is to establish a mobile business that sells work uniforms from a cube van or delivery truck. Both options have drawbacks and benefits in terms of the business. However, the second option of being a mobile retailer of work uniforms will be less costly to establish, as well as to operate on a monthly basis. The types of uniforms and work clothing that can be sold include work overalls, healthcare uniforms, fire and police service uniforms, food service uniforms, and school sportswear. Also stocking and selling specialized work footwear, such as steel toe work boots, can earn additional revenues. Regardless if the business is operated from a fixed location or on a mobile basis, one of the main marketing tools required will be to design and produce a full-color catalog and a web site that feature the work wear available for sale.

WEB RESOURCE: www.naumd.com
National Association of Uniform Manufacturers and Dealers.

USED WEDDING GOWNS
★★ $$+ 🚗

Sell secondhand wedding gowns from home as well as on the internet for a profit. In a nutshell, the main objective is to purchase secondhand wedding gowns and accessories at bargain basement prices and resell these same gowns for a profit. The gowns can be sold from a home-based location as well as on the internet by developing your own web site. In addition to purchasing gowns, you can also accept consignment gowns and retain 25 to 40 percent of the sales value for providing the service. For additional income you could also sell veils, headpieces, garters, and other accessories, both new and used. Advertise your business in your local newspaper and build alliances with (and have links to) wedding planners to promote the business.

SILK-SCREENING SERVICE
★★ $$ 🏠 🕐

The most common use for silk-screen printing is with clothing, especially T-shirts. However, silk-screen printing equipment can be used for printing logos and images on a variety of products such as mouse pads, bumper stickers, heat transfers, shower curtains, binder covers, furniture, and sports items, just to mention a few. Still, it is often better to stick with what traditionally will generate revenues and profits for a business, and in this case that means silk-screening T-shirts, hats, jackets, and sweatshirts for corporate promotional wear, gifts, sports uniforms, and special events. The profit potential is great for a silk-screening business as T-shirts can be purchased wholesale for less than $5 each and the ink used to print the image adds up to only a few cents per printed item. Simply securing orders for 500 printed T-shirts a week and charging only $10 each for the shirt and the printing can generate a gross profit in excess of $100,000 per year—a compelling reason to start your own homebased silk-screening business today.

WEB RESOURCE: www.interchangecorp.com
Distributors of new and used silk-screening equipment.

HOMEBASED TAILOR
★★ $$ 🏠 🕐

Retailers of men's formal and business wear generally do not have an in-house tailor, and typically alteration work is subcontracted to outside contract tailors. This fact creates a more than ample opportunity for the individuals with sewing experience to capitalize by starting a tailoring service that operates right from a homebased location. Once again, the fastest way to establish the service is to offer men's wear retailers your services on a subcontract basis, and you can arrange a certain time of the

day to pick up garments to be altered. Then, return the garments as soon as you have completed the alterations. Additionally, to generate more revenue for the business, consider purchasing tuxedos that can be rented to clients via the menswear stores that currently do not provide their customers with this service. The individual tailor is a lost art today, so market your skills through fliers and local ads to a new generation. You can also increase your profit potential by doing alterations. Since many people look to their dry cleaners to do alterations, you can establish yourself by being available as a subcontractor to new dry cleaners that open in your area.

WEB RESOURCE: www.paccprofessionals.org
The Professional Association of Custom Clothiers, representing custom clothiers working from home.

TIE-DYE CLOTHING
★★ $$ 🏠 🕐

If history has taught us anything it is that it will repeat itself, and that is certainly the situation in terms of tie-dye clothing, as these popular cultural icons of the 1960s are once again returning to favor as a fashionable clothing option. Creating tie-dye clothing is extremely easy and training books and videos on the subject are available through most craft supply stores. The business can easily be operated from home, and clothing to be tie-dyed can be purchased from clothing manufacturers on a wholesale basis. Once the clothing has been tie-dyed it can be sold to clothing retailers on a wholesale basis, directly to consumers via the internet, at flea markets, street fairs, local concerts, and through sales kiosks located in malls.

WEB RESOURCE: www.wholesaleroom.com/Apparel/T-Shirts/index.html
A portal offering various places to buy t-shirts.

SPORTSMEN'S VESTS
★★ $$ 🏠

Manufacturing custom-made sportsmen's vests for hunting, fishing, and boating activities is an outstanding homebased business venture to get rolling, especially for the entrepreneur with sewing skills and experience. The key to success in this type of specialty clothing manufacturing business is to ensure that the sportsmen's vests serve many functions related to the activity they have been created for, as well as ensuring that materials and workmanship used in creating the product are of the highest quality. Once completed, the sportsmen's vest can be sold to national sporting goods retailers on a wholesale basis, or the sportsmen's vest can be sold directly to consumers via mail-order catalogs, recreation trade shows, and even the internet. Furthermore, the business can be started on a part-time basis and expanded to full-time from the profits that are earned. Be sure to seek exporting opportunities for the vests, as American and Canadian sporting goods and sportswear is extremely popular overseas, especially in Japan and Germany.

SECONDHAND CLOTHING STORE
★★ $$$$

There are a few options available to the entrepreneur considering a retail business that sells secondhand clothing. The first and most capital-intensive option is to open a used clothing store from a fixed retail location or storefront. The second option is to sell the secondhand clothing items via a flea-market booth. The third option is to develop a web site and sell used clothing via the internet.

Of course, all three options could be combined into one operating format, and combining all three methods of marketing and distribution would greatly increase potential business revenues and profits. I have even recently heard of a few companies that are now selling secondhand designer clothing by way of home parties and independent sales consultants, which could also be a potential avenue well worth investigating. Aligning yourself with a charity can also draw a great number of people to your store. While the charity will receive a portion of the money, your business will increase, since people will donate clothing and receive a practical tax deduction. Make it very clear how much goes to the charity.

WEB RESOURCE: www.narts.org
National Association of Resale and Thrift Shops

PROMOTIONAL WEAR
★★★ $$ 🚗 🕐

Promotional wear such as hats, jackets, and golf shirts emblazoned with corporate and business logos have become very popular for corporations to purchase and resell or give to valued employees and clients as an appreciation gift. Starting a business that sells promotional clothing is very easy to initiate. Not only can the garments be purchased on a wholesale basis, but also you can enlist the services of local silk-screeners and embroiders to carry out customizing the clothing for your clients, thus greatly reducing the start-up investment needed to get the business rolling. If business is good, you may then opt to purchase your own silk screening equipment. Gaining clients can be as easy as arranging appointments with business owners to present samples of the promotional wear along with reasons why these types of promotional items will benefit their business. Attending local chamber of commerce meetings can give you a one-stop opportunity to meet several potential customers and spread the word around that you are in business to help promote other businesses. Once you establish some corporate clients, you can handle their ongoing need for promotional materials. Once established, a business that retails promotional wear can be very profitable, especially when you consider product markups of 50 percent or more are not uncommon in the industry.

WEB RESOURCE: www.wholesaleroom.com
A portal to help you find the necessary merchandise at wholesale prices.

EMBROIDERY SERVICE
★★ $$$ 🚗 🕐

Recent technology changes in the embroidery industry have made it very easy even for a novice to start an embroidery service. Embroidery machines are now available in single or multihead units enabling the operator to embroider six items at a time or more. Additionally, modern embroidery equipment is computer assisted, meaning that the designs can be created using special software and then automatically transferred to the embroidery machine to complete the stitching of the design. The business can easily be operated from a homebased location. However, there should still be a small showroom established, even if it is in the home, to display items that can be embroidered as well as samples of embroidery options. Marketing the service can be as easy as creating a catalog, marketing brochure or even a flier and distributing the information to potential clients such as sports associations, charities, corporations, and clubs. Furthermore, you can build a simple two- or three-page web site showing your work. As a service business, you can also align yourself with retailers of items that can be embroidered in exchange for promoting the retailers on your site.

WEB RESOURCE: www.embmag.com
Embroidery Monogram Business magazine online.

TEAM UNIFORM SALES
★★ $$ 🏠 🕐

Schools, sports associations, and sports clubs can all be potential customers for a business that specializes in retailing team uniforms. Millions of people across North America participate in amateur sporting events such as football, baseball, hockey, and soccer on a weekly basis. Almost all of these sports teams have one thing in common: the members of the teams dress in a uniform that represents the team. Selling team sportswear with logos, names, and numbers printed on the clothing items is a very easy business to get rolling. You can purchase equipment required to silk-screen and embroider the athletic wear, or you can subcontract this element of the business out to established silk-screen and embroidery companies and concentrate on marketing. Gaining customers can be as easy as creating a catalog of the team uniforms that you stock and setting appointments with decision makers representing the sports teams to solicit business.

WEB RESOURCE: www.brother-usa.com
Click on either "home sewing and embroidery" or "industrial sewing and embroidery" for embroidery machines.

PET CLOTHING
★★ $$$ 🏠 🕐

Any pet owner will certainly understand the outstanding opportunity that awaits the enterprising entrepreneurs that start a business that markets specialty clothing for pets, as the spending habits of pet owners often know no bounds. There are a couple of approaches that can be taken in terms of establishing this type of business. The first is to design, manufacture, and market the pet clothing. The second approach is to simply purchase the clothing from a manufacturer on a wholesale basis for resale purposes or to have a local seamstress design and manu-

facture the clothing for pets. The first approach to establishing the business will be more capital intensive to get off the ground, but with that said, there are also more options in terms of marketing the products, as well as the potential to generate higher sales and profits. Pet products can be marketed directly to local pet stores, sold at flea markets, local fairs, pet grooming salons, and via fliers handed to the many people who are out walking their dogs. Having a web site can increase sales as you can show some of your products and sell online. The more unique and innovative your designs are, the more you can also rely on word-of-mouth marketing, (also known as viral marketing) where people notice dogs in the area wearing your outfit and ask the owners where they purchased it. In fact, giving away a few free samples in residential areas where there are many pet owners can launch this type of highly effective word-of-mouth marketing.

WEB RESOURCE: www.appma.org
American Pet Products Manufacturers Association.

BELT BUCKLES
★★ $$ 🏠 🕐

Are you searching for a truly unique homebased business opportunity with a focus on manufacturing? If so, perhaps you should consider starting a business manufacturing specialty belt buckles. The business can be put into action on less than a $3,000 initial investment, and the long-term profit potential is sensational. The key to success in this type of specialty manufacturing business is to ensure the buckle designs are original and to place a concentrated effort on utilizing many marketing methods to ensure maximum exposure for the business and products. Additionally, consider utilizing recyclable materials such as metals and glass for the raw material to construct the belt buckles. Not only is this a way to reduce the cost of materials, but more importantly, it can be used as a very powerful marketing tool.

HANDBAG DESIGN AND MANUFACTURING
★★★ $$ 🏠 🕐

Creating and manufacturing designer handbags is a terrific new business enterprise to start right from the comfort of home, as not only can the business be run on a part-time basis, but also there is almost no operating overhead to bite into monthly profits. Unique designs and utilizing uncommon materials for the making of the handbags can be your competitive advantage, and completed products can be wholesaled to fashion retailers or placed on consignment in local retail shops. Additionally, the handbags can also be sold directly to consumers by displaying the products at fashion shows, at flea markets and fairs, on your web site, or by renting a sales kiosk in a busy mall on weekends. Furthermore, seek big market opportunities by building joint ventures with established handbag manufacturers that can produce and wholesale your handbag designs under a split revenue agreement. This is another item that can benefit from word-of-mouth advertising, if the bags are unique and stand out. Therefore, make sure to give a few out to friends and family members who will be walking around busy malls.

CHILDREN'S DESIGNER CLOTHES
★ $$$ 🚗 🕒

Calling all seamstresses and hobby fashion designers! It is time to start to profit from your good fashion sense and sewing skills by starting a homebased business that designs and manufactures children's designer clothing. Marketing the finished product can be as easy as hosting monthly fashion shows right in your own home. Children from your local neighborhood can be enlisted to work as clothing models and invitations can be sent to parents within the community to attend the fashion show. At the end of the show, simply collect orders for the clothing the parents wish to purchase and set about making the clothes and planning for the next fashion show. To expand the business you can employ independent sales consultants right across the country to also host monthly fashion shows and split the revenues that are earned on clothing sales.

BATHING SUITS
★★ $$

Custom made-to-order bathing suits retail for as much as $150 each while only costing about $20 in material to make. Thus if you have a flair for design and a skill for sewing, starting your own homebased business that specializes in made-to-order bathing suits for clients seeking the perfect fashion look for the beach may be just the business opportunity that can put you on the road to

financial riches. Once again, the business can be operated from home simply by converting a room into a workspace and showroom to display samples of your work for clients. Gaining clients can be as easy as printing discount coupons that can be distributed to travel agents who present the coupons as a gift to their clients traveling to sunny destinations—not to mention the fact that this is a type of business that will receive a lot of free advertising by way of word-of-mouth referrals.

BATHING SUIT SHOP
★★★ $$$$

If you are anywhere close to a beach, you can set up a bathing suit shop in strip mall or at a booth in a busy indoor mall. By the third or fourth day of a weeklong or two-week beach vacation, nearly half of the travelers are tired of their same two or three bathing suits and ready to spring for a new one. Local pool and beach parties are also good reasons to open a shop for bathing suit sales. If you are not in a year-round warm climate, you may opt to split the year with a winter business such as ski apparel and equipment. This can be your second line of work or you can partner with another business owner who can take over from September through February. There is a great markup for swimsuits; making hot items such as the thong-style bikini requires little material but sales of these suits command big bucks. You can spend between $5 and $35 per item wholesale and sell them for $25 to $125 per item retail, depending on quality, style, and designer name. Also, don't forget to stock cover-ups, towels, inexpensive sunglasses, visors and sun hats, flip flops, sun screens and lotions etc. Someone always forgets to bring some beach accessory on the trip, so you can make a lot of money selling them.

WEB RESOURCE: www.ujenawholesale.com
Swimwear wholesaler.

MOBILE FORMAL WEAR RENTALS
★★ $$$$ 🌐

Take a traditional formal wear rental business, add wheels, and you have the focus of this business opportunity. Who says the customer has to come to you? Why can't you go to them? You can, and that is what makes this a unique business opportunity to pursue. You can offer clients the exact same service and products that a traditional formal wear rental business does simply by converting a delivery van into your operating location. Anyone seeking to rent tuxedos would simply phone in advance and book an appointment for you to go to their home or office. Alterations could even be completed on site if time allows. If not, the tuxedo could be delivered to the client the following day. Establishing alliances with wedding and event planners will go a long way to secure business as these professionals can refer your service to their clients. In a rural area where such formal rental shops are rare, you could be the only game in town.

WEB RESOURCE: www.belltuxedowholesale.com
A wholesale supplier of several brands of tuxedos.

SUSPENDERS
★★ $$ 🚚 🕒

Suspenders featuring colorful and bold designs are hot selling fashion accessories, and starting a business that manufactures suspenders is a very easy business to set in motion. The business can easily be operated from a homebased workspace on a full- or part-time basis. Researching how suspenders are manufactured can be as simple as spending a couple of hundred dollars on competitors' products for closer examination. The complete product can be packaged in a unique style to increase consumer interest and sold on a wholesale basis to fashion retailers or directly to consumers by way of the internet. Another marketing idea is to display the product at consumer-attended fashion trade shows. Manufacturing and selling related fashion accessories such as hats, belts, gloves, and neckties can also earn additional revenues. Once established, the business could prove to be very profitable, not to mention a whole lot of fun to operate.

LINEN SUPPLY SERVICE
★★ $$ 🚚 🕒

What are the basic ingredients necessary to start and operate a linen supply service? A delivery vehicle, a linen inventory, facilities to clean the linens, and good marketing skills. A linen service is simply supplying restaurants, catering services, event planners, hotels, and convention centers with tablecloths, towels, linen napkins, and in some cases entrance carpets. Many clients rent the items

on a regular or irregular basis, and rental rates include delivery, pickup, and cleaning of the items. You can sell linens as well, and they can be custom embroidered for an extra fee. If space permits, the business can be operated from a homebased location. However, if space is at a premium at home, consider starting the business as a joint venture with an established laundromat or dry cleaner.

WEB RESOURCE: www.buy-linens-wholesale.com/google/wholesale-towels.htm
This is one of a number of linen wholesalers.

SAFETY CLOTHING SALES
★ $$ 🚚 🕒

Selling safety clothing and footwear on a mobile basis to customers working in factories, at construction sites, and in warehouses is a great business to get rolling. The business can be operated on a full- or part-time basis and managed right from a homebased location. In North America, millions of dollars are spent every year by workers, companies, and organizations to purchase safety clothing such as vests, coveralls, and work boots. Securing a small portion of this very lucrative market can be as easy as securing wholesale accounts with manufacturers of these items, purchasing a delivery vehicle, and creating a catalog featuring the items for sale and distributing the catalog to potential clients. Aim to achieve yearly sales of $150,000 while maintaining a 50 percent markup, and the result will be a business that is generating a gross profit of $50,000 per year.

MATERNITY CLOTHING
★★ $$ 🚚 🕒

More than four million babies are born each year in the United States. Assuming the average expectant mother purchases five new maternity garments while pregnant adds up to a whopping 20 million maternity garments sold each year in the United States alone. There are a few ways to cash in on this very large and lucrative market. The first is to design, manufacture, and sell the maternity clothing, and the second is to purchase maternity clothing on a wholesale basis and resell the clothing for a profit. While both options are viable in terms of generating profits for the business, the first option has the potential to generate more sales and profits as well as provide more options for the operator in terms of marketing methods. Profit potential will vary; however, markups of 100 percent are not uncommon in this industry. You could also make this a mobile business, making it easier for your customers to see your merchandise.

WEB RESOURCE: www.apparelsearch.com/Apparel_Search_2.htm
The apparelsearch portal includes opportunities to purchase maternity clothing in bulk at wholesale prices.

CUSTOM NECKTIE SALES
★★ $$

Here is an interesting approach to starting a business that sells custom made and even hand painted neckties. Negotiate an exclusive distribution contract with a manufacturer of quality neckties, create a basic marketing brochure describing the neckties along with the retail prices, and distribute samples of the neckties you stock along with the marketing brochures to offices throughout your community. The purpose of this type of direct marketing sales is to leave the samples at offices for a few days along with an order form. Customers wishing to purchase a necktie for themselves, or as a gift for others, would simply complete the order form and leave it with the receptionist for you to fulfill when you return to pickup the samples. It's unique and could prove to be very profitable.

DRY-CLEANING SERVICE
★★★ $$$$

At one time it was said that the dry-cleaning industry had created more millionaires per capita than any other industry. While I am not sure that this statement still holds true today, one thing is for sure: starting a dry-cleaning service is an excellent business venture to set in motion. Ideally, a dry-cleaning service should be strategically located to be able to take advantage of the target market, and the best locations are generally built-up urban areas in office districts or storefronts with excellent parking facilities in suburban strip malls. Additionally, as a method to increase business revenues, consider providing clients with a free pickup and delivery service as well as establishing satellite locations or depots where customers can drop off and pick up their dry cleaning the next day.

Work this into your fee structure to account for the extra time it will take you to go back and forth to these locations. Also, many dry cleaners offer alterations as a way of making additional income. If this is not something you excel at, you can find a tailor or two in the area (whose work you like) and subcontract the alterations end of the business. Dry cleaning businesses are easy to promote through local ads and fliers in the neighborhood.

WEB RESOURCE: www.cleanersonline.com
Directory service listing information and links to the dry-cleaning industry.

LINGERIE SHOP
★★ $$$$ 🌐

In the new millennium, specialization is the buzzword for retail "bricks-and-mortar" businesses, and opening a lingerie shop fits the bill perfectly. Get started by selecting a highly visible store location for your business. Malls are a good choice and you will require less than 1,000 square feet, so the rent should be reasonable. Next you will want to establish accounts with lingerie manufacturers and distributors. Harness the power of the internet to locate these companies. The rest is pretty straightforward; you stock your store and sell your products. In addition to selling lingerie from the storefront location, also consider hiring sales consultants to host in-home lingerie parties as a way to bolster sales and profits. A direct mail campaign, mail-order catalog, and web site can also be used to increase revenues.

WEB RESOURCE: www.lingeriemart.com
The largest worldwide distributor of wholesale lingerie.

FABRIC SHOP
★★★ $$$$

A fabric shop retailing numerous styles and types of fabrics can be opened in a fixed storefront location or even from home, providing you have the space required and the proper zoning in place. Fabric shops have traditionally been very profitable specialty retail operations as the markups applied to fabrics for retail sales can exceed 100 percent or more. The business needs little in the way of specialized equipment, thus keeping the operating overheads to a minimum. To get going in this business you will need to secure supply arrangements with fabric manufacturers, many of which are located outside of North America, so the business will require quite a bit of research and planning. In addition to fabrics, sewing patterns, buttons, zippers, curtain rods, and even sewing machines can also be sold as a method to increase the selection of goods available to consumers as well as increasing revenues.

WEB RESOURCE: www.textileweb.com
Directory service with links to associations, manufacturers, and distributors within the fabric and textile industry.

LEATHER FASHIONS
★★ $$$$ 🎒 🕐

Selling leather fashions is another great fashion retailing business to initiate. Worldwide, there are thousands of manufacturers of leather fashions and accessories, so securing a wholesale source for products should not prove to be difficult. Consider retailing the leather fashions by way of the internet, home shopping parties, and catalog sales. Like many clothing ventures, the profit potential is excellent for a business that retails leather fashions, as many items can retail for as much as $1,000 each and the same item can often be purchased wholesale for less than $500.

WEB RESOURCE: www.leatherassociation.com
Leather Apparel Association.

WESTERN APPAREL
★★ $$$$

Like country and western music, country and western apparel is currently enjoying a rebound in terms of consumer demand and popularity. Starting a business that retails country and western apparel is a sensational new business venture to put into action. In the spirit of being unique, consider opening a retail business selling country and western apparel in a nontraditional retail environment. Try locating the business within an established country and western theme restaurant or club, or establishing the business within a music retailer. Forming this type of joint venture with an established retail business often facilitates a lower capital investment and reduced monthly operating overheads, not to mention the fact

that the business can capitalize on the existing customer base to drive sales.

WEB RESOURCE: www.sheplers.com
Major supplier of western apparel

EVENING GOWN RENTALS
★★★ $$$ 🎒 🕐

Many designer evening gowns now cost $1,000 or more, placing them far outside the financial reach of many consumers, especially those who have limited use for such a gown. This fact creates more than ample opportunity for the determined entrepreneur to start an evening gown rental business, which can be easily conducted from a homebased location. Marketing the business can be as simple as creating a full-color catalog featuring pictures and descriptions of the evening gowns for rent and distributing the catalogs throughout the community where they will generate the most interest in the service including business associations and wedding and event planners. Once established, an evening gown rental business should receive a vast amount of referrals from satisfied customers, not to mention a lot of repeat business. You can also tie it in with tuxedo rentals if you choose and call it a full "formal wear" rental business. Marketing tip: From weddings to proms, there are numerous formal occasions in May and June. Therefore, you should plan (and budget) to boost your marketing efforts as you approach these two months. Also, make sure to take deposits to cover the cost, because you don't want to see your inventory disappear.

SILK SCARVES
★ $$ 🎒 🕐

Genuine silk scarves can retail for as much as $100 each, yet can be purchased in bulk and on a wholesale basis for as little as $10 each from foreign manufacturers. Herein lies the business opportunity. Simply secure an exclusive import and distribution contract with a foreign manufacturer of silk scarves and set about marketing the product. The scarves can be resold in smaller quantities to clothing retailers on a wholesale basis or directly to consumers via fashion shows, sales kiosks, and the internet. Thousands of importing opportunities are available for the enterprising entrepreneur to capitalize on. All it takes is some initiative and a desire to become a successful business owner.

WEB RESOURCE: www.alibaba.com
Search under "silk scarves" and you can find scarves made around the world.

MONOGRAMMED BATHROBES
★★ $$ 🏠 🕐

Are you searching for a unique and interesting business opportunity that has minimal competition and can be operated from a homebased location? If so, perhaps you should consider starting a business that sells monogrammed bathrobes and towels. Clients can include luxury hotels and bed and breakfast operations as well as consumers seeking gifts for loved ones or even themselves. You can contract the embroidery aspect of the business to a local company that specializes in monogramming garments. The towels and bathrobes can be purchased in bulk on a wholesale basis from any one of the thousands of manufacturers of these products worldwide. You should have no difficulties in maintaining markup percentages in the range of 100 percent or more, potentially making this a very profitable homebased business that definitely warrants further research and consideration.

SLEEPWEAR
★★ $+ 🏠 🕐

It's a fact that more than six billion people inhabit this planet and the vast majority of people wear some sort of clothing to bed that was purposely designed to sleep in. That is one gigantic potential marketplace, thus creating an exciting business opportunity. Like many business start-ups featured in this directory, there are various options available for starting a particular business, and in the spirit of uniqueness consider these various options for starting a business that focuses on sleepwear.

- Purchase various styles of sleepwear on a wholesale basis and host in-home sleepwear parties that generate orders for your products.
- Design and manufacture your own line of sleepwear and wholesale your products to retailers.
- Create a sleepwear web site that enables visitors to purchase or create their own sleepwear by selecting style, size, and fabric.
- Design and sell patterns used for creating sleepwear and let consumers sew their own from the patterns they have purchased.
- Secure the licensing rights to popular children's program characters or themes and incorporate them into sleepwear for kids.

WEB RESOURCE: www.apparelsearch.com
Search under sleepwear and find wholesalers at this portal.

CAPS
★★ $$

Baseball-style caps, with the names of sports teams, towns or cities, or even business logos, are extremely popular. A small retail location or a booth at a mall can be your base for selling adjustable caps and even a few visors and sun hats. There are numerous cap styles and you can purchase most of your inventory for $5 or less, buying wholesale, and then sell caps at various price points starting at $9 and going up to $25 or more for caps with professional team names or logos. Stock up heavily on the home teams, world champions, and college favorites.

WEB RESOURCE: www.capwholesalers.com
A wide variety of caps available for wholesale prices.

CLOTHING STORE
★★★★ $$$$ 🌐

Not very unique; in fact, this is a rather basic, straightforward business concept. However, a well-stocked clothing store in a good high-traffic location featuring the latest in styles of men, women and/or children's clothing can make you rich. A full-time, cost- and labor-intensive effort will be necessary to bankroll and open such a store. In time, however, with good marketing and a knack for knowing what styles are on the cutting edge, you can build from a business plan to a very successful business. You will need to consider what type of store you wish to open: high-end designer fashions, off-the-rack sales by volume, etc. In addition, are you going to sell to men and women? Children? All of the above? Are you specializing in sportswear, formal attire, plus sizes, or do you run the gamut? Specialization is usually a plus, as long as you are not so specialized that you will have a hard time building a customer base. A passion for fashion, knowledge of the fashion industry, plenty of competitive research, due diligence, and a location that will draw passersby are all among the requirements to make this business work. But keep in mind that once you get started, you can write off a trip to Europe to check out fashions as a business expense. To build this business, market your store all over the place, have a professional web site, price your merchandise accordingly, and start off with plenty of sales and specials, such as buy-one-get-one-free, or save 25% on accessories if you buy a gown. Finally, remember that repeat business is the key to your success, so ask customers what they want, provide excellent customer service, have a fair return policy, and start up an email (and/or print) newsletter for your customers. This will provide little bits of fashion advice (content) while providing plenty of promotion for your apparel.

WINTER GLOVES
★★★ $$ 🏠 🕐

Why not specialize by selling a product that is much-needed in all of the colder winter regions? Buying in mass quantity, you can secure a very good discount from most manufacturers, allowing you to pay less and make more on your markup while still finding a price point that is lower than most stores. Carry a wide variety of both men's and women's gloves and sell from booths at fairs, a mall kiosk, or in conjunction with a larger store, perhaps carrying winter sporting goods. Promote yourself widely through fliers, ads in local publications, and on the internet. During the warmer months, you can switch over and run a business selling sunglasses or another summer product.

NOTES:

COMPUTER AND HOME OFFICE SUPPORT

Businesses You Can Start

KEY	
RATINGS	★
START-UP COST	$$
HOMEBASED BUSINESS	🏠
PART-TIME OPPORTUNITY	🕐
LEGAL ISSUES	⚖️
FRANCHISE OR LICENSE POTENTIAL	🌐
GREEN BUSINESSES	🍃

BOARDROOM FACILITIES OR BUSINESS CENTERS

★★★★ $$$$

The increasing trend toward conducting business enterprises from a home office continues to grow at a record pace in North America. Due to this fact, an entirely new business requirement has surfaced. What do you do if your business is homebased, yet you require short-term meeting facilities? There is one simple solution to the question if you're an enterprising entrepreneur; you start a boardroom office facility that can be rented and utilized by homebased business entrepreneurs, employees, and traveling business people. The best way to reach your target market, which of course, is homebased business owners, is to join local business associations in your community and start promoting your boardroom rental service. Almost every city and community across North America now has a Homebased Business Owners Association or Chamber of Commerce. Most of these associations host networking meetings and these networking meetings are fantastic forums to meet other business owners and introduce them to your new boardroom service. Likewise, you will want to get the message out to corporate and business travelers that may also require this type of service while conducting business in your area. Many of the larger hotels, including most of major hotel chains, have such facilities, called business centers, available for their guests. An option for you to

consider is to start your business in, or adjacent to, a smaller hotel that does not have such amenities. It will benefit the hotel because they will attract more business travelers and not have to run the facility (that's your job) plus you can also open the business center to non-hotel guests, thus capitalizing on the home office business in that community.

REQUIREMENTS: The boardroom facility, or business center, will have to be well equipped with office fixtures, furniture, and other equipment such as private meeting rooms, computers, wireless internet connections, copiers, overhead projectors, multi-line and function telephone system, stationery supplies, and other related client support services and products. You will need to have access to a catering service, messenger service, and administrative office services. When choosing a location for this business, the following should be considered: a central location, good parking, and at least 1,500 square feet of floor space. Prior to establishing the business, a market study should indicate if the business would be supported mainly by homebased business owners or business travelers; in the latter case, a facility near an airport could be beneficial.

START-UP COSTS: The start-up costs will vary greatly as to the size of the boardroom office rental facility that you intend to open. However, a $30,000 to $40,000 initial investment for equipment, leasehold improvements, and marketing will be sufficient funds to start a medium-size boardroom facility.

RROFIT POTENTIAL: Well-equipped small (6 to 20 people) meeting facilities generally rent for the following rates: $40 to $50 per hour, $100 to $150 per day, $500 to $800 per week. Additionally, you can charge for any special services you provide, such as telephone answering, secretarial services, and catering, transportation, and stationery supplies. Furthermore, to maximize profits you will want to have multiple boardrooms and meeting rooms available for rent. Once established, the profit potential for a boardroom rental facility can easily exceed $60,000 per year or more in a major metropolitan area. All of this will depend on how well you market the service to clients, since you will need to maintain a steady rate of customers utilizing the facilities.

HOME OFFICE PLANNER/DESIGNER
★★★ $$ 🏠 🕐

Functional room design is more important for a home office than you may think. "Where is my…?" "I can't work with all this noise." "My desk doesn't fit through the door!" Many first-time attempts to work from home or operate a homebased business are met with frustration and a feeling of "Where do I begin?" These very common problems are the basis of starting a home office planning/designing service with a focus on assisting employees or business owners to establish, or make the transition to, a homebased office. You would also work one on one with the client to develop successful work and organization plans and programs that are tailored to specific needs. The home office planning service can help determine the most efficient office layout, storage solutions, recycling programs, work routine schedules, computer and telephone integration, as well as suitable equipment requirements and functional furnishings that suit the needs of the home worker. Remember to market this service to corporations as well as homebased business owners, since many employees now telecommute from their homes and many of these people are not familiar with establishing a suitable home working environment.

A home office planning service can be marketed directly to potential clients by all traditional advertising mediums, as well as by joining business associations and promoting the service at networking meetings and events.

WEB RESOURCE: www.yourata.com
This site from the American Telemarketers Association links to articles and information about a large chunk of your market: telecommuters.

HOME OFFICE RESOURCE GUIDE
★★ $$$ 🏠 🕐 🌐

Are you looking to start a business that can be set in motion with a minimal capital investment, operated from a homebased office, and has the potential to be expanded across North America over a very short period of time with unlimited income potential? If so, perhaps starting a community resource guide for homebased business owners and homebased employees is the right business venture for you. The business is very straightforward; simply design a resource guide that features information on local services, products, and associations that will be of benefit to homebased employees and business owners. The resource guide can be published on a semiannual or annual basis and can be supported by two different revenue streams. The first source of revenue for such a guide is generated by way of advertising sales. Local companies can purchase advertising space in the resource guide in the format of an eighth of a page, a quarter of a page, or a full-page advertisement. The second source of revenue for the resource guide is through sales of the resource guide; currently similar small business resource books are selling in the range of $25 to $50 each. The guide can be sold through local business associations as well as on a wholesale basis to local retailers. Additional revenue for this type of business can be gained by also starting or implementing a chapter of a homebased business association that is currently not represented in your community. Overall, this business will take careful planning and research to establish; however, the rewards both personally and financially can be worth the effort.

WEB RESOURCE: www.jbsba.com/content/suites/hb_teleworking/index.shtml
Here you will find the American Association of Home Based Businesses as part of a small business advocate site.

BOOKKEEPING FOR HOMEBASED BUSINESSES
★★★ $$ 🚗 🕐

While most major companies have bookkeepers on staff, homebased businesses have the same needs without the same available help. As a bookkeeper for homebased businesses you can work from their space, or at least gather the materials and handle the bookkeeping duties for several businesses at once from your home office.

REQUIREMENTS: You will first need to train and receive certification as a bookkeeper before you send out a mailing to all homebased businesses licensed in your area. You will need to purchase at least one, if not a couple, of the most common bookkeeping software products, although in an age-old business such as this, you may not need anything too elaborate to meet the needs of many small homebased businesses.

PROFIT POTENTIAL: Bookkeepers can earn anywhere from $20,000 to $100,000 depending on the number of clients you have and work into your regular schedule.

WEB RESOURCE: www.aipb.org
American Institute of Professional Bookkeepers.

COMMERCIAL MAIL RECEIVING AGENCY
★★ $$$ 🚚

Zoning laws can make it difficult for some businesses to operate from homebased locations. Therefore, you can set up a service whereby your business receives packages for other businesses at one set address. You charge a monthly rate and make life much easier for the home business entrepreneur who finds him or herself running back and forth to post office boxes or dealing with neighbors who begrudgingly accept packages when they are not home. Many customers will want to use the services of a Commercial Mail Receiving Agency (or CMRA) for privacy purposes; for example, a person running a homebased business may not wish to divulge his or her home address.

To start off, you will need a small office space, which need not be very elaborate. Once the CMRA address becomes the "business address" for x number of businesses to have items mailed, you are all set. Of course, to keep the business from being overwhelmed by packages—since you are not running a storage facility—you will need to stipulate in a contract how long you will hold packages and how much you will charge beyond that timeframe. In addition, you will need to have a contract that clears you from responsibility for shipments or pick-ups, so that if the carrier does not show up, it is not your fault.

WEB RESOURCE: www.privacilla.org/government/cmra.html
The Postal Service's CMRA regulations.

CUSTOM COMPUTER SALES
★★ $$$$ 🚗

Selling computer systems and equipment is one of the most competitive sectors of the retailing industry. The only way to go up against the numerous retailers and manufacturers who sell computers is to have the ability to build and sell customized computers for specific purposes, such as engineering, medical technology, and advanced technical concerns. If you can put the various components together for clients and build the models they need, you can charge several thousand dollars for such specialized equipment. Such a business requires knowing the industry inside out and staying on top of the latest technology. You also need to provide top-notch customer service to compete in this industry. Such a business can be homebased and marketed at computer trade shows, fairs, online, and by word of mouth through Chief Technology Officers and IT specialists.

WEB RESOURCE: www.outletpc.com
One of several places online to get many of the basic parts you will need.

COMPUTER REPAIR TECHNICIAN
★★★ $$$ 🚗 🕐 🌐

Computer malfunction or a complete computer network systems crash can cost some companies thousands of dollars in lost revenues for every hour that their computer system is down. This fact alone is more than a compelling reason to start a mobile computer repair business. While large corporations have IT professionals on staff, mid-sized and small businesses do not, which is where you come in. Operating the business on a mobile basis means that you will never be more than a cell phone call away when a client calls to inform you that disaster has struck and they are in desperate need of your service. In addition to reliable transportation, a cell phone, and tools to operate the business, you will need computer repair experience and skills, and plenty of it. Of course, if you lack the skills needed to repair the computer systems, you could always concentrate on the marketing and management aspects of the service, and hire subcontract repair technicians to work on an on-call and revenue split basis. You can also convert space in your basement or garage for the tougher jobs that you cannot handle on site.

WEB RESOURCE: www.comptia.org
The Computing Technology Industry Association.

COMPUTER UPGRADING SERVICE
★★ $$ 🏠 🕒

Starting a business that specializes in upgrading existing computer systems with new internal and external equipment is a terrific homebased business to initiate that has great potential. A computer upgrading service is a very easy business to get rolling, providing you have the skills and equipment necessary to complete upgrading tasks, such as installing more memory into the hard drive, replacing a hard drive, setting up a wireless system, building onto an existing network (or setting one up for a company from scratch), or adding a new disk drive to the computer system. Ideally, to secure the most profitable segment of the potential market, the service should specialize in upgrading computers for small business (since most larger companies have IT professional on staff). In addition, you should market yourself to the home-based computer users who often need such assistance. Managing the business from a homebased location while providing clients with a mobile service is the best way to keep operating overheads minimized. Plus you'll potentially increase the size of your target market by expanding the service area, due to the fact the business operates on a mobile format. This can be combined with a repair business as well.

COMPUTER CLEANING SERVICE
★★ $ 🏠 🕒 🌐

Most commercial office cleaning services will not clean computers while cleaning an office. In fact most commercial cleaners will not even dust a desk that a computer is sitting on or near. Why? Simply because they do not want to accept the liability should anything happen to the computer equipment or information and programs stored within. Herein lies the business opportunity. The fastest and most efficient way to establish a computer cleaning service that specializes in cleaning computers used for business is to build alliances with commercial office cleaners so they can recommend your service to their clients. The only requirements for operating a computer cleaning service are to have the proper equipment to clean the computers along with the needed skills and a liability insurance policy.

USED COMPUTER SALES
★★ $$$ 🕒

If you love dabbling in and working on computers, this business may suit you very well. Purchasing secondhand computers and computer equipment by way of auction or surplus sales and reselling the equipment for a profit is a terrific new homebased business venture to put into action. Many corporations, government agencies, and educational institutions upgrade and replace their computer equipment on a regular basis. Often the computer equipment is only a few years old and can be purchased for as little as 5 percent of its original cost. The key is to make sure the computer system is not too antiquated and then sell it to individuals who are looking for second or third computers, or something on which their youngsters can play games or their teens can go to chat rooms. Small businesses that only use basic software for inventory or bookkeeping can also benefit from a previously owned computer at half the price of a new one. Local classified ads, fliers, or posters in busy locations, flea markets, or local fairs are places to market such a homebased business.

WEB RESOURCE: http://dmoz.org/Computers/Hardware/Used
A massive portal of similar businesses to provide you with ideas of what you can do and how you can do it.

COMPUTER DELIVERY AND ASSEMBLY SERVICE
★★ $ 🏠 🕒

A computer delivery and assembly service is a very easy new business venture to set in action. The best way to market the service is to establish joint ventures with retailers of new and secondhand computer systems and equipment. They sell it; you deliver and install it. Furthermore, as a method to earn additional income for the business, consider marketing additional services along with the delivery and assembly service, such as computer repairs or upgrading if you know how to do such tasks or can subcontract the work to someone with the necessary abilities. The amount of income the business can generate will vary as to the services provided. However, even operating a computer delivery and assembly service alone can easily generate a part-time income of $30 per hour or more.

TONER CARTRIDGE RECYCLING
★★ $$ 🚗 🕓 🌐 🌿

Ink or toner cartridges used in many photocopiers, fax machines, and printers are able to be recycled by simply replenishing the ink supply, and this fact creates a terrific opportunity to start a toner cartridge recycling business. The business can easily be run from home, and the only requirements for operating the business is to have transportation, a few basic tools, and the ability to refill the cartridges with new ink. Your competitive advantage over retail operations that sell new toner cartridges for office and printing equipment is the fact that you can offer clients free and fast delivery of recycled cartridges. In addition, clients can save as much as 50 percent by purchasing recycled toner cartridges, as opposed to the cost of new cartridges.

WEB RESOURCE: www.tonerfarm.com
Wholesaler of new and remanufactured printer toners and ink cartridges to businesses.

COMPUTER KIOSK DESIGNER
★★★ $$$ 🚗 🕓

Computer kiosks are popping up everywhere in North America: movie theaters, malls, retail stores, and grocery stores. Starting a business that designs and constructs specialty kiosks to house computer equipment is a fantastic new business venture to set in motion. The main requirements for operating this type of specialized manufacturing business is to have a good working knowledge of construction, as well as the ability to work in various material mediums. The business can be based from a well-equipped home workshop with a truck, van, or trailer for local delivery of the kiosks. Securing contracts for designing and manufacturing the kiosks can be accomplished by building a few samples, creating a marketing brochure, and distributing the marketing material to potential clients in need of this kind of product. Once established, this type of specialty manufacturing business can prove to be very profitable.

MOBILE COMPUTER TRAINING
★★★ $$ 🚗 🕓 🌐

As a rule of thumb, most computer training schools require the student to come to their business location for training classes. However, for companies that have recently upgraded their computers system or have introduced new software into the business, it is often not practical to have ten or more people going off-site for computer upgrade training or to learn how to maximize the benefits of a new software program. Herein lies the business opportunity. Combining your computer, software, and marketing skills and experience, you can start a mobile computer training service. The classes can be conducted at the client's location as well as using the client's computer equipment. Income potential range is at least $50 per hour.

WEB RESOURCE: www.icca.org
Independent Computer Consultants Association.

WEB SITE QUALITY CONSULTANT
★★ $$ 🚗 🕓 🌐

In exchange for a $150 consulting fee, give small business owners the real lowdown on the quality of their web site. In the rush to get online, many small business owners forget that their web site must effectively promote their business and provide quality information and service. In fact, more than 75% of web sites posted by businesses are not generating much business or serving any purpose other than giving a phone number and directions.

As a web site quality consultant you can view a client's web site and submit a full report. The report could include a comparison to competitor sites, a rating on how user-friendly their site is, and suggestions on how the site could be improved, such as practical tips for user-friendly functionality and/or a better design. You can show the business owner ways to provide enhanced visitor services and improve the content, graphics, or navigation, or all of the above. The cost of this very beneficial consulting service is low, but the impact that it could potentially have on a client's site could mean the difference between cyber failure and cyber success. When you put it in those terms, securing clients should not be difficult. Of course, to start such a business, you need to be an expert on what makes up a good, functional, and cost-effective web site for a specific business—and remember, not all businesses will have the same potential clients or needs. A lot of preliminary research will be necessary to conquer the learning curve involved in starting such a business. Note: Once you do get started, make sure to check in and monitor the results of your recommendations and analysis. This is how you can build your business, based on marketing the success stories of those business owners who listened to you and, as a result, saw significantly higher profits.

WEB SITE DESIGN
★★★ $$ 🏠 🕒

Thousands of web sites are launched everyday, and here is your chance to cash in by starting a web site design service. Fear not if you do not know how to design a highly effective web site. You can take courses in web site design at your local community college or, failing that, you can hire a high-tech wizard to design the sites while you concentrate your efforts on sales and marketing. Online competition in web site design and service is steep so you may want to take a more hands-on approach and market the service in your own city or community. Start by designing a few sample sites—one in an e-commerce format and one as an information portal. Next, initiate a letter-writing and follow-up telephone campaign to introduce yourself and your service to small business owners in your community that currently do not have a business web site, or have a very minimal site at best. The goal is to get a presentation appointment at their place of business. Finally, armed with your laptop or notebook computer, you can meet with business owners, present your sample sites and explain the benefits of your web site design service.

WEB RESOURCE: www.iawmd.com
The International Association of Web Masters and Designers.

COMPUTER COVERS, CASES, AND ACCESSORIES
★★ $$ 🏠 🕒

Let's face it, everyone has a computer or two or three, so why not capitalize on that fact by selling all that goes with a computer? It's very easy for consumers to buy the hardware directly from Apple stores, online from Dell, or at one of the major electronics stores. However, without much overhead, you can sell all the add-ons and accessories at reasonable prices, including adapters, notebook batteries, laptop carrying cases and desktop covers, special gaming mouse pads and keyboards, glare guards, and a slew of other gadgets designed to accompany the computer. You can even sell Paw sense, a special devise to protect your keyboard from wandering cats. Stay on top of what the latest "needs" are for computer users and then promote the products to solve those needs. There's an endless stream of goodies coming out for computers, and if you can stay one step ahead you can forge a successful business from a small retail location, a booth at a busy mall, booths at trade shows and a well-planned web site.

WEB RESOURCE: www.pcadapter.com
A wholesale source of computer accessories

COMPUTER SECURITY CONSULTANT
★★★★ $$ 🕒

As of mid-2006 there were over 185,000 listed computer viruses with the number continuing to grow. Add on the problems caused by spyware, adware, phishing, and identity theft and there is clearly a need for online security. While it is unlikely that you will know how to circumvent the vast majority of viruses out there, if you are highly knowledgeable about personal firewalls, multi-layer network and virus protection systems, and the many software applications (from Symantec, McAfee, PC-cillin and various others) you can provide the much needed support and consulting necessary to protect small and homebased businesses against these growing online threats. Market your services through local business associations, the chamber of commerce, in conjunction with computer stores (who can sell the products you recommend and install) and by advertising in business publications, as well as having a presence on the internet through your own site, ads on other sites and reciprocal links. Make sure you stress the point that billions of dollars worth of business is lost every year because companies do not take the time to protect themselves from such threats.

DATA BACKUP SERVICE
★★★ $$$

So many businesses today are dependent upon computers as their lifelines. However, once the technology goes down for a business, all vital data and business records can be lost. The result can be very damaging and even result in bankruptcy. Most business owners mean to backup their database and their computer systems on a regular basis but very few ever actually do so. While large companies have IT professionals handling this task, small business owners do not, and in many cases, if the system goes down they can lose a lot of valuable information. You, however, can be their savior by providing data backup information, consulting, software, backup plans and actual offsite backup on your servers. While you may not need a full-fledged server farm (unless you sign up some major companies) you can have a system in place 24/7 to run backups of databases for businesses in any part of the country. Therefore, if a hurricane such as Katrina shuts down a business for several weeks or months, the data can be maintained and retrieved when the business reopens.

The initial set up costs to handle this business from a homebased location should be about $10,000 for the hardware and software to backup your initial clients and for your marketing purposes. Depending on the amount and complexity of the data, you can start as low as $15 per month for 1 GB of data and go up to 6 GBs. Do your homework first and study up on tape backup sources, hard disk cloning, mirroring and imaging hard drives as well as the different types of offsite backups you can offer such as continuous backup and no-wait recovery.

As threats continue to increase, this is a business that has tremendous potential to make you rich, if you know what you are doing and market aggressively.

COMPUTER AND VIDEO GAME DESIGNER
★★★ $$

Okay, so you have to be very well versed in how computer game technology works to even consider something like this. However, if you are creative in the tech environ-ment, have a firm grasp of game mechanics, and can develop the concept, layout, and design of video or computer games, you can have a fun and lucrative career. Writing and art experience, to go along with basic programming skills, are very helpful in this career. While you can hire someone to handle the higher-level technical chores, creativity will make or break you when it comes to creating original game ideas that will sell.

Once you create a game concept, you will take it to video game publishers who will test and develop the game from the initial stages, hopefully to a fully marketed product. You should study the game market very carefully to know what is out there and what is forthcoming. This is a highly competitive business, and just like getting a movie produced by a major film company, getting a video game on the shelves is quite an accomplishment. If you have some new and innovative concepts, you could make fortune. Note: Copyright any original game ideas before letting anyone else see them.

WEB RESOURCE: www.igda.org
International Game Developers Association.

DATABASE ADMINISTRATOR
★★ $$

Most businesses need to accumulate and store a great amount of data about their inventory, customers, suppliers, vendors, employees and so on; especially businesses that are primarily web based. A database administrator makes sure that all data is properly stored, safeguarded, and can be retrieved as necessary. A thorough knowledge of computer storage systems and software is necessary to succeed in this career. However, if you are well versed in the latest in technology, you can locate many potential clients in small and midsize businesses that are growing. It is these business owners who are looking to outsource some of the data storage responsibilities. You need to make sure you get your business card and a brochure or flier into their hands, and have a web site so they can see your credentials and philosophy on handling sensitive data properly. You also must be prepared to deal with everyone from computer super-geeks to people with no computer background. Trust is a major factor in this business, so your clients will want to meet you personally. In some situations, you may be handling the database at their location, while in others, the data may be electronically and securely transferred to your own systems, which need to be in place with the utmost of security installed.

Note: To be most competitive, you should seek out certification through a computer training program. According to the US Department of Labor, the middle 50 percent of database administrators earned between $44,490 and $81,140 as of 2004.

SYSTEM ANALYST
★★ $$

Essentially, this is a business about helping other businesses get their work done most efficiently. System analysts help business owners and managers determine what hardware and software applications to buy, and how to integrate and maximize their technical capacities for the highest possible efficiency. In short, they help businesses with all of their computer needs. You will need to be a very good listener (which may be your competitive advantage, since many computer experts love to do things their way). Once you assess the problems or needs of the business, you can draw out the solutions on diagrams and charts to show the flow of information, how the network will operate, the means of processing and storing data, etc. Analysts experiment with various plans until they come up with the quickest, easiest, and least costly means by which the client can achieve his or her business goals. Since most of the work will take place at the client's offices or place of business, you should be able to freelance as a system analyst from a homebased location. If you are good and word spreads, you can make $100,000; and with little overhead, other than marketing yourself and advertising, you can keep most of it (except of course what Uncle Sam takes).

TELECOMMUNICATIONS SPECIALIST
★★ $$ 🖥️ 🕓

More and more people are telecommuting, and that means appropriate systems need to be in place to make this means of working from home a smooth process. Telecommunications specialists design voice and data communication systems, supervise installation of these systems, and provide maintenance and service to clients after installation. This can be a simple system set up

between a small business owner and one or two employees, or an elaborate network involving hundreds of valuable offsite workers. Setting up wireless transmissions, voice transmission, data communication, cable-to-modem communication, and satellite communication capabilities are all part of the duties of a telecommunications specialist. If you have the high-tech skills, this is a growing business and one you can cash in on by staying ahead of the ever-changing technical learning curve. Market yourself to new businesses and growing businesses of all sizes. As a telecommunications specialist you can charge $100+ per hour and work from a home base, although you will typically spend the majority of your time in home offices or satellite offices of larger businesses.

NOTES:

33
CRAFT
Businesses You Can Start

DECORATIVE PARTITION SCREEN MANUFACTURING
★★ $$ 🏠 🕒

If you have an entrepreneurial spirit and a creative talent, starting a business that manufactures and sells decorative partition screens may be just the moneymaking opportunity that you have been looking for. Partition screens are commonly used in homes, offices, and even outdoors to add decorative flair or to divide and partition any existing space. To start, you will need to have a basic knowledge of carpentry, artistic talent, and the desire to succeed in this business. Once completed there are numerous ways to market the screens, including selling them to specialty retailers on a wholesale basis, placing them in retail stores on a consignment basis, or selling the screens to residential and commercial interior decorators.

This is truly a unique and inexpensive homebased business opportunity to start that can be operated on a full- or part-time basis. In terms of product pricing, the first step is to check out the competition. A general pricing formula is to take your material and labor costs, which add up to the product cost. Then figure out your markup (anywhere from 50 to 100 percent) and multiply it by your product costs to equal the wholesale or retail selling price.

CANDLE MAKING
★★ $ 🏠 🕒

The popularity of specialty candles has really taken off in the past decade as more and more people are starting to enjoy the relaxing effect that burning scented candles can have. This popularity and consumer demand for specialty candles creates a tremendous business opportunity for the innovative entrepreneur to start a business that manufactures and sells them. A good starting point for learning how to make candles would be to visit the local library, take an evening class, or visit the web site for the National Candle Association. A homebased candle-making business is best suited for the entrepreneur who is seeking additional income on a part-time basis, with a long-term goal of establishing a full-time and profitable business concern. Selling the completed candles can be as easy as renting a table at a local craft show, placing the candles in retail locations on consignment basis, or even establishing wholesale accounts with national specialty retailers. Furthermore, adding fragrance, coloring, and creating artistic details on the candles will definitely increase consumer demand for the product and result in more profit for you.

WEB RESOURCE: www.candles.org
National Candle Association.

CRAFT SUPPLY STORE
★★★ $$$$

Starting a craft supply retail store is a fantastic new business enterprise to set in motion. There are thousands of people across North America working in the craft industry, as a hobby or fulltime, and all of these potential customers need a place to purchase their craft supplies. This is the kind of retail business that will require a substantial initial start-up investment, but the profit potential can easily justify the investment. Ideally, this type of business enterprise will be located in a highly visible and easily accessible location within the community. Furthermore, be sure to carry a wide variety of craft supplies. The key to successful retailing is to build repeat clientele, and the best way to ensure this happens is to have the store well-stocked with products and supplies that represent all areas of the craft industry. Marketing this type of enterprise would be through traditional advertising mediums such as newspapers, fliers, and radio. An innovative approach to generate more income would be to hold instructional seminars after business hours on different crafting techniques such as painting or silk-flower arrangements. Locating wholesalers and distributors for products will not be difficult, and the profit potential is tremendous as product markups can be 100 percent or more.

WEB RESOURCE: www.craftassoc.com
National Craft Association, links to manufactures and distributors of crafts supplies.

POTTERY
★★ $$ 🏠 🕐

Starting a business that designs, produces, and sells pottery items is definitely best suited for the entrepreneur with a creative flair who is seeking a unique homebased business opportunity. Some of the aspects of this business to be considered are:

- *Ability.* Anyone considering this business venture will definitely need the ability to not only create pottery items, but to create interesting and unique ones.
- *Equipment and supplies.* All equipment and supplies required for starting and operating a pottery-making business are readily available in almost every community through craft supply stores that stock the items or order them on an as-needed basis.
- *Marketing.* Pottery items can be sold by renting a table at craft shows or street fair, by selling the pottery to retailers on a wholesale basis, and by placing the pottery items in retail stores on a consignment basis.
- *Business location.* A pottery business is ideally suited to being operated from a homebased studio location. Additionally, if zoning permits, the studio can also act as a retail outlet or factory direct sales outlet for the pottery products. In addition to creating and selling pottery items, you can also generate additional business revenues and profits by holding instructional classes on pottery making and pottery glazing techniques.

WEB RESOURCE: www.amartpot.org
The American Art Pottery Association.

CACTUS ARRANGEMENTS
★★ $ 🏠 🕐

Creating and selling cactus arrangements—what a great and inexpensive homebased business venture to start. As houseplants go, cactuses are one of the most popular. The reason is simple. People love having plants to decorate their homes, but most people do not have the time or the green thumbs required to care for plants. Cactus plants are very easy to grow and require very little in the way of regular maintenance. Purchasing cactus plants and related materials from a wholesale company would be your first step. Be sure to negotiate the best price possible with the wholesaler, and also research the care and requirements for each type of cactus. Now the fun part starts: creating interesting cactus arrangements that will command top dollar. The selling price of the cactus arrangements will greatly depend on the arrangement itself; however, adding product costs and labor time together, plus a 100 percent markup, is not out of line in terms of establishing a retail selling value. Ideally, aim to establish wholesale accounts with retailers to stock and sell the cactus arrangements, as well as selling the arrangements directly to consumers via rented sales kiosks in a busy mall or market.

WEB RESOURCE: www.growit.com
Online directory of nursery wholesalers.

HAND-PAINTED PLANTING POTS
★★ $ 🏠 🕐

Gardening is one of the fastest growing pastimes in North America. For the entrepreneur seeking to capitalize on the huge demand for garden-related products, look no further than starting a business that creates and sells one of a kind hand-painted clay gardening pots. More and more people are searching for unique and interesting ways in which to display their flowers and shrubs, so why not create extraordinary planting pots for these consumers and start making money? Simply purchase clay planting pots from a local wholesale company, and paint and decorate the pots with unique, interesting, and colorful themes and designs. Once completed, the flowerpots can be sold in various ways, including directly to specialty retailers or at garden centers on a wholesale basis and to residential and commercial interior decorators and garden planners. You can also sell them by renting a sales table at a local craft show or flea market and of course directly to consumers by advertising the hand-painted flower pots for sale over the internet.

WEB RESOURCE: www.flowerpots.com
A portal leading to numerous sites for buying pots to paint.

MOSAIC TILE CREATIONS
★★★ $ 🏠 🕐

Creating home decoration items featuring mosaic tile designs is an exceptional business venture to set in motion. Not only can this enterprise be started and run from a homebased location, but also this business is also very inexpensive to initiate. Best of all, interesting home and office decoration products are always in high demand. Create unique mosaic tile designs—everything from tabletops to mosaic tile picture frames. Your only limitations will be your imagination. Mosaic tiles can be purchased ready to install or you can create your own simply by buying discontinued styles and colors as well as collecting broken tiles from local building and renovation companies. Of course, the latter options would be excellent choices, as most could be purchased at a very low or no cost, not to mention the fact that you will be recycling any unwanted waste product. Marketing the mosaic tile creations can through traditional advertising mediums,

as well as by renting a weekend sales kiosk in a market or mall. Additionally, be sure to contact interior decorators in your community to introduce them to your unique decorating product line.

WEB RESOURCE: www.mosaicmercantile.com
Manufacturer and distributor of mosaic tile equipment and supplies.

HAND-PAINTED STORAGE BOXES
★★ $ 🏠 🕐

With so many people looking for unique and interesting ways to organize their personal belongings, home office documents, and family keepsakes, hand-painted storage boxes are sure to fit the bill. The options are endless! Using materials such as wood, metal, and cardboard, you can create designer storage boxes to suit every decor. You will need to have some artistic talent, but with that said, arts and craft classes are available in almost every community in North America. Additionally, consider building the storage boxes out of recycled materials as well as using organic paints to decorate the storage boxes. Not only will you be helping the environment by doing this, but you will also be able to capitalize on an earth-friendly marketing approach.

LAWN ORNAMENT SALES
★★ $$ 🏠 🕐

Not only are lawn decorations easy to make, they are also easy products to sell. Combining these two facts creates a wonderful business opportunity for the innovative entrepreneur to start a business that manufactures and sells them. The first step will be to purchase or make the molds required for manufacturing the lawn ornaments; the rest is very straightforward. Simply practice making and painting lawn ornaments until you are satisfied with the finished product. Next you will be ready to start making money. Lawn ornaments are currently retailing in the range of $25 to $100 each, depending on the size and style of the item. The profit potential is excellent as it only costs about $5 in material to produce the average size precast lawn ornament. The lawn decorations can be sold on a wholesale basis to retailers, or you can even sell them directly to consumers right from your own front yard.

WEB RESOURCE: www.concrete-success.com
Suppliers of lawn ornament molds and equipment.

WOODCARVING
★★ $$ 🚗 🕒

Do you carve wood for a hobby, and are the carvings good? If so, consider starting a woodcarving business that not only lets you work at what you like best, but also makes you some money at the same time. Original, interesting, and unique woodcarvings sell like crazy in the right retail environment, such as arts and crafts shows, and specialty retail shops. Finding retailers to stock and sell the woodcarvings is simple. Why? Because the owners of these businesses know how well woodcarvings sell and how much money can be made selling woodcarvings. Of course, if you want to keep the bulk of the profits yourself, you can always sell your woodcarving creations directly to consumers at flea markets, fairs, on your own web site, or by local advertisements featuring photos of the woodcarvings for sale, or on one of the many online auction sites such as eBay.

WEB RESOURCE: www.chipchats.org
National Wood Carvers Association.

KNITTING
★ $ 🚗 🕒

Do you currently knit sweaters, jackets, and more? If so, perhaps you should consider turning your hobby craft into a profitable part-time business enterprise. The business is to simply create beautiful and unique hand-knitted products from sweaters to a clothing line for stuffed animals. The opportunities are endless; all you need is a creative spirit, knitting needles, some yarn, and you're in business. For the truly enterprising entrepreneur, aim toward developing a web site that features pre-made knit clothing products for sale, as well as a custom made-to-order service where site visitors could simply fill out an order form for the size and style of knit products they want. The income and profit potential will vary in this type of unique crafts business. However, there should be no problem in attaining a part-time income level of $10,000 per year or more after expenses.

WEB RESOURCE: www.tkga.com
The Knitting Guild Association

STUFFED ANIMALS
★★ $$ 🚗 🕒

There are a few different approaches that can be taken when considering starting a business that focuses on selling stuffed animals. The first approach is to design and manufacture the stuffed animals yourself. The second approach is to purchase stuffed animals on a wholesale basis and resell them for a profit. The third approach is to purchase antique stuffed animals and resell them for a profit. All three approaches have a great opportunity at business success as stuffed animals, new or old, are always popular and will always be in high demand by collectors and consumers alike. The profit potential is outstanding, especially if you can locate a good source for antique stuffed animals, as it is not uncommon for antique teddy bears to sell for as much as $1,000 each. For new stuffed animals, you can sell at fairs, flea markets, and places that may be holding carnivals as prizes to be won.

WEB RESOURCE: www.toydirectory.com
Directory service listing toy manufacturers.

CRAFT SHOWS
★ $$ 🕒

Do you want to know how you can make an extra $25,000 per year by hosting only four annual craft shows? It is actually quite easy to host craft shows, and in the spirit of being unique, let me suggest a way that you cannot only make an additional $25,000 per year part-time, but you can also have a lot of fun doing it. The business concept is very direct. Simply, secure 100 craft vendors per craft show that you host, and charge each vendor $100 for table rental. Holding a winter, spring, summer, and fall show will generate total business revenues of $40,000 (4 shows x 100 vendors each show x $100 per table booth = $40,000). The next trick is to keep as much of the gross revenues as possible, and seek out ways of promoting the show so craft vendors will receive maximum exposure. Here is how it can be accomplished:

- *Free location for the craft shows.* Finding a location to hold the craft show without having to pay rent is very easy. Simply negotiate with the landlord of the location that shows' admittance fees and concession snack revenue will be retained by the location or landlord. One thousand people paying $1 each to attend and spending only $2 each on snacks will result in a two-day fee of $3,000. As you can see, finding a location for the craft show should not be hard.

- *Free advertising for the craft shows.* Advertising and promoting the craft show for free is also very easy. Start by negotiating with the craft vendors that 5 percent of their total sales will go to a community charity. The next step is to contact a local newspaper or TV station and negotiate a joint venture in terms of sponsoring the craft show and the local charity. Once again, it will not be hard to find a newspaper or TV station that is willing to give away some free advertising in exchange for the goodwill benefits of being a co-sponsor of a community event for charity.

WEB RESOURCE: www.artsandcraftshows.net
Directory service listing arts and craft shows.

QUILT SALES
★★ $$ 🚗 🕒

Quilting has been around for generations and continues to thrive. Like many things today, "Everything old is once again new and popular," and starting a business that sells custom-made one-of-a-kind quilts could be your opportunity to reap big financial benefits. If you are already familiar with quilting, great! If not, simply research the different aspects of quilting by visiting your local library or looking up "quilting" on your search engine and you will find enough information to get started. For those of you not familiar with copyright laws, be sure not to infringe on someone else's creation. Selling the quilts could be as easy as renting a table at local craft shows or selling the custom quilts via the web to a global audience. Additionally, look for opportunities in purchasing antique quilts and reselling the quilts for a profit, as the collector market for antique quilts is hot.

WEB RESOURCE: www.nqaquilts.org
National Quilting Association.

BASKET WEAVING
★★ $ 🚗 🕒

Starting a business that manufactures and sells custom-made baskets is an incredible enterprise to get rolling, simply because people from every walk of life are always searching for the perfect piece of functional home decoration. Utilizing a wide variety of raw materials ranging from rattan to wire will provide you with not only the material required to make the baskets but also result in a varied and interesting product line. If you do not know how to basket weave, don't worry; you can always take a few instructional classes or locate other basket weavers and sell their finished products. Marketing the baskets can be accomplished by establishing accounts with retailers to stock and sell the baskets, as well as by hiring a direct sales force to host home parties that feature the complete basket product line for sale.

WEB RESOURCE: www.weavespindye.org
Handweavers Guild of America Inc.

DRIED FLOWERS
★ $ 🚗 🕒

Growing, processing, and selling dried flowers could put you on the path to self-employment independence, and financial freedom. One of the best aspects about setting this business enterprise in motion is the fact that it can easily be started right from your home, using your own garden as the initial source for the flowers to be dried and sold. Once the business is ready to be expanded there are a couple of options in terms of the required flowers. The first is to lease vacant land to increase flower production and the second is to purchase flowers. While the second option is easier, it will also reduce the amount of available profit. Once dried and packaged, the flowers can be sold to retailers on a wholesale basis. Profit potential range is $5,000+ per year part-time.

ARTIFICIAL PLANTS
★★ $$ 🚗 🕒

Designing, making, and selling artificial plants is a terrific homebased business venture to put into action, as the demand for artificial plants is strong and will continue to be strong in the future. Artificial plants are easy to make, and the raw materials required are available in almost every community through craft supply stores. Additionally, many of these same craft stores also stock books and instruction videos on how to make artificial plants for profit. Marketing the artificial plants can be accomplished in a number of ways, including selling the plants to retailers on a wholesale basis, placing the plants at retail locations on a consignment basis, and selling the plants to interior designers and event planners at discounted prices.

SEASHELL JEWELRY
★★ $ 🏠 🕐

Do you live near the ocean and take daily walks on the beach? If so, you could be walking past thousands of dollars in potential profits and not even realize it. Starting a small homebased business that designs and sells seashell jewelry is not only an easy and inexpensive business to set in motion, it also could prove to be very fun and interesting. The business opportunity is to collect various sizes, shapes, and colors of seashells right from the beach and create beautiful jewelry. Once completed the jewelry can be sold to local retailers on a wholesale basis, placed in retail stores on a consignment basis, or sold at street fairs. A seashell jewelry manufacturing business is not only easy to start and run, but it could also generate an extra income of $10,000 per year or more. It's also a great business to start if you have kids, because they can help you find your supplies along the beach. Be sure to check local regulations before collecting shells; many areas have restrictions.

CHRISTMAS DECORATIONS
★★ $ 🏠 🕐

Each year, billions of dollars are spent on Christmas decorations worldwide, and securing a portion of this very lucrative market is easy. This new business enterprise is very straightforward and can be initiated by anyone, as it does not require any special business experience or skills. Simply design, produce, and sell custom one-of-a-kind Christmas decorations. Go for the high end of the market where consumers are willing to pay $25 or more for one Christmas decoration that will become a family heirloom. The decorations can be made from almost any type of raw material, in almost any popular Christmas theme. The key to success is that the Christmas decorations must be unique and appealing. The decorations can be sold to specialty retailers on a wholesale basis or directly to consumers via renting a sales table at art and craft shows. Hint: While this is obviously a seasonal business, don't be fooled and wait too far into the year to get started. You should be ready to start selling in September, October at the latest. That means start making decorations by February.

PLASTER CASTS
★ $ 🏠 🕐

Now a few of you reading this may be wondering how you can start a profitable business that creates and sells plaster casts. Probably many more of you are wondering why someone would purchase a plaster cast. Amazingly enough, there are businesses that not only survive producing plaster casts, but also earn very substantial profits for doing so. Annually, millions of plaster casts depicting people, animals, and objects are sold as home decorations. The materials needed to make plaster casts are inexpensive and readily available at most crafts supply stores. Many of these same stores also carry information, books, and videos about how to make plaster casts and, in some cases, even conduct classes on the subject. The potential to earn an income or generate a profit from this very unique business enterprise will obviously vary based on a number of factors. However, providing you can tap into the right marketing and distribution mix, there will be no reason why you cannot only create an income but also a profit, as others have already proven that this can be accomplished.

FLOWER ARRANGEMENTS
★ $ 🏠 🕐

Millions of flowers are purchased each year for every kind of occasion imaginable, and all of these occasions have one thing in common: the flowers have to be arranged once they arrive at the event. The opportunity for making money by creating and selling flowers arrangements are endless—everything from creating small bouquets and large center pieces to establishing joint ventures with interior decorators and event planners. You can even simply supply real estate agents with thank-you flower bouquets delivered to their clients who have recently purchased a home. Gaining new clients for the business can be as easy as preparing samples of your work and hand delivering them to potential clients with a full marketing presentation outlining the value and benefits of your service. This is a great part-time homebased business opportunity to set in motion, and the spin-off opportunities to earn a substantial yearly income are almost unlimited.

WEB RESOURCE: www.aifd.org
American Institute of Floral Designers.

CUSTOM BUTTONS
★★★ $$ 🏠 🕒

Are you searching for a unique and inexpensive home-based business opportunity that has little competition and a real chance of succeeding? If so, consider starting a business that specializes in manufacturing and selling custom one-of-a-kind buttons for clothing. The buttons can be manufactured from just about every type of raw material including wood, metal, seashells, and glass. The key to success in button manufacturing is two-fold. First, the buttons must be unique in design and appearance; and second, the marketing of the buttons must be well thought out. Consider the following:

- Establish accounts with specialty retailers to purchase the buttons on a wholesale basis.
- Sell the buttons to manufacturers and designers of custom clothing.
- Sell the custom clothing buttons directly to consumers via the internet.

POTPOURRI SALES
★★ $ 🏠 🕒

Starting a business that makes and wholesales potpourri products is an excellent homebased business venture to set in motion. The potpourri can be made from dried flowers, pine cones, and bark mulch with fragrant essential oils added. Once packaged, the potpourri can be sold on a wholesale basis to specialty retailers or directly to consumers via a sales kiosk or craft show. One important aspect of the business that should not be overlooked is packaging. The packaging for the potpourri should be unique to your business as a method to separate your product from the competition. Additionally, be sure to use recycled materials for the packaging of the products, as this will not only help the environment, but also it can also be used as a fantastic marketing tool.

WEB RESOURCE: www.pioneerthinking.com/potpourri.html
One of several places on the web to find potpourri recipes.

IRON SCULPTURES
★ $ 🏠 🕒

Calling all talented artists with welding skills and a home workshop. It's time to start profiting from your talents by starting a business that produces iron art sculptures. The raw materials required for the sculptures can be purchased from metal recycling facilities for low or no cost. Once completed, the sculptures can be marketed directly to art-loving consumers and art collectors on a web site through local art shows and at galleries. Furthermore, along with artistic sculptures, you can craft iron sculptures that have functional value such as weather vanes, coat racks, and partitions.

WEB RESOURCE: www.sculptor.org/Foundries/IronSteelSculptors.htm
A good place to get information on iron sculpting and see the works of other sculptors for inspiration.

LAMPSHADES
★ $ 🏠 🕒

Are you searching to start a part-time business that has virtually no competition? If the answer is yes, then consider starting a business that manufactures and markets custom-made lampshades. The key to success in this very unusual manufacturing business is to ensure you create unique lampshades, not only in appearance and design but also in your choice of raw material used in the construction. Market the lampshades by contacting local interior decorators and setting appointments with them to introduce them to your unique product. Additionally, aim to sell the lampshades to retailers on a wholesale basis or place the lampshades into retail stores on a consignment basis.

WEB RESOURCE: www.lampshop.com
Supplies, tools, and information on making lampshades.

WINE RACKS
★ $ 🏠 🕒

Are you searching for an inexpensive business start-up that can be operated part-time from home? If so you may want to consider activating a business that focuses on manufacturing and wholesaling custom-made wine racks. The business is easy to establish and only requires basic woodworking skills and woodworking equipment. In addition to constructing the wine racks from wood, you could also build the racks from a metal or, even better, all recycled material such as scrap metal and used building material that can usually be acquired for free with a little bit of detective work. Once you have designed and constructed a few wine racks, they can be wholesaled or consigned to wine stores, furniture stores, liquor stores, u-brew-it wine shops, and even restaurants. The key to success in wine rack manufacturing is to have a unique product that consumers are compelled to purchase for themselves or as a gift for others.

WEB RESOURCE: www.uniqueprojects.com/projects/winerack/ winerack.htm
A free plan for a wine rack.

DESIGNER PILLOWS
★ $ 🏠 🕐

Turn your sewing machine and skills into a part-time profit center by creating custom-designed pillows. The pillows can be completed on a made-to-order basis, or you can develop standard designs and themes and sell the pillows on a wholesale basis. Be sure to establish alliances with interior decorators, as these decorators could become your best customers for custom-designed pillows. Additional income can also be earned by designing and manufacturing custom pillow and cushion slipcovers with elaborate themes. Stick with standard sizes or custom made-to-order designs for this side of the business.

WEB RESOURCE: www.upholster.com/howto/pill.html
How to make pillows and cushions.

STAINED GLASS
★★ $ 🏠 🕐

Stained glass lampshades, sun-catchers, window inserts, and light panels are extremely popular home decoration products. In almost every community across North America there are classes available that offer training about how to make stained glass items. Additionally, the materials and equipment needed to start this part-time business are very inexpensive. Completed stained glass creations can be sold by way of craft shows, home and garden shows, on your own web site, on retailer's web sites, or by renting a sales kiosk in malls on weekends. The profit potential is outstanding, as stained glass lampshades alone can retail for as much as $1,000 or more.

WEB RESOURCE: www.anythinginstainedglass.com
Wholesale source for supplies and equipment.

CORSAGES
★ $ 🏠 🕐

Corsages are used as a fashion accessory for hundreds of special occasions, and one of the best aspects about starting a business that makes them is the fact that the business can be started for peanuts. A small amount of research and practice will be required for to train yourself in the art of making corsages. This information can be obtained at local libraries, craft shops, or on the internet. Once completed, corsages can be sold to local flower and gift shops on a wholesale basis. Additionally, be sure to build alliances with wedding and event planners in your community, as these special occasion planners can utilize your service themselves or refer their clients to your service.

WEB RESOURCE: www.save-on-crafts.com/cormakbas.html
Instructions on how to make a corsage.

METAL JEWELRY MAKING
★★ $ 🏠 🕐

Most jewelry makers have experimented with different materials and styles before finding their niche. If you have discovered that you like working with metals, you can design and sell jewelry at craft shows, flea markets, fairs, and booths at malls and make some good money—if your designs are original and you know how to sell. If you have a good eye for detail you can not only make metal jewelry, but also repair jewelry for additional income. Before getting started in this as a business, have an inventory to show your work and get a feel for pricing from visiting other crafts fairs and flea markets. You can also sell to retailers by setting up appointments. Practice your sales pitch and, if possible, take pieces you may be able to reproduce easily, in the event that your work sells immediately and the retailer calls you for more pieces just like the ones you just sold.

WEB RESOURCE: www.cooksongold.com/indexgb.html
Information on the metal jewelry field.

NAPKIN RINGS
★★ $ 🏠 🕐 🖋

You see them in gift shops, on dining room tables, and in the finer restaurants. Napkin rings are fairly easy to make from wood or metal and decorate in any of various manners. To successfully launch such a business, you will want to make your napkin rings unique and market them to home stores, gift shops, and other local stores and/or sell them at home shows, flea markets, fairs, and other such events. You can also use scrap metals or recycled materials to create the napkin rings, such as old film canisters, and even get the family into the business with youngsters making some napkin rings from paper maché. While you probably won't end up with a retail napkin ring shop (although it would be unique), you can make some additional income from a homebased napkin ring making business.

SOAP MAKING
★★ $ 🏠 🕐 🖋

Homemade soaps are rapidly becoming a favorite of the ecologically aware "green" generation. Books and web sites abound with soap making recipes. However, while many people find that the homemade soaps smell great and are healthier for the skin, few people take the time to make them. That is where you come in. By taking the time to make, package, and market homemade soaps, you can make a nice income. Market to home and bath retail stores, body shops, health shops, at craft fairs, and through your own web site. While the scent is a big marketing plus, so are the packaging, the name, and the story of how the one-of-a-kind soaps are made. It's a personal item and therefore should be marketed at a personal level.

WEB RESOURCE: www.soapcrafters.com
Scents, flavors, molds and everything else you need to begin soap making for fun and profit.

ARTS & CRAFTS INSTRUCTOR
★★★ $ 🕐

If you are good at making things, you owe it to yourself to teach the next generation (or even the previous one) how to make things. Children, adults and seniors can all enjoy arts and crafts classes and you can teach anything from soap making to origami. Schedule courses in conjunction with a youth group, community center, after school center, senior center, evening adult ed program, or in affiliation with a church, temple, association, or even a corporation as a means of stress reduction. Your costs will be renting the space, promoting the courses, and for materials, although it is usually advisable to charge a small materials fee. If you can team up with various other crafters, you can list several courses in one brochure. If not, make up a flier for distribution at wherever you arrange to hold the classes, as well as all local public gathering hot spots for the demographic groups you are seeking.

NOTES:

_____

_____

_____

_____

_____

_____

_____

_____

_____

_____

_____

_____

34
DESKTOP PUBLISHING
Businesses You Can Start

SPECIALTY GREETING CARDS
★★★ $$

Millions of greeting cards are sold annually in the United States, and starting a business that designs and produces one-of-a-kind custom greeting cards for clients is a terrific desktop publishing business to set into action. However, today you are competing against greeting card software and numerous online greeting card opportunities. Therefore, you need to offer a higher quality card and sell your ability to design and create something original and distinctive for your customers. In addition to a high-quality color printer, you will also need top-of-the line computer design software. Ideally, marketing efforts should be focused on potential customers that would send a lot of greeting cards each year, as well as clients who would benefit the most from sending customized greeting cards. Give them some ideas of what you can do for them that is conceptually above and beyond the basic online cards. Potential customers would include corporations, associations, organizations, professionals, and individual consumers who would be prepared to purchase the specialty greeting cards in minimum orders of 50 at one time. Potential income range is $20 to $30 per hour.

WEB RESOURCE: www.greetingcard.org
Greeting Card Association.

COMPANY NEWSLETTERS
★★★ $$

Designing and printing newsletters for companies, salespeople, and stockbrokers is a fantastic low-investment business start-up that can generate a great income. Monthly newsletters are a terrific way for salespeople and business owners to stay in contact with clients, promote monthly specials, and help secure new business. Many businesses and organizations still prefer a newsletter you can hold in your hand rather than an electronic newsletter (although you can offer both). The key is to show business owners that you have the time and ability to do a newsletter for them. To succeed in this type of venture you will need the following:

- Creativity and writing skills
- Computer aptitude and desktop publishing software
- Strong marketing and presentation skills
- A well-equipped home office
- Clients

The first four requirements are easy to acquire or learn. However, it is the last that is the most important—without clients there is no business. To secure business, you should pre-design three newsletter mock-ups, or samples, featuring local companies, then set presentation meetings at these companies to explain the values and benefits of your newsletter service. This type of marketing and presentation system is extremely effective. However, you'll need to have patience with the process because, as with most new business ventures, you are only as good as your reputation and that has yet to evolve.

WEB RESOURCE: www.newslettersonly.com
Industry information, resources, and links.

COUPON BOOKS
★★ $$ 🚗 🕐 🌐

Community coupon books are hot, and starting a business that designs and produces coupon books is a sensational new business endeavor to set in motion. The concept is very straightforward. Simply secure 50 to 100 businesses throughout the community that would like to be featured in the coupon book free of charge. Of course, the catch is they must be prepared to provide consumers with a discount on their products or service, either in the form of a percentage discount or a fixed amount of discount on a particular product or service. Once they have agreed to this, remind them to let all of their employees know, since it's bad for business when customers come in holding coupons and the person behind the counter has no idea that that he or she is supposed to honor it… and this does happens very often. Revenues for the business are gained by selling the coupon books to consumers within the community, so the larger the advertised savings the better. Suppose the discounts offered in the coupon book add up to a total of $5,000. You would want to advertise that fact by promoting a coupon book that costs $10, but will save the purchaser $5,000 on products and services they purchase on a regular basis within their own community. College towns are a great market for this type of savings book.

WEB RESOURCE: www.couponpros.org
Association of Coupon Professionals.

HOLIDAY DRINK GUIDES
★★★ $$$ 🚗 🕐 🌐

Holiday drink books are simply small guides that are published twice per year in the winter and summer and feature recipes for alcoholic and nonalcoholic drinks. The holiday drink books are distributed throughout the community free of charge and are supported by selling display-advertising space in the guides to local companies wishing to advertise their products and services. Starting this type of desktop publishing business is very easy, as the business can be operated from home and requires little in the way of start-up investment or special skills. Furthermore, to gain additional year round income, consider expanding the business to include publishing and distributing community coupon books as well as a free classified advertising community paper. Both of these opportunities are also featured in this chapter of the directory.

PACKAGE DESIGN SERVICE
★★ $$ 🚗 🕐

Most manufacturers realize that product packaging can be just as important as the product itself in terms of sales and the overall success. This is why many manufacturers enlist the services of a professional when it comes time to design or redesign of packaging for their products. This is a terrific opportunity for enterprising entrepreneurs (with a design background) to capitalize on by starting a packaging design service. Once again, potential clients can include just about any manufacturer that is introducing a new product to the marketplace or any manufacturer that is seeking to redesign existing packaging of a product. As a method to get started, consider redesigning packaging for a product that is produced locally in your area and that you feel could use a makeover in terms of the packaging appeal. Once completed, present your concepts and ideas to the manufacturer of the product along with a presentation of the possible benefits that can be gained by altering or changing the packaging entirely. You may be pleasantly surprised by the outcome of the meeting. Don't forget to ask for the business.

WEB RESOURCE: www.flexpack.org
Flexible Packaging Association.

LOGO DESIGN SERVICE
★★ $$ 🚗 🕐

Company or product recognition is a very important aspect of the overall marketing of a company or product. Logos build consumer recognition and brand name image in terms of identifying a particular logo with a business, product, or service. To reinforce this statement look no further than the Nike swoosh or the golden arches of McDonald's. This fact formulates an outstanding opportunity for the enterprising entrepreneur to capitalize on by launching a logo design service. A logo design service can be operated on a full- or part-time basis right from home, and the only requirements needed to succeed will be a creative artistic ability and a computer. Marketing this type of service can be as easy as designing sample logos of fictional companies and distributing the logo designs along with a presentation describing your service to advertising agencies, marketing companies, and at business networking meetings. Be careful to search and make sure that none of your logos have already been granted copyrights by other businesses. The service will require time in terms of establishing a client base. However, once established, a logo design service can easily generate an income in excess of $50,000 per year for the owner.

INVITATIONS
★ $$ 🏠 🕒

Are you searching for a desktop publishing business opportunity that can be operated from home and started with a minimal investment? If so, consider starting a business that designs and produces custom made-to-order invitations. Not only can this business be started for literally peanuts, but there is also gigantic consumer demand for custom-designed invitations. Marketing the business can be as easy as contacting event and wedding planners in your community and presenting them with samples of your work. Additionally, providing your handwriting is excellent, you can also add calligraphy as an option. Since there are invitation-making software products available, you need to use your creative design and graphics skills in conjunction with top-of-the-line software to create invitations that are clearly of a higher quality than that which your clients could make at home.

BUSINESS PRESENTATIONS
★★★ $$ 🏠 🕒

A business presentation or proposal is not only judged on the information contained within, but also on the format, appearance, and the overall flow of the presentation.

Due to this fact, many business owners realize the importance of having a business presentation or proposal professionally created as opposed to creating it themselves. Starting a desktop publishing service that specializes in creating and producing business presentations and proposals is a fantastic new venture to get rolling. Marketing this type of business can be as simple as designing sample presentations and distributing the presentations at business functions and networking meetings. The business can easily be operated from a homebased location on a full- or part-time basis, and the only skills needed to make the business successful are computer skills and knowledge of what makes a top-notch business presentation. Once again, you are selling skills, abilities, and the fact that you are saving the company the time necessary to create the presentation package.

HOME SAFETY GUIDES FOR THE ELDERLY
★★★ $$ 🏠 🕒 🌐

Here is an outstanding desktop publishing venture to start in your community. Every year in the United States thousands of the elderly fall victim to crime or suffer injuries right in their own homes. Starting a desktop publishing business that focuses on creating and distributing monthly home safety guides for the elderly is not only a great way to operate your own business, but it is also a fantastic way of providing a valuable and much needed community information service. The home safety guides can feature tips on how to make a home less of a target for crime, as well as how to prevent needless accidents around the home and what to do in case of an emergency. The safety guides can be distributed free of charge throughout the community and supported by display advertisement sales. Additionally, be sure to build an alliance with local police and fire protection agencies, as this can be a way to gain credibility for the business, as well as useful information and tips for the safety guides.

CATALOGS
★★ $$ 🏠 🕒

Millions of catalogs are designed and produced each year in the United States, and securing just a small portion of this very lucrative market can make you rich. The key to success in this industry is not to have all the skills required to produce the catalogs yourself, but to have excellent marketing skills and a good contact base of professionals who can assist in the creation and production of the catalogs from start to finish. In terms of marketing the service, you first must produce sample catalogs to act as marketing tools. The next step would be to simply show potential customers the sample catalogs whenever and wherever possible. Additionally, aim to join local business associations in your community, as the members of these associations can be a great source of business for your service or as a referral source to lead you to potential business.

WEB RESOURCE: www.catalog.org

A catalog portal featuring numerous catalogs to provide ideas and inspiration.

MARKETING BROCHURES
★★★ $$ 🏠 🕒

Like business presentations, marketing brochures are more than a few words on a page accompanied by a glossy picture. The importance of effective marketing brochures cannot be overstated in terms of attracting new business for many companies. This fact creates a terrific opportunity for an entrepreneur with a sales and marketing background to capitalize by starting a desktop publishing business that creates and produces highly effective marketing brochures for clients. Once again, this business can be operated from home on a part-time basis and expanded to full-time as the business grows. Potential clients can include just about any business that relies on marketing brochures to generate all or some interest in their business, products, and services. Potential income range is $35+ per hour.

WEB RESOURCE: www.stocklayouts.com

Click on brochures for software and templates.

EVENT PROGRAMS
★ $$ 🏠 🕒

Seminars, auctions, plays, trade shows, and business conventions generally have one thing in common. They require event programs to be distributed to the people in attendance to let them know what's going on, what's for sale, and what's coming up next. Starting a desktop publishing business that designs and produces event pro-

grams is a very easy new business enterprise to launch. A computer, a quality printer, scanner, and excellent desktop publishing software are some of the equipment that you will need to get started creating event programs until the business is established, at which point you may want to consider the addition of a binding machine and high-speed photocopier. Furthermore, specializing in short production runs, personalized customer service, and quick turnaround time will give you an advantage on competition, as the larger and more established printing firms typically require larger runs to bring their quote down. They also cannot provide the customer attention that you can. Market this business to schools, community theater groups, and local associations.

BARTER-AND-SWAP PUBLICATION
★★ $$ 🏠 🕒

Barter-and-swap publications have become very popular in the past decade, as people seek more creative ways to get rid of items they do not want or need, and trade it for useful items they would like to have. Herein lies an outstanding opportunity to start a community barter-and-swap publication. The publication can be published on a bimonthly or monthly basis, and in addition to featuring thousands of barter and trade classified ads, the paper could also feature puzzles, games, and facts on local history or trivia. Revenue can be generated in three ways or a combination of any of these methods that include:

- Distribute the paper for free and charge for the barter or swap advertisement.
- Give the barter and swap advertisements away for free and charge for the paper.
- Do not charge for the paper or the ads, and sell display advertising space to local merchants.

INSTRUCTION MANUALS
★★ $$ 🏠 🕒

Worldwide, millions of products are manufactured that require that an instruction manual is included in the packaging to describe assembly methods or how to use the product. This fact creates an outstanding opportunity to start a desktop publishing business that designs and produces instruction manuals. On the surface this business opportunity may seem somewhat limited in terms of potential clients and profitability. However, consider the following: securing just ten manufacturing clients that produce a total of 100,000 products annually can potentially generate a gross profit of $250,000 per year for your business, simply by maintaining a mere 25-cent markup on each instruction manual that is sold to the manufacturers and included with their products. I bet that you now see the potential of this business in an entirely different light. If the client is supplying you with all of the written material, you can handle the layout and printing only. However, if you are asked to write the instructions, you should either have a technical writing background or access to someone with such experience who you can hire as a freelancer. Instruction writing is often not as easy as it looks (which may explain why instructions are often so hard to follow).

RESTAURANT MENUS
★★ $$ 🏠 🕐

Starting a desktop publishing business that specializes in designing and producing restaurant menus is a fantastic new enterprise to set in motion. Restaurants can be ideal clients to work with, due to the fact that menus regularly change and generally only a short production run of the menus are needed, thus excluding many larger commercial printers. Furthermore, this type of desktop publishing business is also ideally operated on a part-time basis, and it would only require a handful of regular clients to produce a substantial part-time income. In addition to a computer, you will also need a color printer that can produce larger menu pages up to 11-inches by 17-inches. Additional revenues can also be earned by creating and producing restaurant paper placemats and menu inserts describing daily specials.

BUSINESS DIRECTORIES
★★ $$$$ 🏠

Manufacturers, charity organizations, business organizations, wholesalers, printers, publishers, homebased businesses, tour operators, and engineering professionals are only a few examples of the numerous business directories that can be created by a desktop publishing business that specializes in developing business directories. Generally, revenues are earned in two ways in this type of business. The first is to charge companies, organizations,

and individuals a fee to be listed and featured in the directory, and the second way to earn revenues is to sell the directories to companies, organizations, and individuals who are seeking these types of business directories for information, marketing, and resource purposes. The profit potential is good, and a business directory publishing business can be operated from home.

WEB RESOURCE: www.adp.org
Association of Directory Publishers.

BUILDING HISTORY GUIDES
★★ $$ 🏠 🕐 🌐

Are you seeking to start a very interesting and potentially profitable desktop publishing business that can be operated from home on a part-time basis? If so, perhaps you should consider starting a business that specializes in writing guides about local historical buildings in your community, as well as features display advertisements promoting community businesses. The building history guides can be published each month and distributed free of charge throughout the community. Revenues to support the business would be earned by selling advertising space in the guides to local merchants wishing to promote their products and services. Furthermore, local residents can supply most of the historical information and pictures featured in the guide, thus greatly reducing the amount of time it will take to create the monthly publication. Such a guide will be of particular interest in areas known for their historic past. They can be sold through local realtors in exchange for a small commission.

WEB RESOURCE: www.oah.org
Organization of American Historians.

BUSINESS FORM TEMPLATES
★★ $$ 🏠 🕐

Business form templates are simply blank business documents and forms in print format or on CD-ROM or floppy disk that have been specifically designed to be used in a particular business industry, such as automotive sales, manufacturing, or home renovation. The purpose of the business forms and documents are to make it easier for business owners to establish operating and record keeping systems for their businesses. The business forms and documents can include items such as monthly expense reports, estimate forms, work orders, purchase orders, sales receipts, bookkeeping forms, packing slips, and sales reports, just to mention a few. Business form templates can be packaged and sold to specialty retailers on a wholesale basis, or directly to consumers via the web.

RESUME SERVICE
★★ $$ 🚗 🕐

It is very competitive world when seeking a job in any field and having a resume that looks and reads in a professional manner can give you the inside advantage. The key here is not just being able to print high quality resumes, but in knowing how to present the information in a clear and concise manner that jumps off the page. A good resume service can include the writing and layout as well as the printing. Once established, repeat business and word-of-mouth referrals will keep the service hopping. However, to initially market the service there are a few methods that can be employed, such as posting information fliers describing the resume service on community and company bulletin boards, taking out a small print classified ad in a community paper, linking to employment web sites, aligning yourself with headhunters and employment agencies, and networking with people at career expos.

WEB RESOURCE: www.nrwa.com
The National Resume Writers Association.

FREE CLASSIFIED AD PUBLICATION
★★ $$$ 🚗 🕐 🌐

Are you seeking to start a homebased desktop publishing business that has the potential to earn you a six-figure income? If so, perhaps you should consider starting a free classified advertisement publication in your community, also known as a Pennysaver. The business concept is very basic and can be easily run from a homebased office. People from within the community with cars, furniture, houses, or just about anything for sale could advertise their items for free in the paper. The paper would be distributed free of charge throughout the community and published on a monthly or bimonthly basis. Revenue for the business would be generated by selling larger display advertising space to local merchants and service providers wishing to promote their products and services.

FOR-SALE-BY-OWNER KITS
★★★ $$ 🚗 🕐

Millions of cars, boats, homes, and businesses are sold each year in the United States privately by the owners of these items. This fact creates an outstanding opportunity for the innovative entrepreneur to capitalize by starting a desktop publishing business that specializes in creating For-Sale-by-Owner marketing kits. These kits should be created specifically for the purposes of marketing one particular item (such as a car), and include a guide on how to maximize profits from the sale, sales and marketing tips for that particular product, and offer to purchase and contract forms in template form. The kits can be in print format or on CD-ROMs, and sold to retailers on a wholesale basis or directly to consumers via mail order or on the internet. Once established, the profit potential for this type of unique desktop publishing business is outstanding, as the market for the product is unlimited.

CORRESPONDENCE AND TRAINING MANUALS
★★ $$ 🚗 🕐

Every year in North America, millions of people take part in correspondence and training courses at home, and starting a desktop publishing business that designs and produces correspondence and training manuals is an outstanding new business venture to set in motion. Clients for the business can include all levels of schools, companies with employees that work from home, government agencies, and just about any other business or organization that requires manuals to be produced on a yearly basis. This is the type of desktop publishing business that will take time and patience to establish, plus some technical writing experience or access to technical writers. However, once the business is established, many clients will potentially become yearly repeat clients. By providing attention to detail and quality customer service, you should be able to maintain steady clients.

PUZZLE AND GAME BOOKS
★★ $$ 🚗 🕐

Here is a great homebased desktop publishing business to activate in any community. Trivia, crossword puzzles, and word search games are hot, and starting a business that creates puzzles and game books combined with coupons featuring discounts on products and services provided by local merchants has the potential to make you rich. The booklets could be sold locally through participating retailers that have advertisements and discount coupons featured in the book. Additionally, as a method of increasing sales and interest in the game booklets, consider establishing an alliance with a local charity, wherein a portion of the revenues generated by book sales goes back to support community charity programs.

WEB RESOURCE: http://thinks.com/webguide/crossword-software.htm
Distributor of software used to create crossword puzzles and games.

EMPLOYMENT AND CAREER PUBLICATIONS
★★ $$$ 🏠 🌐

Producing a monthly employment and career guide can provide a fantastic new business venture. The business can be operated from a homebased location and even has the potential to be expanded nationally on a franchise or license-to-operate basis once established. The paper can be distributed throughout the community free of charge and supported by charging companies advertising fees to list their employment and career opportunities. Additionally, the paper should also include useful information and tips for readers on subjects and topics pertaining to securing gainful employment. The tips could include information on how to prepare for a job interview, ten secrets to a winning resume, and more.

SMALL BUSINESS GUIDE
★★ $$$ 🏠 🕐

Small businesses drive the economies in both the United States and Canada. In fact, small business is responsible for 80 percent of all new and existing employment in both countries. Starting a desktop publishing business in your community that specializes in creating a monthly small business guide is a terrific new business venture to set in motion. The small business guides can be distributed free of charge to small and homebased business owners throughout the community and supported by selling advertising space to local companies wishing to advertise their products and services in the

guide. Furthermore, the information and articles featured in the monthly guide can include tips for improving the performance of a business, legal issues pertaining to business, and other information small business owners would find useful. You can also have people subscribe to an online version of the guide.

COMMERCIAL REAL ESTATE GUIDE
★ $$$$ 🚗

Creating a monthly publication that features commercial real estate for sale or lease is a terrific homebased desktop publishing business to put into action. In addition to commercial real estate listings, the paper can also include business and franchise opportunity advertisements. Advertising clients can include commercial real estate agents and brokers, property development companies, and franchise and business opportunity companies. Securing revenue for the monthly paper can be accomplished two ways. The first is to charge consumers to purchase the paper through retail distribution channels by print or electronic subscription. The second method of revenue is selling the advertising space to agents and brokers. The key to doing this successfully is aligning with area brokers and making sure to update the listings as soon as new real estate becomes available.

BUSINESS PLAN SERVICE
★★★ $$ 🚗 🕐

Did you know that a recent survey of new business owners revealed that less than 25 percent of the 250 owners surveyed had created a business plan for their new venture? When asked why they had not created a business plan, the number one reason given by the business owners was simply that they did not know how. Approximately 700,000 new businesses are started each year in the United States; this fact creates an outstanding opportunity for starting a service that creates business plans for prospective entrepreneurs and owners of new business ventures. Of course, first you will need to take some time to study how business plans should be formatted, by utilizing the web, books, magazines and taking seminars and courses on the subject. Once you have gained some degree of expertise, you are ready to roll. Keep in mind that there is stiff competition in this business, so you should have a few sample plans written and ready to show prospective business owners. You should also focus on some broad categories of businesses, such as retailers or manufacturing only or in the service industry. Finally, marketing this type of specialized service will take some clever planning, in terms of promoting the service and getting the word out. However, consider the following marketing methods:

- Join local business associations and attend networking meetings to promote your service.
- Obtain a list of all new applicants for business licenses through your local business service center.
- Build alliances with business training schools to market your services to the students.

CAMPUS NEWSPAPER
★★ $$$ 🚗

The fact that most universities and colleges already have campus newspapers does not mean that they are good papers, or that there isn't room for another one. Starting an unofficial campus newspaper is the focus of this business opportunity, and creating and producing it is very straightforward. The paper can be published on a weekly or bimonthly basis and distributed free of charge throughout the campus (with the permission of the school) and throughout the community. Information and articles featured in the newspaper can focus on campus issues and events, and most of the information can be obtained for free from students, readers, and freelance hobby writers. Selling classified and display advertising space to local businesses wishing to gain exposure to the paper's readership base would support the paper. In a town or region with several schools, you could start a newspaper focusing on campus life in general, including the happenings at all of the universities and articles of interest to the broad student population. This will increase readership, and therefore raise advertising rates.

WEB RESOURCE: www.studentpress.org/acp
Associated Collegiate Press.

DIGITAL PRINTING SERVICE
★★★ $$+ 🚗 🕐

The printing industry has been revolutionized with the advent of digital technology. No longer are business owners and consumers at the mercy of print shops to create their short run marketing brochures, event programs, and invitations as these types of printed items can now all be printed in full-color digital format in quantities of one or more without the expensive print plate making charge. A digital printing service can easily be operated from home and the main requirements to get this business rolling will be a good PC, design software, a high quality digital printer capable of 11-inch by 17-inch printing, and of course the ability to use this equipment efficiently. Once again, you will want to concentrate your marketing efforts on customers that are seeking short run printing services. Potential customers will include business owners, consumers, schools, government institutions, clubs, and associations. The equipment will let you print professional full-color items such as newsletters, invitations, business cards, marketing brochures, event programs, restaurant menus, booklets, and guides. Advertise and promote your digital printing service by joining local business associations to network for clients. Short run digital printing is becoming extremely popular with business owners that routinely change prices, promotions, and products. Once the word is out about your service, the business will easily be supported by referrals and repeat business. The key is to be very good at layout and have top-of the-line equipment that exceeds what your clients could do on their own. Quality customer service is also a big plus, since many people are unsure of the look they are seeking.

WEB RESOURCE: www.printusa.com
Directory of new and used digital printing equipment, dealers, and supplies.

COLLECTIBLES GUIDES
★★ $ 🚗 🕐

From antique fishing lures to Star Wars memorabilia, there are guidebooks listing the going rates for a wide range of collectibles. By aligning yourself with local chapters of fan clubs, associations, and both dealers and collectors of such collectibles, you can gain plenty of printing work on these guides. Typically the books contain more price listings than articles, but the right combination, featuring accurate data from those who are immersed in the field, can be the start of a small publishing venture with plenty of potential growth, since there are numerous collectibles. Typically such specialized publications can retail for upwards of $40, so if you are able to access the data without much difficulty, you can make a good profit on your guidebook business.

CONVENTION AND CONFERENCE LITERATURE
★★★ $$ 🚗 🕐

Conventions and conferences may only be in town for a short time, but they typically have a high volume of printing needs. If you can specialize in marketing to, and meeting the needs of, convention and conference planners, you will have the makings of a potentially profitable desktop publishing business. Look for associations, universities, organizations, and groups that will be having conventions or conferences in the upcoming year. You want to reach the organizers of these events well in advance to put in your printing bid. In some cases you will be fortunate enough to reach the planners well before they have even considered their printing requirements, while in other situations they will be using the same printers for the tenth straight year. Have samples of programs, journals, invitations, and any other printed matter that a convention would need, and offer various price points. In addition, make it clear that you can be ready and on call during the convention for the many printing needs that will arise.

SCHOOL PHONE DIRECTORIES
★★ $ 🚗 🕐

More and more schools, from grade schools to colleges, are publishing their own phone directories. While colleges may list the student's numbers in dorms and apartments, grade schools through high schools list the phone numbers of school personnel and of the parents of all the children attending the school. The books are handed out to each student early in the school year. You will need to bid early in the school year to do the book the following school year. This will mean contacting the school administration and finding out who is in charge of assembling the directory. Some districts will handle the directories for several schools. Since schools typically do not have large budgets for such printed materials, using a desktop publisher like you rather than a pricier printer

will likely be in line with their thinking. Get a feel for their budget and determine if you can meet that price and still make a profit. You can build steady business if you can do the job quickly and accurately for the upcoming school year.

SCHOOL CALENDARS
★ $ 🚗 🕐

A great part-time idea to make some extra money is to get in touch with the local school boards in various areas and put together calendars for the school year indicating days off, half-days, special school events, report card time, graduation rehearsals, year-book photos, graduation day, etc. School photos can be included as well. Typically, most school districts have this information on hand in advance but often they don't take the time to compile it on one yearlong calendar, instead sending papers home with students with each bit of information. Local advertisers can pay for the calendars if the schools are facing budgetary constraints, which is often the case.

CHILDREN'S MAGAZINE PUBLISHER
★★ $$ 🚗 🕐

Millions of adults remember reading the Weekly Reader as a child. Today, there are several magazines geared for young readers, but as we encourage kids to embrace reading, it seems that there is always room for one more. If you can compile or write interesting non-fiction stories in areas that are fascinating for young minds, then you can start up a successful children's magazine, or several. You can focus on one or several subjects and include artwork and photos from young artists and photographers. Games, quizzes, comics, word puzzles, and other fun and even educational materials can be included. To support the publication, you can sell advertising space and/or ask for sponsorship from a major corporation. You can distribute the magazine through the schools, libraries, local book or magazine stores, and through your web site, where you can also sell subscriptions. Do a mock-up or dummy copy or two and give them out for free to generate interest from kids, parents, teachers, and advertisers.

WEB RESOURCE: www.magazine.org
Magazine Publishers Association.

KEY

RATINGS	★
START-UP COST	$$
HOMEBASED BUSINESS	🏠
PART-TIME OPPORTUNITY	🕐
LEGAL ISSUES	⚖️
FRANCHISE OR LICENSE POTENTIAL	🌐
GREEN BUSINESSES	🌿

39
ENTERTAINMENT
Businesses You Can Start

DUNK TANK RENTALS
★★★ $$$$ 🏠 🕐 🌐

This certainly is not the first thing that jumps to mind when you start the process of thinking about the various types of business opportunities you can start and operate. However, for anyone who is seeking something a little bis out of the ordinary in terms of a new business venture, a dunk tank rental business does have a lot of benefits to be considered, including limited competition, low start-up investment, ability to be managed from a homebased office, flexible business hours, no inventory, minimal overheads, and great profit potential. Potential customers will include sports associations, charities, business associations, schools, fund-raising consultants, special event planners, caterers, kid's party planners, and community organizations. Generally a group, club, organization, school, or charity will rent the tank in conjunction with a fundraising carnival, party, or sports activity night and then charge people in attendance a fee to attempt to dunk the unfortunate soul who has been chosen to take the wet seat. With that being the case, what better way than a dunk tank to raise the money? It is very important to ensure that the dunk tank is safe for all participants. This can be assured by either buying a dunk tank that is already made, or having one made with careful planning, research, design, construction practices, and material choice. Designing a dunk tank should be left to a profes-

sional engineer, as a typical dunk tank contains over 3,000 pounds of water once filled. Furthermore, the tank should also be professionally built.

Your other concerns will be suitable indoor or protected outdoor storage area for the dunk tank when not in use, transportation capable of securing and towing the trailer mounted dunk tank, and liability insurance for the business. Make sure this is reviewed by your attorney so that you are covered for all potential accidents, including moving and setting up the tank. One-day rentals can easily bring in $350 to $500 depending on how far you need to travel to the client.

WEB RESOURCE: www.twisterdisplay.com
Manufacturers of dunk tanks and equipment.

EXTRAS-ONLY AGENT
★★ $$$$ 🏠

The film and TV production industry is booming, and starting an extras-only casting agency can potentially secure you a portion of this multibillion-dollar industry. Extras casting is simply supplying people to act as background performers in a film production. Typically extras or background performers represent every walk of life in terms of race, age, gender, size, and appearance. The first step to successfully compete in this very competitive industry is to build and maintain a good contact base and working relationship with film producers, directors, and other casting agencies. These are the people and companies that will call upon your service to supply extras for film work.

The second step is to have the photos and phone numbers of at least 100 extras that fit all races, sizes, shapes and ethnic groups at the ready and on your computer to email, send, and/or phone immediately when a call comes. You need to have people who are readily available to go on day-long shoots on a fairly regular basis or you will lose credibility in this on-demand business, as producers will start calling someone else. In terms of revenue generation for the business, an extras agent retains 10 percent of the extra's wage as a commission, so it is important to work in volume, as extras generally make in the area of $30 to $100 for a full day shoot, possibly more if they are in a performer's union.

USED CD MUSIC SHOP
★ $$$

Do you want to open a business in the fast-paced music industry that really has the potential to earn big profits? If so, perhaps you should consider starting a retail sales business that buys and sells secondhand musical compact discs. The business can be established in a storefront location or at flea markets or local fairs. The latter is probably the best way to start until you have enough of an inventory and following to graduate to a retail location. To initially establish an inventory of compact music discs for the business, place classified advertisements in the local community newspaper offering to purchase whole or partial compact disc collections. Currently, secondhand music CDs are retailing for $5 to $10 each.

JINGLE WRITER
★ $ 🚗 🕓

Do you have a musical talent for creating catchy little tunes and rhymes? If so, the time has never been better than now to start a jingle writing service, as advertising in all mediums are booming thanks entirely to the dot-coms. Potential clients for a jingle writing service can include radio producers, advertising agencies, and small business owners who cannot afford pricey big advertising agency rates. The key to success in this unique business is to go out and ask for business. Select local companies in your community that now have a radio presence, but not a catchy jingle for their advertisements. Have some sample jingles recorded and ready to provide on CDs, by email or on your web site. If the business owner likes what he or she hears, have a contract that says that you will provide a jingle for x amount of money. Get a retainer, or some money up front, so that you are not working on spec. Next, create an original jingle and set an appointment with the owner of the business to present your work. Don't forget to sell the clients on the need for a catchy jingle to promote the business name. Since this is a very subjective business, you need to be flexible and willing to rewrite your masterpiece to meet the needs of the client. One catchy and successful jingle and you will not only get more business from that client but, hopefully, word of mouth business as well. Remember to copyright your work. FYI: Barry Manilow started out as a jingle writer.

ENTERTAINMENT HOTLINE SERVICE
★ $$ 🚗 🕓

Just about any determined entrepreneur who is willing to work hard and practice good business skills can tackle starting and operating an entertainment hotline service in your community. Simply start an entertainment hotline service that features various events taking place in the community on the specific day and week. Callers to the free entertainment hotline would be able to choose from an index of categories that could include movie listings, community events, restaurants, concerts, and plays. Additionally, if any of the businesses featured on the hotline service wanted to offer discounts or special pricing for events on the service, they would be encouraged to do so. Revenues for the business would be earned by charging the companies featured on the entertainment hotline service a monthly fee for membership to the service. You could also get a sponsor whose name is mentioned in the welcome and sign-off of each call. Providing 100 to 150 companies could be secured and featured on the entertainment hotline, the business could prove to be very profitable. Just make sure to update the listings very often and market the phone number all over town.

STREET ENTERTAINER
★★★ $$$$ 🚗 🕒

Do you possess a special entertainment talent such as miming, juggling, or walking on stilts? If so, perhaps you should consider applying that talent to becoming a professional street entertainer, or busker, as many buskers can earn more than $1,000 per week. Becoming a street performer is very easy. However, there are two potential drawbacks. First, you will typically need to find busy locations where you will find tourists. The second potential problem is that many communities in the United States and Canada are starting to regulate street performers by issuing licenses or permits to conduct the performances, and generally the permits are awarded on a lottery basis, so research is vital to avoid getting fined or even arrested. Another avenue to explore is performing at fairs, community events, auctions, and other specific gatherings with the approval of the event planner. Even some retail stores, hotels, or other business will hire you to perform in front of their establishment or in their lobby if you are unique and your act is tasteful.

MYSTERY DINNER PARTIES
★★★ $$ 🚗 🕒 🌐

Organizing and hosting mystery dinner parties is not only a sensational business venture to initiate, but it could also prove to be a lot of fun. "Who done it" or murder mystery dinner parties have become an extremely popular entertainment service in the past few years, and there are many benefits to starting this unique and fun service including:

- The business can be managed from a homebased office and operated on a full- or part-time basis. Plus, the initial start-up investment is less than $3,000.
- The demand for the service is high, and clients can include individuals wanting to host an interesting dinner party, corporations seeking a fun social function for their employees and customers, and event planners searching for something out of the ordinary in terms of a unique entertainment experience for their clients.

The theme of the party can be created or you can use a popular mystery theme or story that people are familiar with. Currently, mystery dinner party services are charging rates in the range of $15 per person plus the cost of a catered dinner.

WEB RESOURCE: www.killerscripts.com
Licensing rights to murder mystery dinner scripts.

REHEARSAL SPACE RENTALS
★ $$$ 🕒

Musical bands and performers have always had a difficult time securing space for rehearsing their acts and numbers, and starting a business that rents rehearsal space to musicians and other performers (such as theater troupes) by the hour, day, week, or month is a fantastic new enterprise to get rolling. Ideally, the business will be established on leased premises in an industrial building so that noise will not be a concern or become a problem. Additionally, the spaced that is leased for the rehearsal space should also be subdivided into a few smaller rehearsal rooms to accommodate more than one customer at a time. Current rental rates for rehearsal rooms start as low as $10 per hour and can go much higher depending on the location and whether or not there is any equipment included in the rental costs. With the okay of the facility owner, you can also hold wrap-up parties and receptions after the run of a play, a film shoot, or concert, and charge $65 and up per hour, plus more for food and drinks.

RECORDING STUDIO
★★ $$$$

The investment required to start a sound recording studio is gigantic. However, the profits that the business can potentially generate are even larger. Starting a sound recording studio is much easier than it was at one time, simply because of the advancement in technology. Many recording studios that specialize in voiceovers for radio advertising, compact disc recordings, and videocassette recording are even homebased operations. Any one who does not have experience in the recording industry is well advised to stay clear of this particular business opportunity—unless the business is approached or established as a joint venture enterprise with a person or company that has the necessary industry background, but lacks the financial backing or business experience to ensure the enterprise succeeds. A recording studio can potentially exceed $100,000 per year in profit after wages, expenses, and taxes.

WEB RESOURCE: www.1212.com
Directory of products and services for the sound recording industry.

WEDDING SINGER OR WEDDING ENTERTAINMENT BOOKER
★★ $$ 🚗 🕑

Unlike the movie, many wedding singers actually do possess a great musical and singing talent, and starting a wedding singer service may be just the new business opportunity that you have been searching for. There are a few options available in terms of starting a wedding singer service. The first option is of course, if you have the talent, then you can be the wedding singer and market your services. The second option available is to start a service booking wedding singers, bands, and DJs in your area. The second option will be more costly to initiate, however, it has the potential to generate higher sales and potential profits for the business, as you would be representing multiple wedding performers and retaining a portion of their performance fee as your commission. Profit potential range is $20,000+ per year. You will need to locate at least a half-dozen good singers and bands that have the versatility, wardrobe, and availability to play weddings, and then market the business to wedding planners, catering halls, and bridal shops.

RED CARPET SERVICE
★★ $$ 🚗 🕑

A red carpet service includes individual services such as valet parking, ushers, event planning, and professional emcees all wrapped up into one service for clients. The market for a red carpet service is huge in every city across North America, and clients can include event and wedding planners, business owners hosting special events, catering facilities, seminar and trade show companies, and even political and sports organizations for award ceremonies. Once established, this is the type of business that will be kept very busy by way of repeat clients and word-of-mouth referrals. As there are numerous variables, the profit potential for the business will fluctuate.

However, even on a part-time basis the business is capable of $20,000+ per year.

CHARITY CASINO ORGANIZER
★★ $$$$ 🚗 🕑 ⚖

There are two options available for generating revenues and profits by starting and operating a charity casino business. The first option is to simply rent casino equipment to charities for their events. The second option is to completely organize the event and supply the equipment, dealers, staff, and the location. The first option will be less costly in terms of establishing the business, but with that said, the amount of revenue the business is capable of generating will also be less than the second option. Additional aspects to consider prior to establishing the business will be local government regulations in regards to operating a casino business and demand for the service from local charities.

WEB RESOURCE: www.gamblersgeneralstore.com
Casino equipment and supplies distributor.

MUSIC FEST PROMOTER
★ $$$ 🚗 🕑 ⚖

Music festivals are extremely popular entertainment events across North America, and becoming a music festival promoter is an outstanding opportunity for the entrepreneur that is seeking to start a part-time business. The business concept is basic and you can get started by first deciding what type of music festival or festivals you want to promote: country and western, jazz, rock, or folk. Consider the following seven-step process to establishing the business.

1. Secure a suitable location for the music festival such as a park, beach, outdoor arena, or farmland.

2. Apply for and secure all required permits from local government agencies.

3. Secure performers and vendors for the festival.

4. Build alliances with co-sponsors for the event, such as TV and radio stations.

5. Assemble a volunteer workforce to assist in operating the event. This can usually be accomplished by joining forces with a local charity that receives a portion of the admission sales.

6. Print tickets.

7. Promote very heavily in a variety of ways, including on your own web page.

There is a great amount of research and planning required to organize and host a music festival. You may start by building up a reputation by promoting a small local concert series in a park or a local venue before daring to move on to larger promotional events.

SINGLES-ONLY PARTIES AND DANCES
★★ $$ 🏠 🕒

How big is the potential market for a business that organizes and hosts singles-only dances? Very big, and to back up this statement, consider the following two facts:

1. People are waiting longer than any other previous generation before they get married.

2. The United States and Canadian divorce rate is at a staggering 40 percent.

Initiating a business that organizes and hosts singles-only parties and dances is not only an easy business to get rolling, it is also a business that can be started from home and operated on a part-time basis. The fastest way to get started is to form a joint venture with a local club on the following basis: You supply the people for the event and keep the ticket revenues, while the owner of the club profits from the refreshment sales. Of course, you will need to market the events heavily, pick themes that draws singles of specific age groups, and start off charging very little to hook people into coming to your events. If you have good food and offer a great party or dance club environment, word will spread and you can build a very successful business.

ALCOHOL-FREE CLUB
★★ $$$$ ⚖️

There are numerous benefits for starting a dance club or nightclub that does not serve alcoholic beverages, as opposed to a nightclub that does. The benefits include:

- Less investment capital required to start and operate the business

- Fewer government regulations, and substantially lower liability insurance premiums

- Less competition within the industry, and a clear definition of the target market

- Increased choices in terms of operating location.

In addition to the aforementioned benefits, many people are also starting to lead a healthier lifestyle that does not include consumption of alcoholic beverages, making this a very timely business get going. You can also provide this type of club for teens, 15 and up, who are not of the legal drinking age. This can ensure that they are in a safe, well-managed environment where they can dance and have fun. Safety is a key issue—if parents are comfortable knowing their kids are secure at your club, you've got it made.

MIDWAY RIDES AND GAMES
★ $$$$ 🕒 ⚖️

Starting a business that owns and operates midway rides or games is a very straightforward business to initiate. The carnival and fair circuits in North America operate on a seasonal basis, starting in May and ending in October. In spite of the numerous entertainment diversions that can keep a family busy, carnivals have fared well, though not as popular or numerous as they once were. A well-promoted carnival or exhibition still receives a good turn out. This type of business does require a lot of traveling and is certainly not a business opportunity meant for the masses. However, if traveling and the bright lights of a carnival appeal to you, a very good income can be earned in the industry, and some ride and game operators are earning as much as $100,000 in a six-month season.

WEB RESOURCE: www.vendingconnection.com/ypcarnival.html
Directory of carnival supply and ride dealers.

VOICE OVERS
★ $ 🏠 🕒

Perhaps your voice is your greatest asset, but you do not yet realize it. Do you sound like a silky smooth DJ and can you do multiple impersonations of celebrities and cartoon characters? If so, you may have a well-paying career ahead of you by starting and operating a voice-over service. Clients for your vocal abilities can include film producers, advertising agencies, radio commercial producers, radio stations, publishers of audiotaped books, and corporations for prerecorded telephone messages. At a local level you could supply a much-needed service for small business and local media. Currently people who specialize in supplying their voice for voice-over work for various projects are charging rates for the service in the range of $50 to $75 per hour. Joining a national performers union (if you have the necessary qualifications) is also recommended, as the union performers can make $600 and up per job. However, the farther up the ladder you climb, the more you will encounter fierce competition. You will need a very good demo tape (which can cost anywhere from $500 to $2,000) to send to advertising agencies, commercial producers, and radio station managers in larger markets. It is highly recommended to take voice-over classes.

WEB RESOURCE: www.aftra.org
American Federation of Radio and Television Artists

WEB RESOURCE: www.sag.org
Screen Actor's Guild

BUSKERS SCHOOL
★★★ $$$

What is a busker? It's a term that means street entertainer, and what could be more interesting and fun than starting and operating a school that trains students to become buskers? There probably is not a correct answer to that question, as it is a matter of personal preference. It could be a wonderful business for any determined entrepreneur that is seeking to start a unique business with great potential to be both fun and profitable. Fun aside, all new business opportunities still require careful planning and research regardless of the opportunity, and starting a busker training school is not an exception to the rule. Potential students can include both people seeking busker training to become a professional street entertainer and people who are simply looking for a way to learn a fun hobby such as juggling. Furthermore, the teaching staff can include both retired and actively performing street entertainers who would be prepared to work on a revenue split basis. A busker's school is definitely a business opportunity that deserves further investigation and consideration.

OLD-TIME RADIO PROGRAMS
★ $$$$

History always has a way of repeating itself, and old-time radio programs from the 1930s and '40s are no exception to the rule, as these radio programs are once again becoming very popular. Try to purchase the rights to re-record old-time radio programs onto compact discs. Once complete, the CDs can be sold to retailers on a wholesale basis, or directly to consumers via mail order, the internet, or by local advertising, particularly in magazines and newspapers read by seniors. Providing you can secure the right radio programs to re-record and that demand is high for the programs, the profitability of the business could be outstanding as it only costs a couple of dollars each to mass produce the CDs.

SHORT RUN CD-ROM PRODUCTION
★★★ $$$$

Are you searching for a unique business opportunity in the fast-paced technology industry? If so, consider starting a business that produces compact discs for clients that are only seeking 100 copies or less, as the market demand for the service is gigantic and growing by the second. Anyone who has ever tried to locate a company that is willing to produce a short run for compact disks can certainly tell you it is very difficult, due to the fact that most companies specialize in large runs that produce thousands of CD copies a day. This fact creates a terrific opportunity for the creative and technologically experienced entrepreneur to capitalize by providing clients with a short-run compact disc production service. The start-up costs for the business are high, but once the business is established, the profit potential is outstanding.

DVD RENTALS AND SALES
★★★ $$$$

Opening a store that rents DVDs (digital video discs) is a very exciting business opportunity that continues to thrive despite the increase in on-demand cable movie channels. The key is to stock the latest titles, and have numerous plans to keep titles rented. Many rental shop owners (formerly of VHS rentals) have failed to see the logic in lowering rental prices on older titles. Each day a rentable DVD sits on your shelf you make no money from it. Therefore, be creative with two-for-one discounts, inexpensive microwave popcorn, movie parties, half-price weekly theme rentals, and any other marketing trick you can think of to empty your shelves each day. After all, unlike sales, where you need to restock inventory, this inventory keeps coming back. Remember, you need to gain a competitive edge over on-demand cable movies. Additionally, as a method to further reduce initial start-up costs for the business, consider establishing the business in an existing retail store such as a large food market. This type of location for the business can have many benefits, including sharing monthly overhead costs, capitalizing on an existing customer base, and forming a joint advertising and promotional program.

ENTERTAINMENT BOOKING AGENT
★ $$ 🚗 🕐

If you are looking for a business opportunity that could prove to be both fun and profitable, look no further than starting a business as a freelance entertainment booking agent. A booking agent is a person that actively books entertainers into venues. This can include actors into theatrical productions; singers, bands, comics, and other performers into clubs and films, and so on. The key to being a booker is contacts, and you will need two lists of very good ones. The first list is that of anyone likely to hire a performer, whether it is a producer, club owner, or party planner. The other list is of good, reliable, talented performers who have demo tapes, DVDs, resumes, bios, headshots—whatever is necessary. Your business will then work out the deals and details between the performers and the venue managers, producers, and so on. Generally, an entertainment booking agent does not represent or act as management for entertainers, but merely builds alliances with entertainers and retains a portion of the fees which the talent receives. A background in, and familiarity with, contracts and current rates for performers is very important.

DISC JOCKEY SERVICE
★★ $$$ 🚗 🕐

One of the best entertainment businesses that can be started is a disc jockey service, as not only are DJ services in high demand, but the business can also be initiated on

less than a $10,000 investment and the monthly operating overheads are virtually nonexistent.

There are basically four ingredients required to start and operate a successful disc jockey service:

1. An excellent and varied music selection
2. Top notch DJ equipment and reliable transportation
3. A talent for public speaking, an outgoing personality, and MC skills
4. Very good marketing skills.

Potential clients for a disc jockey service can include event planners, wedding planners, tour operators, nightclub owners, and the individual consumer seeking to secure disc jockey services for a celebration or event. In many parts of the country, the modern disc jockey service also features dancers and numerous party favors when doing sweet sixteen parties, Bar Mitzvahs, graduation bashes, and other parties for kids or teens. DJs with the full package of one to five dancers, party giveaway items, video screens, and various other tricks and gimmicks to offer garner $1,000 to $6,000 for a single party in major markets. With two or three other DJs on staff, doing two parties per weekend at $3,000 each will bring in over $300,000 a year. Of course, you will be paying for the dancers, the party goods and for all of the equipment and its maintenance. However, when you are done, you can walk away with close to $100,000. Also, if you are good, word of mouth advertising will make it almost unnecessary to spend money on marketing.

WEB RESOURCE: www.adja.org
American Disc Jockey Association.

SINGING TELEGRAM SERVICE
★★ $$ 🚗 🕐

Would you like to start a singing telegram business, but your singing abilities are best left to the shower where no one can hear you? Fear not. Starting a singing telegram service is easy, even for those of us who cannot sing. A singing telegram service is a fantastic choice for a new business venture, especially for entrepreneurs with limited capital available, as this homebased enterprise can be put into action for less than a few thousand dollars. Furthermore, there are numerous accomplished singers in every community across North America that will be more than happy to exercise their singing talents for a fee, so locating the singers should not prove difficult. Budding actors, actresses, and dancers are often happy to make some extra money as performers. In fact, in many cases, the latest in o'gram performers often reads, raps, or performs comedy instead of singing. To be competitive in the field and provide a variety of options, you should have performers ready to appear in costume as Elvis, a gorilla, a giant chicken or any number of popular characters. Make sure you have a long list of talents on hand before marketing your service. Once established, repeat business and word-of-mouth referrals will become the main marketing and advertising source. However, until the business is established, fliers, faxes, and a web site will be a good starting point in terms of marketing.

COMMUNITY ENTERTAINMENT DIRECTORY
★★ $$ 🚗 🕐 🌐

Calling all aspiring publishers! Are you seeking to start a homebased publishing business that has the potential to generate a great profit, as well as be started on an initial investment of less than $10,000? If so, perhaps you should consider launching a monthly entertainment guide that services your community. The entertainment guide can be distributed free of charge and feature articles and information about local entertainment events, movie listings, concert listings and reviews, and horoscopes. Selling display advertising space in the entertainment guide to local merchants can support the business. Once again, this is an ideal publishing business to be operated from a homebased office.

The key is to establish ties with all local entertainment venues and keep up with their upcoming calendar of events. You will likely have to do a few versions as samples to gain a reputation in the community for having the most up-to-date listings and information.

BAND MANAGEMENT
★★ $$ 🚗 🕐

There are a few approaches that can be taken in terms of starting a musical band management service. The first approach is to start and operate the business on a part-time basis from home and perhaps only represent one or two musical bands or solo musical performers. The second option is to start a full-time management agency that represents multiple bands or solo performers at one time. Both approaches to establishing and operating the business have their pros and cons; however, careful research will determine the best approach for you. Additionally, be sure to follow current or popular music trends when seeking a band or performer to represent, as the likelihood of success will be much greater. The key to success in this business is largely based on who you know and what you can provide—make sure you have bands that you believe in and get to know as many local music industry people (local club owners, DJs, etc.) as you possibly can.

INDEPENDENT MUSIC LABEL
★★ $$$$

Independent music labels are popping up everywhere across North America, and the rise in numbers of independent music labels rest solely with the creation and subsequent popularity of the internet. Independent music labels now have the ability to level the playing field with their larger and better-financed competition by marketing new bands, performers, and music via the internet. Furthermore, never before has there been such a wide variance of musical styles available to suit everyone's musical tastes—everything from jazz to hip-hop and back to good old rock 'n roll. The key to successfully starting and operating an independent music label will rest squarely in your ability to secure the right musical acts and performers to sign, market, and promote. The start-up cost is high for this unique entertainment venture, but the profit potential is also very high.

WEB RESOURCE: www.musicindie.com
Association for Independent Music.

MODELING AGENCY
★ $$$ 🚗

Some of the world's most profitable and famous modeling agencies started on a shoestring budget. The key to success in this industry is not having deep pockets, but good contacts and knowing how to capitalize on those contacts. When you stand back and analyze a modeling agency, what you find at the core of the business is simply this: a modeling agency represents people of various appearances, shapes, sizes, races, etc., who are used to promote or display a product or service for a paying client. Nothing more. This gets back to my first point, which was industry contacts. Contacts are very important in this industry for a few reasons, including the fact that the industry is very competitive or even cutthroat. Reliability is essential, and new modeling agencies find a lot of closed doors unless they have a contact inside. Once established, a modeling agency can be very profitable, making this a business opportunity that is definitely worth investing some time into researching the possibilities further. The key is to start small and grow. Look for small local businesses that are doing commercials and print shoots so that you can build a portfolio for your models and for your agency.

WEB RESOURCE: www.models.com

SATELLITE DISH SALES AND INSTALLATIONS
★ $$$$

Mini-satellite dishes are in demand by consumers, as many of these systems offer a better deal than basic television cable service. There has never been a better time to start a business that sells and installs mini-satellite dishes, as the product is proven, the price is competitve, and there are many locations that do not have accesss to cable lines and service. The first step to establishing this type of business is to secure a sales and installation contract with one of the many manufacturers and subscription providers that represents a geographic area. The next step is to effectively market the product and installation service, and this can be accomplished by building a direct sales team to represent the products and services, as well as utilizing all traditional advertising mediums to gain consumer interest in the business.

THEATER PRODUCTIONS
★ $$$ 🏠 🕐

Producing a theatrical play is not as easy as it looks. It is, however, a lot of fun, althoughvery often not extremely lucrative. The old joke is that theater is the only business in which if you invest money and come out even, you're considered a winner. Besides putting the money behind the show or gathering backers, as a producer you need to

secure a director, a venue, and a technical team. Once everything is in place, many minor details will arise and everyone will turn to you to save the day. You will need to know a little something about the theater and theater management, even if you are able to find enough people to run everything for you. One major benefit of producing local plays is that often the performers, directors, and stagehands will work for little or no financial compensation. The fact that they are taking part in the play itself is an opportunity for them to enhance their skills and build up their credits. Additionally, many venues for performances can also be secured for free, providing there are benefits for the owner of the venue such as refreshment sales or product sales. The key to making some money in producing a community play for profit is to retain as much of the ticket revenue as possible while seeking out ways to reduce or eliminate production costs without sacrificing the integrity of the performance. Selecting a well-known musical is often the best way to start. Popular musicals can generate the most ticket sales, higher prices, and are familiar to performers and the audience. This makes them easier to rehearse and to market. A good director who can make a familiar show seem fresh, with an original interpretation, can be also be very helpful.

WEB RESOURCE: www.comunitytheater.org
Comprehensive site featuring articles, discussion boards, theater links and more.

KARAOKE DJ SERVICE
★★★ $$ 🏠 🕐

Karaoke singing has become wildly popular in the past decade, and to back this statement up you do not have to look any further than your own community, as I am sure there is a local karaoke club or karaoke singing night. The requirements for starting a karaoke DJ service are basic: you need karaoke equipment, a good music selection, and reliable transportation. Of course, a fairly decent singing voice is not going to hurt business either. You can market your service to event and wedding planners as well as to local nightclubs, restaurants, and pubs that may entertain the idea of a weekly karaoke singing contest.

WEB RESOURCE: www.adja.org
American Disc Jockey Association.

MUSICAL INSTRUMENT SALES
★★ $$$$ 🌐

Retailing musical instruments is a fantastic business venture to set in motion for the musically inclined entrepreneur that is seeking for a way to capitalize on their skills and interests. Ideally this type of specialty retailing is best suited to be established and operated from a retail storefront. However, for the financially challenged entrepreneur wishing to start this type of venture, the business could begin on a part-time basis from home or as a joint venture with an existing retailer within the community, such as a CD music shop or home electronics retailer. In addition to retailing musical instruments you can increase revenues and profits by providing instrument repairs, instructional classes, instrument rentals, and sales of related products such as sheet music. Also be sure to establish relationships with schools, music teachers, associations, and clubs in the community. This can be a fantastic way to promote the business, products, and services you provide quickly as word-of-mouth advertising and referrals really work.

STAND-UP COMIC
★ $ 🕐

First, it's important to know that it's not as easy as it looks to get up and perform comedy. While you may make your friends laugh, it does not mean you can get up on stage and make a roomful of strangers laugh. That being said, if you are good at it, it's an incredible feeling when you stand on stage and hear the laughter. Conversely, you feel quite naked up there when you bomb. It's all part of the career. First, to dispel a very common myth: Comics do NOT wing it and make up their routines as they go along or simply play off of people in the audience. Instead they work long and hard to create a polished, well-rehearsed act that sounds extemporaneous after hundreds, if not thousands, of hours of honing and perfecting. Like acting, there is very little money to be made until you have proven yourself. This means performing at any local comedy club in which you can get stage time. A good five- to ten-minute act will suffice at first, but keep on writing as you want to have twenty or eventually forty-five minutes of solid material. If you get to be a regular at a local club, work there as much as pos-sible until your act is top notch, then get a video or CD made to send to bookers of colleges or paying clubs.

Hint: Watch a lot of comics and try to establish something that makes you unique. What will make people remember you? Your look? Your character? A catch-phrase? It may take some time to find, but most of the great comedians of the past 100 years have had something that made them distinctive from one another. If you can get the paying bookings you will spend plenty of time out of the road, but in the right markets, such as colleges, you can make good very good money. You will also want to find a manager and agency representation to get to the media.

MAGICIAN
★★ $ 🕐

Kids love magicians, and adults enjoy them as well. There are schools in which to train and plenty of books and CDs available for honing your skills. If you can find a few tricks that are not in the repertoire of your competitors, you can stand out from the crowd and get more bookings. If you can market yourself as a character, you have an even better opportunity to generate more attention, and more work. From local kids parties to regular sold out bookings in Las Vegas, the opportunities for a magician are vast. Start by marketing yourself to party shops, party planners, at family oriented restaurants, and on your web site. Much of your business will emerge from word of mouth, providing you are not only good at the tricks you perform, but know how to entertain and please the crowd.

WEB RESOURCES: www.magictricks.com
Plenty of magic tricks to get you started.

ENTERTAINMENT PUBLICIST
★★★ $$ 🏠 🕐

Whether it is a performer, a film, or a theatrical production, someone needs to spread the word in order to sell tickets. Entertainment publicists charge clients monthly fees to do just that. In fact, it's not uncommon to charge several thousand dollars a month to get the name of the performer, the show, or a book as much publicity as possible, meaning blurbs, articles, or mentions on television, radio, the internet, and in newspapers and magazines. The key is being very well connected in the media and having a knack for finding the selling point for your clients. What makes this talent or this upcoming book unique? Can I tie it into a news story or popular trend? Can I get the artist, performer, or writer onto Oprah or the other talk shows? In the course of publicizing talent, films, television shows, and/or books you will find yourself writing press releases, handing interview requests, setting up press conferences, and arranging opening night parties and other such events. It's a marvelous career for someone outgoing, organized, and with a knack for schmoozing. It's also easy to start from a home office. Just start off by building up the media contact list.

LOCATION SCOUT
★★★ $ 🏠 🕐

Can you find the perfect setting for a film, television program, or commercial? A location scout works with production companies, advertising agencies, and film studios to find locations for shooting. The locations need to match what the director or producer has in mind, and be accessible and safe. In addition, the owner of the land or property must be okay with the idea that his or her property will be used in a commercial or industrial shoot. To start out, you will once again need to establish contacts in the business, so that producers, directors, and advertising agency reps know they can contact you to find what they need. You also need to use your camera and take photos of numerous possible locations from back alleys to majestic waterfalls. Descriptive, panoramic photographs or videos of numerous locations can help you present many options to your clients. A location scout typically has a great number of categorized photos and CDs with all sorts of location possibilities. If you are really good, you will be able to tell clients the best times of day for specific shoots and have the local information available, such as where the cast and crew can park, eat, and so on. While the locations manager does make the deals regarding how much the film company or advertising agency will pay for the location, he or she does need to assure that the property can be used so as not to waste the time of the producers when they come to check it out. You earn money by being hired to scout and find a location. Hint: Since it's hard to find all locations yourself,

you can employ some local photographers to take photos of interesting potential locations. If the place is used, you can the give them a commission from your earnings.

WEB RESOURCE: www.afi.com
American Film Institute.

PRODUCTION COMPANY
★★★ $$$ $ 🏠 🕐

"Lights, camera, action!" If you've always wanted to say those words and have some inkling of how to write, direct, shoot, and edit a film, commercial, or television program, starting a production company might be the way to go. To start out, you can work from a basement or garage-based studio, or simply use a home office for your business activities and shoot on location. For $50k to $75k, you can put together enough first-rate equipment to launch the business and pick up some regular clients for corporate video shoots, local commercial work, and short web-based projects. Hopefully, you will impress a few clients and they will provide you with regular work. The first years of a production company usually mean putting the money back into the business to continually upgrade equipment, seek studio space, and build the business. In time, you can branch out from commercial shoots to more entertainment oriented and creative works, although this is typically more risky, so you will usually want to build up your steady client base before starting on your first great independent film.

WEB RESOURCE: www.aicp.com
Association of Independent Commercial Producers.

SCHOOL OF BROADCASTING
★★★ $$$$ 🏢

Getting in front of a microphone and reading copy, following a script, or talking to phone callers is not as easy as it looks or sounds. If you have a background in broadcasting or can reach out and attract several key DJs, newscasters, talk show hosts, actors, or other on-air personalities, you can start training the next generation of broadcasters. The basis of such a business is imparting the collected wisdom of your teaching staff to students through a well-crafted curriculum. In time, you can gain accreditation, but more significantly, you can gain respect and clients by getting your students placed in on-air jobs. For this, you will need to train your students well and have connections in the industry so that you can get demo tapes to the right people. For each student who ends up on air, you can attract fifty to one hundred new students who want to follow in his or her footsteps. While you will eventually want to have your own facility from which to hold classes, you can start out by affiliating with another learning institution and leasing space from which to hold classes. You can also accommodate students online.

WEB RESOURCES: www.nab.org
National Association of Broadcasters.

FAN CLUB MANAGEMENT
★ $ 🚗 🕐

From country singers to soap opera stars, fans love their celebrities. With this in mind, you can start a fan club management business whereby you hook up with up-and-coming performers of all types and set up their fan clubs via a web site and plenty of promotional materials. If you can start "authorized" fan clubs, you can get all of the inside information and you will have access to special merchandise, blocks of tickets, and other perks in conjunction with the performer's publicist. If you start unauthorized fan clubs, you will have to work harder to provide news and collectibles, but you can generate a fan base more quickly if you are dealing with a somewhat well-known performer or a team.

You can also start a regional fan club for someone who already has a national fan club. The larger you can grow the club, the more attention you can potentially generate from the celebrity or team. You make money by selling items featuring the celebrity, having a membership with various perks, and promoting contests and possibly celebrity auctions, as well as holding parties and ongoing get-togethers. A good fan club management business can run several fan clubs and be a very successful and fun business venture.

NOTES:

40
FINANCIAL AND PROFESSIONAL SERVICE
Businesses You Can Start

CHECK CASHING SERVICE
★ $$$$ ⚖️ 🌐

A payday loans and check cashing service is a very good business to start. Consider the following: Typically, a check cashing service will charge customers 3 percent of the total as a service fee to cash a check. While 3 percent might not add up to a lot over the course of a week, it sure can over the period of a year. If you started with a mere $1,000 and cashed a check for that amount every day, at the end of the year your $1,000 initial investment would have generated $1,095 in check cashing service fees, or a 1,100 percent return on investment. Now imagine 10, 20, or 30 times that amount on a yearly basis. Furthermore, an even higher rate of return can be earned on short-term payday loans, making this a financial service to seriously consider as a new business venture.

LEASING AGENT
★★ $$ 🏠 ⚖️

In most areas of the United States and Canada, a special license is not required to match clients with lending institutions that specialize in providing financing solutions on a lease basis for purchases ranging from automobiles to computer equipment for business use. Operating this service is very easy. Simply secure clients wishing to lease a product and complete and submit the lease documents to two or three leasing companies or financial institutions. The lenders that reply with the best lease rates and terms for your clients are the companies that will earn your clients' and your business. Revenues for the service are earned by charging the financial lenders a fee or a commission based on the value of the total lease amount. Income and profit potential range is $40,000 to $100,000 per year.

BUSINESS FOR SALE BROKER
★ $$$$ ⚖️

The financial investment and training time required to secure a commercial realtor's license enabling you to start a real estate brokerage specializing in listing and selling businesses and commercial investment properties will be well worth the effort. It is common for business brokers to earn $250,000 or more per year after expenses, provided they have the right skills to find and sell businesses in good locations and with potential to be profitable for their new owners. Additionally, consider specializing in a particular kind of business sales, such as marketing, manufacturing, or retail businesses. Specialization in the commercial real estate industry is the fastest way to become known as an industry leader and gain valuable referrals. Marketing listings can be by way of the internet, trade specific publications, and a wide network of contacts within the industry.

WEB RESOURCE: www.ibba.org
International Business Brokers Association.

EQUITIES DAY TRADER
★ $$+ 🏠 🕐

With the advent of the internet, an entirely new home-based self-employment opportunity has surfaced. This business has the potential to generate six-figure incomes for everyday Americans who become day traders of equities and commodities. However, this opportunity is considerably risky, as the potential is as great to lose money as it is to make it, especially for the novice and inexperienced trader. The key to successfully earning an income as an equities day trader is to gain as much knowledge about the industry as possible. Specialize in a specific type of stock or commodities trading, have considerable investment capital to get rolling, and most importantly nerves of steel and an understanding of what goes up must come down. Remember, most day traders go for short gains, buy in early, and sell out the same day. Holding overnight is too much risk, especially for heavily invested traders in unstable market conditions. Of course remember the golden rule of stock and commodities trading: "Never risk more than you can afford to lose."

TAX PREPARATION SERVICE
★ $$ 🏠 🕐 ⚖️

An accounting background is highly preferred; however, there are training and certification courses available that will enable you to start your own income tax preparation service as a qualified professional. As in any business, the more you know and the better your skills are, the more you will potentially earn. Though tax preparation is a seasonal service, additional income can also be gained by providing business clients with year-round bookkeeping services. Once established, word-of-mouth advertising and repeat business will support the service. However, to initially secure clients for the business, consider offering a two-for-one special for your first year of operation. Prepare one tax return for the regular fee, while a spouse or partner receives the service for free.

WEB RESOURCE: www.nattax.com
National tax training school.

LICENSING SPECIALIST
★★ $$$ 🏠 ⚖️

As a licensing specialist, you can seek out opportunities to secure the exclusive rights to use a popular name, product, service, or operating system or formula, and sell sublicenses to qualified business owners wishing to utilize the license in a business venture, product, or service. An example of a licensing situation is as follows: A popular motorcycle is being manufactured and you secure the master license to use the name of the motorcycle to promote products and services. You sell a license to a clothing company to use the motorcycle name, image, and logo on their clothing line and charge a one-time fee plus ongoing royalties based on the success of the clothing line. You sell a license to a corporation that wants to establish a chain of restaurants using the motorcycle's name, logo, and image. These are only two examples; there are literally hundreds if not thousands of ways to profit as a licensing specialist. Start by learning as much as possible about licensing and the applicable laws.

WEB RESOURCE: www.licensing.org
Licensing Industry Merchants' Association.

USED ATM SALES
★★ $$ 🏠 🕐

A few years ago, laws governing ownership and operation of ATMs (automated teller machines) were deregulated, paving the way for entrepreneurs from every walk of life to own and operate ATMs as a business concern. Since deregulation of this industry, millions of new ATMs have been sold, and a secondary market is now emerging, which is the sales of secondhand ATMs. While a very lucrative income can be earned by purchasing ATMs and reselling them for a profit, the gigantic profits are made by purchasing secondhand ATMs, locating the machine in a public place where it can generate revenue, and then selling the secondhand ATM as a going business concern. The potential to earn $250,000 per year is attainable for the determined entrepreneur who initiates this very basic business concept and places the ATM in the right location.

BOOKKEEPING SERVICE
★★ $$ 🏠 🕐

Bookkeeping is simply the procedure of recording financial transactions, or put differently, a record is made every time money changes hands. Providing you possess accounting or bookkeeping experience and skill, a substantial income can be earned by running a bookkeeping service. Clients will largely consist of business owners that do not have the time or ability to set up and manage a bookkeeping system for their business. Recent technological advancement has made operating a bookkeeping service very straightforward, as there are many types of small business bookkeeping and accounting software available that will not only make your job easier, but also enable you to service many clients at one time. Typically, bookkeeping services charge clients a monthly fee to record and update their financial records on a regular basis. Averaged, this fee translates into $25 to $35 per hour.

WEB RESOURCE: www.aipb.org
American Institute of Professional Bookkeepers.

COLLECTION AGENCY
★★ $$ 🏠 🕐 ⚖️

If you have had past experience in the field of debt collection, than a logical new business venture for you to start is a collection agency operating from a homebased location. Generally, the duties of a collection agency focus on collecting financial debts typically owed to a company or business in a non-harassing manner and utilizing the telephone and official-sounding letters as your main debt collection tools. Securing clients for the service is extremely easy, due to the simple fact that you will not be paid for your service unless you are successful in collecting the debt owed. Rates for the services are based on a percentage of the amount of money that is collected, and the longer the debt has been outstanding, the higher the fee charge to collect the debt. Typically, a 25 percent fee would be charged on successfully collecting debts that have been in arrears for up to 180 days. Beyond 180 days the fee could increase to as much as 50 percent of the total debt collected.

WEB RESOURCE: www.collector.com
American Collectors Association.

IMAGE CONSULTANT
★ $$ 🏠 🕐 🌍

Many business owners and corporate executives realize that a book is often judged by its cover and thus have no hesitation enlisting the services of a personal image consultant to ensure they are keeping up with current fashion

and social trends to maximize a favorable public image. Beyond assisting clients with wardrobe and etiquette tips, image consultants also assist clients in selecting the best social events to attend. They also help them keep up with current social and political issues. Most importantly, they coach clients on how to avoid situations or conversations that can potentially damage their careers or business. Potential income range is $30 to $50 per hour.

WEB RESOURCE: www.aici.org
Association of Image Consultant International.

VENTURE CAPITAL BROKER
★★ $$

A venture capital broker is simply a person that brings two parties together that share a common goal. This goal, generally and ultimately, is to create a profit. One party is the entrepreneur that is seeking capital to start or expand a business. The second party is a venture capitalist who lends entrepreneurs money for business financing in exchange for a high rate of return on the investment or a combination of company shares and a return on investment. The venture capital broker that successfully brings the two parties together is remunerated by way of commission based on the total amount of financing that was secured. Depending on the amount of money secured, the commission rate will range from a low of 5 percent to a high of 15 percent. Securing clients for the service is as easy as scanning local newspapers for business financing-wanted classified advertisements, and taking over the task of locating suitable capital for the venture. However, finding a source of financing can be very difficult, so be sure to only represent clients that have a viable business concept accompanied by a completed business plan that reinforces the business concept.

WEB RESOURCE: www.nvca.org
National Venture Capital Association.

TENDER RESEARCHER
★★ $$ 🏠 🕐

A tender research service is an outstanding new business opportunity to put into action for the entrepreneur that is seeking to own and operate a homebased business that has the potential to generate an income of $50,000 per year or more. Simply put, a tender research service does exactly that, researches tender information from across North America, and in some cases even the world. The best method for operating a tender research service is to simply charge all clients the same fee, say $50 per month. In exchange for the fee, clients would receive by way of e-mail or fax all tender information related to their business or industry. The main requirement for operating a tender research service is to have excellent research skills. Locating tender information can be accomplished by surfing the web, as well as subscribing to daily newspapers and trade publications from around the globe. One hundred clients each paying a mere $50 per month for the service will result in business revenues of $60,000 per year.

FRANCHISE SPECIALIST
★★ $$$$ 🏠 ⚖️

Forming a joint venture with a lawyer who specializes in franchise business law could be your first step toward building a successful business as a franchise specialist. A franchise specialist service seeks opportunities in two ways. In the first way, the specialist looks for small, independently owned and operated businesses that are ideal candidates to be expanded nationally, on a franchise basis. The second, and more common, manner of operating this business is as franchise specialist looking for companies that have already gone through the lengthy and costly franchising legal requirements process, and are now ready to begin marketing the franchises to qualified owners or operators. In both cases, the goal of the franchise specialist is to market the franchises, retaining a large portion of the franchise fee in exchange for providing the service, and in some cases, even securing a portion of the company's shares.

WEB RESOURCE: www.aafd.org
American Association of Franchisees and Dealers.

LICENSING OPPORTUNITIES
★★ $$$$ 🏠

Licensing is somewhat different than franchising and by definition means "an individual, corporation, or enterprise that has been granted a license by another individual, corporation, or enterprise." Generally the license allows for the licensee to conduct business utilizing the license holder's formulas and procedures, and in some cases logos and names. However, this type of online venture would operate similarly to an online franchise directory. The main objective would be to bring together corporations and individuals seeking to grant licenses with corporations and individuals seeking to acquire licenses. Once again, the site would be supported financially by charging fees to have information pertaining to licensing opportunities featured on the site.

PUBLIC RELATIONS
★★ $$ 🏠 🕐

Many public relation firms are chosen by companies not based on what they know, but whom they know. A good PR person representing an individual, business, product, or service can be the equivalent of having a person in your corner that can pick lottery numbers before they are drawn. Public relations agencies promote their clients, including their new products and services offered, new store locations, and/or any such company news, in a positive manner. The goal is to get them media coverage, exposure, and recognition. Good PR agencies also find ways to do "damage control," which means finding ways to deflect or reverse negative press that has been levied at their clients. Promotion techniques include creating press kits and press releases for clients, organizing media gatherings (such as press conferences) as well as special events, doing placement (which means calling, e-mailing and pitching your client to all types of media), and networking on the client's behalf. Getting started in the business can be difficult, given that the public relations industry is fiercely competitive and depends very much on your list of media contacts. However, as an entry point consider starting small and representing one or two clients on a local basis until you have mastered the fine art of public relations. Most small businesses cannot afford the big, pricey PR firms. You can capitalize on this by charging a small monthly retainer of a few hundred dollars, or only billing them for specific services, such as $50 per hour for placement or to set up a special event for the client such as a party to celebrate the opening of a new store. You can also charge $100 for a press release (read up on the proper way in which to write one), or $500 to put together a full media kit comprised of several press releases featuring different aspects of the business, photos, bios of the owners, and recent stories, all included in a professional presentation folder.

WEB RESOURCE: www.prsa.org
Public Relations Society of America.

EMPLOYEE TRAINING
★★ $$ 🏠 🕐 🌐

The demand from employers for specialized employee training is enormous, and starting a home-based employee-training service is a terrific new business venture to set in motion. The key to success in this business is specialization, and your service should focus on one particular training style or method that you have mastered or can quickly master. Popular employee training course topics include customer service, working without direction, money handling, making the workplace a safe and secure environment, and coping with stress. The training courses can be conducted on the client's site. Marketing the service can be accomplished by attending business networking meetings to promote your service or designing a marketing brochure explaining the service and course curriculum and distributing the brochures to potential clients.

HEADHUNTER SERVICE
★ $$ 🏠 🕐

Unlike an employment agency, a headhunting service does not wait for potential employees or career seekers to send in a resume for a job listing. A headhunter goes out and actively searches for the ideal candidate. This usually means the first stop is at the client's competitors. Securing clients for a headhunting service is very straightforward, simply due to the fact that the clients only pay for the service if and when the ideal person is located and hired. Fees for the service are paid by the client that is seeking to fill an employment position, and are typically 4 to 8 percent of the employment position's annual salary, which is paid in full at the time of hiring or after a few months (as negotiated between you and your client) to make sure the person hired has worked out. In addition to competitor companies, potential employees can also be located at business networking meetings and by surfing the web for situations wanted ads. Even some small business owners

can be lured back into the corporate world if the offer is lucrative enough.

FUNDRAISING CONSULTANT
★★ $$ 🏠 🕐 ⚖️

Acting on behalf of charities as a fundraising consultant can be a profitable and very rewarding business, providing you have the skills and abilities to raise significant funds for the charities that your service represents. The first step required for establishing a fundraising service is to build alliances with local or national charities. Should they hire you as a fundraising consultant, the next step is to establish a fundraising program for the charity, similar to a business plan. The plan or program should outline how the funds will be raised, as well as the fee you will charge for your service. Typically, fundraising consultants charge a commission for services based on a percentage of the total amount of money raised, and the commission rate will vary. You might charge 10 percent on amounts in excess of $100,000, and a higher percentage for smaller amounts raised. Be careful, because if you are looking to take too high a percentage of a small amount raised for charitable purposes, the charity will axe you and go with volunteers. The best way to start off and build a reputation is to start small, running this as a side business by raising funds for a few smaller local charities. As is the case with many businesses, you are only as good as your track record, and you will need to establish one here.

WEB RESOURCE: www.afrds.com
The Association of Fund Raisers and Direct Sellers.

SALES TRAINING SERVICE
★★ $$ 🏠 🕐 🌐

Are you a sales professional who is recognized as a top producer in your industry? If so, in addition to your six-figure yearly commission earnings, you can add another $100,000 simply by training other sales professionals to also become perennial top sales producers. The sales training can be taught at the client's site or in a home-based classroom atmosphere. The course curriculum can be developed by amassing your sales experience, techniques, trade secrets, and methodology into a study guide utilized and practiced by students. Gaining clients for the classes can be as easy as creating a marketing package.

This promotional package should describe the sales training program, highlight your own personal sales achievements, and explain the benefits and value that this type of focused and specialized coaching can have in terms of turning sales order takers into sales order makers. The marketing presentation can be presented to business owners and corporations that rely on a direct sales team to drive business revenues and profits.

WEB RESOURCE: http://ga.salestraining.com
Portal linking to numerous sales training information sites.

INDEPENDENT SALES CONSULTANT
★★★ $$ 🏠

Some of the highest earning professionals in any industry are independent sales consultants working on a freelance basis for clients. Freelance sales consultants represent companies that sell products and services ranging from manufactured goods to home improvement services, and just about everything in between. Securing clients to represent is easy, simply because freelance sales consultants generally supply all the tools of the trade such as transportation, communications requirements, and computer equipment that may be needed to acquire customers and conduct business—not to mention the fact that many freelance sales consultants also generate their own sales leads. Or, put differently, clients have little, if anything, to lose by having freelance sales consultants representing their business. Remuneration for products or services sold is always by way of commission, which will range between 10 and 25 percent of the total sales value.

SEMINAR SPEAKER
★ $$ 🏠 🕐

Corporations, associations, and event planners are on the constant lookout for interesting speakers to lecture at corporate events and seminars. If you possess the ability to speak in public and hold the attention of your audience, while combining interesting life experiences with industry specific information, then an outstanding opportunity awaits you by becoming a seminar speaker. Initially to secure speaking engagements, create a resume outlining your experience and related skills, and distribute this information to event planners, seminar organiza-

tions, and corporations along with a demo tape, CD or DVD of you speaking in some public forum. Hint: Do a couple of volunteer speaking engagements to get a good demo, along with some practice. This is the type of service that is built on word-of-mouth referrals, and if your speeches and lectures are good, you will soon be in demand for speaking engagements across North America, and perhaps the world.

WEB RESOURCE: www.nsaspeaker.org
The National Speakers Association.

PROSPECTING AGENT
★★ $$ 🏠 🕐

In a nutshell, a prospecting agent generates and qualifies sales leads for their clients. However, the service should not be confused with a telemarketing service, as a prospecting service never attempts to close a sale or go beyond qualifying a sales lead for their clients. Prospecting agents are paid for each lead they generate, and the higher the value of the client's products and service, the larger the fee for supplying qualified leads. Additionally, some prospecting agents also generate sales leads first, and then sell the leads to the highest bidder. An example of this would be a prospecting agent that sets up a display booth at a home and garden trade show and collects names, addresses, and contact information from people that are considering a home improvement renovation. The type of renovation they are considering will dictate what kind of home improvement company the prospecting agent will approach to purchase the leads he or she has obtained.

RETIRED PRESIDENTS SERVICE
★★ $$ 🏠 🌍

How many novice entrepreneurs would benefit from consulting meetings with business veterans that have 20 years experience or more in the business world? Almost all. The business concept is very straightforward. Simply, retain the services of retired company presidents, corporate executives, and small business owners to work on a consulting basis, as needed, coaching new business owners in their field of specialty, such as sales and marketing, management, or financial and tax manners. Clients could pay for the business coaching services on an hourly basis, or you could develop a complete program consisting of a guidebook and multiple hours of coaching, and the revenue earned could be split with the retired business consultants.

DEMOGRAPHIC DATA BROKER
★★ $$$ 🏚 ⏰

Once a business determines who their target market is for a product or service they will be selling, they have to know where the target market is, how many potential customers are in the target range, and what the trends are in terms of their target market. Starting a demographic data brokerage service will enable you to fill the demand for corporations, organizations, and small business owners looking for such data. Simply set up a database on your PC that can be used for compiling and storing demographics information. The data can be researched and acquired for free, in most cases, via government agencies, the internet, and with reprint permission rights from publishers of almanacs, encyclopedias, and population directories. The quickest way to secure paying customers that require this type of demographics data is to contact companies that are new or coming into a region to see if they need such demographic data for the area. It's advantageous for you, as a service, to compile data on certain areas or in specific categories, and sell the same data to various companies, rather than having to constantly be compiling new data—unless, or course, you are specifically requested (and hired) to do so.

WEB SOURCE: www.census.gov
The Census Bureau is often a good starting point for data gathering.

GRAND OPENING SERVICE
★★★ $$$$ 🏚 🌐

According to the U.S. Small Business Administration, more than 700,000 new businesses open each year in the United States. This fact creates a fantastic opportunity for the enterprising entrepreneur to start a business that specializes in providing clients with various grand opening services. Grand opening services can include celebrity visits for special events, a red carpet service, ribbon cutting service, and a press release service, just to mention a few. As a unique way of marketing the grand opening

service, consider initiating a direct-mail advertising campaign explaining the various services your business provides. The campaign can be targeted at owners of businesses that have recently opened or will be opening in the very near future. To obtain this type of contact information for the direct-mail advertising campaign, simply contact your local business licensing center and ask for a list of people that have recently applied and been issued a business license.

CONTRACT NEGOTIATIONS SERVICE
★★ $$ 🏚 ⏰

The ability to successfully negotiate a business contract can mean the difference between prospering in business or failing in business. Many business owners are quick to realize that contract negotiation skills are an art form and often best left to professional contract negotiators. If you possess a high degree of business ethics, have exceptional communication, negotiation, and closing skills, then an unmatched opportunity waits in starting a contract negotiation service. Securing clients for the service is best approached by creating a marketing package that explains the service, but more importantly includes your accomplishments in terms of successfully negotiating contracts. Don't be shy. If you have a track record of negotiating multimillion dollar contracts in your past corporate life, let potential clients know. Once the marketing package has been completed, set appointments with companies and business owners that you feel would benefit by utilizing your service and negotiations experience.

OFFICE PROTOCOL CONSULTANT
★★★ $$ 🏚 🌐

The time has never been better than now to start a business as an office protocol consultant. Disputes between employees or between employees and management based on allegations of sexual harassment, racism, and abusive behavior within the office environment can not only morally bankrupt a business, but also financially bankrupt a business as a result of successful litigation. Acting as an office protocol consultant you can advise clients on issues pertaining to these subjects, as well as create a training program for employees and management on how to avoid and react to any potentially unfavorable situation that may arise within the office environment. The business concept is very straightforward, and the demand for this type of consulting service is gigantic, as thousands of corporations rush to retain the services of a protocol consultant as a proactive measure to ensure they are not caught in politically and socially inappropriate situations reflecting negatively on corporate image. Make sure you are up to date on the latest in employment law before advising clients.

MARKETING CONSULTANT
★★★ $$ 🏠

Without marketing a business cannot survive, simply because marketing is a combination of sales, advertising, promotion, and publicity. Put differently, marketing is an activity initiated by business to generate revenues for the business. Top-notch marketing consultants are in high demand from every size corporation and business across North America. Many marketing consultants will specialize in one particular aspect or element, while the more experienced consultants tackle the full range of marketing activities for clients. Securing clients for the service can be accomplished in numerous ways including promoting the service at business networking meetings, initiating a direct-mail advertising campaign, or by setting up meetings with potential clients to present your services. Additionally, if you possess skills and experience in marketing products or services via the internet, be sure to capitalize on this ability, as marketing consultants that specialize in online marketing are earning as much as $100 per hour.

WEB RESOURCE: www.the-dma.org
The Direct Marketing Association.

ORGANIZATION SERVICE
★★ $$ 🏠 🕐

Helping people to become and stay organized can earn you as much as $40 per hour, and best of all the business can be put into action for less than a few thousand dollars in start-up capital. The main focus of an organization service is to assist clients to develop a system to organize their home, office, business, or whatever else needs to be organized and put in place. Gaining clients for the service can be as easy as designing a marketing brochure explaining the service and distributing it to potential customers via direct mail or personally handing out the marketing material at business networking meetings. The key is to clearly explain how you can help others stay organized so that they will have more free time and be able to be more productive. Clearly, organizational skills are necessary to succeed at this career. Practice organizing the offices or homes of friends and neighbors. Once established, this is the type of personal service business that will receive a lot of word-of-mouth referrals and repeat business.

WEB RESOURCE: www.napo.net
The National Association of Professional Organizers.

ASSOCIATION MANAGEMENT SERVICE
★★ $$$

An association management service is a service that provides office, staff, and management solutions for associations, organizations, and trade unions that are too large to rely on volunteers within the association or organization to carry out the administrative and management duties required to maintain the association. Conversely, the organization may be too small and lack the financial backing to hire full-time staff and management. The duties of an association management service can include answering telephones, managing accounts receivables and payables, filing documents, corresponding with association membership, and just about any other task required in the day-to-day management of an association. Establishing billing rates service will depend on the various services provided for each client, and typically a quote is submitted reflecting the costs for providing the management services in a one-year period. The business can be operated from home, providing the intentions are to only manage a few associations. Larger services will require office space with boardroom facilities for association meetings.

WEB RESOURCE: www.marketingsource.com/association
Directory service listing more than 5,000 associations.

SURVEY SERVICE
★★ $$ 🏠 🕐 🌐

Starting a homebased telephone survey service is a terrific new business venture to set in motion. A few of the best aspects about starting this type of business are that it involves:

- A homebased business opportunity with very flexible operating hours
- A growth industry, proven and stable, with no previous experience or special skills required
- Low initial start-up investment and minimal monthly operating overheads

Once established, referrals and repeat business should drive the marketing. However, gaining clients to establish the business can be as easy as developing a direct-mail marketing program and distributing a marketing package to potential clients. The marketing package should include the various benefits that clients receive with your service, as well as a complete description of the service, which needs to be very carefully planned out in advance. Creating, implementing and getting people to respond to surveys is not easy. Therefore, you need some "survey" due diligence prior to starting such a business. Of course, since many people are besieged today with telemarketers, you need to make it clear upfront that you are conducting a survey and not selling anything. Design the surveys around the needs of each client and keep them relatively brief. The client should also provide the caller list and demographic group they want surveyed. The client is also responsible for paying for the phone calls.

CAREER EXPOS
★ $$$ 🌍

Career expos are simply trade shows that bring potential employers and employees together under one roof and in one venue. Career expos serve two functions. The first is that they give corporations a chance to blow their own horns and explain to potential employees why they are the industry leaders and, more importantly, why working for their company has advantages over selecting the competition. The second function that career expos serve is that they give people looking to start, change, or upgrade a career an opportunity to network, hand out resumes, and explain to the corporations exhibiting at the expo how they can benefit the corporation and what they can bring to the table. As you can see, there is a whole lot of horn blowing going on at career expos, but without question they are an excellent opportunity for both potential employers and potential employees to come together and seek mutually beneficial working

relationships and opportunities. You need to serve as the organizer, bringing together the companies and the job hunters under one roof, while charging both sides to attend. Securing a good location for the day may be your biggest expense. Beyond that, market, promote and advertise all over the place, using all available media sources.

EXPENSE REDUCTION CONSULTANT
★★ $$ 🏠 🕐

Calling all business managers, controllers, and operations managers! You can profit from your business and budget management skills and experiences by starting your own expense reduction consulting service. Expense reduction consultants provide clients with services such as developing long-term budgets, analyzing fixed and variable overheads, controlling product and service costs, and developing expense reduction strategies to suit individual client needs. The objective of the expense reduction exercise is to uncover costs associated with doing business that can be reduced or eliminated while still maintaining the efficiency of the business in terms of operations, customer service, and profitability. Potential clients will largely be small- to medium-sized businesses, but you can also target your marketing efforts toward professionals, nonprofit associations, and privately run institutions. Additionally, many of these consulting services will specialize in a particular type of business or industry such as fixed location retailing or manufacturing. Get started by developing an expense reduction manual. The manual should be representative of the type of business or industry you will target and include an index of categories you will analyze, such as business location, employees, communications, etc. The purpose of the manual is to act as a road map to guide you through each client's business. You can then tailor the manual to a specific client's business and enter subcategories for each business component that you analyze. Expense reduction consultants present each client with an extensive written report at the end of their investigation. This report typically outlines the consultant's suggestions in terms of reducing costs, including relevant supporting data and statistics. Fees for the service vary. Some consultants prefer to charge an hourly rate, while other prefer to charge a percentage based on the amount of money they can save a client. The percentage can range from 10 to 50 percent of first year's saving. However, this can be risky in the event the clients do not implement the plan immediately or correctly. Therefore, it is usually much better to get paid by the hour. If you have a strong financial background, and people believe in you based on your business philosophy, then marketing the service can be as easy as joining business associations to network with small business owners.

EMPLOYMENT AGENCY FOR SENIORS
★★ $$ 🏠 🕐 🌏

Ask any older person seeking employment what the most difficult challenge they face is and nine times out of ten the response will be their age. Opening an employment agency geared toward helping aging members of our society find gainful employment may just be your opportunity to build a successful and profitable business. No special training or education can replace good, old-fashioned experience, and this can be your most powerful marketing tool for recruiting small businesses and corporations to become clients and post job openings within their firms suitable for seniors with your agency. There are two methods for generating revenues for this type of business. The first is to charge would-be employers a fee to post a job listing and for you to find a suitable candidate to fill the job. The second option is to charge the person seeking employment a fee when employment is gained through the efforts of your agency. Additionally, you will also want to consider specialization in terms of the types of industries your agency will work in. Choices include a temporary work placement agency, high-level executive recruitment, tourism and hospitality, and just about any other industry wherein the needs of the employer can be suitably matched to the needs of the aging employee. Given the fact that people are living longer today than at any other time in history, the timing to initiate an employment agency for seniors could not be better.

EXPERT WITNESS SERVICE
★★ $$ 🏠 🕐

Starting an "expert witness for hire service" is a very unique and interesting business opportunity for the innovative entrepreneur to tackle. The idea is you represent expert witnesses that can be retained by lawyers to give professional testimony in court or legal proceedings. These expert witnesses could include medical doctors, gun and ammunition experts, transportation and automobile experts, private investigators, or just about any other type of professional that can be deemed an expert in their field or industry. The challenge is to find, and build a database of, professionals who are willing to serve as expert witnesses. Once you have such a list, the service would work very much like an employment agency, but with extremely high security measures in place to protect both clients and the expert witnesses. You can set presentation appointments with lawyers to introduce them to your service and discuss their needs in terms of experts needed to testify at trials. In exchange for providing the service, you would charge clients a commission based on the amount of money received for providing expert testimony. This is the type of business that will take very careful planning in order to establish. Partnering with a lawyer may be a consideration. However, the effort and expense to properly research and establish this business could be well rewarded financially, as expert witnesses can receive as much as five-figures in some situations to provide professional testimony.

PERSONAL DEBT AND BANKRUPTCY COUNSELING
★★★ $$ ★ 🏠 🕐 ⚖️

Personal debt is running rampant and as a last resort some individuals need to file for bankruptcy. Most people have no idea if there are any other alternatives and no idea what the process entails. Debt and bankruptcy counseling is, unfortunately, a rapidly growing industry. You will need to study debt management and bankruptcy laws, and in most cases, be accredited by the state. A background in banking and, or, personal finance is a plus. The key to this field is to find solutions for people who are otherwise out of control with spending or in serious debt for any number of reasons. You job is not to pass judgment, but to create means by which they can settle debts, curb spending, and hopefully avoid personal bankruptcy. If, however, they have no other choices, you will then walk them through the bankruptcy process. Debt counselors can typically make $50 per hour.

CORPORATE TRAVEL MANAGEMENT
★★★ $$ 🖥 🕐

Business travel is a multi-billion dollar industry and this is your opportunity to cash in. Corporate travel managers arrange trips for several companies at once and by booking in bulk they are able to provide better rates for corporate clients. The selling point: Having one central business handling all of the many travel details makes life easier for corporate executives. This is certainly a business you can start from a homebased location since you will spend most of your time on the phone and on the computer making arrangements for your clients with airlines and ground transportation. A background in travel management is a big plus; you can also take courses through many schools or the National Business Travel Association.

WEB RESOURCE: www.nbta.org
National Business Travel Association.

SPEAKERS BUREAU
★★★ $$ 🖥 🕐

Gather up as many business professionals as you can and send them off to do some public speaking. While it's not quite that simple, it's not much more difficult. Experts and possible public speakers are easy to find—in fact almost anyone who has a book, article, blog or simply an opinion wants to be heard. You therefore need to be discerning and select those individuals whom you feel can handle a speaking engagement in a professional manner and "wow" their audience. Your job is not to teach public speaking (see "Instruction" for that career) but to match a good speaker with an appropriate speaking engagement. Market yourself through brochures, fliers, your web site, and networking to colleges, conference planners, and businesses that utilize speakers for courses or training purposes. You can also sell videos about speaking and books on the topic.

EXECUTIVE EXPENSE MANAGEMENT
★★ $$ 🖥 🕐

Top tier executives travel very often, but find very little time to fill out expense reports and manage their travel expense details. This is where you come in. As an executive expense manager, you gather all receipts and organize and create expense reports based on the requirements of the specific companies. You will need to be knowledgeable of the company's travel and expense policies as you manage all of the travel expenses for a specific executive. Part of your duties will be making sure all expenses are reimbursed and if not, following up if there are any problems. Market yourselves to executives through business associations, company newsletters, networking, and through word of mouth. You might contact HR departments and see if they could mention your services.

You can bill hourly at anywhere from $15 to $35 an hour and, since you are working from a homebased location, you can operate with little overhead expense.

BENEFITS ADMINISTRATOR
★★★ $$$$

If you are familiar with the many benefits plans available to employees today, you can start a very profitable business handling benefit plans for various businesses. As a benefits administrator, your business will help companies select the best benefits plans to meet their needs, and you will help design and implement the plans. You will serve as a liaison between the company and the claims adjustors and make sure that employees are aware of their benefit options. In short, you save the business the time and trouble of hiring a full-time staff person to handle all of the paperwork and follow-up details necessary in maintaining health, medical and financial related plans, whether it's COBRA, flex spending, or stock options. Typically, your clients will be small to mid-sized companies with 50 to 150 employees. Since this is not a full time job for any one company, your business can handle such benefit plans for several companies and in some cases use the volume of employees from the companies you represent to get greater bulk discounts, in the event that several companies are satisfied with the same plans.

REQUIREMENTS: Thorough knowledge of employee benefit plans and roughly $35,000 to start up the business, including office equipment, marketing materials, and possibly part-time administrative help.

PROFIT POTENTIAL: This business can, after a few years, see $250,000 or more in revenues. Much of this will go back into the expansion of the business and hiring a benefits administrator, receptionist (should you move from a home base to an office), and upgrading your technology.

64

FOOD-RELATED
Businesses You Can Start

VENDING MACHINES
★★ $$$

Every day, factories, warehouses, office buildings, and recreation centers are being constructed. What they all have in common is the need for easily accessible food and drinks through vending machines. The snack vending business is a multibillion-dollar industry in North America, and continues to grow each year. Entering into the vending industry is very easy. Simply purchase a few vending machines, stock and locate them, and you're in business—right? Wrong. This industry has one of the highest failure rates due to the simple fact that people who start vending routes have often done so at the mercy of vending route business opportunity companies. These companies, in exchange for $10,000 or more, promise huge profits to the operators of these vending routes. Subsequently the vending equipment is inferior and usually ends up in the operator's garage after four or five months of not producing any income while on location. There is no great science to making a vending route or machine pay for itself. The key to success in vending is the same as opening a retail store: location, location, location. Research the right location, get permission to place the machines in that location, maintain and stock them regularly, and your vending machine business will not only make money, it will be profitable for many years. Hint: Some of the larger vending businesses may tie up a well-known route, particularly in major com-

mercial areas, leaving you with little room to get in. Therefore, look for new, growing areas, even those that are not yet open for business, particularly around schools, malls, and tourist areas.

WEB RESOURCE: www.vendingondemand.com
Resource for new and used vending machines.

USED RESTAURANT EQUIPMENT SALES
★★★ $$$

Did you know that starting a restaurant is one of the most common new business ventures? And, did you also know that more than 90 percent of new restaurants go out of business within the first five years of operation? The combination of these two facts is the basis for starting a business that buys and sells secondhand restaurant equipment like grills, fryers, and coffee machines. Simply put, when one restaurant goes out of business you purchase their equipment, and when another restaurant opens you resell that same equipment for a profit. This type of business venture can be started and operated from home initially and moved to a larger location as the business expands. Furthermore, you can specialize in one particular type of restaurant equipment such as deli equipment. The key is to do research and know the quality of the equipment you are buying and the going rate for new comparable equipment. You will also need a place to store some of the equipment that cannot be resold immediately, and a truck (or access to a convenient truck rental service).

Once all of this is taken into consideration, the potential to earn large profits from selling secondhand restaurant equipment is outstanding, and this business opportunity definitely warrants further investigation.

WEB RESOURCE: www.restaurant.org
National Restaurant Association

PREPACKAGED ENERGY FOODS
★★ $$ 🏠 🕐 ⚖️

The increase in outdoor recreational activities such as hiking, rock climbing, and backpacking is fueling the demand for prepackaged energy foods and nutrition bars, creating a terrific opportunity for the enterprising entrepreneur to start a new business venture that packages and sells these types of high-energy food products. You can get started on a part-time basis packaging and selling basic energy food like mixed nuts, dried fruits, and raisins. As the business grows, so can your product line to include energy drinks and full meals. The food items that you package can be sold through retail accounts such as fitness and health food stores, as well as at health clubs and stores that sell outdoor equipment. Furthermore, you can sell the products on your own web site, or by listing your products for sale on other health-related sites as a trade off, whereby you advertise the products of the other site owner.

WEB RESOURCE: www.sfa.org
Snack Food Association of America.

POPCORN CART
★★★ $$ 🏠 🕐 🌐

Here is a great part- or full-time business enterprise that can be started on a small initial investment and return excellent profits. Starting a popcorn cart vending business requires little more than a vendor's license, popcorn cart, and a high-traffic location at which to set up. Excellent locations include weekend flea markets, sports events, fairs, farmers markets, and all other busy community gathering places. New popcorn vending carts can cost as much as $15,000. However, as a way of keeping start-up costs to a minimum, you may want to consider purchasing a secondhand popcorn vending cart, as used carts are currently selling for approximately $2,500 to $5,000 depending on size and condition. The ability to

make a very good living operating a popcorn cart is excellent, and the markup on a bag of popcorn is 500 percent or greater.

WEB RESOURCE: www.snappypopcorn.com/machines.html
Machines ranging from old time machines to Star Wars models.

SANDWICH DELIVERY ROUTE
★★ $$

If you are searching for a very inexpensive business to start in the food industry that has the potential to generate $1,000 per week or more in combined income and profits, then look no further than starting a sandwich delivery route. Ideally, a sandwich route will be established in an office district or industrial district of a city or community, enabling the business to capitalize on sheer volume of people working in these areas. In terms of operating the business, it is as easy as establishing a working relationship with a catering service, a deli, or a restaurant to supply the sandwiches and salads on a wholesale basis, while building a customer base to purchase the lunch meals. Design a menu featuring all the sandwich and salad items available and distribute the menu to office buildings and factories. Customers would simply place their lunch orders in the morning or the day before. Additionally, lunch orders could be placed by way of fax, phone, or e-mail and, of course, delivery would always be free. As long as you are prompt and get the orders right, you can make a lot of money as more and more busy executives eat in, rather than lunching out.

FARMERS' MARKET
★★ $$$ 🕐 🌿

Every community needs a farmers' market, so why not start one in your community? The business is very straightforward to start and operate. Simply secure leased premises large enough to be subdivided into 30 or 40 ten-foot by ten-foot vendor booths. Once completed, the vendor booths can be rented to local farmers, specialty food manufacturers, and crafts people. Current rental rates for booths at farmers' markets are $75 to $125 per day. Assuming you had 30 booths rented once per week, four times per month the business would generate $12,000 per month in rental revenue, prior to operating expenses. The key to success in this type of business venture is to ensure the vendors that are participating in the market have high quality products and any necessary vendor or sale licenses. Signs all around the area and local handouts can promote the fair until area residents are familiar with it.

WEB RESOURCE: www.pma.com
Produce Marketing Association.

COFFEE SERVICE
★★ $$$

Billions of cups of coffee are sold annually in the United States, and securing just a small portion of this very lucrative market can make you rich. We are a nation of coffee drinkers, and to reinforce this statement you do not have to look further than any commercial district to realize there is a coffee shop on every corner. However, a coffee service is not to be confused with a coffee shop, as a coffee service is a mobile business that supplies medium- to large-size companies with free coffee-making equipment in exchange for the company purchasing coffee and coffee filters from the coffee service. The profit potential for a coffee service is outstanding, providing the service operates on a large volume basis and the product is as good or better than the leading coffee emporiums. It's all about buying or making a quality product when it comes to coffee, since coffee drinkers are very particular.

WEB RESOURCE: www.ncausa.org
National Coffee Association.

JUICE BAR
★★★ $$$

A juice bar that serves customers fresh-squeezed fruit juice drinks is an absolutely fantastic new business enterprise to put into action, as more and more people are striving to lead healthier lifestyles. Ideal locations to establish a juice bar include busy tourist attractions and beach areas, food courts in malls, fitness clubs, and public markets. To boost sales and profits, additional items such as sandwiches and salads can also be added to the menu. Furthermore, for truly enterprising entrepreneurs, consider adding a home delivery service that specializes in sales and free home delivery of fresh squeezed juices in larger quantities. The profit potential for a juice bar will vary based on factors such as operating overhead and

total sales. However, an established and well-run juice bar can easily generate profits in excess of $50,000 per year for the owner/operator of the business, and the profits can go much higher by adding additional menu items and delivery services.

ORGANIC FARMING
★ $$$$

Is it time to sell the house in the city and move to the country, but you're just not too sure what you could do to earn a living? Well if that's your dilemma, then perhaps organic farming is for you. In the past decade, organically grown and produced food products have really taken off in popularity and have been scientifically proven to be better for our health. Of course, operating a farm that grows organic foods requires a great deal of consideration and research prior to committing, not to mention an extremely large financial investment. However, the current demand for organically grown foods shows no sign of slowing down and will only continue to expand as the human population continues to become more concerned about maintaining a healthy and balanced diet.

WEB RESOURCE: www.organichub.com
Links to organic farming associations, wholesalers, and retailers.

CHOCOLATE MAKING
★★ $$

Starting a business that creates chocolate candies and treats is a great new enterprise to initiate, and the business can easily be formed as a joint venture with an established catering service or restaurant. The purpose of forming the joint venture is to greatly reduce the amount of start-up capital required to get the business rolling. A joint venture can enable you to utilize the partner's commercial kitchen, and in some cases the existing employee and customer base. The chocolate candies and treats can be sold to specialty retailers on a wholesale basis, or directly to chocolate loving consumers over the internet or at a factory direct outlet. Additionally, be sure to investigate the potential for forming alliances with charity groups, schools, and organizations as the students, volunteers, or members can be enlisted to sell packaged chocolate candies with partial proceeds going back to support community charities and programs. You can also sell special gift candies for the holiday season and special occasions. Just be careful not to eat too much of your inventory!

WEB RESOURCE: www.candyusa.org
Chocolate Manufacturers Association.

PIZZA BY THE SLICE
★★ $$$ ⚖️ 🌐

There are a lot of advantages and benefits to opening a small pizza-by-the-slice takeout restaurant, as opposed to a full-service sit-down pizza restaurant that provides customers with a varied menu and delivery options. These benefits include a smaller initial investment, lower monthly operating overheads, and shorter operating hours. Ideal locations for opening a pizza-by-the-slice takeout restaurant include food courts in malls, storefronts in office districts, and kiosks in large family entertainment centers. Supplying the pizza slices on a wholesale basis to factory and school cafeterias, as well as providing a free lunchtime delivery service of pizza slices in office districts can also be used as a method for boosting sales.

COMMUNITY RESTAURANT GUIDE
★★ $$ 🏠 🕐 🌐

A business that creates and publishes a monthly community restaurant guide is a very straightforward business venture to set in motion. The guide can feature information and articles about community restaurants, restaurant specials,, and coupons, as well as forthcoming community event information. The restaurant guide can be distributed throughout the community free of charge, and revenues to support the business can be gained by charging the restaurants featured in the guide an advertising fee. Additional income can be earned by providing restaurant owners with menu printing options, as well as paper placemat advertising and printing options. Both of these additional business opportunities are featured in this directory.

✈PACKAGED HERBS AND SPICES
★★ $$ 🏠 🕐

Here is a great little business opportunity that can be started on a part-time basis right from a homebased loca-

tion. Purchasing herbs and spices in bulk, repackaging the product into smaller quantities, and selling through local retailers via point-of-purchase (POP) displays is easy to do. The main objective is to ensure the packaging you create for the products is unique. You also need to ensure that the POP displays are located in highly visible areas of the retail stores with which you secure distribution rights. In all likelihood, the POP displays and product will have to be consigned with retailers initially until the product is a proven seller, at which point the accounts can easily be converted to typical wholesale supply accounts. Additionally, consider stocking the displays with cookbooks and recipe guides as well as the packaged herbs and spices as a method to increase consumer awareness and increase business revenues and profits.

WEB RESOURCE: www.garden.org
National Gardening Association.

WEDDING CAKE SALES
★★★ $ 🏠 🕐

Designing and creating one-of-a-kind wedding cakes is truly an art form. For the creative entrepreneur that possesses this talent, an incredible part-time business opportunity awaits by starting a business that makes and sells wedding cakes. Many wedding cakes retail for $500 each or more and generally only cost about 20 percent of the retail value to make. Building alliances with wedding planners and caterers is the fastest way to establish the business, even though it will probably mean splitting the revenue or selling the wedding cakes on a wholesale basis. Additionally, be sure to check local requirements in terms of operating this business from home, as health board permits may be required. If the business cannot be operated from home, inquire at local restaurants to see if a commercial kitchen can be rented on an hourly basis during non-business hours. Operating this type of specialty food business can generate an income of $300 or more each week on a part-time basis, making this a business opportunity well worth further investigation. You will also find that if your cakes are truly unique, you can benefit by word of mouth, particularly if you spread your name around in the local wedding industry—which means making sure wedding musicians, DJs, florists, and photographers have all tasted your creations.

ROADSIDE VEGETABLE STAND
★ $$ 🕐 🍃

A roadside vegetable stand is a fantastic seasonal part-time business to get rolling, as the start-up costs are minimal, the profit potential is great, and the demand for fresh in-season vegetables is high. The key to success in this type of food retailing is to secure a good location from which to operate the vegetable stand. Excellent locations include gas station parking lots, industrial parks, and main highways in and out of busy tourist areas. Make sure to get all necessary approval or licensing. Furthermore, in addition to a highly visible roadside location, be sure and have large and colorful signs made to advertise the stand. Generally, the season for fresh vegetables starts in early June and ends in early September. You can extend your season a month or more by selling cider, apples, chrysanthemums, and pumpkins in the fall.

SUBMARINE SANDWICH SHOP
★★ $$$$ ⚖️ 🌎

Submarine sandwich shops are popping up everywhere across the country, and starting your own sub shop may be just the new business opportunity that you have been searching for. The great thing about starting a sub shop is that operating this business does not require a lot of previous business experience or skills, making this a business opportunity that just about any determined entrepreneur can tackle. Like any restaurant business, the key to success lies in selecting the right location for the business, providing top-notch customer service, and serving good food at reasonable prices. Additional revenues can also be earned by expanding the menu to include salad and soup options, as well as a free home delivery service for food orders over a certain dollar amount. Subs are known as hoagies, wedges, heroes, and by other names in different parts of the country, so know the familiar jargon in your neck of the woods. Since there are two major franchises that sell such sandwiches nationwide, it is up to you to provide something they do not offer to gain the competitive edge, whether that means desserts, beer, waitress service, a salad bar, or something else that will set you apart from the familiar fast food eateries.

GOURMET FRENCH FRY STAND
★★★ $$$ ⚖️ 🌐

French fries are probably the most popular fast food product sold in North America, and starting a gourmet french fry stand may be just the new business opportunity that you have been searching for. Ideally, a french fry stand should be located in busy areas of the community such as mall food courts, beach areas, town squares, or city parks. What separates a gourmet french fry stand from a common french fry is the choice of toppings and sauces that are available. Toppings can include cheese, chili, salsa, gravy, or just about any other type of sauce that is currently available or that you want to create. Also, french fries should be freshly cut from potatoes on site to be considered the best. As a method to keep start-up costs to a minimum, consider purchasing used restaurant and commercial kitchen equipment, as secondhand equipment such as fryers and potato chippers in good condition can often be purchased for half of the cost of new equipment.

HOT DOG CART
★★ $$ 🕐 ⚖️

The biggest challenge to overcome in terms of starting a hot dog vending business is to secure a vendor's permit in your local community. However, even if a vendor's permit cannot be obtained, you can still operate a hot dog cart on privately-owned property and cater to functions such as flea markets, auction sales, sporting events, and fairs. Currently new hot dog vending carts are retailing in the range of $4,000 to $8,000 each, depending on the features. However, as a method to reduce business start-up costs, consider purchasing a secondhand hot dog vending cart, as they are typically half the cost of a new one. This is a terrific business to operate on a full- or part-time basis. Providing you can secure a good location or various local events to cater to, hot dog vendors regularly earn $4,000 per month and more.

WEB RESOURCE: www.topdogcarts.com

✗ CATERING SERVICE
★★★ $$$ 📷 🕐 ⚖️

A catering service is one of the best food businesses to start. Not only is the demand for catering services at an all-time high, but the catering industry as a whole has been proven to be very stable and definitely a growth industry. Additionally, one of the best aspects about starting a catering service is the fact the business can initially be operated on a part-time basis from a home base, and expanded to full-time as demand for the service increases. Securing clients for a catering service can start with building alliances with wedding and event planners. You will also want to develop a marketing package that can be presented to corporations that have catered meetings, seminars, parties, and banquets. Charities, associations, and even schools and universities all use the services of caterers. Your web site should list various catering packages and show some of your food presentations, since presentation is a big part of the sale. Many catering companies specialize in one particular segment of the industry such as corporate parties, and this may be a good practice to embrace, at least until the business is established.

WEB RESOURCE: www.icacater.org
International Caterers Association

COTTON CANDY
★★★ $$$ 🕐

Equipment needed to make cotton candy can be purchased secondhand for as little as $2,000, and starting a part-time business that makes and sells cotton candy is a great little business to tackle. In addition to the cotton candy-making equipment, a small trailer converted into a booth for sales will also be required to get the business up and rolling. Once the trailer has been outfitted with the equipment, supplies, and advertising signs, there are numerous locations to set up at in every community. Excellent locations include flea markets, sporting events, public markets, fairs, beach locations, parks, community events, carnivals, and parades. A cotton candy sales cart, trailer, or kiosk can be operated on weekends only and still generate sales of $1,000 per day.

WEB RESOURCE: www.cottoncandy.com
Portal that includes cotton candy making machines.

FRESH PASTA MAKING
★★ $$$

Does your favorite Italian restaurant make pasta fresh daily or purchase pre-made pastas? If the answer is the latter, then consider proposing a joint venture business opportunity to the owner of the restaurant. You make the pasta at their location, and they use the pasta for meal preparations for the business, as well as sell fresh pasta to their clients. Alternately, a pasta making and sales business could be established in a food market or farmers' market by renting a small booth, storefront, or kiosk, and additional revenues could also be generated by selling freshly-made sauces and seasonings. Operating this type of food business does require pasta-making experience, or at least a willingness to learn by trial and error. However, for the determined entrepreneur, business and financial success can be achieved by using sound judgment and common sense.

WEB RESOURCE: www.pastamachines.com
Manufacturers of pasta making equipment.

MAPLE SYRUP SALES
★ $$ 🏠 🕐

There's nothing better than fresh maple syrup with your pancakes or waffles at breakfast. Like Maine lobster and fresh Florida orange juice, the best maple syrup is a commodity known to come from a certain region of the country—the northeast—and our neighbor to the north—Canada. Therefore, if you can make a deal with a wholesale distributor in Vermont or import maple syrup from Canada, you can make money selling maple syrup to other parts of the country. By purchasing maple syrup from Canada, you can also take advantage of the higher value of the American dollar when selling your product. Once imported, the maple syrup can be sold directly to consumers at farmers markets, county fairs, by mail order, and from your own web site. Note: When importing maple syrup, be aware of any regulations set by the Canadian Food Inspection Agency or by US Customer other government body.

WEB RESOURCE: www.ontariomaple.com
Ontario Maple Syrup Producers Association.

CANDY STORE
★★ $$$$ 🌐

Candy sales kiosks and vending machines are popping up in every mall across North America, and why not? Starting a business that retails candy is very straightforward. The biggest challenge to overcome is selecting the right operating location. Ideally, a candy shop, or even a candy stand, should be in a very busy area of a community so that it can take advantage of foot traffic, as well as impulse buying by consumers. Also consider offering customers a free delivery service to expand the potential market to include customers who want to send candies to relatives in the hospital, loved ones at holiday time, and business owners seeking to reward clients or employees with their favorite box of chocolates or candies.

WEB RESOURCE: www.candynet.com
Portal to several candy manufacturers.

BUFFET-ONLY "ALL YOU CAN EAT" RESTAURANT
★★ $$$$ ⚖️

One price, all-you-can-eat buffet-style restaurants have become extremely popular amongst the budget-minded dining crowd, especially families with several children, so starting a buffet-only restaurant is a very wise choice for a new restaurant venture. A buffet restaurant has one major advantage for the operator over a typical restaurant—shorter work hours. Typically, buffet restaurants cater to the lunch and dinner crowds, opening at 11:00 AM and closing by 9:00 PM. Based on volume, a buffet restaurant can be very profitable, as the operating overheads are often much lower than similarly-sized restaurants, simply due to the fact that fewer employees are required to run the business. Additionally, wholesale food items can be purchased for a lower price based on volume buying, which all add up to beefed-up profits.

WEB RESOURCE: www.restaurant.org
National Restaurant Association.

EXHAUST HOOD CLEANING
★ $$ 🏠 🕐

In many regions of the country, restaurants are required by health board regulations to have their kitchen exhaust hoods cleaned on a regular basis to prevent bacteria growth and grease fires. This fact creates an ample opportunity for enterprising entrepreneurs to capitalize on by starting an exhaust hood cleaning service. There is specialized equipment available for cleaning restaurant exhaust hoods and filters. However, this equipment can be costly, and as a method to reduce start-up costs you

can always resort to the good old "strong arm" method until the business is established and the equipment can be purchased from the profits. Cleaning rates vary depending on the size, style, and access to the exhaust hood, but averaged out on an hourly basis there should be no problem maintaining $30 to $50 per hour for providing the cleaning service.

SPECIALTY SAUCES
★ $$$ 🏠 🕐 ⚖️

Have you been selected as the guardian of age-old family recipes such as barbeque sauces, salsa, and salad dressings? If so, perhaps you should consider sharing the family treasures with others and start a business that specializes in making and marketing specialty sauces. Once prepared, the sauces can be sold in bulk to restaurants, or packaged in smaller quantities and sold to grocery stores and specialty food retailers on a wholesale basis. The main objective in this type of food processing business is very straightforward. The sauces must taste good, and the packaging must be unique to gain consumer's interest in trying the product. The pricing must be in line with the competition and you need to promote heavily to get shelf space in an otherwise crowded market. Be sure to enlist the services of a product demonstration service to give away free samples of the sauces in the stores that will be retailing the products as a method of promotion, or do some in-store demos yourself.

✗ SOUP AND SALAD RESTAURANT
★★ $$$$ ⚖️

Light and healthy lunches are in, and starting a soup and salad restaurant can potentially put you on the road to financial freedom. Ideally, a small restaurant that serves soups and salads will be located in an office district or office building within a community to take advantage of the lunch crowd. Alternately the restaurant can be located within a mall to take advantage of shoppers seeking a quick meal before going home. If the restaurant is located within an office district, the business will also be able to provide a lunchtime soup and salad delivery service, and orders can come in by way of phone, fax, or e-mail to the restaurant. There are no secrets to success in terms of operating a soup and salad restaurant; select a good location, serve good food at reasonable prices, and provide customers with top-notch service, and the business will flourish.

WEB RESOURCE: www.restaurantsolutionsinc.com
Resource for restaurant kitchen equipment.

EMPLOYEE CAFETERIA
★ $$$ ⚖️

Most cafeterias located within factories, institutions, corporations, and schools are operated under a lease by an outside contractor, and if you are seeking to start a low-investment restaurant venture, then this type of business opportunity may be just what you have been looking for. Securing a lease for such a cafeteria is generally obtained by successfully tendering the service. Typically, tenders for cafeteria services are put up for bidding every couple of years, and the existing operators do not always successfully tender for the services. Be sure to start researching the business and, more specifically, look into the particular cafeteria you wish to operate, before the contract is up. Previous restaurant experience, or some familiarity with the workings of such a large-scale food service business, is highly recommended before trying to win the bid to run such a cafeteria.

DOUGHNUT SHOP OR WHOLESALE SUPPLIER
★★ $$$$ ⚖️ 🌐

Did you know that more than one billion doughnuts are sold each year in the United States? That is more than ample reason to consider a doughnut shop as a new business venture. The first approach is to open a traditional sit-down style doughnut shop that serves customers doughnuts, coffee, and muffins. The second approach is to establish a commercial doughnut bakery that is not open to the public, but specializes in making doughnuts for wholesaling to grocery stores, restaurants, school cafeterias, and catering companies. Of course, you can also combine both operating formats and run a doughnut shop as well as a doughnut wholesale bakery business. The industry is very competitive, so be sure to practice good research and planning skills prior to establishing the business. See what the local franchise businesses are doing so that you can provide some alternatives and gain a competitive edge in your area. Profit potential range is $40,000+ per year.

ICE CREAM STAND
★★ $$ 🕐 ⚖️

Ice cream is a universal favorite, and if you can find a location in need of such a shop, or a small ice cream stand, you can make a lot of money. Good operating locations for an ice cream stand include food courts at malls or beach areas. If you open in a storefront on a popular street, your expenses will go up but so will your potential revenues. The added room can allow you to put in a separate freezer for ice cream cakes, and if you have enough space, you can decorate a section for birthday parties for youngsters. Additionally, an ice cream business can also be started on a mobile basis by converting an enclosed trailer or delivery van into an ice cream stand. A mobile ice cream stand has many benefits as opposed to a fixed location due to the fact that you can transport your business to areas where demand is greatest for the product. The profit potential is outstanding, and it is not uncommon for an established ice cream stand to generate profits in excess of $50,000 and a shop to generate even more. To be competitive with the major chains you need to have a wide variety of flavors, offer interesting toppings, and find some clever sales hooks that attract the attention of the biggest ice cream fans—kids.

WEB RESOURCE: www.nicyra.org
National Ice Cream and Yogurt Retailers Association.

PREPACKAGED VEGETARIAN FOODS
★★★ $$$ ⚖️

Calling all vegetarians! Do you find it difficult to find prepackaged meals at your local grocery store that can be prepared quickly and conveniently, and of course that do not have meat or meat by-products in the ingredients? If so, perhaps you should consider starting a business that makes and packages vegetarian meals that can be sold on a wholesale basis to grocery stores and specialty food retailers. If this sounds appealing as a business opportunity, that's because it is. There are an estimated 20 million vegetarians in the United States, and this number continues to grow on a yearly basis as more and more people are starting to understand the benefits of a vegetarian diet. The business will require careful planning and research to establish; but with that said, prepackaged vegetarian foods are a growth segment of the food industry and provide tremendous upside potential for long-term business success and profits.

WEB RESOURCE: http://fpa-food.org
Food Products Association.

VEGETARIAN RESTAURANT
★★★ $$$$ ⚖ 🌐

There are an estimated 20 million American adults who are vegetarians, and this fact creates an excellent opportunity for the budding restaurateur to capitalize on by starting a vegetarian restaurant. Like any restaurant business, conducting a market survey in the area where the restaurant is to be established will indicate consumer demand, and this step is especially important prior to opening a vegetarian restaurant due to the specialized nature of the business. In addition to serving meatless meals, many vegetarian restaurants also sell food products as well as cookbooks, and this can be a terrific way to increase business revenues and profits. Furthermore, also seek opportunities for a lunch delivery service to offices and homes, as this can also be a way to bolster sales. As a rule of thumb most restaurants operate on a 40–40–20 percent basis, meaning 40 percent of the revenue covers food and consumable costs, 40 percent of revenues covers operating and overhead costs, and 20 percent of revenue is left as the pretax gross profit.

CHUCK WAGON
★★ $$$+ 🕐 ⚖

Purchasing an enclosed trailer or delivery step van that can be converted into a chuck wagon is the first step toward starting your own mobile restaurant business. Chuck wagons or mobile food concessions are everywhere, and initiating this type of business venture is easy. As mentioned, you can purchase an enclosed trailer or step van and convert it into a food concession on wheels by equipping it with commercial restaurant equipment such as fryers and grills. Or, you can purchase a mobile concession truck that has been professionally designed and constructed. Typical, chuck wagon menus include French fries, hamburgers, and hot dogs. One of the best aspects about starting this business is it offers flexibility in terms of operating hours and location. Good locations include outdoor auction sales, parades, beaches, fairs,

parks, sporting events, or any other busy community event. You will need to acquire a vendor's permit and a health board certificate to operate. However, providing the mobile concession stand meets health board codes, these permits are very easy to get. The profit potential is outstanding as it is not uncommon for mobile food concessions to generate sales of $1,000 per day or more in the right location.

CATERING TRUCK
★★ $$$$ 🕐 ⚖

Secondhand catering trucks in good condition can be purchased for as little as $10,000, and this can be the first step taken to establishing a catering truck route, which is a great business to set in motion. Not only are the hours of operation generally limited to 6:00 a.m. to 3:00 p.m., but also the business can also be started for less than $15,000 and can easily generate a combined income and profit earnings of $50,000 per year or more. Additionally, food products can be purchased from restaurants, catering services, and wholesalers and marked up by as much as 150 percent for retail sales. Ideal stopping points for a catering truck route include construction sites, factories, parks, beaches, and sporting events.

TAKE-OUT CHICKEN AND WINGS
★★ $$$$ ⚖ 🌐

Starting a take-out chicken and wings restaurant is a very easy business venture to set in motion. This type of restaurant requires little experience to operate, and the kitchen equipment needed can be purchased secondhand in just about every community across the country. Like many restaurants, a take-out chicken and wings restaurant can be established in a fixed location such as a storefront or in a food court at a mall. The business can also be operated on a mobile basis from an enclosed trailer or van that has been converted into a mobile restaurant and meets all health codes and safety requirements. Assuming the restaurant is operating from a fixed location, be sure to provide customers with a free delivery service, as this can potentially increase the size of your market to include customers that may otherwise not frequent the restaurant. Additionally, operating the restaurant in a take-out format will also help to reduce the amount of space required as well as reduce the amount of start-up capital required to get the restaurant rolling.

DESSERT OR PASTRY SHOP
★★ $$$$ ⚖ 🌐

Dessert-only restaurants have become very popular in the past decade, both as a new business venture and for consumers seeking to satisfy their sweet tooth. The business concept is very straightforward. Simply open a small sit-down restaurant that offers customers varied menu options including cakes, cookies, tarts, pies, ice cream, and just about any other dessert or treats that you can think of, or create. Ideally, the location selected to establish a dessert shop should be in an area that has a large volume of people walking by, including theater districts, malls, and office and financial districts, as many customers will be attracted by impulse buying urges. Additionally, very popular items on the menu can also be made and packaged under the name of the business and sold on a wholesale basis to grocery stores and specialty food retailers throughout the local community. Your success will hinge on the yummy factor, and if customers are happy, they will spread the word. Great dessert shops in high-traffic locations can rake in a lot of dough.

COOKIE SALES
★★ $$$

Do your family and friends tell you that you bake the best cookies in town? If so, putting your cookie baking talents to work for you has the potential to make you rich. Mass producing specialty or gourmet cookies is a very easy business to put into action. Simply rent or secure commercial kitchen space, perfect the cookie baking process, design interesting packaging for the cookies, and you're in business and ready to start profiting. Specialty cookies can be sold to food retailers on a wholesale basis, or directly to the public via a cookie sales kiosk or a small stand at the local mall. Another great means of selling your cookies is at movie theaters and local sporting facilities as a concession business. Once established, the profit potential could prove to be outstanding for the creative and maker of clever and tasty cookies. Just ask Famous Amos or Mrs. Fields! And, if you can add a line or two of low fat but tasty cookies, you can grab the business of

numerous people watching their diets and/or their cholesterol levels.

BAKERY
★★ $$$$ ⚖

A bakery can be established as a retail business from a storefront location selling baked goods to consumers, or as a wholesale business selling baked goods to food retailers and institutions. Additionally, many bakeries will operate both as a retail and wholesale business to increase the size of their potential market as well as revenues and profits. Establishing a bakery is a very straightforward process with one exception: the best bakers possess baker's trade papers, so be prepared to hire a qualified baker, or take the time necessary to become a qualified baker. The profit potential is good for a bakery, especially if the business focuses on both retail and wholesale baked goods. Creativity will help you stand out from the competition, as well as interesting packaging and first-rate customer service. Whether you are selling football-shaped cakes for the Super Bowl, dinosaur cakes for kids, special holiday cakes and pies, or exotic bakery novelty cakes, the more ideas you can come up with for shapes, sizes, and designs of your baked goods, the more customers you can attract.

WEB RESOURCE: www.americanbakers.org
American Bakers Association.

PEANUT AND NUT SALES
★ $$ 🏭 🕐

You can start making money by purchasing peanuts (and other assorted nuts) in bulk, repackaging the nuts into smaller sized bags, and selling the packaged nuts to retailers on a wholesale basis. Alternately, the nuts can be placed into retail stores and sold on a consignment and revenue share basis. Don't overlook the possibility of selling peanuts from vending machines that can be installed at locations like malls, pubs, and sports complexes. The vending machines will initially cost a few thousand dollars to purchase; however, the return on investment is quick, providing the machines are installed in busy areas. You can also have a cart selling the various nuts by the pound in malls and other high traffic locations. Any and all of these possibilities combined can bring you a good profit.

FROZEN YOGURT SHOP
★★ $$$

Frozen yogurt has been a favorite treat of consumers for years, and establishing a frozen yogurt shop as a new business venture is not only proven, but also very stable. Furthermore, for the entrepreneur seeking to work hard for half of the year, while traveling the other half of the year, opening a frozen yogurt shop is a very wise choice. The business can be established in a beach or busy tourist area and a full-time income can easily be earned operating the business on a seasonal basis only. In addition to frozen yogurt, additional treats such as homemade fudge and ice cream can also be included in the menu to appeal to a wider range of potential customers, and of course to also increase sales and profits.

WEB RESOURCE: www.nicyra.org
National Ice Cream and Yogurt Retailers Association.

HERB GARDENING
★ $

A small plot of land in your backyard can easily be converted into a cash-producing herb garden. Dill, parsley, and chives are just a few of the many herbs that can be grown at home for profit. Get started by spending time at your local library and on the internet to learn as much as you can about herbs and herb gardening. The rest is very simple. Plant your garden, grow your herbs, design some herb packages, and set out to establish accounts with local merchants to sell your goods. Like any new business venture there will be a learning curve to climb. However, the rewards of a few extra thousand dollars each year can justify the effort.

WEB RESOURCE: www.backyardgardener.com/herb/index.html
Plenty of backyard herb ideas.

RESTAURANT WASHROOM CLEANING SERVICE
★★★ $

Next to bad food, the number one reason people will not return to a restaurant is dirty washrooms. This fact alone can be used as your greatest sales and marketing tool for convincing restaurant owners and managers that they need your washroom sanitation services. Offer the service for free for the first time as it only takes about 20 minutes to sanitize the average washroom. Managers and owners (not to mention patrons) will be so impressed with the excellent service and positive effects that they will contract with you to return weekly to continue the washroom sanitation program. Income potential once established is $15 to $25 per hour.

GROCERY DELIVERY SERVICE
★★ $

You have a few options available in terms of starting a grocery delivery service. The first is to simply contract with local grocery stores to deliver customer orders for a fee. The grocery store would bill the customer, market the service, and manage the deliveries, and you simply deliver the groceries. The second and more lucrative option is to establish a buying account with a grocery wholesaler and resell groceries to your customers at a profit. This method means you will have to create a catalog of the grocery items you stock as well as market the service. However, once again the potential to generate more profit is greatly increased. Grocery delivery services are often very profitable business ventures, as the convenience of home delivery makes getting customers very easy. Start a web site and you can make this a high-tech venture. The key to success is getting deliveries to customers quickly

SEAFOOD SALES
★★ $$$

Starting a business that specializes in seafood sales and home delivery is a fantastic new business venture to set in motion. Both frozen and fresh seafood products such as fish, lobster, and oysters can be purchased on a wholesale basis and resold at a profit to consumers. You need to purchase or lease a delivery vehicle with a refrigeration or freezer unit and, for the best results, make sure you are able to make contacts with wholesalers who have the freshest seafood available. You can secure customer for the business by designing and distributing a menu or marketing brochure that features a description of the various seafood products that are available. Generally, these types of specialty food sale businesses can really flourish. Fresh high-quality seafood is not always readily available in every community, and the convenience of home delivery can be used as a very powerful marketing tool. Potential profit is $30,000+ per year.

WEB RESOURCE: www.nfi.org
National Fisheries Institute Inc.; links to seafood producers.

✗ PERSONAL CHEF SERVICE
★★★ $ 🏠 🕐 🌐

Take your pots and pans, cooking skills, and love of food mobile and hit the road as a personal chef for hire. Prepare gourmet meals for people hosting house parties, small special occasions such as birthdays or aniversaries, corporate luncheons—basically anywhere there is a kitchen on site that you can utilize for your chef service. Personal chefs are becoming a very popular alternative for people that do not have the budget for a full-scale catered event or for people that are hosting small events that do not require complete catering services. Of course you will need to go to culinary school to succeed in this field or have had experience as a chef in a restaurant, since your competition will likely come from such a background. The other alternative is to be the marketer and "matchmaker," so to speak, and bring personal chefs to such private parties and gatherings. To do this, you need to build up a list of excellent chefs, which may include recent culinary school graduates as well as chefs looking for some additional work outside of the restaurants in which they cook. Next, you need to join business networking clubs and community social clubs to spread the news about your personal chef service. This is the type of business that can easily be supported by word-of-mouth referrals and repeat business once established, leading to a full-time profitable business venture. Typically chef rates are quoted on each job and vary on factors such as the supply of food and the type of menu requested. However, on the average, personal chefs are typically earning of $50 and up per hour. Well-known chefs can make significantly more money and you can work on a percentage basis or simply charge a fee that includes an amount for your services.

PRODUCE SHOP
★★ $$$$

The bland produce shops of days gone by, with their less-than-appealing display methods, boring interiors, and limited product selections, are quickly being replaced by what is now called "Produce Boutiques." A wolf in sheep's clothing perhaps, but today's new age produce shops are specifically catering to consumers that have become more health wise and want a relaxing shopping experience. Many produce shops now offer customer services such as a juice bar, the ability to sample products before they buy, and an area to sit down and relax with favorite snacks and read the paper. This is the type of retailing business that must be located in a densely populated urban center to thrive. Fewer cars and more foot traffic are key location considerations. Furthermore, as a method to increase revenues and profits, be sure to establish supply accounts with restaurants and catering companies that are seeking the best produce available to prepare for their valued customers.

WEB RESOURCE: www.pma.com
Produce Marketing Association.

DELI
★★ $$$$ 🚚

Starting and operating a deli has many advantages over a traditional restaurant, including lower start-up costs, shorter operating hours, and lower operating overheads. The best delis not only sell varied meats, cheeses, and other exotic gourmet foods but also provide customers with a lunch delivery service, a few seats and tables for the sit-down lunch crowd, and take-out catering options including cold meat and cheese trays. Noteworthy is the fact that many deli proprietors choose a theme for their business such as a New York-style, British, or German deli. The ideal operating location for a delicatessen is generally found in office districts and strip malls. The key to success in this type of competitive food business is to provide customers with excellent quality, exceptional service, and varied products that will appeal to a large segment of the population.

WEB RESOURCE: www.restaurantequipment.net
Directory service with thousands of source for new and used restaurant equipment and supplies.

TEXAS BARBEQUE RESTAURANT
★★ $$ 🏠 🕐

Texas-style barbeque restaurants are typically crowd pleasers and a great business start-up for the entrepreneur that is looking for a potentially profitable business enterprise. Hamburgers, steak on a bun, ribs, and hot dogs are just a few of the menu items that can be included. You can operate this type of business from a large tent, and cater to sporting events, corporate functions, parades, auction sales, fairs, and social events such as family reunions. This type of food service business will need licensing in most areas by the health board, but providing you meet and maintain health board requirements, securing this type of license is easy. In addition to a large tent, you will also need a commercial barbeque that operates on propane (or even seasoned wood for the true barbeque enthusiast) as well as other basic equipment such as coolers. You can purchase an enclosed trailer or van to transport the equipment to the event you are catering. This is a great part-time business enterprise for anyone with cooking experience to undertake and operate just a few hours each weekend. This can generate profits of $500 or more at a busy event as these types of food products are typically marked-up by 400 percent or more for retail sale. Market the business by building alliances with business associatißons, event planners, associations, community groups, and various clubs. It will not take long to start generating referrals as long as the food and service you provide is excellent.

WEB RESOURCE: www.bbqsearch.com
Barbeque food service information, recipes, and links to equipment manufacturers and product providers.

GOURMET COFFEE KIOSK
★★ $$$$ 🌐

Millions of cups of coffee are consumed daily in the United States and thousands of entrepreneurs are capitalizing financially because of it, and so can you by opening a gourmet coffee kiosk. Rent a kiosk in a mall or market location and provide customers with the best coffee and tea selections available from around the world. You can purchase, or lease, coffee grinding and packaging equipment and offer free samples to coffee and tea enthusiasts as a method to get them acquainted with your products. Unlike a coffee shop that serves brewed coffees and teas along with pastries and snack items, your gourmet coffee kiosk can specialize in selling fresh packaged coffee and tea products to consumers. Purchase the specialty coffees

in bulk in bean form, grind it on site, and sell it repackaged in smaller quantities. Additionally, be sure to develop your own brand of private label coffee and teas. This can be a method of increasing revenues by establishing wholesale accounts with grocery stores and specialty food retailers to stock and sell your brand name products.

WEB RESOURCE: www.kaldi.com
Wholesale distributors of specialty coffee equipment and supplies.

ROMANTIC CATERING
★★★ $$ 🚗 🕐 🌐

Who needs cupid when they can hire your romantic catering service and surprise that special someone their life with a unique and unforgettable romantic dinner for two. Romantic catering is just that. You plan and play host to a memorable dining experience for clients. The evening could start with a romantic ride in a horse-drawn carriage through a park, complete with wine, roses, and mood-setting music. The ride could end on a secluded beach under the stars where the client would dine on lobster and caviar picnic-style. Of course, your service would provide the gourmet meal, make all the arrangements, supply the transportation, and even serve the meal on the finest china while dressed in exquisite formalwear. Best of all, you do not need to be a chef, have the horse-drawn carriage, or even have the ability to serve the meal. All of these can be contracted to qualified people who posses these abilities and equipment. What is required, however, is the ability to market the service in a creative manner and have the imagination to plan the best possible romantic dinner adventures available. Perhaps a deal can be struck with the local newspaper or entertainment magazine. You provide a romantic dinner full of surprises for a reporter, editor, or publisher and their guest in exchange for a write-up about your romantic catering service to be featured in their publication. This is the type of business that can enjoy a great amount of word-of-mouth referrals.

IN-STORE DEMONSTRATION SERVICE
★★★ $$ 🕐

Whether it is a new product that slices, dices, chops and purees or a sample of the latest foods from a specific vendor, there are great sales advantages to in-store promotions, particularly when tasting is involved. If people like what they eat, they tend to buy it. More often than not, neither the companies, nor the food shops, have the available help to handle such in-store demos effectively and the result is food for tasting but no one to move that taste to a sale. Hence, a small business opportunity. You set up the tables or booth and use your demonstration skills to show off the latest in cutlery or serve up anything from slices of cake to pasta primavera cooked fresh in the store. Offer your services to food vendors, grocery stores, gourmet and specialty shops, and the makers of food processors and other kitchen devices. Hone your skills by watching more than your share of television infomercials and practicing your banter. Offer to supply the scripts yourself for a few dollars more, or use those written by the company or store marketing department. This is a very good business to operate from home, starting on a part-time basis, with great potential and not much competition in most areas.

FAMILY-FRIENDLY RESTAURANT
★★★ $$$$ 🎲 🌐 🍃

Where to take the kids for dinner? It's an ongoing dilemma. Fine dining is out and ethnic cuisine may be an acquired taste. Family restaurants, as in Friendly's, Denny's, and other chains, can prove very affordable alternatives, when home cooking is not in the plans. These are also potential money-making businesses. While you may want to look into a franchise, you also may have the desire to "do it your way," without the corporate regulations. A local family restaurant with good food, children's portions, games on the menus, and drink refills can attract a lot of customers through some promotion and a good location (with plenty of parking). Research the area first and determine what other establishments are in close proximity. Market your business based on serving good family fare but not fast food, and look for a niche. In addition, have specials, such as early-bird deals, free ice cream sundaes on Sundays, or anything else that will draw the family with kids. As is always the case with a restaurant, you will need to have a staff you can count on during the busiest hours, provide good service, and more than meet all health requirements. Restaurants are not

easy to start, and the initial investment can be very high, so being able to entice backers with a good business plan is usually the way to go. Such a business venture can be very lucrative if done right. Hint: A few video games or similar activities for the kids can make you very popular.

✗ COOKBOOK SALES
★★★ $$ 🏠 🕐

One thing about cookbooks—they never seem to go out of style. Whether you have the culinary skills to write your own or are buying in bulk and selling other people's cookbooks, a cookbook shop is a great little business, especially with some food preparation accessories, and aprons with clever sayings to boot. You can also set up a booth at a popular mall and, with a catchy name, (like "Cook This!") you'll generate plenty of attention. To set yourself apart from the competition, surf the web and find lesser-known cookbooks that you can have in stock. In addition, have author signings or even have authors in to cook! The better you promote any specialty bookshop, the more likely you will be able to generate a regular following. You can also sell by means of your web site and by having booths at fairs and special events.

WEB RESOURCE: www.americanbookco.com
American Book Company

RESTAURANT MARKETING CONSULTANT
★★ $ 🕐

Ever wonder why a restaurant you really like is always so empty? It may be that you have discovered a very well-kept secret. And while you may enjoy the cozy and quiet confines of the eatery, it is doubtful that this is the best scenario for the restaurateur. Enter the restaurant marketing consultant. This is someone who is well versed in why there is a 60-minute wait for a table in one restaurant and 60 empty seats in another. It is the marketing consultant's job to determine the best ways in which to build up business, whether it means alliances with nearby hotels, happy hours, free samples at busy locations, or other means of spreading the word. If you have some marketing skills and a good knowledge of the restaurant field (or take the time to learn as much as possible) you can command upwards of $50 an hour to put together a full marketing strategy for each client and implement it as required. Market yourself to every uncrowned restaurant you can find by handing out your card with some basics on what you can do, and (once you are established) what you have done.

WEB RESOURCE: www.marketingpower.com

PRETZEL VENDOR
★ $$ 🕐 ⚖️

Pretzels are easy to make fresh and a great snack while walking around a mall, watching a sporting event, or spending the day at the park. Salted and non-salted, long, traditional, sourdough, seasoned, multigrain, and many other variations can all be part of your selection. A high profile location and service with a smile are two prime ingredients for making a pretzel shop popular. Make sure you meet all vendor licensing and health code restrictions. If you are mobile, you can set up a pretzel stand in various key locations, such as outside of a major sporting event or near a popular tourist location, but make sure that zoning laws allow you to do so.

WEB RESOURCE: www.pretzeldirectory.info

SPORTS BAR
★★★ $$$$ ⚖️

Big screens, plenty of excitement, and lots of business during the Super Bowl, World Series, or the World Cup—that's what a sports bar is all about. There is a lot of money in running such a bar if you do it right! That means good food, good service, a good location, and plenty of sports action via cable and satellite feeds. Before you start, you will need to find out all about liquor licensing in your area. Once you receive the license, the hard work just begins. Running a sports bar is very time intensive, with 50+ hour weeks and many (or most) late nights being part of the package. If you enjoy the late nights at work, you will pass the first hurdle. If not, find someone to run the business for you—but make sure they can be trusted. The next key is making sure you have some financial capital to cover the lean months until you establish a reputation. Paying for satellite television, alcohol, food, wait staff, bartenders, and all of the other amenities, not to mention the rent or mortgage, makes this an expensive proposition, even for a small establishment. Finally, there is the need for extensive marketing at sporting events, through local newspaper and radio advertising and by holding contests,

specials, and events to draw in customers. Remember, besides competing with other bars you are also competing with numerous other types of entertainment, including friends with large screen television in their basements. As mentioned earlier, good food, good drinks, and a fun atmosphere are the keys to making this work.

WEB RESOURCE: www.entrepreneur.com/startingabusiness/businessideas/startupkits/article41460.html
An article with the lowdown on opening a bar or a club.

✗ SOUP RESTAURANT
★★★ $$$$ ⚖️ 🕐

Remember the "Soup Nazi" on Seinfeld? While the character was a bit over the top, the concept of soup restaurants flourished and one in particular, called "The Soup Nutsy," capitalized on the offbeat publicity and took off. Now, a decade later, soup restaurants are still a great little business from which to make big bucks with good marketing and a great location. Soups are a great basis for lunch, with salads, sides, rolls and other offerings. The key to success is having a variety of delicious soups at the ready every day. Since a small-sized kitchen should typically suffice, your options for location are greater than they are for other restaurateurs. Research your potential locations carefully and make sure to market yourself to the lunch crowd through all of the usual methods… and offer free, prompt, delivery.

RESTAURANT GUIDE
★★ $$ 🚗 🕐

There are two approaches to a restaurant guide. One is where you cover an area and, like Zagats, you rate the ambiance, food quality and service, then sell the guide through other retailers, bookstores and online. The second option is to list restaurants based on their payment to be included. In this case, you would encourage some type of discount coupon or special, such as a two-for-one offer or free drinks with entrée. In this case the guides are given away for free, but the restaurateur pays to be included. Either way, you have low overhead, beyond printing and marketing, and if you have good layout skills and desktop publishing software, you can handle the printing yourself. Don't forget the option of handling the business online. Hint: If you go the route of rating restaurants, put your personal tastes aside and be as objective and impartial as possible. This is the type of business that can begin in one location and branch out depending on the possibilities and profits from your first guide.

WEB RESOURCE: www.afjonline.com
Association of Food Journalists.

FOOD TASTING
★ $$ 🕐

If you have discerning taste buds and love to eat, then why not eat professionally? Food manufacturers, chefs, and scientists are constantly creating new flavors and mixing new ingredients to try and win over a larger share of the industry, whether it is packaged foods, fast foods, or gourmet foods. Food tasters can work freelance or be on staff of a food company, often working in the lab or kitchens where various foods are created. A good food taster can discern the various ingredients in the food—the sweetness, bitterness, texture, and product consistency—and determine which he or she likes better. In addition, he or she can tell what is in the recipes of competitors. There is little overhead and you can specialize in certain food groups, while running the business from your home and going to the labs and kitchens when needed. You may also run food tasting focus groups, whereby you gather other people and have them tell you what they taste. You then report back to the manufacturer with your findings. Depending on your appetite and whether you are working full or part time, you could chew your way to anywhere from $20,000 to $70,000. You could also hire additional tasters and run the business by booking tasters with manufacturers, chefs, and labs.

CATERER'S WAIT STAFF SERVICE
★★★ $$ 🏠 🕐 ⚖️

Wherever there are catered events, there is a need for wait staff and often busboys. This opens the kitchen door for you to start up a business whereby you are the one source for caterers—or anyone having a private party—that are in need of servers. Start off by running ads for anyone who is looking for part-time waiting work. This will likely include college students, actors, dancers, and performers of all types who need work

between gigs. Make sure to do some basic training and then maintain their availability in one database. Next, market yourself far and wide to all catering businesses, banquet facilities, and anyplace in which a party, wedding, or special occasion might be held. Make sure to have a web site through which you can also provide party planners with the wait staff they need. The larger the area you cover, the more money you can make running a caterer's wait staff business that can easily be run from home with little set-up cost.

WATER ICES
★ $$$ 🏠 🕐

What could be better on a hot summer day than ices? Kids of all ages love them and ices are very easy to sell. You can opt for a cart or a full-fledged location, which can double as something else in the winter months. Banana, lemon, cherry, mango, chocolate, and more than 100 other flavors are all possibilities, plus there are low-sugar options for the diet crowd. You may also want to sell sherbet and frozen custard. It is important to have a good location, or several prime locations, so that everyone knows where your ices can be found. This is business you can typically start for a few thousand dollars.

SUSHI BAR
★★★ $$$$ ⚖️

Since the mid 1990s, sushi has quickly grown as a lunchtime favorite and with a good sushi chef, you can cash in on the popularity of sushi bars. An advantage of a sushi restaurant over other types of restaurants is that you do not need a large kitchen space, which can be a plus when seeking out a location. A refrigeration unit, sushi prep table and, should you be selling take out orders, a sushi display case, plus tables and chairs and or a counter, and you are all set. As is typically the case with a restaurant of any type, location will be a prime concern and in this case a high traffic business locale or a busy mall are two leading possibilities. The Sushi Chef Institute and Sushi Chef Academy, both in California, are two schools to start your search for a good sushi chef, but also network by asking other sushi chefs if they have any leads.

WEB RESOURCE: www.sushicases.com

EROTIC BAKERY
★★ $$$$ ⚖️

Okay, it is certainly not your mainstream business, but there is a market for some erotic bakery goods, especially for bachelor and bachelorette parties. From specially designed and decorated cakes to an interesting array of chocolates to non-erotic multi-tiered or sheet specialty cakes, you can bring in plenty of "dough" and have some fun in the process. Market the store in a tasteful manner to soon-to-be brides and grooms as well as couples celebrating anniversaries. Along with the visual appeal of your treats, you also need to make sure that your products are tasty or the gimmick will lose some of its luster.

GOURMET SHOP
★★ $$$$ ⚖️

If you enjoy the finer things in life, than why not share that enjoyment with others courtesy of a gourmet food shop? Typically a small retail space in an upscale location will be your best bet, and carrying a variety of cheeses, smoked salmon, caviar, truffles, and hard-to-find delicacies can provide you with a regular clientele that enjoys such gourmet treats. Of course, you can also branch out and spread the taste around with mall kiosks and satellite locations in other food and perhaps even wine stores. Know your products well, provide excellent customer service, and set up access for placing orders on your web site.

NOTES:

29
FURNITURE
Businesses You Can Start

REFURBISHING ANTIQUE APPLIANCES
★★★ $$$

The profits that can be made by turning discarded and abandoned antique appliances into refurbished and functional appliances for today's custom-designed residential kitchens are enormous. One of the best aspects of this business opportunity is that you do not even have to know how to repair or refurbish the appliances yourself, as you can hire skilled employees for this part of the business. The market for refurbished antique appliances is absolutely gigantic. Some appliances sell for as much as $5,000 each to interior decorators and homeowners seeking the ultimate designer touch. When you consider many of these same antique appliances can be found in less-than-perfect condition at garage sales, junkyards, and auction sales for less than $100, that's a very good return on investment even if it costs a thousand dollars or more to restore the appliance. Once refurbished, antique appliances can be sold directly to consumers and design professionals via a display booth at home and garden shows, advertisements in home improvement and antique trade publications, and of course through the internet, including web auction sites such as eBay.

FURNITURE DELIVERY AND ASSEMBLY
★★ $$

Starting a furniture delivery and assembly service is the perfect new venture for the handyperson with a truck and basic tools to get rolling. The business can be managed from a homebased office and the fixed operating overheads are minimal. Get started by contacting local furniture and office supply stores in your community to see if they are currently providing their customers with a delivery and assembly option. If not, strike a deal to provide their customers with the service and you're in business. Moving companies are also a good source of work because, as we all know, there is a lot of furniture assembly to be done after a move. Individual clients will also be interested, since many people purchase items with the intentions of putting them together themselves, only to find that assembly is not as easy as it looks. Outside of a suitable delivery vehicle and moving carts, the only other requirements are liability insurance and the ability to assemble a wide range of furniture.

THEME TOY BOXES
★★ $

Manufacturing theme toy boxes is a wonderful homebased business venture and, best of all, the business can be kicked into high gear for less than a $1,000 initial investment. The key to successfully manufacturing and selling the toy boxes is to ensure that the designs are original, the material used in the construction of the toy boxes is unique, and the finished product is colorful and depicts an elaborate children's theme such as horses, cowboys, or dinosaurs. The toy boxes can be sold to retailers on a wholesale basis or directly to consumers via the internet, trade shows, a mall sales kiosk, or mail order. As an additional source of revenue, and as a marketing tool, also consider making wooden toys and including one wooden toy with each toy box as a surprise bonus gift.

WEB RESOURCE: www.scrollsaw.com
Distributor of construction plans for toy boxes.

FURNITURE STEAM CLEANING
★★ $$ 🏠 🕐 🌐

Are you searching for a business opportunity that can be started for peanuts, operated on a full-or part-time basis, and has the potential to earn $30 per hour or more? If so, perhaps you should consider starting a furniture steam cleaning service. A furniture steam cleaning service is very easy to get started, as the equipment needed is available in almost every community, and the business requires little experience or special skills. One of the best aspects of starting and operating this type of business is the fact that it can be operated on a part-time basis and expanded to a full-time business from the profits earned. Additionally, operating the business from home will enable you to keep monthly overheads to a minimum. This can be an advantage for undercutting steam-cleaning rates of the larger established services. As a quick promotion to start marketing, print and distribute two-for-one furniture steam cleaning coupons.

WEB RESOURCE: www.thebluebook.com
Directory service listing manufacturers and distributors of steam cleaning equipment and supplies.

ANTIQUE FURNITURE SALES

Starting a business that buys antique furniture and resells it for a profit is a terrific new venture to set in motion. The following information covers three various methods for starting and operating an antique furniture sales business.

Homebased
★★ $$ 🏠 🕐

The first option for starting an antique furniture sales business is to establish and operate the business from a homebased location. This is an excellent way for entrepreneurs with limited investment capital to get into antique sales, then later expand the business from the profits earned. If this approach is taken, be sure to utilize any low-cost advertising mediums available in the local community for marketing the antique furniture, such as free penny-saver classified ads. Additionally, spend time scouring flea markets and garage sales to locate antique furniture to resell. Providing you have the skills and equipment necessary, you can even offer customers antique furniture restoration service.

Online
★★ $$$ 🏠 🕐

Once again, there are two options for retailing antique furniture on the internet. The first option is to purchase the items listed for sale on the web site yourself. And the second option is to operate a site as a directory for individuals and antique dealers to list their items for sale. If you choose to promote and operate the web site as an antique furniture directory, you have two methods for earning income. The first is to charge customers a listing or posting fee to feature their antique furniture for sale on the site. The second option is to retain a percentage of the revenues that are generated through furniture sales. Be careful with the latter, because unless all sales go through you, deals can be made without you knowing about them.

Retail Storefront
★★ $$$$

The third and most capital-intensive option for starting an antique furniture sales business is to open a retail storefront. This type of specialty retailing has the potential to generate very large profits for the owner-operator of the business. However, careful planning and research are required prior to opening the store. The key to success in such a business will be the location selected for the store. Customer parking, street visibility, size, and consumer demographics all must be carefully considered when selecting the location. In the spirit of being unique, consider a joint venture—perhaps with a store that retails new furniture or appliances. Joint ventures in retailing have many benefits including shared operating overhead costs, joint cost-saving advertising and promotion campaigns, and the ability to draw from each other's customer base.

Antique and Collectibles Dealers Association.

SLATE TABLES
★★ $$$ 🚗 🕒

Slate and natural stone tables are becoming extremely popular both as functional furnishings for residences and as bold furnishing statements for professional offices. This forms a tremendous opportunity for an entrepreneur with creative design abilities to capitalize upon by starting a business that designs, manufactures, and markets slate and natural stone coffee tables, end tables, desks, and boardroom tables. The main requirements for starting and operating this type of specialized furniture manufacturing business include an ability to work in stone mediums, heavy-duty equipment for manufacturing and transporting the finished products, clever marketing skills, and an industrial location for manufacturing.

WEB RESOURCE: http://pebblez.com
A resource for anything involving natural stone, including maintenance and care, as well as design information.

ANTIQUE SIDEBOARD VANITIES
★★★★ $$+ 🚗 🕒

Antique sideboard cabinets make fantastic washroom sink vanities, especially when used in heritage and Victorian homes. Converting antique sideboard cabinets into washroom vanities is an excellent and potentially very profitable new enterprise to set in motion. The main requirements for successfully establishing and operating this type of unique business opportunity include:

- A well-equipped workshop.
- Carpentry and construction skills and experience.
- Excellent marketing and promotion skills.

Patience will be required, as obtaining the antique sideboards to be used for bathroom vanities could mean spending a fair amount of time scouring garage sales, flea markets, and auction sales. Potential customers or buyers can include custom homebuilders, interior designers and decorators, and contracting and renovation companies. Of course the vanities can also be marketed directly to homeowners by way of home and garden trade shows, print advertising, and the internet. To minimize start-up costs to get the business rolling as well as the skills required to operate the business, consider subcontracting out the installation and transportation aspects of the business to local qualified plumbers and transportation firms.

START-UP COSTS: The following example can be used as a guideline to establish the investment needed for starting a business that builds and sells sideboard vanities.

	Low	High
Business setup, legal, banking, etc.	$500	$1,500
Woodworking equipment and tools	$2,000	$5,000
Initial antique sideboard and parts inventory	$2,000	$5,000
Initial advertising and marketing budget	$1,000	$2,000
Office equipment and supplies	$1,000	$2,500
Working capital	$1,000	$2,000
Total start-up costs	**$7,500**	**$18,000**

PROFIT POTENTIAL: The profit potential associated with operating this business is outstanding, as refinished antique sideboard vanities are currently selling for as much as $3,000 each installed. The cost can be as little as $1,000 to assemble and install. Assuming yearly sales of $150,000 can be achieved, then this very straightforward and unique homebased business opportunity can return the owner-operator as much as $100,000 in pretax income. Once established, the business could even begin to manufacture replicas of the original antique sideboards and establish accounts with national home improvement centers to purchase the sideboard vanity replicas on a wholesale basis.

WEB RESOURCE: www.naadaa.org
The National Antique and Art Dealers Association of America.

CUSTOM FURNITURE COVERS
★★ $$ 🚗 🕒

Calling all seamstresses and homemakers with access to a sewing machine, the time is now to put your sewing skills to work and start to earn a living from creating custom fabric furniture covers. There are many patterns available at fabric shops for creating standard-size furniture covers, or the furniture covers can be created on a made-to-order basis. Successfully marketing the business can be accomplished in many ways including the following:

- Building alliances and joint ventures with interior decorators for referrals.
- Selling ready made furniture covers and taking orders for custom-made ones at craft and home-and-garden trade shows.
- Advertising for business in traditional print media and on the internet.
- Working on a subcontract basis for an established furniture upholstery service or retailer of fine home furnishings.

ANTIQUE FURNITURE REFINISHING
★★ $$ 🔨 🕐

The time has never been better than now to start an antique furniture refinishing and repair business, as consumer demand has skyrocketed for antiques in a good state of repair. Once again, an antique furniture refinishing business can easily be operated right from a home-based workshop. Finding customers for the service can be as easy as attending antique auctions and sales and handing out business cards to people who have just purchased an antique piece of furniture that requires repairs or refinishing. Additionally, the service can be marketed by establishing alliances with antique retailers who can either use your service or act as a referral for your service to their customers. Purchasing antiques in poor condition yourself, refinishing, and selling them for a profit can also generate additional income.

WEB RESOURCE: www.assoc-restorers.com
Association of Restorers: information and links into the furniture restoration industry.

SPECIALTY RUG SALES
★★ $$$ 🔨 🕐

Here are two options for starting a business that retails Oriental, Indian, and Persian rugs and carpets. The first option is to locate and secure a foreign supplier for the carpets and negotiate an exclusive sales and distribution contract to represent their products in the United States. The second option is to purchase secondhand high-quality carpets and resell them for a profit. Choosing the second option requires substantially less capital to start and operate. However, the profit potential for the business is also somewhat limited to the availability of a plentiful product source. Regardless of the way the business is approached and established, the fact remains that handmade Eastern rugs and carpets are in very high demand by consumers and professional decorators, and often one single carpet can retail for as much as $10,000. This opportunity definitely warrants further investigation as the potential for huge profits awaits the enterprising entrepreneur who successfully establishes this business.

WEB RESOURCE: www.orrainc.com
Oriental Rug Retailers of America.

CEDAR BLANKET BOXES
★ $$ 🔨 🕐

Manufacturing and selling custom-built cedar blanket boxes is not only a straightforward business venture to initiate, it also has the potential to generate a comfortable income for the owner-operator of the business. There are many design plans available for constructing beautiful cedar blanket boxes, making them a very easy piece of furniture to build. Of course, the more experienced woodworker's original designs can also be manufactured and sold. Once completed, the cedar blanket boxes can be sold to specialty retailers on a wholesale basis, or directly to consumers via craft shows, trade shows, and sales kiosks. Consider incorporating recycled wood into the construction of the blanket boxes, as this can be used as a powerful marketing tool.

ART HEADBOARDS
★★★ $$ 🔨 🕐

Headboards for beds featuring elaborate art or photographs are beginning to pop up in specialty retail stores across the United States, as well as being featured increasingly in interior decorating magazines and publications. This fact creates a terrific opportunity for the enterprising entrepreneur to capitalize on this new furniture fashion trend by starting a business that designs, manufactures, and sells art headboards for beds. The headboards can feature original art paintings or enlarged photographs that are adhered to the headboard. The art headboards can be sold on a wholesale basis to furniture and decorating retailers or directly to consumers and decorating professionals. Currently, art headboards are retailing for $250 for simple designs and paintings and can retail for as much as $1,000 for more elaborate pieces.

AQUARIUM COFFEE TABLES
★★ $$ 🚗 🕐

Are you searching for a truly unique furniture-related business opportunity? If so, they do not come more unique than starting a business that designs, manufactures, and sells aquarium coffee tables. Aquarium coffee tables are simply a fish aquarium base with a clear glass table placed on top of the aquarium. This type of coffee table makes a welcome addition and conversation piece for any home or office, and has become very popular in the past few years. The tables can be manufactured in standard sizes, or on a custom, made-to-order basis. Marketing the aquarium coffee tables is also very straightforward. The tables can be sold to retailers on a wholesale basis, directly to professionals in the interior decorating industry, or directly to consumers on the internet. Make sure to also sell aquarium supplies, because along with being decorative, this is a functioning aquarium.

WEB RESOURCE: www.aquariumpros.com
Aquariums and supplies.

MAGAZINE RACK MANUFACTURING
★ $ 🚗 🕐

Starting a part-time homebased business that designs, manufactures, and markets magazine racks is not only an easy business to get rolling, it can also be set in motion for a minimal initial investment. The key requirements in order to make this business successful are to have a workshop and tools available, as well as basic woodworking and construction experience. Once the magazine racks are completed, they can be sold to retailers on a wholesale basis or directly to consumers via craft and trade shows. Be sure that the design and construction materials utilized in the magazine racks are unique. Consider using

recycled materials, as not only will this save money on material costs, but it can also be used as a terrific environmentally friendly marketing tool.

PLANT STANDS
★ $ 🚗 🕐

Manufacturing and selling plant stands is not only an economical business undertaking to initiate, it is also a business enterprise that can be easily operated from a homebased workshop, with the potential to generate a sensational part-time income. The key to succeeding in a part-time business that manufactures and markets plant stands for indoor and outdoor use is to ensure that the stands are of an unconventional design and that the construction material used to build the stands is also interesting. Once completed, the plant stands can be sold to specialty retailers and garden centers on a wholesale basis or directly to consumers via craft and trade shows sales kiosk, and even on the internet.

HOME DECORATING GUIDE
★★★ $$$ 🚗 🕐 🌐

In spite of its popularity, we have not turned our world completely over to the internet yet. Good old print publishing is here to stay, at least for the foreseeable future. A publishing business that creates and distributes semiannual home decorating guides can still earn excellent profits. The business concept is very straightforward. Simply design a guide featuring information, articles, and tips on home decorating and furnishing ideas. The guide can be printed and distributed free of charge throughout the local community on a seasonal basis (four times a year) or just twice a year. Revenues for the business would be gained by selling advertising space in the guide to local community businesses, such as furniture retailers, home improvement companies, and interior decorators. As a method of promoting the guide and business on a year-round basis, consider forming a joint venture with a local or community newspaper. In exchange for a weekly home decorating tips column, the paper could promote and print the semiannual home decorating guides. The guide could also be a supplement in a Sunday issue of the newspaper. Joint ventures are a fantastic way to potentially increase the size of your market, while decreasing start-up and monthly operating costs for the business. The key is finding something that benefits both parties in the joint venture. Seek and ask; the worst and most definite answer you will ever get is no. And with careful planning and good presentation skills, a no may very easily become a yes.

JUNKYARD FURNITURE CREATIONS
★ $$ 🚗 🕐

If you are looking for a unique homebased business that has minimal competition and potential to generate a six-figure income, then look no further. Starting a business that manufactures and sells junkyard furniture is a very interesting venture. The key to its success is to create funky, yet functional furniture from discarded items typically found at a wrecking yard or junkyard. The most popular junkyard furniture items are generally couches and chairs that have been partially assembled from antique auto parts, such as a couch fashioned out of the front end of a '57 Chevy. Starting this type of business does have its prerequisites—creative and artistic ability, a well-equipped workshop, and design and construction skills. However, for the innovative entrepreneur who possesses these abilities, a fun, interesting, and potentially profitable business venture is waiting.

SHOWROOM PROPS
★★ $$ 🚗 🕐

Many retailers use props for store displays as opposed to the real product. Using props enables the retailer to keep costs down when establishing or updating a showroom, as well as reduce financial loss in the event of damage or theft of the showroom displays. There are two options in terms of initiating a business that sells showroom props to retailers. The first option is to design and manufacture the props, and the second option is to purchase the props in bulk on a wholesale basis from established manufacturers and add a profit percentage for resale. While both options are viable, the second option is far less costly, and easier, to start and operate. However, the profit potential is also greatly reduced for the second option of operating. Careful research and planning will indicate the preferred method for starting the business for you. An additional

possibility is to sell prop furniture to local production houses doing movies, commercials, or local television shows, as well as to theater companies.

PATIO FURNITURE RETAILER
★★ $$$$ 💲

Installations of custom-built decks and patios have become the hottest new home improvement. All new decks and patios require one thing to complete them: patio furniture. A retail business that sells patio furniture is a very easy business to initiate, as there are no special skill requirements. Patio furniture will pretty much sell itself, providing of course that the prices are fair and the quality is outstanding. Worldwide, there are thousands of manufacturers of patio furniture products, so securing a product line should not be difficult. Additionally, consider stocking an inventory of locally-made cedar or log patio furniture, as traditionally wood patio chairs and tables have always been excellent sellers. Marketing the business can be accomplished by utilizing all local print media, setting up your own web site, and holding a grand opening sale to let potential customers know where you are and what products you stock. Having the latest furniture in stock, making quick deliveries, and providing excellent customer service are all means of giving yourself a competitive edge over similar stores in your area.

WEB RESOURCE: www.furninfo.com
Furniture World magazine online: directory of furniture manufacturers and distributors serving the retail trade industry.

USED FURNITURE STORE
★★ $$$$

Purchasing secondhand furniture at auctions and garage sales and from classified advertisements and estate sales is the starting point for opening a used furniture store, or reselling secondhand furniture right from your home. There are a great number of benefits to starting a business that sells secondhand furniture:

- No special skills or equipment requirements
- Relatively low initial start-up and monthly operating costs
- Great profit potential, as used furniture can be marked up by 100 percent or more

- Very little in the way of government regulations beyond a business license
- Proven stable and profitable retail industry

The key to success in this business is being able to price the furniture when buying it and again when selling it. You will need to do some research to determine how similar furniture would be priced in your area if it was purchased new. It also helps if you have the ability to improve upon the furniture by doing some handiwork and repairs wherever necessary.

ANTIQUE RADIOS
★ $$ 🚗 🕒

Purchasing, refinishing, and selling antique radios is a homebased business that can be started by just about anyone on a full- or part-time basis. Antique radios are highly sought-after pieces of furniture, especially if they are in working order and the cabinets have been restored to their former glory. Many collectors of antique radios are prepared to pay as much as $2,000 for the perfect specimen. The main requirement needed to make this business successful beyond the ability to refinish and repair the radios will be time. It will take a substantial amount of time to scour flea markets, garage sales, and auctions to locate the antique radios to be refinished and sold. Marketing the finished products can be by way of the internet, antique and craft shows, and antique auctions, not to mention word-of-mouth.

WEB RESOURCE: www.antiqueradios.com
A collector's resource.

FURNITURE UPHOLSTERY SERVICE
★ $$ 🚗 🕒

In spite of the fact that we are living in a disposable society, furniture upholstery and recovering is not a dying art. Actually the opposite is true, especially for the upholstery service that specializes in recovering antique furniture. The largest drawback for starting an upholstery service is experience. Furniture upholstery is not an easy trade to learn and this business opportunity is best left tackled by an experienced upholsterer or seamstress. An upholstery service can be operated from a homebased workshop or as a joint venture with an established antique repair or refinishing service, or a furniture

retailer by allowing customers who previously purchased items from the store have the furniture reupholstered. Providing automotive, RV, and boat upholstery services can generate additional income for a furniture upholstery business. Income potential is $40 per hour or more.

WEB RESOURCE: www.upholster.com
Upholster magazine online, directory servicing the upholstery industry.

MATTRESS SHOP
★ $$$$ 🏢

Opening a retail mattress store is an excellent example of specialization in the retail furniture sales industry. Mattresses and bedding products have a definite life span of about five to ten years. This is one of the numerous reasons that starting a retail business selling mattresses and bedding products is such a wise choice for a new business enterprise. Furthermore, consider adding institutional sales to the business, meaning hotels, hospitals, and nursing homes. The addition of institutional sales as a sideline for this type of retail business can add a significant amount of revenue to the overall yearly sales. In addition, selling linens, purchased in bulk from wholesalers, can bring you additional income.

WEB RESOURCE: www.sleepproducts.org
International sleep products association.

UNFINISHED FURNITURE STORE
★ $$$$

Selling "naked" furniture may not be sexy, but it does have the potential to generate huge profits for you. Unfinished furniture appeals mainly to two types of consumers: people on a fixed furnishing budget looking to save a few dollars by staining or painting the furniture themselves or artisans seeking to create a custom-finished look that will match their interior decor. Target your marketing efforts toward one or both of these types of consumers and you can't lose selling unfinished furniture. You can either buy the furniture on a wholesale basis from manufacturers, or from local woodworkers and craftspeople. The selection can include tables, chairs, entertainment units, bed frames, and more. In addition to a showroom or a factory-direct approach to displaying and retailing the furniture, consider providing workspace to your customers for finishing the furniture. Not only will you overcome the "I do not have a place to finish the furniture" objection, but you can also generate additional income by charging a small hourly fee for finishes and/or by selling stains, paints, and accessories. Promote the business through advertising circulars, print ads, and your own web site.

WEB RESOURCE: www.buyunfinishedfurniture.com Directory listing retailers, industry information, and links.

BABY AND CHILDREN'S FURNITURE
★★ $$$$

This can be a big money maker if you do it right. First, you will need to research the industry and determine the best pricing, both for buying wholesale and for selling retail in your market. Then scout demographic areas and locations carefully to first find an area with families and young couples and then to determine whether the area can support a high-end shop or build-it-yourself furnishings or something in between. Finally, seek out a location with at least 2,500 to 7,500 square feet since furniture takes up some space. Since a baby and child's furniture store is a destination location rather than a store where people walk by and decide to stop in, you can do very well in a large non-mall facility. You will need to be easily accessible to main roads, have ample parking and a loading dock. Stock up a wide range of products including children's desks, toy boxes, children's dressers, toddler beds, bunk beds, changing tables, cribs and everything else for the child's or baby's room. Arrange merchandise to illustrate the various possible looks of a room and hire knowledgably sales help. Good customer service is also a big plus, especially when competing with major chains. Start-up costs are obviously high, since the rent on a space of this size will not be cheap. You may want to seek out backers when launching a furniture store. Make sure to list all of your capital expenditures and operating expenses in your business plan and review it carefully. Stocking up on inventory is important, but also establishing a good relationship with vendors and manufacturers is vital so that you can order whatever customers don't see in stock. In time, you will get a feel for which items are more popular and which ones are less important to have in stock. Hint: Make such

a store friendly and decorate in a kid-friendly manner since you will likely have young children in the store with their parents on a daily basis. One store even set up a little area with a basketball net for young children to shoot hoops, while another set up some chairs in front of a large television where they show videos.

DORM AND COLLEGE APARTMENT FURNITURE
★★ $$ 🕐

Let's face it, most college students furnish their dwellings using a combination of stuff they've brought from home, stuff they've found on the street and stuff that was designed for other purposes, such as milk creates. Therefore, if you can find the right price points (cheap) you can create a very successful business in a college town. Look for used, or inexpensive, furniture that you can mark up and sell from a small retail location. Since college students typically have very limited space, you need to focus on space saving furniture, such as modular pieces or those that can be converted to serve multifunctions. Since students spend much of their non-class hours on the internet, make sure you have a well-honed web site that is easy to navigate and from which you can sell your furnishings.

FENG SHUI CONSULTANT
★ $ 🏠 🕐

It has been taught that in ancient times, the cities, villages, and homes throughout China were built based on the principles of feng shui. This ancient art teaches people to create a harmonious balance with that which is around us and has emerged, over the past twenty years, as a means of arranging our surroundings and furniture to enhance our lifestyles. Some people believe in it very strongly and claim that they feel the positive energy in a given room by the way it is designed and arranged. Others dismiss all of the above. If you believe in, and have studied feng shui, you can market yourself to designers and decorators as well as home and business owners. Combining the ancient beliefs with some practical and logical decorating ideas (all of which are part of the process), you can benefit the environments of your clients as well as sustain a successful consulting business.

WEB RESOURCE: www.artoffengshuiinc.com

FURNITURE REPAIR
★★★ $$ 🧰 🕐

There are two ways to approach a furniture repair business. One is to have a furniture repair shop for smaller items that can be brought in and the other is to have a toolbox, excellent repair skills, and go to the homes or offices where the furniture needs repair.

Obviously, having a repair shop is the more costly option. Of course, you can combine the two, which will increase your overhead (having someone watching the shop, while you are out repairing furniture) but can maximize your profits. Most furniture repair can be done in a short time with the right tools. You can, therefore, charge by the hour for your services and tack on travel time. Billing at anywhere from $35 to $100 per hour is possible, with the lower end for homeowners and the higher end for corporations that have the money to pay top dollar. Market according to the region in which you see the most potential business. Also consider marketing yourself through fliers and business cards to moving companies and hotels. Offering restoration, upholstery, and other services will enhance your business.

COMPUTER FURNITURE
★ $$ 🧰 🕐

Whether you manufacture it, buy it wholesale, or combine both means of accumulating your inventory, selling computer furniture can be a lucrative business. You can set up a storefront or take orders from a catalog and/or from your web site. Either way, you need to offer a variety to fit all size spaces and offer quick, reliable delivery. You can also offer custom-made computer furniture that you can make yourself if you are handy and have a tool shop in the backyard or in your basement or garage. Market yourself to home business owners through local business associations and through standard advertising means. Keep tabs on the latest configurations of computer equipment so that you can be ready and your form will meet the function of the equipment. In other words, allow for cables, routers, and all sorts of peripherals.

NOTES:

_____

_____

_____

_____

_____

_____

_____

_____

_____

_____

_____

_____

_____

_____

_____

_____

_____

_____

37
HEALTH
Businesses You Can Start

VITAMIN SALES
★★ $$$$

Owning and operating your own vitamin store could be the answer to your financial and self-employment dreams. The time has never been better than now to start a health-related business as more and more people across North America become concerned about their health in general. Selling vitamins is not only a great way to capitalize on consumer demand, but it is also a fantastic way to help others strive for a healthier lifestyle. You will need a great deal of knowledge of vitamin and mineral supplements, which may require taking some time to do sufficient research. You can also hire experienced staff or a health consultant to help build and market the vitamin product line. Locating vitamin manufacturers and wholesalers for this venture will not be difficult as there are thousands worldwide who will be more than happy to establish wholesale accounts with new businesses. Start-up costs are high, but the profit potential is excellent.

A retail location is one possibility. However, you can cut down on the overhead by establishing a vitamin section in an existing store and possibly going in on a joint venture, or by setting up a booth at a mall. To overcome the online competition, you should provide top-notch personal service, have a well-stocked inventory, and offer health seminars, a newsletter, and/or other sources of information on vitamins.

WEB RESOURCE: www.nutritionmanufacturer.com
Wholesale vitamin supplier.

NATURAL HOME REMEDIES
★★ $$ 🏠 🕐

Every year thousands of people turn to a natural, holistic approach to health, and this fact creates a terrific opportunity to start a natural home remedies business, and capitalize on consumer demand. Natural home remedies have been around for hundreds of years, and only recently has their popularity really taken off in a big way. Research and planning are definite prerequisites for this type of health business enterprise. To find information on natural home health remedies, start at your local library, surf the internet, visit local bookstores, and attend seminars by nutritionists and health professionals. In fact, having a nutritionist as a consultant will help you gain credibility. Finding natural home remedy manufacturers and wholesalers for the business will not prove difficult, as there are thousands in North America alone. Innovative entrepreneurs may be able to create some of their own natural home remedies. Make sure they work and be sure you follow local and federal regulations in terms of product ingredients and product health or benefit claims. To keep start-up costs to a minimum, consider selling the natural home remedies via mail order, on your own website, or in partnership with a health food store.

WEB RESOURCE: http://altmedicine.about.com
A good source for articles and ideas on the topic.

PEDICURE SERVICE
★★ $$ 🚗 🕓

Calling all pedicurists that are tired of working for someone else; the time is now to take control of your financial future and start creating profits for yourself by launching your own pedicure service business! A pedicure service is a great business to start and manage from a homebased location while operating the service on a mobile basis. In terms of gaining clients for the service, seek out unusual opportunities—go to people who can't come to you. Clients can include busy professionals, residents of nursing and retirement homes, long-term hospital patients, and just about anyone looking for a terrific in-home or office pedicure service. Providing your clients with exceptional service will guarantee you a very comfortable income and repeat clientele for many years to come. Potential income range is $25 to $40 per hour, plus the potential to sell foot care products will add to your bottom line.

DIETITIAN
★ $$ 🚗 🕓 ⚖️

Are you a certified dietitian? That is the first qualification for starting this business. Options for operating this sort of health business or health consulting service are almost unlimited. As a certified dietician you could simply subcontract your services out to numerous businesses such as hospitals, nursing homes, weight loss clinics, and fitness centers. As an entrepreneur, you could start up an online dietician service that would provide visitors with diet and fitness information, products for sale, fitness training, coaching, and even fitness evaluations—or a combination of any or all of these products and services. Whether you choose to market yourself as a subcontractor or start an online service, the profit potential for diet consulting services is outstanding and achieving an annual income of $50,000 or more is certainly not out of line. To increase business revenues and profits, aim to develop your own exclusive diet programs, books, videos, and software. In addition, arrange for speaking engagements and seminars in health facilities and schools.

WEB RESOURCE: www.cdrnet.org
Commission on Dietetic Registration

SKIN CARE PRODUCTS
★★ $$ 🚗 🕓

With so much emphasis on "natural" these days, a skin care line devoted to "all natural ingredients" would definitely be a wise decision in terms of product marketing and consumer acceptance. The starting point for the business will be research, which can be accomplished with assistance from the internet, local library, and even the local cosmetics counter. Most cosmeticians will be more than happy to explain the benefits of their products, including what certain ingredients will do for your skin. To keep business start-up costs to a minimum, initially start with basic skin care products (e.g., cleanser, toner, and moisturizer), and expand the skin care product line from there. Good advertising mediums to promote and market skin care products would be the internet, promotional fliers, newspaper ads, and home shopping parties, but your best advertising will be by way of word-of-mouth referrals. If your clients are happy with the products and service, they will tell others and it will not be long before you are well on your way to financial freedom. This type of business enterprise is well suited for a homebased location. To jump start the business, offer free skin care analysis to customers along with free samples of the natural skin care products that you sell.

MEDICAL BOOK SALES
★★ $$ 🚗 🕓

There are a few approaches to starting a business that sells medical books, guides, and journals. The first approach is to source publishers of medical books and become an authorized distributor by establishing mail order sales, online sales, and direct sales to consumers via a kiosk established for selling medical books. The second option is to compile information on medical and health issues, write the books, and self publish the books on these topics. Of course, you will need to be a skilled researcher and writer for the second option to work. The market for medical and health publications is gigantic, but there is a lot of competition. Therefore, you might want to focus your attention on a specific area and sell books on that health topic. If you can market books with cardboard display racks, you can have them on the counters in pharmacies, health food stores, and similar retail outlets, which will make it much easier than trying to compete with bookstores and with Amazon.com and other web book retailers.

DAY SPA
★★ $$$$ 💲

With everybody leading such busy and stress-filled lives these days, starting a day spa is an excellent choice for a new business venture. The initial investment to get a day spa up and rolling is substantial. However, the income potential is outstanding. Location is probably the most important aspect of this new enterprise, so be sure to carefully research the area where you intend to open for business. Providing day spa clients with a wide variety of services such as manicures, seaweed wraps, aroma therapy, and massage options is guaranteed to make the business a popular destination for new and repeat clients. You should have no problem charging top dollar for your services, providing you offer exceptional personalized service to your clients. You can market a day spa service through traditional advertising mediums. Be sure to print and distribute two-for-one discount coupons for the initial grand opening. You may have to sacrifice some revenues, but discount coupons are a terrific way to gain interest from potential customers quickly. The income and profit potential will greatly depend on a number of factors, such as services offered, customer volumes, and business location.

WEB RESOURCE: www.clubspausa.com
Day Spa Association.

ORGANIC HAIR CARE PRODUCTS
★★ $$ 🏠 🕐 🌿

Have you always dreamed about starting your own successful business that can be operated from home? If so, consider starting a venture that specializes in developing and producing natural hair care products. One option is to create, manufacture, and sell natural hair care products such as shampoos and conditioners made from100 percent natural organic ingredients. Of course, there will

be a steep learning curve in terms of developing the hair care products. However, utilizing research tools such as libraries and the internet should prove quite useful in this endeavor. If you create your own products, make sure you meet government health requirements and keep the word hypoallergenic in mind. The other option is to buy such products from various distributors and well them to customers through your website, local beauty salons, and even by direct mail.

HOME-CARE SERVICE
★★★ $$ ⚖️

Starting a home-care service is a great business enterprise to initiate, as people are living longer and, more importantly, living longer on their own. This type of new business venture would best suit a person with a background and training in the health-care industry. For those who do not have such a background, home-care training is available in almost every community across North America. Generally, there are two types of home-care providers, and the training required for each is very different. The first type of home-care service is one that focuses on assisting people with everyday tasks such as cooking, cleaning, errands, and personal hygiene. The second type of home-care service can include the aforementioned with the addition of medication administration and, in some cases, therapy. This will mean advanced training and in some states may require certification. Income potential will range from $20 per hour to as much as $50 per hour depending on services provided and skill levels required.

WEB RESOURCE: www.nahc.org
National Association of Home Care.

MEDICAL BRACES AND SUPPLIES
★★ $$ 🏠 🕐

"Brace Yourself" could be your business name or company motto if you're planning to start a business that specializes in retailing medical braces. There are literally hundreds of various types of medical braces used for hundreds of different types of medical conditions—everything from braces for a bad back to knee braces for sports injuries. There are thousands of manufacturers of medical braces worldwide, so securing a wholesale source for the products should not be difficult. The braces can be sold to consumers in a few different ways, including a small retail outlet, a joint venture with a local pharmacy, or directly to hospitals and doctors and online. In addition, crutches, walkers, and other personal medical supplies can be sold to enhance your profits. If you can utilize the services of an authorized/licensed fitter to make sure the products are best suited for each individual, then you can use that as a selling point to attract more business.

WEB RESOURCE: www.hospital-technology.com
Directory service listing medical equipment and supplies manufacturers and distributors.

HAIR SALON
★★ $$$ ⚖️

There are numerous approaches that can be taken should you consider starting a hair salon as a new business enterprise. The first approach is to establish a hair salon that operates from a fixed storefront location. The second approach is to start a mobile hair salon, which is covered in the special services chapter of this business start-up directory. Prior to starting a hair salon, consider the following aspects of the business.

- *Location.* Is there a suitable location available for the business in your community? Good locations can include a homebased hair salon (providing the proper zoning is in place or can easily be secured), an indoor mall, a strip mall, or even in the lobby retail area of a large office building or complex.
- *Competition and price point.* How much competition is there in the local market, and is there room for another hair salon? What is the competition charging for services? Can a profit or reasonable return on your investment be accomplished? What can you do to gain a competitive edge?
- *Services provided.* Manicures, pedicures, facial treatments, hair removal, and other services are also provided in a full-service salon along with hair cutting and styling.
- *Quality of service.* While most businesses benefit heavily from repeat customers, this is especially true with a hair salon. If your haircutters and stylists are professionally trained, provide excellent cuts, and

have a good rappor t with the customers, you can generate a lot of return business, since many people rely heavily on the same person to take care of their hair on a regular basis. Make sure to hire certified stylists or haircutters.
- *Environment.* Whether the look of the business resembles a nightclub or has a homey atmosphere, a salon can benefit from the right ambiance. Know your demographic market and decorate accordingly.

Once all of these va ri a bles fall into place, you can be very successful owning such a salon. If your customers like the styles and their look when they walk out , t h eywi ll tell fri ends and word-of-mouth is significant in this business. To generate additional revenues and profits, sell hair care products at the salon such as shampoos, conditioners, and other related products. For the really innovative entrepreneur, seek to develop your own hair care products line, as there are many manufacturers of hair care produ cts who do priva te label manu facturing. This means that the manufacturer will place its product in your packaging, under your product name. Private label packaging is a fantastic way to not only give your business the look of professionalism and success—it is also a way to wholesale your products locally at first and eventually nationally on a well designed website

WEB RESOURCE: www.beauty-salon-equipment.com
Wholesale hair salon furniture and equipment.

COSMETICS RETAILING
★★ $$ 🚗 🕐

The sales of cosmetics generate billions of dollars every year worldwide, and starting a business selling cosmetics is just about as straightforward as a new business venture can get. There are numerous ways to sell cosmetics and make a profit. However, in the spirit of being unique we will analyze one segment of the cosmetic sales industry that can generate huge profits in a few different ways. The business can be set in motion for less than a $5,000 initial start-up investment. Locate a manufacturer of cosmetic products who does not have representation in your community, state, or even your country. Negotiate an exclusive contract to represent and distr ibute their cosmetic products in the desired area. Once the distribution contract has been secured, the cosmetics can be sold to retailers on a wholesale basis. Or, you can hire a direct sales team whose main focus is in-home sales of the cosmetics. Both approaches have the potential to generate enormous sales and profits.

WEB RESOURCE: www.icmad.org
Independent Cosmetic Manufacturers and Distributors, Inc.

HAIR REMOVAL SERVICE
★ $$ 🏛

Hair removal or waxing is a popular procedure that both women and men have done to rid themselves of unwanted body and facial hair. Starting a hair removal service is a good business to set in motion, providing of course that you or a staff member has training and certification as required. The easiest, and least expensive, way to get the service rolling is to form a joint venture with an established business, such as a hair salon or day spa. A joint venture can reduce the investment needed to start the business, and you can also capitalize on your partner's existing client base to jump-start the business.

MEDICAL EQUIPMENT SALES
★★ $$$$

Millions of dollars worth of medical equipment is sold each year in the United States, and securing a portion of this very lucrative industry is not difficult, especially for the entrepreneur who carefully researches and plans their entry into it. There are a few different approaches that can be taken in terms of medical equipment sales. The first approach is to establish a retail store that sells medical equipment to customers as well as to online shoppers via the store's web site. The second approach is to become an independent sales consultant who represents various manufacturers of medical equipment. The main focus would be to sell medical equipment to hospitals and health centers by soliciting or using the tender process in which hospitals and medical centers routinely ask for bids to replace their current equipment. Tenders are usually featured in newspapers or you can call the hospital to inquire about their current situation and when you could put in a bid. You can also market medial equipment to clinics and doctors for office procedures. Profit potential range is $50,000 to $150,000 per year.

WEB RESOURCE: www.medicalsuppliesplus.net
Distributor of wholesale medical supplies to the public.

MOBILE HEARING TESTING
★ $$$$ 🏛

In many areas of the country, workers' compensation boards and workers' insurance and benefit programs require workers to undergo annual hearing tests as part of an ongoing workers' safety program to ensure that industrial noise is not damaging workers' hearing. This fact creates an opportunity to start a business that conducts hearing tests on a mobile basis. Be forewarned that the equipment needed for this type of unique health service is expensive, and the hearing technician to operate the equipment must be certified. However, this is a business opportunity that has amazing growth potential as health issues are at the forefront of all levels of governments and industry. This is also a business that can be promoted to school boards, since children's hearing is routinely tested. The profit potential is outstanding, and this is definitely a business venture that deserves and warrants further investigation.

MASSAGE SALON
★★ $$$$ 🏛

Starting a massage salon or a career as an independent masseuse requires you to have professional certification or hire staff members with professional certification. However, the training to become a certified masseuse generally takes less than one year and costs less than $10,000, making a massage salon venture attainable to just about everyone seeking to start this business. There are a couple of ways to operate a massage therapy business. The first is to work from a fixed location or massage salon, and the second way is to operate the business on a mobile basis where you go to the client's home or office. Both approaches to operating the business have their pros and cons. A mobile massage therapy business is by far less costly to establish and operate, but also generates less revenues and profits than a salon until you build up your clientele. If you are known to give excellent massages, your reputation can lead to a full schedule very quickly.

WEB RESOURCE: www.amtamassage.org
American Massage Therapy Association.

MEDICAL SEAT CUSHIONS
★★ $$ 🚗 🕒

Millions of people commute back and forth to work each day in agony, suffering everything from back problems to hip and joint problems. Starting a business that sells specialty automotive medical seat cushions may prove to be very profitable and make you a superstar with commuters. The business is very easy to establish and operate. The first step is to locate a manufacturer of medical seat cushions. This can be accomplished by harnessing the power of the internet for research purposes or by acquiring a manufacturers directory. Once you have found a few manufacturers, aim to secure an exclusive distribution contract for their products in the area your business will operate. The seat cushions can be sold directly to consumers by way of mail order and the internet, as well as by setting up a sales booth at car shows, automotive trade shows, or even at a busy train station. The profit potential for this type of enterprise is excellent, as the seat cushions can easily be marked up by 100 percent or more for retail sales.

TANNING SALON
★★ $$$$ 🌀

The quest for the perfect suntan has come under fire in the past decade, as health concerns about skin damage and diseases caused by the harmful ultraviolet rays of the sun have been splashed across the headlines of every newspaper and TV news report. People seek the perfect suntan, but health concerns prevent many of us from sunbathing. Herein lies the business opportunity. Start a tanning salon business and capitalize not only on consumer demand for suntans, but also on public concerns. A tanning salon is a very easy business to get rolling. Make sure you meet any local health requirements and stay on top of the latest in tanning methods. Since there are an abundance of such salons opening, you need to price your services accordingly and create an ambiance that sets you apart from your competitors. You can also sell tanning lotion, bronzers and anything sun related from tanning goggles to sun glasses.

As is the case with most storefront walk-in businesses, whether they are service or product oriented, you need a good location, so consider:

- Good street visibility, easy access, and customer parking.
- The size of the location—you do not want to give the appearance of being too cramped, too small, or too empty.

Advertising and marketing suggestions:

- Build alliances with all the local travel agents and brokers in your community. The travel agents can provide clients who are traveling to sunny destinations with 10-percent-off coupons for your tanning salon to get a jump-start on their vacation tans. And, you can provide all of your clients with travel points, meaning that every time they use the sun tanning salon you give them one travel point. Each point can represent $1 towards the cost of a vacation booked through a travel agent or cross-promotion partner.
- Print and distribute two-for-one sun tanning coupons for the initial grand opening promotion.
- Provide customers with a multi-tanning pass option, meaning that clients could have the option of pre-buying ten tanning sessions for the price of eight.

WEB RESOURCE: www.sundash.com
Distributors of salon tanning equipment.

PERFUME
★ $$ 🚗 🕒

Creating, packaging, and distributing your own perfume line can make you rich. Developing your own perfume, or perfume line, will take some careful planning and a lot of research. A background as a chemist, or working with a chemist can be very useful for this type of business endeavor. However, the hard work could really pay off, especially if you can secure national accounts with well-recognized specialty retailers. In terms of the type of perfume your business develops, consider an all-natural approach to the ingredients as increasing consumer awareness and acceptance of all-natural products is without question the wave of the future. The perfume can be sold to retailers on a wholesale basis, directly to consumers via the internet, or by establishing a perfume sales kiosk set up in high-traffic community gathering places. For mail-order sales, advertise the perfume in specialty publications. Make sure to secure a patent on any new creation before marketing and selling it, or you could lose your exclusivity.

MASSAGE OILS
★★ $$$ 🚗 🕒

Like developing your own perfume line, developing your own massage oil line also has great potential. In fact, the two products could be developed together and wholesaled to the same retailers. Given the current popularity of all-natural products it would be a wise decision to develop the massage oils from natural and organic ingredients. Seek out joint venture business opportunities with established companies that can assist in the development, marketing, and distribution of your products. Often joint ventures mean that you will lose some control and a portion of the profits of the business. However, having a percentage of something big is better than having all of something small.

HEALTH SEMINARS
★★ $$$ 🚗 🕒

Starting a business that promotes and hosts free informational health seminars can make you rich. The key is getting top professionals in the health field to speak on a variety of different topics. To make money, you can either charge an admission fee to attend the seminars or get sponsorship from a health facility for holding the seminars. You can promote individual seminars or set up a health seminar series at a local hospital, library, school, or other easy-to-access evening location. Hot topics include weight loss and healthy diet, natural childbirth, alternative medicines and medical treatments, and age-related health issues. It is not unusual for as much as $10,000 worth of products to be sold at health topic seminars, so you can see how this business could become quite lucrative. Hint: Be sure to book and confirm your speakers and your space well in advance before doing any marketing.

NUTRITION GUIDES
★★ $$$ 🚗 🕒

Most health experts agree a healthy diet is the key to a healthy and long life. Starting a business that creates and distributes nutrition guides is a fantastic new venture to

set in motion. There are two approaches that can be taken with this business in terms of generating revenues and profits. The first approach is to sell the nutrition guides through bookstores and specialty retailers. The second approach is to distribute the nutrition guides free of charge throughout your community and support the business by selling advertising space in the guides to local businesses that would benefit from this type of advertising exposure. Good choices for potential advertisers in a nutrition guide would include vitamin stores, doctors, health professionals, organic food growers, and health food restaurants. If you choose to adopt the second option in terms of operating the business, the nutrition guides could be published twice per year, making this a potentially very profitable business opportunity.

STAIR LIFTS
★★★ $$$$

Are you searching for a unique and interesting business opportunity that has little competition and the potential to make $100,000 per year or more in profits? If so, perhaps you should consider starting a business that sells and installs specialty stair lift chairs. There are many worldwide manufacturers of stair lifts, so finding a wholesale source should not be difficult. Market the stair lifts using all traditional advertising mediums, as well as by establishing alliances with custom homebuilders and renovation contractors to act as sales agents for the product. Be sure to design a stair lift display that highlights the beneficial features of the product. The display can be set up and used as a sales and marketing tool to collect sales leads from potential customers at home and garden trade shows.

WEB RESOURCE: www.medcatalog.com
Medical supply portal.

PERSONAL CARE PRODUCT VENDING
★★ $$$ 🚗 🕒

Starting a vending business that specializes in personal care products is a great choice for a new business venture. The vending machines can be located throughout the community in locations such as public washrooms, restaurants, factories, and all other high-traffic community gathering places. Products sold can include condoms, aspirin, feminine hygiene products, and even disposable baby diapers. The key to success in the vending industry is to secure good locations for the vending machines, and to make sure you carefully watch wholesale product costs. The profit potential is excellent in this kind of vending business, and each machine could easily produce yearly sales in excess of $5,000.

WEB RESOURCE: http://buyritevending.com
This vending machine distributor's site includes a section for personal care products.

WIGS
★★ $$$ 🧰 🕐

Many surgical procedures and medical treatments result in patients losing or having their hair removed. While the hair loss is generally short-term, many people still turn to wigs as a way to provide a solution to the problem. The first step in establishing the business is to secure a wholesale or product supply source for the wig, which should not be difficult as there are thousands of wig manufacturers worldwide. Marketing the wigs can be as easy as establishing alliances with hospitals and medical centers to act as a referral source for the business. The wigs can also be sold directly to consumers via the internet. Once established, this unique business can generate a very substantial yearly income.

WEB RESOURCE: www.wigmasterassoc.com
Wig portal.

MOBILE FOOT MASSAGE SERVICE
★ $$ 🕐

It is a proven medical fact that foot problems that are not corrected early can result in additional medical problems later down the road. And this fact creates a terrific opportunity for the budding entrepreneur to capitalize by starting a mobile foot massage service. The target market for a mobile foot massage service is obvious: people who spend a lot of time on their feet. In the spirit of being unique, consider the following method of marketing to gain new clients and generate business revenue. Prepare a full marketing presentation that highlights all the benefits of foot massages, such as happier workers equals increased productivity. Once the marketing presentation is complete, set up proposal meetings with medium- to

large-sized companies in your community that have employees who are on their feet for most of the day. The pitch to the business owner of why he or she should consider starting a foot massage program for workers will of course be the fact of increased productivity and the possibility of fewer missed work days as a result of foot-related health problems. Once again, a mobile foot massage service is unique and will take some time and careful planning to get rolling. However, once established, an income level of $40 per hour or more should not prove difficult to achieve.

HEALTH TAXI
★★ $$$ 🚐

Starting a health taxi service in your community may be the unique new business enterprise that you have been searching for. The business concept is simply this: Purchase, lease, or rent a suitable mode of transportation such as a passenger van. Set up accounts with local doctors, dentists, and health professionals in your community to provide their patients with a way of getting to and from the doctor's office or clinic via your health taxi service. The doctors would pay a flat fee for every patient that your service taxied to the doctor's location. Not only will the patients benefit from a free taxi service, but the doctors will also benefit by ensuring that patients can get to them to receive proper medical care. Be sure to check out all the legal aspects of the business in terms of liability insurance and special driving permits prior to establishing a health taxi service in your community.

ALTERNATIVE HEALTH-CARE CENTER
★★ $$$$

Do you want to start a business related to alternative health-care, but you lack skills or experience in the industry? You can still be part of this multibillion dollar industry, by starting an alternative heath-care center. Start by leasing a large professional office space and subdivide the space into smaller offices for alternative health-care practitioners to lease, and in effect, you can own and manage an alternative heath care center. Attracting heath care practitioners to sublease the smaller individual offices should be no problem, providing you offer services such as a centralized receptionist, parcel shipping, central record keeping, and additional services that the practitioners would typically require for the operation of their alternative health-care services. In addition, you will handle the marketing end of the business, making people aware of their services. Services housed within the center could include massage therapy, aromatherapy, herbal medicines, and any other alternative health-care service that is available. Make sure that all necessary licensing is taken care of and that practitioners either have their own liability insurance or join together to get the necessary coverage.

WEB RESOURCE: www.alternativemedicine.com

HEALTH FAIR
★★ $$$ 🏠 🕒

Across North America there are thousands of health-care professionals and companies that produce products designed for sale in the health-care industry. These health-care professionals and industry-related companies could potentially become your clients if your intentions are to start a business that promotes, and hosts, two-day health fairs. A health fair is the same as a trade show or crafts show. The major difference is that all of the vendors or exhibitors are in the health-care industry. This unique health-care related business has a chance to become a profitable business concern, given the recent increased demand by consumers for health-care information, products, and services. Charging admission for attendees, as well as charging the exhibitors fee for a booth at the fair, are ways to earn revenues. The key is finding a good location and making sure to spread the word with enough lead time so that newspapers and magazines (some of which need two or three months advance notice) can be contacted for stories, plus you also want to place advertisements. Your web site could post the times, locations, and fees for all upcoming fairs.

HEALTH-CARE NEWSPAPER
★ $$$ 🏠 🕒 🌐

Another business in the health-care industry is that of a health-care newspaper, published on a monthly basis. The paper can feature stories and articles about health care in general, as well as new health-care procedures and products that are being introduced. Local health-care

professionals covering all segments of the health-care industry can supply the information featured in the paper, which can be written by a few good freelance journalists. The paper could be distributed free of charge throughout the community, and supported by selling advertising space to interested local health-care professionals and companies. Profit potential once established is $25,000+ per year, while expenses can be kept low if you can find a good desktop publisher and low-cost distribution service. You could also start this as an online publication, which would save even more money.

INFANT CAR SEATS
★ $$ 🏠 🕒

This is a business you can start from home with some good marketing to anyone with a new baby on the way. There are a wide range of models to choose from, so it is important that you become an expert by getting to know the various brands and helping parents learn the often frustrating process of properly installing and removing the seats from their vehicles. You can make additional money from selling other baby-carrying products and bike seats.

WEB RESOURCES: www.aap.org/family/carseatguide.htm
Car seat safety guide from the American Academy of Pediatricians

LOCAL HEALTH-CARE DIRECTORY
★★ $$ 🏠 🕒

When new homeowners move into a neighborhood they are typically unfamiliar with the medical services and providers in that area. A perfect business to start from home is creating a local health-care directory, listing doctors and dentists by specialty plus chiropractors, personal trainers, and local pharmacies. You can print the guide using a good desktop publishing software program and distribute it for free in various retail locations, medical waiting rooms, and at libraries. To generate income, you can sell advertising space to all local doctors and health-care professionals and facilities. Even at $50 per ad, for 50 ads you can make $2,500 for a semi-annual guide, minus your printing costs. By making up such guides for various communities, you can build this endeavor from a part-time to a full-time business.

YOGA CLASSES
★★ $ 🕒

Yoga has been shown to lower stress and anxiety, improve moods, reduce pain, and increase mental and physical energy. For that reason, yoga classes are extremely popular. To teach yoga, you need to rent a space, supply mats, have some music available, and train to become a yoga instructor. You can then promote classes for all ages. Find a convenient location and place ads in local papers, hand out fliers, and put up posters. Early evening and weekends are ideal times for courses, especially for the nine-to-five set. You can also approach businesses, as corporate yoga classes have become popular during lunch hours or after work. In time, if you are filling up classes regularly, you may be able to open your own yoga studio. However, with community centers and numerous facilities available in most towns, you may find it easier and more cost effective to rent space, partner with a health club, or run classes on site at corporate locations.

WEB RESOURCE: www.yogasite.com/wholesale.htm
Wholesale mats, props, books, music and more.

MOBILE HEALTH SCREENING SERVICE
★★ $$$$ 🕒 ⚖

Many large corporations today are offering medical screenings to their employees. If you can get doctors and nurses involved and market the service to local companies, you can start such a mobile screening service, whereby you will go to various locations and set up shop using an RV or in space provided by corporation such as a conference room. Glaucoma, cholesterol, blood pressure, and women's health screening are among the many possibilities. Your job, which can be done from a home office, is to arrange to bring in the medical staff to each corporate office on a specified date. You will need to coordinate and have doctors and medical professionals who are affiliated with the appropriate medical plans. The company pays for the screening in conjunction with their medical providers and you do not charge the employees. If you are well-organized and connected with the medical community, this is a business you can start with several phone calls.

HEALTH ADVOCATE
★★ $$ 🏠 🕒 ⚖

The impersonalization, inconsistencies, and inaccuracies in the health care industry have created a unsettling feeling for many people today. There is great concern over what is and is not covered under a health plan or by an HMO and because of specialization, most individuals have numerous doctors for various needs. Because of this complexity in the medical industry, becoming a health advocate for companies as well as individuals can be a rewarding and lucrative business. If you have a background in nursing health administration, this is a business opportunity to consider because you probably are familiar with the workings of a hospital, insurance company, or private physician's office. As a health advocate, you handle the health needs for a client or for many clients working for a company. This includes helping them get through to their insurance providers, getting answers, making doctor appointments, finding specialists if necessary, locating doctors in other towns and cities, and generally staying on top of all health related concerns—which might even include researching and finding appropriate diets. If you know how to get the inside track, cut through the red tape, and simplify the medical maze—particularly for seniors—you can build up a very steady business. You can operate this business from home since your phone, your computer, your network of contacts, and your medical savvy are the main tools of this exciting trade.

MEDICAL BILLING SERVICE
★★ $$$ 🏠

It is estimated that nearly 30% of claims to insurance companies remain outstanding for more than 90 days, with some never resulting in payment. Add to this the number of late payments from non-insured patients. The result is that medical practices are losing a significant amount of their income and rates must go up to cover these outstanding receivables. For this reason, many busy medical practices are turning over their billing practices to medical billing services. You can save medical facilities a great amount of time and effort by handling the billing process and tracking down the unpaid claims. If you can run an efficient office and stay on top of outstanding bills, you can start a successful medical billing business. It helps to have a background in the healthcare field and to understand billing procedures and the insurance industry before venturing into such a business. However, with a lot of determination and less than $15,000 for office expenses, you can launch this as a homebased business. Design a brochure spelling out your plan for billing, following up, and collecting payments and circulate it to doctors' offices and medical groups. Since you are new, you might work at first in a collection capacity chasing down overdue payments but in time, as you prove successful at collecting and dealing with insurance companies, you can take over the entire billing process. Note: It is very important to stress patient privacy and use a secure data system with encryption codes so that no one can get access to patient data.

ELDERCARE AGENCY
★★ $$$ ⚖️

Thanks to medical technology and new research, the population today is living longer. In fact, it is anticipated that by the year 2020 there will be more than 90 million people over the age of 75. Yet, while the population is living longer, there are still many things that seniors cannot do entirely by themselves. This opens the door to eldercare, which is a rapidly growing business in North America, particularly with the population spread out and many families no longer living in close proximity to one another. Eldercare workers assist seniors with cleaning, cooking, grocery shopping, laundry, making appointments, taking medicine, and numerous other activities. They also provide companionship. To run such a business, you need to hire a good, trustworthy, responsible staff that can accommodate the diverse responsibilities. While they do not need specific accreditation, you need reliable individuals and typically they should be bonded. If transportation is included, you should also carry liability insurance. To develop a client base, you should market your services with social service agencies that come in contact with the elderly, as well as physicians and hospitals. Advertising in mainstream publication, particularly health magazines read by adults can be advantageous, since you will want to reach family members as well as seniors.

NOTES:

60
HOME IMPROVEMENT
Businesses You Can Start

ATTIC VENTILATION AND INSULATION
★★★ $$

Most homes built prior to the mid-'70s energy crisis were not properly insulated. The homes that were built after this period until the late '80s suffer from being sealed so tight as not to allow enough air circulation, especially in the attic areas. The bottom line: The market for attic ventilation and insulation installation services is absolutely gigantic. Attic ventilation can be achieved in a variety of installation methods including installations of soffit vents, mechanical and non-mechanical roof vents, ridge vents, and gable vents. Recent studies have indicated that the preferred method of attic insulation is a fiberglass batt format vs. blown-in cellulose insulation, which can shift and/or compact. Checking with local experts, building codes, and building centers will give you the best understanding for which procedure may be required in your region. The business can be marketed through home improvement shows, traditional advertising mediums, meeting with contractors, and flier distribution. The business is quick to set up and expand based on a word-of-mouth advertising and referral basis.

REQUIREMENTS: Along with experience in home repair or renovation, you will want to learn all of the local building codes in terms of proper ventilation and insulation specification, and stick to, or exceed these requirements to ensure that the work has been properly completed. This business requires a few basic tools, such as a van or covered truck, step and extension ladders, protective safety gear, and a few hand power tools.

START-UP COSTS: An attic ventilation and insulation installation service can be started for $7,000 to $10,000. This amount of investment would be sufficient capital to acquire a basic truck or van, tools, a small inventory, and provide for an initial marketing budget.

PROFIT POTENTIAL: You can add gigantic markups onto the wholesale costs of the ventilation products, as well as the insulation. In terms of installation rates, there are two methods of billing for this service. The first is to charge an hourly rate that would typically be $40 to $50 per hour for one person, and $70 to $80 dollars per hour for two people. The second method is to calculate a per-square-footage charge; this can be done by way of estimating your time, adding in the product cost plus a markup, then dividing the total number by the number of square feet you will be covering.

FENCING INSTALLATION
★★ $$

The desire to keep kids and pets inside a property, and unwanted trespassers outside, has created a big demand for companies that provide property fencing installation services. The starting point is to first determine the fencing material(s) and style of fencing your service will be installing. There are various types of material used in fencing including cedar wood, pressure-treated wood, stone, brick, steel or cast iron, recycled plastics, cedar rail, chain link, vinyl, and aluminum. Likewise, there are also various methods that can be employed to promote and market a fence installation service, such as subcontracting for construction and renovation companies, direct retail sales via advertising, and "installations only" for home building and renovation centers. Perhaps your fence installation service could be different from competitor's by offering the service of installing the fence posts only and supplying the pre-built fencing panels for the homeowner to complete the installation. This method would save the homeowner money, while having the difficult portion of the job, which is the installation of the fence posts, completed professionally.

WEB RESOURCE: www.fencinglistings.com
Fencing supplies and materials.

WINDOW INSTALLATION
★★ $$ 🚗 🕒

Replacement windows rank sixth as the most frequently completed home improvement renovation, and demand continues to grow. Modern manufacturing methods and materials can be accredited for this booming industry. Today's windows are constructed from maintenance-free vinyl and aluminum extrusions that have excellent insulation value, and come in a full range of designs and operating features. People with a construction and renovation background will find this business start-up to be of particular interest. Market yourself in conjunction with retail outlets that sell replacement windows as well as through local ads in Penny Savers and by way of handouts at home expos or trade shows. Study this rapidly growing business and get to know the differences in the many types of windows available and how they need to be installed.

CERAMIC TILE SALES AND INSTALLATION
★★ $$ 🚗 🕒

Here is another great little business venture that you can start for a very small investment and manage from a homebased office. Ceramic tiles will always be a popular choice for a flooring finish, due to their low maintenance

and high durability features and this type flooring is also very attractive and adds value to any home. To be successful in this venture, you will need experience and knowledge in the installation of ceramic tile flooring, or have access to qualified tradesmen to do the actual flooring installations. Operating as a subcontractor service for construction and renovation companies is the logical starting point for this business and as a method of keeping the initial business start-up costs to a minimum.

WEB RESOURCE: www.floorbiz.com
Directory service listing ceramic tile distributors and flooring industry information.

SIDING INSTALLATION
★★ $$ 🚗 🕒

Siding sales and installation are about as straightforward as a home improvement business start-up can get. Sell the siding, and install the siding. Pricing for siding products and installation is generally based on a per-square basis (one square equals 100 square feet). There are, like any home improvement or renovation service, upgrades to the standard package that can be made available to the consumer. Computer software can allow you to scan in a photo of the current siding, as it looks before your work, and then you can show what it will look like in an "after" photo to give the client an idea of what you can do. You can show the homeowner a multitude of finished looks that could be achieved by installing new siding. Again, use a variety of marketing methods from a web site to handouts and Penny Saver ads to reach homeowners inn your area.

DISPOSAL BIN SERVICE
★★ $$$$

The home renovation and construction industry creates an enormous amount of waste each year that has to be disposed of into landfill sites or taken to recycling facilities for a renewed lease on life. There are a few different approaches that you can take in terms of starting and operating a disposal bin service. The first and more traditional approach is to own and operate your own roll-off or winch truck that is used in the transportation, delivery, and pickup of the disposal bins. The second option is to own only the disposal bins and subcontract the delivery and pickup service to a trucking firm. The second option is less expensive in terms of start-up capital requirements. However, it will also generate less revenue and profit for the business. The third, and maybe most interesting approach is to use tandem-axle trailers, which can be purchased secondhand relatively inexpensively, and can be towed behind any one-ton pickup truck. This third option enables you to enter into a waste disposal service with less money, while controlling all aspects of the business and revenues. Disposal rates are generally charged on a flat fee basis that is based on distance traveled, plus the cost of disposing of the construction waste. Check to make sure that you have all necessary permits or licenses for this type of business and that you have authorization to unload at specific locations.

CARPET INSTALLATION
★ $$ 🚚 🕒

Not unlike siding sales and installation, carpet sales and installation have been going strong for more than 50 years. The main requirement for this type of home improvement business start-up is to have the ability to properly install carpeting or have access to qualified installers. The key to building up the business is showing your work, which may mean doing a few jobs for free in exchange for taking photos of the work to show potential customers, and/or using the recipients of the free installation as referrals to get you going. Once you have demonstrated your work in a few locations, you will get word-of-mouth referrals. Also use local marketing and advertising to spread the word of your business. Carpet installers can make upwards of $25 an hour.

CAULKING AND FLASHING SERVICE
★★ $$ 🚚 🕒

What makes a caulking and flashing service such a fantastic business start-up is the fact that this business venture can be launched for as little as $500 of investment capital, requires little experience, is a unique service, and has a minimal amount of competition. Caulking and flashings have a definite life span and have to be replaced in order for their intended purposes to be effective. Furthermore, the uses for caulking and flashings are varied and required on just about every standing structure.

The simplest method to get rolling and promote your business is to distribute information fliers door-to-door in your community. The promotional fliers should describe all the benefits that replacing caulking and flashings will have for the owner's home. Likewise, residential and commercial property management and maintenance companies can also be a great source to gain new and repeat business.

WEB RESOURCE: www.thebluebook.com
Directory service listing that includes caulking manufacturers and distributors.

DRYWALL INSTALLATION
★★ $$ 🚚 🕒

Drywall installation and finishing is messy work that not many people enjoy doing; which is great for you, if this is the type of new business you wish to start. The drywall trade does require some practice to master. However, if you are patient, you can master the drywall trade quickly. The fastest way to establish and expand a drywall business is to market the service directly to homebuilders and renovators. Additionally, market the drywall service to home painters and fire and flood restoration companies, as these businesses can also provide you with plenty of work. Drywall repair is an essential part of their service. These companies typically subcontract this work to an outside drywall contractor. At the time this directory was written, drywall rates were $50 per hour plus material for repairs and $1 to $1.25 per square foot for new, finished drywall installation. However, you will have to conduct your own market survey in your local area to establish drywall installation and finishing rates.

WEB RESOURCE: www.thebluebook.com
Directory service listing that includes materials for a drywall business.

DECK BUILDING
★★★ $$$ 🚚

One of the fastest growing segments of the home improvement industry is designing, building, and installing custom sundecks. Many of the sundecks now retail for as much as $15,000 and include features such as built-in planters, areas for sunk-in hot tubs, glass or cast iron handrails, and custom manufactured wood furniture to match the sundeck's design. The most profitable way to operate the business is to sell the sundecks directly to the end consumers. However, this method of operating is also the most expensive to launch and establish. Additional ways to get rolling in your own sundeck installation business also include subcontracting for established building and renovation companies, establishing alliances with designers and architects, and marketing the sundeck sales and installation service directly to consumers via a showroom or through trade show displays.

REQUIREMENTS: In most areas of the country, the installation of a sundeck requires a building permit, which must be issued prior to installation. There are building codes in place for the construction specifications and they must be closely adhered to. Starting this sort of venture requires a great deal of construction experience. In terms of equipment, power tools such as table saws, handsaws, and posthole diggers will be required. Be sure to find out if a builder's license is required in your local area for this type of construction business.

START-UP COSTS: The total start-up costs to get going will vary greatly depending on the types of sundecks built and installed. However, an investment in the range of $15,000 to $20,000 will be sufficient to purchase the required equipment and leave enough working capital to fund the business for a few months.

PROFIT POTENTIAL: Once again, the profit potential for a sundeck sales and installation service can greatly vary as to the type of deck manufacturing and installation services that are provided to customers. Potential profits range: $30,000 to $100,000+ per year.

WEB RESOURCE: www.deckindustry.org
Deck Industry Association.

CLOSET ORGANIZERS
★ $$ 🏠

Selling and installing closet organizers is a very inexpensive business you can start and make a pretty darn good living at. Closet organizers are very popular and relatively easy to install. All that is required are a few basic hand tools and reliable transportation. You can market your service to homebuilders and home renovators, as well as directly to consumers through advertisements,

home expos, on your web site or even at fairs. There is a lot of competition in this industry, so you may want to specialize in one particular brand of closet organizer. If you are creative and have building skills, you can design and create your own line of closet organizers and, for more money custom design them to fit the needs of your clientele. The potential profit range for this type of home improvement business will vary. However, an income of $40,000 per year is easily attainable.

WEB RESOURCE: www.thebluebook.com
Directory listing closet organizer manufacturers and distributors.

REFITTING HOUSES FOR THE DISABLED
★★★★ $$$$

Millions of people living with disabilities often find that life's simplest tasks can become stressful and even daunting chores. The housing needs and requirements for people with disabilities are much different from those for people without disabilities. Doors must be wide enough to accommodate wheelchairs, light switches have to be lower, and electrical outlets have to be higher. Kitchens and bathrooms often have to be completely customized, and ramps and other safety items have to be installed in the home. Starting a business that specializes in refitting homes to accommodate people with disabilities can be both a profitable and personally rewarding venture to initiate. One effective way to market this type of renovation service is to construct a showroom that reflects the alterations and improvements that can be made to a new or existing home to make the house more functional and user-friendly for the disabled person. Alternatively, if your budget does not allow you to implement this type of showroom display, you can still market your services with the use of brochures and a web site that illustrates what you can do for your clients. Another option is to do one job for a very low fee, eating much of the cost yourself, in exchange for taking photos to post on your web site and in brochures to show the finished work. This is a very specialized type of business, and it requires experience in contracting and building, so it helps to have experience working with the disabled population.

REQUIREMENTS: This type of service has many requirements that have to be carefully considered, such as liability insurance, business licenses, skilled trades people or sub-contractors and an operating location.

PROFIT POTENTIAL: For any home improvement business to be financially viable, you should always strive for a 50 percent markup on all material and labor. If you follow this pricing structure then you will have a 33 percent gross profit margin on all work completed. Depending on sales volumes, 50 percent of your gross profit will be used to cover the cost of operating overheads, leaving approximately 15 percent of your total sales as pretax profits.

WEB RESOURCE: www.aapd.com
American Association of People With Disabilities.

PET DOORS
★★ $$ 🏠 🕐

There are estimated to be more than 30,000,000 house pets in North America. And if you have a dog or cat, then you are well aware of the fact that they may have to get outside for a host of reasons. Unfortunately, once in a while our schedules conflict with our pets' call to nature. Enter the solution: the installation of a pet door enabling dogs and cats the freedom to enter the safety of a fenced yard regardless of the time of day. The best way to get this business moving is to market the installation service through all the pet stores in your community. This marketing method can be a great way for you to kick start your new business venture into action. The pet stores should have no reasons not to assist you, as they will be selling the doors and retaining their retail markup. You could also supply the pet doors; or even better, manufacture, retail, and install the pet doors, for maximum profit returns. To assist in researching the business, I contacted three pet stores; all are well known and established in my community. Two of the stores offered pet doors for sale, however none of them offered the service of installing them. Conclusion: Check in your local area, and if your research draws the same conclusion as mine, then this business may be a good opportunity for you to start and operate your own fun, profitable, and independent business. Of course, you can also offer a combined rate whereby you provide and install the doors.

REQUIREMENTS: Other than a very basic knowledge of operating power tools, your only other concern will be meet-ing building codes and getting any necessary permits.

START-UP COSTS: A pet door sales and installation service can easily be launched for less than $1,000 including the required tools, product samples, and a small initial advertising and marketing budget.

PROFIT POTENTIAL: Charge a flat fee for the installation of the door with the only variable being the type of door you will be installing. Should you encounter situations that require the pet door to be installed into wall areas instead of a door, I would suggest that this service be priced on a time plus materials basis. You can charge in the $25 to $40 per hour range, plus a product markup on any and all pet door sales.

WEB RESOURCE: www.petdoors.com
Distributors of pet doors and parts.

STORAGE SHEDS
★★ $$$ 🕐

Building and installing backyard storage sheds is a little known business that generates gigantic profits for the owners of these businesses. Sheds are an affordable method for a homeowner to add additional storage space, workshop space, an art studio, or guest accommodations to a home without having to get plans and permits from local government. Working from a small industrial space you can build shed kits for homeowners to buy and install, build the sheds in a controlled environment and transport them to the site to install for the purchasers or you can construct them at the site. The business only requires basic construction knowledge and equipment to implement, and the profits that can be generated are outstanding. An elaborate sample shed can be built and displayed in a high-traffic area in your community with proper signs identifying your business. This type of advertising and promotion would be an excellent way to gain attention and attract new customers. The key to making this business successful is providing service that customers will not get when simply purchasing sheds over the internet. Do your research, become an expert, and help customers choose the shed that best fits their needs.

WEB RESOURCE: www.shedtownusa.com
Makers of sheds, shed kits and accessories.

SKYLIGHT INSTALLATION
★★★★ $$ 🚗 🕐 🌐

The old plastic bubble style skylights are out, and demand is booming for the new high-tech skylights that are now available. Some skylights not only open and close with the push of a button, they also have sensors that will automatically close the skylight if it begins to rain. Some have additional features like smart heat reflective glass, custom shades, and are available in a multitude of shapes and sizes. I talked to one skylight installation company, aptly called "Skylights Only." The owner told me that demand was so great for skylight installation, his company was booked for the next six months straight, and demand showed no signs of slowing down. This business opportunity gets four out of four stars, as not only is there high demand, but the entire venture can be set in motion for less than $5,000. Once again, the income and profit potential will vary. However, skylights have a good gross profit margin, and installation rates average in the range of $35 to $50 per hour. Combined income and profits for a business that sells and installs skylights could easily reach $100,000 per year or more.

WEB RESOURCE: www.thebluebook.com
Directory service listing manufacturers and distributors of skylights.

INTERIOR AND EXTERIOR HOUSE PAINTING
★ $$ 🚗 🕐

The business of painting houses has been around for years, and will continue to produce excellent profits for the owners of house painting services for many years to come. Why? Simple. Fear of heights and/or working from ladders, and slow tedious work can scare off even the most hardcore of do-it-yourself homeowners. House painting is a very simple business to set in motion and requires only a small investment to get going and even a smaller learning curve to master. Like most labor-intensive business ventures, you can pretty much be guaranteed of work regardless of economic conditions. Providing a free value-added service such as cleaning the gutters or windows while on the job site, is a great way to separate your company from the competition. Often small free value-added services will increase the numbers of referrals your business will receive. Your skill as a

painter and ability to do both preliminary work and clean up in a reasonable amount of time, will help make this a profitable undertaking.

WEB RESOURCE: www.pdca.org
Painting and Decorators Contractors of America.

GARAGE ORGANIZERS
★★ $ 🚗 🕐

Starting your own garage organizer service requires no special skills or equipment other than some basic hand tools. Ideally, you can start close to home by providing the service to family and friends, while building a sound referral base. Garage organizers are typically various shelf configurations and/or storage bins. You can buy such items wholesale and provide them with free delivery and installation or you can construct some original designs yourself if you are creative, handy and innovative. Home improvement trade shows will also be a valuable source of leads, and a "before and after" display can generate an enormous amount of interest in your products and services. Such a display can cost less than $1,000 to set up. If you can also provide organizational ideas and help people with the task of clearing out and arranging their garage space, you can earn more as a consultant. The lack of competition in this industry should allow you to mark up your products such as shelving and storage cabinets by at least 40 to 50 percent, while maintaining an hourly rate for installation in the range of $25 to $30 and more for organizing and arranging the garage for maximum efficiency.

WEB RESOURCE: www.thehardwarehut.com/garage-organizers. php

MIRROR INSTALLATION
★ $$ 🚗 🕐

Mirrors are required for just about every residential and commercial washroom application, and a mirror sales and installation business can easily be operated from a home garage. All that is required is a truck with a basic glass rack, a few tools, and the ability to cut glass (or hire an assistant who can cut the glass). The current rate to install bathroom mirrors is in the range of $5 to $7 per square foot, while the wholesale cost of the mirror is only $2 per square foot. Your math skills do not have to be good to know that leaves around $4 per square foot just for installing the mirror. For example, if the average installation job is four mirrors with an average size of nine-square feet per mirror, then this would leave you and a helper $150 for installing the mirrors, which would take about an hour to do. Once you have established the business, you can begin to market the services to commercial and residential construction companies, and it should not take long to build up a solid customer base.

WEB RESOURCE: www.glasslinks.com
Directory listing information and links to the flat glass industry.

PATIO COVERS
★★ $$ 🏠 🕑

Patio covers are a great low cost, high value home improvement project, as not only can a patio cover be an attractive add-on to any home, more importantly it can provide protection and relief from the heat of the sun. The first step to marketing this type of home improvement business is to establish the target market for the product. Potential customers will include residential homeowners with southern exposed yards and patios, as well as commercial businesses such as cafés. A display booth set up at a local mall or home and garden trade show that shows the benefits and value associated with the patio covers will be the best approach to attaining qualified sales leads.

REQUIREMENTS: Most manufacturers of aluminum patio covers ship the finished product as a kit including an instruction guide on how to install the product. Due to this kit format, there is not a lot of technical or construction experience required to assemble and install the patio covers. Additional requirements will be power tools, ladders, and a van or trailer to transport the patio covers to the installation site. Most areas of the country do not require a building permit to be issued for the purpose of installing a patio cover. Of course, you will always need to check local regulations.

START-UP COSTS: An initial investment of less than $10,000 will kick this new business venture into high gear.

PROFIT POTENTIAL: The following is a suggested retail pricing formula.

1. Installation time should be based on a minimum of at least a rate of $30 per man-hour.

2. Add wholesale product costs to labor costs. Remember to include consumables, such as screws, nails, caulking, and all flashings.

3. Add the labor and materials and then add on 50 percent of that number, which will give you the retail or contract selling price. Maintaining this pricing formula will generate a 33 percent gross profit margin prior to operating overheads being factored.

WEB RESOURCE: www.thebluebook.com
Directory service listing patio cover manufacturers and distributors.

WOODEN SCREEN DOOR MANUFACTURING
★★ $$ 🏠 🕑

Old-fashioned decorative Victorian wooden screen doors are all the rage for an inexpensive home improvement. You can capitalize on the demand for such Victorian screen doors by starting a business that manufactures, sells, and installs them. The business can be established and operated from a garage or basement workshop. All you will need is woodworking equipment and some screen door patterns to get rolling. Once again, marketing the doors at home improvement shows and mall kiosks will probably be your best bet, in terms of attracting customers to purchase the finished products. Additionally, check with local homebuilding centers to see if they stock the old-fashion style screen doors. If they do not carry this item, then you will have a great opportunity to set up retail distribution accounts with them.

GAZEBOS
★★ $$ 🏠 🕑

Sales and installations of garden gazebos is a wonderfully inexpensive way to start your own business enterprise. Gazebos have become very popular, especially for those used to house hot tubs. The business can be started for a very modest investment, and has the potential to return big profits. You can design your own line of gazebos to sell and install, or you can purchase plans for gazebo construction and use these designs to get started. You need to be good at constructing things to make this work. Another option is to build an alliance with an existing gazebo manufacturer that specializes only in sales. This would allow you to carry out the manufacturer's installations and capitalize on their customer base. Restaurants, catering facilities, hotels and other places where weddings or other special occasions take place are also prime locations for gazebos.

PROFIT POTENTIAL: part-time $10,000+ per year; full-time $25,000+ per year.

WEB RESOURCE: www.niagaradesigns.com
Design plans for gazebos and garden structures.

HOT TUB INSTALLATION
★ $$ 🚗 🕐

Hot tubs make a great addition to any home. However, the focus of this new business opportunity is not aimed at hot tub sales, but at the installation of hot tubs. In order for a hot tub to properly work and be safe for the occupants, it must be installed correctly, including the electrical hook-up and a solid foundation base. Starting your own business that specializes in the delivery and installation of hot tubs is a great little business venture to launch. You can charge a flat fee or hourly rate for the installation service. Potential customers can include hot tub retailers who require additional installation contractors and homeowners who are moving and require their hot tubs to be relocated. For additional profits you can also sell accessories, such as pumps, covers and the necessary chemicals to keep the tub clean. You can also provide a hot tub cleaning service as well, which can benefit from steady repeat business.

WEB RESOURCE: www.hottubsdirectory.com
A directory of hut tub information.

SAFE INSTALLATION
★★★ $$ 🚗 🕐 🚚

Crime is on the rise, and people are now more proactive in terms of protecting themselves and their families from becoming victims of crime and against the loss of their valuables or personal property through crime. Therefore, a business that sells and installs safes can be lucrative. Safes typically come in two forms. The first is the traditional floor model safe that can be cemented into place as an additional safety measure. The second is wall-mounted safes, which are generally concealed behind furniture or installed in unlikely places, such as attics and closets. In the research of this business, I interviewed a former locksmith who now exclusively installs safes into residential homes. In an average week he installs four to six safes with a profit margin after expenses of $150 to $200 per safe. That is an excellent income level to achieve for a one-person business that operates from home with virtually no overhead. The only system he uses to market his business is directly through homebuilders and renovation companies. These contractors sell his product and service to their clients as an upgrade feature. In return, the contractors keep 20 percent of the total sales value.

REQUIREMENTS: Installing safes does not require any special certificates, with the exception that the person who is carrying out the installation should be bonded for insurance purposes. First find out all of the necessary regulations in your area. You should also have dolly equipment capable of moving heavy items and a few basic power tools to be used for the safe installations.

START-UP COSTS: The total capital required to activate this venture is in the range of $2,000 to $5,000, excluding transportation requirements.

PROFIT POTENTIAL: The safe installer mentioned above, charges a flat fee of $200 to install a floor or wall-mounted safe. Additionally, he adds 30 percent markup to the wholesale cost of the safe. Even if you allow for commissions to be paid to a third party for initiating the sale, this is still a very profitable business to start and operate.

DOOR INSTALLATION
★★ $$ 🚗 🕐

Like windows, doors also rank high among the most frequently completed home improvement renovation. Once again, modern manufacturing methods and materials have helped to fuel the desire for this type of home improvement. Newly installed doors not only have better safety and insulation features, these doors are also highly attractive and can improve the appearance of the home for a relatively small investment. Due to the fact that this is a competitive industry, you may want to consider specializing in one particular type of door or become an exclusive agent or representative for one door manufacturer. Specialization in any industry will generally result in lower wholesale product costs and higher returns, in terms of both product and service demand. Do not overlook the apartment or condominium market for this product.

WEB RESOURCE: www.wholesaledoorsource.com
Suppliers of a wide variety of wholesale doors.

INTERIOR DECORATING SERVICE
★★ $$ 🏠 🕒 ⚖️

Starting an interior decorating service is the perfect business enterprise for the person that has artistic abilities and a creative flair. Generally, certification from a recognized institution in the field of interior decoration and design is required. While the service can be launched without the certificate, it will be much better received by potential clients as a professional service with proper accreditation. Start-up investment is very low, since this business relies more on your personal skills than on manufacturing, repairing, or selling specific goods. It is very easy to operate an interior decorating business from a homebased or shared office location. Most interior decorators prefer to specialize in providing either a commercial or residential decorating service. Residential decorators establish alliances with new homebuilders and renovation contractors as a method to gain access to their clients. Commercial decorators generally build alliances with commercial property managers and commercial contractors and architects. It is important to be able to show photos of your work, whether in a portfolio, on a CD-ROM or on your web site. Therefore, you can do a couple of jobs gratis and take digital photos. This is a business that will also require you to get to know people in the industry who can help you get what you need at low rates. Networking is very important. Home and garden trade shows are also a fantastic forum to promote the service and collect sales leads. Establishing yourself in this business will require a great deal of patience and time, but with good business and design skills utilized, the determined entrepreneur can establish a very rewarding and profitable business providing interior decorating services.

WEB RESOURCE: www.iida.org
International Interior Design Association.

BATHROOM AND KITCHEN VENTS
★★ $ 🚗 🕒

Prior to building codes establishing mandatory installations of kitchen and bathroom ventilation systems for all new construction projects, many houses were built without such systems. This fact creates a fantastic opportunity for an inexpensive homebased business venture that has the potential to generate a very lucrative income. Installation of ventilation systems generally requires only a few hours of time and basic tools and materials that can be purchased at any local building center. Designing simple door-hanger fliers and distributing them throughout your community can help promote the service. It won't take long for the phone to start ringing, as anyone who does not have kitchen and bath vents realizes the damage it causes in terms of mold, mildew, and odors. Total start-up costs will be less than $1,000, and an income level of $600 per week is easily attainable.

ROOFING INSTALLATION
★★ $$+ 🏠 🕒 ⚖️

The best aspect about starting a roofing service is that unlike a new kitchen, a new roof is usually a need, not a want. Residential and commercial roofing manufacturers use many different materials such as asphalt, steel, cedar, and composite materials. The first step to setting the business in motion is to decide on what type of roofing and building you will concentrate your marketing efforts. Regardless of whether you choose residential or commercial, a roofing service will always be in high demand. To get business you can start by subcontracting for a new homebuilder. You can also advertise to consumers directly.

REQUIREMENTS: Depending on the type of roof replacement service you will be operating, the requirements will vary in terms of skilled staff, equipment, regulations, and operating location. In many areas of the country, a builder's license is required to carry out roofing installations. Make sure to look into obtaining all types of necessary licenses and certificates. Liability insurance is also an absolute must, regardless of the type of roofing installations you specialize in.

WEB RESOURCE: www.nrca.net
The National Roofing Contractors Association.

GLASS TINTING SERVICE
★★ $ 🚗 🕒

Glass tinting is a very affordable business enterprise to launch, and with a little bit of practice it can be mastered by just about anyone. The best aspect of the business is the fact that it can be operated on a year-round basis, regardless of weather conditions, right from a mobile installation vehicle. The market for glass tinting is endless in terms of residential, commercial, and automotive applications, including cars, boats, house windows and skylights, retail store windows, and recreational vehicles. A fast start method to get rolling in this business is to build alliances with used car dealers, boat brokers, and commercial property managers, as these businesses can offer glass tinting options to their customers.

CUSTOM FIREPLACE MANTELS
★★ $$ 🚗 🕒

One of the hottest home improvements right now is upgrading or installing new gas fireplaces. Most newly installed fireplaces have one thing in common: they require a mantel to suit the fireplace. Building and installing custom fireplace mantels is a great business to start for a person who has expertise in construction, or more specifically, cabinetmaking. This sort of business can easily be started for less than $1,000 and be operated right from a truck or van. In terms of marketing the mantels, there is an endless supply of potential customers who can provide you with work, including homebuilders, interior designers, renovation companies, gas fireplace retailers, architects, and utility companies.

SOLAR TUBE INSTALLATION
★★★ $$ 🚗 🕒 🍃

Solar tubes are a low-cost alternative to installing skylights. These mini-skylights are available in a few different sizes and are packaged complete with roof flashing, expandable tunnel, interior finishing ring, and all required installation hardware. What makes this a terrific business start-up is the fact that solar tubes are easy to install, require no permits or special tools, and cost the homeowner less than $600 for the complete installation, including the product. The benefit of the solar tube is that they can add a tremendous amount of natural light to

areas that are normally dark, such as closets, stairways, bathrooms, and hallways. The market for solar tubes is unlimited for both residential and commercial applications. Solar tubes are a relatively new product to enter the home improvement market. The potential growth is excellent and current competition is limited. The best way to promote the product and your installation service is to build a mobile showroom on a trailer, keeping it completely free from light inside the trailer with the exception of a solar tube. Both you and your customers will be amazed at the amount of light that is generated by the solar tube, which of course is a great sales tool.

REQUIREMENTS: Only basic construction knowledge and power tools are required to install solar tube skylights. Currently there are no regulations for the installation of solar tubes, but check with local building officials in your area. Note: A few of the solar tube manufacturers have a night light option. If you are considering providing this option to your customers, ensure that you are, or you have access to, a licensed electrician to complete the electrical hookups.

START-UP COSTS: A solar tube sales and installation service can be established for less than $5,000 including the cost of tools, inventory, and a mobile showroom display. Once you have established contact with manufacturers, attempt to acquire exclusive installation rights for your community, as this will often reduce wholesale costs you pay for the product.

PROFIT POTENTIAL: This is a great one-person business that can easily generate an income in excess of $60,000 a year for the entrepreneur who is willing to go for it.

WEB RESOURCE: www.thebluebook.com
Directory service listing solar tube manufacturers and distributors.

HOME IMPROVEMENT DIRECTORY
★★★ $$$$ 🚗 🕒 🌐

The basis of this business opportunity is straightforward. Home improvement contractors pay you a fee to advertise and promote their services and products in your annual home improvement directory. You create the directory in print or CD-ROM format and distribute the directory free of charge in the community that the home improvement directory is intended to serve. As another option, you can offer the directory online by using the same basic concept. A printed directory can be distributed via home and garden shows and a local promotion tied in with a newspaper or TV/radio station, while an online directory can be promoted in traditional manners as well as on other web sites. This new business venture could not only prove to be very profitable, but it also lends itself perfectly to expanding into various other communities, once a working model has been proven successful. Start-up costs will vary depending on factors such as print or electronic directory format, etc., but this venture should not require more than $20,000 in initial capital to get started. The key is in your ability to sell advertising space, coupled with some layout, design, and editorial skills. Aligning yourself with experts in the field and including content with the listings and advertisements can increase interest in the directory. Remember, the larger the circulation, the more you can charge for advertisements.

PAVING SERVICE
★ $$+ 🏠 🕒

Starting a full-scale paving contracting business is extremely investment capital-intensive. However, starting a business as an independent paving consultant is a very inexpensive business to get rolling, and can generate an income in excess of $100,000 per year. What you do to start such a business is market and sell paving services, and subcontract the paving to a qualified and well-equipped paving contractor while retaining 10 to 20 percent of the contract value. Fliers, ads in Penny Savers and other typical means of spreading the word throughout the community will best accomplish marketing such a service. Additional income can be earned by providing a driveway sealing service, and driveway sealing work can be subcontracted to a qualified contractor. Maintaining yearly gross sales of $400,000 will produce a pretax income of $40,000 to $80,000 per year.

WINDOW BOXES AND SHUTTERS
★★ $ 🏠 🕒

Sales and installation of exterior window flower boxes and decorative window shutters is a fantastic little business to get going that can be started for peanuts and oper-

ated right from home on a full- or part-time basis. You can design and build your own products or purchase pre-built window boxes and shutters. All that is required to install these items are a few basic tools and a ladder. These window boxes and shutters can be sold to homebuilders, architects, and homeowners. You might try offering free boxes and shutters to a homeowner in your community in exchange for allowing you to use their home as a show room or reference home. This method will allow other potential customers to drive by to have a look at the dramatic difference that installing window flower boxes and shutters can have on the appearance of their homes. As mentioned earlier, in other listings, giving away a few hundred dollars worth of installed products may return you thousands of dollars in profits.

WEB RESOURCE: http://mo.essortment.com/gardenwindowbo_rwrn.htm
One method of building a window box.

CUSTOM FRENCH DOORS
★★ $$ 🏠 🕒

Starting your own business that manufactures, retails, and installs custom-made interior French doors is an excellent way to be self-employed and generate very lucrative profits. There is very little competition in this business; yet the demand for high quality and unique French doors is very good, especially in the higher-end markets, such as expensive homes and professional offices. A great way to market the French doors and installation service is to work with homebuilders who are prepared to offer your French doors to their clients as an upgrade finishing option. Design tip: To make your custom French doors unique and different from your competitors, you may want to consider a few of the following: Gold-plated or solid brass hardware, stained glass or sandblasted glass lights, stainless steel or mosaic tile covers, and curved or shaped tops. One thing is for sure: this business will allow you to be creative in your designs, which can assist you in building a solid reputation and client base.

FLOORING INSTALLATION
★★★ $$ 🏠 🕒

Laminate flooring that is manufactured to resemble hardwood flooring is an incredibly popular alternative to the high cost of installing real hardwood flooring. Laminate flooring is available in a wide range of finishes and is virtually impossible to damage or destroy. Best of all, laminate flooring is extremely easy to install even if your knowledge of flooring installation is limited. Of course, from a home value standpoint, hardwood floors increase the value of a home and have a distinctive appearance that surpasses most laminate options. From your vantage point, the ability to install either would clearly give you a wider option as a business professional. To set this business in motion, first check to see if the home improvement centers in your area provide an installation service of this product. If they don't, then it's a marriage made in heaven. They sell it, and you become a service provider for that retail location. Unless you sign an exclusive contract, you can work for several stores as a subcontractor. Most retail suppliers today also set up customers with installers. You can also talk to interior decorators and designers to promote your service and establish an additional client base. If you are looking to work with commercial enterprises, you can approach the business in a similar manner, aligning yourself with the suppliers as well as with various businesses that are looking to purchase new floors. As is always the case when providing a service, the quality of your work will speak volumes. It's not always as simple as it looks to lay floors, especially when dealing with the many unique configurations of homes. Therefore, you will need to learn the craft or have experienced employees. You will want to familiarize yourself with local building codes and safety regulations. Also, if you are using compressors or other equipment for installing hardwood floors, you will need to make sure the circuitry in the home can handle the equipment so you don't blow out the electricity—believe me, it happens! Selling and installing new baseboard moldings while you are on the job site can earn additional business revenues and profits.

START-UP COSTS: Total business start-up costs, including tools, sales samples, brochures, and liability insurance will be well under $3,000 providing that you already have suitable transportation, such as a truck, van, or station wagon.

GLASS BLOCK INSTALLATION
★★ $ 🚗 🕐

Glass block is back in vogue for two reasons. The first: Having glass block windows installed is a cost-effective way to beautify your home and add real designer flair. The second reason is that installing glass block into basement window areas is a great way to let the light shine in, and at the same time burglarproof windows. Starting your own glass block installation service does not require a lot in terms of investment or expertise. Almost all home improvement centers will now make up glass block windows on a custom order basis to fit any size opening. However, the installation techniques still do require some experience, but this can be self-taught starting with your home, or the home of a friend or relative.

MOLDING INSTALLATION
★★ $$ 🚗 🕐

The fastest and least inexpensive way to improve a home's interior appearance is to install decorative baseboard, crown, and door moldings. The market for interior moldings and installation services is absolutely huge, both for home renovations and new construction. You can market your products and services to homebuilders, interior decorators, or directly to consumers seeking to upgrade their homes.

MARKETING TIP: Building contacts with window and door installation companies is the quickest way in which to launch your own molding installation business. These companies often will subcontract the molding installations, which have to be completed after the windows and doors have been installed. Alliances established with two or three of these companies can easily supply you with more work than a single owner-operator in this business can handle. The total investment to start your own molding installation business will be less than $2,000 including all required tools and equipment. This business can be managed from a homebased office and operated from an installation vehicle.

WALLPAPERING SERVICE
★ $ 🚗 🕐

The demand for residential wallpapering has been on a steady decline for the past decade, with the exception of wallpaper decorative ceiling and wall borders. However, the demand for commercial wallpaper applications is on the rise, due to the fact that a wallpaper finish as opposed to a paint finish, lasts longer, is easier to maintain, and, calculated over a usable life span, is half the cost of painting. Specializing in commercial wallpaper applications is a very inexpensive business venture that you can initiate. It can return a comfortable living for many years. Commercial builders, renovators, and property managers can be your best source of leads to secure work.

CABINET DOOR REPLACEMENTS
★★ $$ 🚗 🕒

The average new kitchen costs in the range of $20,000 to install, not including appliances. Not everyone can afford this expensive home improvement; however, it only costs a few thousand dollars to update a kitchen's look with new cabinet doors and hardware. Starting this business does not require a great deal of expertise or capital, and you can generally be completely ready to roll for under a $5,000 investment. Capitalizing on the wave of home improvement reality television shows, you might opt to hold a contest where people send in pictures of their kitchen cabinets and you completely renovate the worst looking cabinets for free. It's a great means of advertising and promotion, particularly if you contact local newspapers and magazines. Knowing someone who did this, he received more than 100 entries for the contest, complete with name, address, and telephone numbers. Not only did he choose a winner and install the kitchen update for free, more importantly he had a base of more than 100 potential customers that he could now market to, as he knew that they were in the market for his type of service. He was then able to show "before" and "after" photos of the winner's kitchen cabinets.

INTERCOM INSTALLATION
★★ $$ 🚗 🕒

Recent technology changes in intercom systems have made them extremely easy to install, as wireless intercoms are now readily available. Due to these recent changes in the product, starting a business that sells and installs wireless intercoms is a fantastic business opportunity for just about anyone, regardless of construction or business

experience. Intercom systems have a wide range of uses including:

- Installations in baby nurseries
- Business applications for warehouse to office communications.
- Security applications for residential and commercial door entry use.

Overall this is a very good choice for a new low-investment business start-up that has the potential to generate a very lucrative income for the owner-operator of the business.

HOME IMPROVEMENT TRADE SHOWS
★★★ $$$ 🕒

Why not organize and host your own semi-annual home improvement trade shows? Construction and renovation companies do not hesitate in paying as much as $300 or more, per day for a 10-foot x 10-foot display booth, and the attending public will gladly pay at last $10 to get inside to see all the latest home improvement products and services. Marketing tip: Find a major sponsor to co-host and promote the event, such as a radio station, TV station, local building center, newspaper, or construction association. Securing this type of sponsorship can help reduce your up-front capital outlay as well. You can utilize the resources and the marketing department that a sponsor already has in place. Profit potential range is $10,000+ per home improvement trade show that the business organizes.

HOME THEATERS
★★ $$$ 🚗 🕒

Home theaters have become a very popular high-end home entertainment option. Big-screen flat panel televisions, surround sound, computer technology, and state-of-the-art audio components are all helping to fuel the demand for the perfect family entertainment room. Even theater seating and popcorn/refreshment stands are fashionable. Thus, starting a business that specializes in designing and turning a basement into home theater is a fantastic business enterprise that can generate hundreds of thousands of dollars. To keep business start-up costs to a minimum, consider establishing an alliance or joint venture with an existing audio/visual electronics retailer. Your company would provide the room designs and construction, while the retail business would provide the home theater electronics products. This type of joint venture would be very beneficial to both businesses and increase the profit and market share potential overall. The most important step, however, in getting this business off the ground is having people working for you who have expertise in the latest home theater technology (unless you are an expert yourself). Competition is becoming fierce as newer technology creates an increasing demand for innovative home theaters, so you had better know all about the merchandise and the home possibilities. If you can custom install the exact theater the client wants—no matter how high tech—without damaging or negatively affecting the electrical, cable or technological infrastructure of the home, you will be highly sought out for your services. Also, don't forget liability insurance for those occasions when something goes wrong.

WEB RESOURCE: www.hometheatermag.com
Home Theater Magazine.

GREENHOUSES
★★ $$$ 🚗 🕓

In the past decade greenhouses have become a very "hot" home improvement project. As the baby boomer generation slips into retirement, they are looking for ways to keep busy, stay physically fit, and enjoy life. Greenhouse hobby gardening provides them with exactly what they are seeking. There are various approaches that can be taken for starting a greenhouse installation business. These include:

- Designing, building, selling, and installing greenhouses.
- Designing and selling U-Install-It greenhouse kits.
- Selling and installing greenhouses for existing manufacturers.

You could choose to do all of the above and also help people in selecting the plants and setting up their greenhouses. Charge accordingly.

PROFIT POTENTIAL: $20,000 per year part-time and $50,000+ per year full-time.

WEB RESOURCE: www.ngma.com
National Greenhouse Manufacturers Association.

DEMOLITION SERVICE
★★★ $$ 🚗 🕓

If you have never thought about a demolition service, now is the time to start the ball in motion (pun intended). Don't plan on starting a large-scale demolition service, but you can run a smaller one that specializes in residential and commercial renovation projects. What makes this a great business opportunity is simple. Contractors and renovation companies typically will carry out the demolition needed to get to begin a renovation project. The problem, however, is the fact that these companies are often forced to pay over-qualified carpenters' huge salaries for doing the demolition work that could be completed by laborers receiving a much lower hourly rate. The results often mean less revenues and profits for the contractor. Herein lies the business opportunity: Forming a crew of construction laborers and subcontracting to work with renovation companies and contractors for demolition work has the potential to pay off big. Paying the crew $8 to $10 per hour each, while charging the contractors $15 per man-hour can leave you with a profit of $30 per hour based on a five-man demolition crew, and still save the contractors money. Operate two or three crews and the profit potential increases dramatically. Note: Be sure to acquire workers' compensation insurance for employees and general liability insurance to safeguard against the costs of potential accidents. Make sure to find out about, and have, any necessary permits or licenses necessary if required to do demolition work in your area.

WEB RESOURCE: www.demolition-nfdc.com
National Federation of Demolition Contractors.

CONSTRUCTION PROJECT MANAGEMENT
★★ $$ 🚗 🕓

"Have construction knowledge and management skills, will travel," can be the motto of your new business if you start a construction management business. The market for construction project management services is huge and includes residential and commercial projects. However, due to the nature of the construction industry, you would be well advised to specialize on one of the two areas. Currently, subcontract project managers are charging fees based on the construction project itself. Typically, fees are in the range of $300 to $600 per day, and can go as high as $1,000 per day for specialized construction projects.

FIREPLACE INSTALLATION
★★ $$$$ 🏠 🕐 ⚖️

Wood-burning, gas, and alternative fuels—you can sell and install all of these types of home fireplaces if you are considering starting a fireplace sales and installation business. The best way to operate and market this kind of new business venture is with the assistance of a fully operational fireplace showroom. There are hundreds of fireplace options, mantel options, and fireplace accessories for homeowners to choose from, and a retail showroom is the best way to display these products and build customer interest. Considerations for this type of retail and installation business include business location, qualified installation staff, and liability insurance, just to mention a few. To be successful, you need experience as a contractor or in construction and the ability to complete a job (or supervise the completion) in a reasonable amount of time. Be sure to utilize home and garden trade shows for exhibiting purposes, as they are wonderful forums for collecting qualified sales leads. The profit potential will greatly vary for a fireplace sales and installation business. However, there should be no problems maintaining profit margins of 25 to 35 percent on all retail sales.

CONSTRUCTION ESTIMATING SERVICE
★★ $$ 🏠 🕐

Calling all handymen, carpenters, and home improvement gurus. The time has never been better than now to start a construction estimating service, and the possibility to earn more than $100,000 per year is very real. Unlike a home inspection service that provides a detailed report on what is wrong with a home, property, or building, a construction estimating service provides a detailed report on how to fix the problems and what the renovation or construction work will cost. Your key demographic market for this type of service are home buyers, who not only want to know what is wrong with a home, but also want to know how it can be corrected and what it will cost. A secondary market is existing home and property owners who would like to have an initial cost analysis completed in regards to a home improvement or construction project to assess the value of the project. The main requirement for establishing and running this type of unique consulting service is to have a good understanding of all areas of the construction industry and trades. Rates for a construction estimating service will greatly depend on the size and value of the potential project. However, charging a fee of at least $50 per hour is certainly not out of line.

PAINT AND WALLPAPER STORE
★★ $$$$

Starting a retail paint and wallpaper store is a relatively stable retail business venture to start, as there is no real threat from internet sales of these products. However, the big threat comes in the form of big box retailers, so business location, plus good customer service, is of critical importance to the success and survival of this kind of retailing venture. To increase sales and profits beyond just selling paint and wallpaper, also provide customers with unique services, such as after-hours instruction classes in various home decorating mediums and other products and services, such as equipment rentals for do-it-yourself painters. Factoring in considerations such as competition, start-up investment, operating costs, and profit potential, a paint and wallpaper store is a good choice for a new business enterprise, but best left to those of you with retailing experience and knowledge of the subject.

ABOVE-GROUND POOLS
★ $$$$

Above-ground pools have enjoyed a resurgence in popularity in the past few years. This is a business opportunity for the careful and innovative entrepreneur who is prepared to invest both time and money into selling and installing above-ground pools. The first step that needs to be taken for this business start-up is to locate a manufacturer of above-ground pools and negotiate an exclusive distribution and installation agreement for a selected geographical area. Once that has been successfully achieved, the business can be advertised, promoted, and marketed utilizing all the traditional methods. Additional revenue can be gained by providing clients and above-ground pool owners with a pool maintenance service, as well as a pool dismantling and reinstallation service for customers relocating. You can also offer accessories, such as pool filters, covers and even slides. In addition, linking up with someone who builds decks and working a combination deal can be very advantageous.

Here's a unique marketing approach: By throwing a few pool parties at your own above ground pool, and inviting the new families in the neighborhood to bring their children, you can get a lot of potential customers—particularly when the kids start bugging their parents to buy a pool just like yours.

WEB RESOURCE: www.polarpools.com
Above-ground pool wholesaler.

CUSTOM COUNTERTOPS
★★ $$ 🏠 🕐

Laminates, stone, ceramic tile, concrete, or metal—kitchen and bathroom countertops can and are being manufactured from a wide variety of raw materials to suit every interior décor and budget. Designing, manufacturing, and installing custom countertops is a relatively uncomplicated process that requires only basic tools and a homebased workshop. Once again, kitchen and bath renovations rank as the two most common home improvement projects carried out by homeowners, and countertops are an important component of these renovations. Most manufacturers and installers of custom-made countertops work on a subcontract basis, mainly for interior designers, architects, homebuilders, and renovation contractors. However, custom countertops can be sold directly to homeowners by displaying samples at home improvement trade shows and by initiating an advertising campaign locally in the area you service. The key to success in this type of unique home improvement business is to provide clients with exciting designs, material selections, and top-notch installation services. Retail prices of custom countertops vary greatly depending on size, shape, complexity, and materials used to construct. However, installation rates are standard in the industry and generally range from $30 to $50 per hour.

CABINETMAKING SERVICE
★★ $$ 🏠 🕐

Time devoted to learning the craft of fine cabinetmaking could be time very well spent considering professional cabinetmakers routinely charge $40 to $80 per hour for their service. Market your cabinetmaking services to contractors of luxury homes, architects, interior designers, and directly to homeowners by placing newspaper advertisements and by displaying your products and skills at home improvement trade shows. Remember not to limit your marketing efforts only to residential prospects, as there is also great demand for custom cabinets and shelves in commercial applications for store fixtures and professional offices. Get started learning cabinetmaking by enrolling in courses, purchasing books and how-to videos, and by practicing constructing cabinets for your own home and for family and friends. Many cabinetmakers work from a well-equipped homebased workshop as a method to keep start-up costs and operating overheads to a minimum.

WEB RESOURCE: www.cabinetmakers.org
Cabinet Makers Association.

SEAMLESS GUTTERS
★★ $$$ 🏠

Seamless rain gutters are quickly becoming the choice for most contractors, architects, and homeowners simply because they are inexpensive, quick to install, and available in a wide range of designer colors. The best aspect about starting a seamless gutter service is the fact that it requires little experience to start. There are portable roll form machines available that will form the gutters in the desired profile right on the customer's job site. In a nutshell, a coil of aluminum metal in the chosen color is loaded into one end of the machine and the finished rain gutter comes out the other end. Promote the products and services by way of traditional print advertising and by establishing alliances with new home contractors, renovation companies, and siding and roofing contractors. Many gutter installation contractors work exclusively on a subcontract basis for the above-mentioned companies.

WEB RESOURCE: www.knudsonmfg.com
Manufacturers of gutter-making machines.

CONCRETE STAMPING
★★★ $$+ 🏠 🕐

Concrete stamping and coating is one of the hottest home improvements being carried out by homeowners and contractors alike. This just may be the right new business for you to start. Generally concrete stamping is done with installations of new concrete driveways, walkways, and patios. Once the forms are in place, dyes have been added, and the concrete is poured using various tools to create the desired pattern and appearance on the surface as it cures. These patterns can range from a cobble stone look to the look of blue Vermont slate. The advantage of concrete stamping is that it costs much less to create a concrete driveway stamped to look like slate than it does to install a real slate driveway—not to mention the fact that the concrete-stamped slate driveway can be completed in a fraction of the time it would take to install the real deal. Concrete stamping is not limited to new installations, as there are surface coatings that can be applied onto existing concrete surfaces to create various patterns and textures. Learning the art of concrete stamping and coatings will require an investment of time on your behalf in order to master it. However, if you are seeking to start a home improvement business that is in demand and has the potential to generate lucrative profits, concrete stamping is one of the best bets.

WEB RESOURCE: www.stampcrete.com
Manufacturers and distributors of concrete stamping equipment and supplies; also have concrete stamping training courses available.

GARAGE DOOR SALES AND INSTALLATION
★★ $$$ 🏠 🕐

Garage doors and accessories are not difficult to install. In fact, most manufacturers of these products include detailed step-by-step instruction that outlines the installation procedure. This makes a good business opportunity for just about anyone with basic construction abilities and tools. Like many home improvement and repair businesses, the key to success lies with securing a distribution or installation agreement with one or more manufacturers of the product you intend to sell and install. Thankfully, in the case of garage doors, securing this type of exclusive agreement should not prove difficult, as there are hundreds of companies that manufacture garage doors in just about every style, material selection, and price range available. As great as that sounds, however, the real challenge will be marketing the product and service. This can be accomplished by building alliances within the construction and real estate industries. These alliances should include new home builders, renovation and general contractors, home and property inspectors, real estate agents and brokers, and property managers, all of whom can refer your service or in some cases supply you business with subcontract installation work. You can also market to homeowners by way of fliers, ads in Penny Savers and in other local publications. In addition to basic construction skills, you will also need power tools, such as drills, a mitre saw, and transportation like a truck or large trailer capable of moving the product to the installation site. The repair aspect of the business can be equally as lucrative as the sales and installation side. Simply installing a new garage door opening systems can bring in several hundred dollars. As is typically the case with a new business, you need to become well-versed in the many new devises available and how they work, including those with sensory motion detectors and various high tech features.

SUNROOM INSTALLATION
★★ $$$$ 🏠 ⚒️

The addition of a sunroom is a terrific way for many homeowners to increase living space, add an all-season retreat, and increase the value of their home for a relatively low investment. Sunrooms have become popular in the past decade, and this is what makes starting a sunroom sales and installation business a wise choice. There are basically two options available in terms of starting this business. The first is to locate a manufacturer that designs and pre-builds kit sunrooms that can be sold and installed at customers' homes, and negotiate an exclusive dealer's agreement with the manufacturer. The second option is to design and build custom sunrooms to meet customers' needs and requirements. In both cases, a building permit is generally required in all regions of North America for the installation of a sunroom, so be sure to check local building codes and regulations before you get started. Sunrooms are very easy to build and install and only require basic construction knowledge. If you do not have any construction experience, you can always hire qualified subcontractors to carry out the installations while you concentrate on sales, marketing, and management aspects of the business. Home and garden trade shows are fantastic venues to display your products, and more importantly, collect qualified sales leads. Like most renovation and construction ventures, you should strive to maintain a 50 percent markup on all products and services you sell. Using this pricing formula will result in a 33 percent gross profit margin on sales prior to operating costs and taxes.

WEB RESOURCE: www.nationalsunroom.org
National Sunroom Association, industry information and links to manufacturers and distributors of sunroom kits, parts, and plans.

DRAPERY STUDIO
★★ $$$ 🚗 🕐 🌐

Starting a drapery studio is a fantastic new business venture to put into action, and there are three excellent options for operating this home decoration business. The first option is to run the business on a mobile basis wherein you travel to clients' locations equipped with samples of fabrics, rods, and accessories and conduct the presentation on site. The second option is to open a small boutique where customers come to you; or a combination of in-home presentations and boutique presentations. The boutique can even be operated from home providing you have the space and zoning will permit. The third option is to partner the business with an existing interior designer or decorator within the community and utilize their office or showroom for display purposes. Of course all three options can be combined to make it as easy and convenient as possible for customers to do business with you. Once again, like many businesses where a product is manufactured on a custom basis, you can subcontract seamstresses and installers if you lack the ability to create and install the drapery products. Utilizing qualified subcontractors will enable you to concentrate on the sales and marketing aspects of the business. Also, be sure to use internet to seek out a wholesale source for curtain

rods and drapery accessories. The profit potential is excellent in this business simply due to the custom aspect, and you should have no problem maintaining a 100 percent markup on all products sold and installed.

CEILING FANS
★ $$ 🕐

Using less electricity, ceiling fans are cheaper in the long run than having the air conditioning system going strong all summer long. You can team up with a local retailer or sell the fans at flea markets, home shows, booths at malls and other locations, keeping your costs low. You can then install fans for a $25 an hour fee and sell an inexpensive service contract on repairs. Since it's easy to buy a ceiling fan (like anything else) online, the key to your success is having models on hand and saving the buyers time by having installing them quickly and properly. Have liability insurance and make sure the ceiling is equipped to hold the fan before installation. Safety should be of prime concern.

WEB RESOURCE: www.ceilingfanwholesalers.com
As the name implies, a place for buying fans wholesale.

RESIDENTIAL LANDSCAPING
★★ $$$$

If you have some background in gardening and architecture, plus an understanding of landscape design, you can start a landscaping business. Residential landscapers build patios, fieldstone walls, stone walks, and plant perennial gardens, foundation plantings, herb gardens and anything else to beautify the grounds around a home. In addition, a landscapers find solutions for problem areas that don't get enough sun, get too much sun, are too rocky, or are simply visually unappealing. Doing research and learning as much as possible about planting and maintenance, grass, turf, fertilizer, mowing, trees, water damage, winter damage, and anything else that can beautify or ruin the land, should be your own personal training prior to setting such a business in motion. Since you are working outdoors most of the time, you can start such a business from a homebased office.

Marketing is best done through homeowners associations, real estate brokers and at home shows. Good photographs of your work in a brochure and on your web site are your primary selling tools and will get you business, along with satisfied customers. Expenses are primarily the tools and equipment that you need to shape land and move dirt. When starting out, the larger equipment can be leased as necessary.

PROFIT POTENTIAL: Varies greatly depending on your expertise, geographic region, and your marketing efforts. However, a good landscaping business can bring in $100,000.

CUSTOM CLOSETS
★★ $$$$

There are three reasons why people will contact a custom design company. First, they need more room and better designed closet space. Secondly, they know that custom closets can pump up the value of their home. Third, they want to be the envy of their friends. Building new closets and expanding, or reconfiguring, current ones, are part of the custom closet business. A background in carpentry is helpful for starters, or at least you should be very good at building. However, the other key aspect of such a business is having the vision to create and design closets so that they are more functional, and even multi functional. If you are building closets off-site and transporting them, you will not only need the tools, but the workspace and transport. For all of this, your startup costs may be in the $90,000 range. If you are primarily working on-site and rebuilding and reshaping existing closets, you can start up the business, with the tools and your marketing costs running under $30,000. The key to this business is giving the client what he or she wants. If you can design the closets of their dreams, not only will you be well compensated, but word will spread throughout communities.

WINDOW TREATMENTS
★★ $$$ 🕐

Selling verticals, drapes, curtains, and other types of window treatments can be a lucrative business. There are numerous possibilities today beyond the usual horizontal blinds and by carrying an assortment of such products you can meet the needs of homeowners from a home-based business. Market yourself through ads and fliers and make arrangements to visit the homes of potential clients with a brochure or catalog of possibilities. Make suggestions, based on the décor and your product line, and help the customers make selections. You can work as a representative for one manufacturer or carry the product lines of several. Once you order what the customer wants, you can then provide installations. The markup is very high for such products and word will spread quickly if you provide good, prompt service.

WEB RESOURCE: www.windowtoppers.com/wholesale.html Window treatment wholesaler.

NOTES:

_____

_____

_____

_____

_____

_____

_____

_____

_____

_____

_____

KEY

RATINGS	★
START-UP COST	$$
HOMEBASED BUSINESS	
PART-TIME OPPORTUNITY	
LEGAL ISSUES	
FRANCHISE OR LICENSE POTENTIAL	
GREEN BUSINESSES	

37

HOME REPAIR

Businesses You Can Start

GRAFFITI REMOVAL SERVICE
★★★ $$$ 🏠 🕐 🌐

Starting a graffiti removal service does not require a great deal of working experience, and the market for this service is unlimited, untapped, and it appears that graffiti vandalism shows no sign of slowing down or stopping. The equipment required for this business enterprise will be a portable pressure washer and a portable sandblaster, both of which can be conveniently mounted on a trailer for easy transportation to job sites. Successfully marketing a graffiti removal service is best accomplished by visiting businesses that are often the victims of graffiti vandalism and offering the business owners a low-cost graffiti removal solution. Provide the business owners with a monthly graffiti removal option; basically, for a fixed monthly fee, you will check in on the business once per week to see if there is any new graffiti to be removed. If new graffiti is present, you would simply remove it. If no graffiti is present then you would move on to your next client's location. A graffiti removal service could easily generate sales in excess of $6,000 per month, which could be achieved by securing only 100 customers paying an ongoing monthly fee of $60 to ensure that their business never has to worry about unsightly graffiti on their buildings. Additionally, a graffiti removal service could be marketed to schools, libraries, and all locations that have problems with graffiti vandalism.

MOBILE SCREEN REPAIR
★★★ $$$ 🏠 🕐 🌐

Every year millions of window and door screens have to be repaired or replaced. Starting a mobile screen repair business could put you on the road to riches. Activating a mobile screen repair service only requires a few basic tools and materials such as a miter saw, screen rollers, various screen materials, and screen replacement parts. The business can be operated from an enclosed trailer or truck to provide shelter from inclement weather. The key requirement in marketing a mobile screen repair service is to establish alliances with companies and individuals that require window screen repairs and replacements on a regular basis. These companies can include residential and commercial property management firms, strata corporations, government agencies, and community associations like recreation centers and schools. The profit potential for a mobile screen repair service is excellent, as there is limited competition. Furthermore, screening materials are very inexpensive to purchase; yet the retail selling price of window and door screen repairs and replacements is typically five to eight times as much as the material costs to produce the screens. The income that can be earned in this business venture will vary as to the total number of screen repairs. However, a well-established mobile screen repair service can generate sales in excess of $100,000 per year provided the service can cover a wide-ranging area.

WEB RESOURCE: www.thebluebook.com
Directory service listing manufacturers and distributors of screening material and parts.

DRIVEWAY SEALING
★★ $ 🚗 🕒

Here is a great new business start-up for the university student seeking part-time business earnings to help offset the high cost of attending school. Starting a driveway sealing service is just about as easy and straightforward as any new business venture can possibly be. As mentioned earlier in this chapter, there are an estimated 75,000,000 building structures in the United States, and it's probably safe to assume that at least 25 percent of these buildings have a pavement or asphalt driveway. If this is the case, there are approximately 18,000,000 potential customers for a driveway sealing business. To keep initial start-up costs to a minimum, simply use asphalt driveway sealer in a bucket as opposed to purchasing expensive asphalt spraying equipment. You will find that all the necessary supplies and equipment required for this business are available at any local home improvement or building center. Income potential starts at about $20 per hour.

WEB RESOURCE: http://landscaping.about.com/od/driveways andwalkways1/ht/driveway_sealer.htm
Quick how-to information and tips for applying driveway sealer.

ROOF REPAIRS
★★★ $$ 🚗 🕒

Wherever there is a roof, at some time it will need repair. This fact gives you a very large potential market for a roof repair business. You will need to study up on the various types of roofs in your area and start marketing your business to all building owners (residential and/or commercial) by distributing promotional fliers or by utilizing traditional advertising mediums such as newspaper and yellow page advertisements. You could also subcontract your roof repair services to home repair associations and clubs who already have an existing membership base that can utilize this service. Establishing alliances with residential and commercial property management and maintenance companies and providing 24-hour roof repair services is also a way of marketing your business.

The main requirement necessary to operate this type of business is experience in roofing repairs, or a staff of employees that has experience in roof repairs. Secondary requirements include liability and workers' compensation insurance, and a few basic tools and roofing safety equipment.

START-UP COSTS: The following example can be used as a guideline to establish the investment required for starting a roof repair service. You will need to add on liability insurance, which will depend on how much coverage you elect to purchase.

	Low	High
Service vehicle (used)	$5,000	$12,000
Tools and equipment	$1,000	$2,500
Business setup costs	$500	$1,500
Initial advertising and marketing budget	$1,000	$5,000
Working capital	$500	$1,500
Total start-up costs	**$8,000**	**$22,500**

PROFIT POTENTIAL: Will vary based on several factors, including the types of roofs that need to be repaired, the urgency of the situation, the competition, and how expansive you make your marketing campaign.

WEB RESOURCE: www.roof.com
Plenty of information on roofs, including a link to roof repair products, services, etc.

HANDYMAN SERVICE
★★ $$ 🚗 🕒 🌐

Handyman services have been around for hundreds of years, and will continue to be around for hundreds more, simply because there is a demand for the service and this type of business venture can make money. The main requirement for starting a handyman service is, of course, the fact that you are a handy "jack-of-all-trades" type of person. Currently, handyman billing rates are typically in the range of $30 to $80 per hour, plus materials and a markup on the materials cost. The service can be promoted and marketed to both residential and commercial customers through all means of traditional advertising mediums, such as the yellow pages, home maintenance clubs, newspaper advertisements, and flier distribution. The key is to be able to get to a job, assess the situation and needs of the customer in a timely manner, and provide a reasonable estimate of time and total cost involved. Customers like to have everything explained so that they are not surprised by the final bill. To make substantial money, you will want to hire reliable, responsible people who specialize in different areas, such as tiling, drywall, and so on. You then need to train each employee to represent your business in a professional manner. Often, students working their way through college, retirees, and other people looking for part-time work have specialties they can provide as part-timers for your business. Word of mouth can make or break you; as one co-owner of a handyman service said, "If you do a great job the customer will tell ten friends, if you do a terrible job, they will tell twenty friends." So make sure you (and your staff) do good work. Note: You will need a good amount of liability insurance to run this and many other types of repair businesses.

WELDING
★ $$$$ 🏠 🕒 🚗

The main and most important requirement to starting a welding service is that you must have a welding trade certificate. Providing you do, and have some welding skills, owning and operating this type of business can be very profitable. A welding service can operate from a fixed location or on a mobile basis. Establishing a billing rate for welding is accomplished in two formats. The first billing method is to charge per job, which means that you will give your client a cost estimate prior to starting the work. The second and more common billing method is to charge an hourly rate for welding services. The current welding rate ranges between $45 and $65 per hour. All raw welding materials should be marked up by at least 50 percent to establish a retail selling value. Overall, a well-established welding service can easily generate yearly profits in excess of $70,000.

WEB RESOURCE: www.amweld.org
American Welding Association.

HOME STORAGE SOLUTIONS
★ $ 🏠 🕒

There are hundreds of home storage solution products on the market, and you can profit by starting a business

that specializes in selling and installing these products. The business does not require a lot of investment capital to set in motion, and can be very profitable, as you can charge an hourly rate to install these products as well as add a markup onto all the products that are sold. Search the internet and directories for manufacturers of these products. Next, simply contact them and inquire about becoming a sales agent or representative for their products in your community. This is the type of business that, once established, can grow by word-of-mouth and referrals. It is also the type of business that can benefit from your "expertise." Rather than just selling products, if you can help people determine how to best utilize their space, you can become more highly sought after. Expertise in a field can typically increase the profit potential of a business as you can become a consultant and are called in more often.

ZINC STRIPS AND MOSS REMOVAL
★★ $ 🚗 🕒

If you are living in a wt region of the country, you can start a zinc strip and moss removal service, since moss accumulations on rooftops can cause building and structure problems. This business is very easy to set in motion. Simply put, this business venture involves removing moss from rooftops and installing moss preventative zinc strips and flashing. The fastest and most economical way to market this service is to design a highly effective informational flier explaining the benefits of moss removal and prevention, as well as your service. Distribute the fliers to homes and businesses in your community that have a visible moss problem. Providing you have included the right information in the marketing flier, it will not take long for the phone to start ringing and profits to start coming in. Potential income range is $20 to $30 per hour, plus a markup on installed moss prevention zinc products, such as ridge strips and flashings.

MOBILE PAINT SPRAYING
★★ $$ 🏠 🕒

Prior to researching information for this book, I did not even realize that there was such a business as a mobile paint spraying service. However, there is, and it can be a very profitable business to start and manage. The business, in a nutshell, is just as it sounds: providing paint spraying services to clients on a mobile basis. The best way to run such a business is to transport the paint spraying equipment in a smaller truck or trailer and paint items outside, utilizing portable walls that, when erected, form a mini paint-spraying booth. Mobile paint spraying services can be marketed to both residential homeowners and business owners by using all of the traditional manners of advertising and promotion. The following examples are just a few that can be included in your promotional brochures as items that can be spray painted.

- Fencing
- Garden equipment
- Handrails
- Metal roofing
- Patio furniture
- Signs
- Construction equipment
- Outdoor toys
- Wood siding
- Appliances
- Flagpoles
- Store fixtures
- Steel boats
- Trailers
- Concrete floors
- Parking lot lines

PROFIT POTENTIAL: The companies I contacted that provided mobile paint spraying services all quoted rates in the range of $35 to $50 per hour, plus the cost of the paint.

GUTTER PROTECTION
★★★ $ 🚐 🕐 🌐

Do you want to make $50,000 or more per year, and be independent within a week from now? If so, then starting a gutter protection business may be exactly the type of new business enterprise that you have been searching for. What is a gutter protection business? Gutter protection is a product that quickly snaps into place over the top of four- and five-inch gutters. Once installed, gutter protection allows water to pass into the gutter, but not debris, such as leaves and small branches.

The value of such a business is that many homeowners do not even realize that this product is available. To effectively market this product and service, you will want to design and distribute a promotional and informational flier, which should highlight all the benefits of having this product installed, as well as include your contact information. A demonstration booth, which can be assembled for use at home and garden shows and at malls, is a fantastic way not only to demonstrate the product benefits, but also to generate sales leads from potential customers.

START-UP COSTS: There are various brands of gutter protection systems available on the market, all of which are stocked at just about every home improvement and building center. This means you will only have to carry a small amount of inventory. Providing that you already have an installation vehicle, the business can be started for less than $1,000. Additionally, you will need a few ladders and basic power tools, such as a cordless drill and jig saw. It is also important that you purchase liability insurance whenever you are doing repairs at someone else's home or business in the event that your work is later considered the reason someone was injured.

REACH TRUCK SERVICE
★★ $$$$ 🚐 🕐

Starting a reach truck service is a fantastic small business for someone who is seeking to operate his or her own business on a part-time basis. The service is very straightforward: you purchase a used small bucket reach truck in good mechanical condition, and rent your services out for small residential and commercial building and structure repair jobs that are not easily or safely reached by a ladder. The possibilities are endless as to the variety of services you can provide with this type of equipment. You can include window washing, painting, gutter cleaning, and sign maintenance. You can rent your services to construction and renovation companies who need to install, repair or remove items from second and third floors of buildings that do not otherwise have good ground or working access. This kind of unique service has little competition, and you should have no problems commanding $50 to $60 per hour for your service. Market yourself through ads and other traditional manners and also by advertising on the vehicle itself. If you paint the truck in a colorful manner, you will attract attention while you drive around. Have handouts available.

FIRE AND FLOOD RESTORATION
★★ $$ 🚐 🕐

A small kitchen fire or a burst plumbing pipe are common occurrences for homeowners. Starting a fire and flood restoration service means that you may soon be able to assist these homeowners in repairing the damage resulting from these unfortunate circumstances. The main duty of a fire and flood restoration service is to go to the job site and carry out immediate, sometimes temporary, measures to limit any further damage to the home. These measures can include boarding up broken windows, covering roofs that have been damaged, and removing water that may have accumulated inside the buildings. The secondary duties can include repairing the damage to floors, walls, and the structure of the building. If you have expertise in construction, you may do the work yourself. If not, or should you have several jobs to handle, you will need to hire experienced subcontractors to repair the damage. The largest requirement in successfully establishing a restoration service is to build contacts with insurance companies and brokers, as insurance companies will authorize the repair work in 90 percent or more of all fire and flood restoration situations. Be sure you are insured. Quote each job based on the specific work necessary to rectify the damage. If you gain a reputation for bailing people out, so to speak, you can benefit from word-of-mouth referrals.

WEB RESOURCE: www.ascr.org
Association of Specialists in Cleaning and Restoration.

ATTIC ROOMS
★ $$$ 🚗 🎰

There are millions of homes in North America that have some usable attic space that could easily be turned into a home office, organized storage room, or just a small reading corner. Starting a business that specializes in the installation of small and basic attic rooms may be the business opportunity that you have been searching for. Providing that you have a good working knowledge of construction practices, as well as the most common types of home construction in your community, there is a good chance that you will be able to create the basic designs for such rooms. You can then custom build the room and install a pull-down ladder for easier access. You will charge for your time and for the materials used. It is very important that you take all safety measures into account, as well as making sure the attic is constructed in such a manner to accommodate the weight of building materials and furnishings. Prior to starting this type of home improvement venture, you should check with local building officials in terms of compliance with building code regulations. Also buy liability insurance.

MASONRY REPAIRS
★★ $$ 🚗 🕐

Calling all masons, it's time to put all of your job experience to work for you and start earning profits in your own masonry business. Starting a business that specializes in small masonry repairs can be extremely profitable. Many of the larger masonry companies cannot service smaller masonry repair jobs, as their overhead requires larger contracts to provide adequate cash flow. This fact creates a terrific opportunity to capitalize by specializing in the small jobs such as concrete step and sidewalk repairs, and the installation of stone and brick fireplaces. You can subcontract your masonry services to construction and renovation companies or, market your business directly to residential and commercial customers by utilizing traditional marketing and advertising formats. While operating a small masonry repair business may not make you a millionaire, it can provide a comfortable living with a yearly income that can easily exceed $50,000.

FENCE REPAIRS
★ $ 🚗 🕐

Fences are very easy to repair, and securing work for a fence repair service is even easier. Design a standard fence repair estimate form, leaving a blank area for the description of the repair to be completed. Once you have printed 50 or so of these estimate forms, simply start driving around your community in search of fences that are in need of repairs. The completed fence repair estimate can be left attached to the homeowner's mailbox with a business card and brief cover letter explaining your fence repair service. Aim to close 25 percent of the fence estimates that you complete, and I will guarantee that you can make more than $25,000 per year repairing fences, which is not bad for a business that can be started for less than $1,000.

CEDAR SHAKE RESTORATION
★★ $$ 🚗 🕐

There are millions of cedar shake and shingle roofs in North America, and the average lifespan of a cedar roof is about 15 years. However, if cedar roofs are restored prior to reaching their life expectancy, they can last for 25 years or more. The process of restoring cedar roofing is not complicated. The roof is first pressure washed to remove all accumulated moss and debris. Once this has been accomplished and the roof dries, a coat of wood preservative is sprayed over the entire roof surface. The average-sized cedar roof costs $10,000 to replace; however, the same cedar roof can be restored to give the roof an additional life of five or more years for approximately $1,500. This fact is what makes this such a good business to start. Not only can you save homeowners a considerable amount of money, you can also use this cost savings analysis as your main marketing tool. The equipment required for the business venture is a few ladders, a pressure-washing unit, and a couple of backpack spraying units that are the same type as those used in lawn fertilization. To keep start-up costs to a minimum this equipment can even be rented for the first few jobs, until the business is established. Current rates for cedar roof restoration are in the range of $1.50 to $2.00 per square foot. Additional revenues can be generated by providing clients with gutter and skylight cleaning options while on the job.

WINDOW AND DOOR REPAIR SERVICE
★ $ 🏠 🕐

The target market for a window and door repair service is owners of older homes that have wooden sash doors and windows. The reason to target these homes for this type of business is due to the fact that old wooden windows and doors require yearly maintenance, such as new putty, paint, and removal and installation of storm windows. The demand for this type of repair service will always be strong, as many of these homeowners would not consider replacing the wooden windows and doors because of the heritage value they add to the home's appearance. Potential income range is $20 to $35 per hour. You need to be familiar with how to repair all common windows and doors and be able to do so in a short time frame. If not, run the business, do the marketing, and find the jobs, then hire someone who is good at repair work. Don't forget liability insurance.

AWNING CLEANING
★★★★ $$ 🏠 🕐 🌐

More and more business owners are switching to commercial awning signs as opposed to the traditional box

sign for advertising their business. All of these awnings have one thing in common. They need to be cleaned on a regular basis in order to project a good image for the business they are promoting. This fact creates an enormous opportunity for an entrepreneur to cash in and profit by starting an awning cleaning service. The best way to market, promote, and gain clients for this business is to simply start visiting any place that has an awning out front. Have a brochure with your services and rates and make sure to leave it with an owner or manager. Explain the benefits of keeping the awnings clean and maintained, as well as the benefits of using your service. This may seem to be an old-fashioned and time consuming marketing method. However, if you set a goal of visiting ten potential clients per day and can close two of these presentations, you will then have 40 new clients in a month's time and be well on your way to establishing a solid and profitable business concern.

START-UP COSTS: The following example can be used as a guideline to establish the investment required for starting an awning cleaning service.

Power washer with all cleaning attachments	$1,000
2 10-foot stepladders, 2 small extension ladders	$500
Miscellaneous equipment, such as buckets	$250
Business setup, stationery, and marketing materials	$1,000
Total set-up cost to establish business	**$2,750**

PROFIT POTENTIAL: The key to a successful and profitable awning cleaning service is to secure steady clients that will be using your service on a regular basis. It is much easier to establish the business and generate a profit from 400 regular clients who use your service four times per year than it is to find 1,600 new clients each year. Remember, once a business is established (and this goes for nearly all businesses), 80% of the income will typically come from return customers and 20% from new customers. Assuming the average awning is $70 to clean, and you have 400 regular clients and you clean their awnings four times per year each (1,600 cleanings or about around 30 per week), the business could generate gross sales of $112,000 per year. Of course to do 1,600 cleanings, you would need to hire people whom you know will do a good job and do it in a timely manner.

SANDBLASTING SERVICE
★★ $$ 🚗 🕐

There are two approaches that can be taken should you consider starting a sandblasting service. The first approach is to operate a sandblasting service from a fixed location. The second approach is to purchase a van and operate the service on a mobile basis. The second option is less costly to establish. Operating a mobile sandblasting service will also enable access to a larger variety of sandblasting work. The cost to purchase the basic equipment is minimal, and the required equipment is generally available at industrial supply centers. There are many different types of sandblasting work that can be secured in every community. However, in the spirit of being unique and in an attempt to limit competition and seek a niche, pinpoint one particular sandblasting specialty, such as headstone sandblasting.

WEB RESOURCE: www.sandblastingequipment.org
A directory of sandblasting related links.

HARDWOOD FLOOR SANDING
★★ $$ 🚗 🕐

Many do-it-yourself homeowners are more than happy to stain hardwood floors. However, when it comes to sanding new hardwood floors or sanding off old finishes and scratches from hardwood floors, that's another story entirely. Let's face it, sanding hardwood floors can be a backbreaking task, not to mention the fact that it requires a certain amount of experience, skill, and ability to sand the floors correctly. However, with practice on your own hardwood floors, this skill can definitely be learned in a relatively short period of time. To keep start-up costs to a minimum, you can rent the required floor sanding equipment as needed until the business is profitable and established. Generally, floor sanding is billed on a per square foot basis, so you will want to check current rates in your local area. Successfully marketing a hardwood floor sanding service can be achieved by promoting your service to the end user or by subcontracting your services to local construction and renovation companies. Once the business is established, the owner-operator of this type of specialty construction service should have no problems in creating a yearly income in the range of $40,000 to $50,000.

HOUSE NUMBERS ON CURBS
★★ $$ 🚗 🕐

Here is a fantastic moneymaking venture that just about anyone can start for less than $100. The business is simply painting addresses in reflective paint on the road curb in front of the house. The purpose of having the house number painted on the curb in reflective paint is so that in the event of a 911 call the emergency personnel can locate the house easier day or night. Additionally, address numbers often become hidden by overgrown trees, shrubs, or simply because they are too small and hard to read at night. Having the numbers clearly and professionally painted on the curb makes life much easier for home deliveries, such as the Friday night pizza. The only equipment requirements to set this venture in motion are a set of good quality vinyl number stencils and a paintbrush. To market the service, simply design an effective door hanger marketing brochure that details all the benefits of your low-cost service, and start hanging them on every door handle in the community. This is the type of business that can literally be summed up as a numbers game, meaning the more door hangers you distribute, the more house numbers you will paint. Typically, this method of marketing will result in a two to three percent closing rate. However, given this valuable service is a particular fear sell, and because this service is also unique, there should be no difficulty in securing a five to ten percent closing rate from the door hangers. Make sure that there is no community restriction against such painting on the curbs. You might also approach tenants committees, neighborhood associations, as well as property management companies for townhouses and condos. Providing you secured ten clients per day and charged each one $20 for the service, the business could generate revenues in excess of $50,000 per year for what could be a part-time job.

APPLIANCE REPAIR SERVICE
★★★ $$$ 🚗 🕐 🔧

Stoves, washers, dryers, and dishwashers—repairing home appliances is a service that has been and will always be in high demand. There are many instruction courses available that can train you to become an appliance repair technician, and some instruction courses take as little as one year to complete. That's a very strong argument for starting an appliance repair service, especially given the fact that appliance repair rates are now in the range of $50 to $80 per hour. A friend of mine in the appliance repair business generates a yearly income of more than $100,000. This is not bad, considering he only has two regular customers, works from home, and has no employees. How does he earn so much money with only two customers, you may ask? Easy. Prior to starting the business ten years ago, his research into the industry revealed that most large property management companies did not have a full-time appliance repair technician on staff, even though these same companies would routinely contract for appliance repair services 100 times per year or more. The next step was easy; he simply designed a professional marketing presentation that explained his service and started to solicit all of the large residential property management companies in the area for work. To secure exclusive service contracts for appliance repairs, he provided these firms with a 10 percent discount on labor and would use refurbished parts whenever possible. Of the five residential property management companies he initially approached, two said yes, and after ten years remain his only customers. You could find a similar situation, working with community developments, condos, co-ops or project management companies. You could also specialize in working only on certain appliances and spread the word through marketing that you are the expert to call for air conditioner repair or refrigerator repair. There are so many high-tech appliances today, many with computers within, that it is important to stay on top of the latest developments in the appliance industry by reading and studying up on the new innovations.

WEB RESOURCE: www.nasa1.org
National Appliance Service Association.

BATHTUB REGLAZING
★ $$$$ 🏠 🕐 🌐

The popular colors for bathtubs in the '70s were pink and blue; brown in the '80s; white in the '90s; and now black in the new millennium. Not all homeowners can afford to replace their bathtubs just to keep up with new and popular remodeling trends. However, many of these same homeowners can certainly afford to have their bathtubs reglazed as a method of inexpensively updating their bathroom's appearance. Starting a bathtub reglazing service requires very little working experience, and the equipment is readily available through paint and industrial supply stores. The service is best marketed by establishing alliances with industry-related businesses, such as construction companies, contractors, and property maintenance companies who can utilize the service for their clients. The bathtub reglazing can also be marketed to end consumers via a display and demonstration booth that can be set up at home and garden trade shows to collect sales leads.

PROFIT POTENTIAL: It will vary greatly in this business and be determined by factors such as material cost markup, number of bathtubs reglazed, and operating overhead. However, once established, the business can easily generate an income in the range of $40 to $50 per hour and make an excellent part time business venture, provided you study and practice the art of reglazing.

WEB RESOURCE: www.otsm.com/links.htm
Directory listing bathtub refinishing equipment and opportunities.

CARPORT CONVERSIONS
★ $$ 🏠 🕐 🚗

Did you know that most carports share the same footprint size and dimensions? While this may not seem important to most people, it is very useful information if you plan to start a business that specializes in converting carports into garages. Due to the fact that so many carports share the same dimensions, it creates a terrific opportunity for the innovative entrepreneur to pre-design and build standard carport conversion kits that can be sold on a you-install or we-install basis. This type of business is ideal for starting from home on a part-time basis until the business is established and profitable. To gain customers, simply design a promotional marketing brochure describing your unique product and service, and distribute these brochures to all of the homes in your community that have carports. Prior to initiating this kind of business venture, check local building codes and regulations to ensure that your carport conversion kits will comply with all building code regulations.

CHIMNEY REPAIRS
★★★ $ 🏠 🕒

Providing you have basic masonry skills and experience, starting a chimney repair service can be a very profitable business to own and operate. Brick and stone chimneys all require maintenance in order to stay structurally sound and perform to their design specifications. The best types of chimney repairs to focus on are repairing or replacing damaged rainpots, rebuilding crowns, installing new base and counter flashing, and repainting and sealing brick and stone chimneys. The tools and equipment necessary for repairing chimneys are also very basic and include ladders, roof jacks, stone chisels, and a few hand tools. Providing you already have a vehicle, the business can easily be started for less than $1,000. Chimney repair services can be marketed to homeowners by designing and distributing door hangers and fliers describing your service. You can also work as a subcontractor, providing roofing companies and home renovation contractors with chimney repair services for their clients. The raw and manufactured materials required for chimney repairs are extremely inexpensive and available at most building centers. Visiting used building material yards can supply you with all the old and various colored bricks that will occasionally be required to replace broken or missing bricks while repairing chimneys. A chimney repair service can be a very profitable business to operate. There should be no problem in maintaining a billing rate of $50 per hour to provide chimney repairs, as well as a markup of at least 50 percent on all the material required for the chimney repair.

WEB RESOURCE: www.chimney.com
Directory listing links to equipment and supply manufacturers in the chimney industry.

GARAGE WORKBENCHES
★★ $$ 🏠 🕒

Starting a business that manufactures and sells garage workbenches requires very little investment capital and only basic carpentry skills. The business can be operated from home utilizing a basement or garage workshop for manufacturing and assembling the workbenches. The key to success in this type of manufacturing venture is to include as many custom design features as possible, such as tool racks, clamp-on vices, and locking casters that allow the workbenches to be easily moved. The workbenches can be pre-built and sold through retail accounts, or they can be manufactured on a special order basis. Make sure to approach new homebuilders in your community, as they can offer the workbenches to their customers as an upgrade option.

BASEMENT REMODELING
★ $$ 🏠 🕒

Launching a new business that specializes in basement remodeling is the focus of this business enterprise. The main requirement for successfully operating this sort of business is to have considerable construction knowledge and practical experience. The business can specialize in one particular type of basement remodeling, such as recreation rooms, or it can deal in basement remodeling in general. The profit potential for a basement remodeling business can be excellent once the business is established and has a good client referral base. To start out, you might work on finishing basements for a couple of friends and relatives, as well as your own. Take "before" and "after" photos, make a brochure, and start up a web site, featuring the photos. It is important that you are versatile and can handle the various needs of different homeowners. You will require liability insurance and can benefit greatly by having a good contact list so that you can call in electricians, plumbers, or any other experts or professionals if and when necessary.

WATERPROOFING SERVICE
★★ $$ 🏠 🕒

Starting a waterproofing service for residential homes means that you can specialize in one or two particular types of waterproofing, such as concrete foundations or solariums. Or, the service can focus on waterproofing solutions in general for residential homes. Waterproofing services can be promoted and marketed to both residential homeowners and property management companies by employing traditional advertising and marketing mediums and methods. The service can also be offered to renovation and construction companies on a subcontract basis. The key to success in this type of repair business is to have a good working knowledge of construction practices and the ability to properly assess water ingress problems. As this type of repair business is highly specialized, true professionals will have no problem in creating a business income that can easily surpass $100,000 per year. A great additional revenue source for the service is to also become an exclusive agent representing manufacturers' waterproofing products. Many of these types of specialized waterproofing products can be used in your business, as well as sold to architects, contractors, and the general public.

WEB RESOURCE: www.nawsrc.org
National Association of Waterproofing and Structural Repair Contractors.

STUCCO REPAIR SERVICE
★★ $$ 🏚 🕒

A stucco repair service is perfectly suited for the person with a minimal amount of construction knowledge and investment capital, but who is seeking to be independent by operating a home repair business. The tools and equipment necessary for this venture are readily available at home improvement centers, as is the material required for completing stucco repairs. Owners of this type of home repair service should have no problems in generating an income in the range of $30 to $40 per hour. Plus, you will be able to add a markup onto the materials that are used in the stucco repairs. The business can be marketed to homeowners by all traditional advertising mediums, as well as to home renovation companies on a subcontract basis.

ILLUMINATED HOUSE NUMBERS
★ $ 🏚 🕒

Starting a business that sells and installs solar-powered illuminated house numbers is not only a very inexpensive business venture to set in motion, it also does not require any special repair or construction skills, and you can be very sure competition will be minimal. The solar-powered illuminated house numbers can be purchased from various manufacturers on a wholesale basis and resold to homeowners. The business can be marketed by designing and distributing promotional fliers or by displaying the product at home and garden trade shows. The product can be sold via the internet or mail order to do-it-yourself homeowners who can install the product themselves.

While this business enterprise may not make you a millionaire, it is a great business to start and operate part-time from a homebased office, and can generate substantial extra income.

WEB RESOURCE: www.mahvelousmailboxes.com / accessories/ numbers/illuminated_house_numbers.htm

DRAINAGE REPAIRS
★ $$ 🏚 🕒

Prior to the 1970s, many ground drainage systems were primarily constructed from clay tiles. Over time, these clay tiles can be damaged by tree roots or collapse under compacted weight or corrosion. These facts create a terrific opportunity to start a new business that specializes in repairing and replacing ground drainage systems for residential houses. The business can be initiated on a small capital investment. Most of the equipment that is required for this home repair service can be rented on an as-needed basis. The materials to carry out drainage repairs, such as big 'O' perforated and non-perforated plastic piping, are available at almost any home improvement center. To successfully operate a drainage repair service does not require a great deal of special skills or construction experience. However, research on the subject of drainage and drainage systems should be completed prior to establishing the business.

CONCRETE CUTTING SERVICE
★★ $$ 🏚 🕒

Starting a part-time concrete cutting service is a terrific way to earn additional income and gain valuable business experience. Potential customers for concrete cutting services will include construction and renovation companies, homeowners, property maintenance companies, and driveway installation companies. Simply put, the best way to gain clients and promote the business is to start knocking on doors and soliciting for business. Be sure to establish alliances with plumbing contractors, as they often have to cut concrete basement floors to repair or add additional plumbing pipes, and they will generally subcontract out this work to a concrete cutting service. Current rates for concrete cutting are in the range of $30 to $50 per hour, making this an excellent choice for a new business venture.

VICTORIAN MOLDINGS
★★★ $$$$ 🚚

Restoring heritage and Victorian homes has become the major focus of homeowners and community leaders across North America. And the time has never been better than now to start a business that manufactures, installs, and sells exterior reproduction Victorian moldings. The business can be operated in the following formats:

- Manufacture, retail, and install reproduction Victorian exterior moldings and decorations.
- Manufacture and retail the Victorian moldings via retail accounts, the internet, and mail order.
- Manufacture Victorian moldings and decorations on a custom per-piece basis.

The options for this type of specialty business are unlimited for the enterprising entrepreneur.

START-UP COSTS: The major requirement to set this business in motion will be woodworking equipment. The following list represents some of the required woodworking equipment, as well as the current retail selling prices and additional business start-up costs.

Professional table saw	$2,000
Band saw	$1,000
6-inch joiner	$1,000
12-inch planer	$1,000
Drill press	$750
Radial arm saw	$1,500
Air compressor and accessories	$1,500
Compound miter cut-off saw	$500
Various hand power tools	$2,000
Sawdust collection system	$1,000
Miscellaneous equipment	$1,000
Fixed and portable workbenches	$1,000
Installation equipment	$1,000
Installation truck	$10,000
Total equipment costs	**$25,250**
Business start-up expenses	$2,000
Marketing budget	$2,000
Working capital	$5,000
Business setup costs	$2,000
Total start-up investment required	**$36,250**

The business can be started for less than the above-mentioned amount providing that you already have the required equipment, or you purchase good-quality used woodworking equipment.

PROFIT POTENTIAL: While the profit potential will greatly vary in this particular business due to a number of factors, such as local market demand and competition, volume of completed work, etc., overall, this can be an extremely profitable business to own and operate. Not only can you charge a healthy markup percentage on all completed products you manufacture, you can also charge installation rates which start in the range of $30 per hour and go up from there, based on the complexity of the work being performed.

DRAFTPROOFING SERVICE
★★★ $$$ 🚚 🕐 🚗 🌐 🪶

1. Save homeowners money.
2. Help the environment by reducing energy consumption.
3. Create a more comfortable living environment for homeowners.
4. Build a successful and profitable business.

To get started, simply employ current technology and equipment to first assess where the drafts are originating from and what measures can be taken to reduce or eliminate the source. You can then write up a document detailing recommendations and solutions. If the customer is in agreement and wants you to proceed, you can then carry out the necessary repairs. You will first charge for the assessment. Then, if you fix the problem, will charge for the work and necessary materials for the draft proofing repairs. These repairs could include increased insulation and ventilation, caulking, installation of door and window weather stripping, replacement of electrical wall receptacles to "draft-proof" versions, and even replacement of doors and windows to new high-efficiency models. Providing you have the experience and tools required, you can carry out these repairs. If not, the repairs could be contracted to a local qualified handyman or renovation contractor. Ideally, draft-proofing services are best marketed by establishing working relationships with utility companies, real estate brokers, home inspectors, contractors, and property management firms. Of course, you can also spread the word to homeowners through a brochure explaining what you can do—expect a lot of word of mouth business if you solve the draft problem.

MILLWORK SHOP
★★ $$ 🏠 🕐

Working on a part-time basis from a homebased workshop you can earn a tidy sum by operating a custom millwork shop. Custom millwork shops service renovation contractors and homeowners that are looking to restore or duplicate a piece of antique molding, handrail, spindle, or any other type of wooden ornament while renovating or restoring a home. Additionally, millwork shops often duplicate larger items for customers such as hardwood floor planks, wooden sash windows, fireplace mantels, and interior doors. The two main requirements for operating this type of business are woodworking experience and a well-equipped shop. Tools required will include joiners, planers, table saw, miter saw, band saw, drills, clamps, and all other equipment commonly found in a woodworking shop. Market the service by contacting renovation companies in your local area that specialize in restoring heritage homes. Also contact antique dealers and auction services, as both can also refer your service for restorations and repairs of antique building products and furniture to their clients. Typically billing for this type of specialized work will be done on a per-job basis. However, on average the fee will equal approximately $35 to $50 per hour, plus materials.

FABRIC RESTORATION
★★ $$ 🏠 🕐 🌐

Fabric repair and restoration is big business in North America, and securing a portion of this very lucrative market may be easier than you think. Get started by learning the trade. This can be accomplished in a few ways. You can purchase books and videos on the subject, take training courses, or you can even purchase a franchise or business opportunity in the fabric restoration industry that includes a full training program. Types of fabric repair and restorations include leather repair and dying, fabric repair and dying, and carpet repair and dying. For anyone entering this business I would suggest

offering clients a wide variety of repair and restoration services until the business is established and can be supported by repeat customers and word-of-mouth referrals. Advertise your services in local newspapers, fliers, postings on local bulletin boards, and through local furniture dealers. Additional sources of revenue can be generated by providing other services, such as blind cleaning, carpet cleaning, and furniture steam cleaning.

PATIO AND DECK REPAIR
★★ $$$ 🏠

Over time, Mother Nature can take its toll on your patio and deck, not to mention the chlorine from the pool, spilled drinks from your parties or cookouts, and other stains and discolorations. Some carpentry skills and a knowledge of deck finishes, paints, and wood deaning chemicals, and a few thousand dollars in start-up costs (mostly for tools and such finishes and paints) can get you started in the patio and deck repair business, which can be run from your home office. Fliers, direct mailings, and a presence at home and garden shows can help you build up dientele to whom you can offer a three-year service contact. Make sure you are up on the latest in waterproofing and UV protection when starting out. As is the case with the repair business, become an expert on that which you are repairing and you can do a good business.

NOTES:

_____

_____

_____

_____

_____

_____

_____

30
HOME SERVICE
Businesses You Can Start

POWER WASHING SERVICE
★★★ $$

There are many benefits for the person who is considering a power washing service as a new business enterprise, including low initial investment, proven consumer demand, and no inventory to warehouse. There are literally hundreds of items that can be cleaned using power-washing equipment. To get you thinking, the following are a few suggestions:

- Driveways
- Recreational vehicles
- Mobile homes
- Signs
- Awnings
- Headstones
- Cars
- Boats
- Decks and patios
- Construction equipment
- Metal roofs
- Bricks and siding
- Outdoor furniture

The key to success will lie in your ability to secure repeat customers. It costs 100 times as much to find 100 clients, as opposed to finding one client who uses your service 100 times. Focusing marketing efforts on compa-

nies and individuals that could become regular customers is the best approach, and potential repeat customers could include the following:

- *Construction companies.* Power washing heavy equipment on a regular basis.
- *Cemeteries.* Power washing headstones yearly.
- *Retail stores.* Power washing signs and awnings three or four times per year.
- *Boat dealers.* Power washing their land displayed boats monthly.
- *Trucking firms.* Power washing fleets on a weekly or biweekly basis.
- *Residential and commercial property management companies.* Power washing underground parking lots, decks, driveways, and patios on an annual basis for their clients.

Start-up costs should range between $6,000 and $15,000. Meanwhile, this type of service can be extremely profitable, and the only fixed overheads are a telephone, liability insurance, and transportation. The income level that can be achieved will depend on a great number of factors, such as volume of customers, overhead, and pricing structure. However, a well-established power washing service can easily provide the owner-operator of the business with an income in excess of $40,000 per year, after business operating expenses.

DO-IT-YOURSELF WOODWORKING SHOP
★★ $$$$

A do-it-yourself woodworking shop is a fully equipped woodworking shop that customers rent on an hourly basis to complete personal projects. This type of business is ideally suited to be located in any area where people are unlikely to have access to a home workshop, such as a major city. The business can be marketed to potential clients by initiating a direct-mail campaign and by distributing promotional fliers and discount coupons throughout the community. Approaching organizations and associations like sports clubs, retired persons organizations, and other community groups and offering discounts to their members can also be a fantastic way to market the business. Also market your service wherever woodworking equipment is sold. While this type of new business venture is very easy to start, additional business requirements that are of critical importance will include acquiring general business and liability insurance as well as installing on-site safety and first-aid equipment. One means of making more profits is by having woodworking classes and contests.

HOUSESITTING SERVICE
★ $$ 🚗 🕒

Students, bachelors, and seniors are all ideal candidates to start a housesitting service. Millions of North Americans go on business and pleasure holidays each year, often departing with an uneasy feeling that their unoccupied homes are prime targets for potential disasters, like burglaries and fires. To start a housesitting service, build alliances with travel agents who can refer or recommend your housesitting service to their travel clients. Be sure to compile a reference list to hand out to potential clients, as well as having yourself bonded as an extra precaution, to give clients the peace of mind of knowing their homes are well taken care of in their absence. Be sure to very carefully screen all potential housesitters to make sure they are trustworthy and reliable. Depending on various factors, such as looking after pets, rates will vary, but you can charge on a sliding scale, depending on the length of the stay and any other requirements. While a housesitting service will not make you rich, it can create a few hundred extra dollars each month.

RUBBISH REMOVAL SERVICE
★★ $$ 🚗 🕒 🌐

The first step in establishing a rubbish removal service is to ask yourself, who are my potential customers, and how do I effectively target my marketing efforts? While there are many potential customers for this type of home service, one particular segment of this group is certainly new homeowners, or people who are preparing their homes to be sold. Gaining access to this particular group of potential customers can come from building alliances with real estate companies and sales people to refer or recommend your rubbish removal service to their clients. Equipment requirements will include a truck, van, or trailer, garbage cans, and a few shovels and rakes. Make sure that other agencies do not have licenses to handle specific areas and also adhere to zoning laws and other ordinances that dictate where you can dump the rubbish once you've removed it.

ROOF TUNE-UP SERVICE
★★★ $$ 🚗 🕒 🌐

A roof tune-up service should not to be confused with a roof repair service or roof replacement contractor. Roof tune-ups are a proactive maintenance measure as opposed to a reactive measure, such as repairing a leaking roof. The average roof now costs in excess of $5,000 to replace, and repairs can cost as much as $1,000 to correct a leakage problem. A roof tune-up service is simply carrying out an annual roof inspection and correcting minor problems, such as recaulking a chimney flashing before it becomes a major leakage problem. Clients can include both residential homeowners and managers of commercial buildings. A great method to gain customers year after year is to provide clients with a one-year warranty on their roofs. The warranty would be provided to clients on the basis that should a roof that has been "tuned-up" should not leak within one year from the date of inspection. If it does leak, then the roof would be repaired free of charge. Warranty exclusions or terms and conditions should include situations that would not be covered under the warranty, such acts of nature like hurricanes or tornados, defective manufactured material, and damage caused to the roof by objects (such as a satellite dish) or unusual foot traffic. Creating a warranty for this type of service is an incredible marketing tool, as it gives customers and potential clients additional security in terms of the perceived value of the service.

PROFIT POTENTIAL: Charging customers a mere $125 for the annual roof tune-up, and securing only two roof tune-up jobs per day, can generate yearly sales in excess of $65,000. And best of all, almost all of that is profit. The operating overheads for the business are minimal, and only around 5 percent of the service charge will be needed to cover consumable items, such as caulking. Once established, hiring qualified subcontractors to service the accounts on a profit-share can substantially expand a well-managed roof tune-up service.

POOL AND HOT TUB MAINTENANCE
★★ $$ 🚗 🕒

There are millions of swimming pools and hot tubs in North America, and they all have one thing in common— they must be cleaned and maintained on a regular basis in order to work properly and be safe for the occupants to use. A pool and hot tub maintenance service can be marketed in all traditional advertising mediums. However, as a fast-start method to gain customers quickly, consider distributing fliers or coupons throughout your local community. The fliers or coupons should feature free pool and hot tub water safety tests for owners of these items. The safety test would simply be checking the water for toxins and recommending any corrective measures that can be taken to fix the problem. The true purpose of the free water safety test is, of course, to gain clients for the service on a regular monthly basis. Although seasonal in some areas, this business can be very profitable during certain months—in fact, if you can hire and train a good, reliable staff, you can enjoy some very busy times during the hotter months of the year.

WEB RESOURCE: www.epoolsupplies.com
Directory of pool supply manufacturers and distributors.

FIRE EQUIPMENT TESTING
★★ $$ 🚗 🕒 ⚖

Many communities across North America have regulations that require residential and commercial fire-safety equipment, such as alarms and extinguishers, to be tested and inspected on a regular basis. Providing that you have

experience in fire safety equipment testing (and possible certification in some areas), starting a business that conducts fire-safety equipment inspections can be a terrific, and potentially profitable, business to get rolling. Additional revenues for this type of business can also be gained by selling fire-safety products and equipment to residential and commercial clients, as well as installing the equipment that is sold to customers.

WEB RESOURCE: www.nfpa.org
National Fire Protection Association.

CHIMNEY CLEANING SERVICE
★ $$ 🚗 🕒

Anyone who suffers from fear of heights should skip this business opportunity. But for those of you who do not have "high anxiety," read on. Cleaning wood-burning fireplace chimneys and oil-burning furnace chimneys is very straightforward, and the equipment necessary for this task is available to be purchased in almost every community. Currently, chimney-cleaning rates are in the range of $50 to $175, depending on the size of the chimney and on how complicated the cleaning job will be to complete. To get business, consider building alliances with local firewood and oil delivery companies to initiate a cross-promotional campaign. You would recommend their businesses to your clients, and they could include a discount chimney cleaning coupon with their monthly invoice mailings that promotes your service. You can also do a direct mailing, or place fliers under the doors of all homes in your area with chimneys.

WEB RESOURCE: www.chimneys.com
Directory listings of chimney sweep associations and industry information.

HOME CONSTRUCTION CLEAN-UP SERVICE
★★ $$ 🚗 🕒

Starting a construction clean-up service not only has the potential to generate profits in excess of $60,000 each year, but the business can also be set in motion on an investment of less than $1,000. Each year thousands of new homes are built in the United States, and all of these new homes have to be cleaned prior to the new homeowners moving in. A construction clean-up service should be all-inclusive—meaning that the windows are cleaned, the entire house is dusted and vacuumed, and all leftover construction debris is removed from the site. This type of service is very easy and inexpensive to promote. Get started with your marketing by simply setting presentation appointments with all property developers and contractors in your community and giving an in-depth explanation about your construction clean-up service and why it would greatly benefit their company and clients.

MOVING SERVICE
★ $$+ ⚖

The investment needed to start a moving or a moving and storage business can be very large and will vary depending on the size and operating format of the business venture. However, a small moving service that specializes in short-distance residential moves can be launched for less than $10,000 and has the potential to generate an income of $30 to $50 per hour for the owner/operator of the business. The best place to start such a business is in a community with a potentially transient population, such as a college town or an area with many rental apartments. Put together a flier or brochure and get in touch with real estate agents, seek out "for rent" signs, look for landlords of apartment buildings, talk with directors of college housing and property management firms. The idea is to make sure people have your information and your business cards readily available when someone is looking to move and needs only minimal help, rather than an eighteen-wheeler. Make sure you have adequate insurance, and being bonded is certainly a plus. Before you start, draw up a list of what you will and will not move—or be responsible for—such as pets or certain rare or highly breakable antiques, and hand this out with your signed moving agreement. If you can gain a reputation for making moving a simple, stress-free experience for your clients, then you can generate a lot of business. To be successful, you need to be very confident in your abilities and know the best way to pack and move. Also offer to pack for $25 an hour and/or sell packing materials.

HOME SERVICE CLUB
★★★★ $$$$ 🌐

A home service club is a business or association that provides its members with a referral service for locating reputable companies that provide home improvement, home repair, and additional home services, such as lawn maintenance. Your next question is probably, why would homeowners and contractors pay a membership fee to belong to this type of club? Because each year, thousands of homeowners find themselves caught in situations or even scams where they have paid. in part or in full, for home renovations or services only to find the company that is providing the service has not honored their contract obligations, or the work completed has not been done properly. Likewise, firms that provide these home services would also be happy to pay a membership fee because they would have limited competition for the contracts, and the leads would be pre-qualified by the home service club. The basis for operating a home service club is simple. In exchange for a yearly membership fee, homeowners receive access to reputable contractors who provides an automatic 5 to 10 percent discount on all labor and materials, as well as written warranties on all work completed. Contractors who are members in the home service club, receive access to the membership base with limited competition—meaning that there are only two or three firms represented in each category, such as two lawn-maintenance firms. Additionally, the leads that contractors receive have been pre-qualified by the home service club.

Marketing a home service club is best achieved by using two different methods. The first is to set up a display booth at malls and home and garden trade shows to attract homeowner members. The purpose of the display kiosk is to provide potential members with information about the home service club, as well as to close the sale on site. Closing the sale on site can be accomplished by providing a value-added product or service like reduced first-year membership fees or a free monthly club newsletter. To gain contractors for membership in the club, simply set presentation appointments with the owners of these firms or hold a general invitation meeting and present the benefits of club membership to a large group of contractors at one time. Marketing a home service club can also be done by hiring subcontract sales consultants to promote and sell memberships. While this marketing method reduces the overall profitability of the company, it can provide a faster approach to establishing the needed homeowner and contractor membership base.

Once a home service club has been established, the business has the potential to generate very large yearly profits as the cost to operate the business is minimal. The business can be started and operated from a homebased office. Providing a home service club can be successful, and once all the operational bugs have been ironed out, this type of business lends itself perfectly to national expansion on a franchise or license-to-operate basis.

NONSLIP SURFACES
★ $$ 🏠 🕐

Thousands of people are injured each year in North America as a result of falling due to a slippery floor surface. This is fact, and starting a business that supplies and installs floor and surface coating can not only prevent a great number of these accidents, it can also make you rich. Trying to manufacture, invent, or produce your own anti-slip products and coatings is not the best approach to this business start-up as it will cost thousands of dollars in research and development. Instead, locate a manufacturer of these products and coatings and become their exclusive representative in your community, state, or even country. Not only will this arrangement enable you to devote time solely to marketing products, it will also cost you a lot less investment capital to get the business rolling.

To find and source manufacturers of these types of products simply enlist the services of the internet for research purposes or use one of the various manufacturer directories that are available to find a manufacturing source. Once a distribution agreement is in place with a manufacturer, you can begin to market and install the anti-slip products and coatings.

Potential customers will include all commercial and residential building owners and, more specifically, those who have the most to lose by a resulting accident at their place of business. Any product that can be effectively used to reduce potential liabilities resulting from a fall at a business place is the perfect product to be sold on a "safety precaution" basis, which is always a good business practice to pursue. Or like they say in the life insurance business, "If you do not already have this product (life insurance) it may already be too late." One of the benefits of becoming an authorized distributor and installer of a product or products on an exclusive basis is that it allows you the potential for larger markups to be placed on the product for retail sales purposes, especially if the product performs well.

DUCT CLEANING SERVICE
★★ $$$ 🏠 🕐

Cleaning furnace and air-conditioning ducts has become a routine home maintenance practice for many homeowners. Duct cleaning is relatively inexpensive, and the health benefits are numerous, as anyone suffering from allergies or other breathing-related health problems will tell you. Perhaps these facts are what makes starting a duct cleaning service such a good choice for a new business venture. A duct cleaning service can be set in motion on a modest investment and does not require a great deal of special skills or knowledge to operate, which makes this a very attractive business opportunity for just about anyone. Establishing alliances with related firms, such as heating contractors, real estate agents, and property management companies can go a long way in establishing a client base for a duct cleaning service.

WEB RESOURCE: www.extractionsystems.com
Manufacturers and distributors of duct cleaning equipment.

STORM WINDOW INSTALLATION AND STORAGE
★ $ 🏠 🕐

Anyone seeking a part-time low-investment and easy business start-up may find this opportunity to be of particular interest. Starting a business that provides residential homeowners with a service of installing storm windows in the fall and removing the storm windows in the spring is a very straightforward business to initiate. While this business will not make you rich, it can provide a great seasonal income of $15 to $25 per hour, with the potential for additional income if the storm window installation service also provides homeowners with optional window cleaning and repair services. The equipment necessary to get rolling includes a few ladders and basic tools, such as hammers and screwdrivers. Ideal customers for this service are owners of Victorian and heritage homes, as wood storm windows often do not open or provide air circulation in the summer, requiring them to be removed and reinstalled later.

BLIND CLEANING SERVICE
★★ $$ 🚗 🕒

More and more residential and commercial property owners are now using window blinds as opposed to window curtains, and this fact creates a fantastic opportunity to capitalize by starting a blind cleaning service. There are a couple of different approaches that can be taken for starting a blind cleaning business. The first is to remove and label customers' blinds and take them to a central cleaning location. The second option is to clean the blinds on site using cleaning tanks that can be mounted in a truck or trailer, or cleaning the blinds on site by hand using dusters and cleaning agents. Both operating formats will cost approximately the same to establish and it may be in your best interest to be able to do on and off-site cleaning. It is important to know the various blinds available and what is the best manner of cleaning them. As new products come out, it is up to you to research and learn as much as possible. Market yourself through fliers, both handed out and on local bulletin boards, to property management companies and at home trade shows as well as to neighborhood associations and stores that sell blinds.

WEB RESOURCE: www.omegasonics.com
Manufacturers and distributors of blind cleaning equipment.

HOUSE CLEANING SERVICE
★★ $$ 🚗 🕒 🌐

A good-old traditional residential house cleaning service is still a very good business enterprise to set in motion, as there will always be a demand for such services. Best of all, this type of service can be started for peanuts. The equipment needed to operate such a cleaning service is not costly and can be purchased in any local community hardware store. Currently, house cleaning rates are in the range of $25 to $50 per hour. You can collect as much as 25%, but be careful, if you get greedy your house cleaners may decide to leave and find their own work. The key to building up a staff of housecleaners is to be very good at finding work for your employees and making sure clients do not take advantage of them. On the other side of the business, you will need to market your service to homeowners, homeowner associations and property management companies by way of advertising and having a web

site with hours, rates, etc. Let it be known that your cleaning people are the best around; well-trained, bonded, and reliable. To back up your claim, do training sessions with your house cleaners and explain that in the service industry, being cordial and accommodating always helps. Along with your business license, you will need liability insurance. Once you get started, this can be a very lucrative business if you have good organizational skills and can keep a steady number reliable house cleaners working regularly.

WEB RESOURCE: www.stretcher.com/stories/01/010507b.cfm
Information on starting a house cleaning service.

ROOF SNOW REMOVAL SERVICE
★ $ 🚗 🕒

Every year thousands of building structures collapse under the weight of snow and ice, and simply put, there are only two ways to prevent this from happening. The first is to build all buildings with roof pitches so steep that snow and ice cannot accumulate. The second, and more viable method, (as the first will never happen) is to simply remove the snow and ice from the roof before it can accumulate and cause potential weight problems for the building structure. The best time of year to promote and market a roof snow removal service is in the summer or fall, as this will enable you to build a customer base prior to winter. Ideally, customers should be charged a predetermined flat rate to clear snow from their roofs. A written or verbal contract should also establish at what point the roof would be cleared in terms of snow accumulation. On the surface this may seem to be a business that cannot provide a very lucrative income. However, with careful planning and research, you will soon see that it is very possible to create an income in excess of $20,000 per snowy winter, which is not bad when you consider the business can be started for less than $300.

AIR CONDITIONING SERVICE
★★★ $$ 🚗 🕒 🔧

Calling all air conditioning service and repair trades people, it is time to stop making money for the boss and become the boss. For those of you who are worried about job security and income…don't. Simply pre-market your service and build a customer base prior to leaving your job. Design a presentation package that outlines your abilities and special skills along with air conditioning repair and service rates, and begin to circulate the package to potential clients, such as residential and commercial property management firms as well as directly to residential and commercial building owners. You may be surprised and encouraged by the results, as a small home-based repair business such as this can really compete with larger firms, especially when it comes to service rates, product markup, and service response time.

WEB RESOURCE: www.acca.org
Air Conditioning Contractors of America.

DE-ICING SERVICE
★ $ 🏠 🕓

Here is another great part-time seasonal business opportunity that would go hand in hand with a snow removal service, a roof snow removal service, or both. Starting a de-icing service is about as easy as a business start-up can get. The basis for the business is simply sanding or salting sidewalks, driveways, and steps to prevent people from slipping on ice that may accumulate in these areas in the winter. While salting or sanding trucks can cost a hundred thousand dollars or more to purchase new, it certainly is not required if you plan to focus your marketing efforts on owners of residential homes and small commercial properties for a de-icing service. A truck or trailer can be used to transport the sand or salt, and shovels or small mechanical salting machines can be used for spreading it. Aim to secure long-term repeat clients, and a de-icing service can potentially be a profitable seasonal business to start and operate.

PEST CONTROL
★★ $$$ 🏠 ⚖️ 🌐

Starting a pest control service does require some careful planning and a license in most areas of the country. However, for an enterprising entrepreneur, this can be a small sacrifice to make, as a pest control service can be extremely profitable to own and operate. There are various types of pest controls that can form the basis of the business, such as insect or rodent control, or the business can specialize in providing all pest control services. There are also various methods now being used to control pests, such

as chemical-based sprays and organic-based sprays. This will also have to be a consideration in terms of the types of methods your business will utilize. Overall, a pest control service can be a very profitable business venture and can easily generate profits in excess of $75,000 per year.

WEB RESOURCES: www.pestworld.org
National Pest Management Association, Inc.

HOME INSPECTION SERVICE
★★ $$ 🚗 🕓 ⚖️ 🌐

Providing you have construction experience, and you are also prepared to invest some money and time into an instruction course that will enable you to become a certified home inspector, then you can earn a very good living from owning and operating your own home inspection business. Millions of homes are bought and sold each year in North America. As a condition of sale, or subject to the sale, most of these homes have to be inspected by a professional home inspector to make sure the home does not have major structural or mechanical problems prior to completion of the purchase. Currently, home inspection rates range from $150 for a small and basic residential home to more than $1,000 for large commercial buildings. The business can be managed from a home office, and the monthly fixed overhead costs are minimal, making a home inspection service a great choice for a new business start-up venture.

WEB RESOURCE: www.nahi.org
National Association of Home Inspectors, Inc.

WINDOW WASHING SERVICE
★★★★ $$ 🏠 🕓 🌐

Window washing is the granddaddy of all home service businesses to start. Some of the reasons why are as follows:

- Proven consumer demand with millions of potential repeat clients

- Low start-up investment and low fixed operating overheads

- No special skills or business experience required, and the business can be managed from a homebased office with or without staff

- Flexible full- or part-time hours, no inventory to stock or warehouse

- Can be operated on a year-round basis offering interior and exterior window cleaning
- Potential sales in excess of $50,000 per year
- Unlimited growth potential and even franchise expansion possibilities.

Individually, each one of these reasons represents a good argument for starting a window washing service. However, when you combine all of these reasons, it creates a very strong argument for launching a window washing enterprise. Marketing a window washing service is simple. However, be sure not to overlook residential and commercial strata properties (a cooperative of owners, such as a condo building), as these corporations usually budget for window cleaning once or twice per year, and securing a few of these contracts can really beef up yearly sales and profits. Access to the strata corporation market can be gained by establishing contact with property management firms. These firms will indicate where and when window washing contracts are becoming available and the tendering or estimating process that will be used to award the contract to a qualified contractor.

START-UP COSTS: The following example can be used as a guideline to establish the investment needed to start a window washing service. If you already have a van for transportation and/or ladders, your start-up costs will be less.

	Low	High
Transportation (used)	$2,500	$10,000
Equipment, ladders, squeegees, buckets, etc.	$250	$500
Initial advertising and marketing budget	$250	$3,000
Business setup, banking, legal, office, etc.	$250	$2,500
Working capital	$250	$1,000
Insurance	$1,500	$5,000
Total start-up costs	**$5,000**	**$22,000**

PROFIT POTENTIAL: A large or a small window washing service can both potentially be very profitable. Additional revenues can be generated by providing clients with optional power washing or gutter cleaning services. A well-established and managed window washing service can easily create an income in excess of

$50,000 per year after all business expenses, prior to income taxes.

WEB RESOURCE: www.window-cleaning-net.com
Window Cleaning Network featuring a directory of window washing equipment suppliers.

GARDEN TILLING SERVICE
★ $$ 🏠 🕐

During the off season when you're not installing Christmas lights or removing snow from roofs, why not start and operate a garden tilling service, as this service is in demand and the business is very inexpensive to get rolling. The terrific thing about many small seasonal business start-ups is the fact that they do not require a great deal of investment or practical business expertise. And a garden tilling service falls into this category. The equipment needed to operate the business can be purchased new or used, or even rented on an as-needed basis to keep start-up costs to a minimum. Furthermore, a garden tilling service is very easy to market and only requires a little bit of marketing ingenuity, such as creating and distributing fliers and door hangers throughout the community promoting the service. You can also establish and build contacts with garden centers and landscape companies that can refer your service to their clients. This business opportunity is not guaranteed to make you rich, but when you consider the low start-up investment, a seasonal income level of $20 to $30 per hour is excellent. You can also make additional income by selling soil as well.

CHRISTMAS LIGHTS INSTALLATION
★ $ 🏠 🕐

A roof snow removal service was featured earlier in this chapter, and a good fit with that business is to also provide clients with a service that installs Christmas lights, as well as taking the lights down after Christmas. Even though millions of people decorate their own homes each year with Christmas lights, there would probably be millions more, if it was not for the fact that a lot of people simply do not have the time to install Christmas lights, not to mention the old problem of the lights being installed 20 feet off the ground. This is why starting a service that installs and removes Christmas lights is a great small business venture to set in motion. While this business is not guaranteed to make you rich, it can create an extra income of a few thousand dollars each year just when we all seem to need it the most. Since the owners of many stores and businesses also decorate the exterior or their facilities, you can also approach them. Many simply do not have time to do the decorating themselves. In addition, if you can buy some decorations at wholesale costs, you can sell them to make additional income.

WEB RESOURCE: www.bronners.com
Bronners has a wholesale section for resellers only where you can stock up on decorations.

BUDGET DECORATING SERVICE
★★ $$ 🚗 🕐

Starting a budget interior decorating service can be profitable as well as a whole lot of fun, especially if you like to spend your free time scouring flea markets and garage sales for the perfect, interesting, and unique home decoration items. The business can easily be set in motion on an initial start-up investment of less than a few thousand dollars and operated from a homebased office. Potential customers for a budget decorating service can include just about anyone seeking to decorate their home or office, especially for people or companies on a tight or fixed decorating budget. In addition to the revenue that is earned by providing decorating tips, guidance, and products, budget decorating instruction classes can be held for homeowners wishing to learn the trade secrets on how to find, and place, that perfect home decoration. Of course, you need to first take the time and make the commitment to learning and honing your cost effective decorating skills.

WEB RESOURCE: www.thebudgetdecorator.com
One of several sites with ideas on inexpensive decorating.

SKYLIGHT MAINTENANCE SERVICE
★★ $ 🚗 🕐

There are literally millions of skylights installed in residential homes and commercial buildings across North America. In fact, having skylights installed ranks as one of the most popular home improvements today. However, most homeowners never stop to consider how they will maintain these skylights once installed. That's why start-

ing a business that specializes in skylight cleaning and maintenance is such a fantastic new enterprise to get rolling. A ladder, some cleaning equipment, basic tools, a little bit of construction knowledge and comfort working in high places, is all you will need to set this money making service into action. There are a few methods to marketing the service. The first is to establish alliances with companies and other service contractors that can supply you with work or refer your service to their customers. These companies include property managers, window cleaners, and house painters. The second method to marketing the service is to simply design promotional brochures describing your service and drop off these brochures to every house in your community that has skylights. Either marketing method will work for one simple reason; skylights are generally 20 feet in the air, thus many people will have absolutely no desire to risk life and limb to clean or repair them. Don't forget to get insurance.

ODOR CONTROL SERVICE
★ $$ 🚗 🕐

Believe it or not, odor control and elimination is big business. Insurance companies and homeowners spend millions of dollars annually in North America to rid their homes and buildings of less-than-favorable odors. Fires, floods, leaky roofs, and pets are a few of the culprits in terms of the origins of these bothersome odors, and eliminating these odors can earn you big profits. The best method for marketing an odor control and elimination service is to establish working relationships with insurance companies and fire and flood restoration companies, as these sources can potentially supply you with more work than you can handle.

WEB RESOURCE: http://cor-pro-inc.com
Odor control systems.

CARPET CLEANING SERVICE
★★ $$ 🚗 🕐 🌐

There are nine major reasons why a carpet cleaning service is a great business start-up.

1. Low investment

2. Proven consumer demand

3. Great profit potential

4. No inventory

5. Homebased

6. Excellent growth potential

7. No special skills

8. Flexible business hours

9. Minimal operating overheads

As a fast-start marketing method to promote a new carpet cleaning service consider printing and distributing coupons featuring a free carpet cleaning offer. The catch: have one carpet cleaned at the regular cost and receive free carpet cleaning for another room of similar size. You can also market the service directly to commercial and residential property management firms for apartment and office carpet cleaning Before starting this type of business, make sure to learn the best, safest and least expensive methods of carpet cleaning since you need to provide fast, reliable, and quality cleaning to build up this kind of business. Also, you will make more money if you are able to clean all types of carpets from plush indoor to automobile carpeting.

WEB RESOURCE: www.carpetcentral.com
Directory listing carpet cleaning equipment manufacturers and business and franchise opportunities.

WIRELESS INSTALLATION AND HOME COMPUTER NETWORKING
★★★ $$ 🕒

The world of wireless comunications has arrived and more and more homes are utilizing wireless internet connections, opening up a whole new business for someone adept in configuring such networks. The key is to be able to set up the best locations in the home for wireless transmission and knowing how to install the wireless router and adapter and how to configure the system. You also need to know how to network home computers for maximum use. This means determining what the various computers will be used for and setting them up accordingly. For example, the home office computer and those used for homework and video gaming may be in separate rooms and share a common printer, but not have files accessible to other users. Password protection and a strong knowledge of home computer networking can get

you started and marketing yourself to existing homeowners and new buyers is advantageous.

MOVING ORGANIZER FOR SENIORS
★★ $$ 🕒

Whether it is down sizing to a smaller location or moving into an assisted-living facility, there is a need to assist seniors when in the stressful situation of moving. Typically, family members are thrust into the position of trying to arrange and coordinate a move which the often have little time to do. The needs and concerns of the senior are often lost in the shuffle. As a moving organizer for seniors, your job is to help make all of the arrangements and make the time to carefully follow the needs and wishes of the senior involved. Therefore, instead of a son or daughter packing up quickly and tossing out what he or she deems unimportant, you can help the senior determine what to pack and what to discard. In addition, you arrange the dates and times for the movers, help with packing, arrange with the superintendent or local rubbish removal service for garbage pickup, coordinate with charities for donating items, and most importantly give a senior some piece of mind during the stressful moving process. Some organizers even arrange the new facility to look as close as possible to the previous location to help a senior familiarize himself or herself with the new setting. This is a specialized job that requires great attention to detail along with patience and good listening skills. Let the family members know that it is easier to work with you, even if it costs some money to avoid the strain and angst between family members who are emotionally tied to each other and to things in the move. You can be objective.

33

IMPORT/EXPORT AND MAIL-ORDER

Businesses You Can Start

IMPORT/EXPORT MICROGUIDE

There are a great number of considerations prior to starting an import/export business or a combination of the two. However, the following six steps are the golden rule for successfully establishing an import/export business.

1. Research

Every new business venture has to be carefully researched, in terms of its ability to succeed. However, research is the single most important aspect of starting an import/export business, and the very likelihood of survival will greatly depend on the amount of initial, and ongoing, research used to establish the business, product line, transportation methods, suppliers, agents, legal requirements, and so on. Simply put, research is the backbone of an import/export business, and ongoing research will remain an important aspect of the business, even after you are established.

INTERNET RESEARCH SITES
- International Business Forum: www.ibf.com
- Trade Port: www.tradeport.org
- U.S. Department of Commerce International Trade Administration: www.ita.doc.gov
- Internet International Business Exchange: www.imex.com
- Import Export Coach: ww.importexportcoach.com

2. Supply and Demand

Research will establish the demand for a product, however supply is often overlooked in the research process. Consider the following:

Supply:
- Stability of foreign suppliers, backup, or contingency suppliers
- Stability of foreign government
- Stability of foreign economies and workforce
- Stability of foreign currency, and possible effects on pricing
- Supplier's ability to fulfill orders, and quality of product
- Supplier's ability to meet time lines and deadlines

Demand:
- Projected lifespan of product
- Increasing, decreasing, or stable consumer demand and acceptance of product
- Competition, locally and internationally
- Seasonal or year-round product demand, and demand beyond North American Markets
- Ability to manufacture the product within the United States or Canada
- The economic climate at home

3. Legal Requirements

It is very important to learn the laws, rules, and regulations in all aspects of the industry, as well as in the countries you intend to do business with, as not all countries have the same import/export rules and regulations. Furthermore, additional legal requirements can include:

- National and international employee laws
- Protection from legal liability
- Government product approvals
- Customs policies and procedures

4. Contacts and Alliances

Never overlook the importance of good contacts and related business alliances, especially if you are considering starting an import/export business. The following are contacts and alliances that should be established and maintained, nationally and internationally:

- Lawyers
- Accountants
- Transportation firms
- Import/export agents
- Marketing specialists
- Suppliers
- Wholesalers
- Retailers
- Distributors
- Import/export brokers
- Travel Specialist

5. Transportation

How will you be transporting the products? You need to consider this on three levels: locally, nationally, and internationally. Transportation to an import/export business is like a law degree to a lawyer, you must have a clear and concise transportation plan with a backup transportation plan for your business, otherwise you may be doomed.

Additional transportation considerations include choosing freight forwarder, cargo insurance, product packaging, and product lifespan (if applicable).

6. Profitability

Profit is not a dirty word; businesses must be able to generate a profit in order to stay in business and continue to provide valuable products and services to fill consumer demand. The gray areas that can arise in the import/export industry can make the profitability of the venture strained at the best of times. Transportation delays, union strikes, economic factors, and government and political unrest can all have an effect on the profitability of your import/export products as well as your business. Once again, the greatest tool you have in your business arsenal to help you ensure the profitability of import/export products and your business is doing solid research.

WEB RESOURCE: www.smallbizbooks.com
Business-specific start-up guides and books.

◆ ◆ ◆

IMPORT-EXPORT BUSINESS VENTURES: IMPORT AGENT

Do you have excellent and numerous business contacts in North America? If so, why not capitalize on your contact base and become an import agent? An import agent is simply a person who represents products from a foreign country and works as the middleman to get these products distributed to wholesalers and retailers. Once again, the key to success in becoming an import agent is having the ability to build a business contact base. Manufacturers and exporters from foreign countries will want assurances that their product will be receiving the best exposure possible in the North American market. Researching for products, companies, and manufacturers to represent in North America is very straightforward. A good starting point is to join the WTO (World Trade Organization) for research purposes, or start surfing the internet for import opportunities.

TOYS

As previously mentioned in this directory, it is possible to earn a six-figure annual income importing low-cost toys and wholesaling or retailing these toys for gigantic profits. It is not uncommon for a $1 toy purchased abroad to sell in North America for 10 to 15 times that much. Be sure to obtain exclusive import or export rights for the products you are dealing with as well as exclusive distribution rights, even if you intend to sell the products to national wholesalers, retailers, or distributors. Furthermore, be sure that the exclusive contract states the distribution contract can be sold, as this is goodwill that you have developed for your business and this goodwill should be protected.

CONSTRUCTION EQUIPMENT

Thousands of dollars in profits can be made on one single transaction in construction equipment. Look for depressed areas with a weak dollar. The same construction equipment that can be purchased in these slow economies at bargain basement prices can often be resold at a profit in countries with a strong economy or where the construction industry is booming. Entering into the construction equipment import/export industry requires a great deal of knowledge about construction equipment, as well as knowledge about the import/export business, plus patience, as one single transaction can take up to a year to complete. However, as with all well-devised business plans, the wait can be well worth the effort, as it is possible to make $250,000 or more per year dealing in used construction equipment worldwide.

BUILDING SUPPLIES

Building materials and construction supplies are an excellent choice of products to be imported or exported. Once again, following world economies and world news can be the basis of importing and exporting building materials. I have heard stories of common $100 exterior doors being sold in unstable "feuding" countries for as much as $1,000 each. Building products to consider include lumber, windows and doors, roofing material, construction sealant, flooring, siding, and specialty woods.

CLOTHING

Importing and exporting clothing is a terrific venture to pursue. The key to success is to source exclusive and unique apparel products that will have mass market appeal. Once again, the internet can be used as a fantastic research tool. Seek small independent clothing manufacturers from around the world as well as in North America and simply contact them concerning their policies in terms of import/export representation. Additionally, be sure to follow market trends in terms of popularity of

clothing types. See what is popular abroad and know that very often the "hot" fashion in Italy or France will be the "hot" fashion in the United States six months later.

AUTOMOTIVE EQUIPMENT

According to the Automobile Manufacturers Association, there are more than 130 million cars and trucks registered in the United States. Finding the right automotive products to import cannot only be the start to building a successful business, it can make you rich. As with any product that is imported for the purpose of resale for a profit, the product must have mass appeal and be in demand, or a demand for the product must be effectively established. Finding the right automotive product to import into North America may indeed take time, substantial financial investment, and careful research. However, once again, North Americans have a love affair with the automobile. There are 130 million potential customers in the United States alone, making this an importing venture certainly worth further investigation.

COMPUTERS

In North America we generally think nothing of replacing our computer equipment every few years to keep up with changing technology, or just to have the latest and greatest toys. However, rapid computer upgrading is certainly not practiced worldwide, as people in many different countries simply cannot afford to do so. This situation creates a tremendous business opportunity for an exporting business with a focus on used computer equipment that can be sold around the world. The best aspect about this type of exporting business is the fact that computer equipment in North America that is two years old has no value here and can be purchased extremely inexpensively, or in some cases can even be acquired for free. This same equipment can still command excellent wholesale and retail prices in certain countries that are behind in technological advancement.

FOOD

Every person on the planet needs it to survive, and until a new pill is invented to supply us with the nutrition we need, food will always remain a solid product choice for an import/export business. Regulations and health codes are very strict, however, about transporting foods and plants in and out of countries, so you need to research carefully what you can and cannot send abroad or import from other countries.

IMPORT/EXPORT CONSULTING SERVICE

Phrases such as "global marketplace" and "world business community" are just that—phrases. Generally these phrases are loosely used when describing internet technology and electronic business opportunities. Unfortunately, however, they have very little real impact on the average small business that wants to pursue importing and exporting opportunities. The reality is that there are a lot of details to pursue and, as mentioned earlier, a lot of research that needs to be done to enter the import/export business, and most small business owners do not have the time to do this. That is where an importing/exporting consultant comes in. He or she can provide solutions and programs for companies interested in doing business in the "global marketplace." Corporations need to know how to import or export, where opportunities exist, what the competitive advantages are, and the legal and cultural information about countries with which they intend to do business. Starting and operating an import/export consulting service will require previous experience in this industry, or a great deal of research to be conducted in order to be considered an expert in the field.

◆ ◆ ◆

MAIL-ORDER MICROGUIDE

Simply put, mail order is a means in which a product is purchased by a consumer and delivered to the consumer via the mail, by courier, or even by fax machine or over the internet. To initiate a mail-order purchase, a consumer has viewed, heard, or read an advertisement about the product that they are ordering, and rather than picking up the product at a distant location, they are having it sent to them.

While it might appear that the internet has all but eliminated the traditional idea of mail order through catalogs, guess again. Catalogs and fliers still result in a large buying market, often in conjunction with online businesses. The famous Spiegel catalog, along with catalogs from Sears, Lands' End, Chadwick's, Lillian Vernon, Victoria's Secret, and numerous trade manufacturing businesses, all generate millions of dollars worth of sales. Numerous other businesses are still predominantly mail order, even if they also have a web presence.

Why Start a Mail-Order Business?

Starting a mail-order business will always remain a popular choice for a new business venture, as there are many benefits to starting this type of new business enterprise, including:

- Low initial start-up costs, and high potential profits.
- Can be operated and managed from a homebased location.
- Few special skills are required, other than some marketing skills.
- It's a proven and stable industry.
- Very little regulation or licensing requirements, and flexible work hours.
- Great growth potential by way of adding additional products.
- Can maintain and build an inventory based on orders and not have to store a large inventory, as is the case with a retail business.
- Traditional mail order through catalogs appeals to shoppers concerned about buying online, particularly with the rise of internet identity theft.

What are the Advertising Mediums Used for Marketing Products to be Sold Via Mail Order?

There are various advertising mediums used to attract interest and produce orders to be shipped. The most successful marketing includes:

- Print advertising, newspapers, magazines, and trade-specific publications.
- Home shopping TV clubs and infomercials.
- Flier and catalog distribution.
- The internet, including web sites and advertising on other sites.

Why Sell Via Mail Order?

While almost anything can be sold by mail order, it is also a means of selling products that are unique and not offered in most "bricks-and-mortar" locations. In addition, you can reach markets that do not have access to certain products and people who are not internet savvy or comfortable shopping online. Products to be sold via mail order should have some of the following qualities:

- A large markup and profit potential.
- Easy and inexpensive to pack and ship.
- A product that serves a purpose with mass appeal.
- A product that people need but often never stop to buy, such as a home fire extinguisher. By selling via traditional mail order (fliers, mailings, and catalogs) you are bringing the product to the people, rather then requiring them to go out and look for it or search for it on the web.

Additionally, keep profit in mind. If you are selling a tangible product, do not try to sell a $5 item via mail order, as the cost to market the product will likely be more than the potential profits that can be generated by sales of the product, even in large volumes. A good price point for mail-order products is between $25 and $100, with a wholesale, manufacturing, or production cost of 10 percent to 20 percent of the retail selling price.

What Are the Steps Involved in Starting a Mail-Order Business?

Investigation

- Research the industry.
- Research the legal aspects.
- Research products.
- Research start-up and operating costs.
- Research profit potentials.
- Research the best marketing practices used, and taught, by mail order gurus.
- Research tax laws regarding selling to various states or countries.
- Research the costs of mailing a catalog.

Setup

- Create a business plan.
- Create business identity.
- Establish business management, warehousing, and a shipping location or locations.
- Establish product source, contacts, and alliances.
- Develop operations manual and business procedures.
- Establish shipping methods and payment terms, including credit card processing with banks.
- Research and find the best photographers, layout artists, and/or an art director to help present your products in the best light possible.
- Create and develop methods of advertising and advertising copy.

Action

- Research and develop a major mailing list.
- Secure some level of inventory.
- Place ads, print and send a catalog, fliers, and/or start a web site.
- Fill orders.
- Establish customer service procedures and contact information.
- Search for additional products and mail-order opportunities.
- Review entire business process and operating methods.

WEB RESOURCE: www.entrepreneur.com/startingabusiness/businessideas/startupkits/article37946.html
Article covering how to start up a mail-order business.

MAIL-ORDER BUSINESS VENTURES: KITCHEN ITEMS

Kitchen products have always been popular items to sell via mail order simply because they meet the criteria: small and easy to ship, mass appeal, and the potential for very large product markups. Many mail-order entrepreneurs have become multimillionaires by selling kitchen gadgets via late night TV infomercials. The key is to source or design the right kitchen products to sell. The internet can be of great assistance to source these types of products, especially from foreign manufacturers. Additionally, seek joint ventures with companies or individuals who may already have designed and developed a great kitchen gadget, but need an entrepreneur with exceptional marketing skills to assist them in bringing the product to market.

SEWING PATTERNS

Sewing patterns are a terrific product to be sold via mail order. They cost very little to produce and they can be grouped together and sold for fantastic profits. The best types of sewing patterns to market and sell are as follows:

- Sewing patterns for children and teen clothing.
- Sewing patterns for popular celebrity fashions.
- Sewing patterns for comfortable casual wear.

The sewing patterns can be marketed by placing advertisements in related trade magazines, by placing advertisements throughout the Internet, and on your own web page.

CLOTHING

From Chadwick's to Victoria's Secret, you'll find mail order catalogs selling everything from high-end clothing to sexy lingerie. The photographs need to clearly show the clothing items, list the styles, pricing, and sizes offered. Make sure to have a very straightforward returns and exchange policy that works without hassles, since customers who think they are a size 3 may really be a size 5, but don't like to admit it.

Customer service is essential in the mail order business, since this is a very trusting business. Consumers are trusting that you will receive their payment and send them a product in a reasonable amount of time.

Therefore, if the size, color, or style is wrong, they also trust that you will exchange it or provide a credit. Failure to do so in a simple manner will lose customers and garner a bad reputation.

HOW-TO BOOKS

How-to books, tapes, and software can retail for as much as $50 each and cost as little as $3 each to buy wholesale or produce, and that is what makes how-to books, tapes, and software such great mail-order products. Many publishers, authors, and companies sell master copies of these products with reprint rights, which means that you can place ads and receive orders before you even have to spend money on printing or production costs and inventory. Popular "how-to" titles have always been anything related to business, relationships, child raising, crafts, health and fitness, and self-improvement. Catalogs can easily be produced featuring many titles on these subjects, and with purchased mailing, fax, and e-mail lists you can be in the mail-order business and filling customer orders in a matter of weeks.

CHILDREN'S BOOKS

Books are a great product to sell by mail order since nobody has to try them on and they are easy to package and inexpensive to ship. Children's books are particular favorites because they can make it easier than browsing the shelves at your nearby bookstore. Books should be categorized by subject, fiction or non-fiction, and age group. Add short blurbs so that the buyers know what the books are about and offer a volume discount should someone be buying five or six at a time. You might also use email alerts to let people know when the next book in a series is coming out. Remember, once you get a regular customer, you want to try to maintain that customer, and since they won't "pass by your store" every few days, you need to make an extra effort.

VITAMINS

Mail order vitamin distributors can provide discounts and save shoppers the trouble of trying to find the vitamins they want at local stores. Working closely with vitamin distributors and adding on organic products can prove very successful with the right marketing approach.

Since vitamins aren't very "eye catching" or "sexy" as products, you may want to add some catchy names and utilize appealing packaging. In essence, by "spicing" up the product presentation in a mail order business, you can make up for the inability for consumers to see it on the shelf.

SPECIAL FISHING LURES

There are more than 20 million fishing enthusiasts in North America alone, and with that many potential customers, it's no wonder that millions of dollars of specialty fishing lures are sold by mail order every year. Fishing lures are best sold by creating a fishing lure kit that "guarantees results." The kits can include lures for all types of fishing and can be advertised and promoted by all the traditional mail-order marketing methods. Locating fishing lures to sell is very straightforward, as there are more than a thousand companies and individuals in North America alone that specialize in designing, manufacturing, and wholesaling fishing lures. To locate the manufacturers and wholesalers of fishing lures, use the internet, Yellow Pages, and manufacturers directories for researching purposes.

BUSINESS OPPORTUNITY GUIDES

By far the number-one selling mail-order product is anything related to business opportunities: guides, books, and success formulas sell in the millions every year by mail order. Business opportunity guides can be developed, or business opportunity guides can be purchased on a wholesale basis from the thousands of publishers that handle these types of products. The competition in this sector of the mail-order industry is very heavy and well seasoned. However, with careful research, solid business principles, and by developing or providing an excellent product there is absolutely no reason to fear, as this segment of the mail-order industry continues to expand and double in size every decade.

BUILDING PLANS

Building plans for homes, additions to homes, decks, and garden sheds are terrific products to sell by mail order, and you have two ways to generate revenues and profits. The first way to make money selling building plans is to create a book containing 50 to 100 building plans on various building topics (homes, decks, etc.).

The books will costs around $3 to $6 each to have printed in bulk and can easily be sold for $15 to $25 each. The second way to generate revenues is to sell complete blueprint plans from the book of plans, meaning once a customer has received the plans book they can order the specific blueprint they like from the book. The blueprint plans can include the complete materials list, as well as a scaled building plan. This method of marketing is terrific, as about one-quarter of the customers who initially ordered the plans will submit an order for specific and complete building plans for the project or item of interest.

GOURMET FOODS

Maine lobster, French mushrooms, Italian olives, and more gourmet foods are sold daily via mail order and the more rare and unique food items are, the higher the profits can be. One of the best aspects about starting a mail-order business that markets gourmet food is the fact that many gourmet food manufacturers and processors will warehouse and drop ship the products directly to your customers. This distribution system is fantastic, as you can reduce start-up costs by not having to purchase and warehouse inventory. Additionally, look to create a catalog featuring many types of gourmet food, dealing with a variety of food producers and manufacturers. Of course, the catalogs will be sent free of charge to all interested potential customers. Be careful, however, when shipping, or arranging to ship products outside of the United States. Consumables can be slowed down or not permit to pass through customs. Make sure you are up on the latest in customs laws and regulations

ASTROLOGICAL PRODUCTS

Charts, guides, and astrological symbol products sell like crazy through mail order, and while a few of you may be asking why, remember as entrepreneurs: "Ours is not to question why; only to supply, if there is a demand." There are thousands of manufacturers producing various astrological products; so finding a source to purchase wholesale items should not be difficult. Seek a product that must be updated and repurchased by customers on a regular basis, and once again, with astrological products, this should not be difficult to achieve.

VEGETARIAN COOKBOOKS

It is estimated that 5 percent of the United States population are vegetarians, and 5 percent translates into approximately 15 million people, which are a lot of potential customers for any business to focus on. Selling vegetarian cookbooks via mail order is a relatively simple business venture to start and operate. The books can be written and developed by you, if you have some writing and cooking skills or you can work with an experienced cookbook author. Another option is to purchase the cookbooks on a wholesale basis and sell to customers at a profit. Like many mail order products, there are thousands of publishers and book distribution companies that will gladly warehouse and drop ship books directly to your customers. Most of these companies work on the same basis—you market the product and receive customer orders, and the company ships direct to your clients and bills you for the inventory on 30-day terms, once credit has been established.

HEALTH AND BEAUTY PRODUCTS

Health-care products such as home remedy guides, health-care books and manuals, as well as products that assist the disabled make terrific items to be sold by mail order. In addition, products that bring out the individual's "beauty" can be very popular sellers.

A catalog describing all the products that you sell can be developed and distributed for a minimal cost. Due to the unique and one-of-a-kind nature of many home health-care products, the markups or profit margins can be fantastic, because there is usually little, if any, competition to compare the product to for pricing purposes. However, be warned that trying to develop your own health or beauty care products can be very costly and a disaster if they are not easily accepted. You are much better off marketing and selling existing products in this field.

MILITARY GOODS

Military goods, such as uniforms, outdoor survival gear, and training guides are fantastic products to be sold via mail order for the simple reason that there is always a demand for these types of items, and the supply is usually very limited. The best method to acquiring the products to be sold is to tender for a government contract selling the decommissioned goods or to purchase the items at the many auction sales that take place each year featuring these items. Once again, the profit margins can be excellent, as an item that can be purchased for $5 or less can often be resold for as much as $50.

CAREER GUIDES

Career guides have always been hot mail-order sellers. We have all seen the advertisements: "Hundreds of cruise ship jobs available. For the complete information package send…" These types of guides are very inexpensive to create and print and can retail for as much as $30 each. The following are career guides that traditionally have been great mail-order sellers:

- Cruise ship and airline jobs
- Construction flag persons training and jobs
- Overseas hotel personnel jobs
- High-tech careers
- TV and film production positions

ACNE MEDICATIONS

Teens and adults who have facial acne problems will spend any amount of money for a potential cure, and that is why selling acne medications by mail order is a terrific business enterprise to launch. Acne medications, acne home remedies, and guides to curing facial acne all sell very well. The key to success is, like most mail-order products, the product is secondary and marketing is king.

STAMPS, COINS, AND COLLECTIBLES

Selling coins, stamps and other collectibles by mail order is a very easy business to set up and run. The coins and stamps that sell the best and have the most profit potential are the average, not rare, coins and stamps that are from various countries, creating a mystery or sense of increased value. The coins and stamps should be sold in a limited-offer set or collection to maximize profits. Other collectibles, including sports cards and even movie posters also need not be those that are extremely rare, but simply limited editions of what collectors will want. Make sure to sell in minimum orders of $10 or $15 so that you do not have tons of $5 orders to fulfill.

LEFT-HANDED PRODUCTS

An estimated 5 percent of the world's population is left-handed, while an estimated 99.5 percent of the world's products have been designed and developed for right-handed people. Starting a mail-order business that specializes in selling products specifically for left-handed people is not only a great business venture to set in motion, but also a business venture that makes a lot of sense, given the discrepancy in the aforementioned numbers. Locating left-handed products to sell, such as golf clubs, should not prove difficult, as there are still thousands of manufacturers worldwide who specialize in manufacturing products specifically for left-handed people.

MAGNETS

Claims for the healing power of magnets range from curing cancer to helping arthritis sufferers rid themselves of the painful disease, and whether true or false, magnets sell by the thousands every day. Initiating a mail-order business that specializes in selling healing or health magnets is very easy to establish and only requires a business start-up investment of around $3,000. Currently there are numerous types of magnets available including magnets that you wear as bracelets, in your shoes, as a headband, etc. Locating a source for the magnets should also prove effortless, as there are thousands of manufacturers and wholesalers of these products worldwide. The best aspect about selling magnets by mail order is the simple fact that one health magnet can be purchased wholesale for as little as $2 and sold retail for as much as $20, or ten times the cost.

HOME SAFETY PRODUCTS

This is an example of something people need, but often do not bother to go out and buy. However, by sending out a mailer, you are bringing the offer to them. Fire extinguishers, smoke detectors, protective fences to keep young children from going into the kitchen, or too close to a stairway, and plenty of other such items are excellent to sell via mail order.

CHILDREN'S TOYS AND GAMES

A colorful kid-friendly catalog is a great, and simple, way for parents and kids to sit down together and make up a wish list for Santa Claus, or for a birthday or any other special holiday or occasions that merits a gift. While kids may circle everything in the catalog, you, as a parent, can find some good deals on popular kid favorites. Many large toy and game stores do considerable business through their catalogs, and you can compete with a catalog that offers some fun activities on colorful pages.

SPORTING GOODS AND EXERCISE EQUIPMENT

Athletes love buying the latest in sporting equipment for their favorite activity. And, if you can align yourself with manufacturers of items not found in most neighborhood sporting goods stores, you can score some big points. Home equipment such as pool tables and ping pong tables are good choices, with color photos and measurements, since these may not be items typically picked up while shopping. In addition, by including plenty of golf and tennis accessories, you can lock into the popularity of these sports—especially golf—and the appeal of buying something the player wants but never remembers to pick up, which could be as basic as golf balls. Keep your price points lower than the pro shops and you're all set.

GIFT ITEMS

From candles to soaps to picture frames, gift items are often easier to shop for from the comfort of your own home. Mail order makes this easy, especially around the holidays. Customers appreciate not having to stand in long lines to pay for items or having to carry heavy shopping bags full of gifts through a crowded store. By providing a wide range of gift items at reasonable prices, with some special discounts, coupons, and perks, your web site can be the hit of the holiday. Heavy marketing featuring the above mentioned benefits can pay off with good quality products and excellent customer service.

COLLEGE APPAREL

Yes, we mentioned clothing earlier, but this is a more specific mail order venture that focuses on getting the rights to market clothing with the logos and names of specific colleges, their teams, slogans and colors. Current students and, more significantly alumni, who typically will not find more than the football team caps can be a major market. If you can gain access, legally, to the alumni mailing list, you can build up a very successful business working with just a few of the thousands of colleges in the United States and Canada.

A POPULAR CHILDREN'S CHARACTER

This is not an easy business to start and typically will work best for those with an inside track to the entertainment business. However, if you can get the rights to market products of a popular television or movie character you can make a fortune, especially by sending out small catalogs to families. From the Sesame Street gang to Barney, Batman, Dora the Explorer, Rug Rats, and SpongeBob, children's characters have brought in millions of dollars in revenue. Having a piece of the action and selling dolls, toys, clothing, bedding and anything else with the right character on it can be a marvelous business until the popularity of character runs it course – by which time you may be ready to retire to easy street. The problem is that few characters have the potential and gaining the rights to be the marketing genius for that character is not easy unless you get in during the developmental phase.

NOTES:

54

INSTRUCTION
Businesses You Can Start

KEY

RATINGS ★
START-UP COST $$
HOMEBASED BUSINESS
PART-TIME OPPORTUNITY
LEGAL ISSUES ⚖
FRANCHISE OR LICENSE POTENTIAL 🌐
GREEN BUSINESSES 🌿

HOME SCHOOLING
★★ $$ 🏠 🕐

Thousands of parents each year in the United States are making a decision to remove their children from the public school system in favor of home schooling. This fact creates a fantastic opportunity for an individual with a teaching or education background to start a consulting business that assists parents in establishing a home-schooling educational program for their children. The home-schooling programs can be designed to specifically meet the educational needs of children at various ages and stages of development, as well as feature subject testing, educational field trips, and recreational and social interaction activities. The business can focus on developing and marketing home-schooling programs for children and parents. Or, the business can focus on in-home consulting on a one-on-one basis with parents to specially design a home-schooling program for their individual children. This type of unique consulting service is best marketed directly to parents who are presently home schooling their children or who are considering it in the near future. The best way to gain access to this market is to join home-schooling associations and utilize the associations' memberships or roster lists as a basis for a direct mail campaign for your home-schooling consulting business. The following are two such home schooling associations:

United States

National Home Schooling Association
P.O. Box 327
Webster, New York 14580
513-772-9580
www.n-h-a.org

Canada

The Association of Canadian Home Based Education
P.O. Box 34148, RPO Fort Richmond
Winnipeg, MB R3T 5T5
815-366-5342
www.flora.org/homeschool-ca/achbe

BALLROOM DANCING
★ $ 🕐

Ballroom dancing is back in style, and starting a business that teaches students this fine style of dance may be just the type of business opportunity you are looking for. If you've mastered your ballroom dancing skills, you can embark on this as an independent venture or in conjunction with a recreation or community center in your area. Students wishing to learn how to ballroom dance would pay a course fee and attend the classes on nights and weekends. Typically, these types of instructional courses cost in the range of $75 to $125 and are held once per week for four or five weeks in duration. The best means

197

of doing this is to find a studio space in advance (typically running about $35 per hour to rent) and rent it two or three nights a week for three hours at a stretch for classes and some private lessons. Renting a studio for nine or ten hours would run you no more than $350 per week or $1,400 for the four week course. If you have a total of 30 students in your three classes, at $100 per student or per couple, you would bring in $3,000 with a profit of $1,600. Even after spending $300 per month on advertising, including posters, fliers, and a couple of inexpensive print ads, you would clear $1,300 per month.

WOODWORKING CLASSES
★★ $$ 🏠 🕐

Calling all craftsmen and woodworkers. It is time to put your woodworking skills to work and start an instructional business teaching students how to use woodworking equipment and complete woodworking projects. The business can be operated from a homebased workshop or from a small industrial rental location. Woodworking classes can be taught in a group format or a one-on-one basis. Additionally, you can provide various levels of classes ranging from beginners all the way to an advanced course for the serious woodworker seeking to master the required skills to complete more complicated woodworking projects. Additional revenues for a woodworking instruction service can be gained by providing students the option of purchasing wood for their projects, as well as purchasing woodworking tools once they have completed the course. Your only other requirements to teach this course are being very skilled at woodworking and taking all possible safety precautions—and making sure your students do the same.

STOP SMOKING CLINICS
★★ $$$ 🕐

According to the U.S. Department of Health and Human Services, 25 percent of Americans smoke cigarettes. Even with the assistance of nicotine patches, gums, and pills, smokers often need additional guidance and support to be able to kick the habit. Starting a stop smoking clinic or counseling service is not difficult. The classes can be conducted in a group format or a one-on-one in-home consulting basis. The business is obviously best suited to be started by an ex-smoker, as they can better understand their clients' situation. The best way to approach this type of instruction business is to develop a course manual: "A Guide to Quit Smoking." The manual can be the basis of the stop smoking program that is offered to clients.

ICE SCULPTURE CLASSES
★★ $ 🕐

Who would possibly want to learn how to make ice sculptures? The answer is thousands of caterers. Providing you have the skills and abilities to produce ice sculptures and can teach other people, then you have overcome the first hurdle in establishing a new business venture that teaches students how to make ice sculptures. Ice sculpture classes are best suited to being marketed directly to restaurant and catering company owners by arranging a presentation appointment to display and demonstrate your service. The business does not require an operating location, as you can travel to your client's business location and teach the ice sculpting classes on-site. This is an inexpensive business to establish and there should be no problems charging clients $50 per hour for the classes. Just don't teach such classes outdoors in July!

RIVER RESCUE INSTRUCTION
★★ $$ 🏠 🕐 ⚖️

On the surface, starting a business that specializes in training students river rescue techniques may not seem to be a very viable business opportunity. However, if careful thought is given, you soon realize how important and profitable this business can be. Did you know that more than 4,000 people in the Untied States drown each year? The leading category of drowning deaths is fishermen who are swept away in moving water—often witnessed by others. Many of these deaths could have been prevented had the witnesses of these drownings been taught river rescue techniques. The business requires the instructor of the program to acquire a river rescue instruction certificate, which can be gained by successfully completing a practical and written examination. Equipment such as throw bags, ropes, and safety harnesses will also be needed to conduct the instructional courses. Most of the equipment is available for purchase at recreational outdoor retailers.

Potential clients for a river rescue instruction service include police and fire departments, sports clubs and organizations, fishermen, search and rescue teams, canoe and kayak associations, and all other outdoor enthusiasts.

WEB RESOURCE: www.nasar.org
National Association for Search and Rescue.

GOLF INSTRUCTION
★★★ $$ 🕐

Golf is one of the most popular sports and recreational pastimes in the United States, and millions of people hit the links on a weekly basis. If you have golf expertise and a lot of patience (since many hackers learn to improve their game at a very slow pace) you can start an instruction business that teaches people to play golf, or to improve their game. Most public and private golf courses have on-staff golf professionals who teach golfing lessons to members and visitors. However, this should not be viewed as a negative for starting your own golfing instruction service. There is a multitude of ways to start the business without being stationed or located within an existing golf course. Local golf pros give lessons from their own backyards or at driving ranges. The business can be started on a small capital investment and can be managed from a homebased office. In addition, you can teach the basics of the game to the young golfers of tomorrow by offering your services to schools for their after school activity programs. Golf pros charge anywhere from $40 to $200 per hour for a lesson. Typically packages of five or six lessons are sold, since one lesson is rarely enough to help or teach any golfer, especially newcomers. Therefore, if you charge $100 for a one-hour lesson, you might offer five lessons for $425. Additional revenues for this business can be gained by manufacturing custom golf clubs, as well as repairing golf clubs for clients.

WEB RESOURCE: www.spiritofgolffoundation.org
Spirit of Golf Foundation: Coaching and mentoring junior golfers.

STRESS MANAGEMENT COURSES
★★ $$

Between long work schedules and numerous family and community responsibilities, many people are experi-
encing increased stress. Without question, starting a business that assists people in learning how to cope with stress and how to avoid stressful situations is a business venture with an unlimited number of potential clients. However, seeking corporate clients for stress management courses may be a preferred approach, as you would have the ability to gain perhaps as many as ten clients with the same amount of marketing effort and costs put toward gaining one individual client. The business can be conducted from a homebased or rental office location, or the stress management classes could be held at the client's business or home location. One means of developing an instructional business is to create a manual for your clients to use and follow. By developing your own program, you become the owner of the information, and you should copyright your program and the manual. The key to creating stress management courses is being knowledgeable about the common causes of stress and being familiar with easy-to-explain means of relieving stress. Essentially, you need to become an expert in the field, which may mean taking some courses, doing plenty of research, and attending seminars. Once you are well versed in stress management you can run seminars and charge people to attend.

WEB RESOURCE: www.aboutstress.com
Stress Management Institute.

TRUCK DRIVING SCHOOL
★ $$$$ ⚖

The trucking and delivery transportation industry is enormous. To gain employment in this industry drivers must first acquire a special drivers permit or endorsements on their driver's license to enable them to become professional truck drivers. In most cases, the applicant must successfully pass a written test and a practical road test before acquiring these special driving permits. Make no mistake, the written examination and practical road test are difficult and, due to this fact, most people who are seeking a career as a truck driver enroll in a truck driving instruction program prior to attempting to obtain the required permits and licenses. Starting a truck driving school necessitates a very large capital investment to establish and operate the business. However, the profit potential is excellent for this type of business endeavor, as truck driving instruction programs cost as much as

$3,000 for each student to attend. Further revenue for this business can be generated by providing transportation companies with yearly refresher driving courses for their employees. The benefit to the companies for participating in this type of program is simply the fact that their employees can become improved drivers, which can reduce road accidents, missed work days, and damage to vehicles, which in turn, can increase productivity and yearly profits—and reduce insurance costs.

This is an opportunity best served by former truck drivers who are up-to-date on the latest information that will appear on the written tests and the road tests. You should also know all current laws and safety regulations that apply to truck drivers.

THEFT PREVENTION
★★ $$ 🏠 🕐 🌐

Shoplifting, employee theft, delivery trucks that mysteriously lose their cargo along the way, and the latest nemesis—identity theft—combine to cost companies billions of dollars in lost revenues and profits each year, eventually leading to higher product prices to help offset theft losses. Initiating a consulting service that trains business owners and staff how to prevent thefts and what to do in the event of a theft is a very good venture to set in motion, especially for individuals with a law enforcement or security background. The instructional classes can be taught in a group format that would include the business owner, management, and staff at the client's location during non-business hours. Many theft prevention firms specialize in very in-depth and costly theft prevention programs as a method to separate their service from potential competitors. A lower-cost, but highly effective theft prevention program could be developed and marketed to business owners who are on a restricted budget, such as owners of small businesses. This type of condensed program could be marketed at an affordable price—say $159—and could include two hours of on-site instruction for the owner and employees, as well as a theft prevention manual that has been specially developed for the program. A shortened instructional program such as this could be marketed by enlisting the services of a tele-marketing firm to promote and sell the service. Alternatively, designing and launching a direct mail pro-

motional campaign, aimed at small business owners and companies with less than twenty employees, could market the program. You can also network and meet business owners at meetings of the local chamber of commerce or gatherings of business association members.

SURVIVAL TRAINING
★★ $$ 🏠 🕐 ⚖️

What would you do if you were trapped on a mountainside, in subzero weather, with an impending blizzard approaching? This may not seem to be a likely scenario for many of us. However, to the millions of outdoor enthusiasts who take part in recreational activities such as hiking, skiing, and rock climbing, this is a very real and dangerous threat. Teaching survival training can be marketed directly to potential customers by establishing alliances with recreation-related businesses, clubs and associations, such as hiking clubs and rock climbing schools. Using brochures, posters, and fliers, plus in-person speaking engagements, you could easily spread the word to your niche audience. In addition to recreational enthusiasts, survival training courses can be offered to police forces, fire departments, and forest service employees. The main requirements for this type of business venture are that the trainers will have to be highly skilled and experienced survival training instructors, as well as hold a first-aid instructor's certificate. The survival training course could be instructed over a week-long period with the theory aspect of the course being conducted weekday evenings, and the practical aspect of the course held the following weekend. This type of instruction business should be accompanied by a survival training manual that includes all facets of the complete training program.

WEB RESOURCE: www.nasar.org
National Association for Search and Rescue.

HOW-TO BOOKS
★ $ 🏠 🕐

There are thousands of people who specialize, or have an interest in, a craft, trade, hobby, sport, art medium, or method of doing a particular task or job. And many of these people would love the opportunity to put their experiences, skills, and know-how into print and by writing a book on their subject of expertise. What is stopping these gifted individuals from writing a book? The answer is simple. They don't know where to start or what to do next. Starting a business that teaches people how to write "how-to books" is a terrific venture to put into action if you have a background in publishing or are an established writer or author yourself. Classes can be held on nights and weekends, enabling the operator of this business venture to manage a daytime business or work a daytime job. The how to write a "how-to book" instruction class should include details and practical tips on information such as popular topics for the books, writing styles and formats, publisher contacts, research techniques, and organizational and time management skills, as well as additional information and guidance to assist students in reaching their "book-writing goals." This type of instruction course is ideally promoted in conjunction with a community institution such as a college, recreation center, or continuing education program.

ACTING CLASSES AND PRIVATE LESSONS
★★ $$ ⏱

Acting instruction can take on many forms, as you could specialize in acting for television, theater, and film, or teach general techniques. Training classes and seminars could be held on an independent basis or be provided to students in conjunction with community programs or after-school programs. This type of instruction business is very inexpensive to establish, yet the income potential, even on a part-time basis, is outstanding. Along with being well trained in the field of acting, it is important to teach with the understanding that most people will not excel and become professional thespians. Therefore, you are trying to get your students to reach their highest potential and not aspire to some level above and beyond their own personal limitations. To increase visibility and encourage your performers, you could look into staging a production at the end of an 8-, 10-, or 12-week class period. You can earn additional money by selling the videos of the final class performance and by teaching those interested in learning more on a private basis. Also, if you have a "final show" you can sell advertising in the program to generate additional money.

START-UP COSTS: This should not be much more than rental of your teaching space and perhaps some handouts that you may need printed.

PHOTOGRAPHY COURSES
★★ $$ 🏠 ⏱

A photography instruction service can train students in both traditional print film photography as well as in digital-imaging formats. Courses could be provided for students from a homebased photography studio, or the business could be operated as a joint venture with a community center, adult education center, or after-school program. One marketing method may be to approach retailers that sell cameras and offer a free two-hour photography course for all of their customers who purchase a camera. Of course the objective of this type of free promotion is to have a large percentage of the students who take advantage of the free class sign up for extended photography courses and training (on a paid basis).

COOKING CLASSES
★★ $$ 🏠 ⏱

Does everyone tell you what a good cook you are? If so, perhaps you should consider starting your own business that teaches people how to cook. The business can be started on a shoestring budget, yet has the ability to generate a yearly income in excess of $40,000. If you can secure the necessary zoning and licensing, the business could be established from a homebased location. Alternatively, it could be established as a joint venture with an existing retail store that sells cookware and housewares or a restaurant. This option draws people into their establishment who will likely want to come back as paying customers, plus they get free advertising as you teach your class. There are so many different styles of cooking possible that you could give several courses offering various cooking styles during off-hours (for the restaurant) such as late mornings. You could also serve as a coordinator and bring in various chefs as guest speakers, thus raising the interest and profile of the course. Having a cook-off at the end of the classes could draw some great local publicity for your cooking venture as well as the restaurant.

Establishing a business as a joint venture with an existing business that is already successful is a terrific way to minimize start-up investment, capitalize on an existing client base, and share overhead costs. Joint ventures and amalgamations are without question the business trend of the future.

WEB RESOURCE: www.iceculinary.com
The Institute of Culinary Education.

GARDENING CLASSES
★★ $$ 🏠 🕐

Teaching "how-to" gardening classes can be a fun and profitable instruction business to start. The classes can be conducted right from home, utilizing your own garden as the basis of the instruction class. Successfully marketing this type of instruction business is best achieved by establishing alliances with local garden centers that can refer your "how-to garden" classes to their customers. Additionally, writing and publishing a gardening newsletter (or e-newsletter) featuring local gardens, gardeners, and gardening tips is also a fantastic way to increase business revenues and profits. Securing a mere 20 clients per week, each paying $50 for a day-long "how-to garden instruction course" will result in yearly business sales of $50,000. Of course, this is only practical in areas where you can garden year-round. In some locations this will be a seasonal business.

HOME RENOVATION CLASSES
★★★ $$$

Home renovations have become a national craze and a hobby practiced and enjoyed by millions of American homeowners annually. There are various approaches that can be taken when starting a business that teaches home-owners home renovation skills and techniques. The first is to establish an independent school and charge students a fee to learn a specific home renovation trade such as "how to paint." The second approach is to build an alliance or joint venture with a local building or home improvement center and hold the classes at the building center. The classes can be free, which are then supported by the retailer, or there can be a fee charged to the students for the class. In both cases this is a truly win-win-win situation. The students receive practical and helpful training to improve their homes and save money by not having to enlist the services of a contractor to complete the renovation. The retailers where the training classes are conducted receive fantastic exposure and a lot of long-term future clients. The innovative entrepreneur that establishes the home-renovation training program can capitalize on the building center's existing client base as a quick-start method to attract students, as well as utilize the building center's infrastructure and resources to reduce start-up investment and overheads.

FLYING SCHOOL
★ $$$$ ⚖️

The wide availability and relatively low cost of small prop and ultra light airplanes is fueling a craze for people wanting to learn how to fly a plane, and starting a flying school is the best way to capitalize on this craze. Without question there are a lot of hurdles to overcome, both financial and regulatory, if you consider starting a flying school as a new business venture. In addition to generating revenue for the business from training students, small airplanes and pilots are in high demand for the film industry and are commanding as much as $1,500 per day for supplying themselves and the planes for film work. Additional considerations for starting a flying school include securing the availability of a small local airport, as well as liability insurance, equipment, and marketing your lessons. Although this business will take some time to get started, an experienced pilot can make good money once they get the business off the ground, so to speak.

WEB RESOURCE: www.nafinet.org
National Association of Flight Instructors.

CAMPING AND HIKING CLASSES
★★ $$ 🕐

Camping is an outdoors recreational pastime enjoyed by millions of people across North America. Thus, starting a "how-to camp" instructional business that teaches novice campers and hikers practical information and tips on how to safely go camping is an extremely low-cost business start-up that can potentially generate fabulous profits. One of the best aspects of starting this business is the fact that the classes can be held outside, in most cases, without having to pay a fee or rent for the class location. The business can be marketed directly to potential students by distributing fliers and informational brochures through local retailers such as outfitters. The business can also be marketed through a partnership arrangement with community and recreation centers. For someone who loves the great outdoors, this is a very good low-investment start-up choice that also promises to be a whole lot of fun.

SKIING INSTRUCTION
★★ $$ 🏠 🕐

Downhill skiing, cross-country skiing, and snowboarding have become popular winter sports that are enjoyed by millions of participants in North America each year. Starting a business that trains people in one or all of these terrific outdoor sports is a fantastic seasonal business enterprise to set in motion. The business can be established as a joint venture with an existing ski resort or even an equipment manufacturer. Another option is to start the business as an independent venture with a mixture of in-class theory training and outdoor practical training. Once established, a well-managed small- to medium-size "ski school" can easily generate a seasonal income for the owner in excess of $25,000.

WEB RESOURCE: www.psia.org
Professional Ski Instructors of America.

DOG TRAINING CLASSES
★★★ $$ 🏠 🕐 ⚖️

Becoming a dog trainer and starting a business teaching people how to train their dogs can be both a personally rewarding lifestyle and a profitable business to operate. There are millions of dogs in North America and, while a great number of them are well trained, there are an equal number of dogs and owners that would certainly benefit from participating in a training or obedience instruction program. As the owner of a 90-pound, extremely strong and stubborn Rottweiler, I can personally attest to the many benefits that both myself and my dog Dana have received by enlisting the services of a professional trainer who ran both of us through the trenches, so to speak. The starting point for launching a dog training business is to first become a professional certified trainer. While this is not an expensive or difficult certificate to acquire, it does require you to have a love for dogs and a desire to assist dogs and dog owners

to lead a more rewarding and enjoyable coexistence. The training classes can be conducted from a fixed training location or on a mobile basis wherein you go to the client's home. In both cases the current rates for one-on-one training are in the range of $30 to $40 per hour, while group rates (up to six) work out to approximately $5 to $10 per hour per student. Selling books on training and obedience topics to clients, as well as specialty dog foods and equipment such as leashes and collars, can also generate additional revenue.

WEB RESOURCE: www.nadoi.org
National Association of Dog Obedience Instructors.

MUSIC LESSONS
★★★ $$ 🏠 🕐

Do you play a musical instrument, and play it well enough to teach other people how to play? If so, why not start your own business providing lessons to the thousands of people who take up an instrument each year. This is a simple business, as you can teach from the students' homes or have them come to yours for lessons, thus minimizing overhead costs. However, if you want to build a larger business and generate more profit, you can team with five or six other music instructors and run a music school. This could begin as a homebased venture, whereby you do the marketing for yourself and promote the other teachers for their music lessons (for a small marketing fee). In time, this could lead to an office location from which to run the business or a studio in which various teachers could provide individual lessons and classes. From individual lessons to a well-respected music academy, the opportunities are wide ranging and there is great moneymaking potential. Don't forget to include voice lessons for singers by finding some good voice teachers.

WEB RESOURCE: www.mtna.org
Music Teachers National Association.

SAILING SCHOOL
★★ $$$$ 🕐 ⚖️

Sailing is a sport and recreational pastime that is enjoyed by thousands of people across North America, with thousands more joining the ranks each year. Many of these novice sailors share a common bond: they have enrolled, or will in the near future enroll, themselves, spouses, and family into training courses to learn all the vital techniques and skills required to safely operate and sail a sailboat. Providing you have sailing experience and, better yet, a sailing instructor's certificate, then the business is very straightforward to set in motion and does not even require you to have your own sailboat, as you can provide sailing training for students who already have a sailboat. Generally sailboat instruction courses are comprised of two elements: classroom theory, such as basic navigation, and practical on-the-water training. Additionally, courses are generally conducted over a two- to three-day period on a full-time basis, and a two- to three-week period on a part-time basis. Securing only 20 to 30 clients per year can generate an income, prior to taxes and overhead expenses, in excess of $30,000 per year.

WEB RESOURCE: www.asa.com
American Sailing Association.

SCUBA DIVING INSTRUCTION
★★ $$ 🕐 ⚖️

Like sailing, scuba diving is a sport and recreational pastime enjoyed by millions of Americans, and like sailing, thousands more people are taking scuba-diving lessons each year so they too can enjoy recreational diving. The number one requirement for starting a scuba diving instruction business is, of course, to be a certified scuba diving instructor. There are many training facilities in the United States. However, the best and most recognized scuba diving instructors' program is one that is provided by PADI (Professional Association of Diving Instructors). The course will take a few months to complete and will cost a few thousand dollars. Once certified, scuba diving instruction classes can be marketed directly to potential students via all traditional advertising and marketing mediums. Or, the business can be partnered with an existing scuba equipment retailer or charter boat operation. The bottom line is that you can have a lot of fun, make a decent income, and really enjoy your work.

WEB RESOURCE: www.padi.com
Professional Association of Diving Instructors.

FIRST-AID TRAINING
★★★ $$ 🏠 🕐 ⚖️

Make no mistake, starting an instruction business that focuses on teaching first-aid training has the potential to generate profits in excess of $100,000 per year. Best of all, the business can be managed from a homebased office and started for less than a few thousand dollars. Clients can include construction companies, warehousing and distribution companies, and clubs and organizations. Furthermore, the first-aid courses are best taught on the customer's site in a group-training format, as this can keep the cost per student to a minimum while keeping business volume and profits to a maximum. Additionally, be sure to offer all clients yearly refresher courses for their employees. The first-aid refresher courses can be slightly discounted as a method of ensuring a 100 percent yearly retention rate. Marketing first aid training services is as simple as designing a high-quality presentation brochure and setting appointments with potential customers to explain all the benefits to their firms by having employees receive occupational first-aid training

WEB RESOURCE: www.redcross.org
American Red Cross.

LOG HOME BUILDING CLASSES
★★ $$ 🏠 🕐

Thousands of North Americans dream about owning their own log homes. If you have home building experience, why not teach them how to build such a home away from home? This unique business venture can be advertised in all of the traditional print media as well as promoted and advertised on the internet to attract the attention of potential students around the world. The requirements for starting this type of business are numerous and the investment is large. However, as a method of reducing start-up costs and sharing expenses, a possible consideration is to start a joint venture with an existing log homebuilder.

WEB RESOURCE: www.loghomes.com
Directory service listing log homebuilders and industry information.

FLOWER ARRANGING CLASSES
★★ $$ 🏠 🕐

Thanks in part to craft gurus like Martha Stewart, flower arranging and dried flower products have become extremely popular as home decorations, gifts, and as a hobby. Starting a flower arranging instructional business can be fun, and easily operated from home. The business requires only a minimal investment to get things rolling. Students are currently paying as much a $50 to $75 for one three-hour course, making this a potentially very profitable business venture. Building alliances with flower shops, garden centers, and retail gift stores is a great way to market the business initially, as these types of businesses can act as a referral source or even a joint venture partner, with the flower arranging courses being conducted nights and weekends from their locations. Securing only ten new students per week, and charging a mere $60 for the flower arranging course, will create business revenues of more than $30,000 per year.

DANCE STUDIO
★★ $$$ 🌐

Starting a dance instruction school is a wonderful new business venture to set in motion, as dance schools have been proven financially sound for decades. The business can focus on dance instruction in general, or on specific dance styles such as tap or swing. If you are not a dance instructor yourself, professional dance instructors can be hired on an as-needed part-time, revenue-sharing basis to conduct the instruction classes. The innovative entrepreneur who starts and operates a dance school can also increase revenues and profits by videotaping the instruction classes and selling the videos by way of mail order and the internet. For additional income, you can offer private lessons for the more serious dancers as well as selling tap shoes and other accessories. Holding dance contests and/or having students perform in a recital for friends and family is a great way to generate attention and market your classes. The potential to create a six-figure yearly income by starting and operating a dance studio is very achievable, providing sound business and marketing judgment are practiced and you have a good, easily accessible, safe location—plus insurance. By making lessons

fun and dance steps easy to learn, you could be the next Arthur Murray!

WEB RESOURCE: www.dma-national.org
Dance Masters of America.

EDUCATIONAL TUTORING
★★ $ 🏠 🕐

Many children fall behind or have difficulty in school keeping up with the fast-paced curriculum and over-emphasis on testing as (unfortunately) mandated by school boards and government policies. Tutoring is, therefore, a growing means of helping students of all ages keep up with their educational requirements and even excel. There is one main requirement for starting this type of instruction business; you have to be an expert in the field in which you intend to teach or tutor. Typically, that is why this business is best left to teachers, ex-teachers, student teachers, and professionals with expertise in a specific field (such as mathematicians or scientists) who know how to explain their area of expertise clearly and in a way that students will understand. Beyond that, the business is very simple to start. The business can be operated on a mobile basis going to the client, or a tutoring business can be operated from a homebased office with the client coming to you. Building a customer and referral base for this type of business can be accomplished by networking with school personnel, parent teacher associations, and advertising locally. Tutoring is a very competitive industry and to gain the upper hand requires explanation and disclosure of credentials firsthand, plus references. Current rates for a professional tutor typically vary from a low of $25 per hour to a high of $90 per hour depending on course material and complexity. If you are good—meaning you relate well to students and they respond to your teaching methods—word can spread quickly, as this is very much a word of mouth business.

WEB RESOURCE: www.ntatutor.org
National Tutoring Association.

STAINED GLASS
★★ 🏠 🕐

Launching a business that focuses on teaching people how to make stained-glass items, such as lampshades and sun catchers, is a terrific low-investment business opportunity to initiate. The business and instruction classes can be operated from a homebased workshop, or the classes can be provided for students and operated in conjunction with a community institution, such as a college, recreation center, or community center. One of the main requirements for starting a business teaching others how to make stained-glass products is, of course, being skilled at the craft yourself and having patience when teaching novices. Beyond that, the business is very simple to start. Selling students the materials required to make the stained-glass items, such as art glass, cutters, and glass grinders, can earn additional income.

WEB RESOURCE: www.stainedglass.org
Stained Glass Association of America.

AUTO MAINTENANCE COURSE
★★ $$ 🏠 🕐 ⚖️

Calling all certified mechanics! Put your automobile repair skills to work for you and start a business that teaches students how to do general maintenance on their cars and trucks. The auto maintenance courses could be conducted in association with a community or educational facility, such as a community college, or on an independent basis by leasing a small work and training space. Course instruction can include how to change your oil, change a flat tire, and carry out regular brake and steering checks, as well as any other small automotive related maintenance tasks. Providing you can secure ten paying clients per week for a three-hour auto maintenance class and charge the students $50 each, this great part-time business would generate sales in excess of $2,000 per month.

MARTIAL ARTS
★★★ $$$ ⚖️ 🌎 🕐

The martial arts as a sport is second only to golf in terms of number of new participants over the past decade. Typically, a martial arts school will focus on one particular type of training such as kung fu or kick boxing. A martial arts school can be an expensive new business venture to set in motion. However, the average cost now paid by a student per year for martial arts training is in excess of $600. Providing the business could train 200 students per year, this would result in revenues exceeding $120,000, based on an average of $600 per year per student. Needless to say, this type of specialized instruction can be very financially lucrative, provided you are an expert in the field (such as a black belt in karate) or hire an expert or two to teach classes while you handle the business. In addition to group training, one-on-one martial arts training is also becoming popular for the serious student who is prepared to pay $40 or $50 per hour or more for an intensive training session. Make sure you cover all safety precautions and have significant liability insurance before starting such a business.

WEB RESOURCE: www.mararts.org
United States Martial Arts Association.

JEWELRY MAKING INSTRUCTION
★★ $$ 🏠 🕐

Starting a jewelry making instruction business could prove to be very profitable and fun. To keep initial start-up costs to a minimum, build alliances with local businesses such as craft stores, clothing retailers, and community centers. By establishing these alliances, you can hold the jewelry instruction classes on the site of your new business partners and split the sales revenues with the owners of these businesses—not to mention the fact that this will also provide you with the opportunity to capitalize on the business's existing customer base to attract new students for the jewelry making classes. A mere four classes per week with ten students paying $20 each will create business revenues in excess of $40,000 per year.

DRIVING SCHOOL
★★ $$$$ 🏠 ⚖️ 🌎

Training new drivers how to be good drivers is a multimillion-dollar industry in the United States. The main requirement for starting a driver training school is to be, or have on staff, professional driving instructors. Many driving instruction schools now subcontract out the driving instruction to trained professionals who supply their own automobiles, insurance, and gas in exchange for a percentage of the revenue paid by their students. Using this type of operating format can be a terrific way to reduce the overall start-up and operating costs for the business. Currently, revenue split rates range from a low of 60 percent for the instructor and 40 percent for the driving school to 75 percent for the instructor and 25 percent for the school. This is a very competitive industry and the only way to succeed is to secure contracts with high schools providing driver education courses for students. The contracts for this service are usually awarded on a tender-for-service basis every one to three years.

WEB RESOURCE: www.driving.org
The Driving Instructors Association.

SEWING CLASSES
★★ $$ 🏠 🕐

A sewing instruction business can be set in motion for less than $5,000 and has the potential to easily create an income in the range of $25 to $35 per hour or more. Sewing classes can be marketed directly to students via all traditional means of advertising. You can also initiate a joint venture with a local fabric store to hold the classes evenings and weekends or even as a joint venture with a community or recreation center. Joint ventures are a fantastic way to reduce the overall start-up capital to open a business, as well as capitalize on the partner's existing customer base. Overall, it's a great little business that can generate additional revenue by selling sewing patterns to students, as well as by mail order.

WINDSURFING SCHOOL
★ $$ 🕐

The popularity of windsurfing is again on the rise. This is mainly due to the fact that once the equipment and training have been paid for, windsurfing is a very inexpensive sport to participate in, not to mention the thrill of gliding over waves at 30 miles per hour. The first step in starting a windsurfing training school is to be a windsurfer or to hire professional instruction staff on a revenue-split basis. The business is best established in a busy tourist area: one that preferably draws year-round crowds to the beach. In addition to the equipment requirements, it is well advised to seek out liability insurance, due to the nature of the sport and the potential for serious accidents. With the right training location, additional revenues can be generated by renting windsurfing boards to tourists on an hourly and half-day basis.

Overall, this can be a great new business venture to establish, providing you have the right location. The profit potential for a seasonal wind surfing training school is in the range of $20,000 per season, while a year-round training school could easily generate profits two to three times that number. The revenue generated by the rental aspect of the business could add an additional $10,000 to $15,000 per year, bringing the total potential profits for a year-round operation to $50,000 or more.

WEB RESOURCE: www.pwaworldtour.com
Professional Windsurfers Association.

BUSINESS START-UP INSTRUCTION
★★ $$$ 🏠 🕐 🌏

A recent survey conducted by the U.S. government indicated that a full 40 percent of American adults wanted to start and own a business. With 100 million potential clients waiting, there has never been a better time than now to start a business that trains people how to start and run a business. The business start-up instruction courses could be conducted over a week-long period and the classes could be held at night. Of critical importance for this type of instruction business is to design and develop a course manual that will be used for training purposes, as well as form the backbone of the business. To expand the business beyond any particular geographical area, consider broadcasting the training classes over your web site. This would enable potential clients and students to partake in the business start-up training courses from around the country, as well as increase the profit for the business. The only requirement is that you have a background in, and/or extensive knowledge of, how to start up a business. This includes an understanding of how businesses are financed, the legal requirements for each business type, and the research necessary for a start-up —particularly in conjunction with determining the amount of competition and the ability to establish a market share. Also you must know how to write a business plan and be able to clearly explain its structure and the benefits. For additional income you could sell books (such as this one) and videos on starting a business.

WEB RESOURCE: www.sba.gov/starting_business
United States Small Business Administration: leading resource on opening a small business.

FASHION DESIGN SCHOOL
★ $$$$

Starting a fashion school is very straightforward. However, there certainly is one main requirement: you or your instructors must be fashion designers! There are many approaches that can be taken when considering a fashion school as a new business venture. The first approach is to start a full-service fashion school that is recognized by fashion designers and clothing manufacturers. A less costly and less complicated approach to starting a fashion design school is to target students who have an interest in starting their own fashion label or clothing manufacturing business. The training provided could be over a shorter period of time and could be less costly than traditional fashion school courses. Additional revenues can be created by selling the fashions designed by the students through your own fashion shows, as well as over the internet via your own web site. This type of business is costly to establish. However, the potential to generate a six-figure yearly income is certainly within reach for the hard-working entrepreneur.

PUBLIC SPEAKING INSTRUCTION
★★ $$ 🕐

Public speaking is an art, and unfortunately many business owners and corporate professionals do not realize the importance of being able to project a positive image of their business and themselves, whether it is speaking in front of one person or a group of 500 people. Starting an instruction business that specializes in training business owners, managers, and employees to become effective public speakers is a great new business venture to set in motion. The best way to market this type of instruction service is to design a complete marketing presentation and distribute the presentation to the most likely potential clients, and include a CD or DVD. A good segment of the market to focus on is businesses and companies with medium to large sales forces. Furthermore, the training courses can be conducted right at the client's location, eliminating the need for costly office rental. Aim to secure three clients per week for a specialized half-day public speaking course, and you can be well on your way to earning $100,000 per year. A great way to market such a course is by wowing them with your own expertise. Try to book short speaking engagements in which you discuss the power of being a good speaker in a well-honed presentation that is both informative and entertaining, and leaves your audience wanting to learn more. Private coaching before major presentations can also generate additional income, as can selling books, videos, and CDs and DVDs of instruction for specific situations.

WEB RESOURCE: www.toastmasters.org
Toastmasters International: Worldwide public speaking organization.

FIREARMS TRAINING
★★ $$ 🕐 ⚖️

As the saying goes, "Guns do not kill people, people kill people." This clearly indicates why a person who owns a gun should learn how to safely use, store, and maintain the gun. You must be a certified instructor in order to provide clients with firearms training, thus this will be the first step you need to take to start the business if you are not already a certified instructor. Marketing your firearms training courses is best accomplished by building an alliance with a gun club or shooting range. You can also hold free seminars in your community with a "gun safety" theme and discussion. These types of seminars are a terrific way to collect leads from potential customers interested in participating in a complete in-depth firearms training and safety program.

CUSTOMER SERVICE TRAINING
★★★ $$ 🏢 🕐 🌐

In an increasingly impersonalized world, there is a growing concern about customer service. The public has made it clear that they will no longer tolerate businesses that treat customers poorly, as evidenced by numerous reports to local Better Business Bureaus and an increasing number of complaints to management and senior corporate officials. Rude and poorly trained employees cost companies millions of dollars each year in potential future business and referrals. The companies that benefit from this type of training are the ones that take proactive measures to ensure their staff has received proper customer service and appreciation training. You can earn an incredible income by starting a consulting service that provides companies, organizations, and associations with various customer service training programs that have been specifically designed to meet their individual needs and that target how to become a good, helpful, and customer-appreciative employee. To get started, decide if your instruction program will focus on one specific industry for training, such as food servers, or be a general instruction program that trains all service employees, regardless of the industry or position they work in. Once you have chosen an operating format, the next step is to design, and or utilize, specific programs that are well researched and proven to be effective. You might then design a short training manual (which can be in CD or DVD form) to accompany the course. A less expensive approach is to have your data on a password protected web site available to course members. This eliminates the potentially high cost of getting the materials printed. It also limits the potential that others will copy your course materials and sidestep taking your course. The program (and accompanying manual) should be designed in such a way that it is a comprehensive "A to Z" approach that covers all the bases in customer service and customer appreciation training and can be easily and quickly customized to meet individual client needs. The training programs can take place at client locations during non-business hours in a group or one-on-one format.

A prerequisite for starting this type of business is to be a customer service specialist. While this does not mean that you must possess a specific certificate, it does mean that you must possess a great deal of customer service experience, common sense, and a creative imagination to develop role playing situations for the training purposes. Market the service by joining local business groups to network for clients, as well as build alliances with other types of employee training services that do not presently provide clients with customer service training options. Fees for the service will be in the range of $40 to $100 per hour.

SELF-DEFENSE TRAINING
★★ $$ 🏚 🕐 🌐

Self-defense training is a booming multimillion dollar industry in North America, and this business opportunity will appeal to anyone with a military or police service training background. Once again, providing that you are qualified to teach self-defense, an excellent income can be earned by doing just that. The classes can be conducted in a one-on-one basis at clients' locations, or alternately you can offer the training classes in conjunction with a community center, school, or fitness center. Also, do not overlook the possibility of marketing the classes directly to medium- and large-sized corporations. If you choose this route, you can develop a complete self-defense and personal safety program for your client's employees and even conduct the classes at the corporate location during non-business or office hours. Expanding the business is as easy as hiring other qualified instructors to conduct the classes, and you can even add additional types of instruction courses, such wilderness survival, and river rescue to your roster. Unfortunately, women are often the target of attacks and violent crime, so be sure to pay extra attention to marketing the classes to this segment of the population. Fees will vary depending on your background, degree of instruction offered, and whether or not you are traveling to the student's location. Hint: Research competitors' fees in your area.

WEB RESOURCE: www.awsda.org
American Women's Self Defense Association.

TIME MANAGEMENT CLASSES
★★ $$ 🏚 🕐 🌐

Unlike the hit song of the '60s, time is not on our side! Hectic work and home schedules can leave even the most organized members of our society in a state of constant chaos. The 60-hour workweek, little league games, social commitments, and even simple grocery shopping all are the villains that make managing time near impossible for some. Here is where you can come to the rescue and build a successful business at the same time. Provide clients with time management training that can teach them how to manage their time better, identify time wasted, organize their daily routines, and build a system that is more productive when working and get more enjoyment when not working. Classes can be taught on a one-on-one basis, or in group format. Group format training can be marketed to small- and medium-sized businesses and corporations. The individual classes can be targeted to high-level executive positions and professionals. A prerequisite for starting and operating this business is to have experience in the field and, more importantly, excellent organizational and management skills. Additionally, be sure to develop a standardized time management manual that can be customized quickly and easily to suit individual client needs (perhaps create it on a web site, accessible via password to students only).

SPORT COACH TRAINING
★★ $$$ 🏢 🕐 🌐

At almost any amateur sporting event, you will find plenty of enthusiastic youngsters, a wide range of parents from supportive to pushy, and (unfortunately in far too many instances), a few coaches who simply do not "get it." A good coach puts his or her own needs aside for the betterment of the athletes who, in 99% of the cases, are kids simply looking to have fun and perhaps improve their skills. The heavily promoted idea of "winning is everything" should not be the goal of youth coaching and slowly the public is beginning to catch on. Thus, you have a growing market for this type of business that does not teach coaches how to be better in their particular sport, since in most cases they already have a vast knowledge of the sport already, but how to be better coaches and mentors in terms of interacting with players on the team and their parents, spouses, and game and league officials. The idea is to organize, market, and conduct seminars for sport coaches with specialized management, interaction, and social responsibility themes to help train them to be better mentors and teachers. You can enlist the services of professionals, such as motivational speakers, psychologists, and management specialists to speak at the training seminars and hand out printed material on the subject they are teaching. The seminars can be marketed directly to amateur sports associations, clubs, leagues, and organizations by initiating a direct mail campaign.

WEB RESOURCE: www.nscaa.com
National Soccer Coaches Association of America: a sports coaching site with very good information on proper ways to coach kids.

ADULT LEARNING CENTER
★★★ $$$$ 🌐

If you know ten to fifteen people who would make excellent instructors in their fields of interest, you could start an adult learning center. Major cities in particular are typically home to such learning environments, advertised by distributing course directories widely with short write-ups of the specific course offerings. Hobbies, yoga, fitness, business classes, and the arts (such as singing or dancing) are all popular topics taught in four-week courses. The teacher and the school divide up the fees to take the classes. Usually you need to make an arrangement whereby you pay a school to use their facilities in the evenings. This can come off the top before the money is divided between the instructors and you. Some learning centers run numerous one-night seminars, which are really evenings in which someone is promoting their latest book. Nonetheless, you benefit from people signing up. Seek out interesting, trendy courses and run the business from a homebased office, so other than printing the course booklets, your start-up costs will be minimal. Students can sign up by filling out an admission form in the course booklet or online, once you have set up a web site for the learning center.

Hint: Make sure you interview prospective teachers or seminar speakers and screen them in advance. While they may make extra money selling their books or signing people up for private lessons (have clear policies on this), you need to make sure that any "hidden" agendas do not become not too obvious and that, as teachers, they act in a professional manner and focus on imparting knowledge first and serving their own needs last. Any poor ethics or credibility of your instructors will reflect badly on the learning center and you can lose your business in the process.

WEB RESOURCE: www.learningannex.com

AEROBICS INSTRUCTOR
★★ $$ 🕐

If you are in good shape and excel in aerobics, you can become a certified aerobics instructor. Certification courses are easy to locate and this can be the starting point for a new business venture. All you need is a location, such as a gym at a school, plus some mats, music, and marketing, and you are ready to go. Fees will be commensurate with the length of the course, typically calculated at about $7 or $8 per class, making a six-week course in the $40 to $50 range or a ten-week class in the $70 to $80 range. To draw a wider range of students you should offer classes for different levels, such as beginner and advanced. Having classes for kids, teens and seniors is a drawing card, as well as different types of classes, whether it is hip hop, step, or the popular low impact aerobics.

WEB RESOURCE: www.afaa.com
Aerobics and Fitness Association of America

BOXING LESSONS
★ $ ⏱

Boxing provides a great physical workout and can be a lot of fun. The emphasis, of course, should be on fitness and sports and not on violence. Using the right precautions and setting up mats, or even a boxing ring, in an established facility, which could be a community center or similar location, can provide you with a place from which to run such classes. Based on $10 or $15 per class, you can set up classes in groups of 8 or 10. Kickboxing is also very popular and could be an additional consideration. Before you start out, make sure you have liability insurance, account for all safety and precautionary measures, and get certification as a boxing instructor.

SAND SCULPTING
★ $ 🏠 ⏱

No, you don't have to be at the beach to sculpt sand. If you are creative and have enough sand and available space, you can not only make sand sculptures, but also teach classes for kids, teens, adults, and seniors on sand sculpting. Other than the materials and leasing space in a community center, school, after school or senior center, you have little overhead when starting this type of class. You can also teach clay sculpting, which takes some slightly different skills but is also a popular favorite with all age groups. Classes can range from a one time course for $30 to a three or five week class for $125, plus a fee for supplies. While you will probably not get rich off such classes, you can make some steady income if you market the course widely and generate word-of-mouth marketing.

CPR LESSONS
★★ $$ 🏠 ⏱ ⚖

CPR is something that everyone should know since it can mean saving a life, but most people do not. To become certified, you need to take courses, which are given at hospitals and through the Red Cross or from American Heart Association sources. CPR courses are typically given at hospitals, schools, YMCAs, daycare centers, churches, temples, community centers or any other easily located site (with parking) where you can rent some space to teach.

WEB RESOURCE: www.americanheart.org
American Heart Association

SWIMMING LESSONS AND WATER SAFETY
★★★ $ ⏱ ⚖

If you have a pool at your disposal through a local facility, a university, or even a town or community area, you can make some extra income by becoming a swim instructor. Once you master the skills yourself—not just swimming, but how to teach people to swim—you can give individual or group lessons for different levels from non-swimmers to more advanced levels. Since one lesson typically does not suffice, you can set up between five to ten private lessons for anywhere from $200 to $500, or charge less for group lessons. At $300 for six (one hour) lessons, or $50 per lesson, you could teach ten lessons per week and earn $25,000 for a side business. In addition, swim instructors stay in very good shape!

TENNIS INSTRUCTOR
★★ $$ ⏱

If you excel in tennis—and you need not be a pro— you can give tennis lessons at a country club, on community courts, at local tennis centers, or even on the private courts of the rich and somewhat athletic. You can work out a deal with the court owners or the director of a facility and teach from one primary location, where students come to you, or you can be mobile and teach from wherever someone is seeking lessons. Advertising means primarily posting signs and posters anywhere they are permitted and doing some local advertisements. Word of mouth will also get you interested students if you are a good teacher. As is the case with most types of athletic instruction, it takes more than one lesson to get results. Therefore you can sell lessons by the package to individuals or groups. To teach tennis, not unlike golf, you need not only to be a very good player yourself, but also have:

1. A firm understanding of the basics of the game (i.e., the right way to grip the racket for forehand and backhand, serving techniques, etc.)

2. Patience to work with people who will get it wrong far more times than they will get it right

3. The ability to teach people based on watching them and seeing what they do wrong, or right.

A lot of people can play tennis well, but not all of them can teach it—in fact most cannot! So hone your skills and you can have a successful tennis instruction business.

WEB RESOURCE: www.usta.com/coaches
United States Tennis Association, coaching section.

FENCING INSTRUCTOR
★ $$ ⏲

Fortunately it is the 21st century because in the 13th and 14th century, at least in Europe, dueling and fencing schools were forbidden by law. The unique sport of fencing has drawn increasing interest in the past decade and continues to be taught in many universities throughout North America. To be a successful fencing instructor you must be highly skilled and able to lead both classes and individuals in lessons. You should know how to make instruction fun while teaching proper technique and correct form. Introduce safety rules in the first lesson, and continue to emphasize safety during every session. To teach fencing, you will need to find a location that provides enough area for all students to participate while giving you room to instruct. You also need to have liability insurance and be ready to handle any injuries that may arise.

WEB RESOURCE: www.usfca.org
United States Fencing Coaches Association

PILATES INSTRUCTION
★★★ $$ ⏲

The Pilates Method, (a.k.a. Pilates) has become a widely popular system of physical fitness. Originally developed in the early 20th century by Joseph Pilates, the method encourages the use of the mind to control the muscles. It is an exercise program that focuses on the core postural muscles, teaching awareness of breath and align-

ment of the spine, which is important in alleviating back pain. There is a great opportunity for Pilates to be taught in evening programs or in conjunction with established fitness clubs. Pilates is often taught in conjunction with yoga, so you may work with a yoga club as well. Typically, certified Pilates instructors can earn $40 to $60 per hour and depending on your abilities as an instructor, you can fill your schedule of classes largely by word of mouth. This is an inexpensive career path, as you will need only a few thousand dollars for certification and to promote yourself, once you secure a teaching location.

WEB RESOURCE: www.afpafitness.com
American Fitness Professional Association

HIP HOP DANCING
★★ $$ ⏲

If you know the latest steps, you can start up classes teaching hip hop and other exciting dance moves for fun and for profit. All you need is to rent a studio space, get the music, and get your groove on, so to speak. Advertise at high schools, colleges, and everywhere the younger generation will see your fliers, posters, and ads. Keep your pricing reasonable, in the $45 to $70 range for four or five classes, and know that different students will start at different levels. Rather than over-booking classes, hire additional dance teachers as your business grows and schedule more classes.

NOTES:

_____

_____

_____

_____

_____

_____

_____

62
MANUFACTURING
Businesses You Can Start

PATIO FURNITURE MANUFACTURING
★ $$

Custom-designed and manufactured cedar patio furniture is highly sought after by homeowners who enjoy comfortable and fashionable outdoor patio furniture. Launching a business venture that builds custom cedar patio furniture is a relatively inexpensive enterprise to establish. The business can be run from a garage or basement workshop and requires only minimal woodworking equipment such as a table saw, band saw, planer, basic power hand tools, and sanders. There are thousands of design plans available to assist in constructing the patio furniture, or the seasoned carpenter can certainly manufacture his/her own custom designs. The patio furniture can be sold on a wholesale basis by establishing accounts with garden centers and designers. Or, the custom patio furniture can be sold directly to consumers by marketing the products at home and garden trade shows.

WEB RESOURCE: www.scrollsaw.com
Design plans for patio furniture.

KITCHEN CUTTING BOARDS
★ $

Kitchen cutting boards are easy to make, and there is a strong market demand for the product from both homeowners and commercial kitchen chefs. Once you have mastered the art of producing high-quality kitchen cutting boards you can then move on to butcher block tables, as the market demand for this specialty product is huge and a well-made butcher block table can easily sell for $1,000 or more. This new business venture is ideal for someone who wants to start from home on a part-time basis. Not only can you enjoy the benefits of earning extra income, you will also be gaining valuable business experience that can be applied when it's time for the business to expand. Potential income range is $5,000 to $10,000 per year part-time.

BOOKENDS
★★ $

Manufacturing bookends? Why not? They fall into the category of a great gift for someone who has everything. And best of all, the business can be set in motion for less than $500 and operated right from home. One of the key elements for this manufacturing venture to take off and fly will be your ability to design and create unique products. One idea may be to capitalize on the ever-increasing environmentally friendly theme and manufacture all the bookends out of recycled materials. If this route is chosen, be sure to include the fact that your products are manufactured from recycled materials in all packaging and promotional material, as this is an attractive feature to green consumers and supporting a green business is very much in vogue today. The finished product can be sold through retail stores such as gift shops and bookstores, at trade fairs, flea markets, and on the internet.

WEATHER VANES
★★ $$ 🏠 🕐

Weather vanes adorn millions of homes worldwide. These functional and attractive features add charm to any home and hearken back to the days of old. Manufacturing weather vanes can dearly be accomplished by utilizing a garage or basement workshop, and the vanes can be manufactured from a whole host of materials, such as copper, iron, wood, and plastic. Weather vanes best suit the architectural style of Victorian and heritage homes. Gaining access to owners of theses types of homes can be achieved by advertising the weather vanes in heritage home and antique publications, as well as at antique shows. Additionally, the weather vanes can be sold through the traditional channels, such as establishing accounts with retailers and displaying the vanes at home and garden trade shows. A good starting point for this venture will be to acquire a few antique weather vanes to be used as the templates for constructing replicas and for inspirations for new designs.

WATERBEDS
★ $$ 🏠 🕐

Waterbeds helped form the social culture of the 1970s and although they are not as popular as they once were, if history has taught us anything, it is that it will always repeat itself. Starting a business now that manufactures and sells waterbeds may just put you ahead of the competition when waterbeds once again become all the rage. Parts for waterbeds, such as liners and heaters, are available from numerous manufacturers on a wholesale basis. You simply design and construct the waterbed frames and assemble the other parts to fit. Waterbeds are still in demand and can be sold directly to consumers via placing advertisements in all traditional mediums, as well as selling the beds through the internet and at furniture trade shows.

WEB RESOURCE: www.waterbedreplaceparts.com
Wholesale source of waterbed parts.

CUSTOM PICTURE FRAMES
★★ $ 🏠 🕐

Manufacturing and wholesaling custom-designed picture frames is another great part-time homebased business opportunity. Ideally, the picture frames will be manufactured from a unique material, such as copper, molded clay, plastic, or wood. The more interesting the materials and more unique the design of the picture frames, the better. Consumers are always attracted to different and one-of-a-kind products, especially if the item is going to be given as a gift to a friend or family member. Establishing wholesale accounts with photography stores, photo finishing stores, gift shops, and other specialty retailers is the best avenue to market the custom picture frames. The picture frames can even be placed into these stores on a consignment basis to really get things moving fast. While consigning products is not always the best marketing method available, it does enable a business owner to get the product established in retail stores much more quickly.

WOODEN SIGNS
★★★ $$ 🏠 🕐

There are a few methods of manufacturing highly attractive and functional wood signs. The first is to use a router to remove wood and leave the message or words raised, or concave. The second method requires a design stencil and sandblasting equipment to remove the wood around the message or words. This manufacturing method can also produce a raised or concave appearance to the sign. Initially, a novice wood sign maker should have the wooden blanks for the signs produced by an outside firm, unless you have the required woodworking skills and equipment to construct the sign blanks. All types of businesses and professional services can utilize wooden signs. Such signs are still extremely popular with bed and breakfast lodgings, lawyers, accountants, doctors, antique shops, cafés, gift shops and various other businesses, particularly in suburban and country settings. Currently, high-quality wooden signs are selling at prices starting at $500 each and up depending on size, complexity, and the type of wood used for the sign.

WEB RESOURCE: www.signsupplyusa.com
Distributors of wholesale sign-making equipment.

WOODEN SASH WINDOWS
★★★ $$ 🏠 🕐

Many owners of Victorian and heritage homes will never make the change to new windows manufactured from aluminum or vinyl, regardless of the condition of their original wooden windows. This fact is why starting a business that manufactures, sells, and installs wooden sash windows is such a wise choice for a new enterprise. As mentioned before, most owners of heritage homes would never even consider installing new windows manufactured from aluminum or vinyl. However, almost all would gladly replace the old windows that are in poor condition with new ones that still retain and reflect the home's original appearance and charm. The main qualification for launching this venture is to possess a good deal of carpentry experience and knowledge. The wooden windows can be marketed directly to homeowners or to home renovation companies and contractors on a subcontract basis. A well-established wooden window manufacturing business can easily generate profits in excess of $75,000 per year.

WEB RESOURCE: www.thewindowmaker.com
A site with information on wooden sash windows

BIRDHOUSES
★★ $ 🏠 🕐

While building and selling birdhouses may not make you rich, it can provide a good source of additional part-time business income. The only requirement for starting a business that manufactures birdhouses is to have basic woodworking equipment and skills. There are birdhouse design plans available, or you can design and build your own birdhouses. The finished products can be sold at craft shows, flea markets, and to community merchants. The choices are unlimited in terms of how the birdhouses can be marketed. More important is the fact that this is a good homebased business venture that can be started for peanuts and produce a good part-time income.

WEB RESOURCE: www.scrollsaw.com
Design plans for birdhouse construction.

WIND CHIMES
★★ $ 🏠 🕐

Seashells, glass, metal, or bells—wind chimes can be manufactured from almost any kind of material. Starting a business that manufactures wind chimes can be a great way to turn spare time into extra income. The wind chimes can be sold to retail stores, garden centers, and gift shops on a wholesale basis. Or, the wind chimes can be sold directly to the end consumers via a booth at a busy flea market, at outdoor fairs, or on the internet. While there may not seem to be a lot of potential for profit in this type of manufacturing business, consider the following: 50 retail accounts that sold only four wind chimes each month would produce total unit sales of 200 wind chimes. A $10 gross profit on each wind chime sold would produce gross profits of $2,000 each month for the business venture.

SAUNAS
★★ $$ 🏠 🕐

Designing, manufacturing, and wholesaling custom-built easy-to-assemble sauna kits is a fantastic business venture to set in motion. You can design, manufacture, and package the saunas complete with assembly instructions for delivery all around the world. Parts such as the heater boxes are available on a wholesale basis. Additionally, milling your own cedar boards for the sauna construction can be an effective method in keeping manufacturing costs to a minimum. In addition to establishing accounts with national retailers to stock and sell the sauna kits, you can also sell the sauna kits directly to consumers by displaying the saunas at home and garden trade shows, on the internet and by setting up a sauna display on weekends in busy community malls. You can also install the saunas for local customers for an additional fee.

WEB RESOURCE: http://ga.esaunakits.com
Sauna kit resources and information.

PROTOTYPE DESIGN
★★ $$ 🏠 🕐

Do you want to start a truly unique manufacturing business that has unlimited potential for growth and profits? If so, perhaps starting a business that designs and constructs manufacturing prototypes is the right enterprise for you. Designing and building prototypes is a highly specialized business that requires a great deal of construction knowledge, ability to work with various mediums, and all required equipment necessary for building a host of various products. The following steps can be taken to establish and market this type of new business enterprise:

1. Decide if the business will focus on designing and building manufacturing prototypes in general or cater to a more specified segment of the manufacturing industry, such as mall kiosks.

2. Design a complete marketing and promotional package including previous experience, capabilities, and specialized equipment and know-how.

3. Determine a range of rates and the approximate timeframe for each of several types of jobs. While this is difficult considering the vastness of this business, you can set bottom line hourly rates for your time and work.

4. Join manufacturing and business associations.

5. Acquire membership lists of the associations and initiate a direct mail and introduction telephone call campaign utilizing the newly designed promotional package.

6. List your company in manufacturing directories and trade-related publications.

7. Start a well-designed, professional looking web site that details how you work.

Following these seven steps will place you in front of your potential market for this type of business venture. Generally, clients will want an estimate for their projects prior to awarding the contract, and this can be extremely difficult given the nature of prototype design. However, this is one of the few industries that allows for a certain percentage of gray area, in terms of a cost estimate. The objective is to always enter into the contract with a clear and concise estimate that includes a scope of work, product details, manufacturing time lines, and the potential pitfalls associated with the client's project.

ROOF TRUSSES
★★ $$$$ ⚖️

Most new home construction now utilizes pre-engineered and built roof trusses, as opposed to traditional rafter framing to form the roof structure of the house. This type of framing construction is faster and generally costs less money to install than rafter framing, making it a popular construction choice for contractors. While this is one of the more costly manufacturing businesses featured in this chapter, it also has the potential to be one of the most profitable. The target market for this product is general contractors, home renovation companies, and architects. Setting up introductory meetings with the owners of these firms is the best route to take in promoting and marketing the business. Additional considerations in establishing a business that manufactures roof trusses will be business location, equipment requirements, and most importantly, learning local building codes and regulations.

WEB RESOURCE: www.sbcindustry.com
Wood Truss Council of America.

FLOATING DOCKS
★ $$ 🏠 🕐

Building floating docks and swim platforms is a manufacturing business that can be started by just about anyone with construction knowledge and a well-equipped woodworking shop. Most of the components that are required to build a floating dock, such as the floats and anchors, can be purchased on a wholesale basis from the manufacturers of these products. To locate manufacturers of dock floats, etc., simply refer to one of the many directories available for a detailed listing of parts suppliers or go online. The market for floating docks includes marinas, waterfront campgrounds, homeowners, and government agencies, such as the local Parks Department. While this business enterprise may take some time to establish and build a solid customer base, the potential financial rewards can be well worth the wait.

CANOE PADDLES
★ $$ 🏠 🕐

Millions of people around the world enjoy canoeing as an outdoor recreational sport, and as a canoeist I can attest to the fact that the search for the perfect paddle is a never-ending quest. A business that manufactures wooden canoe and kayak paddles can be established right from a homebased garage workshop, and requires only a small investment into woodworking equipment to get going. The canoe paddles can be sold on a wholesale basis to recreation retail stores, as well as directly to consumers by displaying the paddles for sale at outdoor and recreation trade shows. Additional revenues for this type of manufacturing business can also be gained by manufacturing and selling related canoe and kayak products such as yokes, canoe replacement seats, and custom wood gunnel trim kits.

CD RACKS
★★ $ 🏠 🕐

Like many of the products featured in this chapter, manufacturing CD racks is a very easy and inexpensive business venture to set in motion. The CD racks can be manufactured from wood, plastic, or iron in various shapes and sizes and CD storage capacities. Like many manufactured specialty products, the design and type of materials used will often dictate the products' popularity and lifespan, so be sure to give this aspect of the business careful consideration and be creative. Ideally, the best method of marketing and distributing the finished CD racks is to establish wholesale accounts with both CD and furniture retailers to stock and sell them. You can also sell them at local fairs and flea markets.

ART EASELS
★ $ 🏠 🕐

Hobby artists rank in the millions, and starting a business that builds and sells art easels is a very easy and inexpensive enterprise to get rolling. The business can be operated from a small home based workshop, and the art easels can be sold to art supply stores on a wholesale basis. Furthermore, once the business has been established and all of the manufacturing bugs have been ironed out, approach various manufacturers of all-inclusive painting kits to check out the viability of including an art easel with these painting kits. Another option is to approach schools, after-school centers, community centers, senior centers, and other places that may have art classes and are in need of new easels. Doing this could provide you with twenty to thirty or more easels to build, keeping you very busy while generating a very nice income.

PICNIC TABLES AND BENCHES
★★ $ 🏠 🕐 🪶

Building and selling picnic tables is about as easy as a manufacturing business start-up can get. The business needs only basic construction knowledge, and can be readily operated from a small homebased workshop. In the spirit of being unique and as a method to separate the business from competitors, consider adopting a different method of manufacturing the picnic tables or a different type of raw construction material, such as beach driftwood or recycled building materials, making you a "green" business, which is environmentally friendly and excellent for marketing. The key to success in business often lies with the ability to carve your own niche in a proven, and existing marketplace. Market your picnic tables to parks, universities, local schools, historical sites with significant grounds, or any place else where you think picnics could be held—including the backyards of homeowners.

WEB RESOURCE: www.kitguy.com/#PLANS
Plans for all sorts of things, including picnic tables.

WOOD MOLDINGS
★★ $$$

One of the most popular and least expensive ways to upgrade a home's interior appearance is to install new wood trims and moldings. Starting a business that manufactures custom wood moldings with standard profiles, as well as made-to-order wood moldings, is a terrific business start-up for the skilled and well-equipped carpenter to initiate. Customers can include home renovation and construction companies or sell the moldings on a wholesale basis to local home improvement centers. Additionally, to capitalize on the heritage home renovation market, antique replica wood moldings can be manufactured from recycled wood and sold directly to do-it-yourself homeowners via product advertisements placed in newspapers and related trade magazines. To gain additional revenues and profits for the business, a wood molding installation service can also be offered to clients. Potential profits for a molding manufacturing business will vary based on a number of factors, such as sales volume, overhead, and product markup. However, a well-established wood molding manufacturing business can easily generate profits in excess of $100,000 per year for the business owner.

PACKING CRATES
★★ $$ 🏠 🕐

Designing and building custom made-to-order packing crates is a great business to initiate and has an almost endless supply of potential customers. Every year millions of products are manufactured and shipped in packing crates that have been specially designed and built to protect the cargo. The easiest way to get new clients for a packing crate manufacturing business is to simply design and distribute a promotional package to all the manufacturers in your community. The information package should outline and give details about your specialty service as well as include all vital contact information. Additional revenue for the business can be generated by manufacturing and selling wood shipping pallets to business clients. Once again, try to include recycled wood materials into the finished product.

WEB RESOURCE: www.nwpca.com
National Wood Pallet and Container Association.

STORE DISPLAY CASES
★★ $$ 🏠 🕐

Starting a manufacturing business that specializes in custom-designed and constructed store display cases and fixtures is a fantastic business that can be set up and conducted right from a homebased workshop. There are many pre-designed and pre-built display cases available to retailers. However, often merchants require display cases and store fixtures that have to be specially constructed to highlight their inventory. There are a few marketing techniques that can be used to promote the business including joining retail business associations, networking with the association members to gather potential leads, and establishing alliances with companies that specialize in commercial store openings and renovations. Both can become an excellent source for new business and business contacts.

FUTONS
★★ $$$

Futons are a functional, yet inexpensive, piece of furniture that can serve a multitude of uses. A futon

manufacturing business can be setup and managed from home. However, renting a small industrial location can serve not only for a manufacturing location, but also a "factory outlet" for retail sales of the futons. Books that feature futon design plans and construction tips are readily available. These books can be used as a valuable guide for assisting in the design and construction process of the futons. Futon cushions and mattresses are also available from a number of wholesale suppliers, which can be found listed in various manufacturing print and online trade directories. Overall, this is a good choice for a manufacturing business start-up, especially if the factory outlet route is chosen.

WOODTURNINGS
★ $$ 🏠 🕐

Fruit bowls, candlesticks, stair spindles or baseball bats—there are literally hundreds of different products which can be manufactured simply by purchasing a wood-turning lathe and mastering the art of wood turning. While the finished products can be sold directly to consumers, a better choice in terms of merchandising the wood-turning products is to arrange accounts with retailers, such as gift shops, to stock and sell the products. On a recent visit to a gift shop, I was amazed to find out that wooden bowls made from exotic hardwoods were selling for as much as $300—and even more surprised when the shop owner told me that he routinely sold one or two a week. Some quick math will tell you that just a dozen or so accounts with retailers like this can generate a very comfortable living manufacturing and wholesaling wooden bowls.

WEB RESOURCE: www.woodturner.org
American Association of Wood Turners.

WINDOW SASH MIRRORS
★★ $$ 🏠 🕐

Every year millions of old wood windows are replaced in houses, and these old and often discarded wood window frames have the ability to generate incredible profits, providing they are turned into beautifully refinished wooden sash mirrors. The mirrors are very easy to make. Simply remove all the glass and putty from the window frame, and sand and refinish the frame in a stain or natural finish. Once this has been accomplished, place clear or tinted mirrors into the wooden window frame, and presto!—you have a highly saleable product ready to command top dollar. The mirrors can be sold at flea markets, craft shows, and through retailers, such as antique shops and gift stores, on a consignment basis. This is an ideal business venture to be started by someone who is seeking a low-investment homebased business opportunity that can generate a fantastic part-time income and still allow you to maintain a full-time job.

MAGNETIC SIGNS
★ $$$ 🚗 🕒

Magnetic signs are an incredibly handy advertising tool, especially for the business owner or sales persons that uses their automobile for both business and pleasure, as the signs can be quickly installed or removed for storage in the trunk. Magnetic signs are also very easy to design and produce, making this an ideal business venture for just about anyone seeking to start a homebased business enterprise that requires little in the way of start-up capital and experience. The signs are actually manufactured from a vinyl material with a magnetic backing, which enables the signs to be lightweight and pliable. The signs are then cut to size and shape, and vinyl letters are placed on them to finish the sign making process. The only equipment required for manufacturing the signs is a computer, page layout and design software, a vinyl printer, and a plotter that cuts the letters. Required equipment can be purchased used or new in most communities through printing and sign supply companies. Currently, small to medium magnetic signs are retailing for $30 to $60 each and cost about $8 to $12 each to make.

MAILBOXES
★ $ 🚗 🕒

"Wanted: craftspeople to build custom-designed mailboxes. Flexible homebased work hours and a wage of $20 per hour offered." If this is the type of employment advertisement that would attract you, then why not start your own mailbox manufacturing business? The business can be launched on an initial investment of less than $500 and operated on a part- or full-time basis right from home. The completed mailboxes can be sold on a wholesale basis

to retailers or directly to consumers via a booth at a busy weekend flea market or craft show. Remember, the financial goal of operating a business does not always mean that you necessarily desire a $100,000 per year income. Sometimes just the fact that you are making a few extra dollars operating your own business is all you need.

SILK-SCREENED MOUSE PADS
★★★ $$ 🏠 🕒

Purchasing silk-screening equipment and a few hundred blank mouse pads is all that is necessary for starting your own business that produces mouse pads emblazoned with printed images, logos, and slogans. The business can be operated from home and does not require a great deal of special skills or investment capital to establish. The silk-screened mouse pads can feature generic images and slogans and be sold to retailers on a wholesale basis. Or, since mouse pads are so often "giveaway items," you can create them for companies that use them for marketing purposes, with corporate logos printed on each one. Blank mouse pads can be purchased in bulk for about $1 each, and the cost of ink to silk-screen an image will also be less than $1. Providing you can sell 1,000 mouse pads each week at a wholesale price of $3, the business could potentially generate profits in excess of $1,000 per week, prior to overhead and taxes.

WEB RESOURCE: www.printusa.com
Distributor of equipment and supplies for screen-printing mouse pads.

STAIRCASES
★★ $$$$

Starting a business that manufactures and installs residential and commercial staircases not only has the potential to generate enormous yearly profits providing you have the necessary skills and equipment. You can build and install staircases made from various construction materials, such as hard and soft woods, steel, concrete, or any combination of these materials. The stairs can be sold directly to homeowners who are renovating their homes or building new homes. However, a more suitable marketing approach is to establish alliances with contractors, architects, and renovation companies, and sell your staircase building services to these firms, as well as install the stairs on a subcontract basis. A staircase design and manufacturing business can be operated as a company that manufactures staircases in general, or the business can specialize and manufacture specific styles of stairs, such as spiral, pull-down attic stairs, or rolling staircases for warehouse applications. Make sure to adhere to all safety regulations and building codes, and don't forget to have liability insurance.

PORCH COLUMNS
★★ $$$

Manufacturing decorative porch columns can be a very profitable business once established, especially if the main focus of the manufacturing business is to design and build Victorian porch column replicas. The porch columns can be manufactured from fiberglass, wood, or compressed injection foam. A good starting point in terms of manufacturing the antique replica porch columns is to purchase a few porch columns to be used as the template for designing and building the new columns. The antique porch columns can be purchased at used building materials yards. There are many different approaches that can be taken for marketing this type of unique specialty building product, including selling the porch columns to local and national building centers on a wholesale basis as well as construction and renovation firms. Or, the porch columns can be sold directly to do-it-yourself homeowners by advertising the columns for sale in newspapers and trade publications and displaying the columns at home and garden trade shows.

THEME BUNK BEDS
★★ $$ 🚗 🕑

Bunk beds are extremely easy to design and build, and right now children's theme bunk beds are hot sellers. The key to success in this type of manufacturing business is to choose the right theme and make the beds unique and colorful. Theme bunk beds can be manufactured to resemble race cars, space ships, tree houses, or just about any other popular theme that sparks the imagination of children and gets parents to open their wallets. The theme bunk beds can be sold to furniture retailers and children's retail stores on a wholesale basis. Or, the finished product can be sold directly to parents via traditional advertising

mediums, the internet, and product display and demonstration booths at home and garden trade shows. If you can secure the rights to use a popular children's television character you can command a lot of money and sell the beds to children's furniture stores. You can also offer other types of beds such as loft and captain's beds.

WEB RESOURCE: www.conceptsamerica.com
For bunk, loft, and captain's bed plans, click on "bedrooms."

FIRST-AID KITS
★★★ $$ 🚗 🕑

Two of the best aspects of starting a business that assembles and markets first-aid kits are the facts that the business can be set in motion for less than a $3,000 investment and first-aid kits are in high demand. The kits can be assembled, packaged, and sold to retailers on a wholesale basis or they can be specially designed and marketed to specific industries, such as construction and transportation. There is an additional market for schools, associations, sports facilities, and numerous other locations that should, but often do not, have such kits readily available. Manufacturing and warehousing firms are also an excellent place to market your products since both are required by law to have first-aid kits on site. Providing you can maintain a 100 percent markup on the first-aid kits that you assemble, and achieve $100,000 per year in gross sales, this inexpensive and simple business start-up can generate profits of $50,000 per year, prior to overhead costs.

CHRISTMAS ORNAMENTS
★★ $ 🚗 🕑

Starting a business that manufactures Christmas ornaments can provide you with a fabulous part-time seasonal income just when you need it the most—Christmas time. Christmas ornaments such as tree decorations and door wreaths are very simple and inexpensive to make, and can be sold in various ways including to retailers on a wholesale basis or directly to consumers at a sales kiosk in a mall, at craft shows or from your web site. The business is ideally operated from home and the overheads are virtually nonexistent. While manufacturing and selling Christmas decorations on a part-time, seasonal basis may not make you rich, it can potentially generate an extra income of $5,000 to $10,000 per year. Hint: Start early in the year and prepare to fill orders in the early fall.

CUSTOM DOORSTOPS
★★ $ 🚗 🕐

Now here is a unique and interesting business opportunity. Manufacturing custom designer doorstops is a very easy and straightforward business venture to set in motion. The key to success in this type of manufacturing venture is that the doorstops must be unique in design, and the marketing methods employed must be innovative and clever. The doorstops could be fashioned after antique doorstops, or they could be manufactured from 100 percent recycled materials. The options for manufacturing doorstops are endless and only limited by imagination. Marketing methods that can be utilized are to establish wholesale accounts with national retailers, and the custom doorstops can also be sold directly to high-end homebuilders, architects, and interior designers.

WEB RESOURCE: www.ahma.org
American Hardware Manufacturers Association.

WOOD CLOTHES HANGERS
★ $ 🚗 🕐

Designing and manufacturing custom wood clothes hangers for high-end, expensive men's and women's fashions is a terrific little business enterprise to set in motion. Typical clothes hangers can destroy expensive clothes, so the potential market for custom-made clothes hangers to specifically fit one particular item of clothing is huge. The coat hangers should be made from aromatic cedar wood and stainless steel for the curved hanger. Marketing the coat hangers should not be difficult, given there are thousands of retail clothing boutiques that specialize in high-end custom-made fashions.

MOLD MAKING
★★ $$ 🚗 🕐

Thousands of different products require a mold in order to be manufactured. Canoes are made from a mold, lawn ornaments are made from a mold, many car body parts are made from a mold, and these are just a few examples. Initiating a business that specializes in making manufacturing molds for clients is not a hard business to establish. However, there is definitely one main requirement: you or an employee must be able to design and build numerous styles of molds. Typically, molds used in manufacturing are constructed from fiberglass, so a well-vented workshop will also be a requirement for this business. You will also need to adhere closely to health codes. Gaining clients can be as easy as purchasing a manufacturers directory and soliciting the manufacturers for mold-making contracts, as molds have a predetermined lifespan based on the number of times they are used. The profit potential in mold making is very good, as a single mold can sell for as much as $10,000 for a small product and over $100,000 for a large product, such as a sailboat.

TRADE SHOW DISPLAYS
★★★ $$$ 🚗

Trade shows are a multibillion-dollar industry in North America. All companies and organizations that display or promote products and services at trade shows each year have one thing in common. They all need to have an exhibit display designed, constructed, or rented in order to display and promote their products and services. And the best way to capitalize on the demand for trade show displays is to simply start a business that manufactures custom one-of-a-kind trade show displays as well as off-the-shelf, mass-produced, generic trade show displays. This type of manufacturing business is very easy to establish, as the components needed to build trade show displays are readily available from a wide range of manufacturers. Additionally, a homebased workshop is more than sufficient space to construct the displays, at least initially. To market yourself you can use business directories and the internet to find out about as many trade shows as possible for the next couple of years. Then, well in advance, start a direct mailing campaign to all of the leading players in the industry. For example, when attending a huge annual book trade show, you could easily see that many of the publishing companies took time to plan out their displays. To reach this market, you would contact every publishing house that you could reach well in advance of their annual trade show. As is the case with most custom-designed products, you should have templates and display items ready to view on your web site. Therefore, you need to start by making sample trade show displays for small, medium, and larger needs and have them prominently featured on your web site. Profit margins are excellent for this type of product, especially on the custom one-of-a-kind orders, and finding clients should not be difficult, due to the simple fact that there are an estimated 100,000+ trade shows each year in the United States alone.

WEB RESOURCE: www.edpa.com
Exhibit Designers and Producers Association.

SNOWBOARDS
★ $$$$

Since the introduction of snowboards about a decade ago, there has been no looking back for the sport, as snowboarding now rivals skiing in terms of popularity and appeals to just about every age group, from 5 to 100. Manufacturing snowboards is not a difficult task. The work lies within the design and composition of the snowboard, making a snowboard manufacturing business best suited to individuals with a manufacturing and designing background. However, with that being said, experienced staff can always be hired or brought in on a consulting basis to help implement the design and manufacturing process. The snowboards can be sold on a wholesale basis to national retailers, as well as directly to consumers via the internet and at sports and recreation trade shows. One important aspect of the business that should not be overlooked is to secure a spokesperson for the snowboards who is a recognized person in the world of snowboarding. Building this type of public exposure will be one of the best marketing tools that can be implemented.

RUBBER STAMPS
★★ $$ 🚚 🕐

In spite of the popularity of easy to make and print computerized labels, there will always be a market for rubber stamps that are used for business purposes, as well as in the hobby craft industry. Starting a business that manufactures pre-designed rubber stamps is as easy as one, two, three.

1. Research the industry, market, and business.

2. Establish a manufacturing process, and secure retail accounts for the stamps.

3. Manufacture the stamps and ship to retailers.

The key to success in manufacturing rubber stamps is to be unique and make the stamps interesting. In addition to the traditional business rubber stamps, also manufacture stamps for use in crafts and for personal use. Right now, animal stamps are very popular and feature just about every kind of animal.

CLOCKS
★ $ 🚚 🖋

If you've got the time, this could be a very good business endeavor, since start-up costs are low and unique clocks can bring in profits of $50,000 per year or more. The components needed to build the clocks can be purchased on a wholesale basis from manufacturers of these items, while the housing for the clock itself can be manufactured by your business. The key to success is to make clocks that are different and appealing to consumers. Be creative and try making clocks for kids, teens, or other specific demographic markets. Perhaps use an antique style, or a modern art theme, or maybe a sporty look. Use recycled materials and become known as the environmentally friendly "green" clockmaker. The possibilities are endless as long as the clock works. You can sell to retailers, through advertising, from your web site, or through home fairs, trade shows, and flea markets. Personalized clocks with the faces of the people buying them as the clock's face can be a unique and interesting gift item.

WEB RESOURCE: www.klockit.com
The world's leading supplier of clock-making parts for more than three decades.

BROOMS AND BRUSHES
★ $$ 🚚 🕐

Manufacturing brooms and brushes is another business opportunity that just about anyone can tackle. The business has the capability to produce a very substantial income for the owner-operator. The brooms and brushes can cater to one specific industry that may use a specialty broom or brush, such as the chimney sweep industry, or you can manufacture a wide variety of types. Of course, the largest market is ordinary brooms and brushes used in everyday household cleaning. Once established, this type of manufacturing business is easily capable of producing yearly sales exceeding $100,000.

WEB RESOURCE: www.abma.org
American Brush Manufacturers Association.

WINDOW SHUTTERS AND BLINDS
★★ $$ 🚗 🕒

Manufacturing interior and exterior wood window shutters is a very simple business to establish and run. Best of all, only a small homebased workshop is required for manufacturing space. The demand for exterior wooden window shutters used for home decoration and shutter replacements for heritage home renovations is very large. The completed shutters can be sold to national home improvement center retailers on a wholesale basis, or the window shutters can be sold directly to homeowners on a custom order and installation basis. The profit margins can be terrific on this type of product, as there is not a lot of competition in the industry that focuses on manufacturing wooden window shutters and blinds exclusively.

TREEHOUSE KITS
★ $$ 🚗 🕒

Time to mix childhood memories, business, and profits. That is exactly what can be achieved by starting a business that manufactures tree house kits for the do-it-yourself homeowner to purchase, assemble, and install. The tree house kits can be packaged and sold to retail outlets on a wholesale basis or directly to consumers via advertising the tree house kits for sale on the internet, in newspapers and other publications, and by establishing a display model that can be exhibited at trade shows. Seek to build a joint venture with companies that are already in the business of manufacturing and wholesaling children's toys and playground equipment, as there will be the possibility to capitalize on their customer base, distribution channels, and business expertise and experience.

STORE DIRECTORY BOARDS
★ $$ 🚗 🕒

Large retailers, office buildings, malls, and sports complexes all use directory boards to show visitors where they are, where items can be found, and where the various departments are located. Manufacturing store and office directory boards is a very artistic process, simply because the requirements for each location varies. This means that in most cases you do not have to compete against mass-produced directory boards. However, this is still a very competitive segment of the manufacturing and sign industry, so be sure to take a unique and innovative approach to the manufacturing process and appearance of the finished product. Recently, some companies have been selling and installing electronic flat screen directory boards for free in high-traffic locations. Of course, the catch is that the boards also feature advertising, which is sold to local businesses that serve the community. This may be a route to consider.

PLASTIC DISPLAYS
★★ $$ 🚗 🕒

Brochure holders, publication holders, point-of-purchase displays, menu racks, etc., are just a few of the display holders that can be manufactured from plastics. The market demand for custom designed and manufactured product and information display holders is gigantic, and starting a business that specializes in manufacturing plastic displays is very easy. The business can easily be operated from a small homebased workshop. The finished displays can be sold in numerous ways including establishing wholesale accounts with national office products retailers, direct to companies via a direct sales team, or by designing and distributing a product catalog featuring all the various designs and displays your company manufactures. The plastics used to construct the displays can be purchased inexpensively on a wholesale basis, and the equipment used for the manufacturing process is also very inexpensive and available at all glaziers supply stores.

OFFICE AND ROOM DIVIDERS
★★ $$ 🚗 🕒

Starting a business that designs and builds office dividers is a fantastic homebased manufacturing business to get rolling. The latest trend in office layout is no walls; only dividers to create a really communal workplace. This means the time has never been better than now to start this type of manufacturing business. The office divider designs could incorporate handy features, such as adjustable shelving, built-in waste and recycling receptacles, and built-in message and white boards. Once established, this is the kind of manufacturing business that has the potential to survive and generate a substantial income for the owner. In addition, home dividers are also becoming increasingly popular, especially for setting up homebased offices and this is an avenue for more business.

DOGHOUSES
★★ $ 🏠 🕒

A workshop, woodworking equipment, and basic carpentry skills are all that you will need to start building doghouses for profit. You can build doghouses from your own plans or purchase design and construction plans. Consider incorporating recycled materials into the construction process, as you can play upon the benefits of recycling for marketing purposes. The completed doghouses can be sold to retailers on a wholesale basis or you can opt to sell them directly to consumers via pet fairs and craft shows. Be creative in your designs and include features that normally would not be found in a doghouse. Remember, when it comes to pets, many people know no limits in terms of spending money on their pampered pooches. For the indoor pooches in apartments, consider also manufacturing and selling doggie beds.

WEB RESOURCE: www.woodcraftplans.com
Distributors of doghouse construction plans.

JEWELRY BOXES
★★ $ 🏠 🕒 🍃

Jewelry boxes can retail for as much as 10 to 20 times of what it costs to build them, making this a potentially very profitable homebased manufacturing venture. This is the type of manufacturing business that will let you be very creative in design and in the materials selected for the construction process. Or in other words, "think outside the jewelry box." Consider using materials that normally would not be used for building this product, like recycled items, seashells, glass, or plastic, and use your environmentally friendly approach to increase your marketing efforts as a successful green business. You can market the boxes by renting tables at crafts fairs and flea

markets or teaming with the many jewelry sellers at such outdoor venues. You can also sell them to retailers on a wholesale basis, or on your web site, and on the sites of other manufacturers. The sky's the limit.

FENCE PANELS
★★ $$ 🏠 🕒

Almost all new wooden fences that are being installed today are constructed from pre-built fence panels in four, five-, and six-foot heights. Typically, these pre-built fence panels are constructed from pressure-treated wood or from cedar wood, and are available in a wide range of styles. To get started building and selling fence panels, you will need a homebased workshop, basic power and hand tools, and some design plans, but that's about it. The fence panels can be sold to fence installation companies, landscape contractors, do-it-yourself building centers, or directly to homeowners by placing advertisements in your local newspaper. Once established, and the manufacturing bugs have been worked out, there should be no problem averaging $20 to $30 per hour for building the fence panels.

GARDEN ARBORS
★★ $$ 🏠 🕒

Garden arbors have become a very popular landscape feature that thousands of homeowners are opting to include in their gardens. This creates a terrific business opportunity for the innovative entrepreneur to capitalize on by starting a homebased business that manufactures and sells garden arbors. If you have the ability, you can design your own trademark arbors. Or, if you are lacking in design talent, plans are readily available at most building centers for constructing garden arbors. Only a small workshop space and basic tools will be required for this endeavor. Establishing alliances with architects and landscape designers will enable you to capture the custom made-to-order arbor market. Or you can opt to create standard arbors that can be sold to building centers wholesale. Do not overlook the power of the internet in terms of marketing the arbors, as this is the type of home improvement product that is not readily available in every community, so some people will seek out the product via the web.

LATTICE
★ $$ 🏠 🕒

Wood, vinyl, and metal lattice has become an extremely popular landscaping and interior design building product in the past decade. There are many uses for lattice including decorative interior partitions for residential and commercial applications, exterior garden partitions and design features, and interior and exterior hand railing components, just to mention a few. Manufacturing custom lattice can easily be conducted right from a homebased workshop with minimal tools and experience, making this an excellent business start-up for entrepreneurs with minimal available start-up capital. Sell the finished product to building centers on a wholesale basis or directly to contractors, landscapers, and interior designers. The key to success will be in your ability to separate your product from that of competitors. Seek to create interesting lattice designs, sizes, and shapes that are not usually available. Most lattice products generally are sold in standard sizes, material selections, and designs. Venturing from the norm in terms of the design and appearance of your finished product can be your competitive advantage.

DRIFTWOOD AND LOG FURNITURE
★★ $$ 🏠 🕒

One of the best aspects about starting a business that designs and manufactures driftwood and log furniture for the home and patio is the fact that much of the raw manufacturing materials can be acquired for free or for very little cost. There are literally hundreds of different household and patio furniture products that can be manufactured from driftwood, rough cut logs, or even waste wood. These furniture products and home decorations can include coffee tables, benches, serving trays, side tables, chairs, planters, storage boxes, bunk beds, and picture frames; and these are only a few examples. One unique product that is very easy to manufacture is the driftwood coffee table. Basically, all that is involved is to locate a suitable piece of driftwood, clean with bleach, level and sand as required, and add a shaped glass top. Presto!—a highly saleable and unique piece of functional furniture. Once created, you can sell your furniture and decoration items by renting booth space at home and garden shows, flea markets, and even a kiosk in a mall on

weekends. Be sure to contact interior decorators in the area to introduce them to your unique furniture product line. A basic homebased workshop and tools will be required to get started, as well as some creative design abilities, but that is about all that is needed to get this business off the ground and earning profits for you.

AIR FRESHENER MANUFACTURING
★ $$ 🏠 🕒

Gel packs, mist sprays, scented products, and air fresheners can come in many forms. Manufacturing air fresheners is simple, and there are many books dedicated to the subject. Utilize the internet for research purposes to locate books and how-to manuals for creating air fresheners. It will be best to shy away from using chemical compounds in creating the air fresheners and stick to natural and organic ingredients. The air fresheners can be sold to retailers on a wholesale basis or directly to consumers by displaying your products at home and garden shows, as well as automobile shows. The start-up costs are low for this business. It can be operated from a well-ventilated home workshop, and through trial and error you can potentially create an air freshener product and scent that will appeal to a mass market.

ALUMINUM DOORS AND WINDOWS
★★ $$$ 🏠 🕒

Manufacturing aluminum storm windows and doors is a relatively simple process that can even be conducted right from a well-equipped homebased workshop. This business start-up will appeal to entrepreneurs with some construction and mechanical aptitude. Once again, aluminum storm windows and doors are easy to manufacture as the material required is referred to as extrusions. It is a simple process of cutting the window framing rails to length, wrapping the glass in a rubber gasket, and attaching the rails that are screw-fastened in the corners. The same basic procedure is used for constructing both aluminum storm windows and doors. Additionally, glass cutting experience will also be required. However, this is also an easy trade to master and most stained-glass retail shops even offer glass cutting courses on nights and weekends. Equipment requirements include a compound miter saw, flat glass-cutting table, a few basic hand tools, and, of course, a small initial inventory of aluminum extrusions, glass, and mechanical parts to get started. One of the best aspects about this business is that the start-up costs are low and only a minimal inventory must be stocked, as all the window orders will be custom sizes, and doors can also be manufactured on an ordered basis.

You can sell the storm windows and doors directly to homeowners by initiating an advertising campaign in your local newspaper, as well as displaying products at home and garden trade shows to collect sales leads. Additionally, be sure to establish alliances with contracting and renovation firms as these types of companies can become very good customers. You can measure and install the finished product yourself, or hire subcontractors to carry out the installations. As a general rule, storm windows and doors are sold on a united inch basis (U.I.), meaning you add the height of the window to the width of the window and multiply the sum in inches by the U.I. price. Check with other manufacturers and glass shops in your area to find out what the current U.I. price is, and providing your overhead structure allows, you should be able to offer clients a similar product at a cost that is less than that of the competitions.

WEB RESOURCE: www.thebluebook.com
Directory service listing manufacturers and distributors of aluminum extrusions, equipment, and supplies used in the manufacturing of aluminum windows and doors.

AWNING MANUFACTURING
★★ $$$$ 🏠

A terrific full- or part-time opportunity exists in an awning manufacturing business for entrepreneurs with good marketing skills and design and mechanical abilities. Providing you have the workshop space and zoning permits, you can even manufacture awnings right from a homebased location. There are basically two types of awnings: residential and commercial. Residential awnings are generally constructed from an aluminum or steel frame and covered with a canvas or vinyl fabric shell. Often residential awnings are mechanical, meaning that they can be manually or electrically extended and retracted to suit weather conditions and the user's needs. Commercial awnings are also constructed using an aluminum or steel frame and covered with a canvas or vinyl

fabric shell. Most are stationary, and many also act as signage for the business or office and are often electrically backlit to illuminate the sign at night. Skills required for this business include welding of both aluminum and steel pipe, commercial sewing, basic electrical knowledge, and good design skills. Of course much of the manufacturing work can be completed by employees or subcontractors. Equipment requirements will include a suitable workspace, transportation capable of moving large awnings, a welder and welding supplies, power hand tools, a chop-off saw, and pipe-bending machinery. In addition to sales and installations of awnings, you can also increase revenues and profits by offering clients additional services, such as awning cleaning and repairs.

WEB RESOURCE: www.thebluebook.com
Directory service listing manufacturers and distributors of awning manufacturing equipment and supplies.

GARDEN WORKBENCHES
★★ $$

Designing, manufacturing, and retailing garden workbenches is the focus of this new business start-up. Gardening has never been more popular than it is today. Well-organized and serious gardeners love to utilize professionally designed and manufactured multipurpose garden workbenches for various gardening tasks, such as potting plants and storing garden implements and fertilizers. The garden workbenches can be designed to include many handy features, such as an easy-clean surface, drawers and bins with rollers, and casters on the bottom of the workbench to enable the user to move their new garden workbench to various areas of the yard. The workbenches must also be manufactured from durable and lightweight construction materials. The garden workstations can be marketed by establishing wholesale accounts with national garden centers, as well as displaying the product locally at trade shows.

AWARD PLAQUES
★★ $$

Manufacturing and selling award plaques is a great homebased business opportunity that really has earning power. Every year across North America, thousands of award plaques are given to thousands of deserving recipients for a job well done, most valuable player, or in recognition of a special event. The business can easily be established from a homebased workshop, and the award plaques can be manufactured from any type of raw material in just about any style and size. Marketing the award plaques can be accomplished by a few different methods including creating a catalog with pictures, costs and descriptions of the plaques available and distributing the catalogs to large companies, sports associations, and school boards. Additionally, a unique approach to marketing the plaques would be to develop a web site that features all the available designs, so that customers can order and customize the award plaques right online.

LAMPS
★★ $$ 🔒 🕑 🌐

It's not hard to make a lamp; in fact, for $25 you can purchase a lamp-making kit. The goal here is to start a business that does not utilize the kits but allows you the creativity to design lamps, and shades in particular, that literally "light up the room" with both illumination and personality. Whether you hand-string glass beads, use imported fabric, or color the shade in a myriad of pastels, you can create a lamp business from your own converted basement, attic, or garage. Market lamps at local fairs or flea markets, set up a booth at the mall, and sell to local lighting retail stores. Create a web site to promote your work, and make sure to get your business card with your web address and a brochure or catalog in the mail to local interior designers. You can create some unique lamps for under $40 and sell them for over $100, so if you have the creative flair, this is a business you can embark upon for little money and make a nice profit.

WEB RESOURCE: www.lampmaking.com
Links to lamp making tools, instructions, and accessories.

REMOTE CONTROL HOLDERS
★ $$ 🔒 🕑 🌐

Millions of people waste countless hours every year looking for their remotes. For this reason, remote control holders have become increasingly popular, especially ones that can hold drinks or even have pockets for other accessories, like pens or paper or even your reading glasses. You can design several models made out of wood, metal, or

any of a variety of materials. As long as they hold the remote—or remotes—and either sit on the coffee table, attach to it, or go on the arm of a chair or couch, they will serve the purpose of keeping harmony in households throughout North America, while helping you launch a potentially lucrative business. Along with all of the usual marketing methods, see if you can align yourself with television and electronics stores as well as home theater businesses, where you can sell in greater quantity.

Depending on the materials, and various other pockets or compartments included, you can sell remote control holders for anywhere from $10 to $50, marking the product up close to 100% above your costs. This too is a business that can be run from your homebase.

BREAD BOXES
★ $$ 🔒 🕑

Hi-tech kitchenware move over—the truth remains that the best way to keep bread fresh is in an old-fashioned bread box. And, this is a business that can help you bring in the dough. Unless you know how to work with metals, stick with the basic wooden bread boxes and develop several styles that you can make on a regular basis in a workshop. From pine to driftwood and from to oak to bamboo, you can use almost any type of wood to make a marvelous product line. With a little practice, you can learn to make a roll-top bread box and add it to your inventory. Use a natural finish and you can sell the boxes for anywhere from $35 to $60. Team up with all kitchen supply dealers and market to home stores as well as sell through local home fairs and kitchen trade shows.

MANUFACTURER'S REP
★★ $ 🕑

If you cannot think of something that you would like to manufacture, then why not help other manufacturers take their products from the workshop to the showrooms and web pages of retailers. As a manufacturer's representative, you are an independent agent of sorts, serving as the liaison between the manufacturer, creators, and inventors and the retail stores, mail order businesses, and web sites. It is to your advantage to have some selling experience and be comfortable dealing with a wide range of personalities, since you will be in a position of constantly dealing with people. There is little start-up cost for this type of business, since you are selling a service to manufacturers who do not always have the time or qualified sales people to get their products the visibility necessary to make them top sellers. It will take time to get established and carve a niche, since many major retailers buy directly from manufacturers. But once you have found enough quality products to represent, you can build up this type of business and earn in the $100k to $175k range. Of course, with so many high tech and unique new products on the market, you will also need to learn a lot about the products that you rep and, in some cases, spend time training company personnel so that they can adequately sell the products to customers.

WEB RESOURCE: www.manaonline.org
Manufacturers Agents National Association.

WINERY
★★ $$$$ ⏱ ⚖

While it may not be your traditional manufacturing business, with a workbench and plenty or tools or machinery going, a winery is a marvelous means of manufacturing a product, while having a marvelous time doing so. Of course you will need to be well versed at the art of making wine but like anything else today, this can be learned. The first step, however, is buying or leasing the land on which to grow grapes and finding a place, such as an old barn, garage, or similar location in which to make the wine. Next, you need to experiment with numerous recipes until you find the ones that you believe are most marketable. Finally, you can start making and bottling wines, and then selling to retailers, directly from the winery, over the internet and through various festivals. The more room you have, the easier it will become to market your product through wine tasting events. Of course, if you have limited space, you can arrange with restaurants to hold wine tasting night, while the restaurant benefits from the sale of food and the publicity. Obviously, with the need for land, equipment, bottling and promotion, this is not an inexpensive endeavor by any means. This business also depends heavily on the climate in which you are planning to start a business and any local laws and, or ordinances regarding wine making. However, a winery

can bring in large sums of money if the product is excellent and the marketing is good.

WEB RESOURCE: www.wineryowners.org
Winery Owners and Managers Association.

COMMERCIAL DOORMATS
★ $$

This is an easy business to start. Simply design doormats for commercial business applications that have a real promotional message, such as "Welcome to…" and "Thanks for shopping at…." The doormats can be manufactured from different types of materials and have many different types of messages. The profit potential is excellent for this type of unique business enterprise, and there is limited competition due to the fact that each doormat is custom designed for the client. Market yourself to all small businesses that have a significant amount of foot traffic as well as to business professionals who see clients or patients in their offices.

KEY

RATINGS	★
START-UP COST	$$
HOMEBASED BUSINESS	🏠
PART-TIME OPPORTUNITY	🕐
LEGAL ISSUES	⚖️
FRANCHISE OR LICENSE POTENTIAL	🌐
GREEN BUSINESSES	🌿

48
OUTDOOR SERVICE
Businesses You Can Start

FLOWER KIOSK OR STAND
★★ $$ 🕐 🌐

Starting and operating a flower kiosk or flower stand can be a very profitable business to set in motion, providing you set yourself up in a highly visible and high-traffic area of your community. Various types of flowers such as roses, mums, and carnations can all be purchased on a wholesale basis from flower suppliers. The markups that are applied to flowers for retail purposes can exceed 200 percent, which can make this a very profitable business to run. A flower business can be operated on a year-round basis, providing you have the right location, such as an indoor mall, busy farmers' or food market, airport location, or in the lobby of a large office tower complex. You can also save money by growing some of your own flowers, if you have room for gardens and a green thumb. The key to success is to constantly have fresh flowers at the ready, especially leading up to holidays such as Valentine's Day and Mother's Day. If you can sell vases and perhaps stock some greeting cards, since flowers are often purchased for a special occasion, you can increase your income.

WEB RESOURCE: www.flowersource.net
Directory service listing flower growers and distributors.

LAWN MOWING SERVICE
★★ $ 🏠 🕐 🌐

Calling all high school and university students! Do not work for someone else this summer for minimum wage—start your own lawn mowing service. Mowing lawns is not an extravagant business to run. Providing you already have transportation to move yourself and equipment from job to job, the start-up investment needed to get a lawn mowing service rolling will be less than $1,000. For those of you on a really tight budget, you can do it for half of that amount if you are willing to take the time required to locate and purchase good quality, secondhand, lawn-mowing equipment. Marketing a lawn mowing service is as easy as knocking on doors in the neighborhood or designing and distributing fliers in the community describing your service. Likewise, a good source for potential clients is to contact all residential and commercial property management companies in your area to acquire a list of upcoming tenders for required lawn mowing services. The tender process can take some time, so be sure to start researching this potential market early in the year, prior to the kick-off of the lawn care season. To do well in this business you need to provide prompt, reliable service. Don't just mow randomly, but make sure to leave a lawn in a manner that shows that you have evenly cut all of the grass and eliminated the weeds. Also, don't expect a lawn mower to last forever. Clean the mower periodically (being very careful) and provide necessary maintenance, since this is the key to your business. Buying a leaf blower will allow you to offer another service as a means of increasing your revenue.

WEB RESOURCE: www.lawnmowers.com
Links to lawnmowers and accessories.

PARKING LOT LINE PAINTING
★★ $ 🚗 🕐

For the university students who are not going to start a lawn mowing service, perhaps you should consider starting a parking lot line painting service. It costs about the same to start this business and can produce a similar income to lawn mowing. The main necessity for starting this type of service will be to design stencils that will be used for painting the lines and symbols. The stencils should be cut out of quarter-inch plywood, which will make them sturdy but still light and easy to move. The stencil selection should include straight lines, straight arrows, turning arrows, handicap parking only, no parking, reserved parking, loading zone, and one way. Customers will include any property owner who requires well-marked parking and driving instruction painted on to their parking lots to reduce the chance of accidents and liability claims. Approach owners of newly constructed buildings with adjoining parking lots as well as those with existing lots where lines are no longer clearly visible.

SNOW REMOVAL SERVICE
★ $$ 🕐

There are a few methods for removing snow including a plow mounted on a four-wheel drive truck, a self-propelled or standard snow blower, and a good old snow shovel. Assuming you are not working out for the Olympics, I suggest that you stick with the snow blower or snowplow as your choice of equipment for this business venture, though you will want to have a shovel available for handling walkways or areas you cannot get to with the larger equipment. While a snow removal service is not likely to make you rich, it can generate an income of $30 per hour or more when the service is in season. Additional revenues for the business can be gained by providing a roof snow removal service for homeowners, as well as a sidewalk and driveway de-icing service. You can also stock up on salt for roads and driveways. Snow removal services can be offered to both residential and commercial customers.

WEB RESOURCE: www.plowsunlimited.com
A leading snowplow dealer.

FIREWOOD DELIVERY
★ $$ 🕐

In spite of the rising popularity in gas fireplaces, wood-burning fireplaces will still be around for some time to come. All wood-burning fireplaces have one thing in common—they need wood to burn. The only requirement for starting a firewood delivery business is to have, or purchase, a truck capable of delivering the firewood. Due to the weight of firewood, I would suggest that you purchase a one-ton pickup truck or a heavy-duty tandem-axle trailer for this task. While there are a few approaches to starting a firewood delivery service, the least costly and quickest to establish is simply purchasing split firewood in bulk and having it shipped to your yard or location. Once this has been completed, you can go about selling and delivering the firewood to customers in smaller quantities.

ROCK AND GEM SHOP
★★ $$$$

Rock and non-precious gem collecting is an outdoor hobby enjoyed by millions of people around the world. Starting a rock and gem retail store that stocks equipment used by these hobbyists, such as picks, shovels, gold-panning equipment, and informational books can put you on the path to financial freedom. The main requirement for starting a rock and gem shop is to have an interest in the subject as well as working experience. Beyond retail sales, additional income can be earned by conducting evening and weekend instructional classes on the subjects of rock and gem collecting, as well as how to successfully locate valuable rocks and gems. A rock and gem shop is certainly not the right new venture for everyone. However, specialty retailing, such as a rock and gem shop, can often produce better profits than traditional types of retail operations where you are up against more competition.

SPECIALTY TREE SALES
★★★ $$ 🚗 🕐

Selling rare specialty trees such as the Black Arkansas Spur, Anna Apple tree, or the Mexican Dwarf Banana tree can make you a lot of money. The market for these types of specialty trees is literally every household in North

America, as many specialty trees and shrubs can be grown indoors and outdoors. The key to successfully starting this business is to establish a source of growers for the types of trees that you will be selling, and in some cases, importing and exporting. The business does not require a great amount of investment capital to set in motion and can easily be conducted right from home. A well-designed informational presentation describing your business and the specialty trees and shrubs can be distributed to potential clients such as architects, custom homebuilders, and landscape design companies. With the right trees and shrubs, and a well-planned marketing program working for you, it should not take long for the telephone to start ringing and orders to start rolling in.

WEB RESOURCE: www.growit.com
Directory service listing tree growers and distributors.

STUMP REMOVAL SERVICE
★★ $$ 🚗 🕐

The fastest and most efficient way to get rid of a tree stump is to grind or cut it out. Purchasing a stump grinding machine is the first step on the way to starting a stump removal service. The cost of a new stump grinding machine starts at a few thousands dollars and generally requires a trailer or truck to be used for transporting, as the machines are very heavy. Contacting and soliciting firms, such as construction companies, landscape companies, architects, and property maintenance companies for stump removal work will generally secure all the business that a one-person stump removal service can handle. Currently, tree stump removal rates are in the range of $35 to $50 per hour. The more difficult stump removal jobs are usually estimated prior to starting the job. Make sure you know how to work this type of machine and take all safety precautions (which includes getting insurance) prior to starting such a business.

WEB RESOURCE: www.alpinemagnum.com
Distributor of stump grinding machinery.

PATIO LIGHTING
★ $$ 🚗 🕐

This business is inexpensive to initiate, and patio installations and upgrades are one of the leading home

improvement projects undertaken by millions of homeowners each year. The key to success in this business is to seek a manufacturer of high-quality patio lighting products, and become the manufacturer's exclusive distributor and installer for the lighting products in your area. The lighting products and installation service can be marketed to the end consumer, or you can provide your services to architects, homebuilders, and pool and patio contractors on a subcontract basis. Installing patio lighting can easily produce an income of $25 per hour or more, and the lighting products can be marked up by at least 25 percent to generate additional revenue and profits.

WEB RESOURCE: www.outdoorlighting.learnabout.info/patiolights.htm
Plenty of information about patio lights plus some links to distributors.

TREE PLANTING SERVICE
★ $$ 🖋

On the surface, starting a tree planting service may not seem like a very lucrative business to operate. However, each year forestry companies cut down thousands of trees and replant thousands more. Typically, the task of replanting these trees is left to subcontractors who either have successfully tendered for the job or have established a working history and relationship with forestry companies to provide tree-planting services. A good starting point in this industry is to compile a list of all forestry companies and commence contacting them to inquire about forthcoming tenders and the status of their particular tree-planting programs. Providing you are successful in securing tree planting contracts, be prepared to work hard and form a crew of tree planting laborers. The work is physically demanding and usually requires the operators of these businesses to be away from home for extended periods of time. However, it is common for tree-planting contracts to exceed $100,000 in value.

LANDSCAPING SERVICE
★★ $$ 🚗 🕐

Depending on the region of the country that you are living in, launching a seasonal or year-round landscaping service is a terrific way to stay physically fit, and potentially financially fit. A basic one-or two-person landscaping service can be set in motion for less than $10,000, while a full service landscaping design and installation service can costs ten times that amount to start. A lot of the skill and experience can be learned on the job. However, operating a landscaping service still requires some past landscaping knowledge, skills and experience to initiate and to give clients peace of mind. Potential customers for a landscaping service include commercial property owners, residential property owners, and subdivision property developers. While an established landscaping service can complete work for all three of these types of customers, a new landscaping service should focus on one particular type of customer until the business has established a successful performance record. Most landscaping contracts are completed based on an estimate for services prior to starting the work, so be sure to practice your estimating skills, as it is very easy to underbid and overbid, both of which can be very costly in terms of bottom line business profits.

WEB RESOURCE: www.landcarenetwork.org
Planet: Professional Land Care Network.

PATIO PAVING STONES
★★ $$$ 🏠 🕒

Paving stones have become a very popular choice for use in the construction of walkways, patios, and driveways and starting a business that installs patio paving stones can be a very profitable venture to own and operate. The business can be marketed through all traditional marketing and advertising channels including yellow pages, newspapers, flier distribution, and radio and television advertisements. For entrepreneurs on a tight marketing budget, consider offering your service to construction, renovation, and landscape companies on a subcontract basis to supply and install the patio stone for their projects. While subcontracting for other firms will substantially reduce profits, it is a quick-start method to get the business established and generating cash flow.

WEB RESOURCE: www.pavestone.com/retail/pavers_faq.html
Tips on patio paving stones so you can gain expertise in the field.

LAWN SPRINKLER SYSTEMS
★★ $$$ 🚗

At one time the installation of an underground lawn sprinkler system was reserved only for the wealthiest of homeowners. However, times have changed and new installation techniques and mass-produced plastic pipes have brought the costs of supplying and installing underground sprinkling systems down to a point where they are now within the financial grasp of almost all homeowners. Starting this business requires that the installers of the sprinkler systems be experienced and knowledgeable. Equipment used in this business can be very expensive. However, equipment and tools can be initially rented as a way of controlling start-up costs, and experienced staff can be hired and paid a slight premium as a way of guaranteeing quality work. The service can be marketed directly to consumers via all traditional ad mediums or the service can work for homebuilders and property developers on a subcontract basis, allowing you to include such systems prior to the landscaping of the community. In addition, some parks, ball fields and other outdoor locations can benefit from sprinkling systems, so market to these potential customers as well.

WEB RESOURCE: www.thebluebook.com
Directory service listing equipment and supply manufacturers and distributors.

WISHING WELL PLANTERS
★★ $ 🏠 🕒 ✒

Utilize your carpentry skills and start a business that manufactures and sells wishing well planters. The business can be conducted from home and requires only a minimal amount of capital to get rolling. The wishing wells can be displayed and sold at flea markets, gardening trade shows, or by establishing accounts with merchants to stock and sell the wishing wells. Utilizing recycled construction material for building the wishing wells has two benefits. The first is obvious: You will be joining the "green" team of environmentalists. The second benefit is the fact that utilizing recycled material in construction of any product creates a fantastic platform for a promotional campaign. And in the case of a wishing well, perhaps the slogan could be, "Wish for a Healthier Planet: All materials used in the manufacturing are recycled."

GARDEN PLANNING SERVICE OR GARDEN CONSULTANT
★ $ 🚗 🕐

Many people, myself included, would love to have a vegetable garden and enjoy fresh in-season vegetables in our daily meals. However, the only problem with this is the fact that most people, once again myself included, do not know the first thing about how to grow vegetables and maintain a productive vegetable garden. Assuming you have both the gardening skills and some basic marketing skills, there is a better than average chance that you would succeed in starting and operating your own garden planning service. This type of specialized service certainly does not require very much investment capital to get started and can be managed from a homebased office. You provide your gardening expertise and experience on an in-home consulting basis for people who are seeking to establish a productive vegetable garden. The service could be marketed and promoted by establishing alliances with garden centers that would refer your service to their clients in exchange for supplying you and your clients with the required seeds, plants, and gardening equipment. Depending on the region of the country the business is located in, a seasonal or year-round income of $20 to $25 per hour could easily be charged for the garden planning service. You could also expand and teach gardening classes from your own garden or from a gardening center, where people could then purchase necessary materials.

WEB RESOURCE: www.nationalgardenwholesale.com
National Garden Wholesale

GOLD PANNING
★★ $$ 🕐

"There's gold in them thar hills," or at least that's what you can tell your clients. Providing you live in an area of North America that is known for gold panning and gold mining, you already meet the first requirement for starting your own "How to Gold Pan" instructional business. The business can focus on teaching people who are serious about wanting to learn how to successfully pan for gold, as well as tourists seeking a fun and entertaining outdoor experience while on holidays. The business can be broken into two categories and fee schedules. Serious

students could be provided with a weeklong gold-panning course, while the fun-seeking tourist would be offered a two-hour instructional course. This type of enterprise can certainly be set in motion on a minimal capital investment, and the potential earnings for the owner-operator could be fabulous, once the business has been successfully established. For the tourist angle, milk it. Buy the old-fashioned gold panning outfit, give your course a fun name, gather some pertinent facts, and make it a fun family experience so that your course becomes one of the "things to do" for tourists in the area.

WEB RESOURCE: www.goldprospectors.org
Gold Prospectors Association of America.

STONE SALES FOR LANDSCAPING
★★ $$ 🚗 🕐

Natural stone is used every day for landscaping, both for retaining walls and just for an attractive garden feature. The best aspect of starting a business that supplies landscaping stones to contractors and garden supply centers is the fact that the stones can be acquired for free. A short drive into the countryside will reveal that natural fieldstones are everywhere, and simply striking a deal with a few farmers to provide a free stone removal service will provide you with an ongoing and unlimited inventory of stones to sell. The main piece of equipment required for this business is a good-quality used flatbed truck with a hydraulic cherry picker. A cherry picker is a mechanical arm that is controlled by an operator, enabling heavy items to be picked up and moved easily. Additional revenues can also be gained by offering a delivery service for the stones, as well as a stone removal service for property owners.

BOBCAT® SERVICE
★★★ $$$$ 🚗 🕐

Bobcats are a small version of large bulldozers and earth moving machinery. They can be used for a number of landscaping and construction tasks, including snow removal, topsoil moving, tree planting, excavating earth, digging postholes, removing tree stumps, and clearing brush and debris. The key benefits to owning a Bobcat is the fact that they can easily be maneuvered in small work areas. They can cost as much as one quarter of the amount necessary to operate larger earth moving machinery. A Bobcat service can be offered directly to the end user, such as a homeowner who wishes to have a hole dug for a small addition to their home or the service can be provided to building contractors and landscape installation companies on a subcontract basis. Bobcats are relatively easy to operate and can certainly be mastered by a novice operator with only a small amount of practice. However, as easy as the machines are to drive, they are not easy to repair, and repairs can be very costly. Be sure to purchase a secondhand Bobcat only if it has had a full and independent mechanical inspection. One of the main requirements to operate a Bobcat service is to acquire liability insurance to protect your assets in the event of an accident.

START-UP COSTS: The following example can be used as a guideline to establish the investment required to successfully start a Bobcat service. For the purposes of providing an example of investment requirements and as a method of minimizing start-up costs, costs shown reflect current prices of used equipment.

	Low	High
Heavy-duty truck or van	$5,000	$15,000
Tandem-axle trailer	$1,000	$2,500
Bobcat, including various equipment attachments	$7,500	$15,000
Safety equipment and miscellaneous tools	$500	$2,000
Business setup, banking, legal, etc.	$1,000	$2,500
Liability insurance coverage	$500	$2,500
Initial marketing and advertising budget	$1,000	$3,000
Working capital	$1,000	$5,000
Total start-up costs	**$17,500**	**$47,500**

PROFIT POTENTIAL: The profit potential for a Bobcat service is outstanding, and currently rates for the service are in the range of $50 to $80 per hour and $350 to $500 per day. Securing a mere 25 hours of work each week can produce business revenues in excess of $80,000 per year. Additional business income can also be gained by providing topsoil, sand, and gravel sales and delivery, as well as furnishing clients with an optional rubbish removal service.

WEB RESOURCE: www.bobcat.com
Ingersoll-Rand Inc. Manufacturers of Bobcat construction equipment.

LEAF RAKING SERVICE
★ $ 🏠 🕐

Wherever there are leaves on residential or commercial property, they need to be raked and bagged. Hence, you have the start of a part-time business. While you won't be raking in big bucks, if you can hire the local teens and set up a service whereby you send them to homes, office parks or other facilities that need raking you can have the makings of an easy-to-run homebased business. Schools and government buildings can also utilize your services if you are able to network with the local powers that be. For private homeowners, your marketing will consist primarily of fliers and posters in local shops.

WEB RESOURCE: www.homeownernet.com/articles/leavescleanup.html
Informative article on autumn leaves clean-up.

SPORTS COURT INSTALLATIONS
★★ $$$$ 🌐

Installation of multipurpose sports courts are the latest rage to enter into the home improvement industry. All-in-one courts include features that enable the court to be quickly reformatted to suit alternate sports, such as tennis, basketball, hockey, badminton, and racquetball. This is one aspect of such a business, or you can supply the materials for (and build) courts, specifically designed for the individual sports. Courts may feature high fencing, durable impact-resistant playing surfaces, and even changing room facilities in some cases. Generally, these courts are constructed for outside use, although indoor outdoor options are possible – for a lot more money. Sports courts can be marketed in various ways. You can design an elaborate demonstration display model that can be set up and exhibited at fitness, recreation, and home improvement trade shows or displayed on your web site. You can also form alliances with home builders that can now offer sports court optional upgrade packages to their clients. Other markets for the sports courts include clubs, associations, and corporations. Along with designing such courts for homes, you can market your services to condo or co-op housing developments as well as community centers and hotels. A simple method to establish a retail selling price for the sports courts is to calculate the total cost of material and labor that will be required to complete the installation, and add a 40 to 50 percent markup onto the base labor and material costs. Utilizing this pricing formula will result in a 28 to 33 percent gross profit margin on total sales volumes, prior to subtracting operating overhead and taxes. Of course to start such a business you will need some experience in building and familiarity with the surface requirements of such courts. You will also need to know the building codes and be sure that any such zoning ordinances do not prohibit the construction of such outdoor courts. Liability insurance will also be necessary. To make additional money, servicing and providing upkeep of the courts can prove very valuable, since the surfaces do not always respond well to wear and tear, or the elements if they are outdoors.

SEED PACKAGING
★ $$ 🚗 🕒 ✎

Vegetable and flower seeds can be inexpensively purchased in bulk from numerous seed suppliers and packaged into smaller quantities for retail sale purposes. The best method of marketing the seeds is to design and build a point-of-purchase marketing display that can be located inside retail stores, such as garden centers, food markets, and flower shops. Some retailers may request that the POP displays be stocked on a consignment basis. If possible, try to provide the retailer with a larger wholesale discount as a method of enticement not to consign the seeds. This is a business that requires a high volume of sales to produce generous profits. However, the business should expand quickly once a few POP seed displays have been placed and they start to generate revenues and profits.

WEB RESOURCE: www.amseed.com
The American Seed Trade Association.

MINIGREENHOUSES
★ $$ 🚗 🕒 ✎

Starting a business that manufactures and installs minigreenhouses is a terrific business venture to launch. Minigreenhouses are smaller versions of their larger

counterparts, and typically are around 25 to 30 square feet in total size. These minigreenhouses can be constructed to be free standing or be built onto the side of a shed, garage, or house. Design plans are available for the construction of minigreenhouses, or of course, you can design and build your own if you have some construction experience. The business is best marketed by establishing alliances with a local garden supply center that will allow you to construct and assemble a minigreenhouse display model on their site. Once completed, the pint-sized greenhouses can be sold to homeowners on a "you install kit" basis, or "we install for you" basis. You can also market via a web site and through traditional means, including Pennysavers, local newspaper ads, etc. Make sure to meet all building codes and have liability insurance. A background in plants and planting is also helpful in this "green" business.

WEB RESOURCE: www.greenhouses.com
Supplier of greenhouses, greenhouse accessories, and greenhouse kits.

GARDEN CURBING
★★ $$ 🚗

Cement curbing machines are available that produce fast, easy, and inexpensive curbing for gardens, walkways, and driveways. Curbing machines are available in two styles: self-propelled, and not self-propelled, which require the operator of the machine to maneuver it manually. The neat aspect of curbing machines is that they have interchangeable extrusion heads that can form the concrete into various curbing profiles. Currently, installation rates for on-site curbing start at about $3 per linear foot. Extra costs are charged to customers for preparing the ground for the curbing, as well as for creating elaborate curves and curbing designs. A curbing service is ideally suited for the individual who has landscape installation and design experience, as well as general construction knowledge. While the profit potential will greatly vary because of the amount of curbing that is sold and installed, a well-established residential garden curbing service can produce monthly sales exceeding $6,000.

WEB RESOURCE: www.borderlinestamp.com
Manufacturers and distributors of curbing equipment.

ORGANIC LAWN AND GARDEN FERTILIZER
★★ $$ 🚗 🕐 ✎

As the green movement of environmental correctness sweeps the country, an increasing number of people are now using organic lawn and garden fertilizers as opposed to chemical fertilizers, and the trend toward switching to environmentally friendly lawn and garden products is on the rise. This fact alone should be enough reason for anyone who is considering starting a new business to take a serious look at initiating a business that wholesales and retails organic lawn and garden fertilizer products. With careful research and development practices being implemented, a recipe can be achieved to produce an effective organic fertilizer. However, locating an existing manufacturer of organic lawn and garden fertilizer products and negotiating an exclusive distribution contract may better serve an entrepreneur who is new to this industry. Once the distribution agreement is in place, the organic lawn and garden products can be sold to retailers to stock and sell in their stores. The potential for profits and growth are excellent for this business venture.

WEB RESOURCE: www.ota.com
The Organic Trade Association.

CHRISTMAS TREES SALES
★ $$ 🚗 🕐

Yes, it's seasonal, but it is a big business for two months every year. Christmas tree sales is a terrific part-time seasonal business to initiate that can produce excellent profits for a few months each year. The first step is to secure a supply of good-quality evergreen trees that are approximately 4 to 6 feet high, that the grower has already potted individually into inexpensive plastic pots. The next and very critical step is to secure a visible indoor or outdoor location, such as a busy parking lot, mall, food market, or recreation center, to setup and sell the Christmas trees. Without question, environmentally concerned consumers will gladly pay out a few extra dollars for a Christmas tree that can be planted in the back yard when Christmas is over, as opposed to a tree that will end up shredded or in the landfill. The key to this business is making sure to have plenty of trees on hand when approaching the holiday season and, no matter how you do it, sell them all before Christmas Eve. If you do, you could make upwards of $10,000 each Christmas season, which can buy some pretty nice gifts for your family and friends.

WEB RESOURCE: www.christree.org
National Christmas Tree Association.

TREE TRIMMING AND REMOVAL SERVICE
★★ $$$ 🚗 🕐

Starting a tree trimming and tree removal service is a great business enterprise to activate, especially if you have past work experience or knowledge in this field. The equipment needed to successfully operate the service includes a truck, ladders, safety gear, chainsaws, and pruning shears. A number of measures can be used to gain customers, such as designing and distributing promotional fliers, placing advertisements for your service in newspapers and the yellow pages, as well as competing for tree trimming and removal contracts and tenders. One aspect of the business that must not be overlooked will be to make sure the operation is covered by a suitable amount of liability insurance, as well as disability insurance for the owner and employees.

LAWN AERATION SERVICE
★ $ 🚗 🕐

The easiest way to keep a lawn in tiptop condition is to aerate the lawn twice per year. Starting a lawn aeration service in your community is very straightforward. The equipment necessary is available at most industrial supply centers and is relatively inexpensive to purchase. The most effective way to market a lawn aeration service is to simply design and distribute promotional fliers throughout the community. Once again, this is not the type of business that should be started if your goal is to earn $100,000 per year. However, a realistic earning potential is certainly in the $25 to $30 per hour range.

HAMMOCK SALES
★ $$ 🚗 🕐

While hammocks are certainly easy enough to manufacture, a better route to starting this business is to import the hammocks from a manufacturer located outside the country. Manufacturing hammocks is a very labor intensive job, and countries that maintain a lower wage structure for workers can generally (not always) produce a product for a fraction of what it may cost to produce in the United States. To source an international supplier for hammocks, simply consult foreign trade commissions or research the topic on the internet. Both methods will quickly produce a manufacturer who may be more than happy to enter into an importing agreement with a U.S. company. Once an importing agreement has been secured, the hammocks can be sold on a wholesale basis to specialty retailers such as outdoors and recreation stores and leisure shops. The hammocks can also be sold directly to consumers over the internet or at busy flea markets, local fairs, or at camping and recreation trade shows.

WEB RESOURCE: www.nationalgardenwholesale.com
Hammock wholesalers and information

FISH POND INSTALLATION
★★★ $$ 🏠 🕒

Many people are now including fish ponds in their home landscape designs. These ponds are not only an attractive landscape element, they can also provide hours of relaxing time spent watching the fish. The ponds can be designed for interior and exterior garden spaces, and can be stocked with a multitude of various fish species. Top-notch fish ponds always include recirculating water pumps, rocks, water plants, and pond ornaments. There are many books available on the subject of how to design and create basic and elaborate fish ponds. These books will be an invaluable source of information and assistance for anyone considering starting this type of business. In my opinion, there is only one way to market this type of business. Create an award-winning fish pond display highlighting as many features as possible, and assemble the display at home and garden shows, as well as at malls on weekends to collect sales leads from people who are interested in purchasing such a pond. Having some design abilities will help you to offer customized and creative sizes and shapes of ponds for homeowners or landscapers.

MANURE SALES
★ $$ 🕒

A quick trip to the garden center will tell you that manure is a popular choice for garden and plant fertilizer.

Providing you are in close proximity to farms, you can certainly get enough "raw materials" to get you started in the business of packaging and selling manure-based fertilizer products. To keep the family happy, I strongly suggest this business not be established at home! Perhaps a partnership could be negotiated with a farmer to enable the product packaging to be conducted on the farm site and to meet the demand. The largest expenses to establish a manure sales business will be in the design and manufacturing of the packaging and you will need a truck for hauling the packages. Unless you have the ability to design an outstanding package, this task is probably better left to a professional designer, as this is a very important element of the business. You can sell to garden centers on a wholesale basis both locally and nationally.

WILDFLOWER GARDENS
★ $$ 🏠 🕒

Thousands of homeowners are turning away from traditional flower and shrub gardens, in favor of low maintenance and inexpensive wildflower gardens. There are many benefits to a wildflower garden over a traditional garden, including lower regular maintenance and less costly yearly maintenance to keep the garden in top shape. Additionally, native wildflower gardens have gained in popularity because of their environmental value and varied appearance. Working as a consultant, you can provide clients with wildflowers, garden design tips, seeds, and even the complete installation of the garden. Establishing a billing rate for the consulting service will greatly depend on the various requests of the clients. However, a base rate for the consulting aspect of the business should be set at $25 to $30 per hour.

WEB RESOURCE: www.onr.com/wildflowers.html
National Wildflower Research Council.

WATER WELL DRILLING
★ $$$$ 🏠 🚗 ✎

The average water well now costs in excess of $5,000 to drill, and while starting a water well drilling business certainly requires a large capital investment and a lot of practical well drilling experience, the profit potential can be enormous. The first step to establishing a well drilling service is obvious: the business must be located in a rural area as opposed to an urban center. Additional considerations for establishing this very specialized business will also be local weather conditions, quality of local ground water, the availability of experienced local well drilling labor and local laws regarding where you can drill. All of these things can have an impact on the business. You can market such a business in all traditional methods, as well as directly to homebuilders that specialize in developing country properties.

WEB RESOURCE: www.nda4u.com
National Drilling Association.

CHAIN SAW SERVICE
★★ $$ 🏠 🕐

There are literally hundreds of chain saw jobs, such as stump removal, tree and brush clearing, tree removal, and building demolition. Every community could use a reliable person with a chain saw service. The service can be marketed directly to homeowners by placing small classified advertisements under the "work wanted" section of local newspapers. You can also provide your chain saw services on a subcontract as-needed basis to property maintenance firms and landscape contractors. A chain saw service is not likely to make you rich. However, it is still a great low-cost business start-up that can produce a part-time income of $25 per hour or more. Be sure you are skilled at working with a chain saw, have liability insurance, and take the necessary safety precautions.

WEB RESOURCE: www.chainsaws.com
Links to numerous chainsaw manufacturers.

WILDLIFE CONTROL SERVICE
★★ $$ 🏠 ⚖️

Raccoons, squirrels, and other small critters cause millions of dollars worth of damage to homes and properties each year. New wildlife control policies are springing up across the country, which enable operators of wildlife control companies to trap and relocate these unharmed animals into rural areas outside urban centers. The first requirement to starting this business will be to check local regulations in terms of licenses that may be needed to operate the business. Additionally, be prepared to work long and irregular hours, as this type of service typically provides customers with a 24-hour, seven-days-a-week

service by way of an emergency hotline. The equipment needed to start this business includes animal traps, baiting and handling gear, and a service vehicle. Once established, this type business has the potential to earn the owner-operator an income that can easily exceed $50,000 to $60,000 per year. Make sure to take necessary safety precautions, know all about the traps you are setting, and have insurance.

RETAINING WALL INSTALLATION
★ $$ 🏠 🕐

Designing and installing retaining walls for residential and commercial landscaping projects is not only a great business to start, it is also guaranteed to keep you fit. There are various types of materials used in the construction of retaining walls including cement blocks, pressure treated lumber, and reclaimed railroad ties. The simplest construction materials to work with are the new style of concrete retaining wall blocks that systematically lock into each other. This business can be marketed directly to residential and commercial clients, or the business can work with contractors on a subcontract basis. Installing retaining walls is a relatively straightforward building task. However, the entrepreneur considering starting this type of business should possess construction and landscaping knowledge and practical experience.

SOIL TESTING SERVICE
★ $$$ ⚖️

There are many potential customers for a soil testing business including commercial farmers, property developers, and homeowners, just to mention a few. The main requirement needed for this type of service is to be experienced in soil testing, or hire employees who have such experience. Beyond that, the rest of the requirements are the same as any new business enterprise. Soil testing is the sort of business that does not explode out of the blocks so to speak; it can take many years to build a client and referral base. With that in mind, be sure you have both the time necessary and the patience required for starting this type of business. Due to the types of chemicals used in soil testing, this business is not suitable to be a homebased business and should be located in an industrial rental unit.

WEB RESOURCE: www.homeharvest.com/soiltesting.htm
Soil testing kits.

FISHING LURES AND TIES
★★ $$ 🔧 🕐

Calling all homemakers, retirees, students, and anyone else looking to earn extra income from a part-time business venture. If this describes you, maybe starting a business venture that makes specialty fishing lures and fishing ties is the business oppor tunity that you have been searching for. The market for fishing lures is absolutely gigantic, and the potential to earn $30 or more per hour from making and selling fishing lures is not only achievable, it is being done by thousands of people around the world right now. Getting started in this business only requires research into the construction of fishing lures and ties. Currently, there are hundreds, if not thousands, of books available on this subject so there should be no difficulty learning the trade. Once the fishing lures and ties have been designed and produced, there are numerous ways to sell them. The first method of sales and distribution is to sell the fishing lures to retailers, tackle shops, and fishing camps on a wholesale basis. The second method of sales and distribution is to sell the fishing lures and ties directly to fisher men, and this can be accomplished by mail-order sales or going directly to the source and establishing a sales kiosk that can be set up at fishing and outdoor trade shows. Given the fact that this business can be set in motion on an initial investment from as low as $500, the profit potential is excellent and can well exceed $30 per hour.

WEB RESOURCE: www.oldfishinglure.com
Background information and links to antique fishing lure retailers.

SAND AND GRAVEL DELIVERY
★★ $$ 🕐

Ideally a sand and gravel delivery service should be established in a densely populated area in order for this type of micro delivery business to be successful. A small storage yard and suitable delivery transportation, such as a one-ton dump truck, will be needed. Sand, gravel, and topsoil can all be purchased in large quantities on a wholesale basis from a large producer. These same products can then be resold to consumers and business clients in smaller portions at a profit. Clients for this type of service and product will include homeowners, landscaping firms, and garden centers. Maintaining a 100 percent markup on all products sold and deli vered, as well as achieving annual sales of $200,000, will result in gross profit for the business of $100,000 prior to taxes and operating costs.

WEB RESOURCE: www.quarryworld.com
Directory service listing sand and gravel producers.

FISHING BAIT SALES
★★ $$ 🔧 🕐

There are an infinite number of options available to an entrepreneur in terms of starting and operating a business that involves stocking and selling fishing bait. My wife's family successfully operated a bait and tackle shop and a complete fishing tourist camp for more than 20 years. The following list highlights a few of the options for operating a business that stocks and sells fishing bait:

- *Minnows.* Bait minnows, like shiners, can be caught in rivers and creeks by using minnow traps or a seine net. Bait minnows can also be raised in ponds. The key to keeping the minnows alive and healthy is to have a good oxygen aeration system in place. The minnows can be sold on a wholesale basis to local bait shops or directly to fishermen, providing you have retail space and facilities. A license to catch or trap bait minnows is generally required, so be sure to check local regulations.

- *Dew worms.* These are also commonly called night crawlers and are also excellent fishing bait that can be raised or picked for a bait supply business. Raising dew worms requires worm boxes to be constructed and the soil used in the boxes must be nutrient rich and changed on a regular basis. Dew worm picking is best accomplished by forming a crew to pick the worms from the ground. Golf courses are ideal locations, as the worms will come out at night, especially after a light rain. Worms can be packaged in flats and wholesaled in bulk to fishing bait shops, or packaged in smaller quantities and sold directly to fishermen.

- *Leeches.* They can be caught or raised for a fishing bait business, and the leeches can be sold on a wholesale basis to bait shops, or they can be packaged in smaller quantities and sold directly to fishermen, providing you have a retail bait and tackle shop.

Like any new business start-up, careful planning and research prior to establishing a business will always increase the chances for success, and starting a fishing bait supply business is no different. The business can be operated from home under the right conditions, or the business can be established in a rental location, which can include enough space to allow for both retailing and wholesaling bait and possibly fishing tackle and fishing equipment. As mentioned previously, there are an infinite number of options available in terms of starting a fishing related business, and with careful planning and research, a fishing bait supply business can be extremely profitable for the innovative and creative entrepreneur.

RV WASH SERVICE
★ $$ 🚗 🕒

Many campgrounds, overnight RV parks, and even some hotels have RV wash centers right on site, but not all, and the ones that do not are the ones that you want to aim your marketing efforts toward. Simply establish alliances with campgrounds and overnight RV parks to provide their visitors with an optional RV wash service. You can joint venture with various locations and set specific days of the week that you will be on site to offer the service. This is a really beneficial service for campgrounds that do not have an RV washing area, thus they will be more than happy to build the alliance and promote the service. In terms of equipment, all that's required to get started is a portable power washer, a few buckets, and a ladder. You should have no difficulties charging in the range of $15 to $25 dollars to wash the exterior of the average-sized RV and this will only take 30 minutes or less to complete. This is a good business opportunity for someone that is looking to start a business with a minimal investment and on a part-time basis.

CHIPPER AND MULCH SERVICE
★★ $$$$ 🚗 🕒

Starting a portable chipper and mulch business is a terrific venture that can keep you busy on a full- or part-time basis earning a great income. Portable chippers are simply a trailer-mounted wood chipper that is gasoline powered and used to chip branches, brush, and waste woods into saleable mulch. Some chipper models can even accept branches up to 12 inches in diameter, but like any piece of heavy equipment, the bigger the capacity the higher the cost to purchase. Money is earned two ways in this business. The first is to charge customers a fee to turn brush and branches into mulch, and the second is to sell the mulch. The mulch can be sold to landscape contractors, garden centers, and farmers. In addition to a chipper, you will also need a large truck to pull the chipper trailer and to act as the bin for the mulch that gets blown out of the chipper. The business can be costly to start. However, chipper fees are in the range of $45 to $60 per hour for operator and equipment. Potential clients will include landscape contractors that do not provide this service, government contracts for cleaning brush from the sides of roads, and property developers. Of interest is the fact that some chipper services are also starting to work with re-roofing contractors that specialize in cedar roofing. Instead of sending the old shakes to landfill sites, they are chipped on site and the mulch is sold providing the shakes have never been chemically treated. It's a great idea, it's good for the environment, and it's a good way to earn extra profits.

WEB RESOURCE: www.woodchuckchipper.com
Manufacturers of wood chipping equipment and machinery.

CADDIE TRAINING AND BOOKING
★ $$ 🕒

Yes, many of the finer golf courses at resorts and at private clubs still have caddies. While the year-round full-time professional caddie is hard to find today, there are plenty of college kids, home from out-of-town schools for the summer, who know that caddying pays more than life guarding and also gives them the opportunity to play some marvelous courses. These are your customers for teaching the job of caddying. The job of the caddie is more than simply carrying a golf bag. The well-trained caddie helps the golfer determine the distance from the ball to the green, considers potential hazards along the way, and help the player select the right club for a shot. He or she also helps golfers maintain their equipment, find lost balls, navigate the course, and maintain a steady pace of play. If you are well versed in the game of golf and possibly even caddied when you were young, you can start a business whereby you train caddies in golf etiquette and the art of being a caddie. If you can ingratiate yourself with club owners, you can also help them find the best young staffers for their caddie needs. In time, you may even build up an accredited caddy academy. There is minimal cost to start up the business since it is primarily imparting knowledge, providing training, and serving as an employment service of sorts to golf courses. This may be a part-time business in many parts of the country, but in Florida, Arizona, or other golfing Meccas, you could do very well with this business on a full-time basis. Market yourself to colleges as well!

FULL CAR WASH
★★★ $$$$ 🚗

Setting up and maintaining a full car wash can be costly, but without much local competition, big profits can be made. Hand drying, interior cleaning, and other low-cost, quality service features go a long way toward building up business. You can also offer detailing if you have the experience, or hire someone to handle such detailing, which can include polishing and buffing or waxing.

START-UP EXPENSES:

Legal	$500
Marketing: Brochures and advertising	$1,800
Insurance	$500
Rent (2 months)	$ 4,000
Expensed Equipment	$4,200
Signs	$700
Building Materials	$1,300
Building Labor	$1,000
Total Start-up Expenses	$14,000
Cash needed	$12,000
Total Requirements	**$26,000**

This is a rough estimate of getting a full car wash started. The first step to starting this business may be securing backers, and with a good business plan, this can be inviting, since a car wash is a tried and true business.

At full car washes you can expect to make from $15 to $35 per vehicle depending on services. At a part time venture, $5 to $10 is certainly fair enough, and charge the high end if half of it is going for a good cause.

COMMERCIAL LAWN CARE
★★ $$ 🕒

Apartment complexes, medical facilities, office parks, and shopping malls—these are just some of the facilities that require ongoing lawn care and can be the basis of a potentially substantial market. If you have expertise in what it takes to care for a lawn, you can establish regular clients and make significant money. The cost to start up such a business will be primarily the tools of the trade, which should cost you under $15,000, plus advertising and marketing. Beyond mowing grass, there is the need for trimming hedges and caring for shrubs and bushes. Pest control is also typically part of the picture. Like many businesses, this service will depend largely on how far you, and your staff, have made it around the learning curve, since the more you can solve lawn problems, the better chance you have of getting and maintaining clients. Make sure to get all necessary licensing (particularly for using pesticides) and liability insurance and consider joining the Professional Lawn Care Association of America. One of the keys to success is being able to listen carefully to the needs of your clients and then meeting their needs, plus applying practical solutions to problems that arise.

WEB RESOURCE: www.grolawnplus.com/plcaa.html
Professional Lawn Care Association of America

GOLF COURSE MAINTENANCE
★★ $$ 🕒

Unlike other types of landscaping, golf courses require some unique care. The course is not only designed to look good, but is obviously an integral part of the game. Therefore, someone looking to start this type of highly lucrative, and competitive, business needs to become very familiar with the various intricacies that are involved in caring for a golf course. Fast greens, casual water, and thick rough are golf expressions that are all directly related to the course, which other lawn care specialists need not understand. In addition to knowing how to operate the necessary equipment for performing turf and golf course maintenance, the course needs to be properly irrigated, and maintaining the irrigation system is crucial to play on the course. Other responsibilities include minor course repair, daily maintenance, and reporting course conditions to the starter and the course superintendent. Learning is a combination of taking course turf management courses and on-the-job training. Once you are well versed in all the necessary skills and practical applications, you will want to hire a reliable, credible, hard-working staff. Beyond equipment, some of which is supplied by the course, there are limited start-up costs. This is the type of business that needs experience in the field (literally) to get off the ground. Therefore, before embarking on such an endeavor, you should work for a golf course maintenance service for a year or two, gain valuable experience, and meet the people in the golfing industry in your town. They will be your potential clients.

METAL DETECTOR BUSINESS
★ $$ 🎒 🕐

Metal detecting is a very popular hobby, with clubs meeting weekly, going on hunts, and/or holding contests all over North America. Starting a business that sells metal detectors can be lucrative if you can ingratiate yourself into the world of metal detection. Equipment can run from $150 to $1000, as well as accessories, including travel bags, chargers, rechargeable batteries, headphones, digging tools, flashlights and more. You can also provide information on local clubs and even start up a subscription newsletter with content from various club enthusiasts. Of course, you will need to have an interest in metal detection and learn as much as possible about the detectors and the industry/hobby. Since the business centers around a hobby, your best bet would be to set up a kiosk or booth at a mall, utilize mail order, a good web site and/or align yourself with a sporting goods or hobby store. You'll pay the owner a commission to allow you to handle your section of the business since, in most cases, he or she will not be versed in this area.

WEB RESOURCES: www.fmdac.org, www.detectordept.com Federation of Metal Detector and Archeological Clubs and discount metal detectors.

NOTES:

KEY

RATINGS	★
START-UP COST	$$
HOMEBASED BUSINESS	
PART-TIME OPPORTUNITY	
LEGAL ISSUES	
FRANCHISE OR LICENSE POTENTIAL	
GREEN BUSINESSES	

43

PET-RELATED

Businesses You Can Start

DOGGIE WASH OR SALON

★★ $$$$

When I think of a doggie wash, visions of Dana (my 90-pound Rottweiler), soaking wet, shaking like mad, and on the run in my home jump to mind. Dog owners like myself share a common dilemma—when it's time for the dog to have a bath, where do you bathe the dog? The solution is a doggie bathhouse, and starting one of these businesses in your community can put you on the road to financial independence. The business is similar to a coin-operated car wash, except instead of washing the car, you wash your dog. Dog salons have become the more fashionable means of dog washing and can also allow you to charge higher prices for the more "fashionable phrasing." The business can be established in a retail store location of approximately 800 square feet, which would allow for the installation of at least four dog washing booths and a small retail area at the front for product sales. A quick-start marketing method is to distribute free dog wash coupons throughout the community, as this method of promotion can be excellent for letting potential clients know where you are located as well as introducing them to your very unique business.

START-UP COSTS: The following example can be used as a guideline to establish the investment required for starting a doggie wash business.

	Low	High
Lease requirements (F&L)	$1,500	$5,000
Leasehold improvements	$5,000	$10,000
Equipment and fixtures	$5,000	$10,000
Inventory	$2,000	$4,000
Business setup, legal, banking, etc.	$1,000	$2,000
Promotional material	$500	$1,000
Initial advertising and marketing budget	$1,000	$2,000
Working capital	$3,000	$6,000
Total start-up costs	**$19,000**	**$40,000**

Profit potential: The profit potential can be excellent for this type of business venture, as people usually wash their dogs every four to six weeks. Additionally, you can sell related products such as pet shampoo, dog food, books, pet toys, treats, walking collars, and leashes as a way to increase sales and profits. The key to success in this type of business is to have the doggie wash located in a densely populated urban area that is comprised mainly of apartment and condominium residences. Most dog owners will be more than happy to pay $10 to have the ability to wash their dogs in a safe and friendly environment. Since big city rents may be more than you bargained for, you might join forces with a pet store, kennel, or other such existing pet related business.

WEB RESOURCE: www.appma.org
American Pet Products Manufacturers Association.

MOBILE DOG WASH SERVICE
★★ $$+ 🚗 🕒 🌐

The purchase of a secondhand van or enclosed trailer is the first step toward starting a mobile dog wash service. You will have to outfit the truck or trailer with a water tank and some other basic equipment such as a hose and brushes. You can market a mobile dog wash service by creating promotional fliers and placing the fliers on display at pet retailers, vets, and the local ASPCA. Like many pet services, word-of-mouth referrals will become your main marketing tool so be sure that a quality service is what you are providing. Also seek to build an alliance with a local charity, as they can host monthly dog washes as a method to generate revenues for the charity and you can provide the service for a 50 percent split of revenues generated.

DOG WALKING SERVICE
★ $ 🚗 🕒

A dog walking service is perfectly suited for the person who has the time, patience, and a love for dogs. Best of all, this business venture can be initiated for less than $100. There are various styles of multi-lead dog walking collars and leashes available that will allow three or more dogs to be walked at the same time without becoming tangled in the leash. Acquiring this equipment will be important to your new business, as it will reduce frustration and enable you to walk multiple dogs at the same time, thus increasing revenues and profits. Of course, you need patience and some training at handling dogs before you try to walk large groups at once. To secure clients for the service, simply design a promotional flier that explains your dog walking service and qualifications. Distribute the fliers to businesses that are frequented by dog owners such as grooming locations, kennels, pet food stores, community animal shelters and town halls. Once word is out about your dog walking service, it should not take long to establish a base of 20 or 30 regular clients. At just $12 per dog per day, or a weekly discounted rate plan of $55 for five days (assuming dog owners won't need you on the week-

ends) with 25 regular daily pooches in three groups you could make over $1,375 per week or more than $70,000 a year. And you'll get exercise to boot. Remember to adhere to local ordinances regarding cleaning up after dogs.

PET TAXI
★ $$$ 🚗 🕒 🌐

A pet taxi service could be a difficult business to operate for a profit, unless you are located in a very densely populated urban center. However, a pet taxi service that is operated in combination with another business, such as a delivery service, can be a fantastic way to diversify and profit. The main requirements for operating a pet taxi service is to have suitable transportation such as a van or station wagon and a good communications system to enable you to quickly respond to customers' calls for pet pickup and delivery. Using a cellular telephone for incoming and outgoing calls and inquiries can easily fill the communication requirements. A pet taxi service can be marketed and promoted by using all the traditional marketing methods such as print media. Furthermore, a well-designed and informative promotional brochure that explains the service and pricing structure displayed in local pet-related businesses and retailers can go a long way to securing new and repeat customers.

DOG RUN SALES AND INSTALLATIONS
★★ $$ 🚗 🕒

Initiating and operating a business that focuses on manufacturing and retailing pre-designed and constructed dog runs can be a very lucrative enterprise to start. Dog runs are not only easily designed, but equally easy to build. Once the dog runs have been constructed, they can be disassembled and packaged for convenient shipping and fast installation on a customer's property. A key requirement in the design process of this type of product is to separate your product from the competition. In the case of dog runs, this could simply mean installing a sunshade or building in a food and water dish. Dog runs can be sold through local or national retail accounts, such as pet stores and animal shelters. Furthermore, this type of specialty product is also suited to internet marketing, mail-order sales, and related exhibition trade shows. The profit potential will greatly vary on a number of factors including product pricing, number of units sold, and market demand. However, dog runs are a necessary piece of equipment for many dog owners with sufficient property as well as breeders, and kennels, and the market has already been proven and established. Parks also install dog runs, so you may check with local parks and recreation departments to see if they are interested and can fit a dog run into the budget.

CUSTOM COLLAR AND LEASH MANUFACTURING
★ $$ 🚗 🕐

Starting a business that manufactures and sells custom dog collars and leashes could prove to be a very profitable business venture to get rolling. The only requirement to set this enterprise in motion is a sewing machine and the ability to sew. Nylon webbing, leather, and the required collar and leash hardware can all be purchased on a wholesale basis. The next step is to simply design the collars and leashes and begin to manufacture and market your products. While the potential to get rich from this type of business is not great, there should be no problem establishing a very lucrative part-time income that, with some clever promotional ideas, could even be turned into a full-time and very profitable homebased business. Market your products at dog shows, pet shops, veterinarian's offices, kennels, with dog walkers, and by simply handing out fliers to all of those people you see walking their dogs.

PET GROOMING
★★ $$$ 🌐

The main requirement for starting a pet grooming service is obvious. You, or an employee must be a pet groomer. Many pet groomers are not officially certified, however, those who take the time to register and complete a pet grooming certification course will be doing themselves, their clients, and their customers (the pets) a great favor. A pet grooming service is very inexpensive to start, and has the potential to be extremely profitable, as pet grooming for medium-sized dogs now costs in the range of $30 to $100 per visit. Additional revenue can be gained for the grooming service by selling related pet grooming products such as flea powders, shampoos, and even specialty pet foods.

WEB RESOURCE: www.nauticom.net/www/ndga
National Dog Groomers Association of America.

BEST WALKING TRAILS BOOK
★★★ $$$ 🚗 🕐 🌐

Using the internet can enable you to write books about the best pet walking trails for every community across North America. How? Simply visit as many web sites as possible that focus specifically on pets or dogs. By utilizing chat rooms, you can ask site visitors questions that pertain to the best pet walking trails and areas in their specific community. The information gathered can become the basis for a "best pet walking trails" book. While this won't make you rich, it can bring in some profits, especially if you provide some places where people who are limited by local laws can now walk their dogs, and particularly let the dog off the leash. A series of books can be self-published and distributed for sale through retail outlets such as book stores and pet stores or you can sell the guides as an ebook, downloadable from your web site. You could also approach a publisher of outdoor, animal, or pet-related books with a sample of your work to see if they are interested in publishing the book (and distributing it) for you. Additional revenue for this type of unique business venture can be gained by soliciting advertising from pet-related businesses in the communities that the book serves, and for a fixed cost you can promote and highlight their business in the book.

HOUSE SAFETY SERVICE FOR PETS
★★ $$ 🚗 🕐 🌐

It is extremely important for households with young children to put safety measures in place so that children cannot open cabinets and gain access to potentially harmful products and chemicals. It is equally important for households with pets to take these same safety measures and precautions. Starting a business that focuses on securing households to prevent pet injuries can be a very personally rewarding and profitable business to initiate. The service is best marketed by designing and distributing information fliers about this unique service to local pet-related businesses and organizations in the community, such as the ASPCA, pet food stores, and veterinarians' clinics. You can charge clients a fee for the in-home pet safe consulting visits, as well as sell products that may be required to make the home pet safe.

ENGRAVED PET TAGS
★ $$ 🕒

Engraving pet name and identification tags is a terrific little part-time business that anyone can start and successfully operate for a profit. Engraving tags requires no special skills or experience, and only basic metal engraving equipment that can be purchased at industrial supply stores will be needed. Ideally, an engraving service is best promoted and marketed by designing a portable sales kiosk that can be set up in malls and flea markets on weekends and during holiday times to engrave and sell the pet name tags. Currently custom-engraved pet name tags sell for $5 to $20 each, depending on the type of metal tag used and the amount of engraving that has to be completed. The retail selling price leaves a lot of room for profit, as the blank tags can be purchased in bulk on a wholesale basis for less than $1 each. This type of specialty retailing gives the operator a lot of flexibility in terms of working hours, operating location, and expansion potential, which can all add up to a fun and profitable part-time business opportunity.

PET DAY CARE
★★★ $$$$ 🌐

Day-care centers for dogs are becoming extremely popular as more and more caring dog owners are starting to realize that money spent on doggie daycare while they are at work is money well spent. Dogs, like people, are social creatures and need to have contact with people as well as other dogs to become better behaved and more confident family pets. A doggie day care is the perfect place for Rover to learn important and beneficial socialization skills. This type of business venture should not be confused with a kennel service, which is featured elsewhere in this chapter. This is a pet day-care center, and dogs are dropped off in the morning and picked up the same day with no overnight stays. To market the business, simply establish alliances with all local pet-related businesses in your community, such as pet food stores, pet grooming shops, and vets. A pet day-care center is not suitable as a homebased business venture, unless you have

the space and the proper zoning. Ideally, the business location would have 2,000 to 3,000 square feet of indoor space and the same amount of outdoor space. To really give your clients the feeling of security and reassure them that they have made the right choice in terms of pet day care, install a digital web cam and broadcast live images of the day-care center activities over your company's web site. Imagine, pet owners at work could simply log onto the pet day-care web site and check on their dogs any time they wanted to. This can be used as an amazing marketing tool for the business as well.

START-UP COSTS: The following example can be used as a guideline to establish the investment needed for starting a pet day-care center.

Leased operating space:

2–3,000 square feet (F&L)	$4,000
Leasehold improvements	$10,000
Kennels and fixtures	$5,000
Office equipment	$5,000
Marketing, promotion, and advertising budget	$2,500
Working capital	$10,000
Business setup, legal, accounting, banking, etc.	$2,500
Total start-up costs	$39,000

PROFIT POTENTIAL: Currently rates for dog day care are from $14 to $20 per day, which generally includes two walks, one meal, and a drop-off time of 6:00 AM and a pick-up time of 6:00 PM.

PET MEMORIALS
★★★★ $$$ 🏠 🕒 🌐

The basis of the business is very straightforward. Select four various styles of rocks or monuments that are approximately one foot square. They do not have to be expensive. Once you have selected the stone that will be used for the memorial, select an artist to draw ten designs that will be used as the standard for the memorials. The only part of the memorial that will be customized will be the pet's name and possibly a date. Next, you will want to set up accounts with retailers such as veterinarians, pet food stores, and pet grooming salons, who will act as the authorized distributors of the pet memorial. All the distributors should have an order catalog as well as a sample of the memorial on site. These retailers will simply take orders from their customers and fax a completed order form for the pet memorial to your office. You can subcontract the sandblasting of the memorial to a local firm as well as the delivery. Aim to establish 100 accounts with local pet-related stores and it will not take long to build a very solid and profitable business.

EVERYTHING FOR BIRDS
★★ $$$$ � 🕒

The title of this business opportunity may have a few of you confused. What exactly is an "everything for birds" business venture? The business opportunity is simply this, bird watching, feeding, and bird ownership in the United States is big business that generates millions of dollars each year in related sales. An everything for birds business is a retail operation that sells everything to do with birds, both wild and domesticated, except the birds. The store can be setup and located in any one of the following retail sales formats: a mall kiosk, an individual store, or kiosk within an existing retail business such as a supermarket. The focus of the business is to purchase bird-related items such as bird feed, birdhouses, and books on bird watching on a wholesale basis, add a generous markup, and retail these items to consumers. The profit potential for this type of specialty retail operation is terrific, as the overheads can be kept to a minimum and the markups that can be applied to these types of product for retail sales are in the range of 100 to 200 percent.

In addition to retail sales from a fixed location, the innovative entrepreneur could also sell bird-related products over the internet. Finding products for the business can be accomplished by purchasing one of the many manufacturing directories that are available. These directories focus on information such as the type of product, the uses for the product, manufacturers contact information, and the person to contact within the company. Manufacturing directories are available for North America or worldwide. Once established, this type of specialty retail business is an ideal candidate for franchising nationally to qualified operators or franchisees. Aim to achieve yearly gross sales of $200,000 in an everything for birds store and the business can easily generate gross

profits in excess of $100,000 providing you can maintain a 100 percent markup on products sold.

PET TRICK BOOKS AND VIDEOS
★★ $$$$ 🚗 🕒

Pet owners are always searching for ways to teach their pets new and interesting tricks, and this is the basis of this new business start-up. You can work with established pet trainers to produce your own pet trick videos and sell the videos through retail merchant accounts, mail-order catalogs, and web sites. You can assemble this same information and put it in the print format of a book, which can be sold utilizing the same retail channels as the video sales. Additional revenues for this type of venture can be sought by soliciting national pet food and pet equipment manufacturers for advertising purposes in the videos as well as in the book. You can also set up pet training classes if you have a local trainer who is interested or if you have learned the techniques yourself.

PET EMERGENCY KITS
★★ $$ 🚗 🕒

Are you seeking to start a business that only requires a small initial investment to get rolling, yet the profit potential is extremely good? If so, perhaps you should consider starting a business that manufactures, assembles, and wholesales emergency first aid kits for pets. The business does not require any experience, and the only skill requirement is the ability to be an effective marketer. The kits should include simple products and medications that can assist in a pet emergency, such as a cut paw. The kits can be sold to pet-related businesses on a wholesale basis, as well as directly to consumers via mail order and the web. The key to success in this type of business enterprise is to make the packaging of the kits very effective, as well as establishing as many wholesale accounts as possible.

WEB RESOURCE: www.avma.org
American Veterinary Medical Association.

PORTABLE SUNSHADES FOR PETS
★★ $$ 🚗 🕒

The sun and pets are generally not a suitable match, and that's why a portable sunshade business for pets is a great idea. Portable pet sunshades are perfect items for any pet owner to purchase and take along on vacations or a trip to the beach with Rover. Ideally, the pet sunshades would be manufactured to be smaller than a traditional sun umbrella, but larger than a rain umbrella. The sunshades should feature colorful images of pets, as this can create an emotional type purchase from many pet owners. You can sell this product to pet retailers and veterinarians on a wholesale basis, as well as sold directly to consumers via the internet, mail order and at fairs and flea markets. This is also a business that will sell by viral marketing (a.k.a., word-of-mouth marketing) whereby you give away some samples of the product for free to people who will be out and about with their pets. The visibility of a unique product attracts attention and generates sales through word of mouth. Look at how well it worked for iPods! This is a terrific small homebased business concept that really has the potential to grow and become very profitable.

WEB RESOURCE: www.avma.org
American Veterinary Medical Association.

SPECIALTY FISH SALES
★★★ $$$ 🚗 🕐

Becoming a specialty fish breeder is easier than you might think. The only requirements to get this business in motion are to purchase large breeding tanks or construct breeding ponds. Then purchase additional equipment, such as water and air circulatory machines, a few various species of breeding tropical fish, and you're in business. Some tropical fish breeds sell for as much as $100 each, so once established a specialty fish breeding operation can become very profitable. Marketing the specialty fish is also very straightforward. Simply establish accounts with local pet stores to purchase the tropical fish on a wholesale basis and look for local tropical fish collectors. Note: To do this effectively, you must read up on how to care for tropical fish. It's very easy to lose more fish than you breed if you do not know what they require.

WEB RESOURCE: www.tropicalfish.com
Excellent tropical fish resource.

DOG SADDLE BAGS
★★ $$ 🚗 🕐

Activating a business that manufactures and wholesales saddle bags for dogs may just be the kind of unique

business enterprise you have been seeking to start. The dog saddle bags could be manufactured with comical messages printed on them such as "Dog-in-Training," or "I'm with Stupid" with an arrow pointing at the walker. The saddle bags could feature various compartments that can be utilized by the pet owners for carrying items like water, dog biscuits, and balls. This business would not take a lot of investment capital to get rolling and could easily be operated and managed from a homebased location. The options to marketing the saddle bags are limitless and include accounts with pet retailers, mail-order sales, e-commerce through your web site, and by displaying and selling the saddle bags at flea markets, fairs, and dog shows. Try the viral/word-of-mouth approach to marketing marketing as discussed earlier.

INTERIOR AND EXTERIOR PET FENCING
★★★ $$ 🚗 🕐

Manufacturing and wholesaling portable pet fencing is a very inexpensive business venture to launch and operate. The business can be run from a homebased location and also requires very little in the way of special skills or requirements. Basically, the business features pre-assembled fencing for pets that can be used inside and outside the home, as well as easily packaged and transported for the occasion when pet and owner are on vacation and a detainment system is required. The key to success in the portable pet fencing business is that the fencing must be durable, well designed, and constructed to allow for easy assembly, shipping, packaging, and portability. The market for this type of product is limitless, and a good starting point once the fencing has been designed and a prototype built is to market the product to a major national pet retailer, with an objective to secure national retail distribution accounts.

WEB RESOURCE: www.optionsplus.com
All sorts of information on pet fencing.

PETTING ZOO
★ $$$$ 🚛

There is something special about a petting zoo that lures both children and their parents. Starting and running a petting zoo is certainly not for everyone, as a petting zoo requires a great deal of knowledge and special handling skills in terms of the animals. Additionally, this type of business can be somewhat costly to start and operate and you need proper licensing, land, and a good location. No, this is not a good homebased business. However, a properly established and managed petting zoo can be both a personally and financially rewarding business to own and operate. Traditionally, popular animals featured in a petting zoo have always been sheep, goats, deer, ponies, and rabbits. You can also do this on a portable basis with a large truck housing several animals which you can bring to carnivals, fairs, and other events and set up an outdoor area with proper fencing. Of course you will need plenty of insurance and have to take all safety precautions prior to starting such a business, which includes making sure animals have any required shots.

WEB RESOURCE: www.pettingzoofarm.com
Directory service listing nationwide petting zoos and industry information.

PET FOOD STORE
★★ $$$$ 🐾

More than one billion dollars worth of pet food is sold every year in North America, thus opening your own pet food store may just put you on the road to financial freedom. There are various approaches that can be taken to launch a pet food store. The first is to open a store that sells all types of pet foods. The second approach is to open a store that sells organic pet foods only, and the third approach is not to open a retail store but provide customers with pet food catalogs and free home delivery. The third approach is by far the least expensive to start of the three. Profit potential will vary as to the operating approach that is taken with opening a pet food store or supply business. However, maintaining annual sales of $200,000 and 100 percent markup will create annual gross profits of $100,000.

WEB RESOURCE: www.appma.org
American Pet Products Manufacturers Association.

PET FOOD BOWLS
★ $ 🚗 🕑

Designing, manufacturing, and wholesaling pet food bowls is a great homebased business venture to get rolling. The key to success in this type of business is for the pet food bowls to be interesting, constructed of a unique material, and perhaps serve a specific need, such as bowls that are higher than normal for dogs with arthritis. The pet food bowls can be sold to pet stores, veterinarians, and pet groomers on a wholesale basis, as well as directly to consumers via the internet and mail order. Additionally, utilizing a mall kiosk, pet names can be silk screened directly onto the pet food bowls for customers right on site. This type of kiosk is very inexpensive to construct and sales could easily top $1,000 a day.

PET NAME BOOKS
★ $$ 🚗 🕑

Writing a pet name book is almost guaranteed not to make you rich, but it is guaranteed to be a whole lot of fun. There are many different approaches that can be taken with a pet name book. The book could focus on one particular type of pet, such as cats or dogs, or feature historical pet names or celebrity pet names and how they came to be. Other items to consider are whether you will self-publish the book or have a commercial publisher take on the project. Self-publishing will add additional start-up costs to have the book printed and distributed, however the profit potential is also greater if you can get out there and market and distribute it yourself. If you have good desktop publishing software, you can save yourself some money in the long run. If you choose to go the commercial publishing route, you will need to look up publishing houses that might print such a book (houses that handle pet and name-related books) and send a sample with a book proposal. The current commission or royalty rate is typically 4 to 8 percent of the total gross volume of book sales.

TROPICAL FISH AND AQUARIUM RENTALS
★★ $$ 🚗 🕑

Gigantic profits can be earned by starting a tropical fish and aquarium rental business, and best of all, this unique enterprise can be set in motion for less than $5,000 and managed right from a homebased office. At this point I am sure you're wondering—exactly who would rent tropical fish and an aquarium? The list is very long, and if you think about waiting rooms, the list of potential clients can include doctors, lawyers, restaurants, and business offices. The concept behind the tropical fish rental is this: People who must wait in a waiting room need something to keep them occupied, and believe it or not it would be less expensive for businesses and professional offices to rent tropical fish every month than to supply customers and patients with costly newspapers and magazines. Once a regular clientele base has been established for a tropical fish and aquarium rental business, the yearly profits that can be earned could well exceed $50,000 or more.

PACKAGED CATNIP
★ $$ 🏠 🕐

Cats go crazy for catnip. Starting a business that produces catnip or purchases it in bulk and wholesales the catnip in smaller quantities is a homebased business venture that just about anyone can tackle. The prepackaged catnip can be sold to pet food stores, pet retailers, veterinarians, and pet grooming companies on a wholesale basis. This is a product that can be marked up by 100 percent or more, even for wholesaling. Providing you can achieve gross yearly sales of $100,000, the business would generate a gross profit before taxes and expenses of $50,000, which is not bad for a low-investment business venture.

WEB RESOURCE: www.appma.org
American Pet Products Manufacturers Association.

KENNEL
★★ $$$$ 🏠 �

Starting a dog kennel has numerous and varied requirements that must be carefully planned for and researched prior to starting the business. The investment needed to establish a dog kennel from the ground up can easily exceed $150,000, making this business venture one that should only be tackled by a seasoned business pro with experience in the pet industry. However, having said that, I have a close personal friend who has successfully operated a professional dog kennel for more than 15 years, and the business never fails to generate a pretax income of less than $80,000 per year after expenses. Additional revenues for a dog kennel can be earned by also providing customers with services, such as training instruction for their dogs, and selling related products,

such as dog foods and leashes. Profit potential range is $25,000 to $150,000 per year.

WEB RESOURCE: www.abka.com
American Boarding Kennels Association.

PET TOYS
★★ $$ 🏠 🕐

Designing, manufacturing, and wholesaling pet toys could put you on the path to financial freedom, and best of all this is a business opportunity that can be started part-time from home on a minimal initial investment. There are literally thousands of different pet toys on the market and this is definitely a situation where it is not important that you build it first, only better. The toys can be sold on a wholesale basis to pet retailers, or even directly to consumers via the internet and mail order. I purchased two glow-in-the-dark balls for my dog from a man who was selling them right out of a knapsack in the park. The key to success in this type of business is to have a high-quality toy and the ability to get the pet toy in front of as many potential customers as possible. Remember, pets are like children to most people and generally people will spare no expense when it comes to the happiness of their pets. That is why starting any new business that involves pets, or that is related to pets in any way, has already got a head start on the road to financial success.

PET TRAVEL KITS
★★ $$ 🏠 🕐

Starting a business that prepackages everything an owner will need for a long car trip with their pet is a terrific small homebased business to get rolling. Pet travel kits can include water, a sunshade for the car windows, and plastic bags for treasures, messes, and treats. The travel kits for pets can be sold on a wholesale basis to pet store retailers, truck stops, veterinarians, and pet grooming companies. In the world of business ventures there is not a lot that can be started for less than a few thousand dollars that has the potential to earn profits of greater than $25,000 per year. However, this business opportunity is one of the very rare as it can be started for less than a few thousand dollars and selling a mere 5,000 car kits for pets per year with a gross profit of $5 each will generate an income of $25,000.

PET FURNITURE COVERS
★ $$ 🚗 🕐

Calling all homemakers with a sewing machine and sewing skills! Put your sewing experience to work for you and start making made-to-order furniture covers for pet owners. This type of specialized service can be marketed through pet stores, furniture stores, and veterinarians. Simply design and distribute information and marketing brochures that highlight all the benefits of your custom-made furniture covers. The furniture covers can be sold by mail order, over the internet, and directly to interior designers. Additional revenues can also be earned by creating made-to-order pet clothes for clients seeking something a little bit different for their pets.

PLAY CENTER FOR DOGS
★★★ $$$$ 🌐

Anyone who owns a dog will tell you how frustrating it is try to find a suitable and safe area that the dog can run off-leash, play, and socialize with other dogs. More and more communities are banning dogs from parks, beaches, and playing fields, making it an almost impossible to find an off-leash area for dogs, especially if you live in a densely populated urban center. A play center for dogs would be a welcomed in any community by both dog owners and non-owners. The play center could be conducted from an indoor or outdoor location and feature grassy surfaces, ponds, and a lot of running space for dogs and their owners. Customers would pay an hourly fee for using the play center and for the really hardcore customers, a discounted monthly pass could be offered for sale. The business can be marketed by distributing promotional fliers and discount trial offer coupons throughout the community. Don't spend too much money on initial advertising because word will spread very quickly. Dog owners are quick to tell other dog owners about unique and beneficial services for their pets. Once established and proven profitable, this business is an outstanding candidate to be expanded on a national basis by selling franchises to qualified operators.

PET GROOMING KITS
★★★ $$$$ 🚗

Are you looking for a pet-related business start-up that has the potential to make you rich? If so, perhaps you should consider starting a business that designs, packages, and wholesales pet grooming kits. Simply package pet grooming supplies into one convenient kit. The kits should be animal-breed specific and include a booklet on grooming tips for the particular breed as well as grooming equipment and supplies, such as brushes, shampoos, and nail clippers. The pet grooming kits can be sold to pet store retailers nationally on a wholesale basis, as well as directly to consumers via the internet and mail order. Providing careful planning, research, and marketing skills are practiced, this type of business concept has the potential to generate millions of dollars in annual sales.

BREED BOOKS
★ $$ 🚗 🕐

Thousands of new pet owners have numerous questions after purchasing or adopting a new pet in terms of the particular breed's habits, health needs, dietary needs, and training tips. Starting a business that publishes and distributes breed-specific pet books is a terrific home-based business venture to initiate. Fear not if you do not have the skills required to write the books yourself, as you and the business will be better served by having professional dog breeders and trainers write the books on the breeds they specialize in. Once the books are complete and printed, they can be sold on a wholesale basis to pet stores, pet breeders, veterinarians, and even the SPCA. This type of new business venture will require a substantial amount of investment capital, planning, and research in order to be successful, however, the potential financial rewards could be well worth the effort.

WEB RESOURCE: www.adba.cc
American Dog Breeders Association.

POOPER SCOOPER SERVICE
★★ $ 🚗 🕐

Believe it or not, you can make a very comfortable living by starting a doggie pooper-scooper service in your community. The business is extremely easy to set up and has no special requirements in terms of skills, equipment, or business experience. As crazy as this may sound, how difficult would it be to find 200 customers willing to pay a mere $30 each per month to ensure that all little treasures have been cleaned up and removed on a weekly basis from their yards? The result would be creating an income of almost $75,000 per year from a not-very-glamorous, but necessary business that can be put in motion for less than $1,000. This type of service can be marketed through veterinarians, pet food retailers, and most of all, word-of-mouth.

WEB RESOURCE: www.pooper-scooper.com
Directory listing hundreds of pooper scooper services in North America.

SCRATCHING POSTS
★★ $$

Scratching posts—cats love them, and cat owners love them even more. Starting a manufacturing business that focuses on building cat scratching posts is probably the easiest manufacturing business featured in this chapter. This enterprise requires virtually no special skills and only basic hand or power tools. Logically, the best venue for selling this type of product will be to local pet stores and at cat shows. Purchasing a few scratching posts can give you a good idea in terms of how this product is constructed and the various types of materials required. Once again, if possible try to incorporate recycled materials into the construction of the posts, as it will serve as a good marketing tool and, of course, help the environment. This potentially "green" business venture is ideal for the person who is seeking a few extra dollars each month from their own homebased business.

PET BREEDER
★ $$ 🚗 🕒 ⚖️

If your motivation for starting a pet breeding business is purely for profit, then forget it. The last thing the world needs are more puppy mills. However, if your motivation for starting a pet breeding business is because you have a keen interest in a particular breed of animal and you also have a keen interest in ensuring that the animal is sold to a caring family, then this is the business for you. Chances are you are going to have a very rewarding business future both personally and financially. Additional considerations for starting a pet breeding business include qualifications, business location, registration, association memberships, and marketing skills and abilities. Once established, a professional animal breeder might not need

to advertise, as word-of-mouth and referrals spread fast in this industry.

WEB RESOURCE: www.adba.cc
American Dog Breeders Association.

PET MATS
★ $$ 🚗 🕒 🌐

Selling dog and cat specialty mats is a fantastic home-based business to start that really has the potential to earn some serious cash. You can purchase the pet mats in bulk relatively inexpensively and silk-screen on the customer's pet name in bright colors. The mats can be sold directly to consumers via a specially designed sales booths that can be setup on weekends at malls and flea markets. This business has the potential to generate sales in excess of $1,000 per day, and best of all, the entire business can easily be set in motion for less than $5,000. Additional revenues can be earned by silk-screening pet names for clients on other types of products, such as pet clothes.

PET FAIRS
★★ $$$ 🕒

Starting a pet fair trade show business is a great new enterprise to set in motion that has the potential to earn you a very comfortable six-figure income every year. The business concept is to simply host pet fair trade shows and charge vendors a fee for table or booth rental, as well as visitors an entrance fee into the pet fair. The show can feature retailers of pets, pet clothing, pet toys, pet foods, and just about any other product or service that is related to pets. The shows should also feature workshops on pet training, as well as pet shows for entertainment, such as trained dog routines. The great aspect about a business that organizes and hosts pet fairs is it can be started small on a local basis with an annual or a semiannual pet fair in your community, and expand into various geographic regions of the country from the profits the business generates.

PET SITTING
★★ $ 🚗 🕒

There are many pets that cannot be boarded or left with friends or family for various reasons. Enter the pet sitter! An excellent money-making business, you need to simply match people who love pets and have some spare time with those who are heading out of town and cannot bring Fluffy, Muffy, or Mr. BoJangles along. Retirees and students are often your best candidates for pet sitting employment. You do, however, need to carefully screen that the individuals are highly reliable and understand the needs of the pets and their owners. For dogs, a pet sitter will typically visit three times a day for feeding and walking, plus perhaps some time for grooming. For cats, perhaps a visit of an hour a day will suffice for feeding, possibly brushing, and cleaning out the litter box. For other pets, feeding and any other necessary needs will be provided. Since pet sitters are being trusted to enter and leave private homes, bonding your employees is a good idea. Market your pet sitting service widely throughout your community and in all places that pet owners would be found, including pet stores, veterinarians offices, and through dog walkers or groomers. Since most often a pet sitter will be hired for a short time frame, you need to establish hourly rates that are commensurate with any competition in the area. The pet sitters typically make anywhere from $10 to $20 per visit, so you can expect to charge $15 to $25 per visit. Therefore, if you have 10 sitters each making 20 visits in a week, or a total of 200 pet visits per week, you can collect $4,000, of which you will make $1,000 per week.

WEB RESOURCE: www.petsitters.org/index.cfm
National Association of Professional Pet Sitters

DOGGIE SWEATERS AND CLOTHING
★ $$ 🏠 🕒

Wanna make a fashion statement in the canine world? By designing, manufacturing, and/or buying doggie sweaters and other pet clothing items wholesale, you can launch your own doggie clothing business from the comfort of your own home. Sweaters, rainwear, hats, even goggles are all part of the well-dressed doggie ensemble, so you can carry a full line of products. Your minimal start up needs would include sewing equipment, creative marketing, and a web site to show your goods. Along with marketing your clothes to pet shops and making yourself known to groomers, vets and anyone else in the doggie community, make sure to get some products out and about on the dog runs and in other places where the well-dressed dog is seen by his or her peers, and more impor-

tantly, by their owners. Word of mouth can generate a lot of sales, since dogs are not as fussy as humans about being caught wearing the dame outfits. Also, by making customized sweaters you can make more money.

PARTY ANIMALS
★ $$ 🕒 🚗

No we're not talking lamp-shade on the head party animals, but instead real animals for kids parties. If you love animals and know how to handle them, you can start up a business that brings a small menageries of kid-friendly favorites to parties for young children. Among the favorites are snakes, lizards, bullfrogs, bunnies, baby ducks, parrots and, if the backyard is big enough, ponies. Typically, the handler (you or someone you hire) brings the animals in to the party and explains a little about them, and lets the kids pet them, or in some cases feed them. Ponies can provide rides as well, for those with big backyards. Of course the expense is in housing the animals, which can be in conjunction with a local petting zoo or with the help of friends and neighbors who want a some pets. If you want to take the business up a notch, you can create a full traveling petting zoo, and, for one hour parties (plus set up and take down) you can charge $300, including goats, sheep and other larger animals. If, however, you are working with more of the "indoor" smaller house variety of animals, you might charge $150 for an hour "show" or display of the animals for the kiddies. Some fun kid-friendly jokes and puns always work well with a prepared presentation on your part.
Market yourself to anyone with young children.

GOURMET DOGGIES TREATS
★★ $$ 🏠 🕒 🌐

People love to pamper their pets, especially dogs, so why not start off a business that feeds into that mindset. Healthy dog biscuits and those made from the finest ingredients can command big bucks as the public becomes more and more aware of their pet's dietary concerns than their own. All you need are some healthy and, or, gourmet recipes, biscuit molds, unique packaging and a marketing plan and you are on your way. Pet shops, pet fairs, and even standard gourmet shops are targets for such top-of-the-line doggie delights.

WEB RESOURCE: www.gourmetsleuth.com/recipe_dogbiscuit.htm
Gourmet dog biscuit recipes to start off with

PET TRANSPORTATION SERVICE
★★★ $$$ 🕐 🚚

More and more people today have pets, with approximately 70 million cats and roughly 60 million dogs in private homes in North America. Pet transport services are therefore becoming much more in demand as a means of safely relocating pets to their new homes. Clients want to trust that you can help move pets safely and comfortably whether it is a local move or hundreds of miles to another part of the country. Custom carriers, necessary food, toys, supplies, emergency medical attention, and all other details need to be taken into consideration by such a business. In addition, you can also make arrangements for comfortable air transportation by learning all about the best and safest options for pet air travel and handling all arrangements, including providing the pet owners with the necessary paperwork. The start-up costs can be high since you will need a vehicle or two for transport. Such vehicles must be equipped with proper ventilation. Along with having great familiarity with moving animals comfortably, you will want to make it a policy that animals have necessary shots prior to transit. Also, make sure all transport equipment meets the criteria of the Independent Pet and Animal Transport Association. Hiring experienced pet handlers can be a valuable asset in building this business from a small operation into a large-scale, potentially international pet transport business. Transport rates for animals can vary widely (much as they do for airline tickets for people) and depend on the size of the animal and length of the journey. In time, with good handlers and a knack for knowing how to get pets safely to any far away location, you can generate well into the six-figure income range with a well-managed business.

WEB RESOURCE: www.ipata.com
Independent Pet and Animal Transport Association

PET SHOP
★★ $$$$ 🚚

Obvious perhaps, but why not start your own pet store if you love animals? A pet store can be a wonderful boost to a family friendly community and a great business opportunity. The keys to success are knowing all about animals and about running a retail businesses, since the bulk of sales will be pet food, pet toys, carrying cases, aquariums, cages, leashes and other many other accessories. Prior to starting such a business, you will need to do some research to determine how much inventory to stock, based on your location and the popularity of certain products. If you can find some vendors selling unique pet products such as gourmet goodies, health foods for pets or clever pet-friendly gadgets, you can gain a competitive edge over any local competition.

And then there are the pets. Depending on the size and location of the store, and your connection with breeders, you can determine which animals to sell. Remember, the more animals you commit to selling, the more responsibilites, and potential costs, you will have for feeding, boarding and overall care, including health concerns. Only if you believe you can provide puppies with a fair amount of space, should you sell them. Likewise kittens also need opportunities to climb, so only have them if you can provide them with adequate living conditions until someone takes them home. Bunnies and ferrets are popular as well, but also need some room. Smaller pets, such as hamsters, gerbils, chameleons, lizards, fish, tortoises, parakeets, cockatiels and other types of birds are all possibilities depending on your knowledge of the animals, or upon hiring someone who is able to care for them. You also need to be in contact with a local vet or two and work only with breeders whom you know and can trust that they are giving you the animals only once it is safe to remove them from their mothers. Licensing rules, safety and animal concerns, vaccinations and other regulations must be complied with, making this a detailed business to open. However, if you are good with animals and truly enjoy finding homes for pets, this can be a marvelous (and eventually, lucrative) business to start. Some pet shops even have parties for young children as a way of making money and marketing.

WEB RESOURCE: www.entrepreneur.com/magazine/entrepreneur/1999/august/18128.html

39
PHOTOGRAPHY
Businesses You Can Start

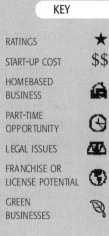
CONSTRUCTION PHOTOGRAPHY
★★ $ 🏠 🕐

Do you have $1,000 to invest in a new business enterprise that can potentially earn you tens of thousands of dollars in profits each year? If so, coupled with basic photography skills, you can start a construction photography service. What exactly is a construction photography service, you may ask? The answer and the business opportunity are very straightforward. Each year thousands of new homes are built in North America, and a construction photography service is providing new home owners with a complete photo album of their home's construction, right from the hole in the ground to the moment the moving truck arrives. The photography service can be provided in traditional film format or by using digital photography, which allows you to email photos directly to your clients. There is only one way to market this business. Go after the real estate market, which includes homebuilders and property developers. Why? Simply because many of these companies build hundreds of new homes each year, and not only will securing photography contracts with these companies generate a handsome profit for you, it is also goodwill and a great marketing tool for the construction company. From a practical perspective, photos allow clients to see their homes progressing. Such photos may also be used to confirm the home building is conforming to building code regulations and

can be used later on if there are concerns. Homebuilders can make sure everything is going as planned so that they will not have to backtrack and make changes later. In addition, it illustrates how they build homes, which is excellent for marketing purposes.

WEB RESOURCE: www.nahb.org
National Association of Home Builders.

PET PHOTOGRAPHY
★★ $$ 🏠 🕐

I am going to share an interesting business concept with you that involves photographing pets. My wife and I were out walking our dog Dana in a local waterfront park. It was approaching dusk and as we were standing there admiring the sunset a man approached us and asked if we minded if he took a few pictures of Dana and us with the sunset as a backdrop. Assuming he was a tourist or a photographer for the local newspaper we said sure. Once he was finished he asked for our address so he could mail a few of the pictures to us. Once again we said sure and gave him our mailing address. Approximately two weeks later we received a large brown envelope in the mail. Upon opening it we found a beautiful 8 by 10 photograph of Dana and ourselves, along with the photographer's business card and order form for additional prints of the photograph. Having our picture taken with our dog is something that never even entered our minds. However, that day my wife called the photographer and ordered six more prints of that picture in various sizes, and then booked an appointment with the photographer to take further pictures of Dana. In the end the photographer spent about $8 dollars on a gamble that paid off—in our case to the tune of $200. I am certainly not implying that this type of marketing is suitable for everyone or every business or service. However, once again, the creative and innovative entrepreneur can create market demand when there is none. A good pet photographer knows how to keep animals in a comfortable environment and can catch the gleam in their eyes. The more you practice, the more you will find that special look for great photographs. Pet lovers will tell you which are their favorite photos and which ones capture their pets in the best light. You can go to the homes of pet owners and/or have your own photography studio.

PHOTOGRAPH SALES
★★ $ 🚗 🕐

Selling photographs as art for home and office decorations to consumers is a very easy task to accomplish, providing the photos are very good, unique, and interesting. Not all photographers have that special knack for taking such striking photos that others will spend money to purchase. Therefore it is to your benefit to take classes and read some books on photography and learn about the importance of light, form, and structure. To market your work, framed or unframed photographs can be sold at art or craft shows, home and garden shows, to stock photograph services, at galleries, from your web site or to retailers for resale purposes. Photographs can be featured in restaurants to enhance the décor and sold on a consignment basis. While it is not easy to make a living in this manner, it is certainly a way of combining your hobby and skills with a part-time business venture. And if you are really good at photography and marketing, it can become a successful business.

SPORTS PHOTOGRAPHER
★★ $$ 🚗 🕐

Millions of people worldwide are participants in adventure or extreme sports, and starting a photography business that catches the sheer terror and thrills of these sports is sure to be a profitable and fun business to launch. The photographs can be sold directly to the people involved in the sport, or they can be sold to advertising agencies, newspapers, magazines, and as collectable art. The biggest prerequisites for starting this type of photography business are to be a very good action photographer and to be knowledgeable about and enjoy the sports that you will be photographing. You can also be a photographer of traditional sports including baseball, basketball, football, and soccer. Start out at a local level, catching college and high school teams in action, and eventually you can branch out to regional teams and even professional teams. The most important aspect of this type of photography is knowing when to take the shots capturing the right moments. You also need to have the right equipment for this type of business. You can market sports photography to local newspapers, sporting goods stores for sale or to decorate their walls, and as framed photos for sale to sports enthusiasts. Plus, you can have great fun doing this.

REAL ESTATE PHOTO SERVICE
★★ $$ 🚗 🕐

A real estate photography service is a terrific and inexpensive homebased business to start and operate. Thousands of real estate agents and homeowners simply do not have the time, equipment, or skills necessary to take professional photographs of a home or building they are selling or listing to be sold. The best method of marketing a real estate photography service is to simply arrange appointments with real estate agents and present a portfolio of homes, buildings, and properties that you have photographed. Ideally the service should be provided to clients in both film and digital image format. Amazingly, photographing a mere 50 homes per week, and charging only $25 for each home photographed, will produce sales in excess of $50,000 per year. Of course, you will need to practice, practice, practice to make sure your photos capture the homes in the best light—no pun intended. Also, if you can learn how to make a virtual tour of the homes, you can make a lot more money in this business, as such virtual home tours are very much in demand.

WEB RESOURCE: www.amarasoftware.com
Makers of software used for slideshows and virtual tours.

VIDEO EDITING SERVICE
★★ $$$ 🏠 🕐

Millions of North Americans now own camcorders or digital camcorders and use them on a regular basis for filming important family milestones, vacations, and special events. Starting a video editing service that takes a client's raw film footage and turns it into a fantastic video production including music, titles, and special effects is a fantastic business venture to put into action. A video editing business can easily be operated from a homebased studio, and the business can focus on both video film editing as well as digital film editing. Market such services in all traditional venues and through camcorder retailers, videographers, and on your web site and those of other entrepreneurs. Starting a video and digital editing service does require special editing skills and equipment. However, like any great business opportunity, hard work, research, practice and planning can pay off in terms of personal and financial rewards.

WEB RESOURCE: www.omegamultimedia.com
One of many distributors of video editing software.

AERIAL PHOTOGRAPHY
★ $$$ 🏠 🕐

There are a few approaches that can be taken when considering an aerial photography business as a new self-employment venture. The first approach is to take photographs of the subject, property, or building from an airplane or helicopter. The second approach is to purchase a remote controlled inflatable that has an automatic camera mounted on it that can be operated from the ground. The second approach has become very popular, as it is a less costly option over the long-term. Potential clients for an aerial photography business can include homeowners wishing to have a picture of their homes from a different perspective, land developers for subdivision and property development purposes, and business owners for a unique outlook on their business that can be used for promotional purposes. Rates vary largely for aerial photography. However, current billing rates for photographs taken utilizing a remote-controlled inflatable are in the range of $150 to $200 per half day, and more than $300 for a full-day rental of operator and equipment.

WEB RESOURCE: www.floatograph.com
Distributor of remote controlled photograph and imaging systems and equipment.

PERSONAL PHOTO INVENTORY SERVICE
★★★ $$ 🏠 🕐

Each year, millions of dollars worth of personal property such as TVs, stereos, home computers, and other household items are stolen from homes and businesses. Taking a series of personal inventory photographs of items in someone's home, office, or business means taking photographs of anything and everything of value so that both the customer can have copies and a copy can be either stored in a safe location for security purposes. Having photos to show what was on the location prior to a burglary, theft, or natural disaster can be valuable for law enforcement officials as well as the insurance company involved. A fantastic way to market this type of unique service is to establish alliances with companies that sell and install home alarm systems. The alarm companies could offer this service as a free added-value for their clients or charge only a small fee for the service. A joint venture such as this would be a win-win-win situation. The home or business owner would receive a terrific service that could potentially save them thousands of dollars or result in the stolen items being returned. Once again, this type of business is very simple to establish from a homebased location, since the work is done on the premises of the client. This type of business does not even require a great deal of photographic skill. You will, however, need to be familiar with storing digital images and for safe keeping you should also back up all of the photos to CDs and store a copy offsite.

HEADSHOTS
★★ $$ 🏠 🕐

Taking photographs of actors and models is a sector of the photography industry that generates millions of dollars in revenues each year. You need to be skilled at taking photos in the right lighting and from the best angles to capture "the look" for actors and models, who are already in a highly competitive business. This business is best operated from a photography studio so you appear as professional as possible and you can share a studio with another photography business as long as it does not interfere with your primary business. You can use a home-based studio when starting out or for handling phone calls. Marketing this type of photography service is best accomplished by establishing alliances with acting and modeling agencies, drama departments of universities, community theater groups, and modeling schools. Word-of-mouth will also be very important since actors and models travel in the same circles – therefore, once one or two get work based on the headshots you have taken, word will spread quickly. Currently the rate for taking actors' headshots is in the range of $100 to $200. Modeling portfolios start at approximately $250 and go up in price depending on their complexity.

PHOTO CALENDARS FOR BUSINESSES
★★ $$ 🚗 🕒

Are you looking for a very unique photography business to start? If so, perhaps you should consider starting a photography business that produces specialty calendars for clients to give away to valued customers as a business promotion. At some point we have all been given a generic calendar from a business, club, or organization. The focus of this business, however, is much different, as the calendars that are produced for each client's business is unique and exclusive to the business. Why would a homebuilder give away a calendar to a client that featured animal pictures? Obviously the calendar should feature photographs of the homes the builder has completed; this would be a far more powerful marketing tool for the business. Likewise, a restaurant calendar should features the foods, the chef, the interior of the restaurant and even the staff. The business is very easy to market. Simply design sample calendars and set appointments to present the product to local companies that you feel would greatly benefit from this type of specialty marketing tool. Providing you have excellent product and presentation skills, there should be no problem gaining customers for this type of photography business.

NATURAL DISASTER PHOTOGRAPHY
★ $$$ 🚗 🕒

There are many different approaches that can be taken, in terms of starting a natural disaster photography service. The first approach is to travel the world and take pictures of the numerous natural disasters such as earthquakes, floods, and fires that happen annually, and use the photos to create a yearly natural disaster coffee table book. The second approach is to use digital camera equipment to take photographs that could then be posted on a web site and sold to news agencies and publishers. Both approaches to this photography business require sizeable investment capital, photography skills, and excellent marketing skills. However, this is a unique and interesting business that has the potential to generate an extremely large income, providing the business can be properly established.

PERSONAL POSTCARDS
★★★ $$$ 🕒 🌐

Once again, this is a business opportunity that could not have been started a decade ago simply because the technology to create instant postcards simply was not yet available. Get started by building a custom sales kiosk and equip the kiosk with computer equipment, software, and a digital camera. Then take pictures of tourists at tourist attractions. The pictures can be produced instantly in the format of a postcard complete with text captions and graphics. Instead of tourists purchasing generic postcards to send home to family and friends, they purchase postcards featuring themselves in front of a tourist attraction or involved in a tourist activity. Outside of having the ability to run the camera and computer equipment, the main business requirement will be a very good and busy tourist location to set up the kiosk in order to take the pictures. Excellent locations can include tourist attractions, amusement parks, sport tours such as white water rafting, busy outdoor parks, and natural wonders.

U-FILM-IT MOVIE STUDIO
★ $$$$

Are you looking for a fun, interesting, and unique business opportunity that has minimal competition? If so, perhaps you should consider starting a movie studio that provides customers with props, clothing, and equipment on a rental basis so they can film and produce their own movies. Additionally, the movie studio can be rented to film production companies, theater groups, acting students producing their own short films and audition tapes, and just about anyone else seeking to film their own movie, play, or commercial for profit or fun. A U-Film-It movie studio will require substantial investment capital for equipment and to get it rolling. However, there should be no difficulties charging rental rates in the range of $150 to $250 per hour for the use of equipment, location, and props.

CORPORATE VIDEOS
★★★ $$$$

Corporate videos have become a very popular marketing and training tool for companies worldwide, and starting a business that films and produces high-quality corporate training and promotional videos could put you on the path to financial freedom. Without question this is another business venture that requires a great deal of planning, research, investment capital, and experience in order to successfully operate. The service can be marketed directly to potential customers, or it can be established as a joint venture with an existing advertising agency or marketing agency. This would be a great business opportunity to start in conjunction with the U-Film-It movie studio, as the corporate videos could also be filmed in the same studio when the studio is not being rented.

CUSTOM PHOTO ALBUMS
★ $$ 🏠 🕒

In spite of the popularity of digital cameras and CD-ROM photo albums, traditional photo albums will always be used to showcase cherished family photographs as they are handy. They can easily be passed around a room full of interested onlookers, and face it, it's tough to pass around a full-size computer or to have a group of ten people crowd around a monitor. The photo albums that you design and manufacture should be interesting and constructed from unique building materials. The completed photo albums can be sold to local and national retailers on a wholesale basis, directly to consumers from your web site, or through traditional advertising and marketing. While creating and selling custom photo albums won't make you an overnight millionaire, it can provide a good part-time income.

PHOTO TRANSFERS
★ $$ 🕒

Starting a part-time business that photographs people and pets and transfers their images onto plates, mugs, plaques, or any number of items is a terrific small business opportunity that does not require a great deal of photographic experience or investment start-up capital to get rolling. This type of business can be operated from a small booth located in a busy area such as a mall on the weekends, or at flea markets, trade shows, carnivals, and outdoor community events. The equipment needed to run the business is available to be purchased new or used and can be found on the web or by special order through photographic equipment supply businesses. If you are considering this type of business be sure to market the service to businesses, clubs, and organizations, as photo plaques make great achievement awards and corporate gifts. In addition, the hosts of parties, communions, Bar Mitzvahs, and other special occasions will be looking to you for photo transferring as a gift item for guests.

WEB RESOURCE: www.printusa.com
Distributor of equipment and supplies for imaging transfers and printing.

COMMERCIAL PHOTOGRAPHY
★★ $$ 🏠 🕒

Every year there are millions of catalogs, marketing brochures, and information pamphlets distributed in the United States, and many of these promotional mediums use photographs of a product, person, or place to highlight the product, service, or information that is being promoted or sold. Starting a photography business that takes professional photographs for commercial use in catalogs is not very easy to initiate. The growing availability and use of digital cameras has many business owners under the (often misguided) belief that they can handle their own photography needs, and there is also a lot of competition for the remaining work. However, a commercial photography service can be an extremely successful business venture if you are good, reliable, and understand the client's needs. Get a portfolio of commercial photographs completed and even do your first job for free to show what you can do for a company. Once you get your foot in the door with one or two jobs, use those photos in a brochure and on your web site to generate more business. Market yourself to retailers directly and to advertising agencies, starting with smaller ones that can hire you on a subcontract or freelance basis.

WEB RESOURCE: www.apanational.com
Advertising Photographers Association of America.

PORTRAIT PHOTOGRAPHER
★★ $$ 🚗 🕐

Calling all hobby photographers! Why not start a part-time business as a portrait photographer and start profiting from your hobby? A portrait photography business can be easily operated from a homebased studio or as a mobile photography service going directly to the client's location. This type of business can be marketed by all traditional means of advertising, as well as by establishing alliances with large retail stores and setting up a portrait photo studio on weekends. The second option of marketing will generate fewer profits as you will have to negotiate a revenue split with the retailer, however, this can be a terrific joint venture as it will enable you to capitalize on the retailer's customer base. Part-time potential income ranges from $10,000 to $25,000 per year.

WEDDING PHOTOGRAPHER
★★ $$ 🚗 🕐

There are a number of different approaches that can be taken when starting a wedding photography business. The first option is to be the wedding photographer, and the second is to start an agency representing wedding photographers. If you choose the first option, hone your skills working with an established wedding photographer (even for peanuts) as an assistant. This will allow you to get an idea of what shots are necessary, how to get the best photos before, during, and after the wedding ceremony and reception, and other tricks of the trade. Once you are ready to strike out on your own, market your services to wedding planners, catering halls, and on your own web site. The second option would mean serving as an agent of sorts, representing local photographers by doing the marketing and getting jobs for them. Make sure everyone you represent is extremely reliable and proficient at wed-

ding photography – an art that includes getting the right photos at the right moments without being a nuisance or in the way. The next step in all wedding photography is putting together the wedding album or albums, which you do once the proofs are ready and the couple has decided upon the photos they want included. You can market various packages which include albums for the parents of the bride and groom, various individually framed photos, and so on. Selling the many variations of photos and photo albums is where you make the real money. Another alternative would be to host a wedding photography service online that includes wedding photographers from all over the country, so that anyone seeking a wedding photographer would simply log onto the site for a list of those found in their area. Revenues for the web site could be generated by charging the photographers a yearly fee to be listed, and from advertising revenue from related businesses such as wedding planners and caterers.

WEB RESOURCE: www.wpja.org
The Wedding Photojournalism Association.

THEME PHOTOGRAPHY STUDIO
★★ $$$

Providing you can secure the right high-profile retail location in a busy year-round tourist area, starting a theme photography studio can be an outstanding business opportunity that has the potential to generate profits in excess of $10,000 per month. The key to success with a theme photography studio is to have a wide and interesting range of backdrops and costumes for customers to choose from for their photographs. Current technology can enable you to produce all the photographs as digital images and augment the pictures for the client. Green screen backgrounds allow you numerous possibilities to put your photographic subjects in any situations. The best places to establish a theme photography studio include beach areas (particularly along a busy boardwalk), amusement parks, in popular resort hotels and on a mobile basis traveling from mall to mall on weekends. Additionally, this type of business can be marketed to clubs and associations seeking fun photographs for their members.

PHOTO BUSINESS CARDS
★★ $$ 🏠 🕐

Designing photo business cards is a fantastic home-based business to set in motion. The equipment needed to operate a photo business card enterprise is inexpensive and includes a computer, scanner, design software, and a digital camera. Potential clients can include any person who is in business, or requires a business card for their job. The most efficient way to operate the business is to simply supply the service of taking the photograph to be used in the business card and designing the layout for the card. Printing the cards should be done by a professional printer as it will cost less to produce mass quantities and the overall quality will be far superior. Currently photo business cards are retailing for approximately $150 to $200 per thousand, and cost around $40 to produce that same quantity. Quick math will tell you that leaves around $100 to design the cards and take the picture, or about $50 per hour, making this a potentially very profitable business venture to start and run from a home-based location

HOLIDAY GREETING CARDS
★★ $$ 🏠 🕐 🌐

Love them or hate them, holiday greeting cards featuring employees of a business or a family standing in front of a fireplace at Christmas are here to stay. Some people find picture greeting cards to be silly, while others swear by them and have them created every year. Starting this type of photography business does not require a great amount of photographic experience as most of the digital images can be improved or cleaned up with basic computer software programs, like PhotoShop. Gaining clients for this type of business can be accomplished with the use of a sales and promotion kiosk that can be setup in malls and trade shows to demonstrate and promote the service. Keep in mind that if you are looking to do a lot of Christmas cards, get them started in August or September because it will take some time to get them printed and shipped. Overall, a photo greeting card business is a good choice for a homebased business opportunity that has the ability to create a part-time income of $20,000 or more each year.

SCHOOL AND BUSINESS YEARBOOKS
★★ $$$ 🏠 🕐

Each year millions of school yearbooks are sold across North America, and business photo yearbooks are starting to become popular for medium to large companies to have produced as gifts to their valued employees. The best aspect about starting a yearbook photography business is the fact that you do not have to be a photographer to make the business work, as the photography aspect of the business can be subcontracted to a professional photographer. The real key to success in this type of photography service is to possess excellent marketing abilities, as this is a very competitive segment of the photography industry. Once again, potential clients for a yearbook service can include grade schools, high schools, colleges, universities, companies, clubs, sports leagues, associations, and charity organizations. As a method to separate your yearbook service from the competition, perhaps you could specialize in digital yearbooks and supply the final product on a CD-ROM or DVD.

WEB RESOURCE: http://pspa.pmai.org
Professional School Photographers Association International.

PHOTO KEY CHAINS
★★ $$ 🕐

Once again, here is a fantastic photography business opportunity that can be started simply by purchasing a digital camera, notebook computer, the right software, and a couple hundred blank key chains. Photo key chains are very popular with tourists, who can't resist a picture of themselves with a loved one while on vacation. The key to success with this type of business venture is to be located in high-traffic areas with loads of tourists. Utilizing the above-mentioned equipment will enable you to produce a finished photo key chain in less than five minutes, and for less than $1 in costs. Considering the photo key chains sell for $10 it is a very good return on investment. Good locations for this mobile photography business include pubs, restaurants, comedy clubs, beaches, malls, amusement parks, sports events, concerts, and just about every other high traffic community-gathering place. You can also sell photos on buttons as well.

LITTLE LEAGUE CARDS
★★★ $$ 🚗 🕒 🌐

Baseball, football, soccer, and hockey each have literally hundreds of thousands of little league teams. Little league photo trading cards, along with team pictures, have become very common for such leagues. You can operate from a homebased location and service the little league teams in your community. The investment to get started adds up to little more than the cost of a good camera and photo supplies. Marketing the service is as easy as contacting amateur sports clubs and associations in your area to present your product.

However, since there is increasing competition, see if you can create some unique card ideas and other sports related items to stand out from the crowd, as this is a business that has really caught on in recent years.

BABY PHOTOGRAPHER
★★★ $$ 🚗 🕒 🌐

No, a baby photographer is not a one-year-old with a camera. This age-old business involves taking portraits of babies and it is not all that hard a skill to master. The business can be managed from home and operated on a full- or part-time basis. Equipment needed is inexpensive, and operating overheads are minimal. If you posses photography experience you are one step ahead of the game. If not, don't worry as there are photography courses available in every community that will put you on the path toward starting this business. There are numerous options in terms of how it will operate. You can go to clients' homes to take the photographs. You can set up a small studio in your own home providing you have the space and zoning permits. Or you can partner with one or more retailers in your community and set up a small photography studio within their store that operates one or two days per week. Of course you can also combine all three options and make it as convenient as possible for your customers to have their baby photographed. In addition to camera and developing equipment you will also need backdrop scenes, props, and a few toy diversions to keep the babies' attention on the camera. One skill required is having great patience—not only waiting for baby to smile, but while dealing with the often overzealous parents.

As a parallel business, baby trading cards are starting to become very popular and this is a service you may want to consider providing to your clients. Baby trading cards are a photograph of the baby complete with the baby's name printed on the front and "baby stats," such as date born, height, weight, favorite food, etc., printed on the back. Parents love to give these baby trading cards to friends and family, as well as receive other cards from parents. The baby trading cards also provide a good opportunity for repeat business as the cards and photographs can be renewed annually, starting newborn and one year-old babies, right up to the teenage years.

ONE-HOUR PHOTO LAB
★★ $$$$

In spite of the increasing popularity of digital imaging, print or negative photography will be around for many years to come. A good income can still be earned by starting and operating a one-hour photo lab. Of course the resourceful entrepreneur will also provide customers with digital imaging services in addition to traditional film development services, plus photo album possibilities. Like any retail business, location will be a major consideration. Good operating locations for a one-hour photo lab include stand-alone booths set up at indoor malls, small storefronts in strip malls, and within existing retail stores such as grocery stores and pharmacies. One-hour photo lab equipment is easy to operate and most distributors of this equipment will include some training when new or used photo lab equipment is purchased. The title of the business suggests that all film developing is completed in one hour or less. This is inaccurate, as it is best to give customers film development options. The faster they want their film developed the higher the costs. There are also incentives that you can offer to secure new and repeat business such as two prints for the price of one, a free roll of film with each three rolls developed, and a free 8 by 10 inch blowup of one picture per roll of film developed. Also to increase revenues, you can establish drop-off and pick-up satellite locations. These locations simply mean that customers can drop off their film at various locations throughout the community and pick up their photos at a later date. You simply drive to these location daily and pick up the film to be developed and drop it off the next day when you return to pick up film again. The key to having various locations is to be very well organized and to make sure satellite locations are also well-situated. Otherwise this option may be more of a hassle than it is worth.

WEB RESOURCE: www.usedphotolab.com
Broker listing secondhand one-hour photo lab and photographic processing equipment for sale.

SAILBOAT RACE PHOTOGRAPHER
★★ $$

Do you have a lust for adventure, good photography skills, and are you seeking to start your own business? If so, then this particular business opportunity will be of interest to you. Every year there are thousands of sailboat races and regattas taking place in the United States. Starting a business that photographs sailboat races, or more specifically a sailboat in action for the boat's owner and captain, is a fantastic new venture to get "sailing." Once again, the only requirements to operate the business will be a good camera and photography skills, a strong stomach, and the ability to rent a boat and captain for the day of the race. Utilizing a digital camera will enable you to show the photographs to the boat owners at the end of the race right on a laptop computer. This is a sensational marketing tool, as you would then be able to take orders and payment for the photographs and mail the finished product to the customer at a later date, or place all of the photos taken onto a CD-ROM and edit in special effects and music. The options are unlimited when you apply technology to a strong business concept.

FREELANCE PHOTOGRAPHER
★ $$ 🚗 🕐

Thanks in part to the popularity of the internet, still pictures are once again in huge demand for media publishing. Why? Simply because there are in excess of ten billion web pages worldwide and many of these pages feature photographs. If that's not enough to convince you that photographs are in high demand, consider that there are millions of print publications distributed every month that also feature photographs. Freelance photographers have various options open to them in terms of selling their photographs. You can sell them directly to brokers who will pay you a one-time fee for the photograph and all copyrights. You can feature your photographs in one or more of the numerous online stock photo services, wherein every time your photograph is downloaded you receive a small fee. You can develop your own online stock photo service, or you can select what you believe to be your best photographs on varying subjects and send them to media publishers in the hopes that they will get purchased. The options for selling the photographs are almost as vast as the number of photographic subjects.

WEB RESOURCE: www.aipress.com
International Freelance Photographers Organization; site contains information about how to earn money as a freelance photographer as well as industry information and links.

HOUSE PHOTOGRAPHY
★ $$

Are you seeking a way to earn an income or extra money utilizing your photography skills? If so, perhaps you should consider starting a house photography service. The business could be started for less than a few thousand dollars and operated right from a homebased studio. The business concept is very basic. Simply photograph houses in your community at the right time, such as Christmas, during sunsets, or during storms. Pictures taken under these conditions are excellent "one-of-a-kind" photos that almost any homeowner would be proud to have and, more importantly, be happy to pay for. Potential income for part-time is $10,000+ per year and full-time is $25,000+ per year.

PHOTO GALLERY
★★★ $$$

Whether a gallery features your photos or those of other photographers, it is a very nice addition to any town. A small gallery location can be both for selling photos as well as for displaying the talents of new or experienced photographers. You make money from photographers looking to exhibit and a commission on the sale of photographs, as well as frames and framing. Photo greeting cards and other items in a gift shop can bring in additional money. In addition, galleries can be very nice places to hold parties and you can make money by utilizing part of the space. A gallery will mean leasing, renting, or buying a space, arranging the lighting to optimally display photos, and then waiting a while before you will see a return on your initial investment – unless of course you have a space available.

PHOTOGRAPHY STUDIO RENTAL
★★★ $$$$

Got a nice size loft space available? Perhaps you know someone with an office facility that is not using a significant portion of their space. A location with high ceilings and some natural lighting can make a great studio to rent out for photo shoots. If you invest in a cyclorama, or backdrop, which can be lit or decorated as necessary, you can increase the value of such a studio for photo shoots. Also, kitchen sets are very much in demand. Washrooms, hair and makeup areas, fax and computer services, secured equipment storage rooms (for shoots of two days or more), blackout shades for the windows, and other options can increase your chances of being booked often.

The more amenities you offer, the more likely magazine art directors, advertising agency execs, and independent or corporate photographers in need of photo shoot locations will rent your space for anywhere from $200 to $700 per day. Some studios have flat fee day rates of $400 or $500 per 12 hour day, while others have half day rates, full day rates for eight hours, and additional hourly charges. Also, make sure you have ample power for lighting purposes and liability insurance should anyone get injured. Market your studio to film studios, print photographers, magazines, web sites, advertising agencies, and through ads to the general public, as you never know who needs to do a photo shoot. An investment of $100,000 is not out of the question to set up and start a full rental photo studio. However, if you can book at $500 per day and fill 20 days per month you can bring in $10,000 monthly, with limited ongoing costs except marketing, maintenance, and rent or mortgage payments. If you already own a space that can be used as a studio (as zoned by the community) you are way ahead, as contracting fees can be around $50,000 to turn your own space into a studio location, or even less if you are handy.

PHOTO ID BADGES
★ $$ 🚗 🕐

Someone has to take those often terrible photos that you see on your identification cards or badges at work, or for membership into a club, association, or organization. You can be that someone, taking (hopefully) decent quality photos of all company employees, students at a college or high school, or members of a high end golf club. Whatever the need, you can fulfill it by taking the photos and making the ID cards, plastic in some cases and electronic in other situations. Typically photo ID badges will cost you less than $3.00 each to make, but you can sell them at $6.50 or $7.00 each, and of course on bulk orders of 25 or more you might bring down your rate to $5.00. The key is to turn the photos around and make up the badges in a short time.

PHOTOJOURNALIST
★★ $$ 🕐

Typically hired by a newspaper or magazine, the life of a photojournalist can be an exciting one and this is a business for people who enjoy the antithesis of the nine-to-five desk job. As a photojournalist you are essentially documenting history with a camera by photographing newsworthy people, places, or events. You are telling the story with your photos. This is not easy work, since you may need to capture such photos when they happen and gain access (legally) to the places where the photos need be taken – often the magazine or newspaper will help get you in the door, or between the bulls they run in Pamplona, or in the eye of the hurricane. You will also need to get the photos developed and handed in to an editor very quickly to meet a tight deadline.

REQUIREMENTS: You will need top-of-the-line photographic equipment and some terrific photos in your portfolio to show your work to editors, producers, publishers, art directors, and/or web content directors. Get your feet wet by taking photos for local newspapers for little or no money until you build up your portfolio. Depending on how aggressive you are and how much your photos capture the essence of the story, you can bring in between $20,000 and $70,000 with little overhead except film and batteries—both of which will be compensated for by the publication once you become established.

WEB RESOURCE: www.nppa.org
National Press Photographers Association.

PRODUCT PHOTOGRAPHER
★★★ $$ 🚗 🕐

"Okay, smile!" These are not words commonly used by product photographers in their line of work. Product photography is an art and one that can pay very well if you know how to get the right lighting, angle, and "look" that the clients want to best represent their products in a very competitive marketplace. You can work for manufacturers directly as well as for advertising agencies and retailers, making the possibilities of gaining clients very far reaching and also making this a potentially highly lucrative business. As is typically the case, you will need a portfolio, which is not particularly expensive since you will not need to pay models. Again, this is a business that you can run from your home. If you can establish yourself as the regular photographer for several businesses, so that all new products are yours to photograph, including catalogs, you can be on your way to having a very successful homebased business.

USED CAMERA EQUIPMENT
★★ $$ 🚗 🕐

Not everyone needs the latest in digital cameras. There is a steady and potentially lucrative business to be built in the buying and re-selling of used photography equipment, including cameras, lenses, filters, tripods, lighting, projectors, various accessories, and even digital products. The key is to know what you are buying and not to overpay, so that you can resell equipment at 50% to 100% markups. A fully-dedicated storefront location might be costly to start with, so you might opt to hook up with another retailer or perhaps set up a booth in a mall. A web site is also a significant manner in which to buy and sell such equipment. Your first mission is to build up an inventory which will require you to seek out cameras and equipment through any (legal) means possible, including auctions, flea markets, garage sales, advertising in local classified sections of the newspaper as well as in photography magazines, reaching out to photography clubs, classes, chat groups, and directly contacting anyone in the field. Follow up on all leads. Once you have a reasonable inventory, you can begin marketing yourself as a seller. Start-up costs should be about $35,000 to $50,000 to build up an inventory, do some marketing, rent a small space, and launch a web site.

PHOTOGRAPHY CONTEST COORDINATOR
★ $ 🚗 🕐

Baby photos? Funniest photos? Best overall photos? Categories notwithstanding, you can start a fun and lucrative business running photography contests. First, make sure you are not breaking any local laws by holding contests and apply for whatever licensing or permits necessary. Contests are most often sponsored by a group, organization, newspaper, magazine, or business of some type. The sponsor puts up the prize and gets a ton of promotion and you run the contest by finding the location or putting together the web pages that will feature the photos. Contest themes, regulations, deadlines for entries, entry fees, judges and/or means of voting are all your responsibility. Awarding the prizes can be at a special event or simply by mail. Market yourself to any business or group that you believe would benefit from a photo contest in terms of marketing, publicity, and possibly some income. Charitable groups might use your services to raise money through a photo contest. You are compensated in one of two ways. First, you can be hired by the business or group to run the contest, and second, you can collect entrance fees, perhaps splitting such fees with a charitable organization. In time, you may be so successful by holding web based contests that you can utilize advertisements to cover the cost of prizes and run contests without any additional sponsorship.

DIGITAL CAMERA SHOP
★★★★ $$$$

From teenagers to seniors, people love digital cameras. So with that in mind, you can open up a shop to sell the cameras and accompanying software, plus lenses, filters, carrying cases, and all of the numerous digital accessories. Battery sales alone can be a lucrative business! Location is always a major factor when opening a retail shop and this is no exception. You will want to be situated in a shopping area with a good amount of foot traffic, since camera buyers may make a special trip but the accessories sell more quickly if impulse buyers are factored into the equation. Photo contests, photo classes, and special gallery-type showings are great ways to market your shop and draw people in. Use all other traditional advertising and marketing means and be willing to go the extra mile for customers by ordering specific items. Your startup costs will depend largely on the size of the location, which can range from a small booth in a mall to a 10,000 square foot location. Expect to spend anywhere from $50,000 to $150,000 for furnishings, equipment, inventory, rent, payroll, insurance, security and other expenses to get a moderate shop off the ground. Also make sure to have enough cash on hand until you get rolling.

WEB RESOURCE: www.wholesalecamera.com
Digital cameras at discount wholesale prices.

BOUDOIR PHOTOGRAPHY
★★ $$ 🏠 🕐

Yes, it's a legitimate business, if you are taking tasteful, yet provocative, photos in your own professional studio. Romantic photos make marvelous Valentine's Day gifts or simply serve as ways to spark a relationship. You need not only be good with a camera, but also know how to work professionally with models to set the mood and establish a trusting atmosphere. The idea is to convey an attitude or "state of mind" with such photos, based on suggestions, such as lingerie, low-cut necklines, and manner of posing models for the desired "sensuous" effects. You can create a homebased studio providing you have the room and the atmosphere, which will mean you can't have kids running up and down the stairs above you during a photo shoot. Other costs are that of first-rate camera equipment, including lighting, and marketing, which needs to emphasize your tasteful and professional approach to the subject at all times. For a one-hour photo shoot, you can charge upwards of $100 and add for re-touching and making presentation pieces such as calendars or photo albums. Once you establish yourself in the field, much of the work will come through word of mouth.

NOTES:

29
REAL ESTATE
Businesses You Can Start

PROPERTY MANAGER
★★ $$ 🏠 🕐

Here is the perfect new business venture for someone who wants to start a business on a limited investment and manage his or her new enterprise from the comforts of a home office. Becoming a property manager is relatively straightforward, provided you understand the responsibilities included in handling and managing a property. The duties of a property manager can include organizing tradespeople to conduct repairs on the building structure, receiving and replying to tenant and owner inquiries, leasing vacant units, and negotiating lease terms and details. A property management service is ideally suited for a person with a real estate background. Working in a property management business to start can familiarize you with the basics; you can then branch out on a part-time basis and begin managing properties on your own. As the business grows, you can hire and train additional people with real estate and property management background to handle properties. To succeed in this type of business you need to be very well organized, understand some construction needs, know both landlords and tenant's legal rights, and be a good listener in order to understand the many needs of the tenants, owners, contractors, and repair people, all of whom you will be dealing with on a regular basis.

WEB RESOURCE: www.npma.org
National Property Managers Association.

COMMERCIAL LEASING AGENT
★★★ $$ 🏠 ⚖

Educating yourself about the laws of commercial real estate leases and contracts can really pay off, especially if you apply this newfound knowledge and become a commercial leasing agent. A commercial leasing agent service can be set in motion for less than $10,000, and can return as much as $100,000 per year in income. The main focus of this enterprise is to source buildings, stores, and offices to list for lease, and find suitable tenants to occupy these locations. In exchange for your services you charge the landlord of the building one month's rent as your fee, or a leasing commission. Should another real estate or leasing agent be involved in the transaction, you would simply split the fee with that person or company. Commercial leasing is very straightforward, but you will still want to extensively research the topic as well as check local regulations in terms of the legalities of becoming a leasing agent in your community.

HOUSE PREPARATION SERVICE
★★★ $$ 🏠 🕐

Every real estate agent will tell you that a home that has been professionally prepared to be listed for sale will sell fast and for top dollar. That is why real estate agents will become your best source of referrals if you are considering starting a house preparation service. There is only one objective to be achieved in this type of service for your clients. Make the home ready, so that it will sell quickly and as close as possible to the full asking price. Best of all, this can be easily accomplished if you place yourself in the shoes of the potential purchaser. How? Look for things that standout and could have a negative impact in the eyes of a potential buyer, such as loose boards on the front porch, a broken pane of glass in a window, dull paint in the living room, or a cracked tile in the kitchen floor. A thousand dollars spent to repair a few minor deficiencies prior to listing a home for sale can easily fetch the vendor ten times that amount in a higher selling price. Why? Deficiencies begin to add up financially in a potential buyer's mind and usually result in a lower negotiated sale price for the home. Charging for your service should be done on a pre-estimated basis. That means you will estimate the job prior to commencing with your services. Additionally, your estimate should clearly state exactly the work to be performed, so there won't be any difficulties arising after the work has been completed. There should be a signed agreement by both parties to govern any discussions or miscommunications. If you are handy, you can handle the repair work yourself and easily command at least $40 per hour for labor, plus a 100 percent markup on all materials that may be required to fulfill the agreement. If you are not handy, but understand what to look for in a home from a buyer's perspective, you can compile a report of what needs to be done and have skilled individuals handle the actual repair work. If you do only the "inspection" reports, detailing what needs to be done, you can charge a flat fee of $100 for the report, or more for large properties. This business can easily be operated from a homebased office. Be sure to have liability insurance and remember to do any actual repair work only once you have a signed contract.

HOUSE FOR SALE BY OWNER PUBLICATION
★★ $$$ 🏠 🕐

Many homeowners are forgoing the services of a real estate agent when selling their homes as a method of saving money on commission fees. This situation creates a great opportunity for business-minded entrepreneurs to capitalize on by starting a "For Sale by Owner" publication in your local community, or on a web site. The publication can be printed and distributed free of charge on a weekly or monthly basis and supported by selling advertising space to owners of the homes for sale. As well as selling advertising to local companies, such as moving and storage firms, consider adding home renovation businesses seeking to gain exposure to potential new clients. As a quick-start method to get the first publication in print and distributed, you can give away the "home for sale" advertising spaces for free. This kind of grand opening promotion not only gets you rolling, but it also builds good will with the free advertisers, of which many will become paid advertisers for the next issue of the home for sale by owner publication. If you opt to run this business over the internet, not only will you be renting low-cost, highly effective advertising space to homeowners selling privately, but you will also be providing them an alternative to high-priced print advertising. You will want to index the site into various sections such as residential homes for sale, condominiums for sale, vacant land for sale, etc. In addition to the advertising revenues created by home seller listings, you can also earn extra advertising income by developing a community service providers section in the site. This section of the site can list local companies in the real estate, home improvement, and moving industry—basically any type of business that is associated with home ownership.

MINI-STORAGE CENTER
★★ $$ 🏠 🕐

The mini-storage industry is booming. Why? Simply because with homebased businesses opening at a record pace, homebased business owners require storage space for products, displays, and equipment. Likewise, the baby boomer generation is scaling down to smaller residences and requires storage space for their personal belongings. The toughest part of this business opportunity is finding enough square footage for storage and an infrastructure to accommodate the security measures you will need. You then need to buy the facility. Insurance is next and that can be costly. Without question, starting a mini-storage business involves an enormous investment on behalf of the entrepreneur. However, the income that can be earned from a well-established mini-storage business can exceed $150,000 per year or more, in time. A possible solution to combat this high investment dilemma may be to form a group of investors to back the business venture financially, helping you to purchase the facility with you as a minority share holder and the operator of the storage business.

WEB RESOURCE: www.selfstorage.org
Self Storage Association.

SHARED OFFICE CENTER
★★★ $$$$

Shared office facilities are very popular, and the demand for low-cost shared office rentals continues to increase right across North America. As an alternative to working from home, many small businesses are utilizing shared office space as a way of keeping monthly overheads manageable, and shared office centers usually consist of 20 to 30 small individual offices housed within one location. Once you find and lease, rent, or purchase a location, you can generate additional revenue from providing your tenants with a wide range of "extra services," such as shared reception and secretarial services, high-speed photocopying, parcel shipping and receiving, wireless internet service, and boardroom facilities. You will also need to find a location that is well-equipped for high tech business needs and safe for occupants. The individual offices can be rented furnished or unfurnished—providing this option to tenants is also an excellent way to increase your business income with furniture and equipment rentals. The most difficult part of this business is securing the space until you find the tenants you need. In an effort to not to pay a lot of money for the facility until you rent out the office space, you might start canvassing your chosen area to determine how many business owners are looking for this type of business office space. This will give you an idea of how quickly (or not) you will be able fill the space you choose. In some busy areas, the right (well equipped) shared office spaces have waiting lists while in other more financially depressed areas, business owners are sitting with unrented space available. Therefore, doing some preliminary canvassing can be very valuable.

REAL ESTATE SIGN INSTALLATION SERVICE
★ $ 🏠 🕒

Installing real estate signs is a very inexpensive way to get into business for yourself. This enterprise requires no special skills, and only a few basic tools are needed to complete the sign installations. Most real estate agents and companies do not install their own signs, as they generally do not have the time or the proper vehicle to transport the signs or the necessary equipment to carry out the installation. A great way to separate your service from a competitor's service in this industry is to provide your clients with not only a fast and reliable sign installation service, but also free regular checks to make sure the signs have not been damaged or removed from the building or property site.

VACATION PROPERTY RENTAL AGENT
★★★ $$ 🏠 🕒

Many people purchase vacation homes in the hopes they will be able to rent the property to tourists for part of the year as a way to reduce the costs of owning and maintaining their vacation property. Unfortunately, rental income often fails to materialize, as the property owners do not realize how much time and work is involved in renting their properties effectively. As a result, the property sits vacant, or is sold due to the lack of rental income. This fact creates a terrific opportunity to start a vacation rental service that could also provide property maintenance and management services for the owners of vacation properties. The business can be managed from a home office and started on a part-time basis while establishing a good reputation for service and reliability in the vacation property rental industry. Some real estate experience is a big plus and good marketing skills are a must, since you will need to tap into the market for people seeking vacation homes. Today, the best way to run such a business is via the internet. Utilizing a web site, categorized by location and type of vacation property, you can either specialize and list vacation homes in one region, or branch out and list homes in several parts of the country with which you are familiar. Be forewarned that if you branch out too far, you may be listing homes in areas you know nothing about, which could destroy your reputation if the vacation homes are not legitimate or are in dreadful shape. For this reason, it is highly advisable to stick to a few key areas with which you are familiar.

In exchange for an annual listing fee, vacation homeowners could receive a link to a web page that gives details and contact information including photographs of the vacation home for rent. Promote the site by placing low-cost classified advertisements in community newspapers under vacation properties for rent. Your ad could read, "Thousands of vacation homes for rent. Check them out at www...." There are advertising programs available that will enable your ad to be featured in as many as 1,500 newspapers per month for less than $1,000. Contact your local community newspaper for details.

PETS-ALLOWED APARTMENT RENTALS
★★★ $$ 🏠 🕐

The most common phrase in house or apartment for rent advertisements is "no pets allowed." If you have a dog or cat, there is a good chance that you have dealt with the very frustrating task of finding a new rental home for yourself and your pet. This business opportunity comes to the rescue of pet owners who are seeking rental accommodations that allow pets. To get going, contact landlords and property management companies in your community to inquire about their particular regulations in regards to renting residential units to people with pets. The landlords who indicate that they do allow pets in their units are the ones who will benefit. Why? Simply because you can save the landlords money in advertising costs by providing free advertising via your pets-allowed property rental service and web site. The money earned in this business is derived from the pet owners seeking the rental accommodations, as they pay you a fee to locate an apartment or a house that allows pets. The most effective marketing method for this rental service is to simply run a classified advertisement under "Houses for Rent" and "Apartments for Rent" in your local newspaper. The ad should run every day and simply read "Hundreds of houses and apartments for rent that allow pets" (plus your telephone number). While this business won't make you rich, it will bring in additional income and help pet lovers find suitable homes.

STUDENT HOUSING SERVICE
★★ $$ 🏠 🕐

Locating suitable living accommodations can be very difficult for students, especially if they cannot arrange dorm or on-campus housing. This business, therefore, focuses on finding suitable apartments or room and board

accommodations for students. Landlords have apartments to rent and individuals living in close proximity to colleges and universities have space in their homes to accommodate students in a room and board situation. This business venture provides the service of bringing these two parties together via a student housing service. The business can be marketed and promoted in all traditional local print publications. You can generate revenue by charging both the landlord and the student a fee if both need your services. However, in most situations, landlords in college towns will not have a hard time renting an apartment or a room. Therefore, you can make more money by providing a specialized service to the college student by finding the right apartment or room in the right part of town, easily accessible to the school, with parking, in a safe environment, etc. Parents are typically paying a tremendous amount of money for their son or daughter's education. An extra $200 or $300 for an expert to find the best off-campus accommodations is drop in the bucket at that point. Before starting this business, however, you need to become that expert, which means aligning yourself with anyone and everyone who could possibly have an apartment or room to rent and letting them know (with a brochure to back up your sales pitch) that you can find college students as occupants... students that will not bring in destructive friends, play loud music at all hours, and skip out without paying rent. If they gain trust in you as someone who can find the right tenant, you are home free as the middle person. Then, you explain to students that you have some rules that need to be followed before you can find them a great home away from home while on campus. Certainly, a student in need of housing will be eager to abide by the rules, especially since mom and dad are likely footing the bill. Thus, you are in business as the middle person, making everyone happy!

REAL ESTATE AUCTIONS
★★ $$$$ 🚗

Real estate auctions are becoming extremely popular, as an auction is a very effective method to sell a property quickly and effortlessly. The main requirement for starting a real estate auction service is that you, a partner, or an employee must be a licensed auctioneer. The business can focus on real estate in general, or be more specific and specialize in one particular type of real estate such as vacation properties or commercial buildings. The business creates revenue by way of a commission percentage that is based on the total selling price of the property be auctioned, and the commission rate charged often varies between 3 and 10 percent. The key objective is obvious: sell the property for as much as possible as this will earn the business a higher commission fee. This will make your client very happy, which in turn helps to build a good reputation in the industry and guarantees future real estate auction clients.

REAL ESTATE PRESENTATIONS
★★★ $$ 🏠 🕐

High-end real estate properties deserve a custom-designed marketing presentation to highlight all the special features contained within these homes and properties. Starting a business that designs and produces specialized real estate marketing presentations is not only a very unique service, it is also a new business venture that requires only a small investment to get going and can be operated right from the comforts of a home office. The requirements for starting a real estate presentation publishing business are very straightforward. You will need computer equipment and presentation design software. The goal here is to maximize the presentations that can be offered for multi-million dollar real estate properties. The presentations should utilize all of today's technologies and include vital information on the property being marketed, as well as colorful images and pictures. Likewise, the presentation should be printed on medium to high-gloss paper and be bound and presented in a creative fashion. Gaining new clients for the business can be very easy: simply design sample presentations featuring local properties for sale and set appointments with the listing agents of these properties to present your sample marketing presentation.

START-UP COSTS: A real estate presentation publishing business can be started for less than $10,000. This should easily cover the costs to purchase a new computer, if necessary, plus the software and printing equipment. One of the greatest benefits of starting this business is that once the equipment has been purchased there is very little additional capital needed to start making money right away.

PROFIT POTENTIAL: An hourly fee of $100 to design the presentation is certainly recommended. Additionally, if each presentation costs $3 to produce, the retail-selling price of the presentations should be two to three times the production costs. Remember that you will be dealing with million-dollar properties, so a few hundred dollars to properly present a high-end property is not out of line. To maximize profits, be sure to copyright the entire presentation that you have designed and produced. Copyrighting these presentations means the real estate agents will not be able to have the presentations reproduced by anyone but you. This will guarantee that each time they require an additional presentation for that particular property you will be making a profit by selling the presentations to the client.

RESIDENTIAL RENTAL SERVICE
★★ $$

A residential rental service can be operated from a small office location, and does not require a lot of investment capital to start. Once the business has been set in motion, the fastest way to get landlords to list their properties for rent with the service is to provide the service for free. This approach saves the landlord money by not having to advertise their properties for rent. It also provides you with a method to acquire a few hundred residential rental listings for the rental service very quickly. A fee paid by the person seeking the rental will generate revenues for the business. This can best be achieved by charging potential clients a membership fee to gain access to your rental listings. The fee would be small, perhaps $100, and the membership would last for a month or two, which should provide the client with ample time to search and secure a new rental accommodation.

MOBILE HOME BROKER
★ $$ 🏠 🕐 🚗

In some areas of the country, working as a mobile home sales broker does not require a real estate license and that is one of the many reasons making this a very good low-cost business venture to initiate, if your state or municipality allows it. The business can be operated from home on a full- or part-time basis, and promoting the broker service can be by way of designing and distributing promotional information pamphlets to all the mobile home parks in your community. You can charge clients a 5 or 6 percent commission upon successfully selling their mobile homes. Becoming a mobile home broker does not require a lot in terms of equipment, and the main requirement to make the business successful will be outstanding sales and marketing skills.

WEB RESOURCE: www.mobilehomeparkstore.com
Directory service listing mobile home associations, parks, and manufacturers.

ARTIST WORKSPACE RENTALS
★ $$$ 🕒 ⚖️

Renting a large warehouse space and dividing the space into smaller sections to rent to artists as work studios is a great way to start your own business and be self-employed. The work studios can be rented on a daily, weekly, or monthly basis, providing they are used for work areas only and not residential units. The business does not require a great deal of investment capital to get rolling, and the monthly profits can be terrific, if you assume a 3,000-square-foot warehouse rented for $2,500 per month, and the same warehouse could be divided into 15 smaller 200-square-foot artists' workspaces and rented for $400 per month each. This simple scenario could create a gross monthly income of $3,500 each month before expenses or about $2,500 afterwards. The main requirement prior to starting this venture is to check local zoning and fire regulations to make sure the venture is legal in your local area. You could make $30,000 per year from one property or $60,000 if you could find two such locations and 30 regular tenants. The problem is finding tenants and making sure they stay put. You should do a lot of advance research to determine if there are enough artists looking for space in the area you have chosen. If there is a space shortage, and many artists seeking studios, hurry and get the business started. Conversely if you find very few artists seeking space, then this is not the supply and demand equation you are looking for.

DEVELOPER HOME SALES
★★★ $ ⚖️

Providing you have excellent sales and marketing skills, a career as an independent new home sales consult-

ant may be right up your alley. In most areas of the country a real estate license is not required to sell new homes, townhouses, and condos for the developer of these housing and subdivision projects. The main obstacle to overcome in establishing yourself as an effective and results-oriented professional is to convince the developer that you are the right person for the very important task of marketing their capital-intensive developments. However, once established, persistence and results are generously rewarded, as top producers in this industry routinely earn six-figure incomes year after year. Marketing your consulting expertise is like marketing any business. Prior to contacting developers to solicit for sales consulting contracts, make sure that you have done all your homework and have prepared a complete presentation as to the projected sales forecasts and marketing methods you will be implementing in the merchandising of their development project.

WEB RESOURCE: www.nahb.com
National Association of Home Builders.

FOR SALE BY OWNER CONSULTANT
★★★ $$+ 🏠 🕒 🌐

Thousands of people across North America attempt to sell their own homes and properties each year. Some are successful but many more are not, creating a business opportunity. Starting a business that assists homeowners in selling their own homes not only is a service that is in high demand, but it is also a business venture that can make you rich. A For Sale by Owner consulting service assists clients with tips and techniques to not only sell their homes, but to do it quickly and for top dollar. The consulting service can include information about how to prepare the home for sale, what the asking price of the home should be, how to advertise and market the home, which web sites to post on, and all legal matters and documents required to sell a home. Additional revenue for this type of consulting service can be generated by publishing a For Sale by Owner publication and a For Sale by Owner web site, both of which can provide substantial sources of advertising revenues and profits.

START-UP COSTS: The following example can be used as a guideline to establish the investment needed for starting a for sale by owner consulting service.

	Low	High
Business setup, legal, banking, etc.	$250	$500
Web site and/or publication	$1,500	$3,000
Office equipment and stationery	$2,000	$4,000
Initial adverting and marketing budget	$2,000	$4,000
Working capital	$2,000	$4,000
Total start-up investment	**$7,750**	**$15,500**

HOUSE TOURS
★★ $$ 🕐

Homes featured on the home tour can include those of historical interest or landmarks, celebrity homes, homes of heritage interest, technologically advanced homes, those of famous architects or of unique architectural styles, and even homes that have had a checkered past, such as the location of a murder or home of a criminal. Starting this type of tour business is very easy and inexpensive to do. Clients can include local residents, organizations, students, and of course, tourists. Additionally, the business could go virtual and offer clients a glimpse of these homes via your web site. Mainly this is the type of business that would really be of interest to tourists, so be sure to establish contacts and forge alliances with hotels, motels, restaurants, and the local tourist bureau. Also make sure that you are not violating any privacy laws by starting such a business, and if you post photos of people's home (and information about the owners or the homes) on the internet, obtain permission first to avoid being sued. The profitability of this type of business will greatly vary as to the popularity of the house tours and the frequencies the home tours are operated. Look for an interesting angle, such as homes of movie stars, multi-million dollar homes, castles, or some such theme to generate interest. The real Cosmo Kramer's reality tours of locations used in the television program Seinfeld was (for a while) a successful business venture in New York City. If you can get 200 clients per week paying an average of $10 for the tour each will create business revenues in excess of $100,000 per year.

FIRST-TIME HOME BUYERS GUIDE
★★ $$$ 🏠 🕐 🕐

Many of us remember, and many more will soon find out, that purchasing your first home is a major decision and a difficult task. The questions that arise about a home purchase are numerous and the answers always seem to be few and hard to come by. Starting a business that writes and publishes an annual guide for first-time home buyers and features information such as mortgage details, home repair tips, and legal matters is a terrific homebased business venture to initiate. The guide should be widely distributed free of charge throughout the community it serves and can be supported by advertising sales made to community merchants and service providers that wish to be featured in the guide. Potential advertisers can include real estate agents and brokers, home improvement companies, landscape contractors, moving and storage firms, and just about any other business that is related to housing or real estate in general. Typically, these types of guides will cost in the neighborhood of $10,000 to $15,000 to publish, print, and distribute on an annual basis, but can easily generate advertising revenues of five or six times that amount. You can also post versions of the guide on the internet and sell downloadable copies.

MORTGAGE BROKER
★★ $$ 🏠 🕐 ⚖️

There are two main requirements to becoming a mortgage broker. The first is to check in your community to see what certification requirements are necessary to legally arrange mortgages for potential clients. The other is to take courses on mortgages, study up on the many types of mortgages offered and learn which are the right ones for specific clients. It is important to understand the particulars like balloon mortgages, ARMS, fixed rate mortgages, the current interest rates, points, credit reports, and weighing the risk of each borrower to the lending institutions. You will need good number skills and salesmanship to excel at this profession, and you will need to be comfortable working with real estate agents, brokers, buyers, attorneys, and of course, the many lending institutions you represent. Providing you can acquire the necessary certification, and learn this complex business, then this can be a very profitable business to launch. You can charge clients a flat fee or percentage of the total mortgage that you arrange for their home purchase.

WEB RESOURCE: www.namb.org
National Association of Mortgage Brokers.

REAL ESTATE ADVERTISING KIOSK
★ $$ 🚗 🕒 🌐

Designing and constructing an unmanned real estate advertising kiosk is a fantastic way to get started in your own business. The kiosk can be located in high-traffic community gathering places such as malls and recreation centers. These same kiosks can feature advertisements for houses that are for sale locally. The advertisements would include a picture and brief description of the property for sale. Charging real estate agents a fee to utilize the kiosk for advertising the properties they have listed for sale could generate revenue. The kiosk would have to be constructed of low maintenance materials and feature lighting and safety glass fronts to deter vandals or tampering with the advertisements. Ideally, the kiosk would be four-sided and have the ability to hold 48 letter-sized ads. The advertising space can be sold for $50 per month, and the kiosk could generate an income of $2,400 per month prior to expenses.

RELOCATION SERVICE
★ $$ 🚗 🕒 🌐

Put your organizational skills to work for you by starting a homebased relocation service. Millions of people in North America move annually, both locally or across the country. For anyone that has undertaken a relocation or two in the past, I'm sure that you can easily identify with the need and demand for a professional relocation service. The main objective is clear. Providing relocation services for a client means you are responsible for coordinating the move, ensuring telephone and utilities connections have been completed, and in some cases providing school and other community services information. Also, most importantly, you remove the anxiety from what can be a very stressful situation. A relocation service can be promoted by a few methods, including direct solicitation of large corporations that routinely shuffle management and employees around, building alliances with moving companies, and by joining your local chapter of the chamber of commerce, as many people will phone the chamber to find out more information about the community they are relocating to. Currently, rates for providing relocation services start at $500 each and can go much higher depending on the size

and complexity of the move as well as unusual or special requests. For the entrepreneurs seeking big market opportunities, specializing in international relocations can be extremely lucrative. Ideally, operating an international relocation service will mean establishing a working relationship with a lawyer that specializes in immigration. You will also want to specialize in a specific country of origin.

REAL ESTATE APPRAISAL SERVICE
★★ $$$ 🚗 ⚖️

Anyone considering a self-employment career as a professional real estate appraiser should begin by receiving the necessary training and securing the appropriate credentials. Additional considerations will also include the type of appraisal service or area of expertise you will provide, such as residential homes, commercial buildings, farms, or income-producing properties. The licensing requirements are different for each field and in each state. Real estate appraisal rates vary widely based on the type of property, the purpose of the appraisal, and the research required. Typically, appraisals start at $150 to $200 and go up from there. Appraisers in the residential field typically earn $40,000 to $50,000 annually, while commercial appraisers can earn as much as $80,000 to $100,000. However, the learning curve is much steeper for appraising commercial properties.

WEB RESOURCE: www.iami.org/narea.cfm
National Association of Real Estate Appraisers.

TRAIN-CAR COTTAGES
★ $$$$ ⚖️

Old railroad freight cars and cabooses make fantastic cottages, guest homes, and studios. Starting a business that converts railroad cars and cabooses into useable living or work space is certainly not a venture that can be tackled by everyone. It requires substantial investment capital, careful planning, and most importantly, clever marketing. However, providing that this business enterprise is properly researched and capitalized, the profit potential could prove to be outstanding. Get started by checking building and zoning codes in the area that you would like to market this type of unique living or work space buildings. Assuming the first step is viable and the train cars can be converted into habitable dwellings that comply with local building codes and regulations, then you will want to start to contact railroad companies and private collectors to secure the rail-cars for their transformation. Initially, to keep start-up costs to a minimum you can provide the rail-car cottages or studios to people who already have land and that are seeking to build a cottage, add a guest home, or create a studio to operate a business or office from. Renovations and refurbishing the railcars can be contracted to local qualified contractors, and in most cases you will be able to pre-sell the railcar and let your customer decide about the features and amenities they would like built in. One thing is for sure, once you have a few train-car cottages on location, interest and demand will soon follow.

WEB RESOURCE: www.caboosenut.com
Information and links about railroad cabooses and transformations into living space.

REAL ESTATE CONSULTANT FOR SENIORS
★ $$ 🚗 🕒

Downsize? Move to a retirement community? Find a home in an easy-to-navigate area? Seniors have specific needs that are not always addressed by busy realtors, brokers, and family members. Therefore, you can tap into a niche market by serving as a consultant to seniors, and/or empty nesters who are trying to decide what to do and where to go. There's little competition in the field and your job is to assess the needs and the current living situation and help individuals make (or not make) such changes. Often, financial planners find themselves in the position of helping make such decisions. However, these decisions are typically based solely on how much money can be saved and not always on the best interests of the parties involved. In this capacity, you can help a couple, or single, decide on what the best living situation might be. You can find a real estate agent or even locate a house or apartment yourself. Should the couple decide that they want to move to a golfing community in Florida, you can help them scout locations, or – if they spend a month there to determine whether or not they like it – you can find them a house sitter. Knowing the most likely options, having a good head for numbers, understanding what the clients needs are, and solving problems is the crux of the

job. You can bill on a sliding scale, starting with a $50 to $100 consulting fee and then adding on based on what you can do.

OPEN HOUSE SECURITY
★ $ 🕒

In a recent episode of a television sitcom, a real estate agent stood and argued with her son-in-law during an open house that they were holding, while in the background the entire house was cleaned out by burglars. Although this is an exaggeration, it is true that a real estate agent trying to sell a house can often be taking a risk when opening the door to someone's home to a parade of strangers. Therefore, you can start a unique part-time business that provides security for real estate agents, who are primarily women. There is a growing problem of theft to the homeowners and personal harm to real estate agents, who have been robbed and molested while showing homes or during open houses. If you have a background in law enforcement or security you can handle this as a one-person business, but if not, or if you are looking to build this business up, you can enlist the help of former security guards and retired officers to help real estate brokers. Carrying a line of secure safety products, such as lock boxes, will also benefit this unique homebased business. You need to align yourself with realtors, brokers, and the agents individually and work on a small monthly retainer. If you personally secure six open houses a month at $125 each, escort six realtors who are uncomfortable showing a home alone in the evening at $25 each, and sell $300 worth of alarms and lock boxes, you can earn $1,200 a month for less than 50 hours of work and little in overhead except the cost of the products, which you can buy wholesale.

RESIDENTIAL REAL ESTATE BROKERAGE
★★★★ $$$$ 🚗

To start, you will need to get your real estate license, learn the business, and then, in time, you can go for your brokerage license, which in most states is a separate license. Brokers oversee several agents who typically work as independent entities from within the broker's offices, and adhere to the broker's parameters. As a broker you can advertise for or in conjunction with the agents, and supplies can be provided or not depending on how you see fit. Keep in mind that by offering your agents training, supplies, some advertising, and even a web page, you are more likely to get the best agents and increase your potential profits.

START-UP EXPENSES:

Legal/Incorporating	$930
Better Business Bureau Fee	$399
Stationery, etc.	$2,000
Brochures	$1,000
Mailings/Postal	$1,000
Advertising	$2,500
Company Yard Signs	$1,300
Insurance	$225
Answering Service	$200
Web Site Design	$840
Utilities Start Up	$250
Rent	$3,000
Expensed equipment/Computer/Copier	$3,000
Office Furnishings/Lease or Used	$5,000
Office Supplies	$1,000
Other/Miscellaneous	$2,000
Business Software	$1,600
Total Start-up Expenses	**$26,244**

Hint: Just as the case with selling real estate, you need to find a good location, where homes are readily on the market and perhaps new homes or condo developments are in the works.

WEB RESOURCE: www.nareb.com
National Association of Real Estate Brokers.

REAL ESTATE INVESTMENT ADVISOR
★★★ $$ 🏠 🕐 ⚖️

Millions of dollars can be made by investing in real estate, whether in land, homes for re-sale, commercial ventures, or real estate investment trusts (REITS). If you have the mastery of real estate investing, you can forge a successful business advising individuals, investment groups, or even investment banks on the best ways to grow their money in real estate, while growing your own as an advisor. The bottom line is being as well-versed as possible in the field, and it helps to have a financial and/or real estate background. You can start by imparting knowledge through seminars, writing articles, and building a web site with real estate investing advice. Once you have demonstrated that you know the real estate investing field inside and out, you can schedule clients to work with you on an advisory basis.

WEB RESOURCE: www.narreia.com
National Association of Residential Real Estate Investment Advisors.

LAND BROKER AND DEVELOPER
★★★ $$$$ 🕐 ⚖️

Land brokers primarily buy and sell land for the purposes of housing, commercial use, and farming. The key, however, to succeeding as a land broker is being able to evaluate the land and produce feasibility studies that demonstrate the potential use for generating income from that land. If you can determine how the land can be best used, you can market it for the best possible uses, whether that means a strip mall or a golf course. You can broker the land as is or serve as a developer, which means overseeing building on the property and/or restructuring the land to better fit the needs of the potential buyers. As a developer you may be involved in the entire process from bidding to construction. A good land broker and/or developer can create a situation whereby the land sells for top value and proves to be profitable for the owner. As a result you can make six-figures turning land around.

REQUIREMENTS: You need to have a very good understanding of the valuation of land, excellent math and economic skills, an ability to sell, good communications skills, and enjoy working outdoors to venture into this high paying, but very specialized, area of real estate. Do plenty of research before making any foray into this business opportunity.

WEB RESOURCE: www.nahb.org
National Association of Home Builders.

31
RECREATION
Businesses You Can Start

PAINT BALL GAMES

★★ $$$ ⏱

If you have ever participated in a paint ball war game, you know how popular these events can be that place you in fun competition with family, friends, and co-workers. The business structure is quite simple. People pay you a fee for transporting them to a site, so they can form teams and use paint ball guns to shoot paint balls at each other in a strategic game of war or cat and mouse. Market the business by going directly to large groups of people who will use a day of paint ball war games as an opportunity to take part in an event that can include a large portion of their entire group. Ideal candidates are corporations, schools, clubs, and sports associations. To really kick things into high gear attempt to enlist local high-profile politicians and business people to take part in a charity game. Place the citizens of the community in direct competition with these high-profile community leaders. Not only will this give you a real shot in the arm in terms of exposure for your new business, it can also raise a great deal of money for a local charity.

REQUIREMENTS: The main requirement for this business venture is a large area of land to operate and host the paint ball game events. Additionally, an enclosed trailer can also be located on the event site to serve as a portable office and for equipment storage. Secondary requirements include liability insurance, first-aid equipment, and emergency action plans. The transportation of the participants can be contracted to a local transportation company to reduce start-up costs.

START-UP COSTS: Including the cost of equipment, advertising, land lease, and a portable trailer, the complete business can be started for less than $15,000. To reduce investment requirements, it may be possible to negotiate a profit-split arrangement with the owner of the land where the games will be played.

PROFIT POTENTIAL: Participants pay a flat fee for the game that usually includes transportation to the site, a basic lunch, and the game itself. The fee can vary between $30 and $50 per person. Participants also pay for the paint balls used in the game. This business, even operating on weekends only, can easily generate profits in the range of $20,000 to $30,000 per year. This venture also lends itself to selling T-shirts, hats, and jackets to the participants at the end of the game. Generally these keepsakes would have captions such as "I survived the Third World War" with your company logo and a business name printed on the item of clothing.

WEB RESOURCE: www.npbs.com
Distributors of paint ball equipment and supplies.

HOUSEBOAT RENTALS
★ $$

There are numerous options available to you in terms of starting a houseboat rental service. The first option is to purchase the houseboats ($20,000 to $30,000 each secondhand). The second and more viable option is to locate houseboat owners and see if they are prepared to enter their boats into a rental pool that is managed and operated by your service. Houseboat rental rates are in the range of $750 to $1,000 per week and the person who is renting the boat must pay for additional operating costs such as gas and insurance. In exchange for the boat owner allowing their houseboat to be used in the rental pool, they would receive 50 percent of the rental revenue and pay no moorage or maintenance fees for their boats. You would keep 50 percent of the rental fee and maintain the houseboat for the owner. Including operating overheads, boat maintenance, and moorage, a pretax net of 20 percent of the total rental fees per year should be the profit. If you have at least ten houseboats in the rental pool that were rented for an average of 25 weeks each per year, this example would leave you a profit of $50,000. The business can be started for less than $10,000 providing you are not intending to purchase the houseboats. With a good web site, and promotion to get people to the site, you can branch out by making this a web-based business whereby you bring people together (boat owners and renters) via the internet. In exchange for a small listing fee, houseboat owners seeking to rent their boats could post an advertisement with a description of their boat, photos, rental rates, and contact information on the site. Visitors to the site seeking to rent a houseboat would simply select a location from an index and start viewing houseboat rental information in that geographic area. Prior to starting such a business, you should to work with an attorney to make sure you have all necessary paperwork that holds you responsible only for bringing the parties together and not for any damages to the houseboat. As is always the case when serving as a middle person, part of your job is to make the best match between the most trustworthy, reputable parties. Therefore you will need to establish some parameters so that you can screen boat owners and renters to some degree. Your reputation will hinge on this factor—and hence your success.

BUNGEE JUMPING
★ $$$$ 🕐 ⚖

Bungee jumping peaked a few years back, yet it is still popular with people who seek adventure. The biggest downside to starting this business is the very high investment to get the business going, and the very high cost of liability insurance to keep it operating. You will easily require an initial investment of $50,000 to start this business. However, at $75 to $150 per jump, you can very quickly recoup your investment plus sizeable profits, provided you have secured a safe location for jumps, have taken all possible safety precautions, and studied up on specifics of this fad. Hint: The bridge must be higher than the length of the cord.

MARKETING TIP: For some very strange reason, nude bungee jumping is the latest craze. I would certainly think that you could charge a $25 premium per jump for anyone who wished to take the leap of faith, the natural way. Of course, you should make sure you are not about to get someone arrested for indecent exposure and that all participants are over the age of eighteen.

MOBILE ROCK CLIMBING
★★ $$$$ ⚖

We all know how popular rock climbing has become in the past decade, and here is a business that you can start based on a successful and proven theme. A mobile rock climbing wall that is mounted on a trailer and designed for fast assembly and dismantling can be used for the following purposes:

- *Instruction.* This aspect of the business is very straightforward. Market the rock climbing instruction classes to corporations, organizations, clubs, and schools who pay a flat hourly, half-day, or full-day fee, as opposed to a per person instruction fee.
- *Fun.* You can rent the use of the wall to organizers of parties, carnivals, fairs, and other fun activities. They pay you a fee for renting the wall for the day and you make money by charging per climb.
- *Business promotion.* This aspect of the business is unique. Companies within the local community hire the mobile rock climbing wall and your instruction capabilities to promote their own business for sales

events, grand openings, and special occasions. Imagine the advertisement, "Climb to the top of the wall, ring the bell, and receive 25 percent off the retail price." The possibilities are endless for this type of unique promotion service.

REQUIREMENTS: You or an employee will have to be a certified rock-climbing instructor. Furthermore, you will also need the expertise to build your mobile rock-climbing wall. Liability insurance and safety equipment are an absolute must in order to run a mobile rock climbing business.

START-UP COSTS: A mobile rock-climbing business can easily be started for less than $30,000, including the cost of designing and building the rock climbing wall, safety equipment, and the trailer.

PROFIT POTENTIAL: Once the business setup is completed, the monthly overheads are minimal and the business only requires one part-time employee. The following is a good example of the rates that can be charged for this service. All rental rates include instructor and assistant, the setup and dismantle time, as well as the use of the required climbing and safety equipment.

- Hourly instruction and rental rate: $150
- Half-day instruction and rental rate: $350
- Full-day instruction and rental rate: $500

Providing the average sale is based on a half-day rate and you are booked 15 half days per month, the business would generate revenues in excess of $60,000 per year.

WEB RESOURCE: www.amga.com
American Mountain Guides Association.

DOG SLED TRAINING AND TOURS
★ $$$+ 🛷 🕐

Provided you are living in one of the colder regions of the country, you can start your own dog sledding school for less than a $20,000 investment. You can operate the business on a year-round basis using sleds with runners in the winter and sleds with wheels in the summer, although there will be far less takers in the warm weather and it's tougher on the dogs. Promote the business by advertising in travel and recreation magazines and on a web site, as well as by establishing alliances with travel

agents and other tour operators and training schools. Additionally, be sure to initiate a direct mail advertising campaign aimed at sports associations and clubs, as you may be able to attract multiple students or guests by providing group discounts. However, keep in mind that starting this type of business will take a great amount of research, planning, and training as you will have to know a lot about dog sledding and how to properly care for northern breed dogs.

WEB RESOURCE: www.sleddog.org
The Alaska Dog Mushers Association.

CROSS-COUNTRY SKIING
★★ $$$+ 🕐

Cross-country skiing is a fantastic way to stay fit while enjoying the great outdoors in the wintertime. A low-cost method to start your own cross-country ski facility is to rent agricultural land in the winter and setup a portable trailer from which to operate your business. A cross-country ski facility can be marketed to just about anyone who is seeking a wintertime activity including sports associations, clubs, corporations, schools, and individuals. To really give this business a shot in the arm, give away two-for-one single-day ski pass coupons or free rental equipment with the purchase of a day ski pass. The intention of this type of promotion is to quickly get as many people as possible acquainted with your business. You will be surprised how many people return as full-paying customers once they realize how much fun and enjoyment they can get out of this sport.

REQUIREMENTS: The first requirement for this business is snow, and lots of it. Locate in the northern climates of the United States or in parts of Canada known for large annual snowfall. The longer the winter season, the more revenue your business will generate. Additional requirements will be obtaining liability insurance, securing rental land for operations, and checking to make sure that the zoning of the land allows for this type of commercial business venture. Furthermore, you will also need someone on staff with first-aid training, and transportation such as a snowmobile for emergency situations and for use in grooming, maintaining, and marking ski trails. The onsite trailer can serve as the office, concession, pro-shop, equipment storage, and classroom training facility. Providing the business is successful and capital is available, the business can be relocated to owned land with service buildings constructed. If the land is owned, the business could operate on a year-round basis offering mountain biking trails, equipment rental, and camping in the summer.

START-UP COSTS: The total cost to establish this type of business and kick it into high gear will be between $20,000 and $30,000. This includes a portable site trailer, equipment, and initial advertising budget. The start-up cost does not reflect the purchase or lease of land.

PROFIT POTENTIAL: The potential to profit in this business is outstanding if you choose the right location and market yourself well. You can operate on very tight overheads and once the rental equipment has paid for itself, it will act as residual income for a great number of years. Revenue can be generated by the sales of day and season passes, equipment rentals, and cross-country ski lessons.

WEB RESOURCE: www.crosscountryskiing.com

BOAT CHARTERS
★ $$$$ ⏱ ⚖

Owning and operating a boat charter business can make you the envy of any burned-out corporate employee. The requirements for a boat charter business are very straightforward. You must own a suitable boat and have a certificate that allows you to operate the charter boat. There are various types of boat charter businesses that can be started, providing you meet the requirements, and they include dive charters, sightseeing, business functions, weddings, whale watching, and fishing charters. Typically, a boat charter will include catering, an itinerary, and often some form of entertainment or social activity. Generally, boat charter rates are calculated and charged on a per-person basis, and the rate will vary depending on the type of boat charter business you are operating and the services or activities that are included, as well as the market in which you are operating the business. The start-up costs for a boat charter business are high—in the $50,000+ range. However, the business can be profitable and afford you a rewarding lifestyle that money sometimes cannot buy.

EXTREME ADVENTURE TRIPS
★★ $$ 📷 ⏱

Does taking a hot air balloon trip over Australia interest you? How about a kayak trip down the Amazon River? You can start a business in which you act as an agent or broker on a local basis for adventure travel companies located around the world. Starting this type of unique business requires very little in the way of investment capital to initiate, and the service can be marketed directly to consumers via your own Adventure Travel Broker web site and/or through traditional mediums of print advertising. Once you have secured a paying customer and all the travel accommodations and activity plans have been confirmed, you would charge the adventure tour company a 20 percent commission of the total trip value. Providing you can maintain yearly sales of $500,000 (which shouldn't be difficult given the fact that many of these adventure tour trips are selling for as much as $10,000 per person), the business would generate gross sales of $200,000, which is outstanding for a homebased owner-operator business. The trick to this business venture is doing a lot of research to find adventure travel companies and establish relationships with the operators of these adventures. You will need to learn all about the most popular excursions and become an expert through your research.

ROWBOAT RENTALS
★ $$ ⏱

Here is a great little business that can be started for peanuts and operated on weekends and holidays on a part-time basis. Secondhand good quality rowboats can be purchased for as little as $500 each, yet the same rowboats can be rented for as much as $10 per hour to fishermen, sightseers, or anyone who enjoys a relaxing afternoon on the water. Obviously the business has one main requirement in order to be operated: water. If the business is established within close proximity to a river or lake, the boats can be rented from a marina location, beach, or even right from a riverbank. A rowboat rental business also requires that you carry liability insurance and the boats are outfitted with safety equipment such as life vests, paddles, and a whistle. You can do very well in a popular tourist location, or market yourself to day camps, associations, and for other types of group outings (provided you have enough rowboats to rent).

CAMPGROUND
★★ $$$$

Campgrounds remain the single largest family vacation destination in the travel industry. North Americans spend billions of dollars at campgrounds and on camping-related products each year. There are various types of campground operations that can be started, including a seasonal campground, a year-round operated campground, tent-only camping, trailer and motor home-only, and campgrounds that cater to one specific industry such as fishing. All of these campgrounds have one thing in common: the greater number of services and products that are offered to the campers, the higher business revenues will be. This means you will want to have a pool or swimming facilities, an on-site store, firewood, washroom facilities, activity centers, laundry, holding tank dean-out facilities, and more. The better and more expansive your service, the better the chance for return visitors and referrals. Furthermore, seek to join campground business owners' associations such as "Good Sam," as being listed in these types of travel associations is a guaranteed way to have campers stay at your campground. The key, however, is to find camping grounds and this is not easy. In many cases, you will need to take over an existing campground from someone looking to give up the business, since finding a location that has yet to be discovered (and is camping friendly) has become extremely difficult. Of course to run a campground, you need to be very knowledgeable about camping, and having a passion for it doesn't hurt either.

WEB RESOURCE: www.allcampgrounds.com
American Campground Owners Associations.

SNORKEL TOURS
★★★ $$ ⏱

Tourists, sun, and water are the crucial elements that will make this business start-up a triumphant success. Starting a snorkel tour business is a fantastic way to earn a potentially lucrative income, and enjoy a personally rewarding lifestyle. How do you get customers for this business venture? Easy. Design a very informative and colorful brochure depicting your fun and relaxing snorkel

tours, and distribute them to all the hotels, motels, campgrounds, and restaurants in the local area where the business operates. Likewise, you will want to establish pickup times with all of these locations, in terms of starting the tour. You will have to pay the hotels a booking fee, but the business can easily generate enough revenue and then some to cover the costs of booking commissions. Also consider enlisting the services of a tour-booking agent, as these booking agents work beaches and other busy tourist areas promoting and enlisting clients into the different tour activities they represent. Good booking agents can easily sign up 100 or more tourists in one day for various activities.

REQUIREMENTS: The requirements for this business enterprise are very specific. You will need general knowledge and experience in snorkeling as well as first aid training and equipment. You will also be required to carry liability insurance and possibly a certificate or registration number identifying you as a tour operator. Any business plan should always include research in terms of legal restrictions and registrations. Not required is a waterfront business location, as the idea of the tours is to pick people up at predetermined locations and shuttle them to one or more locations for the snorkeling. However, to generate business, you will have to find snorkeling locations that are not already the site of numerous other tours. Premiere snorkeling areas in North America include Hawaii, the Florida Keys, Texas, and California. Cold-water snorkeling is also becoming popular in areas such as British Columbia, Washington state, and the Great Lakes. However, keep in mind that you will have to invest in two- or three-millimeter wet suits for customers to wear if you are planning to establish cold-water snorkeling trips. In addition to reef snorkeling, shallow water, surface shipwrecks, and designated marine parks are also popular spots for snorkeling.

START-UP COSTS: Contracting out the transportation aspect of this business to local transportation and boat charter companies will keep the start-up costs for this business to less than $10,000, including the cost of promotional brochure design, equipment, and advertising.

PROFIT POTENTIAL: The profit potential is excellent. A basic format to follow for operating a snorkeling tour business is as follows: Charge a flat fee of at least $40 per person for a half-day snorkeling tour. Include required transportation both by land and sea, the snorkeling equipment, about 30 minutes of basic instruction, and a small bag of fish food. Your total cost to provide this all-inclusive snorkeling tour should average out to approximately $20 per person. If the usual snorkeling tour includes ten people and you have two tours per day three days a week, your yearly profit would be in excess of $60,000. You can make more money if you sell underwater disposable cameras and underwater video footage.

WEB RESOURCE: www.padi.com
Professional Association of Diving Instructors.

ADVENTURE CLUBS
★★ $$$ 🏠 🌐

Establishing an adventure club in your local area is an exciting way to capitalize on the growing popularity of adventure trips, activities, and adventure sports in general. The business concept is to start an adventure club offering members discounts on sporting events, adventure holidays, sports equipment, and sporting activities. The hook is that there is no fee for a membership, as business revenues are earned from companies who wish to advertise in your discount directory and on the club's web site. You will have little resistance from business owners you approach for advertising sales, providing you have a captive market that they want reach also. This business can be fully operational for an investment of less than $15,000 and has the potential to return excellent profits for the creative entrepreneur. Furthermore, the fastest way to get members in the club, even though the memberships are free, is to set up a display booth at an outdoor recreation trade show for a week. This is the target market you want and there should be no problems acquiring a few thousand new members from a busy recreation trade show.

TRAMPOLINE SALES AND RENTALS
★ $$ 🏠 🕐

Trampolines are fun and a good way to get exercise, plus kids love them. Selling trampolines for backyards and local park use is just half of this business opportunity, and the more competitive part, since small trampolines are widely available online and at sporting good stores. The trick is to purchase large trampolines and rent them out for use at parties, fairs, carnivals, company picnics, and other gatherings. Also look at summer camps that may rent trampolines for a couple of days a week. If you can locate a young "master trampolinist" who is good at doing tricks, he or she can be part of the rental package, showing off at such events for more money (which you'll split with the performer). This is a fantastic low-investment business that you can start and operate on a part-time, weekend basis. Market a trampoline sales and rental business through print advertising, product demonstration displays, and the internet. A web site with photos of people having trampoline fun is a good marketing tool.

WEB RESOURCE: www.trampmaster.com
Manufacturers of trampolines and accessories.

RIVER RAFTING
★★★ $$$$ ⚖

White-water river rafting is a low-cost, mini adventure trip that almost anyone can participate in. White-water rafting excursions can be advertised to the general public as well as schools, corporations, and clubs to gain customers. There is no marketing magic here. This is a good business and a fun adventure that does not require a lot of arm twisting to get people excited about paying you to go rafting. With that being said, you will still want to separate yourself from any competition and seek your niche in the marketplace.

REQUIREMENTS: You and your employees that will be operating either the paddle-style rafts or motorized-style rafts will be required to get a license, which is commonly referred to as a river guide certificate. Likewise, all employees will need certification in first aid and river rescue techniques. You will also be required to carry a substantial amount of liability insurance. All of these certification courses are widely offered by outdoor instruction and certification companies. Additional information about these companies can usually be obtained from local police and fire departments. In terms of equipment, there are generally two types of river rafts used in this business venture. The first is a motorized inflatable raft, and the second is an inflatable paddle raft.

All boats and passengers have to be equipped with safety gear such as life vests and helmets.

START-UP COSTS: The start-up costs for a white-water rafting business can vary greatly. However, a good used paddle raft and trailer will set you back approximately $7,000 to $10,000. In terms of total capital requirements you should have in the neighborhood of $30,000 available to properly set this business in motion.

PROFIT POTENTIAL: The three river rafting companies that I checked with were all charging about the same rate for a one-day trip, which was $85 including a light lunch but not transportation to the rafting center. Once again, the potential profit for this type of business will greatly depend on how large your operation is, and your total customer volume.

HORSEBACK RIDING
★ $$$ 🕐

Starting a horse riding stable, training, and boarding facility requires an enormous capital investment, and this type of business start-up is strictly for the experienced horse fanatic, not to mention that you must be a seasoned business veteran. However, if your dream is to teach horseback riding, and rent horses to riders by the hours, you could start out by simply aligning yourself with a local stable or farm and splitting the business profits. From the profits you earn, you may eventually be able to build up to owning a small stable with two or three horses. While you can make more money, you will also incur the higher expense of boarding the horses. Until you build up a busy stable, it will be hard to make a lot of money from this endeavor.

WEB RESOURCE: www.riding-instructor.com
American Riding Instructors Association.

HIKING GUIDE BOOK
★★ $$ 🏕 🕐

Writing your own hiking guidebook for your local area is a fantastic opportunity to earn extra money year after year. Hiking as a pastime, hobby, and sport is extremely popular and millions of people receive a vast amount of enjoyment from participating in this fun outdoor activity. Your "Guide to Hiking" book can include

explanations of all the local trails and hiking areas, as well as information on how to get to the trails, what to look for, and what to watch out for. Once the book has been printed, it can be sold through local retailers via a point-of-purchase display and/or on your web site with a trail directory. You can generate income for a printed guide as well as the online directory by selling advertising to local hiking, camping, and outdoor equipment suppliers. Including a few coupon pages in the book, or download-able discounts online, can generate additional income, and the coupon pages can be sold to local merchants wishing to advertise their hiking or outdoor-related businesses. The book can be published on a yearly basis with an updated and revised edition on hiking. The online version can be continually updated.

PONTOON BOAT RENTALS
★ $$$ 🕐

Once again, this is a great little business venture to initiate. You can purchase used pontoon boats for next to nothing, and rent them out for weddings, corporate functions, or just to people who want to float around and relax on a warm summer day. Pontoon boats do not require much in the way of maintenance and are very economical to operate. You can charge rental rates of $100 per day or more for pontoon boats and moor them at local marinas. Don't forget to get the necessary licenses and liability insurance. Business tip: You can purchase the pontoon boats and let the marina maintain, store, and rent the boats for you. This partnership can work well as it can give you an ongoing income and the marina can generate additional rental revenue without having to spend precious capital purchasing the pontoon boats.

WEB RESOURCE: www.southlandboat.com
Pontoon boat manufacturers.

WATER SKI TOURS
★ $$$ 🕐 ⚖

Sun, surf, and sand. Who doesn't like this combination? For those of you seeking to start a business that will enable you to enjoy the great outdoors, perhaps you should consider starting a business providing water ski tours or rides to vacationers. Purchase a boat and water ski equipment, and charge beach goers and vacationers a fee for 15 or 20 minutes of water skiing up and down the beach. The main requirements for starting the business will be a beach or marina operating location, business license, a boat, and liability insurance. Providing you can satisfy all the requirements, get ready for a lot of fun in the sun that may even earn you a good seasonal income.

BASEBALL BATTING CAGE
★★ $$$$ 🌎

Baseball batting cages have always been, and will always be, a popular recreation attraction. Starting a baseball batting cage business could prove to be financially lucrative and fun. Since it is often hard to secure a batting facility that will generate enough business on its own to pay for the necessary land, you typically find batting cages at amusement parks, indoor family fun centers, and golf driving ranges (also listed here). Therefore, you could start a joint venture with such a business, providing them with someone who will run the batting portion of the business and pay for a part of the land lease or purchase. Beyond securing the space, you need only to purchase (and maintain) pitching machines, batting cages, lighting for night use, aluminum bats (wooden bats splinter or break too often), and batting helmets. You will also need liability insurance. If you can market your batting cages to little leagues, softball leagues, high school and college teams, camps, schools, and associations, you can draw a larger crowd. Earn additional money by selling batting gloves and having photos taken of batters taking swings, which can be sold for fun or for instructional purposes.

WEB RESOURCE: www.sterlingnets.com
Manufacturers of baseball batting cages.

SKATEBOARD PARK
★ $$$$ 🌎

Skateboarding and in-line skating are among the top popular sports and recreational pastimes in North America, and are enjoyed by millions of participants every day. There has never been a better time than now to capitalize on the demand for anything skateboard or in-line skating related. Perhaps one of the best ways to focus on this demand is to start a skateboard and in-line skating park. The park can be indoor or outdoor, depending on geographical location, and can feature areas with obstacles for beginner to advanced skill levels. Additional income can be earned by providing equipment rentals as well as instruction courses for skateboarding and in-line skating. Without question this is an expensive and difficult business to establish in terms of planning, research, and financing. Beyond the basic set-up materials and liability insurance, you can keep the costs down by locating the business in an existing amusement park or local outdoor park, where you can lease the land from the local department of parks and recreation. Since skateboarding and inline skating are very popular, you can make significant money in this type of endeavor and if you hold contests and teach classes you can add to the potential profits. Just remember to make safety a priority.

WEB RESOURCE: www.skateparkequipment.com

BILLIARDS HALL
★★ $$$$

Cash flow best describes this business venture. Starting a billiards parlor that provides customers with pool table rentals, a concession stand, and pool lessons is a great business to operate. Not only can a pool hall generate substantial profits, but the payment terms are great— CASH. The key to owning and operating a successful billiards parlor is location; the business must be located in an area that is likely to attract pool players. Good locations to establish the business include industrial parks, strip malls, and upscale locations in office districts. Additional income can be gained by selling monthly memberships and by starting leagues. Currently pool table rental rates are $8 to $12 per hour for snooker, and $6 to $10 per hour for eight ball tables. A mere ten pool tables can produce as much as $200,000 per year in business revenues.

WEB RESOURCE: www.arcade-equipment.com
Directory service listing billiards and arcade equipment manufacturers.

FISHING AND HUNTING GUIDE
★★ $$ 🏕 🕐

Starting a fishing and hunting guide service is a very low-investment enterprise to set in motion that has real potential to earn a comfortable living. There are a few ways to market a fishing and hunting guide service. Build alliances with motels and hotels in the area where the guide service is located so these types of businesses can refer their clients to your service. Promote the fishing and hunting guide service by placing advertisements in fishing and hunting publications. You can also advertise on the internet, or start a direct-mail campaign aimed at hunting and fishing associations and clubs. Currently rates for this type of service vary depending on factors such as equipment rentals and transportation requirements. However, base rates without equipment and transportation start at $125 per half-day and as high as $400 per day.

PARASAILING
★★ $$$$ ⚖️

Parasailing is a blast and the only thing I can think of that would be more fun than parasailing is owning a parasailing business. Be forewarned—this is not a cheap business venture to set in motion, as professional parasailing equipment is very expensive and used parasailing boats can cost as much as $50,000 alone, plus there is the cost of insurance. However, with that being said, the investment to start the business will seem small compared to the profits that can be earned by a parasailing business, once you have secured the right high-traffic beach to work from. Parasailing rates vary from location to location and also on the amount of time the person is in the air, but typically they are in the range of $30 for ten minutes. In one day, a parasailing business can generate sales of $1,000 or more (with tandem riders), which is excellent for a business that only requires two people to operate it.

WEB RESOURCE: www.parasail.org
Parasail Safety Council.

BOOKING AGENCY
★★ $$

Starting a booking agency for recreation businesses in your area and even those in other parts of the world is an excellent business enterprise to initiate, and best of all it can be tackled by just about anyone regardless of business experience. A booking agency works like this: You promote and sell recreational and travel services for existing companies in the industry and charge a commission on the total sales. The tours and packages you promote and

sell can include services such as hotel rooms, dive tours, snorkeling tours, beach parties, car and Jet Ski rentals, etc. To increase business, you could use a web site to promote these types of activities to would-be vacationers and travelers. Currently recreation and travel booking agencies are charging a 20 to 25 percent commission on all packages and tour services they sell.

SCUBA DIVING CHARTER BOAT
★★ $$$$ 🕐 ⚖️

A financially and personally rewarding lifestyle awaits anyone who starts a scuba diving charter boat business. The two main requirements to get this business rolling are an experienced dive master or instructor on board and a boat. Perhaps you possess one of these requirements, but not the other. This can be the groundwork for a potential business partnership or joint business venture with a company or individual that has what you lack. The business can be marketed by utilizing all the traditional marketing and advertising methods, as well by building alliances with companies and individuals who are already in the travel and recreation industry who can refer your business to their clients for free. Or they can even act as a booking agent for you business and receive a commission for doing so. Ideally, a scuba dive charter boat will be operated in a busy tourist area, or in an area where weather permits year-round scuba diving.

WEB RESOURCE: www.padi.com
Professional Association of Dive Instructors.

LASER TAG
★ $$$$ 🌍

Indoor laser tag is quickly becoming as popular as paint ball games, and starting a laser tag recreation center may just put you on the path to financial independence. Though this is a very costly business to start and operate (well into the six-figure range), the profit potential is outstanding. Revenues are earned by drop-in customers that want to play, as well as by selling monthly memberships to the center. You can also market laser tag games to corporate clients, schools, and clubs, and create special packages that include laser tag games, food, and beverages for corporate and social functions such as birthday parties. Additionally, many operators of laser tag centers also create team leagues and monthly tournaments and give away prizes to the winners. Of course you will also want to have a concession counter on site and sell related products, such as promotional clothing and equipment to bolster sales. The initial objective when you first open is to get as many people as possible to come out and try the game, as a great number of these people will return as regular customers. To accomplish this, give away two-for-one play coupons, and create joint promotions with other businesses in the community.

WEB RESOURCE: www.lasertag.org
International Laser Tag Association. Industry information and links, as well as information about how to start a commercial laser tag recreation business.

PEDAL BOAT RENTALS
★ $$

A fleet of ten pedal boats can generate as much as $30,000 in rental revenue in a single three-month season. Considering the business can be operated by one person and is relatively inexpensive to launch, that is an excellent return on investment. To establish a pedal boat rental business you will need a waterfront location to operate from. The location can be independent or in partnership with an existing business such as a marina. The business can be supported by walk-in traffic as well as two-for-one coupons that can be issued for use on slower mid-week periods. Extra income can be acquired by adding a small catering cart that sells soft drinks and popcorn. This business venture may not make you wealthy, but it can generate a good income and definitely will be a relaxing work environment.

WEB RESOURCE: www.bwmarineproducts.com
Manufacturers of pedal boats and equipment.

BIRDING TOURS AND TRIPS
★ $$ 📷 🕐

You may know it as bird watching, but the current official term is "birding." Call it what you will, there is a large, dedicated following of this quiet pastime. Learning about birding and being able to plan tours and vacations for enthusiasts can result in a nice business venture that has low start-up costs and can put you smack in the middle of nature. Researching the most popular locations for birding and, with luck, discovering some less commonly known ones, can provide you with the starting point from which to branch out. Finding a good location from which to spot a rare species is akin to hitting a home run, since the more devoted birders are often very quick to flock to such a locale. Known as "twitchers," there are many birders who are determined to swoop in to catch as many various rare species as possible. Tours are typically limited to less than ten people and run by experienced guides. It's worthwhile to study web site of the American Birding Association in an attempt to match their guidelines and tour standards, since enthusiasts are looking for such quality birding tours and vacations. Once you know what your goals are, arranging the who, what, where and when of the tours or trips are the next steps, since we already know "why." Finally, you need to promote your tours or trips to the demographic audience through the internet and through magazines, newsletters, chat rooms, and by word of mouth in the birding community.

WEB RESOURCE: www.americanbirding.org
American Birding Association.

NUDIST RESORT
★★★ $$$$ ⚖

While it is a lifestyle that may offend some people, it is a business for those who believe in letting it all hang out. Camping, hiking, boating, volleyball, and numerous activities are all part of the resort atmosphere at clothing-optional facilities that typically sit on several acres of secluded land. Some are even family friendly. Accommodations range from cabins or even trailers to more elaborate suites. You'll need to determine what is available and start by purchasing several cottages or a small hotel and expanding. Start-up costs will be high because you will want to make sure to add amenities and/or upgrade those on the property you purchase. If you are in a warm climate, this can be a year-round business; in the colder climates, you can share the facility with a winter ski resort. Marketing will include advertising in newsletters and on web sites devoted to the lifestyle. If you choose go this route, prepare for negotiations with local town officials and scout out a location very carefully to make sure you are not in violation of anything before you and your campers dare to go bare.

WEB RESOURCE: www.aanr.com
American Association for Nudist Recreation

SKYDIVING SCHOOL
★★ $$$ 🕐 ⚖️

Skydivers are a rare breed of thrill-seeking individuals. Their passion—and possibly yours—is the basis for a new business. However, before you can teach the thrill of freefalling, you need a few key ingredients, starting with an airplane, which you can lease as necessary, and a United States Parachute Association (USPA) certified instructor. These are your main start-up costs, along with a facility in which to sign-up students and from which to run the business. There is a great deal to learn prior to venturing into this business, including the many FAA and USPA safety requirements. You will also need to make sure you have liability insurance and liability releases for students to sign prior to jumping. To increase your income, you can sell the many tools of the trade, or hobby in this case, including goggles, helmets, jumpsuits, and, of course, parachutes.

WEB RESOURCE: www.skydiving.com, www.uspa.org
United States Parachute Association.

MOUNTAIN CLIMBING GEAR
★★ $$$ 🕐

What goes up must come down, but in this case, slowly and carefully. Mountain climbing is a rigorous activity that takes plenty of skill and very reliable equipment. In the right (mountainous) locations you can open up a storefront, and with some steady marketing you will be able to launch and maintain a steady, profitable business, as long as you stock up on the latest equipment. You can also hire well-trained guides to lead expeditions. If you're not located near the mountains, you can offer the same gear via the internet. You need to make alliances with the leading manufacturers and vendors dealing in clothing, gloves, shoes, harnesses, ropes, climbing packs, and accessories. If you opt for a storefront, you might look to team with sporting good store until you launch your business.

WEB RESOURCE: www.johann-sandra.com/mountaindir.htm
A huge mountain climbing site with a mountain of information.

NOTES:

22
RECYCLING AND GREEN
Businesses You Can Start

COMMUNITY RECYCLING GUIDES
★ $ 🏠 🕐 🌿

Do you know where to go to recycle items in your community? Publishing a series of community recycling guides can provide residents with the information they need to know, including what can be recycled, where to take recyclables, where pickups are made and when, etc. You can print these guides yourself or have them printed (on recyclable paper of course) by a local printer. Since this is an environmentally friendly endeavor, you should not have too much trouble getting advertising from local merchants in each community. The guides can be distributed at high-traffic locations in the neighborhoods. While this is not likely a business endeavor that will make you rich, it can provide some steady part-time income. Remember to keep up with changes that will come up regarding the information and print new guides every several months.

BUNDLED KINDLING SALES
★★★ $ 🏠 🕐 🌿

Packaging and selling kindling for fireplace and camp-fire use is a very inexpensive business to get rolling and requires no special skills or experience. This is a great business opportunity for any person with limited business expertise and investment capital to pursue. To locate wood that can be recycled into kindling, look no further than building demolition sites, manufacturers of wood products

(waste wood), and construction and property development sites. To market the kindling, simply shrink-wrap the kindling into five- and ten-pound bundles. Once packaged, the kindling can be sold to gas stations, food stores, campgrounds, and building centers on a wholesale basis.

RECYCLING CONSULTANT
★★ $$$ 🕐 🌿

Taking the time to educate yourself in the subject of recycling industrial and household materials can really pay off, especially if you apply that knowledge and become a recycling consultant. Millions of homeowners and companies now recycle everyday waste material. However, millions more could be, and people that are now recycling could also be recycling various other waste materials except they do not know how or what. This is the point where your recycling knowledge can start to work for you by teaching homeowners, business owners, and employees how to recycle, what to recycle, and where it can be recycled. This is an environmentally beneficial or "green" business that is very straightforward to start; you charge corporations and homeowners a fee to design a specially created recycling plan for their business or home. In addition to creating the recycling program, you can also give a brief instructional course on the recycling program that you have created for them, as well as on the topic of recycling in general. The timing to become a recycling consultant has never been better than now, as the need for every person on the planet to practice recycling measures has never been more apparent. Potential income ranges from $50 to $100 per hour.

TELEPHONE AND HYDRO POLES
★★ $$ 🏠 🕐 🖋

Due to safety and structural integrity concerns, most wooden telephone and hydro poles are replaced after 30 years of service. In many cases these old wooden poles can be acquired for free from telephone and utility companies, or purchased at extremely low prices. On the surface this may not seem like an exceptional business opportunity, unless you take the time to consider that once the telephone poles have been milled into lumber there is enough wood from one single telephone pole to build more than 100 wooden shipping pallets. Currently new shipping pallets are selling for $12 to $15 each, which means each telephone pole that was acquired for free or purchased for a few dollars contains enough lumber to potentially produce $1,500 worth of saleable merchandise. In addition to shipping pallets, the lumber can also be used to build patio furniture or used for deck planks and fence boards. The key to this business is securing a truck to transport the poles before and after their recycling transformation.

USED MATTRESS SALES
★ $$ 🏠 🕐 🖋

Are you searching for a recycling business that can be started for peanuts and has the potential to generate a good part-time income? If so, consider starting a business that purchases good-quality used mattresses and resells them for a profit. There are a couple great sources for purchasing used mattresses at very low prices. The first is hotels and motels, as most replace their mattresses every five to eight years. The second source is retailers of new mattresses as many of these businesses provide their clients with free disposal of the old mattresses. Once the mattresses have been steam cleaned, they can be advertised for sale to the general public. Many first-time homeowners on a limited furnishing budget and students are the prime customers for purchasing a high-quality used mattress. Providing the business can achieve monthly sales of $3,000 and maintain a 100 percent markup on all

used mattresses bought and resold, then this very inexpensive business start-up can generate a gross profit each year in excess of $18,000.

ENERGY MANAGEMENT CONSULTANT
★★★ $$ 🏠 🕐 🖋

Corporations and homeowners combined spend billions of dollars annually on energy to light, heat, and air-condition their homes and buildings. Imagine how much healthier the environment would be, as well how much money each of us could save every year, if we could all reduce our energy consumption by a mere 10 percent? Here is the focus of an incredible business opportunity. Working as an energy management consultant from a homebased office, you can teach homeowners and business owners practical and useful energy management tips about reducing consumption and waste. Successfully activating this business will require a great deal of research, planning, and training. However, with energy costs continuing to soar, the need to take care of the environment and save money is becoming a major concern. This type of venture should have a very favorable future if you are able to spread the word that you are available for consultations and that you have some practical money-saving energy strategies.

RAILROAD TIES
★ $$ 🏠 🕐 🖋

Railroad ties are in great demand for use in landscaping to create retaining walls and planters and are currently selling for as much as $25 each. There are thousands of miles of abandoned railroad tracks that are removed every year, and securing a contract to purchase the old railroad ties can be the start of establishing a business that resells railroad ties for a profit to homeowners and landscape contractors. Additionally, railroad ties can be sold to building centers and garden centers on a wholesale basis. The business can be managed from a homebased office, and as a method to reduce the start-up investment needed to get rolling, the transportation and delivery aspect of the business can be subcontracted to an established trucking firm. Like any business, the key to success will be dependent on a number of factors such as securing a railroad tie source, as well as the volume purchase discount, market demand, and operating overhead costs. If all of these factors can be researched and proven viable, this can be a financially rewarding and unique business opportunity to pursue.

FLEA MARKET HOST OR VENDOR
★★ $$ 🕐 🖋

As a flea market host you can subdivide a large indoor or outdoor area into smaller subsections and rent these spaces to vendors on a weekly, monthly, or yearly basis. The key to success in operating a flea market is to have high-quality, well-priced goods that are in demand. This will mean securing quality vendors with materials that people will buy, and a great location. You then need to advertise that the flea market is open by utilizing all means of local publicity including Pennysavers, local newspapers, fliers, and all local web sites. You can even be creative and ask local musicians who'd like some exposure to play as a draw, or get school children to provide some artwork to put on display to draw their parents. If you are not game for running a flea market, you can always take the approach of becoming a vendor by collecting materials from individuals (paying them for their "junk") and re-selling it at booths at various flea markets. Overall, both are good business opportunities to initiate that have the potential to generate great profits.

WEB RESOURCE: www.fleamarkets.org
National Flea Market Association.

PALLETS
★ $$ 🏠 🕐 🖋

Starting a business building shipping pallets from reclaimed wood is a fantastic way to help the environment and join the ranks of the self-employed. Shipping pallets are very easy to build and only require basic tools and woodworking equipment to be used in the manufacturing process. Pallets can be built from various types of wood, such as telephone poles and wood reclaimed from house and building demolitions. Once constructed, the shipping pallets can be sold to transportation, manufacturing, and warehousing firms. Currently shipping pallets are selling in the range of $12 to $15 each. If the raw manufacturing material can be acquired for free or purchased

inexpensively, this could prove to be a very profitable homebased recycling business to start.

WEB RESOURCE: www.nwpca.org
National Wood Pallet and Container Association.

SECONDHAND BOOKSTORE
★ $$$ 🖋

Opening a retail store that sells secondhand books and publications is a great way to help the environment by recycling a very common and in-demand product, not to mention the fact that many secondhand bookstore owners earn a very good annual income. The following formula can be used as a guideline to establish the wholesale purchasing price of books, as well as the retail selling value of secondhand books. Of course there are variations to the rule such as condition, rarity, consumer demand, and age, but the following formula is widely accepted and practiced by owners of secondhand bookstores. If you are purchasing books, estimate between 10 and 25 percent of original retail value new. When selling books, the price should be about 25 to 50 percent of original retail value new. Make sure to check the condition of books as they come in, and even though you are not ordering copies of books, you should still try to maintain some inventory control so that books don't mysteriously walk away.

SPILL CONTAINMENT SERVICE
★ $$$$ ⚖ 🖋

There are two main types of spill containment services that can be started. The first is a water-based operation that specializes in containing, cleanup, and recovery of liquid or solid material spills (such as oil or chemicals) that occur in open waters, lakes, and rivers. The second type of spill containment service is land-based, with a focus on the containment, cleanup, and recovery of liquid or solid material spills that occur on roadways or land in general. You will need either very deep pockets or a very understanding banker to finance this type of business venture, in addition to government licenses, certifications, and the patience and persistence to go through a lot of red tape. However, as a spill containment, cleanup, and recovery service is highly specialized, the potential profits that can be realized are enormous.

CARDBOARD BOXES
★ $$ 🏠 🕐 ✎

Starting a cardboard collection and recycling business is a very easy and straightforward venture to set in motion. Cardboard boxes can be collected from retailers, grocery stores, and manufacturers and sold to local or state cardboard recycling facilities. Prices paid for reclaimed cardboard fluctuates, as cardboard is a commodity and the price is established on a world supply and demand basis. Still, a part-time income of $1,000 per month or more is easily attainable with collecting and selling reclaimed cardboard boxes. Further information on collecting cardboard boxes and the prices paid for the used cardboard can be found at any local recycling depot, or by contacting local government recycling agencies.

WEB RESOURCE: www.recycle.net
Directory service listing cardboard recycling facilities.

BARN BOARDS AND BRICKS
★ $$ 🏠 🕐 ✎

Thousands of brick buildings and barns are demolished in the United States annually, thus creating a terrific business opportunity by purchasing reclaimed barn boards and bricks at bargain prices and reselling these items for a profit. Reclaimed bricks can be used for landscaping purposes in constructing patios, sidewalks, and driveways, while reclaimed barn board can be used for making antique replica furniture and as a decorative wall treatment. The main requirement for starting this type of recycling business is to have a storage space large enough to hold an inventory, as well as locating a good and constant supply for the reclaimed material. Providing bricks and barn board can be purchased in large enough quantities at volume discount prices, this business can be extremely profitable. These reclaimed items can be substantially marked-up and sold to homeowners, designers, renovation companies, and landscape contractors in smaller quantities.

CEDAR RAIL FENCING
★★★ $ 🏠 🕐 ✎

Antique-style split cedar rails are a hot and valuable commodity sought by urban homeowners for use in building decorative property fences that add a certain country charm to their city oasis. If you have spent any time driving country roads, then you are well aware of the fact that not only are cedar rails plentiful, in most cases they are no longer serving a fencing purpose for the property on which they are located. The best method to acquire the cedar rails is to approach property owners and negotiate to purchase the fencing. Once a supply has been accumulated, the cedar rails can be sold on a wholesale basis to garden centers, landscape contractors, or directly to homeowners on a retail basis. This is a terrific little business venture that can easily generate profits of $25,000 per year or more for a creative entrepreneur.

OIL RECOVERY
★★ $$$$ 🏠 ⚖ ✎

Oil recovery and recycling is a multimillion-dollar industry, and starting a business that specializes in reclaiming various types of oil to be sold to oil recycling firms is a relatively easy business to set in motion and operate. The various types of oil that can be reclaimed and recycled are motor oil, transmission fluids, automobile lubricants, and restaurant cooking oil, just to mention a few. The key to success in the oil reclaiming industry is to establish ongoing exclusive contracts with companies that routinely use some type of oil in the day-to-day operation of their business. This is a business that can generate sizable annual profits, providing the business is operated on a high-volume basis, as profit margins are very tight in this industry. Be sure to check licensing and regulations in your local community in terms of compliance that may be needed to operate an oil recovery service.

SCRAP METALS
★★ $$+ ✎

There are a great number of options open to the creative entrepreneur who is considering starting a recycling business focusing on scrap metals. You can specialize and operate a scrap metal depot that sells various reclaimed metals to metal recycling companies, or specialize in one particular type of scrap metal collection and recycling. Owning a scrap metal recycling business is like having your company traded publicly the day it opens for business. Metals are commodities and the price fluctuates on a supply and demand basis, often based on forecasts for the supply and demand for certain types of metals a year or more in advance. Overall, this is a good choice for a recycling business start-up, and the investment can vary from a few thousand dollars to hundreds of thousands of dollars.

PINE CONES
★★ $ 🏠 🕐 🍃

Calling all hikers. Here is a terrific recycling business start-up that is guaranteed to keep you outdoors and fit. Collecting pine cones is not only easy, but it can also be very profitable. Pine cones can be packaged in one- to two-pound bags and sold to craft stores on a wholesale basis. Currently pine cones are wholesaling in the range of $2 to $5 per pound depending on the size, style, and rarity. Collecting other types of forest products such as willow branches (furniture making) and mushrooms (gourmet foods) can also add additional income to the venture. Overall this is a terrific business to get started on a full- or part-time basis, and keeping busy collecting pine cones can provide you with an annual income that can potentially surpass $25,000.

SAWDUST
★ $$ 🏠 🕐 🍃

Sawdust is readily available and usually free, and this is important information especially if you are considering starting a recycling business with a focus on sawdust. Sawdust has many uses: it can be compacted into pellets and used for fuel for pellet-wood stoves, it can be used for bedding purposes for livestock and pets, and it can also be compressed into molds to create interior trim moldings and home decoration items. Sources for acquiring sawdust can include sawmills, home renovation centers, and furniture manufactures. Additional revenues for this type of recycling venture can also be sought by acquiring wood chips, packaging them, and selling them to landscapers and garden centers on a wholesale basis.

WEB RESOURCE: www.sorbilite.com
Manufacturers of compression molding systems and equipment.

TIRES
★ $$$ 🍃

It is estimated that more than one billion tires end up in landfill sites and tire storage facilities each year worldwide. Recycling and ridding the planet of used tires is one of the largest environmental concerns that all countries face. Recently, innovative companies have been cropping up that have developed technologies for recycling used tires into products such as fence boards and industrial flooring. The time to develop a tire recycling process has never been better, as many levels of government have special grants and loans available for starting this type of recycling business. Starting this type of business takes time, money, and creative development. In spite of this, the individual or company that develops a useful product manufactured in whole or part from used tires stands a better than average chance of business success and financial rewards.

RECYCLED KITCHEN CABINETS
★ $ 🏠 🕐 🍃

Secondhand kitchen cabinets can be put to good use as storage cabinets in the garage, workshop, or basement. They can be outfitted in a summer cabin or cottage or even resurfaced and sold as "new recycled cabinets." Finding a good supply of secondhand cabinets to resell for a profit is very easy, as kitchen replacements continually rank as the number one home improvement carried out by homeowners. Start by contacting kitchen and bath renovation companies in your area and strike a deal to purchase cabinets they have removed. In most cases you can get these cabinets for free simply by agreeing to pick them up and remove them from the site. Next carry out any minor repairs that the cabinets may require and begin to market the recycled cabinets. Advertise the cabinets for sale by placing free ads in your local penny-saver or barter publication. This recycling business may not make you rich, but earning a few thousand dollars each year is certainly within reach for the determined entrepreneur.

PAPER RECYCLING
★★ $$ 🕐 ⚖️ 🍃

Electronic media notwithstanding, there is still a vast amount of paper flooding our homes and offices on a daily basis. In fact, Americans use over 200,000 tons of paper annually and dispose of more than half of it within a day! While this is very wasteful, it is also the basis for a potentially lucrative business, and one that can help to save the environment. Recycling old newspapers, magazines, catalogs, and even computer printouts is a great and rewarding way to earn money. While it may sound too easy, collecting piles of paper from homes and businesses and selling them to a recycling plant in your locale area can add up to a good sum of money, if you are a determined entrepreneur. In fact, paper recyclers have been known to reach the $100,000 income mark for a year of hard work. If you opt for a part-time business, you can certainly collect $500 per week or $25,000 a year by making pick-ups on weekends. In fact, this can be a family business, as your kids can collect smaller loads of paper from their friends' homes and at school. All you need is a pick-up truck or a van. There is no other special training or skill necessary. To make life easier, you can utilize a shed, your garage or a small collection space to store up papers so that you don't need to go to the recycling plant each time you collect. Spread the word through various marketing methods that you are collecting recyclables on a certain day of the week and hit each area on that day. You can also establish a drop-off location in conjunction with an association, school, house of worship, or even a local business looking for some favorable PR. If you pay two cents per pound, or $40 per ton, you can then get $50 to $60 per ton from the recycling plants or at least $10 per ton profit. Fifty tons of newspapers per week gives you $500, and that's not including magazines or high-grade computer paper, which can bring in more that the $50 per ton. If you can spread the word about the value of recycling and get as many people in your community to pitch in, you can build this business quickly through word of mouth and make a difference.

NOTES:

49
RENTAL
Businesses You Can Start

POWER TOOLS
★★★ $$$$

Simply start by purchasing good-quality commercial-grade power tools, design an information brochure listing tool descriptions, and indicate day and weekly rental rates. The rental price list can be distributed to local construction and renovation companies. Your advantage over the competition is that you can advertise that you guarantee free delivery of the rental tool (if in stock) to the job site in one hour. The entire business can be conducted right from a delivery truck with the assistance of a cellular phone for incoming rental inquiries.

START-UP COSTS: The initial investment to set a tool rental business in motion will be in the range of $20,000 to $25,000, plus the cost of a delivery truck or van.

PROFIT POTENTIAL: Providing you can maintain weekly rental sales of $2,000, there will be no difficulties in generating profits of $1,000 per week after overheads, equipment repairs, depreciation, and replacements.

WEB RESOURCE: www.whsletool.com
Wholesaler of power tools representing leading power tool manufacturers.

PERSONAL WATERCRAFTS
★★ $$$$

Renting personal watercrafts like Jet Skis® can be a fun and profitable way to earn a living. A watercraft rental business can be established in a fixed location, such as a marina, or the business can be operated on a mobile basis, setting up daily in busy tourist areas like public beaches. You will need to get permission for the mobile operation, as well as securing liability insurance regardless of whether the business is operated from a fixed location or on a mobile basis. This unique rental business could even be operated on the basis that each watercraft has its own small trailer, and people could rent the watercraft on a daily or weekly basis for extended holidays.

START-UP COSTS: There are numerous variables, in terms of the total investment required to start a personal watercraft rental business including the number of rental watercraft, fixed or mobile operating location, and transportation equipment. However, this type of rental business will require approximately $25,000 to $35,000 to establish.

PROFIT POTENTIAL: Jet Skis generally rent for the following rates: $50 to $70 per hour, $200 to $250 per day, and $600 per week. A well-equipped and established watercraft rental business can easily provide the owner-operator with profits exceeding $50,000 per year. Additionally, the ability to mechanically maintain the equipment will help keep overhead costs to a minimum.

WEB RESOURCE: www.nauticexpo.com
Manufacturers of boats and boat equipment.

MOBILE HOT TUBS
★★ $$ 🏠 🕐 🌐

Portable hot tubs, such as Soft Tubs® and Lite-Tubs® are a smaller version of traditional hot tubs. Portable hot tubs do not require any special electrical hookups, and only weigh about 60 pounds each, making them ideal for such a business. These hot tubs can easily be transported by truck or trailer and it only takes one person about an hour to completely set up a tub. Once established, a hot tub rental business can effortlessly sustain itself through word-of-mouth referrals, and repeat customers.

START-UP COSTS: New portable hot tubs retail for $2,000 to $3,000. However, you may be able to go directly to the manufacturer and receive a volume discount if you intend to purchase five or more at one time.

PROFIT POTENTIAL: While researching this business opportunity I found out that portable hot tubs rent for $150 per day and can also be rented on a weekly and monthly basis. Assuming that you had four hot tubs that were rented an average of 100 days per year each, the business would create gross sales of $60,000 per year with only a part-time effort.

WEB RESOURCE: www.softub.com
Manufacturers of portable hot tubs.

FURNITURE
★ $$$ 🏠 🕐

Renting furniture on a short- or long-term basis can be a very profitable business to start and operate. There are many reasons why people rent furniture, including short-term job relocations, financial restrictions, and as a way to keep business start-up costs to a minimum by renting reception area furniture as opposed to purchasing it. Start-up costs will vary depending on the size of business that you intend to establish. However, as a cost control measure, consider purchasing good quality secondhand furniture as opposed to new furniture, and carry out any repairs or cleaning that may be required prior to renting these items. Additionally, delivery can be contracted to a local moving company to avoid the high cost of acquiring your own delivery vehicle. Investment range is $15,000+.

PROFIT POTENTIAL: A rule of thumb in the rental industry is to try to maintain rental fees of 10 percent per week of the rental item's value, or maintain a percentage as close as possible to 0 percent. Utilizing this type of pricing formula will make your business profitable, and the rental inventory will pay for itself with a mere ten rentals. The key from a marketing standpoint (for any rental business), is to have as much of your inventory rented out at all times. Therefore, unlike a one-time sale in a retail business, you need not hold out for higher prices at the risk of closing for the day with inventory still in house. It's better to rent something for $50 a day for an entire week then have it sit there for the week while you wait for it to be rented for $80 a day. Each day the item sits in your facility, it earns no money for you, while simply depreciating.

WEB RESOURCE: www.ifra.org
The International Furniture Rental Association

KARAOKE MACHINES
★★ $$ 🏠 🕐

Everybody deserves his or her 15 minutes of fame, and becoming a singing sensation with the assistance of a karaoke machine allows anyone to achieve momentary stardom. Karaoke machines can be rented to nightclubs, the general public, aspiring singers, disc jockey services, and event and wedding planners.

START-UP COSTS: Good quality karaoke machines retail for about $2,000. Additionally, you will have to build a music library consisting of a wide selection of rock, blues, country and western, and contemporary music. In total, an investment of $3,000 will be required.

PROFIT POTENTIAL: Karaoke machines rent for $100 to $150 per day. Additional revenue can be generated if you have the ability to act as an event host or emcee. This extra source of income can be as high as $150 per event that you host. Part-time potential profit range is $10,000 to $12,000 per year and can be attained with a little bit of clever marketing and shameless promotion.

WEB RESOURCE: www.totalkaraoke.com
Suppliers of karaoke machines and music discs.

BIG-SCREEN TELEVISIONS
★ $$ 🏠 🕐

Starting a big-screen TV rental business can be a great way to get into business on a minimal capital investment.

Big-screen TVs can be rented to corporate clients for presentation purposes and seminars, TV production companies for props, trade shows for video demonstrations, and to just about any sports fan seeking to watch the playoffs in style. Furthermore, the business can be operated from a homebased location, and the monthly overhead costs to run the business are virtually nonexistent.

START-UP COSTS: The latest big-screen TVs, including flat screen high definition models, can cost anywhere between $1,500 and $20,000 depending on how large you want to go and the quality you are seeking. You will also need a van for deliveries, and good heavy-duty dolly equipment to move the TVs around once at the rental site. You can earn additional money by setting up home theaters for those who cannot afford to buy one but would like to have the full experience for a Super Bowl party, special occasion, or to impress an important business client. This could also mean renting out concession stand equipment and top-of-the line surround sound speakers.

PROFIT POTENTIAL: Once again, the amount of revenue this rental business can generate will depend on a few factors, such as how many TVs you are going to be renting and the rental rates that your local market will bear.

PORTABLE STORAGE SERVICE
★★★ $$$ 🏚 🕐 🌐

The home improvement and renovation industry is booming. Due to this fact, starting a portable storage rental business can put you on the path to financial freedom. Almost all homes that are undergoing renovations have one thing in common: Where do homeowners store furniture and personal belongings while their home is in the midst of the renovation? The solution: Portable storage. I met a very enterprising entrepreneur a few years ago, who realized that there was a need for a portable storage service in his community. Unfortunately his financial situation did not allow him to start this business by way of traditional means of purchasing pre-built portable storage units, as they cost more than $3,000 each at that time. Here is where the creativity and innovative actions of an entrepreneur can really pay off. His solution was to purchase used one-ton and five-ton truck bodies for about $500 each from a local wrecking yard. Once he had the truck bodies at his home he painted and signed them with his company logo and name, as well as welded two rollers onto the front of each box. Welding the rollers onto the front of the boxes allowed the newly-built portable storage units to be picked up and delivered by a traditional roll-off or winch truck. He contracted out the delivery and pickup of the storage units to a local trucking company. In total he had less than $800 into each portable storage container and was able to charge a premium over the competition because his storage units had almost 50 percent more storage room than traditional portable lockers. At the time of our conversation he had already constructed 12 of these low-cost storage containers and was renting them for $200 each per week. He negotiated a flat fee of $50 to the trucking company for the pickup and delivery of each storage container. Thus he had built a business that had sales in excess of $2,000 per week, from an initial investment of only $10,000. This type of portable storage service is best promoted directly through construction and renovation companies, as they already have contact with the people who will require this service. You may even want to consider a profit-sharing deal with these companies that support and help market your business.

CONSTRUCTION EQUIPMENT
★★ $$$$

Beyond power tools, there is a vast amount of construction equipment that is required to successfully complete a building or renovation project. A great deal of this equipment is rented for this purpose, as opposed to purchasing construction equipment. Such equipment rentals can include lift and crane trucks, generators, lighting equipment, ladders, safety equipment, grading equipment, and on-site security equipment. Starting a construction equipment rental business requires a very good working knowledge of the construction industry and of the exact needs and requirements of contractors, in terms of equipment. Additionally, mechanical and equipment repair abilities are an absolute must.

START-UP COSTS: To properly setup and establish a construction equipment rental business you will need a very large investment, in the neighborhood of $100,000 to $150,000. Once again, providing that you have the ability to repair the equipment, you can save a considerable amount of start-up capital by purchasing used construction equipment that is in good mechanical and operating order. However, the name of the game in construction equipment is reliability and speed, and if your equipment is not reliable contractors will rent elsewhere.

PROFIT POTENTIAL: Construction equipment rentals can be extremely lucrative, annual profits can easily exceed $100,000 per year.

MANNEQUINS
★★ $$ 🏠 🕐 🌐

I'll bet that most of you reading this did not realize that new mannequins sell for as much as $2,000 each. Due to the high cost of purchasing mannequins, many retail business owners have to do without the added visual benefits of displaying merchandise on them. Starting your own mannequin rental business means that you can not only come to the rescue of small retailers by renting mannequins, but you can also help even the playing field between small retailers and their larger competitors. The best way to market the service is by simply designing and distributing information brochures to local retail businesses describing your mannequin rental service.

PROFIT POTENTIAL: Once your initial inventory of mannequins is paid for, the revenue that this business can generate is almost 100 percent profit, as the overheads are minimal and mannequins generally do not require much in the way of maintenance or repairs. Suggested rental rates are as follows: per day $20 to $30, per week $80 to $100.

WEB RESOURCE: www.mannequinexperts.com

POOL TABLES
★ $$ 🏠 🕐

Starting your own pool table rental business could literally be your break into the exciting world of business ownership. Pool is a relaxing pastime that unfortunately cannot be enjoyed by all, simply because many people find the cost of pool tables and accessories beyond their financial means. You can rent pool tables for parties, both at residences and for corporate gatherings, so start by aligning yourself with party and corporate convention planners. Marketing such a business might include holding a contest with the winner receiving free use of a pool table for six months including delivery, setup, and acces-

sories. Other means of marketing include brochures, fliers and a well-designed web site.

START-UP COSTS: A complete pool table package retails for between $1,500 and $3,000. Good-quality secondhand pool tables and equipment can be purchased for about half the cost of the new pool tables and equipment.

WEB RESOURCE: www.brunswick-billiards.com
Billiard tables and supplies.

TENT TRAILERS
★ $$+ 🏠 🕐

Between roughing it in a tent and resting comfortably in a luxurious RV, tent trailers are the sensible middle ground for camping enthusiasts. Starting a part-time homebased business renting tent trailers is a wonderful way to cut your entrepreneurial teeth. The business can be marketed by word-of-mouth and referral or by traditional advertising print media methods. Furthermore you can promote your business by attending homebased business owners' association meetings. Renting a tent trailer for a camping holiday is not one of those things that pop directly to mind unless someone plants the seed.

START-UP COSTS: New tent trailers cost in the range of $7,000. However, good used tent trailers can be purchased for $2,000 to $3,000. Investment ranges $3,000 to $15,000.

PROFIT POTENTIAL: Once again, with this type of rental item always strive to rent the item for at least 10 percent of the value. Providing that you have even three tent trailers, which you rent on average of 20 weeks per year, your business could generate sales of $18,000 per year, which is very good for a low-investment business that you can operate from home with a part-time effort.

PARTY TENTS
★★ $$ 🏠 🕐

A party tent rental business can be started as a stand-alone business, or it can make a great add-on to an existing equipment rental business. Additionally, this business enterprise can easily be managed from home on a part-time basis. Potential clients will include wedding planners, caterers, event planners, and charity organizations. Likewise, the party tents can also be rented to community merchants holding outdoor clearance sales.

START-UP COSTS: New large party tents retail for $3,000 to $5,000, while secondhand party tents sell for $1,500 to $2,500. A total investment of $10,000 will secure two or three large, good quality party tents and an enclosed trailer for deliveries and pickups.

PROFIT POTENTIAL: Party tents require about one hour for two people to set up, and about the same amount of time to disassemble. Currently party tent rentals and set-up rates are in the range of $250 to $500 per day.

PARTY SUPPLIES
★★ $$$$

The profits that can be earned by operating a party supply rental company are enough to make anybody celebrate. Parties, special events, and social functions all require certain equipment and supplies in order to comfortably accommodate the people in attendance. Tables, chairs, and banners are just a few of these required party items. There are two types of party supply rental services. First, you establish a fixed location for your party rental supply business and open your doors to the general public. The second and less expensive option is to operate the business from home and deal with only industry professionals, such as caterers, wedding planners, corporate event planners, and children's birthday party services.

START-UP COSTS: The terms of capital required to start a party rental supply service are as follows: Option number one will cost approximately $30,000 to start, including the rental inventory and establishing the business from a fixed storefront location. The homebased option, catering exclusively to professionals within the event planning industry will cost substantially less to start, in the neighborhood of $10,000.

PROFIT POTENTIAL: Like many rental businesses, once the equipment is paid for, the vast majority of rental revenue will be profit. Profit potential range is $10,000+ per year part-time and $25,000+ per year full-time.

WEB RESOURCE: www.partytents.com

MUSICAL INSTRUMENTS
★★ $$+ 🏠 🕐

Millions of people across North America play a musical instrument, or are considering taking lessons to learn how to play one. You can capitalize on demand by starting a business renting musical instruments to students and to people who do not have the financial resources to purchase musical instruments, especially pianos. Additionally, musical bands and entertainers often rent musical instruments while they are traveling. On a small scale, a musical instrument rental business can be operated from a homebased office. However, if your plan is to start big, you may want to consider leasing a retail storefront for the business enterprise.

START-UP COSTS: Once again, purchasing secondhand equipment can be a method employed to keep business start-up costs to a minimum. Additionally, you may also want to specialize in only one particular type of instrument rental, such as pianos. Investments range is from $5,000 to $25,000+.

PROFIT POTENTIAL: Rental rates for musical instruments greatly vary depending on the type of instrument that is being rented, and the following is a rental rate guide that you can utilize for establishing rates.

- Daily: 5 percent of the instrument value.
- Weekly: 10 percent of the instrument value.
- Monthly: 10 to 20 percent of the instrument value.

COMPUTER EQUIPMENT
★★ $$$ 🏠 🕐

Renting computer equipment on a short- and long-term basis is practical for business travelers, companies with limited computer purchasing budgets, businesses with trade show displays, hotels without business centers and students, among others. The key will be to have the latest models and the most commonly available software—because if you don't, someone else will. The renters need to be able to keep up with the business community and, just like leasing a car, they want to rent top models that are out of their budget to purchase. Make sure you take deposits to cover the cost of the computer "walking away" and be forewarned that some may do just that. Also, examine the going rental rates in your area as they will vary greatly depending on economic factors. Your ability to promptly provide exactly the equipment and software required will allow you to charge more money. Expertise is a plus, as renters need to know exactly how the hardware and software work and with what technology they will need to interface. Time is also typically of the essence, otherwise why is someone in such need of a computer? Therefore, you need to be reachable 24/7 or have a part-time staffer to help you get computers in the hands of those who need them very quickly. To increase your income potential, have the latest in A/V equipment at the ready as well. And, don't forget to maintain and upgrade your equipment regularly.

OFFICE EQUIPMENT
★★ $$$$

Desks, chairs, photocopiers, filing cabinets, and telephone systems are just a few examples of office equipment that are required by most businesses in order to function on a day-to-day basis. Start-up businesses as well as those in transition, film companies, or offices set up for a specific short-term event (such as running a two week sales conference) are all your potential customers.

START-UP COSTS: A business that rents office equipment and furniture can be initiated on a small scale, and for less than $10,000. Of course, the business can be expanded later from the profits that are generated. On a larger scale this sort of new rental service would require $30,000 to $50,000 to properly establish.

PROFIT POTENTIAL: Rental rates will greatly vary, in terms of local market demand, and the age and condition of the equipment that is being rented. However, assuming the initial investment into the rental equipment for the business was $15,000, then you should expect rental revenues around $1,500 per month. Office equipment generally rents for 10 percent of its value on a monthly basis, meaning a 20 percent return on investment per year.

CAMPING EQUIPMENT
★★★ $$$ 🏕 🕐

Camping is hugely popular in North America as a recreational pastime. However, there is only one drawback to this splendid outdoor family activity. Many families cannot afford to purchase the required equipment to go camping, especially if they are only going to use the camping equipment once or twice a year. This factual sce-

nario creates a great opportunity for innovative entrepreneurs to start a camping equipment rental business, and fill a large market demand that can line your pockets with profits.

START-UP COSTS: For the purpose of projecting business start-up costs, assume that your new camping gear rental business can supply enough camping equipment for ten families with four family members. The investment would be as follows:

Camping Item	Item Quantity	Item Cost
Sleeping tent	2	$200	$400
Sleeping bags	4	$150	$600
Portable stove	1	$100	$100
Food coolers	2	$100	$200
Miscellaneous items		$200	
Total package cost		$1,500	
Total start-up cost to outfit 10 families			**$15,000**

Additional capital will be required for marketing and promotional purposes. In total a camping supply rental business can be started for less than a $20,000 investment.

PROFIT POTENTIAL: The camping equipment package should rent for 10 percent of the package value per week, or for this example $150. You will be renting single items or multiple items throughout the year. A camping supply rental business can generate profits of $20,000 per year on a part-time basis.

RVS
★ $$$ 🏕 🕐

To avoid investing hundreds of thousands of dollars yourself into starting an RV rental business, you may want to consider launching this enterprise with the assistance of a pool, or group rental system. An RV pool rental system works on the following basis. Owners of RVs allow you to rent their units to your clients in exchange for a portion of the rental revenue. Additionally, as the owner of the business, you may also have to agree to maintain and insure the RVs. However, each rental agreement can be negotiated individually with RV owners. North America remains one of the world's top travel destinations for foreign travelers, and traveling by RV allows them to enjoy and experience a unique and unforgettable holiday.

START-UP COSTS: The total cost to establish an RV rental business using the rental pool format will be approximately $10,000 including a web site and promotional brochures.

PROFIT POTENTIAL: Class "C" RVs rent for $600+ per week plus gas, insurance, and a mileage charge over a certain number of free miles. Class "A" RVs start at $800 per week and go up from there. In the rental pool system, you keep 50 percent of the rental revenue as the operator of the business. One of the easiest ways of running such a business is online, whereby you make the connections between RV owners and those who would like to rent an RV for week or two. In the United States there are more than ten million registered recreational vehicles and many RV owners rent their units when they are not using them. An equal number of people rent RVs annually and set out onto the highways on vacation. What an opportunity to bring these two parties together via your web site! The site could be divided by city or state as well as RV classification. Visitors would simply scroll through the index until they found the type of RV they were interested in renting. You could charge a small posting or listing fee to RV owners. Additionally, to increase visitor interest, develop a camping or RV park directory. Imagine—1,000 RV owners paying a mere $15 a month each to have their rental information featured on the web site will create yearly sales of $180,000. Of course, you need to make it clear that you provide this as a service and that you are not responsible for the condition of the RV. Make sure to have signed contracts that you can email to all parties so that you act ONLY as the middle person and are not held legally responsible for any damages.

WEB RESOURCE: www.rvra.org
Recreational Vehicle Rental Association

STORE FIXTURES
★ $$$ 🏠 🕐

Many retail businesses are started on a shoestring budget and often do not allow for the purchase of new store fixtures. Renting store fixtures such as display cabinets, shelving, and cash registers can be a way that you can get into business in your local community without a lot of previous business experience. Potential clients include businesses that require the use of store fixtures on a temporary basis including inventory liquidators, businesses setting up at local trade shows, and existing businesses establishing secondary satellite locations. A store fixture rental business may not be a good candidate for starting and operating from home due to the storage space that will be required, unless of course you have adequate storage space available at home.

START-UP COSTS: New high quality store fixtures are extremely expensive. However, scanning local newspapers for business closure notices may result in an ability to purchase high-quality store fixtures secondhand for a fraction of their original retail value. Investment range is $10,000 to $25,000.

PROFIT POTENTIAL: The demand is not as high for store fixture rentals as for other rental ventures that can be started. You may want to consider adding sales of used store fixtures and equipment as a method of supplementing rental revenue.

CASINO EQUIPMENT
★ $$$$ ⚖️

Renting casino equipment to charity organizations for fundraising events and to businesses for promotional events is big business. The biggest requirement will be to make sure that you will not be bending or breaking any laws, but legal information, in terms of operating a business that rents casino gaming equipment, is very easy to obtain on a local basis. Review the laws carefully and have an attorney step in to cover any gray areas before you proceed to rent.

START-UP COSTS: To properly establish a casino equipment rental service will be very costly, in the neighborhood of $50,000 to $100,000 to cover the cost of equipment, transportation, and business setup. There are very few short cuts or cost saving measures that can be utilized, as the equipment must be in perfect working condition.

PROFIT POTENTIAL: The casino equipment that you rent can be supplied to charity organizations and companies on a daily, weekly, or monthly basis—whichever will meet your clients' requirements and needs. Additional revenue can be earned by supplying qualified dealers, as well as by having your own "learn to become a casino dealer" instruction school. The profit potential will greatly depend on the type of business venture that you will be operating, and also on how diversified the business will be. One thing that is for sure is that anything to do with gambling and casinos is generally a pretty safe business venture to start and operate, in the right environments.

WEB RESOURCE: www.oneeyedjackgaming.com
Distributor of casino equipment and supplies.

FENCING
★★ $$$+ 🏠 🕐

Renting portable fencing solutions to construction companies and outdoor event planners is a fantastic homebased rental business that can be started on a relatively small initial investment. Most rental fencing is in the form of a chain link that is generally six to eight feet high. Additionally, the fencing is typically installed with barbed wire on top to prevent trespassers into the construction site or event.

START-UP COSTS: Ninety-five percent of the start-up costs associated with this business venture will be the purchase of the fencing material and suitable transportation for delivery purposes. The balance of the start-up costs will be used for a simple marketing brochure and establishing the legal aspects for the business, such as business registration and rental contract forms. Start-up investment range is $15,000 to $30,000.

PROFIT POTENTIAL: Fence rental rates are calculated by the total number of linear feet required for the job. Furthermore, there are additional charges for the complexity of the installation and factors, such as the number of gates and height of fencing required.

CANOES AND KAYAKS
★★★ $$ 🏠 🕐

Starting a canoe and kayak rental business will not leave you up the financial creek without a paddle, as this is one of the best low-investment rental businesses that can be started. A canoe and kayak rental business can be established in a few different operating formats. With the first, you can supply canoes or kayaks to marinas and waterfront hotels and split the rental revenues that are generated. The second option is to operate a canoe and kayak rental business from your own rented waterfront location. For the third option, you can run the business from home, advertising through print media to attract customers who can simply pickup the rental item from you, or you can deliver the rental equipment to the customer. The second and third options will generate the most income for the business, as well as give you the most control over the business and rental equipment.

START-UP COSTS: A canoe and kayak rental business can be nicely established for less than $10,000, or slightly more with the necessary liability insurance. The following is a current retail price list for canoes, kayaks, and accessories.

Fiberglass canoe	$400–$600
Kevlar canoe	$800–$2,000
Ocean fiberglass kayak	$1,500–$2,000
Tandem ocean kayak	$2,000–$3,000
Roto-mold white-water kayaks	$700–$1,000
Paddles	$10–$150

Life vests should be supplied for free as they are generally part of the legal requirements for running the business. Purchase previously owned canoes and kayaks, as they generally sell for half of the cost of new ones. Just make sure they are in excellent shape or you may be cause yourself more headaches and increase your need for higher liability insurance.

PROFIT POTENTIAL: As is the case in many rental businesses, once the inventory has been paid for there are not a lot of overheads associated with operating the business. Canoes and kayaks have a very long and usable life span and only require the occasional repair. Canoes rent for $40 per day and $125 per week, while kayaks rent for $50 per day and up to $200 per week. A well-established and equipped canoe and kayak rental business can easily generate revenues in excess $100,000 per year.

PORTABLE BUILDINGS
★ $$$$ 🏠 🕐

There are many uses for portable buildings to be set up on a location for temporary business and operating applications. Potential clients for a portable building rental business include construction companies, fairs, outdoor auctions, outdoor liquidation sales, movie and TV production sites, outdoor community special events, sporting events, and roadside vending. The biggest requirement for starting a portable building rental business is the ability to move and set up the portable buildings, which are very often modified trailers to suit the client's needs.

START-UP COSTS: The initial start-up investment required to set this business in motion will vary greatly to the number of portable buildings you will be renting as well as the equipment that is supplied or outfitted with the buildings. Investment range is $20,000 to $100,000 or more. Additional cost considerations include transportation, storage, and insurance coverage.

PROFIT POTENTIAL: Portable building rental rates start at $200 per day and $400 per week and go up depending on the size of the buildings and the functionality. Assuming you can meet clients' requirements, a profitable living can be made renting portable buildings.

BOATS
★★ $$$ 🕐

Renting small, motorized, runabout boats to fishermen can be a very lucrative rental business venture to establish in your area. Fishermen travel wide and far in search of the perfect fishing hole. The business can be water-based and operated from a marina or rented dock facility, or it can be land-based and the boats can be rented with a trailer. To get started, design colorful brochures and distribute them to hotels, motels, and tourist attractions. The brochures should contain information about your boat rentals, including rates and the size of boat and motor. The hotels and motels can act as booking agents for the business while providing a great service for their guests. Consider a rental revenue split of perhaps 20 percent for the booking agent and 80 percent for you. This should be more than an adequate financial incentive for any motel proprietor to happily get on board with the program.

START-UP COSTS: Small, secondhand fishing boats with a motor and trailer are selling in the range of $2,500 to

$5,000 each. An initial investment of $10,000 to $15,000 will be suitable to get this venture "floating."

PROFIT POTENTIAL: Small fishing boats rent for about $100 per day and include safety equipment and gasoline. Three rental boats working for you 100 days per year each can produce a gross business income of $30,000.

MOPEDS
★★ $$$$ ⚖️

This rental venture is best served by establishing the business in a high-traffic area that caters to, and is visited mainly by, tourists. The business can be operated from an independent location or in partnership with a hotel or multiple hotels acting as the rental location for the mopeds. A mechanical aptitude will assist with keeping your fleet of mopeds on the road and in good repair.

START-UP COSTS: A fleet of ten new mopeds will set you back about $15,000. Additionally, depending on how you establish the rental operation, an additional $5,000 to $10,000 of working capital will be required.

PROFIT POTENTIAL: Mopeds rent for $50 to $60 per day plus the cost of insurance and gasoline. Once again, providing that your business is located in a busy year-round tourist area and that you have only ten mopeds for rent, you could generate yearly revenues exceeding $100,000. Additional income can be acquired by renting bicycles and in-line skates from the same location. Also, you may act as a booking agent for local tours and tourist attractions, as the commissions earned can really add up and generate excellent additional income for the business. Each year there are numerous serious accidents because people renting mopeds are not familiar with how to ride them. You need to have some stringent rules of the road clearly posted (or handed out to each renter) and all safety equipment available. Provide some basic lessons if need be and remember the saying, it's better to be safe than sorry.

WEB RESOURCE: www.moped.org
Links to moped dealers and clubs.

PORTABLE SIGNS
★★ $$$ 🏠 🕐

Just about every retail merchant holds at least one large sale per year and these sales all have to be advertised and promoted to get the attention of consumers. Starting your own portable sign rental business will allow you to cash in on the retailers seeking to promote their sales. Portable rental signs generally feature a flashing arrow or some other type of attention-grabbing feature. These signs have the ability to change messages, either electronically or with the use of individual letters. To kick this business into high gear, simply check the local newspapers for merchants that are advertising forthcoming sales. You can then call or visit these businesses and present all the benefits that having a portable message sign on site will have in terms of increasing potential revenues for their sales.

START-UP COSTS: Start-up investment range is $10,000 to $15,000.

PROFIT POTENTIAL: Portable message signs rent for $75 per day and $150 per week. Your arithmetic skills do not have to be good to realize that having a few portable signs that are rented on a regular basis can really generate some serious cash flow and profits.

WEB RESOURCE: www.letterperfectinc.net
Manufacturers of portable signs and letters.

VIDEO AND CAMERA EQUIPMENT
★★★ $$$ 🏠 🕐

The absolutely best way to market the business is through local hotels and motels. Simply design a brochure and price list and obtain permission from the hotels, etc., to place this brochure in all of their guest rooms. You can rent the equipment directly to vacationers and business travelers that call you as a result of seeing the brochure in the hotel. Providing your customers with a free one-hour delivery service right to their hotel room is also a valuable method to overcoming any potential resistance to renting the equipment. Of course, you will need to work out a revenue splitting or payment arrangement with the hotels and motels that permit you to post your brochures.

START-UP COSTS: An initial start-up investment of $8,000 to $12,000 can set this business venture into motion.

PROFIT POTENTIAL: Digital camera equipment rents for $30 per day per item and up. This is definitely the kind of rental business that allows you to charge 10 percent of the rental item's value each time the equipment is rented.

MOVIE PROPS
★★★★ $$$ 🏠

Rentals of set or location props are certainly not limited to only the film production industry. Props are also required for trade shows, mall displays, social functions, business presentations, theater performances, and so on. Starting a prop rental service does not mean that you have to invest hundreds of thousands of dollars into unique and interesting props for inventory, although it helps to have some basics on hand such as plants, trees and home furnishings, especially for kitchen sets. If you can specialize in certain types of props you can carve a niche in the market. One Queens, New York company became known for their medical prop rentals, which ranged from gurneys to ambulances.

To expand the possibilities, you can tap into that which other people have available, such as rare cars, antique jukeboxes, and gadgets of every kind, that they would be more than willing to rent for a fee. To serve as such a middle person for these types of rental items, you should start a prop-for-rent web site. Promote the site to those who routinely rent props, including production companies, event planners, etc., and make sure you introduce yourself to local film bureaus, theater companies, advertising agencies, and the drama departments of local universities. The web site can be indexed by category with photos of the harder-to-find items up for rent. To generate revenue for your business, simply charge a 50 percent commission on the rental value of all items. One example might be a rare car that rents for $300 per day for a commercial shoot. You keep $150 dollars for bringing the two parties together electronically. Of course you will have to work out delivery, pickup, and liability issues. Once again, make sure your contract states exactly what you are and are not responsible for, limiting your liability in the event someone gets injured by using a prop they rented through your service.

SCAFFOLDING
★ $$ 🏠 🕐

Almost every building and home service trade needs to rent scaffolding at some point in the course of operating their business. To start this type of business you purchase new or secondhand scaffolding, design a brochure and price list, and distribute the brochure to local home service companies and contractors in your community. Providing a free delivery and pickup service for scaffold rentals will get the telephone ringing and scaffold rental orders coming in.

START-UP COSTS: The investment needed to get the business rolling is very reasonable; $10,000 will suffice initially, until the scaffold rental inventory can be expanded from the profits earned. A secondhand truck, van, or utility trailer can be used for deliveries, or the delivery aspect of the business can be contracted to a local transportation firm. Don't forget liability insurance!

PROFIT POTENTIAL: A small scaffold rental service can achieve profits in excess of $20,000 per year, and additional revenue can be generated by installing and dismantling scaffolding for larger rental contracts.

BOUNCY HOUSES
★★ $$$

The focus of this new business opportunity is the rental of portable, inflatable, carnival-style bouncy houses for children's birthday parties and community charity events. In addition to renting bouncy houses, this business start-up can also include operating the bouncy houses in tourist or high-traffic community gathering places, and charging parents a $3 or $4 fee for their kids to spend ten minutes inside bouncing around with their friends. There are numerous types of bounce houses and bounce castles available today. A "designer" top-of-the-line 15 x 15 foot model costs around $1,800 to purchase. Larger houses cost several thousand dollars and can command more money because they can accommodate more children at one time. For additional income, you can also offer inflatable slides. These generally cost around $4,000 to $5,000, but you can make that back in a very short time when renting units out for parties at $200 for a couple of hours. Other than a vehicle for transport (which can be rented as necessary) and liability insurance, there are not many start-up costs. You'll need to have a place to store the houses, which take up a fair amount of room even when deflated. You'll also need to make sure you learn about (and post) all safety information for parents and children.

FARMLAND
★ $$+

The basis of this rental business is maybe not as the name indicates. The idea is to rent or lease farmland that is not being used by the owner. You can divide the land into smaller tracts and rent it to people who would like to have their own vegetable garden, but cannot due the lack of space or because they are residing in an apartment. The other means of making money by renting farmland is by renting the land for events and activities ranging from concerts to county fairs to carnivals, not to mention film and commercial shoots. If you let farmers know that you can get them some top-dollar for use of their land, they can sign up as clients.

PLANTS
★★ $

Money can grow on trees. Just ask any business owner in the plant rental industry. Renting plants is a pretty uncomplicated rental business. You can operate right from home on a full- or part-time basis, and the delivery and pickup of the plants requires very basic transportation, such as a small economy car. The target market for plant rentals are trade show planners, wedding planners, seminars, product demonstration firms, professional offices, TV and movie production sets, entertainment events, political functions, and every other business or event that requires a professional and appealing appearance on a short- or long-term basis.

START-UP COSTS: A modest investment of a $1,000 or less can get you rolling in your own plant rental business.

PROFIT POTENTIAL: The operating overhead for a plant rental business amounts to the cost of delivery transportation and the occasional plant casualty. The revenue the business generates is basically 100 percent profit. Additional sources of income can be earned by adding a plant care or plant maintenance program service to the plant rental business.

TANNING EQUIPMENT
★★ $$

People love to have a nice tan. That's what makes starting your own business renting in-home tanning equipment such a logical business start-up venture.

MARKETING TIP: This may sound crazy, but working with travel agents to help rent the tanning beds for in-home use is a fantastic way to set this business in motion. The most frequent visitors to tanning salons are people who will be going on holidays to a sunny destination in the near future. The idea is to get a base tan prior to leaving on vacation. Building these alliances with travel agents makes a lot of sense because they know exactly who is going on vacation and when.

START-UP COSTS: An initial investment of $10,000 can get this business underway and working for you.

PROFIT POTENTIAL: Tanning beds can be rented for as much as $200 per week to people seeking the perfect tan. Assuming your rental business had four tanning beds each working just 25 weeks per year would create business revenues of $20,000 per year. To increase sales, add other rental products like portable hot tubs and pool tables. Adding these items can enable you to create "packaged fun rentals" by the week or month that could include multiple rental items and be offered to clients as a discount package rental rate.

SNOWMOBILES
★ $$$ 🚗 🕐 🚜

Snowmobile riding is an extremely popular outdoor wintertime activity that is enjoyed by millions of people in North America. A snowmobile rental business is unique and specialized and requires a sound business and action plan put in place prior to activating the business. One absolute must is liability insurance, due to the nature of the activity.

START-UP COSTS: Starting a business that rents snowmobiles on a seasonal basis can be very costly, as new high-powered snowmobiles can cost as much as $10,000. However, if you are mechanically inclined and have the ability to repair and maintain snowmobiles, you can minimize start-up costs by purchasing good-quality secondhand equipment. Generally, late-model secondhand snowmobiles sell for about half of the cost of a similarly equipped new one. Current snowmobile rental rates are in the range of $30 per hour, and $150 to $200 per day.

APARTMENT LAUNDRY EQUIPMENT
★ $$ 🚗 🕐

Many apartment and condominium buildings are constructed without laundry facilities within the residential units. Most of these buildings have a shared or common laundry room that is generally used by all the tenants of the building. You can start your own business that not only installs and services rental laundry equipment, but also retains a portion of the rental revenues. To launch this type of enterprise you will have to build alliances with landlords and property management firms. Laundry room equipment contracts are often tendered to contractors every few years. Starting now to prepare your business will enable you to not only tender for these very lucrative contracts, it will also allow you to establish your business immediately upon being awarded a contract.

START-UP COSTS: Coin-operated laundry equipment retails for about two to three times the amount of residential laundry equipment. A typical laundry room with three washers and dryers will cost in the neighborhood of $8,000 to $10,000 to outfit properly.

PROFIT POTENTIAL: Profit potential will greatly depend on the number of people residing in the building. However, the industry average is $500 per laundry machine per residential unit per year.

PORTABLE SAWMILLS
★ $$$ 🚗 🕐

Operating a portable sawmill rental business can potentially earn you two sources of income. The first source can be derived by simply renting portable sawmill equipment to customers. Renting the sawmill equipment as well as supplying an operator (you or an employee) to operate the equipment for the customer can earn the second source of income. There are a surprisingly large amount of situations that require a portable sawmill to be used for sawing lumber on site, including creating new dimensions from salvaged lumber, log home building, and clearing fallen trees for property owners and insurance companies.

START-UP COSTS: Portable sawmills retail for $10,000 to $20,000, and are generally situated on a flat bed trailer for easy transportation.

PROFIT POTENTIAL: Portable sawmills without an operator rents for $200 to $300 per day. With an operator the sawmills can be rented for as much as $500 per day.

WEB RESOURCE: www.sawmill-exchange.com
Directory featuring portable sawmills for sale and related information.

GO-CARTS
★ $$$$ 🏎️

At one time go-cart tracks were all the rage for entertainment of kids and adults alike. Starting your own go-cart track may just put you ahead of future competitors. The business does require a fixed location or track to operate. However, with some clever planning and negotiations, you may be able to secure an operating location that can be partnered with an existing amusement or family entertainment business. Partnerships like this often work well, as each independent business works as a drawing card for the other, not to mention reducing overheads by non-duplication of operating requirements and expenses.

START-UP COSTS: As an independent business venture, a go-cart track could easily require an investment in the range of $250,000 (with leased land) to get rolling. However, as a joint venture with an existing entertainment or amusement type business, the business could be started for less than half of that amount.

PROFIT POTENTIAL: Go-carts are rented in two ways: The first is where the rider pays a fixed amount of money for a certain number of laps around the track. The second is when the rider pays a fixed amount of money based on the time they are on the track. In spite of this being an expensive business to start, a popular and well-established go-cart track can produce sizable profits for the business owner that can easily surpass $100,000 per year if you are located in a high-traffic, easily accessible location.

PORTABLE DRESSING ROOMS: TRAILERS
★★ $$$$ 🕐

The movie and TV production industry is booming, and operating a portable dressing room rental business can make you a financial star. However, keep in mind that the vast majority of television and film shoots take place in Los Angeles and New York City, and the studios have plenty of such trailers parked on their lots or in garages. In addition, similar established rental companies will provide very stiff competition in the top markets, having already aligned themselves with the major studios. Therefore, the best way to make this a successful business is to select a region of the country, or large city, and make trailers available not only for major studio productions, but for independent film makers and local advertisers. Nearly every major, and even smaller cities in North America, has a film bureau promoting on-location shooting. If you can service a few cities in close proximity or even be the go-between for hooking up local production companies or advertising agencies with the nearby dressing room facilities that they require, then you can make a go of it in this business. Portable dressing room trailers can be very expensive to purchase or build. However, the rental rates are very lucrative, especially once you have established a solid repeat clientele base. Don't forget to market your dressing rooms to businesses and organizations outside the film industry, including outdoor theater productions, circus and carnival companies and major corporations shooting industrial films. Investment range $50,000 plus. Profit potential of $100,000 per year is attainable in this business, if you make alliances with film bureaus.

OUTDOOR BEACH LOCKERS
★★★ $$$$ 🏠 🕐 🌐

There has always been one drawback to sunbathing at the beach. Where do you put your car keys when your bathing suit does not have any pockets? Even worse, what if you have spent the morning shopping and now you want to go for a swim. If you leave your belongings or new purchases lying around there is no doubt that someone will walk off with them. Outdoor-secured storage lockers can be an amazingly profitable rental business to start. The locations these portable storage lockers can be installed are endless and include beaches, public markets, parks, arenas, fitness centers, trade shows, and sports playing fields, just to mention a few.

START-UP COSTS: This is definitely not a cheap business to start in terms of capital requirements. You can purchase pre-built storage lockers like the ones at airports, or you can design your own lockers to better suit the areas in which you will be installing the lockers. One idea may be to have number pads installed on each individual locker that would enable the user to punch in their own entry code upon depositing the coins. This method of locker access would be great, as it does not require the user to carry (and possibly lose) the locker key. Investment range is $20,000+.

PROFIT POTENTIAL: Assume each locker stand has 30 separate lockers that are used twice a day at a cost of $2. Each locker stand could generate $120 per day. Now, if you had only three of these portable storage locker units in place, your business revenue could be as much as $130,000 annually. Additional considerations may be to arrange a revenue split with the various locations where the storage lockers can be installed. Splitting revenues will cost you money in terms of the bottom line. However, it may be a method that you can use to secure the best possible installation location for the storage lockers.

WEB RESOURCE: www.americanlocker.com
Distributors of multipurpose security lockers.

BEACH EQUIPMENT
★★ $$

Renting beach equipment is not only a fun and relaxing business to operate, it can also be very profitable. The business can be established at any busy tourist beach area, either from a fixed location or a portable one right on the beach with proper permission. Hot rental items always include inflatable inter-tubes, shade umbrellas, snorkeling equipment, and surfboards. Additional revenue can be earned by providing quick surfing and snorkeling lessons. The profit potential is outstanding from renting beach equipment, as many of the rental items will return their initial purchase cost within as few as six rentals. Generally, this business is operated on a seasonal basis. However, if your lifestyle allows, the business can be established in multiple locations in different climates and operated on a year-round basis.

CLASSIC CARS
★★ $$$$

Tourists, vacationers, movie studios, production companies and advertising agencies are all likely candidates to rent a '69 Mustang, '59 Cadillac Eldorado, '49 Lincoln, or '37 Packard complete with running boards. In fact, they also make unique vehicles for newlyweds as they exit the ceremonies or receptions and drive off into the sunset. Whether you are renting strictly old-time classics or a few modern ones as well, this is a business you will enjoy running, while also making very good money.

START-UP COSTS: Other than leasing a lot on which to park the cars, costs will include some basic office equipment, marketing, and of course, the cars. For $100,000, you can likely purchase five such cars after scouting and spreading the word through all available channels that you are buying. Other options are to lease the cars from the owners, allowing you to have the car for x amount of time, or work a consignment deal with the car owners, which will allow you use of a car owned by someone else for a percentage of the rental. These are attractive options because the upfront cash outlay is less and you can get more cars into the business. It also allows you to determine which cars are popular and which ones are not generating much attention. Of course, you will need to pass on all liability to the drivers who rent from you. If you enjoy classic cars, this could be a great business to run and there is money to be made in the right location and with good marketing. Again, you want to have the cars rented out as much as possible, so price accordingly.

KITCHENS
★★★ $$$$

There are two ways of going about the kitchen rental business. One is to have a fully-equipped, state-of-the-art kitchen available for rent for photo shoots, cooking demonstrations, cooking classes, film and television shoots, and so on. The other is to have a mobile kitchen that you can set up wherever needed, including outdoor sporting events (such as golf tournaments), fairs, amusement parks, film and television shoots, parties and at disaster relief locations. The kitchen equipment, which can include walk-in freezers, three-compartment sinks, broilers, ovens, stoves, pizza ovens, grills refrigerators, counter space, etc., can be included as part of the overall package when renting the kitchen, or included on an a la carte basis. Buying or leasing a large truck and purchasing the necessary equipment, plus insurance, can result in $100,000+ start up costs. Of course, you can save some money by purchasing top-quality previously owned equipment. Getting investment backers together will be contingent upon a good business plan that demonstrates your demographic market. Therefore, before starting out, you will want to make a list of all of the places in your area that could rent kitchen equipment. There are likely more than you think.

WEB RESOURCE: www.mobilekitchens.com
The leader in the field can provide some ideas for starting on a much smaller scale.

HOT AIR BALLOONS
★★ $$$$ 🏧

No, this probably won't work in downtown Chicago or New York City, but if you are in Arizona, Colorado, Utah, or any location with some open spaces, you can launch a business that can launch your customers, so to speak. From Maine to Vancouver, hot air balloon companies take people on the ride of a lifetime. Not only are they beautiful to look at and provide a great aerial experience for passengers, but hot air balloons can provide a marvelous means of flight and a great business opportunity.

REQUIREMENTS: The average sport hot air balloon carrying two or three people can be purchased for $40,000 to $60,000. You then need to hire FAA commercial licensed pilots and your business can take off. You also need a location at which to "park" the balloons, plus there is a cost to maintain them. All totaled, your start-up and yearly costs would run you about $400,000 for a fleet of four balloons (which typically need to be replaced after about 400 flying hours), fuel, instructors, marketing, office equipment, insurance and other costs. If, however, you charge $250 per person for an hour flight, $500 for two people per flight, then, at an average of just 20 flights a week, you could make $520,000 a years or a $120,000 profit.

WEB RESOURCE: www.fai.org/ballooning
International Ballooning Commission.

BICYCLES
★★ $$$ 🕐

Bike riding is a great physical activity, a gas-savings means of getting around, and typically a lot of fun. In tourist and vacation locales, people will often rent bicycles to ride along the boardwalk or take in the scenery while in parks. Biking is simply a great way to spend an afternoon.

REQUIREMENTS: You'll need a fleet of bicycles, and the tools to maintain and repair them, and a location, which can be a storefront, a corner of a larger business, or even a small trailer or stand with a couple of bike racks. If you own or lease a truck, you can actually set up and pack up the bikes each night, saving you on overhead costs.

STARTUP COSTS: You should be able to start up a bike rental business for $7,000 to $15,000 with the primary cost being 15 to 25 bicycles at about $250 to $300 each. Market the business by posting signs, handouts, and having the name of the business on the bikes themselves. Always take deposits from renters and get liability and theft insurance. Typically bikes are rented for $10 to $20 per half hour, depending on the demand. You might also rent the bicycles built for two, surreys, and roller blades. Don't forget to provide helmets and padding for free. Hint: Find a good location, preferably one that has little competition from other bike rental shops, plus great scenery and if possible, few roads for cars.

FLOOR CLEANING MACHINES
★★ $$$ 🕐

Sweepers, scrubbers, waxers, carpet cleaners, and similar machines to clean and polish residential or industrial floors all provide the makings for a rental business. For less than $25,000 you can start up a business that can allow homeowners or businesses to do industrial strength cleaning periodically or for special occasions. If you establish regular clients, you can work out contracts where they will rent the equipment every x number of months, saving them from purchasing and storing such cleaning machines. Turbo air carpet and floor dryers are also nice to have in stock for homes in areas where basements tend to flood.

MEDICAL EQUIPMENT
★★★ $$$$ 🏧

There are a number of reasons why people need to rent medical and hospital equipment, from home care to physical therapy to shooting a movie or staging a play. Various types of walkers, electric scooters, wheelchairs and transport devices as well as lifts, traction equipment, humidifiers, whirlpools, and hospital beds should all be part of your inventory of supplies and equipment that can be rented. You will need a van or even a truck available for transporting such equipment to people's homes and a good knowledge of how to operate each piece of equipment. With a good web site and digital photos you may not need a location from which customers can select what they need; instead, they will order from the web site or from a brochure or catalog, if you have enough available products. By ordering directly from manufacturers, and in some cases, buying items that have been previously used, you can get some fair prices when purchasing the inventory, which might cost you $20,000.

UNIFORMS
★★ $$$

Whether your customers are dressing up as a butler or domestic servant for fun or working at a party, the uniforms need to come from somewhere. A uniform rental business can supply clothing for chefs and food servers, lab coats for technicians, medical clothing or any other types of uniforms that may be needed for short-term use by businesses, individuals or production companies. With a digital camera, you can put together a catalog, web site, and/or brochure to best display the variety of available uniforms. Make sure to stock up on a variety of sizes and keep all uniforms clean.

WEB RESOURCE: www.bestbuyuniforms.com
Wholesale uniforms.

HELICOPTERS
★★★ $$$$

For aerial photography or for tourist rides around a scenic location such as the Grand Canyon or around New York City, helicopter rentals can be big business. Of course, the main cost is the chopper, which can range from $100,000 to $400,000 depending on the size and year of the model, and from whom you are buying it. You will also need a licensed pilot, your fair share of insurance, and a place to park your whirlybirds. If you can go

in on a business venture with a helicopter owner whereby you run the tours, arrange the times, and make all the bookings, while he or she provides the helicopter and pilot, you can split the profits as you see fit, and have far less overhead than trying to purchase the choppers yourself. Helicopter tours can cost $150 to $300 (or more) per person for an hour, and in a popular location for tourists, booking 40 flights a week, with two people per flight paying a total of $400, would bring in $16,000 weekly or over $800,000 a year.

WEB RESOURCE: www.rotor.com
Helicopter Association International.

VIDEO GAMES
★★ $$$$

PS2, PS3, PSP, GameCube, Xbox, Xbox360, and so on and so forth. If you are a gamer or have a child, pre-teen, or teenager, chances are you will know what these are. Video games comprise a billion-dollar industry and you can be part of it by renting just some of the endless stream of games on the market. For $40,000 you can stock and launch a small video game rental location. Selling controllers and accessories, as well as some of the previously owned games, can add to your profit potential. It helps tremendously to find a location in or around a mall so that kids can visit while their parents shop. Hint: Keep a close watch on what you are buying. While you may not be familiar with all of the games, you must be aware that some are not for young children and others are strictly for adults. Be selective in what you carry and make sure to read warnings and rent games that are T only to teens or M-17 only to persons over the age of 17. At $5.99 a pop, you can rent games for a week, or for around $9.99 you can rent them out for a month. Make sure to read the trades and stock up on the latest games.

WEB RESOURCE: www.pcgamer.com
PC Gamer, one of the leading magazines in the gaming industry.

72
RETAIL
Businesses You Can Start

COOKWARE
★ $ 🚗 🕐

Hosting home parties that feature cookware and other types of kitchen products for sale is a terrific low-cost homebased business venture to set in motion—and the way that Tupperware became a multi-million dollar business. There are, however, literally thousands of manufacturers in the United States that market their products on this type of basis, and finding one is as easy as researching the subject on the internet. Typically, you can purchase the cookware items for wholesale cost and resell the same items retail at "home cookware parties." In addition to hosting the cookware parties, you can also build a team of cookware party hosts and become a regional manager of sorts, keeping a percentage of the total sales that are generated. Since cookware, like most items today, is readily available on the internet, you need to be clever, find items that are not easily located, and come up with creative packages such as Asian cookware with a wok and other accessories for one combined price. Whether it is Asian cuisine or some other style, cook a meal at someone's home and have him or her invite 20 friends. After dinner, provide your catalog, highlighting the tools used for that meal, and of course you can sell other items as well!

WEB RESOURCE: www.cookware.org
The Cookware Manufacturers Association.

BEER COMPANY NOVELTIES
★★ $ 🚗 🕐

Are you searching for a unique retail business that can be operated from home on a part-time basis? If so, perhaps starting a business that buys and sells beer company novelties will be of particular interest to you. There is an absolutely gigantic market for collectable beer company novelties such as signs, posters, games, coasters, and specialty beer bottles. Scouting garage sales, flea markets, the internet, and newspaper classified ads can be the starting point of acquiring beer company novelty items that can be resold to collectors at enormous profits. Finding buyers for the collectibles can be as easy as posting free classified ads on various internet newsgroups sites, as well as listing the beer company novelties for sale on eBay and other online auction web sites. It is possible to create a part-time income of $25,000 per year buying and selling collectable beer company novelties, providing a 100 percent markup is maintained on all items purchased and resold and yearly sales of $50,000 are achieved.

RESTAURANT AND HOTEL SUPPLIES
★ $$ 🚗 🕐

The hotel and restaurant supply industry is enormous and generates billions of dollars in sales of products such as linen, tableware, and paper products each year. Starting a business that sells restaurant and hotel supplies is a very straightforward business venture to set in motion. To get rolling, simply negotiate a distribution contract with manufacturers of these products and begin to establish accounts with hotels and restaurants to supply them. Initially, the business can be operated on a part-time basis from home until enough accounts have been established and proven profitable to expand the business. Remember, this is a very competitive industry and as a small player do not attempt to win business on price only. Establish value-added services to win business such as free delivery, unique products, and exceptional service.

PAWNBROKER
★★ $$$$ 🗂️

Pawnbrokers sometimes get a bad rap, and unfortunately it only takes a few bad apples dealing in stolen merchandise to give the industry a bad name for all operators of pawnshops. However, like any business venture, eventually the bad business operators will disappear and the good operators will flourish. Starting a pawnshop is a good choice as a business choice for a few reasons, such a relatively low initial investment and excellent profit potential. Utilizing used product pricing, or value guides such as the Blue Book, will take away any guesswork in terms of the wholesale and retail value of products. The key to success for operating and profiting from a pawnbroker business is to keep all transactions legal, establish the business in the right location, deal only in up-to-date merchandise that has real value, and always practice good negotiation skills. If you can overcome the negative image problems by possibly NOT even using the word pawnbroker, you can make this work. You might also try to position and display items in a novel manner as opposed to the typical pawnshop "cluttered" look.

WEB RESOURCE: www.nationalpawnbrokers.org
National Pawnbrokers Association.

USED JEWELRY SALES
★★ $ 🏠 🕓

Purchasing secondhand jewelry and reselling the jewelry for a profit can be a lucrative business. Getting started in this type of retail or resale business is easy. Simply purchase secondhand jewelry from newspaper classified ads that appears to be distress sales. The jewelry can then be resold to individuals who are seeking a particular piece of jewelry for any special occasion as a gift. The one main requirement to make this business work is to have experience in the jewelry business in terms of knowing value, quality, condition, and overall industry expertise. You also need to be personable and win potential customers over in a trusting manner so that you dispel any initial idea that the jewelry is hot. Maintaining yearly sales of $150,000 and a 100 percent profit margin will result in pretax and expenses earnings of $75,000 per year.

SUNGLASSES
★★ $$$ 🕓 🌐

Selling sunglasses is a very inexpensive business startup to get rolling, and the profits that can be earned are excellent. Establishing the business can be as simple as purchasing an initial inventory and selling the sunglasses right from a booth set up in a mall, at a beach, or at a busy weekend flea market. There are thousands of manufacturers of sunglasses worldwide, so there should be no problem finding a source for good quality and inexpensive sunglasses. Providing that the right wholesale-to-retail pricing formula can be established, this simple little retailing venture is a good candidate to expand on a franchise basis and sell franchises to qualified owners-operators nationally in every region of the country. Securing the licensing rights to popular people, products, or themes can help in the marketing of the sunglasses. A pair of sunglasses that feature the name of a popular celebrity printed right on the glasses will sell better and for more money than the same sunglasses without the name or an endorsement.

WEB RESOURCE: www.wholesalesunglasses.com
Distributor of wholesale sunglasses to the retail trade.

WATCH KIOSK
★★ $$$ 🕓 🌐

Retailing wristwatches from a specially-designed sales kiosk is a fabulous low-investment business venture that anyone can own and operate. There are no special skills required to turn this business opportunity into a successful and profitable business enterprise. Watches remain one of the most popular gifts that are given on any number of occasions, such as Christmas, birthdays, graduations, anniversaries, or just for a job well done. Watches can be purchased on a wholesale basis for just a few dollars and marked up 300 to 600 percent for retail sales. Ideally, the kiosk used for selling the watches should be located in a high-traffic area, such as a mall, busy flea market, tradeshow, or public event. The kiosk can be used on a part-time basis and assembled for special events and holidays. If the kiosk has the right location it can certainly be operated on a full-time basis year round. Once this type of unique retailing business has been established and proven profitable, it can be the perfect business model for franchising purposes or expansion by way of multiple corporate locations.

WEB RESOURCE: www.watchwholesalers.com
Wholesaler of wristwatches.

GIFT BASKETS
★★★ $$+ 🎮 🕒 🌐

Gift baskets are extremely easy to assemble. Simply select items such as specialty foods, flowers, or personal health products and arrange them in an attractive wicker basket, and the gift basket is complete. The real secret to success in owning and operating a gift basket service is not in the gift baskets, but in the marketing and sales of them. The following are some suggestions on how to market gift baskets.

- Concentrate your marketing efforts on gaining repeat corporate clients, professionals, small business owners, and sales professionals such as realtors. Hospitals can also become a good client.
- Provide clients with only three pricing options; the first being a nice but economically-priced gift basket in the price range of $30 to $40, the second a more elaborate gift basket still modestly-priced in the range of $50 to $60, and the third option would be very elaborate and retail in the range of $100+.
- Design and create samples of the three gift basket options. Once completed, take pictures of the gift baskets and create a marketing brochure that fully details your business and provides a full description of the gift baskets. The marketing brochure should be in color and printed on high-gloss paper. Furthermore, the brochure should clearly state "keep

in a handy spot, for you never know when you will need to send a gift basket." The desired objective is for the recipient of the brochure not to dispose of the brochure.

- Once the brochure is complete, begin a direct-mail campaign as well as a hand delivery campaign for the marketing brochures. Once again, the marketing should be targeted at businesses, professionals, and salespeople, as these are the most likely candidates to become regular and repeat clients for the business
- Provide clients with free local delivery of the gift baskets. Be sure to arrange delivery for gift baskets that are being sent outside the local area. The key is service. Make this a pleasant shopping experience and the clients will become regular customers.

Maintaining a 100 percent markup on the gift baskets sold and achieving $150,000 per year in sales can generate a pretax profit of $75,000 per year for this terrific homebased business opportunity.

AIRBRUSHED HELMETS
★★★ $$$$ 🕒 🌐

I was introduced to this very unique business venture a few years back while on vacation. A very innovative entrepreneur had set up a retail storefront location in a busy beach area that specialized in selling and airbrushing colorful images on helmets used in a variety of sporting and recreational activities. The way the business operated was pure genius. The shop was bright, colorful, and well located. Airbrushing the helmets on site while the customer waited always guaranteed a large crowd of onlookers. The shop sold pre-painted helmets as well as painting a customer's helmet while they waited. The types they sold included baseball, hockey, bicycle, football, motorcycle, and snowmobile helmets for the vacationing snowbirds. In the two hours that I was there, the shop sold or airbrushed a total of 28 helmets with three artists working. Each helmet took approximately 10 to 15 minutes to complete, and the shop boasted a one-price policy for the artwork of $30 (plus the cost of the helmet). The shop featured binders with pictures and images that clients could choose from for artwork, or customers could provide their own art and supply the artist with a photograph, rough drawing, or even just an idea of what they wanted airbrushed on their helmet. The artists were subcontract employees who were paid commissions based on the total number of sales they generated. The owner told me that in the three years that he had been open, his shop had sold more than 8,000 helmets and painted more than 25,000 images on everything from helmets to beach clothing to motorcycle gas tanks. That is absolutely amazing when you consider this was a seasonal business open only four months a year. Assuming each helmet only sold for $25, the business would have then generated total sales of one million dollars over that three-year period, or more precisely $80,000 for each month that the business was open. The main requirement for starting a business that airbrushes helmets is obvious. You have to have artistic ability or employees in place with the artistic ability to paint the pictures and images. Additionally, the business must be located or operated in a very busy tourist area, or an area with enough local interest to generate sufficient sales.

WEB RESOURCE: www.airheadairbrush.com
Distributor of airbrushing equipment and supplies.

UNIVERSITY BOOKSTORE
★ $$$

New textbooks and course guides are very expensive, especially for students who are struggling to survive on tight education and living budgets. A university bookstore selling new titles along with used books can be the basis of a terrific new business venture. You can set up in conjunction with a university or capitalize with a central location near several. You may not even need a full time location. Just as many H & R Block tax offices set up offices for just tax season, you can set up your storefront during the September and January months just as the semesters are starting. You could also operate such a business by setting up a web site to sell the books as they come in.

For the used books, the trick is to get the books at the end of one semester and store them until the next is around the corner. The other option is to have students bring in their books and use them as trade-in value against the books that they are purchasing. Therefore, if a student brings in a $25 text book, you could give them $8 off a new text book and then turn around and sell the $25 used book for $16, thus making an $8 profit on the

exchange. For new books, you need to gather the book lists for various courses in advance and make sure you stock up on them prior to the start of the next semester. Buying books in bulk will provide you with a discount. Having a local, high-profile location, whether permanent or temporary, will give you the edge over Amazon.com and other online book sellers because you can put the book right in the customers hand, rather than having them waiting a few days—and students are notorious for waiting for the last second to buy books. Plus if the student drops the class, it is easier to return the book.

Good customer service and various necessary school supplies, such as backpacks, notebooks, and calculators can help you make this a lucrative venture, especially in a city like Boston where there is a glut of colleges. Also, market yourself with some good promotional ideas, like holding in-store social events for new students to meet and greet other students in the area.

SILK FLOWERS
★ $$

Starting a business that wholesales silk flowers to retail specialty stores is a fantastic homebased business enterprise to set in motion. One of the best aspects about starting this type of business venture is that it enables you to work as the middlepers on or agent. Simply source people that make silk flowers and agree to sell their products on a wholesale basis to retailers. Amazingly enough, maintaining yearly sales of $100,000 and a markup of 50 percent will generate a pretax and operating expense income of $33,000 per year. This is excellent for a part-time home-based business that can be established with an initial investment of less than $5,000. The silk flowers can also be sold directly to consumers by establishing a sales kiosk that can be setup at malls and flea markets on weekends.

WEB RESOURCE: www.silkflowers.com
Wholesaler of silk flowers.

INVENTORY LIQUIDATION
★★ $$$$

Every year thousands of retail merchants and corporations across North America go out of business, move, reform, and amalgamate, and often this results in billions of dollars worth of stock and inventory becoming available at bargain basement prices. Purchased properly, this same inventory can sometimes be bought for as little as five cents on the dollar. Later you can resell merchandise for as much as five times the purchase price on a wholesale basis, and as much as ten times on a direct-to-consumers retail basis. A good starting point for purchasing bargain inventory (at least until the business builds a reputation and contact base as a liquidator) is to establish alliances with trustees that deal in commercial bankruptcies. Generally the trustee appointed will either arrange to auction off the inventory assets of clients, put out a tender, or offer to purchase the inventory, which usually goes to the highest bidder on a cash basis. Reselling the inventory can be accomplished in a few ways including selling to retailers on a wholesale basis or selling in smaller quantities to other inventory liquidators. On a direct-to-consumer retailing basis, the inventory can be sold through a company-owned liquidation store or by a well promoted web site. Liquidation sales can also be advertised and held over a few days in short-term rental premises. However, there is a down side to this business, which is purchasing inventory that is difficult to sell regardless of price. This is a very common mistake for first-timers in this industry. Traditionally, the best type of products to purchase under inventory liquidation conditions are power and hand tools, books, music CDs, toys, building materials, and electronics. Larger items, such as display cases and furniture, will help you make some real money, however, you need to sell all such items quickly so as not to need a warehouse to store goods. Always stay clear of products that have a limited shelf life, or that have special warehousing and transportation requirements. Once again, this is the type of business where the ability to profit will greatly depend on numerous of factors such as sales volumes, markups, product costs, and being very good at marketing. Having personally dabbled in this industry in the past, I can assure you that it is possible to make $10,000 per month or more, providing a carefully planned and well-researched approach to the business is executed.

DOLLAR DISCOUNT STORE
★★ $$$$ ⚙

Dollar or discount stores are popping up everywhere across North America, and that can only mean one of two things. Competition is too heavy and there will soon be a thinning process, or dollar store owners are making money and expanding into new geographic areas of the country to capitalize on consumer demand. Given the popularity of dollar stores, and the fact that these stores require careful planning and a large start-up investment, my money is on number two. Competition is stiff, but there seems to be unlimited consumer demand for bargains and discount retail stores. The main objective in the discount retailing industry is two-fold. The first is to source and establish alliances with manufacturers of low-cost products, and the second is that the products have to be of reasonable quality and have a useful purpose. The best products to sell via discount stores fit the following profile:

- Inexpensive items, retailing for less than $5
- Kitchen products, toys, and household products
- Less-expensive versions of popular name brand product.

The trick to making this business work is the old retail adage: location, location, location. People are not typically making a special trip to a dollar-discount store, since the gas prices mean they will spend more in transit than at the store. Therefore, you need to be in locations where there is high traffic volume and have window displays of whatever people will pick up on impulse. For example, have $3.00 pairs of sunglasses in the window on the first sunny day of summer or inexpensive earmuffs clearly displayed for the first days of winter. You need to sell in volume to make this type of store work, so also market your merchandise as ideal party giveaways and have a special "Goody Bag" section.

JANITORIAL SUPPLIES
★★ $$$ 🏠 🕐

Every year companies, government agencies, organizations, educational institutions, and associations spend billions of dollars on janitorial and sanitation supplies such as cleaners, paper products, disposal bags, and janitorial equipment. Starting a janitorial supply business to secure a piece of this very big and financially lucrative pie is not difficult to do. Like many wholesale or middleperson businesses, the key to success is to get out and talk to potential customers. This is a competitive industry and waiting for business to come to you is simply waiting to go out of business. Deal with more than one manufacturer in order to negotiate and secure good pricing. Traditionally, profit margins in the industry are tight and usually products are sold for no more than 10 to 20 percent over costs, so it is critical to build high volume repeat customer accounts.

WEB RESOURCE: www.issa.com
International Sanitary Supply Association.

WICKER AND RATTAN SHOP
★ $$$

Wicker and rattan products have always been popular for use as indoor and outdoor furniture as well as home decoration items, due to their low cost, unique appeal, and ability to last a long time. Starting a wicker and rattan retail business is extremely simple. The first step to establishing the business is to decide on the operating format: a retail store, a cyber store, or a mobile sales kiosk. The next step is to locate a good manufacturing source for the wholesale products. This is best accomplished by utilizing the internet or directories to find manufacturers of wicker and rattan products. When you open for business, practice good business judgment and marketing skills.

WEB RESOURCE: www.wholesalewickerfurniture.com
Links to wicker furniture distributors and manufacturers.

NOSTALGIA STORE
★★★ $$$

Everything old is new again, especially collectibles and novelties from the 1940s, '50s, and '60s. Opening a nostalgia store is a great, and unique, retail business enterprise to set in motion. The profit potential is excellent, consumer demand is proven and growing, and the business can be started on a relatively modest investment of less than $20,000. Of course, starting a retail business does not limit you to only a "bricks-and-mortar" operating format. Nostalgia products can also be retailed or sold on the web, a sales kiosk or booth, by mail order, or a combination of all of these marketing or retailing methods. As with many business ventures, success lies within the ability to attract the customer's attention, not within the method of distribution or sales. Overall, starting a

business retailing nostalgia items is a great new business enterprise, and some items depending on their rarity can be sold at tremendous profit markups.

NEWSSTAND
★★ $$$$ 🖐

In spite of the popularity of internet newsgroups and news web sites, the good old-fashioned corner newsstand remains a fixture in all major cities. Starting a newsstand requires getting in touch with one of the many distributors that carry just about every kind of magazine, publication, and newspaper you can imagine so that building alliances with hundreds of publishers is not required. Additionally, most distributors of publications in every form have a buy-back policy, meaning that once the publication is out of date it is returned and there is no charge levied for it. The keys to a successful and profitable newsstand business are diversification and location. The business should provide customers with product selections such as lottery tickets, cigars, and snack items and if possible, stock a few hard-to-find specialty publications. For example, in New York City, certain newsstands carry Back Stage and other publications for aspiring actors. Get an idea of the local market and decide what special interest publications your customers would want. By having a few specialty publications available you can draw people to your newsstand so you are not relying only on passersby. And speaking of passersby, a high traffic area is very important. Seek out locations where people have time on their hands, such as near train stations, bus stops, hospitals, or at the airport.

WHOLESALER
★★ $$$$

A wholesaler is the link between a manufacturer or producer of a product or service and the retailer or reseller of the product or service. There are many different types of products and services that can be sold on a wholesale basis including food items, computers and software, telecommunications services, and even public utilities. Starting a wholesale business is somewhat more difficult than starting a traditional retailing business. Not only do you have to source companies to buy products and services from, you also have to source companies to sell the same products and services to. As competitive as the wholesaling business currently is, the future does look bright, especially when you consider homebased and cyber based business start-ups are increasing at a record pace. Many of these new business enterprises lack the space required to get their products to market, which means they need the services of a wholesaler with distribution channels, warehousing space, and transportation capabilities. Hint: Wholesale products you know something about and do plenty of research to make sure you are getting good deals from manufacturers.

WEB RESOURCE: www.awmanet.org
American Wholesale Marketers Association.

FLAGS AND FLAG POLES
★ $$ 🚗 🕒

Are you looking for a homebased business opportunity in the retail sector that is interesting, has little in the way of competition, and has the potential to generate excellent revenues and profits? If so, why not consider starting a business the sells and installs flags and flag poles. Seek a manufacturer of the flags and flagpoles, and begin to market, especially in advance of Independence Day . Along with the United States and Canadian flags, you can sell flags of other nations, state flags, and custom-made flags for associations or fraternal groups.

WEB RESOURCE: www.flaginfo.com
National Independent Flag Dealers Association.

BUMPER STICKERS
★★ $$ 🚗 🕒

In spite of the fact that most new cars and trucks have plastic bumpers, bumper stickers remain very much a cultural icon. Taking the following five steps to establishing a bumper sticker wholesaling business can put you on the path to financial freedom and self-employment independence.

1. Hire an artist and design ten really great bumper stickers, or locate a manufacturer and choose ten bumper stickers from their collection.

2. Design a point-of-purchase (POP) display that is unique and colorful, and that can feature the ten bumper stickers and hold 20 of each (total 200

bumper stickers for each POP display).

3. Establish wholesale accounts with retailers to stock the POP in their stores in a visible area. At first some retailers may want to take the POP displays in on a consignment basis until the product is proven popular and profitable.

4. Service and maintain existing wholesale accounts and expand wholesale base to include additional retailers. Also seek to establish accounts with national multi-unit retailers.

5. Implement a web site that features thousands of different bumper stickers that visitors can customize and download for home printing on specialty print paper. (Charge $1 to $2 each for the bumper sticker electronic file transfers.)

PROFIT POTENTIAL: The profit potential for this type of unique business is outstanding once established. Bumper stickers can be printed in mass quantities for less than ten cents each, and retail for as much as $4 each. There is, however, a lot of competition, so the key is to be clever and timely.

SOLAR PRODUCTS
★★★ $$$$ 🖋️

More and more North Americans are starting to realize that we must take care of the environment and look for alternate ways to power our lifestyles. You can sell solar-powered products, such as lights and battery systems, as well as wind-powered generators and solar cell storage systems for big profits. Here are a few suggestions to increase business revenues:

• Hire a direct sales team to call on and solicit business from property developers and contractors for sales and installation of solar-powered products for their new housing developments and construction projects.

• Stock and sell solar-powered products that can be of value to all industries and markets, such as solar chargers for batteries as used on pleasure boats.

• Design and build an elaborate display featuring solar-powered products, and use the display to promote the business and sell the products at trade shows, home and garden shows, and community events.

- Seek out manufacturers of solar-powered products and establish an exclusive sales and distribution contract for their products to be handled by your company. The products can then be sold to national retailers on a wholesale basis.
- Establish alliances with various government agencies that would be willing to provide consumers with product discounts for switching from electric to solar-powered household products. Of course, your business would be the supplier of the products for the energy conservation program.

You can also handle such a business successfully from the internet by drawing people to your web site through a major promotional campaign linked to other energy conservation sites. The money you are not spending to house products in a warehouse can be used for such marketing purposes.

WEB RESOURCE: www.seia.org
Solar Energy Industries Association.

VIDEO GAME STORE
★★ $$$$ 🐸

Video games are big sellers, and hot items include those designed for X-Box, Play Station, GameCube, and other formats. Capturing a portion of the video game sales market is very easy to do, provided you find a good location and promote that you have the latest titles. Selling the game consoles, controllers, and accessories will increase your potential profit margin. You can also add a web site through which you can sell games and offer a newsletter, for which enthusiasts can sign up. The fans of these games love to read up on the latest versions, cheat codes, and anything that has to do with the industry.

WEB RESOURCE: www.regalgames.com
Distributor of video games to the retail trade.

FLORIST SHOP
★★ $$$$ 🐸

There are three important issues to address in order for a florist shop to become successful. The first is your business location, which must be in a high-traffic and highly visible area to increase walk-in business. The second concern is delivery. The business must provide cus-tomers with a fast and efficient delivery service. The third important aspect is making sure to have an ongoing supplier of fresh flowers so that you never run out. Hire a part-time flower arranger and market via your web site to local corporations, hospitals, and other key potential clients as the place where people can purchase exquisite arrangements. This can set you apart from the other local flower shops and provide you with regular clients.

WEB RESOURCE: www.ascfg.org
Association of Specialty Cut Flower Growers.

NEON SIGNS
★★★ $$ 🚗 🕓

The investment needed to start a business that manufactures neon signs could easily exceed $100,000. However, starting a business that designs and sells neon signs, while the manufacturing and installation aspect of the signs are contracted to an existing manufacturer, can be set in motion for less than $10,000, and the potential business profits can easily exceed $100,000 per year. Simply go out into your community and take pictures of businesses that are successful, but could definitely use improvement in terms of their business signage. Next, utilizing computer and design software, design a new neon sign for the business that really promotes them and stands out visually. Once the design is complete, build a presentation including the proposed new sign look and set a meeting with the owner of the business. You will be amazed at how the business progresses from that point on.

WEB RESOURCE: www.nassd.org
The National Association of Sign Supply Distributors.

CIGAR SALES
★★ $$+ 🪧

Across the United States millions of dollars' worth of cigars are sold monthly and some of these cigars sell for $250 or more each. Securing just a small portion of this very lucrative market has the potential to make you rich. Once you have secured a wholesale source for purchasing cigars, here are a few ways to retail them for a profit:

- Employ direct sales teams remunerated by way of commission based on their sales.

- Initiate a direct mail and e-mail campaign aimed at corporations to purchase the cigars to give to valued clients and business associates as gifts.
- Open a cigar shop in a small storefront in a mall or a busy downtown location.

SEASONAL GARDEN CENTER
★★ $$$ 🕐 🌐

A seasonal garden center selling trees, shrubs, flowers, and topsoil can return as much as $30,000 in profits in only a three- or four-month operating season. The main requirements, in terms of equipment, will be to purchase or rent portable fencing that can be installed around the perimeter of the garden center. A polyvinyl tent or dome may also have to be purchased or rented to act as shelter for the more delicate plants and as the retail outlet. The inventory can be purchased from various greenhouse suppliers on a wholesale basis, and generally the plants, flowers, and shrubs are marked up by at least 100 to 200 percent. The key to success for operating this type of seasonal retailing business is location. You need a visible location in a high-traffic area of the community.

LUGGAGE SHOP
★ $$$$

Starting a specialty retail business that sells travel luggage and bags, as well as purses, wallets, and briefcases, is a fantastic business venture to start. There are thousands of manufacturers of travel bags and luggage worldwide, so finding a wholesale product source will not be difficult. Additionally, be sure to establish a web site that features the travel gear for online shoppers. Once again, look for the right location. If you are carrying designer names, you can opt for a high-end mall. If not, look for a busy location near clothing stores, travel agencies, and similar storefronts.

WEB RESOURCE: www.luggagedealers.com
The American Luggage Dealers Association.

VACUUM CLEANER SALES
★★ $$$

A vacuum cleaner sales and repair business is a terrific small business venture to put into action, as the business and consumer demand for the product has been proven for many decades. Like any new retail business venture, store location will top the list of special considerations for this new venture, as well as local competition, potential market growth, and local labor force for the vacuum repair aspect of the business if you do not possess this ability. It will be of great importance to the success of the business to establish an exclusive sales, service, and distribution agreement with a manufacturer of vacuum cleaners, as this is the only way to compete in a competitive market, keep wholesale product costs low, and build brand-name recognition. Additionally, be sure to also provide built-in vacuum cleaner sales both to residential clients, as well as to commercial customers such as property developers and construction companies. Expanding the product line to include built-in vacuums can greatly increase business revenues and profits.

DISCOUNT TOOLS
★★ $$$$ 🕐

Tools are one of those things that some people can never have enough of, regardless of how many of them they ever get put to use. Starting a retail business that specializes in selling discount tools is an absolutely fabulous business enterprise to initiate. The start-up investment is relatively low, and the profit potential is outstanding. The best operating format for this type of retailing venture is to hold two or three discount tools sales per month that are very well advertised and promoted in the community where the sales will take place. Good locations for the sales include temporarily renting an empty store in a mall for the week of the sale or having the sale within a large retail store such as a grocery store. There are many excellent locations in every city or community; the key is to secure the best locations in the busiest areas. The tools can be purchased from foreign manufacturers extremely cheaply, especially if the tools are being discontinued or have small flaws. The best types of tools to sell and that have the highest profit margins are tools that retail for less than $50, are small and easy to ship and package, and that are unique.

ATHLETIC SHOES
★★ $$$$

Good-quality sports shoes can cost as much as $200 per pair, which means opening such a store selling athletic footwear is a great retail business. However, since not all families can afford the top of the line models, or want to spend that much on shoes, you should make sure to have a wide range of options including discount footwear available with some incentives and inexpensive giveaway items so that the child or teen who ends up with a $30 pair or sneakers instead of a $150 pair will also feel good. Get in touch with the hottest trends and find inexpensive items that you can use as promotional giveaways.

The question is not will people buy good-quality brand-name sports footwear at discounted prices. That is a given. The real question is how do you purchase the sports footwear at low enough discount prices that will still let you make a profit reselling them? The answer is that you do a lot of research and establish alliances and contacts in this industry, worldwide if necessary. You have to seek out opportunities to purchase manufacturers' seconds, discontinued product lines, and liquidation inventory from out-of-business retailers and wholesalers seeking to sell older stock. Also, seek to expand the product line by also providing customers discounted sportswear and sporting equipment to increase business revenues and profits.

WEB RESOURCE: www.nsra.org
National Shoe Retailers Association.

PINBALL MACHINES
★★ $$ 🏠 🕑

How do you make money selling pinball machines? You buy them at bargain prices and resell them for a profit. Older style pinball machines from the 1960s and '70s are currently riding a wave of popularity, as collectors from around the globe vie to build the ultimate collection of arcade pinball machines. There are really two aspects to the business; the first being the ability to locate the pinball machines, and the second aspect is locating the collectors who are looking to purchase the pinball machines. Locating the pinball machines will take some legwork and time searching classified sections of newspapers, garage sales, flea markets, and the internet. In terms of locating purchasers for the pinball machine, look no further than the web. You can develop a web site featuring the pinball machines for sale, or post advertisements in the various newsgroups. Another option is to market

the old pinball machines to restaurants looking to enhance their ambiance with some fun nostalgia and to theater and production companies doing films shot in prior decades.

COINS AND STAMPS
★ $$$$

Opening a retail store that buys, sells, and trades collectable coins and stamps is a good business venture for the hobbyist coin and stamp collector to get going. The store does not need a great amount of square footage, as the inventory is compact. As a method to reduce start-up and operating costs, consider a joint venture with another retailer. Good matches for this type of shared retail space include pawnshops, comic book retailers, and memorabilia stores. As is the case with any retail venture, the goal is to buy low and sell high, thus you must possess strong negotiation skills and have experience identifying the condition and value of coins and stamps.

MILITARY COLLECTIBLES
★ $$ 🏠 🕑

Purchasing military collectible items at bargain basement prices and reselling them to serious collectors for a profit is a fantastic way to earn a part-time business income. Devoting time to scouring flea markets, garage sales, and classified newspaper advertisements is the first step to finding military collectibles that can be purchased for the right price. Once you have assembled an inventory, there are various methods to resell these items, including display advertisements in specialty collectors' publications, online auction services, and upscale flea markets. Additionally, there are books and guides available that list the high-low value of every imaginable military collectable item. I suggest that a few of these guides be purchased as they are an invaluable source of information and pricing details. Worldwide there are millions of people who collect military items such as helmets, guns, knives, and medals as a hobby and for profit. You can capitalize on this fact and earn money by posting a web site that is devoted to bringing collectors of military items together to buy, sell, and trade. The site can feature a chat room for visitors to exchange information about military collectibles as well as guides that list the value of these items ranked by condition. In terms of creating a revenue stream, your options include:

- Developing a military collectibles auction service within the site
- Charging collectors a fee to post items for sale within the classifieds section of the site
- Selling banner advertising space to companies that want exposure in this type of site
- Selling replicas of military collectibles and other items, such as print-format valuation guides.

GLAZIERS' SUPPLIES
★ $$$ 🚗 🕐

Setting up to wholesale glaziers' supplies from home is a terrific niche-retailing enterprise to get going. You supply local glass shops, stained-glass retailers, and framing stores with products and supplies used in the glazing industry, like specialty glass, glasscutters, grinders, and glass drill bits. This type of unique business venture is ideally suited to be established in a smaller community that is currently not being serviced by a large wholesaler. Additionally, like many specialty products you will be amazed at the profit margins there are in these types of glaziers' products. To get started, simply book appointments with local glass shops and other businesses that rely on these types of supplies and present your product line and prices. Also be sure to ask these business owners what types of products you could carry that they would purchase on a regular basis.

BINGO SUPPLIES
★ $$ 🚗 🕐

Almost every major city across North America has a minimum of 10 to 20 bingo centers operating at any one time. You can start your own business selling bingo supplies to these bingo centers as well as to thousands of regular bingo players. This business venture can easily be operated from home on a part-time basis. Locating manufacturers and distributors of wholesale bingo supplies is as easy as harnessing the power of the internet for research purposes. This type of business is not likely to make you rich, however, once established there should be no problem in generating a few extra hundred dollars in profits each month.

GOVERNMENT SURPLUS
★★ $$ 🚗 🕐

Purchasing secondhand government products and surplus equipment for pennies on the dollar of the original value, and reselling these items to consumers at marked-up prices can make you rich. Every year in the United States, various levels of government offices and agencies sell off used equipment such as fleet vehicles, computer hardware, and office equipment. This surplus equipment is typically sold by way of auction or through a tender process, and providing these surplus items can be purchased at the right price, they can often be resold to consumers for two or three times what you paid the government for them. Using the internet, you can locate these government surplus sales and auctions and begin to purchase surplus equipment. Likewise, the internet can also be used as a powerful marketing tool for reselling these same surplus items by posting classified ads, listing the items with online auction services, and placing notices in newsgroup forums.

HYDROPONICS EQUIPMENT
★★ $$ 🚗 🕐

Indoor hydroponics gardening equipment is becoming increasingly popular, especially in densely populated urban centers where green space for gardening is a luxury that not many can afford. Hydroponics gardening equipment and supplies can be sold right from home. Get started by arranging a dealership or representative agreement with one or more of the hundreds of manufacturers of this type of equipment. Place advertisements promoting your products in your local newspaper, as well as joining community gardening clubs to network for business.

WOODCRAFTS
★★ $ 🕐

If you love to sell, then this is the right low-investment business opportunity for you to start. Most woodcrafts are sold via craft shows and flea market, and the selling aspect is what keeps many people that produce beautiful woodcraft items from ever realizing a profit from their work. If you have sales ability and access to fine woodcrafters, we have a match made in heaven. Find woodcraft artists and use your marketing and sales abilities to promote and sell their products. In exchange for providing this valuable service, charge a 25 percent commission on all products sold. You will be responsible for the costs associated with renting booth space at these shows. However, maintaining sales of $2,000 per show and paying an average booth rent of $100 will still leave you a profit of $400 for a weekend's work.

WEB RESOURCE: www.woodcraft.com
All about woodcrafts and woodcrafters.

GUN SHOP
★★ $$$$ 🔨

In spite of the fact that gun ownership is becoming increasingly restrictive due to government legislation in both the United States and Canada, opening and operating a retail business that buys, sells, and trades guns still has the potential to be profitable. In addition to gun sales you can also sell ammunition and hunting-related products as well as offer a gun repair service. Promote the business by establishing alliances with gun clubs and shooting ranges as well as with firearm instructors, as these clubs and individuals can refer your business to others. Starting this type of retail business will require a substantial investment and you will also have to clear a few legal hurdles before you can open.

LOTTERY TICKET KIOSK
★★ $$$+ 🔨

Providing you can obtain a lottery ticket vendor's permit or state licensing, then operating a lottery kiosk can be very profitable. Ideally the kiosk will be located in a high-traffic area of the community such as a mall, market, or transportation station. The investment needed to start this sort of retail business will be in the range of $15,000 to $20,000, not including the cost of the kiosk. If possible, try to find a location with a kiosk for rent, due to the fact that having a kiosk custom designed and built for the business will set you back an additional $15,000.

LIGHTING SHOP
★★ $$$$

Upgrading or replacing interior light fixtures has become a very popular home improvement project for many homeowners, simply due to the fact that this type of improvement is relatively inexpensive and can have a beneficial impact on the appearance of their homes. Starting a business that sells interior and exterior lighting products is a wise choice for a new business enterprise. This sort of retail operation does not require a lot of floor space and as a method to reduce start-up costs you may even consider forming a joint venture with an established retailer in your community such as a furniture, or paint or wallpaper store. Be sure to initiate a direct-mail marketing campaign aimed at architects, homebuilders, and interior designers, as they can also become customers or refer their customers to your store. You can also market lighting products to small businesses and offices in your area through brochures and a concerted marketing campaign.

WEB RESOURCE: www.wholesalelightingstore.com
One of many lighting wholesalers.

WINE STORE
★★ $$$$ 🔨

Retailing wine can be extremely profitable, and this type of business can even be operated from a well-positioned booth located in a mall or market. In the right location, walk-in customers will keep you busy selling lots of wine. But as a method to bolster sales and profits, be sure to establish alliances with event and wedding planners, catering companies, and business clubs and associations as they can become a great source of repeat business. Like any retail business, seek a competitive advantage, meaning offer your customers something the competition does not, such as phone-in orders with free delivery or maybe a weekly wine tasting night. Also consider a newsletter (or e-newsletter) that talks about the latest wines you will be carrying or vineyards in the area, if there are any, as wine enthusiasts enjoy reading about their passion. The ability to separate your business from the competition can be the difference between business success or business failure.

WEB RESOURCE: www.wswa.org
Wine and Spirit Wholesalers of America.

SPECIALTY BUILDING PRODUCTS
★★ $$+ 🔨 🕐

Based on price, quantity, or selection it is nearly impossible to compete against the big retailers of building products. However, on a smaller scale and with specialization, you can sell building products and prosper. The key to success is to seek out a building product that is specialized within the industry or marketplace. These types of specialty products can range from a new type of slip-resistant flooring to a fireproof house siding. These sorts of building products are out there, but you have to be prepared to invest a lot of time and a little bit of money to find them. Get started researching by harnessing the power of the internet and by attending home improvement trade shows and building product trade shows.

LINEN AND BEDDING SHOP
★★ $$$$ ⊕

Retailing towels, bedding accessories, sheets, and table linens can be extremely profitable, especially when you consider that these products are routinely marked up nearly 100 percent for retail sales. However, like any retail operation, success comes to those operators with an eye for detail and a habit for practicing sound business judgment, and a linen shop is no exception to the rule. Considerations prior to opening will include your business location, local competition, methods of advertising and promotion, and all management aspects including finances, employees, and inventory. Start-up costs for this type of business are reasonable. The bulk of available start-up capital can be used for purchasing moneymaking inventory, and marketing your business.

WEB RESOURCE: www.wswa.org.
Wholesalers of linens and bedding supplies.

KITCHEN AND BATH ACCESSORIES
★★★ $$$$ ⊕

Kitchen and bath accessories shops have become extremely popular in the past decade and are springing up in every city from coast to coast. Like many specialty retailing businesses, a kitchen and bath boutique has the potential to be profitable as it is not uncommon for owners of these businesses to resell their goods for two or three times more than the wholesale costs. In addition to walk-in customers, be sure to promote the store to interior decorators, architects, and contractors, as they can be both an excellent source for business and will generate referrals via word-of-mouth advertising. Stock items that

are commonly found in today's kitchens and bathrooms such as towel racks and stands, spice holders, specialty soaps, custom cabinet hardware, and more. Ideally, the store will be located in a high-traffic area of the community, such as a mall, strip mall, or public market. Cross promotions and advertising campaigns with kitchen and bath contractors can also be used as a terrific promotional and marketing method. In the past decade, kitchen and bathroom renovations have continually ranked as the first and second most popular home improvement projects carried out by homeowners. The future for this type of retail enterprise can best be described as a growth market with huge upside potential.

FLOORING CENTER
★★ $$$$

In 1999, flooring replacements ranked eighth as the most popular home improvement renovation carried out by homeowners in the United States, generating an estimated ten billion dollars in sales. A tremendous opportunity exists to capitalize on this enormous market by opening a retail flooring center that stocks, sells, and installs a wide range of flooring products, including carpets, area rugs, ceramic tiles, hardwoods, laminates, cork, and vinyl. Flooring installations can be contracted to qualified installers on a subcontract basis, and as a method to bolster sales you can hire flooring sales consultants to work on a commission basis. Do not rely strictly on walk-in store traffic; display your flooring products and services at home improvement trade shows and by setting appointments with new home contractors and architects to present the flooring products and installation services you provide. Be sure to build alliances with property management firms of both residential and commercial buildings. On average, flooring is replaced every 10 to 15 years and property managers and interior decorators can be an excellent work and referral source.

WEB RESOURCE: www.woodfloors.org
National Wood Flooring Association.

GREETING CARD STORE
★★ $$$ ⊕

In spite of the increasing popularity of electronic or e-mail greeting cards, there are still more than two billion paper and printed greeting cards sold annually in the United States and Canada, generating some six billion dollars in sales revenues. Securing just a small fraction of this very lucrative market can make you rich. While Hallmark accounts for a large piece of this industry, you can step in with a retail location and cater to a local community with clever and well-designed cards for all occasions. Greeting cards can be purchased in bulk on a wholesale basis very inexpensively. It is not uncommon to retail the cards for two or three times more than wholesale cost. If you can find lesser-known card lines, or even some local artists, you can build a reputation for having more than just the standard cards available. You can also carry paper plates, balloons, and other party related items.

WEB RESOURCE: www.greetingcard.org
The Greeting Card Association.

BATTERY KIOSK
★★ $$$$ ⊕

The wave of the future for manufactured electronic goods is wireless, and manufacturers have but one option to power these products: batteries. Telephones, computers, radios, and more—consumers want electronic goods that are portable and that they can use just about anywhere. For the innovative entrepreneur, an outstanding business opportunity awaits by starting a business that specializes in retailing batteries for consumer electronics products. This type of specialty retailing is ideal for kiosk sales. Get started by having a kiosk professionally designed and constructed and by securing a high-traffic location for the kiosk in a mall or public market. The types of batteries that you can stock and sell are almost unlimited and include batteries for cellular telephones, laptop computers, wristwatches, camcorders, and can even include highly specialized items such as wheelchair and motorcycle batteries. In addition to retailing the batteries from a kiosk location, also be sure to market your products via the internet, especially for the more highly specialized batteries. Securing multiple wholesale sources for the batteries will not prove difficult, as there are thousands of battery manufacturers and distributors worldwide, and harnessing the power of the internet for research purposes is a good starting point. The start-up

costs for this venture will be high, but the profit potential is fantastic. It is not uncommon for batteries to be marked up by 200 percent or more for retail sales.

WEB RESOURCE: www.batteryweb.com
Directory service listing battery manufacturers, industry information, and links.

CONVENIENCE STORE
★★ $$$$ ⊕

In spite of the rising popularity of internet shopping combined with home delivery of grocery and convenience items, starting and operating a "mini convenience store" is still a good business venture that has the potential to generate respectable profits. The name suggests it all. In order to succeed in this segment of the highly competitive retail industry, the store must be convenient. This means an easily accessible and highly visible business location, well stocked with the most popular convenience products, and fast and friendly service. You also need to be able to have extended hours for convenience, even 24/7 if possible, with trustworthy sales help. Remember, if a customer's shopping experience at the store is not convenient then there will not be any repeat business. Stock up on all of the food staples such as milk, eggs and bread. Then add snack items, soda, and paper goods including napkins, paper towels, and toilet paper. You also want to include aspirin or similar over-the-counter health related items, plus lottery tickets, tobacco products, newspapers, magazines, and sundry items like inexpensive sunglasses and tan lotion in a beach area. Some convenience stores offer photocopying, postal stamps, and even fresh-cut flowers for sale on a daily basis. Once again, business location is the key to success. The business must be located with easy street access and good parking, or alternately in an area of heavy foot traffic like a mall, transportation terminal, or office district. Make sure to have tight security measures in place, especially if you are open at all hours. If you sell beer, make sure to I.D. anyone who could be underage. You could jeopardize your business by selling alcohol to minors, and convenience store owners have learned this by paying heavy fines and/or spending a couple of nights in jail.

WEB RESOURCE: www.nasonline.com
National Association of Convenience Stores.

USED APPLIANCE SALES
★★ $$$ 🚗 🕐

A tidy profit can be earned by selling used appliances such as refrigerators, stoves, washers, and dryers, right from a homebased location. Get started by building a resource library of appliance models, manufacturers, and retail selling prices when new. This type of resource library will prove invaluable when buying secondhand appliances for resale purposes. To secure an initial inventory of used appliances to sell, begin by attending auction sales, garage and estate sales, and scanning your local classified newspaper ads for good used appliances at bargain basement prices. Your target market for resale will include people on a budget, owners of secondary homes, and owners of residential rental and apartment properties. Some basic knowledge of home appliance repair will come in handy, as well as a heavy-duty moving dolly and a pickup truck or utility trailer. Aim to maintain a 50 percent markup on all appliances sold and to generate gross annual sales of $50,000 and this simple part-time homebased business will net $15,000 per year.

COSTUME JEWELRY
★★ $$ 🕐 🌐

Billions of dollars worth of non-precious gem and costume jewelry is sold annually in the United States, and staking your claim in this very lucrative industry may be easier than you think. The jewelry can be sold from a kiosk located in a mall, or by renting a booth at a weekend flea market or fair. You can also sell the jewelry by employing independent sales contractors to host home shopping parties. Use the internet to locate wholesale sources and manufacturers and distributors of jewelry items. Additional items that are also very profitable and that can be sold from the same booth or kiosk include watches, sunglasses, and small gift items. It is not uncommon for non-precious jewelry items to be marked up by 100 percent or more for retail sales, making this a potentially very profitable business to operate even on a part-time basis.

AIR AND WATER FILTRATION SYSTEMS
★★★ $$ 🚗 🕐 ✎

Cash in on the clean water and air phenomenon by starting a business that sells and installs air and water fil-

tration systems. The objective for operating this business is crystal clear: Buy your air and water filter products and systems on a wholesale basis and resell them for a profit. Installations will not prove difficult as most air filtering devices are simple plug-in models, and water filters are generally installed inline. Inline refers to a quick attachment of the water filter to an existing water line, whether at the intake source into the home or business or under the sink counter. There are many marketing methods that can be employed to sell the air and water filters. You can display your products at trade shows and in malls to collect qualified sales leads, use a direct mail campaign, and/or have a web site that illustrates the benefits of such systems. Be forewarned this is a very competitive industry and to succeed will require careful planning and clever marketing. However, with that said, air and water pollution is on the rise and the long term prognosis for this industry can only be described as excellent.

WEB RESOURCE: www.ecomall.com
Directory service listing manufacturers and distributors of air and water filtering systems and products.

WEB RESOURCE: www.waterfiltercomparisons.net
A very good starting point for research.

COMMUNICATIONS STORE
★★ $$$$ 🌐

Stake your claim in the multibillion-dollar communications industry by opening a communications store. Stock and sell items such as residential and business telephone systems, answering machines, fax machines, Palm Pilots, cell phones, pagers and intercoms, plus numerous accessories such as cell phone chargers, hand-free headsets, cases, pouches, and so on. The communications industry is very competitive. However, with careful planning, good customer service, clever marketing, and the latest in high-tech communications items, you can earn a six-figure yearly income owning and operating such a communications store. Make sure to have a very good location.

COPY CENTER
★★ $$$$ 🌐

Copy centers typically provide customers with a wide range of services, including both color and black and white photocopying, fax service, laminating, booklet and report binding, and small-run print jobs of business cards, fliers, and business presentations. The key requirements for success in this business are unquestionably location and an understanding of the needs of each and every customer. Customer service and fair pricing can make or break you. The copy center must be located in a highly visible area with excellent parking facilities and/or lots of walk-by foot traffic. As a method to reduce start-up costs, as this type of equipment is extremely expensive, you may want to consider purchasing secondhand equipment or leasing new equipment. The industry is competitive and start-up costs are high, but the profit potential is outstanding, and it is not uncommon for owners of copy centers to earn a six-figure income.

MODEL BOATS
★ $$

Large and elaborate models of sailing schooners and war destroyers are highly sought after by individual collectors and by professionals for office decorations. Starting a business that sells completed model boats is a fantastic new moneymaking enterprise. Don't worry that you do not have the skills to build the model boats, as there are thousands of people who do, and seeking out only a handful of these hobby model boat builders will keep your inventory levels high. As important as the model boat is to the success of the business, of equal importance is the way in which the model boat is displayed. The display cases should be made of clear glass to properly present the model boats, and in the case of larger models it should be tempered safety glass, especially if the finished model will be displayed in an office or public area. The profit potential is outstanding for this type of unique business, as model boats can draw prices of $2,500 each or more.

WEB RESOURCE: www.modelboat.com
Distributor of model boat kits and tools.

CANDLES
★★ $$

Candles serve many purposes, whether they are the backdrop for a romantic evening, used to lower electric bills, serve as backups for blackouts, mask less pleasant aromas, relax the soul in aromatherapy, or are an integral part of a spiritual occasion. You can make candles to sell, or buy them from wholesalers or creative candle makers and mark them up generously. Selling candles can be a homebased business (with good marketing and a web site), or a business you can run from a small shop or a booth at a mall. In addition to selling candles, you can make money selling candle-making supplies including kits, molds, waxes and dyes. Most of this can be sold, especially the candles, at 100% mark up. Candleholders can also bring in a lot more money if you hook up with some original crafts artists.

WEB RESOURCE: www.onestopcandle.com
A good starting point to research and purchase goods.

COSMETICS AND BEAUTY SUPPLIES
★★★★ $$$

The cosmetics industry is huge, and based on the seemingly endless supply of powders, perfumes, and products designed to enhance personal beauty, there is a big business opportunity. From Calvin Klein to Brittany Spears to Mary Kate and Ashley Olsen, there are numerous popular name-brand perfumes as well as lipgloss, nail polish, and much more to market. As is typically the case, you need to study up on the latest products and maintain your inventory. Finding a prime location for walk-in business is important and doing make-up applications, makeovers, and even having parties featuring your latest line of products is to your advantage. There is a good markup and a very wide range of products in the cosmetic business, opening the door to kids-looking-for-something inexpensive to high-end customers. The more you can tailor your business to accommodate the diversity of the market, the more likely you will do very well. Consider a small shop or even a booth at a mall for starting out and make sure you have a web site for taking additional orders.

WEB RESOURCE:
http://databases.cosmeticsbusiness.com/web
A major database of cosmetics manufacturers.

LADIES SHOES
★★★ $$$$

Pumps, sandals, flats, heels, boots—there are plenty of options when it comes to women's shoes and going into this business can be very profitable. A good location is a starting point, followed by quality sales help and first-rate customer service. As is the case with many retail businesses, you are only as good as your inventory, so make sure to stock the latest styles and keep a close eye on your competition, because this is a very competitive market. Carrying hard-to-get sizes and less commonly found lines can give you a competitive edge. A shoe store can cost anywhere from $7,500 to $475,000 to open depending on the location and the inventory, which are the two biggest variables. If you can become a representative for a manufacturer, you can cut these costs out completely, by selling from a web site or a booth at a mall, street fair, or other location. The choice depends on whether you want to get started by going full-force with backers and a storefront or on a smaller scale.

RETAIL CONSULTANT
★★★ $ 🏠 🕒

Where to open a store, how to position the merchandise in the store, how much inventory to stock, how to build a killer web site, how to evaluate the competition and gain a competitive edge, how to keep a retail location secure, and how to price your goods are all questions that need to be answered whenever someone is starting a retail business. If you have a background in retail and have successfully gone this route before, you can pass your wisdom on to new entrepreneurs by becoming a retail specialist, a.k.a a retail consultant. It is estimated that some 44% of retail purchases are no longer made in a typical "store." Therefore, it is up to you to you to help the retail business owner understand the options and determine whether a brick and mortar storefront is the best route in the modern age of electronic shopping and catalogs. To start such a service business within the retail industry, you need to build a proven track record, which might mean some free consultation at first to prove that your methods (and you had better have some methodology up your sleeve) will work. Even if you have been knee deep in the retail world for several years, it is highly advisable to put due diligence at the top of your To Do list prior to sending out your marketing materials. The industry changes quickly and you need to know how to advise retail clients and provide practical solutions that can be profitably implemented and sustained. In many

cases, retail consultants specialize in certain areas, which may be wise since selling shoes and selling houseboats are very different retail businesses. Market yourself to any new store owners as well as existing store owners and managers. Some will toss you card, sure that they know it all, while others will realize how difficult it is to go it alone today and that they could use your help.

WEB RESOURCE: www.nrf.com
National Retail Association

NOVELTY SLIPPERS
★★ $$ 🏠 🕒

Why not cash in on the new fad of funny footwear? A company called "Fun Feet" launched a line of comfy cushioned novelty slippers that are sold either through kiosks or purchased at wholesale prices and resold at stores, fairs, festivals or markets. In fact, if you can stage a few casual parties at neighbors' homes serving desserts and featuring the fun slippers, you are likely to make some sales while in your bathrobe. Other novelty slipper companies are also marketing their footwear and you can certainly shop around. However you get started, this is an excellent part-time, fun business that you can launch for less than $10,000 and make money.

WEB RESOURCE: www.relaxus.com/funfeet.php
The fun feet line of slippers.

CELL PHONE ACCESSORIES
★★★ $$$$ 🕒

The cell phone business is a multi-billion dollar industry dominated by several top players. While you cannot compete with Verizon and some of the big guns, you can certainly do very well selling the accessories from a booth at a mall or fair, a small shop, a shared space with another retailer, and/or from a web site. Car adapters, headsets, cell phone covers, chargers, holsters, and external antennas are among the variety of items you can have in stock. Ring tones can also be very popular from your web site, providing you have permission to market them. Look for wholesalers with the latest, trendiest items to maintain a marketable inventory.

WEB RESOURCE: www.easyaccessories.com
Links to many cell phone manufacturers.

WIRELESS STORE
★★★★ $$$$ 🔧

It's much more than phones and pagers today—wireless routers and WiFi technology is everywhere. You can cash in on the growing technology by handling everything wireless in one location. Sirius radio, satellite network equipment, laptops, Bluetooth products and more are all possibilities once you scale the learning curve and bring your wireless I.Q. up to processing speed. You can start from a small 1,200 square foot storefront location, a web location, or both, maintaining enough inventory to get you started and buying more as you sell. You can also set up a mall kiosk to get off the ground. Make sure you are knowledgeable and can answer customer questions. Secure your premises carefully, since laptops sometimes tend to walk away. For $75,000 you can launch this business with a sufficient inventory, money to cover your rent in the lean months, and some funding left over for operating cash and marketing. A high profile location is advantageous since many consumers don't know they need the latest in wireless technology until they see it.

WEB RESOURCE: www.intertangent.com/023346/ Wireless_Manufacturers/RFID
Wireless resource directory

AUDIO VISUAL TECHNOLOGY
★★ $$$$

A/V products are a major source of business in North America and around the world. With this in mind, you have the starting point for a potentially very successful business venture. First, seek out manufacturers, many of whom are overseas in Asian countries and throughout the world. Establish relationships and do a great deal of research to make sure you know the various components available in the current market. Then, determine where you will be selling and what your demographic market will want. Are you a high-end retailer, or are you carrying a wide variety to meet different pricing demands? Projectors, media players, screens, A/V carts, and connecting cables should all be part of your inventory whether you choose to open a storefront, operate online, or through mail order catalogs, or handle sales with a combination of the three. You should include customization, installation, and even brief tutorials if necessary. Market your products to businesses as well as to universities and schools. Keep an eye on the competition (this is a very competitive business) so you will be able to price accordingly and seek out opportunities to create package deals. Rather than just selling, position yourself as a consultant helping to personally assess the needs of the clients and provide them with answers, and you can make significantly more money. To give you an idea of the potential for such a business venture, one Michigan based AV "solutions" provider (a.k.a. retailer) started in 2003 with an initial $2 million. In 2005, the company did nearly $26 million in sales. If you started with $200,000 and a smaller business with less inventory, at the same rate of return you could see sales of 2.6 million in less than two years. Of course, you need to be on top of what is going on in the industry and what leading businesses need and be prepared to meet their demands.

GLASS SHOP
★ $$$$

Windows, tabletops, and mirrors—the need for glass is everywhere. That's why a glass shop in your community is a good business to start. Operating this kind of specialty business requires experience in glass cutting and glass installation techniques, or glazing; or a person with these skills, called a glazier. Providing you or your staff possess this type of work experience and ability, then opening a glass shop can be a very profitable business to own. There are a great many types of glass installations the business could focus on, and you may want to specialize in one or two specific areas, such as custom glass table tops, or only installing construction equipment glass, such as windshields. This business venture can be costly to establish, as you will also want to have also an inventory of glassware and various products to sell. However, once you have identified the market that you will be catering to, the business can easily generate profits that can exceed $75,000 per year.

WEB RESOURCE: www.gwiweb.com
Directory of wholesale glass and glazier supplies.

TIN SHOP
★★ $$$$

The demand for custom-manufactured tin flashings and products is enormous, and starting a tin shop that fabricates these items can put you on the road to financial freedom. The business can be launched right from a basement or garage workshop and only requires a minimal amount of equipment such as a metal break, tin sheers and a spot welder. Of course, the main requirement for this type of new business venture is that you have to be a tinsmith or have a lot of experience working with tin and various metals. Establishing alliances with roofing and heating companies will supply you with all the work that you need, as these types of construction trades often require custom manufactured tin flashings and products. You can also market tin products to a wider consumer market.

HOBBY SHOP
★ $$$$

Model trains, puzzles, and games of all sorts are big business, and launching a hobby shop retail business can put you on the path to financial freedom. Hobby shops can be operated from a retail storefront or online via your own web site. The possibilities are endless. However, one thing is for sure—the markups added onto these types of products are enormous. The investment required to start a hobby shop will greatly depend on the way in which the business is set up. Likewise, these same variables will also determine your monthly overhead operating costs. Before setting out to start such a venture, familiarize yourself with as many popular hobbies as you can.

LONG-LIFE LIGHT BULBS
★★★★ $$

Do you want to potentially earn a six-figure yearly income from owning and operating your own home-based business? If so, consider starting a business that specializes in selling and installing long-life light bulbs for commercial and residential applications. Long-life light bulbs not only last as much as ten times longer than traditional light bulbs, but they also can consume less than half the energy requirements to run than a standard light bulb. That's good news considering the skyrocketing cost of electricity. These two facts make for a very interesting business opportunity. If you can show home and business owners that they can save utility costs by installing a light bulb that uses less energy and lasts

longer than a standard light bulb, then this is the basis of the business making money. There are many manufacturers of long-life light bulbs, so securing a wholesale source will not be difficult. The only tools required to install the light bulbs will be a couple of ladders and a few basic hand tools to remove light covers. Look to market the light bulbs to potential customers who have the most to gain in terms of cost savings. Good candidates will include retail chain stores, government agencies, school boards, residential strata corporations, property management firms, office buildings, and community and recreational centers.

WEB RESOURCE: www.buylighting.com
Distributor of wholesale light bulbs.

ICE SUPPLY
★★ $$$

There are many good reasons to start an ice supply business. Consider some of the following:

- No government regulations or certifications required.
- Relatively low initial business start-up investment required with a fast return on your investment.
- Proven consumer demand and flexible business hours.
- Can be operated from a homebased location on a full- or part-time basis.
- No special business skills needed to run the business and excellent growth potential.

Starting an ice supply business is a great choice for a new business venture that has limited downside and many benefits. Once the ice has been produced and packaged, there are many options available to market the product, including:

- Selling the ice via ice vending machines located throughout a community.
- Selling the ice to retailers such as gas stations, convenience stores, and food markets on a wholesale basis.
- Selling the ice directly to consumers by establishing the business in a busy beach tourist area.

WEB RESOURCE: www.machineice.com
Distributor of ice-making machinery and supplies.

KNIFE KIOSK
★ $$$$

Retailing products from a kiosk located in a mall, or even within a larger retail store, is a terrific way to keep operating overheads to a minimum, thus increasing the profit potential of the business venture. A great product to sell from a kiosk-based location is a specialty knife. The kiosk can stock and sell all type of knives such as ones used in hunting and fishing, custom kitchen knives, wood carvers knives, and knives for collectors. Additionally, to increase revenues and profits, you can also provide a knife and scissors sharpening service at the kiosk. Due to the unique nature of the product and business, product markups of 100 percent or more are not out of line and are not uncommon in this type of retailing.

ROSES
★ $$

Roses can be purchased in bulk on a wholesale basis for as little as $10 per dozen, and can retail for as much as $5 each or $50 per dozen. Selling the roses is very easy to do. You need only to have a license and set up stands from which to sell. Ideal locations for selling the roses include outside restaurants, movie theaters, and bus and train stations. You can also sell through vendors inside high-end restaurants and nightclubs, providing permission can be obtained by the establishments and vendor licenses are procured. The key to making this business work is having the suppliers who can provide you with roses on a daily basis. Make sure to secure a number of growers before starting such a business. One you get started, there is a tremendous markup on roses, especially around Valentine's Day and Mother's Day.

WEB RESOURCE: www.flowersource.net
Directory service listing growers and distributors of flowers.

SHOWER CURTAINS
★★ $$$

Every home has one shower, or more, depending on how many full bathrooms there are. Add shower curtain liners and bathmats to your business and you can make very good money from showers without even getting wet.

Check out a number of manufacturers and look for affordable and unique products from reliable vendors. Most products allow for a good markup and are easy to ship if you have an online presence along with a small shop or kiosk. Market yourself through advertising to consumers and at home shows. Also consider marketing your products to hotels where you can sell in bulk, still making money on the markup.

WEB RESOURCE: www.teonline.com/home-furnishings/bathroom-furnishings/shower-curtains.html.
Listings of manufacturers of shower curtains and other bathroom products.

BOBBLE HEAD DOLLS
★★ $$$

Yes, bobble head dolls. While this may or may not be a full-time endeavor, these little wobbly-headed collectibles are very popular and selling them from street fairs, mall kiosks, catalogs, by mail order, and/or through a web site can bring in some tidy profits. If you can get the licensing rights to make specific models and get hold of a manufacturer who will do just that, you can make this a serious business, since professional sports often use bobbleheads as giveaways which could mean as many as 25,000 dolls at one ballpark. If you find an importer overseas who makes bobbles, as they're called, you can usually buy them at $5 each. However, you may need to order in a group of 500, so you need to buy very popular characters. You can then turn your $2,500 into $10,000 by selling the dolls at $20 each. Therefore, even if you sell 250, you care doubling your investment, and you can always hold onto the other 250 or donate them to charity.

WEB RESOURCE: www.frontiershowroom.com/bobbleheads.html
This is an idea of how it works from one manufacturer, and there are plenty of others.

RATINGS	★
START-UP COST	$$
HOMEBASED BUSINESS	🏠
PART-TIME OPPORTUNITY	🕐
LEGAL ISSUES	⚖
FRANCHISE OR LICENSE POTENTIAL	🌐
GREEN BUSINESSES	🌿

30
SECURITY
Businesses You Can Start

FIRE SAFETY LADDERS
★★★ $$$$ ⚖

Every year across the United Stated thousands of people are injured or die as a result of fires. Many of these fire-related deaths and injuries could have been prevented had the victims had access to safety ladders enabling them to escape the burning building safely. A business that manufactures, sells, and installs fire safety ladders for residential and commercial applications has the potential to generate profits that could easily exceed $250,000 per year due to an almost unlimited market for the product. The following options are available to the creative entrepreneur that establishes a fire safety ladder business:

- Manufacture and wholesale fire safety ladders; retailers like home improvement centers could act as the distribution channels.
- Manufacture and retail fire safety ladders directly to consumers who carry out their own installation. The fire safety ladders could be sold via the internet and at booths at trade shows.
- Manufacture and sell the fire safety ladders to construction industry companies only, such as new homebuilders. These companies would install the safety ladders.

REQUIREMENTS: In addition to planning and research, also seek to have the safety ladders certified by Underwriters Laboratories (UL). Not only will this likely be required for selling the ladders to consumers, it also provides consumers with peace of mind, as they know that they are purchasing a proven and safe product. Additional requirements will include manufacturing facilities, transportation, and marketing. Also, seek to have the product endorsed by a professional association such as the Firefighters of America. A product endorsement such as this will greatly assist in marketing, as well as acceptance by consumers.

START-UP COSTS: The investment required to start this business will be substantial and could easily exceed $100,000. However, as a method of reducing the start-up costs for this enterprise, the fire safety ladders could be designed in prototype form and pre-sold to national retailers based on the prototype example. Once this has been accomplished, an existing manufacturer could be awarded the manufacturing contract for the product. This is a terrific way to greatly reduce the capital required.

WEB RESOURCE: www.nfpa.org
National Fire Protection Association.

WINDOW SECURITY BARS
★★ $$$ 🏠 🕐

Thousands of homes and businesses are burglarized annually even though many have alarms and other types of theft deterrent devices. Many home and business owners are now installing security bars on windows and doors as a method to deter burglars and prevent property entry and theft. The chances of breaking and entering crimes being reduced or stopping in the near future is highly unlikely, and this fact is what makes starting a security bar manufacturing and installation business such a good choice for a new venture. The business is very straightforward to get rolling and operate. Security bars can be sold to residential homeowners as well as to commercial property and business owners. In addition to using all traditional advertising mediums to promote the business, you can also establish contacts and alliances with companies such as alarm installers, property management firms, and contractors, all of which can refer your security bar manufacturing and installation service to their clients.

REQUIREMENTS: The main requirements for starting a business that manufactures and installs window and door security bars is to have welding equipment, welding experience, and a workshop large enough to properly carry out the work required to manufacture the security bars, unless you are able to purchase them from an outside manufacturer.

START-UP COSTS: The investment required to start a window and door security bar manufacturing and installation business will vary. However, an investment of $20,000 to $25,000 will be sufficient funding to establish a small to medium manufacturing facility, as well as provide for the business setup, initial advertising, and marketing budget costs associated with this type of business venture.

PROFIT POTENTIAL: To establish a retail selling price for window and door security bars consider using the following pricing formula as a guideline. This is a common pricing formula used within the construction and renovation building industry.

**Material costs + labor costs x 1.5 or
50 percent markup on costs.**

Example: material costs are $100 plus labor costs of $50 multiplied by 50 percent markup or $75 equals the total selling price of $225. Providing this formula is utilized and the business can achieve yearly sales of $300,000, the business would generate a gross profit prior to overheads and taxes of $100,000 per year.

HOME ALARM SALES
★★ $$$ 🚗 🕐 ⚖️

There are various approaches that can be taken when starting a security alarm business. The first is to sell and install alarms that are monitored, the second is to sell alarms for residential and commercial applications that are not monitored, and the third approach is to sell security alarm packages to the do-it-yourself homeowner for self-installation. All three approaches have the potential to pay off big in terms of business profits. However, the best approach is to sell and install residential and commercially monitored alarms, which can generate an ongoing residual income by way of monthly alarm monitoring fees, paid by the home or business owner. The first option is the most capital intensive of the three businesses to start, but it also has the potential to return the highest profits. Whichever approach is used to start and establish a security alarm business, one thing is for sure: Crime is not going away, making this a great business opportunity to pursue. Market your alarms through advertising, by distributing fliers, on your web site and at home shows. Make sure that each system is carefully and clearly explained, as a common complaint is that owners of alarm systems don't use them because they cannot figure out how they work. Excellent customer service and knowledge about the industry can make this a successful business venture. Note: Government licensing required.

WEB RESOURCE: www.alarm.org
National Burglar and Fire Alarm Association.

BODYGUARD SECURITY SERVICE
★ $$$ ⚖️

Bodyguards are no longer just hired to protect celebrities, they are hired to protect business leaders, high profile activists, authors, journalists, and just about anyone else in the public eye who is either being threatened or is having his or her life infringed upon by the media or a "fan base." Starting a bodyguard service requires a great deal of careful planning and research in order to ensure business success. Bodyguards can earn $1,000 per day, and, as an agency that retains 20 percent of the rate, it would not take many bodyguards on staff working only a few days per week to generate business sales in excess of

$200,000 per year. Besides hiring experienced bodyguards, you can earn additional income by adding an instruction service focused on training students how to become professional bodyguards. As is the case with any service-oriented business, you must make sure you meet the needs of your clientele with first-rate customer service, meaning that you provide protection whenever and wherever necessary by well-trained personnel. Make sure all clients have signed contracts that are very specific in regard to the services they do and do not want provided. This will limit the potential liability claims that can arise from an overzealous bodyguard. And remember, in the service industry, your reputation is only as good as your staff and their training.

WEB RESOURCE: www.iapps.org
The International Association of Professional Protection Specialists.

RECORDS STORAGE
★ $$$$

Many companies are required by law to retain financial and legal documents and files about their business and clients for long periods of time. In some cases this can be ten years or more from the original date of the information or document. This fact creates a huge opportunity to start and run a record storage facility, since many companies simply run out of space to store their documents and files. Ideally the business will be established in a location or warehouse that will take the following considerations into account: security, fire sprinklers, building condition, pest control, square footage, ease of accessibility, potential for expansion, central high-traffic location, and affordability. Rates for record storage vary greatly to the clients specific needs, in terms of volume of record storage and type of documents being stored. However, a well-planned and managed records storage business can post yearly profits that exceed six-figures.

WINDOW ROLL SHUTTERS
★★ $$ 🏠 🕐

Window and door security roll shutters are a terrific alternative to unattractive security bars, and starting a business enterprise that sells and installs window and door security roll shutters is very simple. You can focus on residential or commercial installations, or both. The first step is to source a manufacturer of the roll shutters and secure an exclusive distribution and installation contract. Marketing could consist of a demonstration and sales booth setup in a mall or at a trade show to generate interest and sales leads for the products. Additionally, establishing alliances with contractors and renovation companies is a terrific marketing approach, as these businesses can offer their existing customers your products in exchange for a commission.

SPECIAL EVENT SECURITY
★ $$ 🏠 🕐 🚗

Every year in North America there are thousands of special events such as concerts that require security staff present to control crowds and make the event safe for everyone in attendance. Starting a business that provides security for special events is very easy to set in motion, and the security staff used can be off-duty or retired police officers or security guards seeking to gain additional income. Contacting event planners and promoters in your community or state to explain the benefits of using your special event security service can help to market this type of security service. Additional revenue for the business can be earned by having the off-duty police officers conduct special instruction classes to students seeking to learn personal security techniques. Overall, a special event security service is a great new business venture for someone with a police or military background, contacts within the industry, and a thorough understanding of crowd control. Hire only individuals that understand methods of crowd control and can provide security without overstepping their roles. The best security is typically that which is unobtrusive and discreet.

SURVEILLANCE EQUIPMENT SALES
★★★ $$$ 🏠 🕐

Millions of small video cameras, emergency service scanners, night vision glasses, and other types of surveillance equipment are sold to consumers worldwide annually. Starting a business that retails these surveillance devices is very easy to do. Simply locate manufacturers of various types of surveillance equipment and purchase the equipment on a wholesale basis for retail purposes. The best method of marketing surveillance equipment, due to the limited market demand, is to establish a web site that features and sells the surveillance products. Additionally, advertisements can be placed in newspapers and trade publications for catalog ordering, enabling customers to receive your surveillance equipment by mail order. For the best results, stay on top of the latest in technology as new cameras and surveillance equipment is constantly being developed. Note: Make sure it is clear in your contracts and sales literature that you are selling and possibly installing the equipment, but that you are not responsible for the usage by the clients.

SECURITY STORAGE LOCKERS
★★ $$ 🚗 🕒

There are numerous approaches that can be taken when starting a security locker business. The first is to manufacture and sell the security lockers, while the second approach is to purchase the security lockers from an existing manufacturer on a wholesale basis and resell the lockers to clients at a profit. Security lockers have a wide range of uses including companies securing office products, pharmacies securing medications, and short-term security solutions for personal property at airports and other stations. This is a specialty product with a limited market. The profit potential is good and could be in the six-figure range for the entrepreneur who is willing to take the time required to plan and market the business properly.

WEB RESOURCE: www.americanlocker.com
Distributors of specialty security lockers.

CRIME PREVENTION TRAINING
★★ $ 🚗 🕒

Crime affects one out of four Americans in some fashion every year, and starting a business that trains people how to prevent themselves from becoming the victims of crime can be a very personally rewarding business venture to set in motion. The basis of the business concept is very straightforward. Simply hold training sessions in a group format for people who are seeking a way of protecting themselves and their families from becoming vic-

tims of crime. The classes can be held in conjunction with community services and groups, or on an independent one-on-one basis. A background in police service or the military will help to establish credibility for running this type of business. The profit potential for a crime prevention training service is excellent, as students should be more than happy to pay a mere $100 to learn more about crime prevention tips and techniques they can use to help prevent themselves and their families from becoming victims of crime. Make sure to stay on top of the latest crime activity, which now includes identity theft.

GUARD DOGS
★ $$$ 🔧

There are a few different approaches that can be taken for starting a guard dog security service. The first approach is to supply guard dogs with security handlers, the second is to provide guard dogs without security handlers, and a third is to combine both options. The requirements for starting the business are obvious. You must have trained guard dogs and either experience at training the dogs or be affiliated with a dog trainer. You also need a suitable operating location. Currently guard dog rental rates without security handlers are in the range of $40 to $60 per eight hours and include delivery and pickup of the dog. Guard dogs with security handlers are supplied to companies and associations for security purposes in the range of $125 to $175 per eight hours. You will need significant liability insurance and may need licensing, depending on the region in which you are doing business. Make sure to include in your plans the cost of housing and feeding the dogs.

SECURITY LIGHTING
★ $ 🚗 🕒 🔧

Calling all electricians! It is time to start earning extra income putting your talents to work by starting a part-time business that sells and installs residential and commercial security lighting solutions. The business can be started for peanuts in terms of investment capital, and has the potential to generate an additional income of $30,000 per year or more on a part-time basis. The best method to market this type of business is to establish a joint venture with home alarm companies. This can be a terrific marketing method as the alarm companies already have the sales force and customer base to assist in building your new business. Simply put, the alarm companies would offer their customers optional security lighting as part of the complete home security system, and you would supply and install the lighting. There should be no difficulties finding an alarm company that would be prepared to go into this type of joint venture, especially when you consider they could earn an additional $2,000 or $3,000 per month in commissions for selling your security lighting solutions.

BOAT ALARM SALES AND INSTALLATION
★★ $ 🏠 🕒 ⚖️

Many alarm companies have skipped installing alarms in boats because there is no effective way to charge a monthly monitoring fee due to the fact that many marinas do not have individual telephone lines to each boat and berth. Starting a business that specializes in only installing boat alarms is a venture that has millions of potential clients and relatively little competition. Marketing a boat alarm sales and installation service can be accomplished by designing and distributing promotional brochures to marinas and boat dealers, as well as setting up a booth at boat shows to collect sales leads. The profit potential is fantastic even as a one-person operation; you could easily surpass $75,000 per year in sales.

LOCKSMITH
★ $$$$ ⚖️

The main requirement for starting a locksmith service is of course to be a certified locksmith. While this may appear as something that will take a long time, it is not—you can become a locksmith relatively easily and the instruction training generally takes less than a year to complete. The best aspect of starting a locksmith service is the fact that this business venture has been proven successful and profitable for decades and is probably one of the most stable business opportunities available to start. A great aspect of this business is that it requires little physical space. Income potential ranges from $20,000 to $80,000 per year.

WEB RESOURCE: www.aloa.org
Associated Locksmiths of America.

SECURITY AND SAFETY MIRRORS
★★★★ $$ 🏠 🕒

In spite of the popularity of security video cameras, security mirrors will always be a popular choice for merchants to purchase and install. Unlike security cameras that may indicate a theft or shoplifting problem hours after the incident, security mirrors enable shopkeepers to keep an eye on their valuable inventory in real time. The market for security mirrors is almost unlimited, as there are millions of potential customers right now, and thousands more retail stores opening for business on a daily basis in the United States. One way to market this business is to simply design marketing brochures and solicit to local shop owners. Providing you can explain all the benefits that the security mirrors will have for customers, you should easily be able to achieve a 25 percent closing rate on all presentations.

REQUIREMENTS: Outside of a business license, there are typically no legal restrictions or certifications that must be complied with in regards to starting a business installing security mirrors. The only equipment needed for this business venture is a couple of good quality stepladders and a cordless drill. The best aspect about starting this business is the fact that there are virtually no special skills required; almost anyone can install security mirrors.

START-UP COSTS: The following example can be used as a guideline to establish the investment needed to start a security mirror installation service.

	Low	High
Installation vehicle (used)	$2,500	$5,000
Installation equipment	$500	$1,000
Initial inventory	$500	$1,000
Business setup, legal, banking, etc.	$250	$500
Initial advertising and marketing budget	$250	$500
Working capital	$1,000	$2,000
Total start-up investment	**$5,000**	**$10,000**

PROFIT POTENTIAL: Even for a small one-person security mirror sales and installation business the profit potential is outstanding. The security mirrors vary in cost as to the size of the mirror and if the mirror is plastic or glass. A small

24-inch security mirror can be purchased wholesale for less than $30, and the current retail price for the same size mirror is $125 for the mirror and installation. Two simple 30-minute jobs per day can create a gross profit of over $4,000 per month. Note: If you branch out and begin selling two-way mirrors, you need to be aware of privacy matters and potential legal ramifications before installing such mirrors.

WEB RESOURCE: www.brossardmirrors.com
Manufacturers of safety and security mirror products.

SECURITY ENGRAVING
★★ $ 🚗 🕒

Are you searching for a homebased security business that can be started for less than a $1,000 initial investment? If so, consider starting a security engraving service, as the business is inexpensive to start and operate. This business can easily be managed from a homebased office, requires no special skills or business expertise, and has the ability to produce a very comfortable income for the owner-operator of the business. Well-concealed security engraving identification numbers and names make it very easy for police to return stolen property to the rightful owners, as well as catch the thief that sells the stolen merchandise to pawnshops and secondhand stores. To get working, simply design brochures and fliers explaining your service and distribute them throughout your community. It will not take long for the phone to start ringing.

WEB RESOURCE: www.gravers.com
Distributors of engraving equipment and supplies.

PERSONAL SECURITY PRODUCTS
★★ $$ 🚗 🕒

Personal safety products and devices, such as pepper spray, mace, stun guns, whistles, and personal alarms, can be purchased on a wholesale basis from the thousands of different manufacturers that manufacture these types of security products, and resold to consumers for a profit. The personal safety products can be sold and distributed in various ways, including through mail order, a retail store, sales booth at a mall, over the internet, and by direct-sales teams. Be careful that all products that you sell are legal in your area. Also consider teaching personal safety courses for additional income, if you have a background in law enforcement.

WEB RESOURCE: www.safetycentral.com
Numerous safety and security devices.

COUNTERFEIT DETECTION EQUIPMENT
★★ $$

Counterfeit currency remains a problem for retailers, and costs all of us millions of dollars each year as a result of retail prices increasing to help offset these financial losses. Selling counterfeit detection equipment to retailers does not require a lot of experience in the industry, but like any sales-based business it does require good marketing and salesmanship skills. The key to success in this type of security business is not to sell to the retailer with one location, but to target retailers with multiple store locations. Additionally, one of the first steps to be taken prior to establishing the business will be to source a manufacturer of the equipment and negotiate an exclusive sales and distribution contract that services your particular community, city, or state. Providing a 50 percent markup can be maintained on all counterfeit detection equipment sold, and the business can achieve annual sales revenues of $250,000 the business would then generate a gross profit prior to taxes and operating costs of $85,000 per year.

CONSTRUCTION LOCK-UP SERVICE
★★ $$$$ 🔐

On any medium-sized construction site there are hundreds of thousands of dollars worth of building materials and tools around at any given time, making construction sites a prime target for thieves. Starting a construction lock-up security service is not only a service that is in high demand, but the business also has the ability to generate profits that are well into the six-figure range. The focus of the service should be a one-stop approach to construction lock-up and security services, and provide clients optional services like security patrols, security storage locker rentals for tools, portable security fencing rentals, and site trailer rentals. A construction lock-up security service will appeal to a wide variety of potential customers including property developers, commercial contractors, home renovation companies, demolition contractors, and even film and TV production companies. The best way to market the security services is to hire sales professionals on a commissioned basis. The sales professionals can solicit business for the security service, as well as up-sell customers into various security services the business offers. Additional revenues can be earned by providing contractors with employee safety instruction, as well as providing road contractors with flag persons and traffic control service.

REQUIREMENTS: There are few legal requirements for starting a construction lock-up security service except any security staff or guards must be certified and bonded. Also, there are the usual requirements such as a business license and liability insurance.

START-UP COSTS: The investment needed to start a construction lock-up service will greatly vary as to the size of the business, and the number of different services the business provides for clients. However, a small construction lock-up service can be started for less than $20,000 while a larger service will cost in excess of $50,000 to start.

PROFIT POTENTIAL: Profit potential range is $25,000 to $200,000 per year.

ELECTRIC SECURITY GATES
★★ $$$ 🏠 🕐

Electric security gates are a popular home improvement upgrade and security feature for many homeowners, strata corporations, companies, and landlords. Starting a security gate business does not require a great deal of practical construction knowledge, as the manufacturing and installation aspect of the business can be subcontracted to qualified professional trades people. However, like almost any business venture, a definite prerequisite for success is certainly an ability to be or become an effective marketing and sales pro. Building alliances with renovation and construction companies is a good start in terms of marketing and getting the word out about your business. Additionally, home and garden trade shows can be an invaluable source for collecting well-qualified sales leads.

GENERATOR SALES
★ $$$ 🏠 🕐

Selling, repairing, and installing emergency generator systems is a fantastic business venture to set in motion. Floods, earthquakes, ice storms, and the more common

power outages are a few of the reasons why this business can flourish as businesses will need stand by (back-up) generators in case their electricity is shut down. Many businesses, especially hospitals, require back up generators to automatically kick in when necessary. Other situations will require the need for power and a stand-alone generator. This could be for anything from a mobile medical facility set-up after a natural disaster to a movie shoot on location. As is typically the case when starting a business, you will need to read up the many details of that industry, such as the various types of generators available, including diesel and gas models, as well as how to determine the power needs of a business. You can also make a tremendous amount of money by selling uninterruptible power supplies (UPS) for home and office computers. Most people know that they should have something in place as a backup, just in case they are on their desktops when a power outage occurs, but few people take the time to do anything about it. This is your opportunity to be at the ready with USPs and surge protectors as well.

CONSTRUCTION SITE SECURITY
★ $$ 🏠 🚗

Millions of dollars worth of tools and building materials are stolen from construction and building renovation sites annually, and this fact is what makes starting a construction site security service such a wise choice for a new business enterprise. This type of security service does not require a great deal of investment capital to set in motion, and the business can easily be managed from a homebased office. Running such a business means combining a knowledge for security with all of the practical elements necessary for a construction site. This includes having several options available, including walls or fencing, alarms, surveillance systems, motion detectors and even guards and, or guard dogs. Gaining clients for a construction site security service is best achieved simply by soliciting construction and renovation companies for business. Set appointments with these firms and explain all the benefits using your security service will have for their companies. The key is to know the business very well. Having a background in security, along with some background of construction sites, is a big plus.

AUTO ALARM SALES AND INSTALLATION
★ $ 🚗 🕒 ⚖️

In spite of the fact that many new automobiles now come outfitted with auto alarms as standard equipment, starting an auto alarm installation business is still a good choice for a new business venture, especially if the objective is to build a small one-person business that can provide the owner with a comfortable annual income. Establishing alliances with used car dealers is a fabulous way to activate this type of security business, as the car dealers can offer their customers optional installations of car alarms provided, of course, by your auto alarm sales and installation service. Overall this is a good business start-up for the technically inclined individual, and the income possibility for an automotive alarm sales and installation service is in the range of $25,000 to $50,000 per year.

PHONE-UP SECURITY SERVICE
★ $ 🚗 🕒

Starting a security phone-up service is a very inexpensive business venture to launch that can be operated right from the comforts of a homebased office. A few of you might be wondering exactly what a security phone-up service is, and how this business can make money. A security phone-up service is a security service that telephones clients on a regular daily basis, as set up by the plan, to make sure that there are no problems in terms of personal security and health. Clients for a phone-up service can include seniors living alone as well as individuals with disabilities. To start, you should set up several plans and present them to potential clients in a brochure and on your web site. The plans will vary in how often calls are made and the necessary response, which can include anything from alerting doctors, hospitals, and police in the event of a serious emergency situation to contacting a family member on his or her cell phone for less significant concerns. Current rates for a phone-up security service is in the range of $25 to $40 per client per month. Securing only regular customers can produce an income greater than $35,000 per year. Additional revenues for this business can also be from providing clients with a custom telephone memo and paging service.

MOTION DETECTION SYSTEMS AND SENSORS
★★ $$$ ⚖️

Cameras are only part of the elaborate world of modern security. You can now make big bucks selling the latest in digital security systems as a dealer for a manufacturer or by establishing your own an independent security business. Full digital set-ups now allow you to pinpoint specific areas in which you want movement detected by using the mouse on your computer to outline parts of the room or rooms in which the detection system is set up. In fact, systems can now work through existing cameras and pinpoint the time and place where a crime was committed, so clients no longer have to search through hours of footage. You can market motion detection systems to offices through direct mailings and follow up phone calls as well as holding security seminars and meetings with local chambers of commerce. You can also sell the more basic analog motion detectors, which you can purchase wholesale for $20 and sell for a 50% mark up at $30. For these, you can spread the word by fliers and brochures around the neighborhood.

WEB RESOURCE: www.cctvwholesale.com
Wholesaler of digital motion detection systems.

BACKGROUND AND PRE-EMPLOYMENT CHECKING SERVICES
★★★★ $$$$ ⚖️

Despite the fact that employers typically ask for background information from prospective new employees, and landlords ask the same of new tenants, very seldom does either bother to check out the validity of such information. This can prove costly, as evidenced by a rise in employee theft and tenant-landlord problems over the past couple of decades. If you have a background in security and are diligent when it comes to doing research, you can start a very lucrative business handling the background checks for which employers and landlords do not have the time or the necessary skill. Your job is to search criminal, previous employment, and credit records and perform due diligence in a short timeframe. You can market such a business through brochures, fliers, speaking engagements, a web site, and well-placed advertising to human resource directors and landlords. The cost of hiring and training employees can typically be over $4000, while the cost to rent an apartment can be nearly as much. It is therefore in your client's best interest to have employees or tenants that stick around awhile. This is the key to your marketing efforts.

WEB RESOURCE: www.virtualchase.com/articles/background_checks.html
How to conduct a background check.

SCHOOL SECURITY CONSULTANT
★★ $ 🕒 📖

The days of schools being safe havens for students to learn are unfortunately gone. While there has always been a need to maintain order among students, increased media exposure to violence, among other factors, has created a generation in which serious violent crime is a possibility in nearly any school. External threats also pose a problem to schools today. These unfortunate realities open the door for someone with a background in security to start a business as a school security consultant. Selling your knowledge and expertise means you can operate from a home office and bill at $60 or more per hour to help examine and analyze the current state of a school. By working with the school personnel and evaluating the infrastructure of the facility, you can create guidelines for crisis intervention and map out safety procedures that need to be put into effect, including lock downs should there be criminal activity in the vicinity of the school. By reviewing crime patterns and policies, the potential for weapons in the school, and current drug policies, you can help schools re-vamp their safety and security procedures. Establishing some basic plans and honing them to fit the specific recommendations based on each individual school will be the focus of your job. Market yourself to public schools, starting with the local school boards, and then move to private schools and parochial schools. You should also commit to an annual review to make sure all safeguards are working and to address any new concerns that have arisen since your previous assessment.

WEB RESOURCE: www.schoolsecurity.org
National School Safety and Security Services

IDENTITY THEFT CONSULTANT
★★★ $$ 🚗 🕒

Identity theft is the fastest rising crime in the world. In the past four years, more than 12 million Americans have been victims of identity theft. These sobering facts mean that an identity theft consultant can be a blessing to the millions of would-be victims out there, which is nearly everyone. In the modern world, we sign up constantly for services and use credit cards in a variety of manners including via the internet and by telephone. This opens the door to an identity thief who can get access to your credit card number, bank account information, and other personal information. To sell your services as an identity theft consultant, you need to become the expert. If you have a background in security, this is to your benefit. If not, you can immerse yourself in study and read everything possible on how identity thieves operate and all of the protective means of stopping them. While you cannot act in a law enforcement capacity, you can provide preventative measures through speaking engagements and personal consulting sessions at businesses to provide information so that they are not responsible for their customers becoming victims. In addition you can counsel victims as to exactly what they should do, since they may be in a state of panic once they find out that someone has cleaned out their bank account, built up tremendous debt, or is even responsible for them having a criminal record. Your levelheaded approach can help the individual contact and work with the authorities, as well as making the necessary phone calls to credit card companies while trying to rectify the situation. Charging $50 to $70 an hour for your services and conducting two-hour seminars can help you build a successful business.

LIFEGUARD SERVICE
★ $$ 🕒

Though in some regions they are primarily needed in the summer months, in other areas of North America lifeguards are needed year-round at beaches and pools. This is where you come in. A lifeguard service provides highly trained and skilled lifeguards to pools and beaches around a community, city or throughout a state. To get started you will first need to accumulate a list of every pool or beach within the region you will serve and then start advertising for trained, certified lifeguards. For newcomers, such as students looking for summer or part time work, you provide the training (or hire someone) so that they can become skilled and certified to handle the lifeguard responsibilities. Depending on the area, you can also hire additional teachers to teach boater and surfer rescue and handle other necessary safety precautions. In addition, you should provide training in how to communicate effectively and handle numerous situations that can arise, such as the use of illegal substances on the beach or around the pool at which they are working. You then promote yourself to the owners of every pool on your list as "the" place at which to find the most competent, trustworthy, skilled lifeguards. Your pay comes from the students if they need to be trained and from the owner of the pool, beach club or resort hiring you. This can certainly be a homebased business with low start-up costs. There are numerous lifeguard positions that need to be filled in any town, not even those by the ocean, making this a potentially successful business venture.

WEB RESOURCE: www.americanlifeguard.com
American Lifeguard Association.

COMMUNITY AND DEVELOPMENT PATROL
★★ $$ 🏠 🕐

Recent years have seen the increase in condo and co-op townhouse developments emerge. These pre-designed communities are marvelous ways in which to sell homes to any demographic group, whether it's primarily young families or seniors. Many of these developments have swimming pools, community centers, playgrounds, and other communal areas that enhance socialization. While they are under the jurisdiction of local police authorities, residents often feel safer when a local patrol is keeping an eye on the premises. If you have some background in law enforcement, this can be a marvelous opportunity to launch your own business for no more than $1,000, not counting a patrol vehicle. Once you have obtained the necessary state or city licensing, you can start seeking out clients by sending out mailings explaining your services to management companies of such townhouse developments. Of course, you will need to have a plan of action

that explains how you will patrol the area and what your policies will be should you find some type of wrongdoing. Naturally, you should be ready to defer to the local police, since you do not have the same level of authority. You will also want to hire guards and train them in the methods of securing the premises while not overstepping their bounds or interfering with the residents privacy. By having patrols in several area developments, you can secure $50,000 from the patrol business.

NOTES:

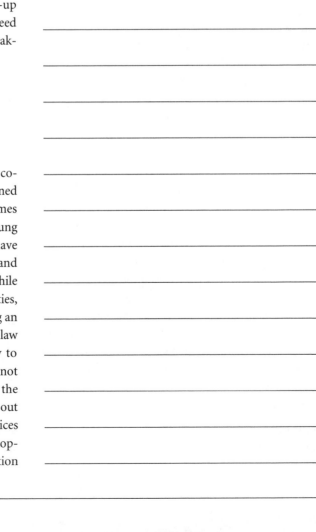

95

SPECIAL SERVICE
Businesses You Can Start

KEY

RATINGS	★
START-UP COST	$$
HOMEBASED BUSINESS	🏠
PART-TIME OPPORTUNITY	🕐
LEGAL ISSUES	⚖️
FRANCHISE OR LICENSE POTENTIAL	🌐
GREEN BUSINESSES	🌿

HURRICANE AND NATURAL DISASTER PREPARATION SERVICE
★★ $ 🏠 🕐

Every year hurricanes and tornados create devastation. Being prepared for nasty forces of nature can save not only property, but also prevent personal injury. The business is quite simple. Start with lumber for boarding up houses to prevent damage to windows and doors. You measure windows and doors, cut plywood to fit these openings, label each board to its proper location, and install quick-fit installation hardware on each piece of plywood. The next time there is a threat of a hurricane or tornado, the homeowner will be prepared. In addition, you can supply home and business owners with battery-powered flashlights, water-resistant boots, backup generators, bottled water, and disaster supply kits. You can even help them back up their computer data to an offsite location so as not to lose valuable business and/or personal data. By providing services, selling necessary goods at a reasonable cost, and including valuable information, you can run a lucrative and rewarding business that helps people survive in the face of danger. The service can also be marketed to owners of vacation properties and to owners of seasonal businesses who want the peace of mind of knowing their buildings will be secure during the off season.

CROWD CONTROL SYSTEMS
★★ $$ 🏠 🕐

Parades, concerts, demonstrations, and fairs all require portable fencing, ticket booths, and barriers to be temporally installed at the site where the event is taking place. You can rent crowd control items by marketing the service to event planners, city management staff, and charity organizations in your community with the assistance of your own specially designed brochure and rental item price list. Likewise, many construction and renovation companies require these same rental items on a periodic basis and these businesses can also be placed on your potential client list. This type of rental business is easily operated from home and you can contract out the delivery of the rental items to a local transportation company in order to keep start-up costs to a minimum.

AUCTION AND AUCTIONEER SERVICE
★★ $$ 🏠 ⚖️

Did you know that it is estimated that more than 75,000 auctions sales take place each year in the United States? Becoming a certified auctioneer is not difficult; the course is less than two weeks in duration, and costs only a few thousand dollars. Like many auctioneers, you may specialize in one area, such as paintings or perhaps sports memorabilia. Typically auctioneers retain 7 to 12 percent of the value of the goods auctioned and in some cases also charge purchasers a bidder's fee that can range from an additional 5 to 10 percent. The focus of this business start-up is to act as the auctioneer at charity, school, or other types of auction, or to match up auctioneers with the need for their services by serving as the middle person and making a commission (15-20%). If you are handling the auctions yourself, you will need to be skilled at auctioneering, so hone your craft. If you are booking auctioneers, make sure they are well trained. However lucrative this may sound, be forewarned that hosting and promoting auction sales can be very costly. You have to pay for expenses directly from commissions, such as wages for employees, transportation costs, sale advertising and promotion, and administrative costs. Securing clients can also be difficult due to the fact that this is a competitive industry and sellers want as much for their products as possible, especially commercial clients. The decision to select one auction service over another is usually based on past performance and experience in the particular goods being auctioned. But if research is completed, careful planning is practiced, and you take the time to build a strong and reputable service, a financially rewarding future can lie ahead.

WEB RESOURCE: www.auctioneers.org
National Auctioneers Association; industry information and links as well as certification programs.

BARTENDER
★★ $ 🏠 🕒

Starting a bartender-for-hire service is a fantastic way to get into business for yourself without breaking the bank. You can market your services as an independent bartender to catering companies, event planners, hotels, and pubs for relief duties. The business only requires a few hundred dollars of seed capital to initiate and can return $150 to $200 per day plus gratuities. Ideally, the entrepreneur who starts a bartender-for-hire service will be an experienced bartender themselves, with outstanding social skills and a knowledge of how to mix drinks. Employing other bartenders on an "as-needed, on-call basis" can generate additional revenue, provided they are good at what they do. Once again, your service will only be successful if your bartenders are responsible and know

what they are doing. A bartender-for-hire service has the potential to create annual revenues that can easily exceed $50,000 or more.

WEB RESOURCE: www.bartending101.com
American Bartending Association.

DRY CLEANING DELIVERY SERVICE
★★ $$ 🏠

Today's lifestyles are hectic and busy with not enough time for simple tasks like dropping off and picking up dry cleaning. That is exactly what you want to hear if you are considering starting your own dry cleaning delivery service. This business is a great low investment option with high potential earnings, little competition, and very low operating overheads. To get started simply build an alliance with an existing commercial dry cleaner and negotiate the lowest possible per item dry cleaning rates that you can. Once you have accomplished this task, you can then create your own marketing brochure and price list reflecting a 100 percent markup on your wholesale dry cleaning cost. The next phase of establishing the business is to solicit clients. This is best achieved by distributing marketing brochures where they will have the highest impact, such as professional offices, companies with uniforms, and government and nonprofit associations. I interviewed one such business owner who in a 12-month period added three subcontract delivery persons and increased total sales volumes to more than $100,000 per month by following this very basic formula for his dry cleaning delivery service.

OFFICE MOVING
★ $$ 🕒 🚚

Unlike moving residential household furniture, moving office equipment and fixtures requires much more planning in order for the move to be successful and allow the business the fewest possible interruptions to their operation. An office moving service can be marketed through property management companies and directly to business owners via brochures and networking at business association functions. The main requirement is to carry sufficient liability insurance and to check to see if a mover's license is required in your community.

BICYCLE COURIER SERVICE
★★★ $ 🚗 🚐

The first step in starting your own bicycle courier service is to check and see if a courier license is required for your vicinity. If a license is not required, or if you can secure one easily, the second step is to begin marketing your new bicycle courier service. To attract clients, simply set appointments with local companies who would require fast, reliable, and local delivery service. Ideal candidates include law firms and design companies. You can charge similar rates for envelopes and small parcels as the motorized couriers charge, with the benefit that your overhead will be a fraction of theirs. One person can easily operate a bicycle courier service with a cell phone for incoming delivery inquiries. The business can then be expanded to include multiple bike couriers with a central dispatch system. Many big cities have a number of bike currier businesses. The keys to this business are:

- Making sure you have reliable riders
- Being able to provide riders with quick routes so that they can make speedy drop offs and move onto their next delivery.
- Having liability insurance
- Training your riders to avoid accidents and collisions

This low-cost business venture can be an excellent way to earn an excellent income while staying very fit.

WEB RESOURCE: www.nybma.com
New York Bicycle Messengers Association.

BODY PIERCING
★★ $$ 🚐

Body piercing started as a fad in the '80s, continued to expand in popularity in the '90s, and is becoming a mainstream industry in the new millennium. Starting a body piercing service does require experience or an experienced staff plus liability insurance, but this business venture can be started for peanuts. You can operate from a fixed location or on a mobile basis in different locations during peak holiday times. An obvious partnership for this kind of unique business is to incorporate your service with an existing business such as a tattoo parlor or hair and nail salon. Business partnerships help to reduce initial start-up costs and ongoing monthly overhead costs. Profit potential will greatly vary. However, once established, this kind of business can easily generate weekly sales in excess of $1,000, especially if you also sell the jewelry items.

WEB RESOURCE: www.tattoospa.com
Industry information and links to licensing requirements.

REUNION PLANNER
★ $$ 🚗 🕐 🌐

What is the best way to start your own reunion planner service? Acquire numerous old high school and college yearbooks and as they approach ten, twenty, or twenty-five years, start a direct mailing to inquire about student's interest in a reunion. If the response is positive and you believe that you can make a go of it (and not lose money), schedule a reunion! Send out the invitations promising great nostalgic memories, plus food, drink and entertainment. You can then charge $60 for individuals or $100 per couple, or more, depending on how extravagant you plan to make the evening. Review your costs in advance and double the total for your profit. You can also make money from commemorative T-shirts, photos, and videos and other such items. Do some research and customize themes to personalize the event for each class. Organizing and hosting just one reunion per month can easily create a part-time income of $12,000 to $15,000 per year.

WELCOME SERVICE
★ $$ 🚗 🕐 🌐

Here is a business start-up that requires no practical business experience and very little capital to activate. A welcome wagon service is simply making new residents of your community feel welcome and explaining all the various services and attractions that are available locally. Local companies pay you a small fee in exchange for promoting their products and services to new residents, thus creating a business income. These small fees really start to add up, especially if you are promoting 30 to 40 local businesses at any one time. To source information about new arrivals in your community, build alliances with landlords, real estate agents, business associations, and schools.

PRODUCT ASSEMBLY SERVICE
★ $ 🚗 🕓

By anyone's estimate, there are far too many products sold that have to be assembled by the purchaser, and these assemblies are never as easy as advertised. A product assembly service can be started for well less than $500 and marketed directly through a retailer who does not currently provide this service to their customers. Of course additional revenue can be created if you also deliver the products that you will be assembling. The business only requires a few basic power tools, assembly skills, and perhaps a van if you intend to provide delivery options. Remember, this business can also work in reverse for people who are moving and have to disassemble products and reassemble these same items after relocation. This aspect of the business can be promoted in conjunction with moving and storage companies.

PRIVATE INVESTIGATOR
★★ $$ 🚗 🔧

When you think of a private investigator, images of Sam Spade may come to mind. However, private investigators today do not sleep in their office, carry a flask of whiskey, or wear trench coats and wide-brimmed hats. Most assignments now handled by private investigators include researching business competitors, spouse surveillance, and insurance fraud investigation. The business does require an investigator license, and a police or surveillance background would be beneficial. A well-established private investigator can enjoy an interesting lifestyle that can be very rewarding in terms of compensation for services.

WEB RESOURCE: www.becomeapi.com
Directory service of industry certification information.

WEB RESOURCE: www.pimagazine.com
PI Magazine, The Journal of Private Investigators.

NETWORKING CLUB
★★★ $$ 🚗 🕓 🌐

Starting a networking club in your community is a perfect way to be self-employed and make a large number of new and valuable business contacts. Networking clubs are a perfect choice for a new business start-up, especially if the kind of networking club or business association that you are intending to start is currently not represented in your community. The purpose of a networking club is to introduce business owners and their products and services to other business owners. Networking meetings are usually very casual and generally take place in the morning as a breakfast meeting, or in the early evening to help each other generate leads through outside people they know. In other words, if one member is an accountant and another is a printer, they will each promote the services of the other individual to all of their friends, business associates, and so on. Typically every week a couple of members get up and talk about their businesses in greater detail. Members pay a monthly or yearly fee to belong to the club and to be listed in the club's directory. You can generate additional revenue by providing various services to your members such as monthly guest speaker seminars and mini-business trade shows that can be open to club members as well as the general public. Usually, a limited number of people are accepted into each club (perhaps 15 or 20). It's highly advisable not to have competing businesses in the same club. Therefore, if you have enough people for Monday, Tuesday, and Wednesday morning clubs, you can spread three accountants, three printers, or three chiropractors out among the different meetings so they are not in direct competition. It is also important to do some reference checks on your members. If someone does not have accountability and your members send their friends, neighbors, and business partners to this person, the credibility of the entire club can take a beating. Also, make sure to get a good idea of the various personalities of the members, since there will always be one arrogant loudmouth in every networking club that can drive away membership faster than you can build it up. Plan carefully!

TELEPHONE ON-HOLD ADVERTISING
★★ $ 🚗 🕓

Millions of business owners are missing out on a prime opportunity to market their products and services every day. How? By not having prerecorded messages advertising their products and services when their call-in customers are placed on hold. For this business concept you create an on-hold advertising message for your clients and hire a professional voice person to record the message in a studio. The client pays for this service on a one-time fee basis or on a monthly contract basis that includes a fixed number of changes to their telephone on-hold advertisement. The profit potential is excellent, especially if you can persuade a few hundred business owners to join your unique advertising service on a monthly billing basis.

ASSOCIATION SALES
★★★ $ 🚗 🕒

Business associations and clubs all have one thing in common. They all require members in order to generate revenue. Acting as an independent business association sales consultant is an extremely low-cost business start-up that can allow you the opportunity to capitalize on your sales abilities. There are literally hundreds of different associations you can contract your sales services to, including boards of trade, chambers of commerce, tourist associations, and networking clubs. Your income will be earned by a commission charged each time you sign a new member into one of the associations that you are representing. A good formula is to charge a 30 percent commission on the first year's membership dues and a 10 percent commission for every year thereafter, providing the member remains active in the association. This billing formula gives you both a real and an annual residual earnings base.

PIANO TUNING SERVICE
★ $ 🚗 🕒

Pianos are everywhere and they all need to be tuned and maintained on a regular basis in order to work and sound perfect. The main requirement is you have to know how to tune and maintain various types of pianos. Providing you have this skill and a few hundred dollars, you're in business as a professional piano tuner. A piano tuning service can be operated right from your vehicle with the aid of a cellular telephone. Operating a piano tuning service is perfect for the person seeking a good part-time income to supplement an existing one. Contacting local music stores and music schools to promote your service will be the fastest way to earn business via referral and word-of-mouth advertising.

WEB RESOURCE: www.pianoworld.com
Directory of piano tuner links and industry information.

GIFT-WRAPPING SERVICE
★ $

You can establish your own gift-wrapping service operating from a booth at a mall during holiday times, or in a partnership with a large retailer who will permit you to set up the business within their store. Either way, a gift-wrapping service can generate as much as $1,000 per day in profits during the busy Christmas shopping season. The business can also be operated on a year-round basis by adding additional services, such as a corporate shopping service, gift basket service, and an errand service, all of which are featured in this directory as business opportunities. Many businesses today, however, provide their customers with free gift wrapping, meaning that you will need to be hired by the stores or even by web businesses to handle this service.

PACKING SERVICE
★ $ 🕒

The least favorite task of any moving job is without question all the packing and unpacking of boxes full of personal items. You can start your own packing service for peanuts and be sure of lots of business, because no one likes this necessary chore. Moving companies will be your best source of work, as they can directly supply the jobs or can refer your services to their customers. This is a great business to be partnered with a product assembly service, as operating the two services in one will assure you of ample demand to keep you working on a full-time basis. Generally for this type of service you would charge on a per-hour rate or on a flat rate for the entire job. Either way you should try to maintain at least $20 per hour for your services. Hint: Make sure to have sturdy packaging materials of all shapes and sizes and practice packing some "odd-shaped" items before starting out.

JACKHAMMER SERVICE
★★ $$ 🚗 🕒

A jackhammer service is a unique business opportunity that has virtually no direct competition. Starting your own jackhammer service is a low-cost way to be self-employed in the construction industry that can easily earn you $30 to $40 per hour. This construction service is required for removal of sidewalks, installation of new plumbing under basement floors, and breaking up small rock formations in the way of construction progress. You can offer your services to construction and renovation companies of every kind on an as-required basis. The business can be operated from home and a cellular telephone. To really keep start-up costs to a minimum, rent the required jackhammer for your first few jobs until you have established that there is a need and demand for a jackhammer service in your community.

COMMERCIAL DOOR MAINTENANCE SERVICE
★★★ $$ 🚗 🕐

Starting a commercial door maintenance route may be your opportunity to earn in excess of $100,000 per year, and with a minimal initial investment. All commercial doors have one thing in common. They all need regular routine maintenance in order to be safe and work properly. Regular maintenance includes adjusting or replacing door closures and pivots, replacing automatic doormats, and lubricating pivots and concealed hinges. The business does require that you have a working knowledge of commercial door systems. However, the learning curve is not a challenge and you can pick up a lot of this knowledge on the job. Additional requirements will be a service vehicle, tools, and an inventory of the most popular types of replacement parts, as these are generally available only through specialty distributors or directly from the door manufacturers. The business is best marketed by providing your services on a monthly service contract basis to business locations with commercial door entrances. Current service rates are in the range of $40 to $60 per hour, plus parts. Commercial property management companies can be your first stop to offer this much-needed service to their existing business customers.

WEB RESOURCE: www.specialtydoors.com
Distributor of commercial door systems, parts, and supplies.

MOBILE MAKE-UP ARTIST
★★ $$ 🚚

Calling all cosmeticians! Why not start your own make-up artist service and start earning profits for you instead of the boss? Providing you have the experience and required credentials, this is a very low-cost business venture to establish. You can market your services to pho-

tographers who specialize in actors' headshots, residents of senior and retirement homes, anyone in the film production industry, soon-to-be-brides and their bridal parties... and the list goes on and on. The business is best suited on a mobile service basis, so that you can take advantage of wherever your services may be required. A make-up artist's service can be activated for less than $3,000, and can return profits far in excess of $30,000 per year for the owner-operator.

COAT CHECK SERVICE
★ $ 🚗 🕐

Providing a coat check service for just one social function per week and charging only $125 for the service will earn you an additional $6,500 per year, plus tips! Best of all it only takes a few hundred dollars and a little bit of legwork to get rolling. You can create your own marketing brochures, complete with pictures of yourself in an expensive tuxedo or evening gown, and distribute the brochures to potential paying customers. Clients can include wedding and event planners, catering companies, and trade show and seminar organizers. This type of event service is always in demand and is a great business start-up for the outgoing businessperson wishing to establish a good part-time income.

BILLING AUDITOR
★ $ 🚗 🕐

How often, as business owners or consumers, do we miss overcharges on invoices that over time can add up to thousands of dollars? This fact is the only marketing tool you will need to promote a bill auditing service. Getting started will not require a large investment, but operating a bill auditing service does certainly require good bookkeeping and research skills. You can base rates on a percentage of money that may be recouped for clients, or on a flat hourly rate charge. The business can easily be operated from home on a part-time basis, and once established can generate revenues in excess of $20,000 per year.

NAIL SALON
★★ $$

There are various approaches that can be taken when considering starting a nail salon. These include:

- An independent nail salon established in a fixed retail location like a small storefront.
- A salon that is partnered with an existing business such as a hair salon or day spa.
- A business that is set up as a mobile nail salon that travels to your client's homes or offices.

Providing you already possess the proper credentials and experience to start this type of business venture, all three approaches to starting and establishing the business are viable. The best of the three is to partner with an existing related business, as you can minimize start-up costs and share monthly operating costs. Likewise, partnering with an established business allows you to take advantage of the client base. Once established, a nail salon can generate profits in the range of $40,000 per year.

WEB RESOURCE: www.nailartstudio.com
Nail art designs and industry information and links.

REMOVABLE TATTOOS
★★ $$ 🕐

Here is a great business venture that can keep you busy earning money on weekends and evenings. Starting a removable tattoo business is economical in terms of needed start-up capital, and does not necessitate any special skills or equipment. The business is best suited to be set up on a mobile or portable basis via your own booth, tent, or cart at busy malls, fairs, or other high-traffic community event. Furthermore, partnering the business with a tourist attraction can be a fantastic way to create instant sales using the tourist customer base. In terms of profit potential for this kind of unique business venture, that will vary greatly depending on the business location and product markup. However, there should be no difficulties in earning $200 per day on a busy weekend, and even more if you are located in a busy tourist area or mall.

BOAT DELIVERY SERVICE
★ $ 🕐 ⚖️

So you're a salty sea dog from way back, are you? Then why not put this experience to work for you and start your own boat delivery service? Depending on your experience you can specialize in sailboat or powerboat delivery. Many boats are sold to novice and inexperienced boaters who are from outside the area in which the boat

was purchased. Utilizing your boating and navigational skills means you can deliver these boats to their homeport for the new owners. Additionally, many boat owners in northern climates like to move their boats to sunny southern climates for use in the winter months. Sailing or powering larger boats to a new temporary homeport is much cheaper than transporting the boats by land. Get started by marketing your boat delivery service to local marinas and boat retailers, as well as by joining boating associations to network for business. The business can be initiated for a very small investment, and return a comfortable living in terms of income. Additional revenue can be generated for this business venture by selling and installing electronics and general marine equipment, as well as by offering a rigging service for sailboat owners and a boat cleaning service for all boat owners.

DISTRIBUTION WAREHOUSE
★★★ $$$$

Homebased businesses and the internet have created a booming market for distribution and warehousing services. Why? Because homebased and cyber ventures generally do not have the infrastructure required to store and ship their products that are being sold. Starting a warehousing and distribution service means that you can act as a warehouse, shipping, and receiving agent for as many as 20 or 30 different companies. This business venture does require a great deal of research and investment capital. However, with careful planning and exceptional organizational skills, this type of business venture is capable of creating a six-figure income per year, all within a very short period of time for the enterprising entrepreneur.

MAILBOX CENTER
★★ $$$$ 🕐

Starting a mailbox center is a very easy business enterprise to activate that requires no special business experiences or skills. The main requirement will be a small retail storefront location; approximately 600 square feet will be more than sufficient. Likewise, you will need individually locking mailboxes and a few pieces of office equipment such as a high-speed photocopier, fax, personal computer, and scanner. The purpose for the additional office equipment is so you will have the ability to provide your customers with extra services like a photo-copying service. Also, try to acquire the rights to act as a drop-off and pickup depot for courier companies, as this service can also produce sizable extra revenues and profits. Selling postage stamps, envelopes, packaging materials, and various other shipping-related items can make this a booming business.

SHOWROOM DESIGNER
★★ $$ 🚗 🕐

Business owners who design their own retail show-rooms waste millions of dollars each year. Why? Because in most cases, the showroom that they have designed themselves (in an effort to save money) is very ineffective and, as a result, can cost their business lost sales and profits. Showrooms must be visually appealing, customer-friendly in terms of traffic pattern and ease of locating a product, and functional for staff. As a showroom designer you can utilize all your creative talent and design experience to build a very successful and rewarding career. The business does not require a great deal of capital to start. However, experience and design knowledge will be required in order for this new venture to succeed. Teaming with commercial interior decorators is a very good entry point into this segment of the design industry. Additional revenue sources include providing clients with a window display service, renting props for showroom displays, and special sales and promotional events. Be sure not to limit your marketing efforts strictly on new store openings, as for every new store that opens there are 100 times as many existing stores that would benefit from having their showroom redesigned and may be more open to this type of service.

ERRAND SERVICE
★★ $ 🚗 🕐

Busy lifestyles dictate that many business owners and professionals do not have time for even the simplest of errands like taking the dog to the veterinarian. Creating a marketing brochure that explains your service can be your best tool to attract new clients. The brochures can be distributed to business owners and professionals. Likewise a few promotional items such as pens and memo pads emblazoned with your company logo, name, and telephone number will go a long way as a gentle reminder of your fast, reliable, and affordable errand service. Attending just a few business association or networking meetings can easily secure a few dozen clients for this service. Remember this is the kind of business that can be supported 100 percent by referrals and word-of-mouth once established. The main objective is customer satisfaction, due to the fact that customer satisfaction is all you are really selling.

LITTER PICKUP SERVICE
★★★ $ 🚗 🕐

Starting a litter pickup service requires a small investment and a few basic tools, such as garbage cans, shovels, and rakes. You can create a low-cost promotional brochure that explains the benefits that a neat and tidy parking lot and entrance can have for a business, in terms of a customer's first impression. Like any service business, your goal should be to establish a monthly service contract with clients. A good rate to charge for your service would be about $60 dollars per month for an average size parking lot and entrance area. In exchange the business owner would receive a weekly visit to their site in which you would pick up and remove all litter, as well as remove any simple stains on pavement and sidewalk surfaces. Each visit should only average about a half-hour in time and this quick and simple pricing formula can earn you $30 per hour.

PORTABLE TOILETS
★★ $$$$

The not-so-sweet smell of success! Implementing a portable toilet business can be very lucrative, especially if you take the time to build a solid contact base. Clients can include event planners, construction companies, charities, sports associations, and just about every other business or organization that holds outdoor events. This is not an inexpensive business to start and operate. The main requirements will be the purchase of the portable toilets and a delivery or pump truck. The truck will be the largest expense, as a new one can sell for as much as $150,000. To keep initial start-up costs down, a second-hand truck in good mechanical condition will probably be a better choice, at least initially. For extra money you might also have a portable sink on hand for additional rental needs.

WEB RESOURCE: www.nuconcepts.com
Manufacturers of portable toilets.

CONSTRUCTION FLAG SERVICE
★ $$ 🏠 🕐 ⚖️

There are literally thousands of road construction projects and special events each year, which require the services of traffic control flag personnel. This business start-up lends itself perfectly to the homebased entrepreneur to manage and supply the required personnel to act as traffic control flag people. You can invoice the construction companies a fixed hourly rate for this service, and pay your employees a few dollars an hour less than what you have collected. If you can maintain ten people working on a full-time basis, this business can easily produce yearly sales of $60,000. The main requirement for this business venture is that you and your staff have taken an instruction course that will certify you for traffic control duties. This requirement could also produce additional sales revenues by charging all employees a fixed instruction course fee, prior to establishing employment with your firm.

CONSTRUCTION EQUIPMENT CLEANING
★★ $$ 🏠 🕐 🌐

You do not often see bulldozers stopping into the local car wash for a quick clean up. It isn't practical, and would cost a lot just for fuel to get there. But contractors need to keep these pieces of equipment clean because dirt and mud can affect the hydraulics and cause damage that can cost thousands of dollars to repair, not to mention the costly down time delays. Investing in portable power washing equipment will give you the ability to start your own mobile construction equipment cleaning service. Market the service by simply stopping into all construction sites and solicit business. You will not have much resistance, as competition is limited for this type of service and all contractors realize the benefits of keeping the very expensive construction equipment clean.

WEB RESOURCE: www.epowerwash.com
Directory service listing power-washing equipment manufacturers and distributors plus industry information.

LIMOUSINE SERVICE
★ $$$$ 🏠 ⚖️

Before starting this business, you will need to check in your local area to see if officials are awarding any further limousine vehicle licenses. If not, find out how much will it cost to secure one of these licenses through a resale opportunity. The next requirement is to secure a chauffeur driver's certificate. This step is relatively simple and only requires a written exam and practical road test to be successfully completed. If you meet these requirements, starting a limousine service is a terrific way to earn a very good living while being your own boss. In recent years many limousine companies have been turning away from the traditional stretch car format in favor of vans and large sport utility vehicles to serve as limousines. There are numerous reasons why this is being done and why you may want to also consider these types of vehicles for your own service. The first is that these vehicles are less costly and more practical; smaller vehicles guzzle less gas and can help keep costs down. The second and perhaps more important reason is using this kind of transportation offers the occupants more privacy and security, which can be very crucial for corporate and celebrity clients. The financially cautious entrepreneur seeking to get into this business can start by working on a subcontract basis as a driver for companies that have the transportation but need drivers. It should be noted, however, that a limousine service is a very expensive undertaking, even with a small fleet of cars. Many have tried and learned the hard way. Between buying or leasing the cars, maintaining them in top condition (hiring a mechanic or two), having a lot of insurance, and paying for gas, a garage for keeping the cars, and an office from which to take reservations and to market the business, you can easily put yourself in the $300,000+ start-up range. Plus you will need to hire a dispatcher, unless you have the skills to handle the job yourself. Unlike other businesses where the start-up costs are high but then the costs to run the business are much more manageable, most of the high costs in this business are ongoing. You'll need new cars every two or three years to stay competitive. You also need reliable drivers. All that being said, providing corporate clients with limousine services, plus limos for weddings, proms, parties, plus airport shuttles can make for a lucrative business... eventually. The business can be marketed by establishing alliances with wedding and event planners, and with hotels, convention centers, business associations, and networking groups.

WEB RESOURCE: www.limo.org
National Limousine Association.

BOOKBINDING AND REPAIRS
★ $ 🏠 🕒

Working right from home, you can bind books in small quantities and repair antique books. Bookbinding equipment is very inexpensive to purchase and there are even construction plans available that will enable you to build your own equipment. Marketing the service can be as easy as establishing alliances with secondhand book retailers and book collector clubs. The ability to bind and repair books can also pay off in terms of finding valuable collectors books yourself, carrying out any needed repairs, and selling the books for a profit.

WEB RESOURCE: www.a1binding.com
Distributors of bookbinding equipment and supplies.

CORPORATE GIFT SERVICE
★★★★ $$$$ 🏠 🌐

Do you have an eye for the perfect gift? If so, starting a corporate gift service can make you a millionaire. For rewarding a valued employee, thanking existing clients, or wooing a potential client, gift giving is essential for most corporations. You can choose a hundred or a thousand perfect gifts that can easily be engraved, customized, or personalized for your corporate customers to give as one-of-a-kind gifts. Once you have selected the items that you will be retailing, create a catalog and web site to display and promote the gift items. The catalogs can be distributed to corporations around the world, and the web site address, with a promotional message, can be e-mailed to every corporate address you can find. The key to success is having gift items that are unique and ready for fast delivery to your customers.

AUCTION BUYER SERVICE
★ $$ 🏠 🕒

Until the day arrives that all auctions take place via the internet, there will always be a need for an auction buyer service. In a nutshell, an auction buyer is a person who takes the place of the purchaser at an auction when the purchaser is unable to attend. An auction buyer's service is very inexpensive to start, and clients can be gained through promoting your service in all traditional print media, as well as electronically over the internet and through e-mails. Remuneration can be by way of a commission on the value of items purchased on behalf of clients, or on a flat-fee basis. Ideally you want to have several clients that you are representing at any one auction. This business start-up will really be of interest to those who have special skills and abilities, such as an art appraiser or antique car appraiser. The more specialized you make your service, the better the chance to eliminate competitors and the greater chance to increase revenues and profits.

PRODUCT DEMONSTRATION SERVICE
★★ $$ 🏠 🕒

Companies often use product demonstration as a method to promote and introduce new products into the marketplace. We have all seen people in grocery stores offering free samples of food or cleaning products to customers. The concept behind this type of marketing is to try and get consumers to like the new product and therefore start to purchase it on a regular basis. The best method of operating a product demonstration service is to hire people to demonstrate the products on a part-time, as-needed basis. Typically, product demonstration services are awarded by companies on a contract basis and include a certain number of demonstration hours and outlets in the contract. Currently product demonstration rates are in the range of $7 to $10 per hour, and the product demonstrators typically receive 80 to 90 percent of the fee. It is vital to the survival of the business that a lot of contracts are secured for product demonstration in order to realize suitable business revenues and profits. The best way to secure product demonstration contracts is not by vying for new or existing contracts with many other demonstration firms, but to go looking for new business by soliciting companies that typically would not use this method of marketing for their products. The reasons for taking this type of marketing approach is that you greatly reduce competition, and that you get to utilize all of your entrepreneurial skills in getting potential clients excited about your service and the benefits it will have for their companies. Profit potential range is part-time $10,000+ per year and full-time $25,000+ per year.

SIGN MAINTENANCE SERVICE
★★ $$$ 🚗 🕐

Look around—signs are everywhere and each one can represent money in your pocket. You can start a sign maintenance service on a relatively small capital investment, and manage the business right from a home office location. All signs require maintenance: light bulbs have to be changed, columns and support posts have to be repainted occasionally, and the signs have to be cleaned. Sign maintenance is most profitable when established on a monthly service contract basis. Clients pay a monthly fee in exchange for ongoing and automatic monthly sign maintenance. The monthly charge for maintenance will be as varied as the signs. New signs can range from $500 to $250,000 to purchase, which means there are no set rates and each individual sign must be priced on its own maintenance requirements. The equipment required for this business venture includes ladders, basic power tools, and a bucket-lift truck, all of which can be purchased secondhand for a fraction of the new cost. Market the service by establishing alliances with sign makers to work on a subcontract basis carrying out sign maintenance for their clients. Also simply create promotional brochures describing your service and distribute the information to commercial property management companies and to business owners with signage that must be maintained. Additional revenues can also be earned by purchasing mobile and inflatable signs that can be rented to business owners wanting to promote sales or special events for their business.

GOLD PLATING
★ $$$ 🚗 🕐

Starting a gold plating business can literally give you the "Midas Touch." The equipment required to operate this business venture is readily available and inexpensive. However, the profits that can be earned are extremely lucrative. The following is only a partial list of items that can be gold plated, and a little bit of creative thinking can expand this list to thousands of items: kitchen and bathroom fixtures, cabinet hardware, automobile emblems, musical instruments, baby items, awards, nameplates, and light fixtures. A great way to establish this kind of business venture is to set up a booth at a mall and gold plate items on site while customers wait. Likewise, building alliances with custom homebuilders and automobile dealers is a great way to network and secure business for your service.

WEB RESOURCE: www.beckerindustries.com
Distributors of gold plating equipment and supplies.

FINDER SERVICE
★ $ 🚗 🕐

Starting a finder service is one of the easiest home-based business ventures to get rolling. A finder service simply means that in exchange for a fee you locate products or services that clients are seeking. These items could range from antique cars to military collectibles to a qualified babysitter prepared to work on holidays. Ideally, you will want to market your service to collectors; it does not matter what collectibles they are searching for, just as long as they are routinely searching. You can base your fees on an hourly rate or you can charge clients a percentage based on the value of the item you have located for them. Additionally, be sure that you are very web savvy, as it will be one of your leading research tools for locating items for clients. By developing your own web site that enables people to post notices about items they are trying to find, you can also run the business as a classified service. In a nutshell, the site would operate like a classifieds web site, but instead of people selling items, people would place ads looking for stuff. You could charge the poster, or providing the site was well promoted and had numerous hits, you could make money through advertisers.

HAIRDRESSER
★★ $$ 🕐 🔧

If you have a hairdressing license, starting your own hairstyling business can be a wonderful way to make some tidy profits. You can open a small salon of your own by finding a good location and doing some local marketing, go into business with another entrepreneur (perhaps a nail salon owner), or start a mobile business whereby you do the hair of people who cannot travel easily, simply do not have the time, or cannot risk traveling with their new coiffure. You can market yourself to the elderly, disabled individuals, busy executives, busy moms with upcoming social plans, brides and bridal party members, actors prior to a performance, and so on. Additional revenues can also be earned by providing clients with manicure and pedicure options. Profit potential can easily exceed $30,000 per year for the owner-operator of the business.

MANUFACTURER'S REPRESENTATIVE
★★★ $$ 🏠

Industry directories are an invaluable research tool, and as a business opportunity a manufacturers directory can put you on the road to earning in excess of $100,000 per year. Utilizing manufacturers directories can help you identify products that are not being manufactured or possibly even sold in your local community. Once you have identified these products and conducted your own market analysis into their viability in your area, you will be able to contact the manufacturers of these products from the information supplied in the directory. Working as a manufacturer's representative means you promote and market the products on a local, city, state, or (in some cases) country basis. Always try to negotiate an exclusive service contract with the manufacturer. This means you will be the manufacturer's exclusive representative within certain geographic boundaries. Remuneration can be by way of a commission charged on total sales, or you can mark up your wholesale costs on the manufactured goods and resell at a higher price. The first method is preferred, as you will not need to warehouse any inventory.

WEB RESOURCE: www.nam.org
National Association of Manufacturers.

SHARPENING SERVICE
★ $$$ 🏠 🕓

A mobile sharpening service is a great business enterprise to start that does not require a lot in terms of special skills or investment capital. Clients can include construction companies, butchers, ice rinks, landscape

contractors, lawn mower repair shops, and just about every other type of company that relies on sharp blades and saws to conduct their business. You can operate the business on a mobile basis right from a van or enclosed trailer converted into a workshop, or you can operate from a homebased location offering free pickup and delivery of the items being sharpened. As a quick-start marketing method consider distributing two-for-one coupons to potential clients.

GLASS ETCHING
★ $$ 🚗 🕓

Glass etching serves a few purposes. First, glass etching can be used as a method to engrave security numbers or names on glass items. Secondly, glass etching is used to create elaborate designs and pictorial themes on glass for interior decorating or artistic expression. Starting a glass etching service does not require a lot of investment capital to get rolling, and a homebased workshop is more than adequate for carrying out the work. Of course, the main requirement for starting this business is to have artistic talent, especially if the business will focus on etching designs for interior decorating. Overall, a glass etching business is a terrific small enterprise that can yield an income of $25 per hour or more.

WEB RESOURCE: http://eglassetching.com
Glass etching sites and equipment.

BABYSITTING SERVICE
★ $ 🏠 🕓

There are a couple of options available to the entrepreneur who is considering a babysitting service as a new business enterprise. The first option is to simply become a babysitter, and surprisingly enough this can really pay off, especially during peak holiday times such as New Year's Eve. The second option is to start a staffing service for babysitters, wherein parents can call one number to get a reliable, screened, and professional babysitter. The service would charge a flat rate—say $17 per hour—and the babysitter would receive 75 percent of the fee while the service would retain the remaining 25 percent. Providing the service routinely achieved total billable hours in the range of 500 per week, the babysitting service could generate revenues in excess of $50,000 per year.

Carefully screen sitters to make sure they are trustworthy and reliable. Also screen clients to make sure they will be home at the time agreed to and that they treat the sitters properly.

MORTGAGE PAYMENT CONSULTANT
★★ $$ 🚗 🕐

Did you know that paying your mortgage in weekly installments as opposed to monthly installments could save you thousands of dollars in interest charges over the life of the mortgage? While this is pretty basic math, many people never take the time to really calculate out how much money they can save by switching to weekly, or even bi-weekly, mortgage payments. Here is your opportunity to let homeowners know the various options they have, which include refinancing for cash value and/or for lower interest rates. Becoming a mortgage payment consultant is easy. Generally there is no special license required and you can operate the service right from home, provided, of course, that you become an expert on the subject of mortgages. You can advertise by direct mail and by local advertising throughout your community, but avoid phone marketing, as more and more people are beginning to despise telemarketers, especially the ongoing calls from mortgage brokers. Consulting appointments or presentations should only require a few hours in time to identify exactly how much the homeowner can save, so a fair fee for the service would be in the range of $75 to $150 per visit.

WEEKEND COURIER SERVICE
★ $$ 🕐

There are two ways to make money operating a weekend courier service. The first is to simply contract your delivery services to established courier companies on an as-needed basis. The second and more profitable method is to secure weekend delivery contracts with local merchants and professionals. You will need reliable transportation in order to operate this service, as well as a beeper or cellular telephone for incoming inquiries. Many merchants and professionals wait until Friday before shipping local deliveries simply because it is less expensive to ship multiple items than it is to ship one at a time. Waiting until Friday enables them to stock pile

deliveries until the end of the week. Joining local business associations and attending networking meetings is a great way to promote your business and secure contracts for the service.

COMMERCIAL EVENT PLANNER
★★ $$ 🚗 🕐

Commercial event planning means putting together seminars, conferences, trade shows, corporate parties, and special activities. The focus of these events includes raising money and/or public awareness, training employees, boosting morale, and encouraging teamwork. To plan events effectively, you must have the goal of the event firmly in front of you and, in a well-organized manner, assemble all of the pieces of the event in a way that fits the personality, image, and brand of the business. You will need to establish a very good contact base so that you can get what you need quickly and at good prices. Corporate planning takes good multi-tasking and communication skills and very good business sense. It is not a business endeavor to go into without doing a great deal of preliminary research or working with a corporate event planner first—possibly as an assistant or partner.

WEB RESOURCE: www.event-planner.com
Directory service listing event planners, information about how to start and market an event planning service, and industry information and links.

PARTY AND/OR WEDDING PLANNER
★★ $$ 🚗 🕐

Weddings, anniversary parties, Bar Mitzvahs and numerous other personal occasions need precise planning and guidance. This can be a fun and very rewarding job for someone who is very well organized and has a knack for putting all of the pieces of an event together. The goal here is making sure that the guests, and most significantly the guests of honor, have a marvelous time. You can specialize in weddings only, or you can handle various types of parties. Weddings and other parties have a common "to-do" list that includes selecting the photographer, videographer, band or DJ, caterer, menu, and flowers; having the invitations done; and, most significantly, booking the room and making sure it is decorated and ready in time. Your contact list is your greatest asset. If you don't know every bridal shop in town (and they don't know you), then you're not serious about wedding planning. You also must have a very flexible schedule so that when the caterer calls with a change of menu items you can be out the door, meeting the nervous couple and tasting the new appetizer selections. The job is dearly more than putting the pieces together; it means getting very involved, if you want to succeed. Your most important skill must be listening. If the bride wants pink flamingos, that does not mean white doves. You also need to immerse yourself in what can possibly be done at weddings and parties of all types, so that you can make numerous recommendations. Personal event planning is a very competitive business, but if you are good at it, you can make a very good living. To start out, do your first two jobs for free if necessary, or work as an assistant for a while, helping an established planner. Referrals are crucial and you must get your feet wet. In fact, if you are intimidated by taking on a wedding, start with smaller parties such as an anniversary or graduation party. Wedding expenses often exceed $40,000 and Bar Mitzvahs can involve more than $25,000. Therefore, you need to price yourself accordingly, based on the amount of work involved and the rates for wedding and event planners in your area.

WEB RESOURCE: www.nawp.com
The National Association of Wedding Professionals.

WEB RESOURCE: www.event-planner.com
Directory service listing event planners, information about how to start and market an event planning service, and industry information and links.

CEILING CLEANING SERVICE
★★ $$ 🚗 🕒 🌐

Starting a ceiling cleaning service is one of those business opportunities that can be either a costly venture to set into action, or a business that can be started for a modest amount of money. In the spirit of shoestring start-ups, let's choose the low-budget approach. Simply purchase a few buckets, a swivel-head cleaning pad with a telescopic handle, and a ladder; get some liability insurance; and initiate a basic marketing program consisting of flier distribution and introduction telephone calls. Build alliances with commercial property management firms and office cleaners, as both can refer your service to

their clients. Prior to jumping right in, practice on the ceilings of friends and neighbors (and their businesses if possible) for free. You need to get an idea of how to do the job quickly and efficiently, and word of mouth can make or break your business. Don't be afraid to get out and knock on doors because a great deal of new business can be secured by simply cold calling on offices and restaurants in your local area and introducing the owner or manager to your service. Ceiling cleaning is a solid choice for a new business enterprise; the industry is stable, there is proven consumer demand for the service, operating overheads are minimal, and the learning curve is quick and easy to master.

WEB RESOURCE: www.icwc.com
Manufacturers and distributors of ceiling cleaning equipment and supplies.

FURNITURE ARRANGING SERVICE
★ $ 🚗 🕒

Launching a furniture arranging and rearranging service that caters to residential and commercial clients is a fantastic new part-time business venture to put into action. The business can easily be managed from a home-based office, requires little in the way of experience or start-up capital, and has the potential to generate an income in the range of $15 to $25 per hour. Target your marketing efforts toward moving companies, real estate agents, interior decorators, and furniture retailers. You can also market the service directly to homeowners by distributing fliers explaining the benefits of your service, as well as the benefits of having their furniture professionally rearranged (i.e., more visually appealing, better use of small living spaces, increased functionality, Feng Shui, etc.). A prerequisite for operating the business is an eye for design and organization, as well as a strong back. Extra income can also be earned by providing clients with additional services, such as a packing and unpacking service and a budget decorating service, both of which are also featured in this directory.

MYSTERY SHOPPER SERVICE
★★ 🚗 🕒 🌐

No mystery here—the title of this business opportunity explains it all. Go undercover and mystery shop at clients' businesses to assess their employees, operating procedures, and customer service policies. In the past decade, more companies, organizations, and retailers have introduced mystery shopper programs into their business than ever before. And for good reason, as mystery shopper programs work very well at uncovering customer service problems and such. Many mystery shopper companies specialize in a particular industry or type of business, such as retail clothing stores and automobile service centers. They can also be employed to scout competition, particularly for new businesses that are just being established and need to know what their competition is up to but don't have the time to stroll through the retail outlets themselves. You may also want to consider specialization for your business. Generally, the mystery shopper will prepare a document detailing their findings, relaying their experiences, and making recommendations to clients upon completion of their visit. Expanding the business is as easy as hiring additional mystery shoppers to work on a "subcontract as-needed basis." The industry is competitive, so the more relevant experiences and training you can bring to the table, the better. These experiences could include managerial training, prior customer service postings, human resources experience, and operations specialists. There are even mystery shopper training courses available that can put you on the path to starting and operating your own business. Once established, the income potential is in the range of $15 to $25 per hour per mystery shopper.

WEB RESOURCE: www.mysteryshopperjobs.com
Industry information and links.

INDOOR ENVIRONMENTAL TESTING
★★ $$$ 🏠 🕐 ⚖ 🌐

The air you breathe at home and work could prove deadly. As sobering as this statement is, there is truth to these words as more and more cases of indoor environmental toxic poisoning are reported each year. Getting started in the indoor environmental testing industry will mean an investment of time and money on your behalf to become a certified technician or, as known in the industry, a Certified Indoor Environmentalist. The Indoor Air Quality Association offers certification training and the basic course requires approximately one week to com-

plete, costing in the range of $1,000. The association also offers further courses designed to certify technicians with more specific training and testing procedures in various environmental toxins. Additional start-up costs will include equipment purchases, marketing and advertising budgets, transportation, and licensing. However, as a method to keep start-up costs to a minimum, once the certification process is complete you can subcontract your services to an existing indoor environmental testing company that requires technicians to service their clients using their equipment. Marketing the service can be accomplished by initiating a direct mail campaign, building alliances with commercial and residential property managers, and seeking government contracts to carry out air quality testing in government-operated buildings and institutions. Fees greatly vary depending on the testing that is being conducted, but the starting rate is equivalent to $30 per hour and can go as high as $100 per hour.

WEB RESOURCE: www.iaqa.org
Indoor Air Quality Association, industry information and links as well as certification programs.

PLASTIC LAMINATING
★★ $$ 🏠 🕐

Investing a few thousand dollars into laminating equipment is the first step toward starting your own part-time homebased plastic laminating business. This is one of those little-known business opportunities that really has the potential to generate excellent profits for entrepreneurs with strong marketing skills. There are numerous items that can be laminated in plastic, including restaurant menus, brochures, business presentations, identification cards, and place cards. There are also heat laminating presses available that will enable you to laminate items up to 48 inches in width. Having the availability to laminate items in plastic to that width opens up further opportunities for profits from laminating movie posters, maps, and charts for boaters and divers. Market the service directly to restaurants and to small print and copy shops that do not currently provide laminating options. Great add-on services to boost revenues include bookbinding and repairs, digital color printing, and a scanner service. Once word is out, the business can largely be supported by repeat business and word-of-mouth referrals.

WEB RESOURCE: www.laminators.com
Distributors of laminating equipment and supplies.

GARAGE AND ESTATE SALE PROMOTER
★★ $ 🚗 🕑 🌐

Excellent profits await the entrepreneurs that possess good marketing and organizational skills and start a business that promotes and hosts garage and estate sales. Garage, lawn, and estate sales are a popular weekend event in every community across North America. You can provide a valuable service by organizing and operating garage or estate sales for clients who do not have the time to hold their own Your duties will include promoting, organizing, displaying, and selling the items, and cleaning up after everyone has gone home. In a nutshell, it's your client's sale, at their location, with their stuff for sale, but with you as the ringmaster who has organized and carried out the event. Of course in exchange for providing this valuable service you receive either an hourly fee for your hard work or a percentage of the total revenues the sale creates. Typically, the commission will be in the range of 20 percent for larger sales, and up to 50 percent of revenues for smaller sales. Generally you won't find many clients that will complain about surrendering a percentage of the sales, simply because if it wasn't for your service there is a good chance that the sale would not take place. However, if the items are simply not very enticing, you can do everything possible and they may not sell, which is why you may simply opt for an hourly fee instead. If you are a good gauge of the items, and perhaps a frequent viewer of Antique Road Show, you will be able to determine which is a better pricing means for your services. The key to success in this type of business is promotion. Once you have secured a client, be sure to canvas the neighborhood and solicit for additional business. Why hold a small sale if you can potentially increase revenues and profits by enlisting neighbors to also provide items to be sold? Market the sale by promoting it in local newspapers that do not charge for classified ads or that do not charge for garage sale notices. Also have large signs made that can be temporarily installed on telephone poles in the area that the sale is being conducted. To secure future business simply hand out promotional brochures and tell people in attendance about your service.

OFFICE CONTRACTOR
★★ $$$ 🚗 🕑 ⚖️

Here is a terrific business opportunity that will appeal to entrepreneurs with a renovation or construction management background. Big profits can be earned operating a contracting business that specializes in office renovations. Having operated a contracting business for many years, I always found that the commercial jobs or office renovation contracts generally produced the highest profit margins—often two times that of residential renovation jobs. The higher profit margins were usually attributed to factors including fewer changes along the way (completion on time), a less competitive marketplace, and a higher grade of products used in finishing (increased average sale).

To truly succeed in this segment of the construction industry will require patience, as often jobs are not put up for tender or bidding and are awarded on the basis of a referral or having completed past contracts for the client. However, once again patience can be rewarded with profits. You can market the service by establishing alliances with commercial property management companies, moving companies that specialize in office relocation, commercial building cleaners, and real estate and insurance agents. In most cases you will find it to be financially beneficial to hire subcontractors to complete the work as opposed to hiring employees. This is simply due to the nature of the construction industry as a whole and trying to maintain employee salaries during the lean times can mean the difference of staying in business or meeting with financial disaster. Additionally, equipment can be rented on an as-needed basis to keep start-up costs in check. Profit potential will vary on a job-to-job basis, but when estimating always try to maintain a 50 percent markup on labor and materials. Using this pricing formula will result in a 33 percent gross profit margin prior to operating overheads and taxes. Aim to generate gross sales of $1 million per year and you can generate gross profits in excess of $300,000.

BRIDAL AND FASHION SHOW PROMOTER
★★ $$ 🚗 🕑

Organizing and hosting bridal and fashion shows can earn excellent profits. The shows can take place four times per year and feature bridal and clothing fashions for that season. You can rent a ballroom or banquet hall to host the event and, with some clever negotiation skills, you may even be able to secure the venue at no charge, providing you can convince management that food and beverage sales will provide a more than sufficient return. Be careful not to swing such a good deal for yourself that you lose the ballroom and do not have a location for your next event. Therefore, if the location is not getting enough money through food and drinks, offer to put up some money for rental costs. Building alliances is important and sometimes it means spending money to make money. Local merchants in the bridal and fashion industry can be easily secured to showcase their products and services, as there is no cost to the merchants to participate in the show and they can have an opportunity to sell. Revenues to support the business and generate a profit are earned by charging an admission fee to the show, as well as by selling advertising space in the event program and in the form of banners and place cards at tables. Additionally, be sure to secure a co-sponsor for each event that can assist in promotion, such as a newspaper or radio station,. Expanding the business is as easy as promoting and hosting the shows in different communities, and for the truly innovative entrepreneurs you can even establish a web site that features a year-round online bridal and fashion show and that whets the appetite for more and draw people for the real thing.

Before holding fashion shows, you need to secure models. This can range from established models, whom you will pay top dollar, to students and aspiring models who work for very little money because they want the credit of having participated in the shows and the photos and video for their future modeling endeavors.

SMALL CAPACITY BANQUET FACILITIES
★★ $$$$ 🚗 🕐

Small banquet facilities that are suitable for a 100 guests or less are becoming very popular. Starting this type of business just might be the answer to the question, "What type of part-time and potentially profitable business can I start?" You can get started by leasing a suitable commercial location and carrying out the required renovations and leasehold improvements to turn the space into a small banquet room. The facility will require washrooms, a small well-equipped commercial kitchen that can be utilized by outside caterers, and fixtures such as tables and chairs. These types of small banquet facilities are perfect for corporate functions, social and family functions, awards ceremonies, stockholder meetings, seminars, parties, and even weddings. The goal is not to become an event planner or host of the banquet, but to supply a well-equipped and comfortable location for clients that wish to rent an event location. Basically, you rent clients the location and equipment they need to host their event. Market the banquet facility by establishing alliances with catering companies, event and wedding planners, corporations, social and business clubs, and local charity groups. If you find a desirable location, with ample parking and the right ambiance, it will not take long until the banquet room is booked well in advance by repeat clients and clients who have heard about the service word-of-mouth. Be sure to check with and conform to local building and health codes prior to establishing the business. You will need a health board license for the kitchen, on-site fire and safety equipment to meet fire codes, and perhaps a liquor or beer and wine license as well. You will also need to provide excellent customer service, meaning you will do whatever you can to make sure the facility accommodates their needs.

SPECIALTY WIRING SERVICE
★★ $$ 🚗 🕐

Put your basic construction and wiring experience to work by starting a specialty wiring service. Computers, built-in speakers, fire and security alarms, and televisions all have one thing in common—most still require hardwiring in order to work. And until the day that all techno toys, gadgets, and home electronics are wireless there will be a huge demand for the services of a wiring specialist. In fact, even setting up WiFi systems is not as easy as most people think. Starting this business does not mean that you need to be a certified electrician, as these types of wiring jobs are non-electrical or low voltage and do not require a certificate to install. However, basic tools and a good understanding of wiring and networking systems are required. You can provide specialty wiring installation for both new construction and retrofitting of homes and offices. It is obviously easier to install wiring cable and products in a new construction situation, but this segment of the industry is also much more competitive. Additionally, some wiring installation contractors prefer to specialize in one or two types of wiring, such as computer networks or built-in sound and speaker systems. Depending on your experience and local competition in the marketplace you may want to also consider specialization. Market your products and services by developing partnerships with builders of new homes, renovation contractors, and residential and commercial property management companies. Also an excellent income can be earned by subcontracting your services to existing businesses, such as alarm companies (certificate or bonding may be required), electronic and computer retailers, TV cable providers, and satellite TV retailers. Currently specialty wiring installers are charging $40 and up per hour for the service, plus materials used.

SMALL ENGINE REPAIR
★★★ $$$$

Repairing lawn mowers and chain saws can be a very lucrative business. Like any business that relies on walk-in traffic to generate sales, the location of a small engine repair shop is critical in terms of the demographics of the area and primary or target markets. Be sure to establish warranty repair services with manufacturers of small engine equipment, as not only does it pay well, but also these manufacturers can send a lot of business to a small engine repair service. Additional income can also be gained for the business by providing customers with optional services, such as saw and blade sharpening, as well as small equipment rentals.

SPECIAL OCCASION YARD CUTOUTS
★ $

You can design and build your own special occasion yard cutouts, such as a stork for birth announcements or a happy birthday caricature. Or you can purchase pre-designed and constructed special occasion yard cutouts to get this unique advertising business off the ground. Clients typically include people that want to surprise other people by having an announcement placed in their front yard to let everyone in the neighborhood know about the special occasion. Yard card rental rates are in the range of $30 to $60 per day including delivery, installation, and pickup. A special occasion yard cutout rental business is not likely to make you rich. However, a terrific part-time income can be earned from this homebased specialty advertising business.

WEB RESOURCE: www.yardcarddirectory.com
Access to information on starting a yard card business.

PERSONAL SHOPPER
★★ $ 🕐

If you love to shop, this is the best way to go. Making money at something you enjoy doing is the goal of most people and, as a personal shopper, you can spend time in stores and earn money being there. Busy executives, socialites, and people who cannot get out to shop because of illness or injury, hire personal shoppers to help them get what they need. While the ease of purchasing on the internet has cut into this profession in some ways, it has also opened the door to browsing online and buying nearby, for the "need it now" executives. The modern personal shopper utilizes the internet and visits the stores on a regular basis, earning $50 to $100 an hour, which makes shopping that much more fun! The value of a personal shopper isn't just as a time saver, but, much like a caddie in golf, as a knowledgeable assistant. Therefore, you need to know where to find items quickly, where to get the best prices and all of the tricks of the shopping trade. Having a background in retail is a definite plus, since it will help put you in touch with the wealth of products and brands available to the modern consumer. Also, make sure you are a good listener and understand that you are trying to meet the shopping needs and tastes of someone else. As you do some research and wind your way around the learning curve, you should accumulate a host of reference guides and make contacts in as many places as you can. Once you've got the knack, you can hire and train others to be personal shoppers too. Market yourself to executives through mailings, well-placed ads and on a web site. Word of mouth will also be a major marketing tool as satisfied customers will pass your business cards around for you.

ESCORT SERVICE
★★ $$$$ 🕹

Alone in a strange town and need company to a party or dinner? Escort services are legitimate ways in which individuals hook up with a companion who will accompany them to any number of events for the evening. The obvious concern when someone mentions an escort service is the potential for illegal activities, mainly prostitution. To run such a service, you therefore need to screen escorts very carefully, seeking college students and others who are looking to serve only as an escort for the evening. You also need to make it clear to customers and the local law enforcement that your service is above board and legitimate and have contractual paperwork that states your parameters. If you can pass the "image" hurdle, you can charge $200 and up per hour for your escort service and spilt the money with the individual escorts. Advertise in all area publications that will allow you to do so and stress your legitimacy.

COLLEGE PLANNER AND CONSULTANT
★★★★ $$ 🏠

Getting into college is becoming more and more competitive as enrollments have increased while few new colleges have opened their doors in the past couple of decades. If you are organized, very good at communicating with teenagers, and able to withstand pushy parents, you could start and run this unique business and make very good money, upwards of $100,000 with enough referrals. A college planner helps students prepare for college, study for the entrance tests, and go through the application process. However, most importantly, you help the student find the college that best suits his or her needs, from an academic and social perspective. You can help them narrow down the choices and select the best schools to which they should apply. To do this, you need to travel to numerous schools, talk to administrators, faculty, and anyone from the dean to the students to find out what makes a school tick. Doing a lot of research and staying on top of the many policies of hundreds of schools makes this a very busy business and in time you may hire assistants to help with all of the research necessary. However, it can be rewarding, as you help shape the futures of young people, and also quite lucrative. Market

in every way possible to families of high school students, starting as soon as they enter high school. Much of the business will come by word of mouth.

FUNDRAISING CONSULTANT
★★ $$ 🏠 🕐

Charities, associations, schools, and religious institutions are always seeking ways to raise funds. And that's where you can come in, if you elect to become an expert on fundraising and sell your expertise. A good fundraising consultant can assess an organization's strengths and weaknesses and help them determine the best means in which to raise funds. Then, you begin working on the details. For example, too many organizations spend the money they are raising before they even have it. Therefore your job will be to help them find low-cost means of raising money by putting in human hours and expertise rather than draining their budgets.

WEB RESOURCE: www.afpnet.org
Association of Fundraising Professionals.

PARTY DJ SERVICE
★★★★ $$$$

What do you think about making $4000 for a DJ service at a Bar Mitzvah for five hours of work? It is not unheard of for DJ services today to command anywhere from $2,000 to $7,000 for parties and weddings. This is your ticket to wealth if you have the DJ skills or the ability to choose quality DJs and book them. The modern packages come complete with giveaway fun items for guests and, of course, the dancers. Packages in New York for a DJ, MC, and two dancers, plus the giveaways, start at close to $3,000, and you can add on additional items, such as special lighting and videos. Start-up expenses are primarily in putting together the promotional packages and disseminating them to the party planners, catering facilities, and any other places in which Sweet Sixteen Parties, graduation parties, Bar/Bat Mitzvahs, and weddings are held and will probably be less than $15,000. You will need a web site with recent photos of your DJs, dancers, and MCs in action. If you are the only DJ or MC, make sure to get some good photos of you doing what you do best while dressed to the hilt! You will also need to purchase the latest in DJ equipment and hopefully have a van or other means of transportation available. Scout the competition in your area (since this is a "hot" growing business) and see what the prices are and what is included in the various packages. You will need to train your DJs and dancers to accommodate the clients as professionally as possible. Listening to the needs and wishes of the clients are very important when creating the entertainment package for a special event.

WEB RESOURCE: www.djkj.com
National Association of Mobile Entertainers.

INTERPRETER AND TRANSLATER
★★ $$ 🚗 🕐

If you are fluent in more than one language, you can provide a valuable service to businesses, universities, and government officials… and make upwards of $50,000 for doing so. Translating written text and oral presentations or speeches in our multi-cultural society is very much in demand. To really succeed with this business, you also need to be able to capture the nuances and understand the cultural difference between languages as well as translating or interpreting the words. This business can be started from a homebase with virtually no overhead beyond marketing yourself and your services. If you are looking to forge a larger business, you can recruit other translators for various languages. In North America, Spanish, Japanese, Chinese, French, Italian, and German are the languages most in need of translation.

WEB RESOURCE: www.atanet.org
American Translators Association.

SET DESIGN
★★★ $$$$ 🚗

If you love theater, film, and the arts, you might opt to start your own set design business, whereby you create the visual backdrop for theater, television shows, commercials, and/or films. The proliferation of independent producers and filmmakers, plus the growth of local and regional theatre, makes this a business with great potential if you know how to work within a budget (for props and scenery), and arrange the scenery and properties (a.k.a. props) to best suit the needs of the producers, writers, directors, and others involved in creating a production. Numerous schools teach set design and after taking courses, you can hone your skills working on local productions. Take photos of your work and have them ready in your portfolio to show producers. Typically, with commercial productions, you can earn $40k to $50k with little operating expense other than marketing yourself, and much of that will come from networking within the industry.

PERSONAL TRAINER
★★★ $$ 🌐

Most Americans know they should start getting in shape, but many need someone to "pump them up" to get them started. If you are in excellent physical condition and know how to guide others in physical fitness, this is a business to consider. The key to success is knowing the right program for each client by assessing their needs, considering his or her age, health status, weight, etc. You can build your business by word of mouth, along with some basic advertising, and spread the word about your physical-fitness expertise at health spas, running, swimming and biking clubs, and other athletic outlets. Personal trainers are very much in vogue, so this is an opportunity time to consider starting such a business. Earnings of $40k to $50 are typical and if you can sell some health-related products you can increase those numbers.

MEDICAL TRANSCRIPTION
★★ $$ 🕐 🌐

From a homebased office, you can start a medical transcription business and make a nice income. Doctors, dentists, chiropractors, physical therapists, and even veterinarians can utilize the help of someone to transcribe dictated recordings of patient information and create electronic patient records. Material can include examination and operation reports, diagnostic studies, ongoing patient progress notes, and even material for seminars, journal articles, books, and printed matter. Using the internet you can receive dictation and transcribe it using digital or analog dictating equipment.

REQUIREMENTS: You will need knowledge of medical terminology, anatomy and physiology, and basic transcription and computer equipment. Certificate and associate degree programs are easily found to help you attain the necessary skills. While 70 percent of the work typically comes from hospitals or private physicians offices, other sources such as medical and diagnostic laboratories, outpatient care centers, and offices of physical, occupational, and speech therapists can also provide you with clients. One of the fastest-growing fields in the United States, with some 100,000+ medical transcribers, makes this a very viable business to embark upon.

WEB RESOURCE: www.aamt.org
American Association of Medical Transcription.

SURVEY SERVICE
★★ $$ 🚗 🕐

Numerous businesses rely on surveys to gather valuable information for future marketing and sales. Creating and distributing a good survey that collects significant data is not as easy as one might think. Through printed forms, by phone or via the internet, surveys must be presented in such a manner that users are comfortable responding with real data. They also must guarantee that no privacy issues are breached. This is where you can step in with a survey business and help companies gather valid and useful information. To start such a business, you need to have some marketing skills and a good knowledge of statistical information. You can charge clients an hourly rate for your time spent creating the survey and honing it to the specific needs of the client. You can then charge for time spent marketing the survey because without a good plan for marketing, the best survey in the world will be rendered useless if no one responds to it. Finally, you can charge for the time spent tallying the results and even assisting with action plans based on the results of the surveys.

MONOGRAMMING SERVICES
★ $$ 🚗 🕐

Monogramming has long been a popular means of personalizing gift items ranging from photo albums to glassware. If you are good at detailed work and can get the latest in monogramming machines, this can be a lucrative business to start. You can market yourself directly to consumers but you will have a better chance of building up your clientele by aligning yourself with gift shops and retailers. If you become the regular monogrammer for one or several retailers, you can find yourself very busy. You should also make sure that stores with gift registries are familiar with your services.

When pricing your services, you need to consider the specific pieces and the necessary time commitment,. Most jobs can be done quickly and if you are working with a store that is sending over a lot of work, you can give them a bulk discount. You simply need to be prepared for the tougher jobs and therefore not set one across-the-board rate. While you may be able to produce quickly, you need to make sure you give yourself adequate time and have plans in which to pick up and drop off the products so that you do not spend too much valuable time in transit.

WORD PROCESSING
★★★ $$ 🚗 🕐

It may not be very exciting, but if you are fast and accurate, there is plenty of potential work as a word processor. Businesses and universities are just two among many places where volume can pile up and your services can be very helpful. As a part-time business, this can be a great choice, since you can work from home and choose your hours. In fact, some word processors enjoy working in the quiet of the night while enjoying other pursuits during the day, after grabbing a few winks. At $3 per page, your potential income can add up. If you can hit the keys at 100 words per minute, the average 350-word double spaced page will take you 3.5 minutes, meaning you can handle 17 pages per hour for $51. If you can then come up with just 25 hours of work weekly, you can secure $1,275 a week or over $63,000 a year! Of course you will need to use some of the remaining weekly hours to secure a good volume of work. You can also bill higher rates, such as $7 to $10 for resumes and other specific documents that need to be formatted in a specific manner.

IMAGE CONSULTANT
★★ $$ 🚗 🕐

Do you have "the look" or know what "the look" is? If you do, you can start an image consulting business, specializing in working with individual and corporate clients on developing the best appearance for success in their fields. You will also consult on behavior and communication skills through individual consultations, coaching, presentations and workshops.

REQUIREMENTS: While image consultants can gain certification, it is not mandatory. You do need to be well versed in fashion, trends, business etiquette, communication, nonverbal communication, and be able to assess the needs of each specific client. Being able to motivate, educate, and play psychologist when necessary, all fall under the guise of a good image consultant.

WEB RESOURCE: www.aici.org
Association of Image Consultants International.

MASSAGE THERAPIST
★★★★ $$ 🌐

In a stressful world, massage therapy is an excellent business to start and profit from. One of the fastest growing fields, massage therapy can be your ticket to a six-figure income if you master the skills and do significant marketing. Today, you'll find massage therapists not only in spas, but working in health clubs and cruise lines. The more methods of massage you master, the larger the market. Swedish Massage, Deep Tissue Massage, and Trigger Point Therapy are among the methods in which you will want to learn and hone your skills, if you intend to handle the business yourself. The other option is to find individuals who are skilled in giving such massages and serve as the business organizer and administrator, linking the massage therapists up with clients for a commission. You may start out doing some gratis massages to generate word of mouth about your skills. This business is part traditional marketing and (a very big) part word of mouth. Once you have gained clients you will want to have them coming to you regularly, so your massage table-side manner is very important.

REQUIREMENTS: Know what licensing is required in your area, since states, provinces, counties, and jurisdictions have different laws. You also need to complete coursework and training at institutions offering massage therapy programs, or make sure everyone you hire has completed such training programs.

WEB RESOURCE: www.amtamassage.org
American Massage Therapy Association; source for continuing education and information resources.

EFFICIENCY EXPERT
★★ $$

Time = Money. That is the theme of this business, and in today's modern high tech world, corporate executives and owners of manufacturing companies will pay big bucks to get your answers to that equation. There is always a faster, more efficient way of getting something done and you need to assess each individual situation and find that new way. Most efficiency experts today focus primarily on technology. However, there are still practical aspects of time management that can be addressed in almost any business. Therefore, if you study means of saving time and creating fluent systems that get work done faster and more efficiently in any type of business, you can be very successful at such a career. Marketing to businesses of all types can be accomplished through mailings and ads in business publications. Keep in mind since many people resent having an outsider come in and tell them how to do things, so you need to bill yourself as a friend not a foe, and emphasize that you are coming to help and not to boss people around. You can bill at $100 an hour, or more and get a lot of work via word of mouth, provided your clients see results, which means "Time = more money."

REQUIREMENTS: Your mastery of time management, plus math, statistical, communications, and people skills will be your most significant tools. Since you can run this business from home and there are few actual tools, your startup costs are low. However, the learning curve is steep, since you need to have a better way of doing things up your sleeve.

BALLOON BOUQUETS
★ $ 🏠 🕒

When sending flowers seems too personal, many people opt to send balloon bouquets. This homebased business is inexpensive to start and easy to run, provided you have a van or SUV, access to inexpensive balloons, and a couple of pumps. You need to market your services everywhere with ads, fliers, and yes, balloons. Make sure you have balloons for all occasions and can arrange bouquets. Include balloons in a box and other unique manners of presentation. A typical balloon bouquet costs only a few dollars to assemble, with balloons, string, and perhaps a box, and you can charge $25 to $40 or more depending on the size of the bouquet.

WEB RESOURCE: www.wholesaleballoons.com

PERSONAL AIR COURIER SERVICE
★★ $$$$ 🚗 🕐

If you love to travel, this is the business for you. As an air courier, you transport items from one destination to another within a specified timeframe. Items may include business documents, medicines, rare antiques, valuable art, or any number of important corporate materials that need an individual to oversee such transport. As long as you are careful to transport only legal goods, you can run a thriving business and see the world in the process. The advantage of having a courier transport valuable items is that the items are far less likely to get lost, broken, or delayed going through customs. Personal attention is worthwhile for a company when handling valuable or time sensitive goods. Since you are providing a unique service, you are not competing with the many "overnight" courier services that ship cargo. Market your services to major companies, galleries, and high-end auction houses. Also, make sure you are listed in the Yellow Pages and have a web site touting your services. In some cases, you may even be asked to accompany a child or a senior when traveling. You can start this business on your own from a homebase. In time, you can branch out and hire additional couriers. If you do so, however, you may need to cut down on traveling yourself so that you can oversee the travel itineraries of the couriers that you have hired.

REQUIREMENTS: There are very few overhead costs, other than marketing materials and advertising. You will need a valid passport, should be in good health, and be highly responsible to start such a business. You also need to be able to pick up and travel whenever necessary.

SECRETARIAL SERVICE
★★★ $$

The time has never been better than now to start a homebased secretarial service. Homebased businesses are starting in record numbers each year in North America and many business owners and employees, working from home, lack the infrastructure and resources that traditional offices provide. The secretarial

services provided can include word processing, electronic filing, scheduling appointments, receptionist duties, etc. Obtaining clients for such a service can be as easy as sending brochures to all local businesses and making follow up phone calls. Also, start and promote your web site heavily, so that it comes to mind when the need for a secretarial service arises.

TICKET BROKER
★★ $$$ 🚗 🕐 🚐

Unlike ticket scalping, which is illegal, you can legally broker tickets for sporting events, theater, and concerts in most cities in North America. You should certainly check to make sure, but if you can legally broker tickets in your area, start by establishing contacts with stadiums, theaters, and venues at which events take place to purchase blocks of tickets, or be on the list to receive tickets to sell on consignment. In addition, you will need to build up or hook into a large network of movers and shakers in your town who just might have tickets to sell. You will also need to be cunning to come up with harder-to-get tickets by purchasing from season ticket holders and advertising for ticket holders willing to sell. If there is a great demand for tickets, you can sell at a significant markup, with in-demand tickets bringing in hundreds and sometimes thousands of dollars. On the other hand, you may find yourself stuck with tickets for events that are not sold out and lack the luster of the latest Broadway hit show. This is, therefore, a very risky business to go into and one that you should start small, with a limited inventory, until you get the hang of the business and the wheeling and dealing that goes on. Market your ticket business to hotels for tourists, since they often do not know where to go for seats and you can provide the solution. Also, try to align yourself with corporate clients who can afford to pay more for good seats at the last minute.

WEB RESOURCE: www.natb.org
National Association of Ticket Brokers.

ROOMMATE REFERRAL SERVICE
★★ $ 🚗 🕐

Definitely a business that will do well in urban areas and college towns, this is a service that is easy to start for less than $1,000 from a home office. All you need is to mix and match roommates based on information gathered about each applicant—in short, your job is to keep Felix Unger and Oscar Madison from sharing the same apartment. This is an excellent business to take to the web to generate applicants. However, you need to make sure to meet people in person because there are some folks who misrepresent themselves on the internet. You get a commission for brokering the match ups. You can set your commission, or charge a fee, based on the area in which you are "matchmaking," and based on the going rate for rentals.

MEDIATOR
★ $$

In most areas of the United States a mediator is not required to be licensed or have certificate training, making this an excellent choice for a new business venture. The duties of a mediator are to bring two opposing sides together and find common ground. A mediation service should not be confused with an arbitration service as a mediator does not rule in favor of either party, but remains neutral. The purpose of mediation is to reconcile differences between parties before litigation or arbitration is required to settle the dispute. Securing clients for a mediation service is best accomplished by building alliances with lawyers so the lawyers can refer your service to their clients. Mediators generally bill by the day for mediation services, and the rates average out to approximately $80 to $100 per hour.

WEB RESOURCE: www.mediatorindex.com
American Arbitration Association.

PERSONAL ASSISTANT
★★ $$

Independent personal assistant services are becoming extremely popular and widely utilized by business owners and corporate executives that occasionally have a need for a personal assistant, but not on a full-time basis. Duties performed by a personal assistant include everything from booking appointments to returning telephone calls and, in some cases, even picking up dry cleaning or buying gifts for friends and family members. Additionally, most personal assistants are required to have computer skills as well as their own laptops. Travel is often required

to accompany the client to trade shows, business functions, and out-of-town business appointments. Good personal assistants can be very valuable to top level executives, or celebrities, in need of someone trustworthy and efficient.

WEB RESOURCE: www.celebrityassistants.org
The Association of Celebrity Personal Assistants.

INVENTORY SERVICE
★★ $$$

In spite of the fact that many businesses have a computerized inventory tracking system in place, most businesses still must conduct semiannual or annual inventory counts for tax and inventory shrinkage reasons. This fact creates a fantastic opportunity to capitalize by starting an inventory recording service. The business concept is very basic, and there are specialized handheld electronic recorders that enable the user to rapidly record and document inventory with a business or warehouse. One of the main marketing tools to utilize is the fact that, in most cases, the inventory counting can be conducted at night. Not disturbing the business or having to pay employees overtime wage rates to conduct the counts, not to mention the fact of accuracy in counting and recording methods, make this service attractive to businesses.

TRADE SHOW VISITOR
★ $

Did you know that many corporations enlist the services of an independent trade show visitor, or researcher, as a method of keeping track of their competition? Starting a trade show visitor service is very simple. The duties of a trade show visitor are to collect information for clients about their competition exhibiting at the show. The information collected might include items such as marketing brochures, display booth designs, pictures, traffic counts, special promotions, new product introductions, and just about anything else a client may request. To make the business more financially viable, most trade show visitors attend shows representing as many as ten or more clients. To establish and operate the service, excellent communication and marketing skills will be needed, and a digital camera and a notebook computer will prove invaluable.

_____ OF THE MONTH CLUB
★ $$$$

Books, toys, tools, CDs, fruit, or just about any product can be the basis of a monthly club. The secret to success in this type of homebased retail business is to offer good quality products at discounted or less than retail cost. This is to build a large club membership base and constantly expand both the membership base and the selection of products being offered for sale. To keep start-up costs to a minimum, there are thousands of manufacturers and distributors of consumer goods that will drop ship products directly to your customers. To build a club membership base quickly, advertise free memberships as well as a free mystery gift as an incentive for people to become members. You then make money as they purchase products or sign other people up for monthly products sent as gifts. Packaging of the products and special features for club members make this inviting for people to sign up.

TEMPORARY HELP AGENCY
★★★ $$$ 🏠

Starting a homebased "temp agency" is a fantastic new business venture to set in motion. Ideally, the agency should specialize in supplying qualified workers on a temporary basis in one particular industry or area of expertise, such as the construction industry. Recruiting workers prepared to work on a temporary basis should not prove difficult, given that many people, such as students and early retirees, have reasons why they do not wish to seek full-time employment, and even homebased business owners often seek to gain some additional income periodically. Marketing the service can be as easy as creating an information package describing the service and workforce, and distributing the packages to businesses and companies that occasionally rely on temporary workers to run their business. Establishing a billing rate for the workers supplied is based on market value for the job being performed, and the agency representing the worker generally retains 10 to 15 percent or the workers earnings.

FILING SYSTEMS
★★ $$ 🏠

Environmentalists once envisioned the computer and its electronic information storage capacities as the absolute final solution for a world that would no longer need to consume paper products. However, as long as an original signature stands as the most binding and unchallenged legal identification for a person, there will always be a need for paper, files, and filing systems. Operating a business that sells and installs filing systems is a great homebased enterprise to set in motion. Not only can you make a profit on the initial sale of the system, but also as your client's business grows and expands you will receive repeat sales of filing supplies. Customers can include businesses and professionals whose business or service is document reliant such as lawyers, doctors, advertising firms, financial institutions, schools, and government agencies. Aim for yearly sales of $200,000 while maintaining a product markup of 50 percent. The results will be a terrific homebased business generating revenues of $70,000 per year.

WEB RESOURCE: www.resources.com/storagma.htm
Directory service listing manufacturers and distributors of filing systems and storage management equipment.

1-800 TELEPHONE CALL CENTER
★★★ $$$ 🏠

A 1-800 telephone call center is simply an answering service that caters to companies that sell products via mail order, classified advertising, and infomercials. They rely on a 1-800 or toll-free line for incoming inquiries and product orders. Furthermore, a 1-800 telephone service can be operated right from a homebased office. Clients can call-forward their toll-free lines to your office for after-hours inquiry, or you can establish toll-free lines and issue clients an extension number for their business and advertising activities. Establishing billing rates can be by way of charging clients a monthly fee for handling their toll-free lines, or by each call that is received. The telephone equipment needed to start this type of specialized communications business is costly, and as a method to reduce start-up costs, consider purchasing secondhand telephone equipment capable of handling large incoming call volumes.

PROFESSIONAL EMCEE
★ $$

Do you possess good communications skills and a knack for public speaking? If so, your skills are in high demand from corporations and organizations from around the globe as a professional emcee. Professional emcees are often hired to host an event, open a seminar series, or act as the master of ceremonies for events ranging from charity auctions to general annual meetings for large corporations. A freelance professional emcee service is a terrific business to operate on a part-time basis to supplement business or employment income. Professional emcees can earn as much as $500 or more for each event they emcee.

RUNNING DISTRESS SALES
★ $

A distress sale is simply a sale based on an item that a person needs to sell. You see the ads all the time in the classifieds section of your local newspaper; "pool table for sale, must sell now, call…." Amazingly enough, money can be earned by purchasing items in a distress sale situation for pennies on the dollar and reselling the same item for a profit. There are basically two methods of buying distress sale items cheaply. The first is to scan your local classified ads early each morning and call what appear to be distress sale ads. Be the first person in line to make a low offer; how desperate the situation is will dictate the outcome of the negotiations. The second method is to collect advertisements of products for sale that interest you and wait at least four weeks. Once four weeks have passed, begin to call these vendors to see if they still have this item for sale. If so, often a low-ball offer will buy it simply because the seller is tired of waiting. You must be a strong negotiator and the item you are buying must be bought cheaply and be an easily resalable item. You can resell items by clever marketing or packaging them in a group, such as several pieces that make up a living room set.

HEAT TRANSFERS KIOSK
★★ $$

You can earn as much as $1,000 per day selling designs, logos, and messages that are transferred onto T-shirts, sweatshirts, bags, and shorts via heat press equipment. Of course the key to success in operating a heat transfers kiosk is location. Excellent operating locations include malls, beach areas, public markets, and special events, such as fairs, music festivals, and sporting events. The business is very easy to operate and the heat transfer equipment is widely available through numerous manufacturers. There are also thousands of clothing manufacturers and distributors who will be more than happy to set up an account to supply your garment requirements on a wholesale basis. Generally, the best way to operate this type of business is to design display boards and pin the available designs, logos, and messages to them. Customers simply select the garment they wish to purchase, choose what they want emblazoned on the garment, and you press it on the garment while they wait. Currently, this product retails for $15 to $25 each and the wholesale cost to purchase the T-shirt and transfer is in the range of $5 to $8, leaving lots of room for profit. All of this adds up to a great business opportunity that can be operated part-time, has the potential to generate enormous profits, and can be started with an initial investment of less than $10,000.

WEB RESOURCE: www.equipmentzone.com
Distributors of transfer equipment, heat presses, and heat transfer supplies.

INVENTOR
★ $+

Are you the type of person who is always thinking of how to do something better? If so, maybe you should give consideration to becoming an inventor. The title is not as ominous as it sounds. Every day, thousands of products, formulas, and methods are being invented to make life's tasks a little easier or to assist mankind in general. Inventions do not have to be earthshaking discoveries, but they do need to have a practical use and be innovative and unique. The potential to profit as an inventor is as varied as the start-up cost of the invention itself. To see first-hand a simple and effective idea of what an invention can be, visit www.lawnbuddy.com. This very enterprising entrepreneur and inventor has a clear and concise understanding of the art of invention. Another option is to become an inventor's consultant, which in many cases is a sounding board off of which to bounce the ideas and provide the feedback to help the inventor work out the kinks in his or her new innovation. You, or anyone you are working with, should patent or copyright all work.

WEB RESOURCE: www.inventions.org
Invention Assistance League.

WEB RESOURCE: www.uspto.gov
United States Patent and Trademark Office.

39

SPORT AND FITNESS
Businesses You Can Start

PUTTING GREEN SALES AND INSTALLATION
★★★ $$$

Without question, golf is one of the most popular sports and recreational pastimes in North America. Golf putting greens can be designed for indoor or outdoor installations, as well as sold to both residential and commercial customers. To avoid installation problems and time delays, it is best to pre-design six to ten different layouts for the putting greens. When designing the greens, however, keep in mind the various objects that could potentially be in the way such as tree roots, gardens, and lawn sprinklers. The best way to market golf putting greens and generate the largest profit margins will be to sell the greens directly to the residential homeowner or a business owner. For the high-end consumer, you can also custom install actual golf holes on larger tracts of land, and charge a lot of money to do so. A landscaping background and knowledge of golf will be essential for designing a full 300-yard par five golf hole on a private estate or for a company. Sales and marketing options include:

- Direct-sales team with company and self-generated leads.
- Setting up putting green demonstration displays at home and garden trade shows, outdoor and recreations shows, and at malls on weekends with the purpose of generating interest and sales leads from potential customers.

- Contacting residential homebuilders and soliciting for businesses to include the putting greens as optional upgrades for their clients.
- Business-to-business networking clubs and associations.

The profit potential for a business enterprise that designs, sells, and installs golf putting greens is tremendous, because elaborate residential golf putting greens are retailing for as much as $10,000, and a full par three or par four golf hole can cost upwards of $90,000.

INDOOR VOLLEYBALL
★★★ $$$$

Are you searching for a fun and interesting sports-related business start-up that has little competition and has the ability to produce a quick return on investment? Search no further, for starting a year-round indoor volleyball center can provide you with that and more. What could be more fun than starting a business that enables customers to have fun and stay fit at the same time? However, with that being said, starting an indoor volleyball center is no different from starting any other business and requires careful planning, research, and good business judgment to be practiced. The business can generate sales and profits in a couple of ways, including selling yearly volleyball memberships and by providing different products and services for members such as a concession stand, clothing sales, and even volleyball training and instructional clinics. Once again, the profit potential for an indoor volleyball center is outstanding, especially when you consider the operating overheads can be kept to a minimum, and a mere 300 members paying only $40 each per month will create yearly sales of $120,000.

WEB RESOURCE: www.usavolleyball.org
USA Volleyball is the national governing body for the sport of volleyball in the United States.

SPORTS CAMPS
★★★ $$$

Every year, thousands of children and adults attend numerous sports camps across North America, and launching a sports camp has the potential to be a very profitable business venture, not to mention a whole lot of fun. The theme of the sports camp can vary from hockey to baseball to gymnastics, and just about any sport in between. The camp can cater to training kids or adults or both, and can be based on a day camp or weeklong format that includes accommodations for the camps' participants. If possible, try to recruit a local sports celebrity or retired player to assist in coaching or training at the camp or at least lend a name to endorse the camp. The amount of income that can be earned operating a sports camp will greatly depend on a number of factors, including seasonal or year-round facility, number of participants trained, operating format, and overhead. Market the camp by ways of traditional print advertising and by initiating a direct-mail campaign aimed at sports and social clubs, associations, and at corporations looking for interesting ways to build a "team player" attitude for employees. For kids, sports camps are big business and you can market your business through little leagues, after-school centers, and at other places where children and teens are typically found, such as at the mall. There are numerous requirements to starting this type of business, including safety and liability issues, equipment and location, special skills, and experience in the chosen sport. However, for the determined entrepreneur, the time spent researching, planning, and setting up this type of business venture has the potential to justify the effort both financially and personally.

WEB RESOURCE: www.sportscampnetwork.com
Directory service listing sports camps.

HOME GYM DESIGNER
★★★ $$$ 🏠 🕐 🌍

When you consider how many Americans are overweight and out-of-shape, this is a very promising business to start. Many people do not have the time to get to the local gym, but could be more motivated to workout if you bring the gym to them. The focus of the business is not only to sell home fitness equipment such as weights and treadmills, but also to design or transform existing rooms into home gyms. In addition, you can also market used gym equipment, as people may upgrade from a stationary bike or a treadmill to a more high-end fitness machine. If you can use your marketing skills and your web site to move that old equipment from seller to buyer, you can make a commission for doing so and have an extra arm of your business.

START-UP COSTS: The following example can be used as a guideline to establish the investment required for starting a home gym sales and installation business.

	Low	High
Business setup, legal, banking, etc.	$500	$2,000
Office equipment, stationery, etc.	$1,500	$3,000
Portable demonstration display	$5,000	$8,000
Initial marketing and advertising budget	$1,500	$3,000
Working capital	$1,000	$2,500
Total start-up costs	**$9,500**	**$18,500**

PROFIT POTENTIAL: Establishing a pricing formula for this business is very basic. Simply multiply material costs, labor costs, and equipment costs by 1.5, or add 50 percent markup onto the wholesale and labor costs. This pricing formula will result in a 33 percent gross profit margin on total sales volumes prior to taxes and overhead costs being applied. Maintaining yearly sales of $200,000 would result in gross profits of $66,000 using this pricing formula.

WEB RESOURCE: www.homegym.com

PERSONALIZED GOLF BALLS
★★ $$ 🏠 🕐

America is golf-nuts. No other sport or recreational past time is enjoyed by more people than golf, and while this is certainly not enough reason to start a business that sells personalized golf balls, it sure is a good start. Personalized golf balls make fantastic gifts, and launching a part-time business that personalizes golf balls can earn you an extra $10,000 per year or more. The equipment needed to print names, messages, or company logos on golf balls is very inexpensive and available at any silk-screening supply store. Golf balls can be purchased in bulk for as little as $4 per dozen, printed, and resold for as much as $40 per dozen. In addition to gifts for the golf enthusiast, personalized golf balls can also be sold to companies featuring their logo to be given to clients, charity and company golf tournaments, and to tourists, with printed messages or images of the place they are visiting. Selling the golf balls can be accomplished by establishing a sales kiosk at a mall or even at busy golf courses with permission of the owners. You can also promote yourself with ads in sports magazines, newspapers, and at local associations and clubs, all of which typically have numerous golfers. Golf balls can also be preprinted with a humorous golf message and sold to retailers on a wholesale basis. Of course, this type of business can easily be marketed on a web site, where you can obviously reach a much larger audience, and sell nationwide or worldwide, as long as the buyer covers the shipping costs.

WEB RESOURCE: www.print-maker.com
Distributors of pad printing equipment and supplies.

SPORTS MEMORABILIA
★★ $$ 🏠 🕐

Buying sports memorabilia, such as team jerseys, autographed sports celebrity photos, and sports equipment, at discounted or bargain prices and then reselling the same memorabilia to collectors and hardcore sports fans at a profit is a terrific business venture to set in motion. Malls all over the country now have at least one store devoted to sports memorabilia, with autographed prints and jerseys of star athletes bringing in hundreds and even thousands of dollars. You simply need to find a mall or street loca-

tion that does not yet have such a store, and align yourself with the local dealers. To reduce overhead costs, you could start this business at flea markets, fairs, or at booths set up in malls. You could also do this online, although there is very steep competition. Most sports memorabilia is bought and sold through dealers specializing in the industry, and, like any other business, you buy wholesale and sell at retail. In addition, you should sell sports cards and other lower priced items to draw in visitors. Board games, such as the sports themed Monopoly and checkers have also become very popular. Another means of generating revenue is to buy collectibles directly from collectors and sell to other collectors. This can be done by auction on your web site, or by devoting a portion of your space to items you have purchased directly from collectors. You need to learn the values of such items before venturing into this aspect of the business or you will get taken for a ride. Typically, this part of the business will be primarily sports trading, since you will not have much luck reselling signed items unless you can verify that the signatures are legitimate. Since this is a very big industry, you should immerse yourself in learning more about the products, the potential for profit, and the competition. Many memorabilia shops have signings of local athletes and charge big bucks for signed photos, jerseys, etc. Also, consider collectibles insurance.

WEB RESOURCE: www.prosportsmemorabilia.com
Sports memorabilia site to check out and get a feel for what is out there.

FITNESS EQUIPMENT REPAIRS
★★ $ 🏠 🕐

Starting a business that specializes in fitness equipment repairs and maintenance is a great homebased business opportunity to set in motion. Potential customers can include commercial fitness gyms and centers, government-operated fitness centers, companies with on-site employee gyms, and homeowners with home gyms and fitness equipment. Fitness is a huge growth industry, and securing your place in this industry could prove to really pay off in the future as more and more expensive fitness equipment begins to age and requires routine maintenance and repairs. The business is very easy to establish and only requires a basic mechanical aptitude to repair the equipment. Ideally, you will want to establish automatic monthly maintenance contracts with fitness facilities; securing only ten contracts at $500 each per month will generate yearly business sales of $60,000.

USED GOLF BALL SALES
★★ $$ 🏠 🕐

Securing contracts with public and private golf courses and clubs to retrieve golf balls from water and other hazards on and around golf courses won't make you rich, but could be a great side business – one in which you could even involve your kids. Every year millions of golf balls are lost in water or high rough around courses across North America, and reclaiming these balls to be resold as used golf balls is very easy to do. The main requirement for this business is having permission from course owners, managers and starters to track down the misplaced golf balls. If you are a certified scuba diver, as well as have scuba-diving equipment you can handle deeper lakes and water that sits on or adjoining the course. In most cases, however, using nets can help you pull golf balls out of the typically shallow water hazards. Reselling the balls to players, for such hazard shots or to a driving range can bring in some profits, although you may have to share the profits with the club owners or managers. If you can fetch golf balls that have been used in a celebrity golf tournament and have the name of the tournament stamped on it, you can get as much as $25 or more per ball. A golf ball that has a celebrity golfer's name stamped on it can fetch as much as $500, depending on the popularity of the person whose name is on the ball.

USED FITNESS EQUIPMENT SALES
★★★ $$+ 🏠 🕐

Are you a fitness buff, and do you have some extra space around the house and extra time on your hands? If so, why not consider starting a part-time homebased business venture that buys previously owned fitness equipment and resells the same equipment for a profit? The time has never been better than now to start this type of business enterprise, as millions of people across North America are striving to become more fit, and obviously fitness equipment plays a major role in that

pursuit. The fitness equipment can be purchased at garage sales, auction sales, and through newspaper classifieds. Reselling the fitness equipment is also very easy, as it can be advertised for free in many community newspapers and community information boards, as well as by designing product information and pricing fliers and distributing the fliers throughout the community on a regular basis. This is the type of business that will be promoted by word-of-mouth, and it won't take long until the telephone is ringing off the hook with people calling about fitness equipment they want to purchase or sell.

START-UP COSTS: The following example can be used as a guideline to establish the investment needed for starting a part-time business that sells used fitness equipment.

	Low	High
Business setup, banking legal, etc.	$200	$1,500
Initial used fitness equipment inventory	$2,000	$10,000
Office equipment and supplies	$250	$2,000
Initial advertising and marketing budget	$250	$1,000
Transportation (used utility trailer)	$250	$750
Working capital	$250	$1,000
Total start-up costs	**$3,200**	**$16,250**

PROFIT POTENTIAL: The part-time income potential associated with this type of unique homebased business venture is excellent, and the key to making money will lie within your negotiation skills. The goal is to purchase good-quality secondhand fitness equipment for as little as possible, while selling the same equipment for as much as the market will bear. Aim to get in the habit of establishing a standard pricing structure, or formula. This means you want to create a system for maintaining profitability. This type of system is easy to develop. The first step is to acquire as much information as possible on fitness equipment in general as well as the original cost of the fitness equipment. This information can be used to develop a resource library. A suggested pricing structure would be to rate the fitness equipment first in terms of condition, and purchase the used equipment at 5 to 25 percent of the original cost new. Establishing a retail selling price for the equipment is aimed at maintaining a 100 percent markup. Providing this pricing structure is used and annual sales of $50,000 are achieved, the result would be a homebased business that is generating $25,000 annually prior to overheads and taxes.

FITNESS EQUIPMENT CLEANING
★ $$ 🏠 🕐

As fitness awareness and the number of participants continues to grow, the future for a fitness equipment cleaning service looks terrific. Additionally, combining a fitness equipment cleaning business with a fitness equipment repair service would be a great way to increase customer services offered as well as business revenues and profits. Once established, this unique service with little in the way of competition should easily generate an hourly income of $20 or more.

MOBILE GYM
★★ $$$$ ⚖

Are you a fitness instructor looking for a way to start a fitness instruction business that has the potential to generate a six-figure yearly income? Starting a mobile gym and fitness instruction business is a fantastic new venture to put into action, as the mobile aspect of the business enables you to go and get the clients, instead of waiting for them to come to you. This type of fitness business is highly specialized and the target market, though large, can be limited due to the prohibitive cost associated with one-on-one fitness training and instruction. The ideal target market or customer for this type of fitness training is the professional in business who does not have time to go to the gym, and who is seeking highly focused fitness workouts and instruction. Good candidates include people such as TV and movie actors and crew who cannot leave the set, people who operate a homebased business that requires them to be in or very close to their homes every day, and people in general who are seeking to gain fast and effective results from an intensive fitness program. A mobile gym business can be operated right from a five-ton truck or large enclosed trailer and feature the same kind of professional fitness equipment that is found in a commercial fitness center.

REQUIREMENTS: The main requirement for starting a mobile gym business is the instructor must be a certified fitness instructor. There are fitness instructor certification courses available in almost every major city in North America, and the length of these training courses are generally less than a year in duration. Additionally, due to the nature of the venture, general business and liability insurance will also be a necessity.

START-UP COSTS: The following example can be used as a guideline to establish the investment needed to start a mobile gym business. The cost associated with becoming a certified fitness instructor is not included.

	Low	High
Business setup, banking, legal, etc.	$250	$1,500
Transportation, five-ton truck or trailer (used)	$12,500	$20,000
Fitness equipment	$7,500	$15,000
Initial advertising and marketing budget	$1,000	$2,000
Office equipment and supplies	$1,000	$2,000
General business and liability insurance	$1,000	$1,000
Working capital	$1,500	$3,000
Total start-up costs	**$24,750**	**$44,500**

PROFIT POTENTIAL: Once established, a mobile gym and fitness training service can generate an incredible income. Currently mobile gym operators limit class sizes to three people at once and charge rates that start at $40 per hour and can go as high as $60 per hour.

WEB RESOURCE: www.body-basics.com
National Association for Fitness Certification.

MINI-DRIVING RANGE
★★ $$$$ 🌐

A mini-driving range is simply a scaled-down version of a traditional golf driving range, with the netting more closely surrounding the tee areas in the facility. One of the best aspects of a mini-driving range is that it can be located just about anywhere. These locations include on top of an industrial building, in the corner of a large parking lot, or even indoors in an industrial warehouse. The concept behind a mini-driving range is that the ball simply will not travel as far because of the space. Players swinging for distance can still get the feel for how well they drive the ball—it simply won't travel as far because of the netting that encloses the facility. It is also a great place for players to work on their accuracy and hone their short game by using irons and wedges. Having a golf pro teaching lessons, on a sub-contract basis, can generate more income. Putting mats can be added and you can sell some of the many golf accessories including tees, balls, and golf gloves. Once established, a mini-driving range could easily generate yearly profits in excess of $40,000.

WEB RESOURCE: www.sterlingnets.com
Manufacturers of golf driving range nets.

TROPHIES
★ $$ 🏚 🕐

Each year in North America, millions of trophies are given to winning sports teams, game MVPs, and to people being recognized for outstanding achievement. Little league baseball and soccer leagues alone hand out several million trophies to kids each year just for participating. The demand for trophies is not only proven, it also continues to increase every year as the population of people and popularity of sports continues to grow. A trophy supply and engraving business can be started for less than $5,000, and purchasing trophies on a wholesale basis should not prove to be difficult as there are thousands of trophy manufacturers worldwide. Furthermore, the equipment needed for engraving name plaques for the trophies is inexpensive and available at most building centers in every community. Profit potential range is $10,000+ per year.

WEB RESOURCE: www.trophywholesalers.com

CUSTOM GOLF CLUB SALES
★★★ $$ 🏚 🕐

Big profits await the entrepreneur who starts a business that builds custom golf clubs on a made-to-order basis, as well as repairing golf clubs. A custom golf club manufacturing and sales business is the perfect business to be established on a part-time basis, from a homebased location, by someone who has expertise in the game and

the manufacturing of clubs. Later the business can be expanded from the profits that are earned. Manufacturing custom golf clubs may not be as difficult as you think, as there are numerous manufacturers of golf club parts, and the parts can be purchased on a wholesale basis and assembled into a finished product to be sold. As previously mentioned, additional revenues can be earned by providing a golf club repair service to clients.

HOME FITNESS TRAINER FOR SENIORS
★ $$ 🕐 ⚖

Americans are living longer and staying healthier than ever before. This fact creates a fantastic opportunity for the certified fitness instructor to capitalize by starting a mobile fitness training service that specializes in fitness training for seniors. The fitness classes can be conducted right on site at senior citizen and retirement homes, and of course the participants of the fitness classes will be the residents of these institutions. The main requirement for conducting fitness-training classes for seniors is to have a fitness instructor training certificate. For those of you who do not meet the requirements for starting this unique fitness service, fear not—a fitness instructor training certificate only requires a few thousand dollars in course fees and about one year's time to secure. Potential income range is $25 to $40 per hour.

WEB RESOURCE: www.aerobics.com
Aerobics and Fitness Association of America.

SPORTS AGENT
★ $$ 🏚

Finding and representing the next Tiger Woods as a sports agent has the potential to make you a millionaire. Be forewarned that competition is fierce and your contact base in the sports industry in general must be excellent. The main duty of a sports agent is to negotiate for their clients the best possible contracts and product endorsement deals. The best way to break into this highly specialized field is to work for another sports agent in a junior capacity before trying to venture out on your own, since nobody will sign to have you as a representative unless you have experience and have been involved in deals – even if that means simply doing the research or typing up the contracts. Also, by working in the field in any capacity, you get to know the team representatives, which is very important since this business is 90% about relationships.

ARCHERY RANGE
★★ $$$$ ⚖

Archery is fast becoming an extremely popular sport in the United States, and starting an archery range is a fantastic way to capitalize on the recent surge in popularity. An archery range can be established as an independent business or as a joint venture with an existing business such as a gun club. In addition to generating revenues from membership dues, the business can also earn revenues and profits by selling supplies and providing instruction. To secure members and customers for a new archery range, offer a grand opening two-for-one special for all new members who sign up in the first month.

WEB RESOURCE: www.usarchery.org
National Archery Association.

FITNESS TRAINING FOR THE DISABLED
★★ $$ 🕐 ⚖

Every industry can be broken down into specialty segments, and the fitness industry is no different. Starting a business that focuses on providing fitness training and classes for the disabled falls into this industry specialization classification. On the surface, fitness training for the disabled may seem to be similar to fitness training for able-bodied students. However, there are numerous differences that must be taken into consideration. The fitness classes will have to be developed to suit various types of disabilities and a minimum of two trainers or supervisors must be present. Class sizes need to be smaller and the location for the classes must be handicap accessible, including parking. Starting this business will take careful planning and research, but with a little bit of innovative thinking, the entrepreneur starting this business can look forward to a personally gratifying future. Experience working with the disabled population is essential.

FITNESS CLASSES FOR DOGS AND OWNERS
★★ $$ 🏠 🕐

Are you searching for a truly unique business opportunity that requires a minimal start-up investment, has

virtually no competition, and has the potential to generate a great income? If so, perhaps you should consider starting a business that specializes in conducting fitness classes for dogs and their owners. The fitness classes can be held outdoors on a year-round basis and can be designed with a dog and its owner in mind. This type of fitness business is unique and may take awhile to catch on in your community; however, the profit potential is great. Imagine, a mere 20 students (ten dogs and ten people) paying only $5 per day to take part in a one-hour fitness class will create an hourly income of a whopping $50. Best of all, there are virtually no fixed overhead costs as the classes can be conducted from any outdoor venue for free, and the advertising will certainly be by way of word-of-mouth referral.

FITNESS SEMINARS
★★ $$ 🕐 🌐

There are multiple ways to make money by hosting fitness seminars that are free to attend.

- Sell fitness equipment, diet and fitness programs, and fitness-related products during and at the end of the seminar.
- Charge companies a fee to be a speaker at the seminars and sell their fitness-related products, equipment, and programs.
- Design and develop a seminar program that is purchased by the people who attend the fitness seminar, as well as selling advertising space in the seminar program to companies that are taking part in the fitness seminars.
- Use a combination of all or any of these revenue-generating techniques.

As you can see there are a few options available in terms of generating revenues from a business that hosts fitness seminars that is free for people to attend. The two key words here are "free" and "fitness." People will attend the seminars because the topic is fitness, and even more people will attend the fitness seminars because the seminar is free. The concept behind the business is to create a captive audience, build excitement, and then capitalize on the excitement and the fact that you have just created a noncompetitive environment in terms of selling valuable products to consumers or to other businesses.

FITNESS CENTER
★★ $$$$ 🌐

In the past 20 years, fitness centers have not only proven to be popular and very much in demand by fitness conscious consumers, but they have also been proven to be very profitable as a business opportunity. Opening a fitness center requires careful planning and research, and the following are aspects of the business that should be considered:

- *Location.* You need a place that is easy to find and in a safe area with ample parking.
- *Size.* How large a facility can you afford to open and manage?
- *Leasehold improvements.* How much will it cost to bring the facility up to speed? Can you assess and handle all necessary repairs and remodeling to bring the business up to meeting building codes? Can you find good contractors do the work in a timely manner and without costing you a fortune?
- *Operating format.* Will the fitness center cater to all people, or will the focus of the business target to a specific group of people? Will the fitness center be full service, meaning optional aerobics classes and one-on-one personal training for clients?
- *Staff.* Can you find, train and afford quality fitness instructors and staff in the community where the center will be located? What is the expectancy of staff in terms of career opportunities?
- *Wages.* Can you afford the going rate for a full staff?
- *Marketing.* How will the fitness center be marketed? Will it be by way of membership drive or a drop-in rate established? What enticements or services will be used as a marketing tool to draw members from competitors' fitness clubs or facilities?
- *Safety, liability, and insurance concerns.* Can you meet safety requirements so that your liability insurance costs do not prevent you from opening such a business?
- *Competition.* How much local competition is there in the fitness industry, and is the competition in the form of a chain fitness center, community-operated fitness center, or independently-operated fitness centers? How much does the competition charge? Is

there the possibility of a price war? Can the proposed business gain enough clients to be profitable? Can you gain a competitive edge?

Clearly, this is a huge business undertaking, that involves a great deal of startup money and there are many aspects to carefully consider prior to starting a fitness center. However, with careful research and proper planning, a fitness center can be a fabulous business to start, operate, and own, not to mention that it also has the potential to be very profitable once established. Consider finding financial backers once you have written a detailed business plan.

SPORTS EQUIPMENT SWAP MEETS
★★ $$$ 🕐

Sports equipment swap meets are basically a gathering of sporting equipment retailers and the general public (with used sporting equipment to sell) brought together in one venue to buy and sell the sporting equipment. There are two approaches for generating revenue from this business. The first is to charge vendors rent for booth display space. The second way to generate revenues is to issue vendor numbers, have one central cashier window, and retain 10 percent of the total value of the sports equipment sold at the sports swap meet, regardless if the equipment was new or secondhand. Starting a sports swap meet business will take some clever planning and marketing. However, sports in general are part of the North American cultural fabric, and demand for a sports swap meet is guaranteed.

CHILDREN-ONLY FITNESS CLASSES
★★ $$ 🕐 ⚖

Like adults, children need regular exercise to stay healthy and fit, and starting a fitness instruction business that exclusively conducts fitness-training classes for children is a fantastic new business enterprise to get rolling. The fitness classes should be categorized by the children's ages as for beginner through advanced levels. Once again, this type of unique and specialized fitness training can be conducted as an independent business venture, or as a joint venture with an existing community fitness program. Additional considerations to research prior to starting a children's-only fitness business include operating location, required certifications, health and safety regulations, and liability insurance.

AEROBICS CENTER
★ $$$$ 🌐

Would you like to start an aerobics training business, but unfortunately you do not have the experience or qualifications required? Fear not, you still can, by starting an aerobics center. An aerobics center is a leased location that has been specifically set up to operate as an aerobics training center. The center can have multiple training rooms that are fully equipped and rented on a short- or long-term basis by qualified aerobics instructors to conduct their classes. Alternately, splitting the instruction course fees paid by students with the instructors can generate revenues. Additional income can be earned by locating a refreshment booth in the aerobics center, as well as selling related products such as sportswear, books, and videos on aerobics training topics.

MINIATURE GOLF CENTER
★★ $$$$ 🌐

Opening and operating a miniature golf center involves first securing property with the holes for the course pre-built or buying the land and having someone design and create the holes. If you are handy and have a passion for landscaping, you can do the design and construction yourself—but be forewarned, it is much harder than it appears. To be successful, you need high-traffic location near a tourist area or popular location where area residents go for family fun. You need lighting for evening play and the basics: golf balls, scorecards, and putters. Many miniature golf courses are built in conjunction with driving ranges and batting cages, and some have go-cart tracks. A place to buy snacks is also a must for success. You may want to team up with other entrepreneurs to split the cost of the land, or get some financing to help you get off the ground. Since consumer demand for miniature golf has been proven to be strong for many decades, making this opportunity a wise choice as a new business venture for all people seeking self-employment independence. You can also have a mobile course, meaning you set up the pre-designed holes at carnivals and other outdoor activities.

WEB RESOURCE: www.miniaturegolfer.com
Directory service with links and information about the miniature golfing industry.

RUNNERS' STORE
★★ $$$$ 🌐

Long distance running, jogging, and cross training are among the top popular sports and fitness pastimes enjoyed by millions of participants across North America. Starting a retail business that caters to recreational runners is a fabulous new business enterprise to get rolling. A runners' store can stock and sell products such as sports shoes, sportswear, and running and training books and videos. Beyond retail sales, the business can earn additional revenues and profits by providing running clinics and running instruction programs. To kick things into high gear (so to speak), be sure to contact the local sports associations in the community to inform them about the new business and the products sold, as well as the services offered. Also be sure to give members of the various sports associations a preferred customer card, meaning that they will receive a discount on purchases at the store when the card is presented.

WEB RESOURCE: www.americanrunning.org
American Running and Fitness Association.

FITNESS EQUIPMENT MANUFACTURING
★★ $$$

Are you searching for a new business opportunity that will enable you to utilize your design and construction skills? If so, perhaps you should consider starting a business that manufactures fitness equipment. The main requirements for succeeding in this type of manufacturing business is to have a well-equipped workshop, design and construction experience, and good marketing skills. The fitness equipment manufactured can include weight benches, weight stands, and squat stands, just to mention a few. Once the fitness equipment is constructed it can be sold on a wholesale basis to national and specialty retailers, or directly to the public via a factory direct showroom, or over the internet. Profit potential, once established is $25,000+ per year.

WEB RESOURCE: www.sgma.com
Sporting Goods Manufacturers Association.

MATERNITY FITNESS CLASSES
★★ $$ 🕐 ⚖️

If you thought we were out of fitness business opportunities, guess again. There are approximately four million children born each year in the United States. While this statistic may not mean a lot to many of you, it will certainly be useful information for anyone who is considering starting a fitness instruction business that focuses on conducting fitness classes exclusively for expectant mothers. Maternity fitness classes can be held in conjunction with an existing business or community association, or as an independent business. Gaining clients for this type of fitness instruction can be as easy as having fliers in OBGYN offices, maternity clothing stores, and retailers of children's and baby products.

WEB RESOURCE: www.association-of-womens-fitness.org Association of Women's Health and Fitness.

BICYCLE REPAIR SERVICE
★★ $$ 🏠 🕐

How profitable can a bicycle repair service be? Just ask any one of the thousands of bicycle repair shop owners who are now making a handsome profit from their business. A bicycle repair service is a fantastic new venture to start for the following reasons:

- The business can be started and operated from a homebased workshop.
- There is low initial start-up investment and minimal monthly operating overhead.
- The proven consumer demand for bicycle repairs increases each year.
- There is the potential of earning $40 per hour or more, and additional profits can be made on parts sales.
- It's a part-time or full-time opportunity that has very flexible operating hours.
- Repair skills needed to operate the business are minimal and can be learned very quickly.

As you can see, there are many benefits to starting a bicycle repair service on a full- or part-time basis. Be sure to establish alliances with bicycling clubs and organizations in the community, as the membership of these clubs can become potential customers of the bicycle repair

business. Also, if you can repair scooters, you can generate additional revenue.

COMMUNITY SPORTS PAPER
★★ $$$ 🏠 🕐 🌐

Starting a business that publishes and distributes a sports paper that features community amateur sports news is a very straightforward business venture to initiate. The information featured in the community sports paper can include team rosters and photographs, game highlights, team stats, and forthcoming sports association news and game schedules. The news and information can be supplied by the various sports associations and clubs in the community, as well as by enlisting the services of a freelance sports writer. The community sports paper can be published on a weekly, biweekly, or monthly basis, and be distributed throughout the community for free. The paper can generate revenues and profits by selling advertising space to local businesspeople seeking to gain valuable exposure for their companies.

BOXING CENTER
★★ $$$$ 🌐

Once a sport for the brutes, boxing and kickboxing are quickly becoming popular fitness activities in North America, enjoyed by millions of participants regardless of age or gender. An interest in the sport of boxing or kickboxing is definitely a prerequisite for starting a boxing center. However, a great deal of boxing experience or training is not a must, simply due to the fact that you can hire certified boxing and kickboxing instructors to conduct classes and oversee the general operation of the business. Build a membership base quickly by distributing two-for-one coupons that entitle the bearer the opportunity to join the boxing center for one month and receive the second month of membership free of charge. You can also add fun and fitness classes to the roster, such as aerobic boxing and kickboxing, self-defense boxing training, and monthly amateur boxing and kickboxing tournaments. In total approximately 4,000 to 6,000 square feet of space will be required to operate the business, and equipment purchases will be expensive, making this a business venture that will require careful planning and research. To bolster sales and revenues beyond classes and training, you can also sell products related to the sport such as clothing, books, and videos. Imagine, only 500 members paying a mere $30 per month each for membership dues will generate yearly base revenues of $180,000. Make sure you have all necessary licensing requirements, liability insurance and safety measures taken care of.

WEB RESOURCE: www.aiba.net
Amateur Boxing Association; industry information and links.

UMPIRE AND REFEREE SERVICE
★ $$ 🏚 🕐

Every weekend, you'll find thousands of amateur, sandlot, high school, and collegian sporting events taking place. Each of these events needs referees or umpires who know the rules of the game and how to act professionally while presiding over the sport. This is the opportunity for you to open a training and placement center for refs and umps and make some money doing it. Since non-professional athletics does not generate enough money to pay the guys in the striped shirts very much, most are doing this on their spare time. Therefore, this does not put you in a position to make the big bucks handling such a service, but certainly provides a nice opportunity for a part-time homebased operation that can bring in some dollars. You can teach newcomers via videos, books, web sites, and by inviting experienced local refs and umps in to speak. You can market your business as the place to call when schools or leagues are looking for someone to work the games for a season or tournament. You will then make money from the school or league for saving them the time and trouble of finding and training officials. Market yourself anywhere in your region or state, but first build up a list of 100 competent, knowledgeable refs and umps.

PITCH AND PUTT GOLF
★★ $$$$ ⚖️

It's not a full-fledged golf course, but not a miniature golf course either. Pitch and putt courses are typically 18 holes ranging from 50 to 100 yards each, allowing more serious golfers to have an opportunity to practice their short game, while also being a family friendly way to play golf without worrying about long drives off the tee. The

first requirement, of course, is several acres of land. You then need to hire a course architect or someone trained in designing the holes for a course, since the greens will look just like those on regular courses (although a little smaller). With hills and hazards, including water and sand traps, you can have a challenge course that players will want to return to often. You will then need to stock up on nine-irons, pitching wedges, putters, have scorecards printed… and buy boxes of tiny pencils. Course fees typically range from $8 to $12 for adults and less for kids under 12. Once the course is operational your only ongoing expense is maintenance, which you cannot neglect or you will lose the steady clientele you've worked so hard to build up. Place local ads and market the course to associations, clubs, camps and even schools. You can also add a special businessperson's box lunch (unless you have an eatery) and nine-holes for a low package rate, to get local business men and woman to come out and play for an hour during their lunch break.

PING PONG
★★ $$$

Millions of people love to play ping pong (or table tennis), but rarely get the chance, since it is not easy to find tables. Clubs, community centers, and associations sometimes have tables in rec rooms, but most often they look like they have been around since the game was invented hundreds of years ago. Pool halls sometimes have tables, but the atmosphere is not typically family friendly. So, why not start either a ping pong center or, rent out ping pong tables for parties, barbeques or other outdoor occasions (or do both)? If you are opening a place to play, pick a high profile location such as a mall, where shoppers, browsers, and kids will want to play for a little while. If renting tables, make sure to have a van or truck for transport and take deposits in case the table is destroyed (unlikely but you need to be covered to some extent)

START-UP COSTS: For $5,000 you can purchase ten $500 tables. You will then need to stock up on snack foods, water bottles and, of course, racquets and ping pong balls. In addition, you will want to hire some staff to maintain the tables and keep the players "on the clock" so to speak. Still, for less than $15,000 you can launch this business successfully.

If you rent tables at $20 per hour, and book 500 hours a month of table use (about 120 hours a week), you can make $10,000 per week, plus $500 on snacks. After the first month, where you will be paying off the tables (plus rent and salaries), you will be making a profit. It's a fun business and one that, in time, can catch on, since you will be one of few places offering ping pong to a large audience of potential players.

TENNIS SHOP
★★ $$$$

While tennis may not be quite as popular as golf, it is a sport in that twenty million enthusiasts in North America take seriously. You can tap into this large demographic market with a well-situated tennis shop, hopefully within close proximity to courts, such as at a resort location. A well-stocked tennis center can have more than $300,000 worth of inventory including rackets, footwear, and apparel. In addition, a good tennis store includes custom fitting and stringing. You can even offer lessons on nearby courts or if you opt for a $40,000 tennis simulator designed to simulate strokes. Clearly, such an undertaking will require significant startup costs and financial backing. Doing a business plan, with all of the particulars, is the first step en route to what can be a very lucrative business, provided you know all about the game and, more significantly, the rackets, shoes, balls, and accessories.

SPORTING EQUIPMENT
★★ ★ $$$$ ⚖

Buying equipment wholesale in bulk and selling it retail can be a highly lucrative business, especially in the billion-dollar sporting goods industry. A well-stocked sporting goods store is one possibility, while selling directly to schools, leagues, camps, community centers, and colleges is another means of making money. Selling skills and a knowledge of sports are the first requirements. If it is a store you are stocking, you need a diverse mix of equipment focusing on the sports that are most popular in your region, so do your homework prior to ordering. Either way, make sure you market yourself to all organized sports programs and if you opt for the shop, find ways of drawing customers in, such as holding contests, or invite local athletes for equipment signings.

WEB RESOURCE: www.sportslife.com
Sporting goods wholesaler with a built-in dealership plan.

WEB RESOURCE: www.nsga.org
National Sporting goods Association

COACHING SERVICE
★★ $$ 🏠 🕐

Whether it is coaching someone for an upcoming marathon or helping a young athlete in his or her quest to make their college soccer team, there is a growing need for athletic coaches. If you excel in some sporting activity and understand the dynamics of coaching, you can start your own coaching service. Unlike a teacher who typically starts out with newcomers, coaches generally work with the skills that the athlete already possesses and helps to improve upon them through coaching methodology, motivational techniques and a program designed for each client or, in this case, young athlete. Coaches can run clinics in their sport of expertise as well as provide individual coaching at selected locations that are convenient for both parties. Another option is to team up with coaches in various sports and start a business that provides coaching in several sports. This is a business you can start from home with a solid marketing plan that includes reaching out to students and local leagues and clubs.

TEE TIME REGISTRATION
★★ $$ 🏠

The popularity of golf has created a backlog in many markets, whereby players are calling and e-mailing to set up tee times through automated services. This is the premise behind a tee time registration business, which can certainly be run from your home with the right phone and computer equipment. The essence off this business is simple. Courses have x number of tee-off times available and they are selling these tee times, much like airlines sell seats. You are, therefore, acting as a sales rep for a number of courses, much like a travel agent sells airline seats. And, also like the airlines, the golf courses are the ones who pay you to help fill these slots, including those that open up from last minute cancellations. To start, you need to make connections with numerous golf courses. You can then run this as a small local business, featuring tee times for local courses, or branch out via the internet and provide tee times for courses nationally. You need to be very organized and able to manage numerous schedules at once, since you may be booking tee times at 100 courses at a time.

BOWLING SUPPLIES
★★ $$$

While it is not very easy to start a bowling alley, you can sell bowling balls, bags and shoes from a mail order business or team up with a sporting goods store, helping them by paying a portion of the rent in exchange for handling this segment of the sporting goods. You can also inquire at bowling alleys about running a small shop in conjunction with the alley, as their "pro" shop, whether you are a pro or not. Customized bowling balls and bags are popular, and you can also sell additional accessories. Market yourself in the bowling alleys, particularly to leagues—in fact you might have specials for members of a specific league at the start of their season.

WEB RESOURCE: www.bowling300.com
Portal with manufacturers, organizations, centers, leagues and more.

NOTES:

53

TRANSPORTATION

Businesses You Can Start

SAILBOAT RIGGING SERVICE

★ $ 🏠 🕐

Each year, thousands of new and used sailboats are purchased by inexperienced sailors. Starting a sailboat rigging service means that you can put your sailing skills to work. Sailboat rigging is not a difficult task for the experienced sailor. However, for the novice sailor, rigging can be a time consuming and frustrating task. A sailboat rigging service is best marketed by establishing joint ventures with marinas, boat brokers, and sailing schools. Sailing clubs can also act as referral sources for the service. Overall, this is a terrific little homebased business venture that can be operated on a full- or part-time basis, and there should be no difficulties in charging and getting $40 to $50 per hour for the rigging service.

HAND CAR WASH

★★★ $$

For an investment of less than $10,000 you can open your own hand car-washing service operating in a fixed location. Strike a deal with the owner of a gas station, car dealership, or mechanic's garage to set up your car wash in a section of their parking lot that is not being used. Offering a few hundred dollars per month for rent should go a long way in sealing the deal. You will need to purchase a small garden shed for equipment storage and a 10-foot by 20-foot tent to wash the cars under. A water

hose can be tied into the building where you establish the business. A small sandwich board sign can be set up at the edge of the lot advertising your car wash. There should be no difficulties in securing a location for the car wash, as it will act as a drawing card for the establishment that you have struck the deal with. Washing only 20 cars per day and charging customers a mere $10 each will generate business revenues of $6,000 per month.

MOBILE CAR WASH

★★★ $$+ 🏠 🕐 🌐

The following are five excellent reasons why you should start a mobile car wash service:

1. The business can be started on a modest investment of less than $10,000.

2. It can produce potential profits in excess of $60,000 per year.

3. Starting and operating such a business requires no special skills, and there are typically no legal regulations or restrictions.

4. You can run the business from a homebased office and operate full- or part-time with flexible business hours, no inventory, no staff, and low monthly overheads.

5. The demand is enormous; there are more than 130,000,000 vehicles registered in the United States.
   A mobile car wash business is perfectly suited for the

entrepreneur who is seeking a simple, profitable, and low-investment business opportunity. The business only requires basic equipment and can be operated from a van, truck, or enclosed trailer. To market the business and gain clients, all traditional forms of advertising and promotion can be utilized. However, the real target market for this type of service is to establish monthly car and truck washing and cleaning accounts with companies, organizations, and government agencies that have a fleet of automobiles. Securing only ten monthly car washing accounts can produce a yearly income of $60,000, providing each client has 20 cars or trucks in their fleet.

START-UP COSTS: The following example can be used as a guideline to establish the investment necessary to start a mobile car wash business.

	Low	High
Truck or van (used)	$5,000	$15,000
Power washer with accessories	$500	$2,000
Business setup, banking, legal, etc.	$500	$2,500
Equipment, vacuums, etc.	$500	$1,500
Initial marketing and promotion budget	$500	$1,500
Working capital	$500	$2,000
Total start-up costs	**$7,500**	**$24,500**

USED AUTOMOTIVE PARTS
★★ $$$$

Starting a business that specializes in used automotive parts is a fantastic business venture to get rolling, especially if the focus of the business is to supply hard-to-find or rare used automotive parts. The business can be operated from a homebased garage location, or a small industrial space can be rented. The used automotive parts can be advertised for sale in traditional media, such as trade-specific publications and newspapers, and by word-of-mouth referral. The profit potential for a used automotive parts business is fantastic, and gross profit margins of 50 percent or more are not uncommon in the industry. A direct-mail marketing campaign targeted at car clubs and owners of rare cars can also be a very effective marketing tool. Keep in mind, however, that all parts must be in good condition. Also, be very careful when buying parts. You do not want to find out that the car they are from was stolen—which means you are selling "hot" goods.

WEB RESOURCE: www.a-r-a.org
Automotive Recyclers Association.

BOAT BOTTOM PAINTING
★★ $$ 🏠 🕐

Boat hulls must be maintained and painted below the water line on a regular basis in order to maintain performance. Generally, a boat bottom will be painted with antifouling paint every three to four years, and sometimes every year if the water conditions are poor. The process of bottom painting is very straightforward. Remove barnacles and debris by scraping the hull or pressure washing and apply the antifouling paint. A brushed on or roller paint job is generally considered superior to a spray paint job. Negotiating an exclusive distributor's contract with an antifouling paint manufacturer is a terrific way to reduce paint wholesale costs and increase the professionalism of the business.

WEB RESOURCE: www.boatus.com/boattech/BottomLine.htm
Information on boat bottom painting.

AUTO FIRST-AID KITS
★★ $$ 🏠 🕐

Automotive first-aid kits should be provided as a standard feature in new vehicles, but they are not, providing a unique sales opportunity. First aid kits for travel should include items such as water, bandages, a towel or two, roadside safety signals, and over-the-counter pills (such as Dramamine) for those who get carsick. The kits should be packaged in a convenient carrying case with a handle. Such kits can be sold on a wholesale basis to retailers, direct to car dealers and automotive service clubs, or directly to consumers via the internet. You can also establish weekend sales booths at flea markets, busy malls, and car and truck shows. Such kits can sell for anywhere from $25 to $100 depending on the contents of the kit.

PORTABLE SHELTERS AND STORAGE
★ $$ 🏠 🕐

Portable storage systems have become extremely popular in the last few years for anyone that is looking to protect a car, motorcycle, or boat from the weather. Generally, these portable storage shelters are constructed from a lightweight aluminum frame, covered with a water resistant fabric, and are quick to assemble and disassemble. They are available in a wide range of sizes to suit cars, RVs, motorcycles, boats, and just about any other type of transportation that needs protection from the wind, rain, and sun. A potentially profitable part-time business enterprise can be based on purchasing these portable shelters on a wholesale basis and reselling them to car, boat, and motorcycle enthusiasts for a profit. Marketing the shelters will not meet with a lot of resistance, as the cost to purchase one is a mere fraction of what it costs to build a carport or garage. The key to success will lie in your ability to negotiate a dealer's agreement with one of the many manufacturers of these types of portable storage and shelter systems. Your objective should be to secure the distribution rights for a protected territory. You want to be the exclusive sales agent for the manufacturer's product within a defined area.

WEB RESOURCE: www.thebikebarn.net
PTI Products: manufacturers and distributors of portable motorcycle storage and shelter systems.

WEB RESOURCE: www.instantshelters.com
A.I.S., Inc.: manufacturers and distributors of portable storage and shelter systems.

WINDSHIELD REPAIR
★ $$ 🏠 🕐

A windshield repair business can generate an income of more than $50 per hour. You need to be adept in the auto window repair process and make sure that you can provide strength and clarity required in a window so that the driver and passengers are safe and so that the car will pass inspection. There is a low initial investment and minimal monthly business operating overheads. Providing zoning laws are not prohibitive, you can start the business from a home base, using your garage. If neighbors complain, however, you will need to find a location, which may mean leasing space at a local service station. This can be a benefit in that it will give you more visibility. Market the business at car washes, car dealers, used and new auto parts stores, and anyplace where you'll find some of the 100+ million licensed drivers in the

United States or Canada.

WEB RESOURCE: www.aegisweb.com
Distributor of windshield repair equipment and supplies.

BOAT BROKER
★★★ $$+ 🏠 🕐

In most areas of North America, certification is not required to start a professional boat brokerage business, and that is extremely good news if this is your type of business venture. Millions of dollars worth of pre-owned motorboats, sailboats, and personal watercraft are bought and sold annually in this country. Securing a portion of this lucrative market is very simple to accomplish. The business could be a general boat brokerage business or specialize in a particular type of boat such as commercial fishing boats. It could also be operated from a fixed waterfront or marina location, or on a mobile basis and managed from a home office. The options for starting and operating a boat brokerage business are unlimited, making this is an excellent choice for a new business venture that really deserves further investigation.

START-UP COSTS: A homebased or mobile boat brokerage business can be started on an investment of $10,000 or less. A full-service boat brokerage operating from a fixed marina location with berth availability will be substantially more costly to start in the range of $50,000 to $100,000.

PROFIT POTENTIAL: Generally, a boat brokerage or boat sales consultant will charge the owner of the boat a 10 percent commission fee upon the successful sale of the boat. However, the rate of commission can be as high as 25 percent for boats that are valued at $5,000 or less, and as low as 3 percent for boats that sell in the million-dollar range. Maintaining a 10 percent commission rate and achieving total yearly sales of $1 million will result in revenues of $100,000 prior to advertising, overheads, and taxes.

USED BOATING EQUIPMENT
★★ $$ 🏠 🕐

There are an estimated 15 million pleasure boats and personal watercrafts in the United States alone, and almost all boats have one thing in common. At some point they break down and require repairs and replacement parts. This fact creates a business opportunity for an entrepreneur to capitalize on by starting a used boating equipment and parts business. As is typically the case, anyone can start such a business with little experience. However, to make the business work, you will need to do a lot of research on commonly purchased boat parts and learn how to tell the difference between quality used parts and those that should be cast adrift. You can then purchase used boating parts and equipment and resell them for a profit. As is the case with automobiles, make sure the parts are not stolen goods! The business can easily be operated on a full- or part-time basis right from the comforts of a homebased office, but is more likely to be operated from a location on or around a marina since you (or your neighbors) may not want strangers with boat parts showing up at your home at all hours.

WEB RESOURCE: www.nboat.com
National Boat Owners Association.

WATER TAXI SERVICE
★ $$$$ ⚖️

Are you looking for a unique, fun, and interesting transportation business venture that will enable you to capitalize on your boating skills and certifications? If so, perhaps you should consider starting a water taxi business. Providing the question of suitable location can be resolved, a water taxi service can be a terrific business venture to set in motion. Make sure to secure any licensing to operate a business on a given waterway and have all necessary insurance. If you find a river crossing where the more commonly used bridge causes long delays, your means of getting across the water can be a very sought after service. You might also have special destination trips, just as a water taxi service in New York City crosses the East River taking fans to and from Yankee Stadium for ballgames. In addition to the taxi service, you can also provide water sightseeing tours. The costs of owning the boat and maintaining and docking it will be your primary expenses. These can be reduced if you lease a boat that is owned and docked by someone else; they will get a cut of the revenues, but it will save you a lot of startup money. Once the business is successful, you can spring for your own boat.

WEB RESOURCE: www.eaglecraft.bc.ca/boats_taxi.html
Eagle Craft boats that can be used as water taxis.

FARM EQUIPMENT BROKER
★★ $$$$ 🏦 🕐

International connections can really pay off, especially if you are planning to start a farm equipment brokerage business. Your international connection can not only assist in the marketing of the equipment overseas but also in locating discounted farm equipment for North American purchasers. The market for good-quality used farm equipment ,such as tractors and hay combines, is huge worldwide. Selling just one piece of equipment per week can generate business revenues of $200,000 per year and more. The key to success in this business is to build and maintain vital contacts and alliances with farm equipment dealers and other brokers of farm equipment, as well as to seek international opportunities with booming economies.

START-UP COSTS: The investment needed to start a business as a farm equipment broker will vary based on factors such as initial advertising budget, business location, and overall operating expenses. However, an initial investment of $25,000 to $40,000 is suitable to get the business venture set in motion. As a way to minimize start-up costs, you can initially operate from a homebased office and market only local farm equipment to local potential purchasers.

PROFIT POTENTIAL: As a rule of thumb, farm equipment brokers charge a 10 percent commission of the total value of the farm equipment that was successfully sold. There are, however, exceptions to the rule. The commission rate will often be higher on lower valued farm equipment, and lower on very expensive farm equipment. Keep in mind that even if a piece of equipment is not sold, the broker is still responsible for the costs associated with attempting to market the equipment, unless a prior agreement has been established with the equipment owner, which is rarely done. Utilizing a web site you can also buy, sell, and trade farm equipment online. In addition to farmers, farm equipment dealers and brokers could also utilize a web listing service. Employ sales consultants in every region of the country to solicit for farm equipment listings for the site. Build a site index that is sectioned into geographic areas and type of farm equipment featured for visitor search purposes. At $30 per month per listing, maintaining only 1,000 listings on a monthly basis would create a revenue stream of $360,000 per year.

TRUCKING
★ $$$$ ⚖️

There are a few approaches that can be taken in terms of starting a trucking business. The first approach is to secure transportation accounts and hire subcontract drivers with their own trucks and equipment to service the accounts. The second approach is to purchase or lease a truck and work as an independent trucker, servicing your own accounts or subcontracting for a transportation firm. Both approaches to starting a business within the trucking industry have their pros and cons. However, be forewarned: The trucking industry as a whole is extremely competitive, and the rising cost of fuel, maintenance, and insurance has resulted in drivers having to work extremely long hours to generate any profit beyond a working wage. Profit potential including income is $50,000+ per year.

WEB RESOURCE: www.trucking.org
American Trucking Association.

AUTO TOWING
★★ $$$$ 🏭 ⚖️

In many areas of North America, obtaining a license to start or operate an automotive towing business can be a frustrating task, as auto-towing licenses are heavily regulated. Some operators of towing companies forego the license entirely and do not provide towing services to the general public; instead they only subcontract their services on an exclusive basis to car dealers and property managers. However, this can still be a risky venture given that it may be difficult to secure proper liability insurance for this type of towing operation. The alternative to waiting to be awarded a towing license is to purchase one from an existing towing operator or company. Purchasing a towing license and tow truck in an urban area can cost you as much as $200,000, with no towing accounts in place. Overall, starting an automotive towing business can be a terrific and profitable business venture, providing a license can be obtained or purchased at a reasonable price.

WEB RESOURCE: www.towservice.net
Towing Recovery Association of America.

BOAT MOVING AND STORAGE
★★ $$$$ ⚖️

Starting a boat moving and storage business requires very careful planning and research in order to be successful. There are a great number of factors to consider, such as business location, type of boat moving and storage service offered, liability insurance, and transportation and equipment considerations. Probably the easiest and least expensive type of boat moving and storage business to start is one that focuses on small pleasure crafts less than 35 feet in length and 10 feet in width. Boats this size do not have special regulation requirements in terms of transporting the boats on public roads. In terms of boat storage, seek to build alliances with public storage centers on a revenue share basis for storing the boats outside. I have a friend who has been in the boat moving and storage business for more than ten years. He operates his business by subcontracting out all moving and storage aspects of the business to qualified contractors, and focuses solely on selling or marketing the service. Perhaps this approach to a boat moving and storage business can also work for you.

CUSTOM AUTO RACKS
★★ $$$ 🌐

Custom auto racks that are designed to carry golf equipment, skis, mountain bikes, canoes, and kayaks are the latest rage in the automotive accessories industry. Small retail shops that sell and install these types of auto racks are popping up everywhere across North America. Selling and installing custom auto racks is a very lucrative enterprise to get going as there are many manufacturers of these products. Becoming an authorized factory dealer and installer is easily accomplished. The racks are easy and quick to install and do not require a great amount of mechanical skill or installation equipment and tools. The business is best operated from a small rental location with a retailing area and a single garage or drive-in bay for the rack installations. Demand for custom automotive racks is enormous, and securing a 50 percent markup on product costs and charging $30 per hour for installation should not be difficult. Overall this small retail business has the potential to generate a six-figure yearly income for the owner-operator.

BOAT WOODWORK REFINISHING
★★ $$ 🏠 🕐

Many power and sailboats have teakwood decks and trim, and anyone familiar with boating knows that the sun and salt water can really take a toll on boat woodwork. Starting a boat woodwork refinishing service is a fantastic small business venture. The business can be operated on a mobile basis and managed from a home-based office. Additionally, the tools and equipment needed for refinishing boat woodwork are inexpensive and readily available at any home improvement center. When marketing a woodworking refinishing service to boat owners, consider the following advertising and marketing options:

- Join boat and yacht clubs and network with boat owners at club social meetings to promote the woodwork refinishing service.
- Hand deliver informational brochures and fliers to boat owners at marinas.
- Subcontract your services to established boat repair yards.
- Make cold calls and talk to boat owners at marinas.
- Place advertisements in specialty boating publications and newspapers.
- Establish alliances with boat brokers and dealers to provide boat woodworking refinishing services prior to the boats being listed for sale or resold.

To promote the business and create a lot of interest in the woodwork refinishing service, consider purchasing an older wooden boat in poor condition. Refinish half the boat to perfection, and leave the other half in its original decrepit condition. The end result will be an amazing "before and after" marketing tool that can be displayed at marinas and boat shows to promote the refinishing service.

CAR STORAGE
★ $$$

Car storage is big business, especially in the cold northern areas of the United States and Canada. The first step to establishing a car storage business is to secure low-cost indoor storage space, such as a vacant warehouse or manufacturing building. The next step is to simply market the business. This is best accomplished by joining automotive clubs and associations and networking for business at the their meetings and social functions. Of course, be sure to obtain insurance for the business, as it will be a necessity and a great marketing tool.

VAN INTERIOR CUSTOMIZING
★★ $$$ 🏠 🕐

Interior customizing of vans and trucks is big business, especially in the commercial sector for delivery and service vehicles. Starting a business that supplies and installs products for van interiors, such as toolboxes and shelving units, is an outstanding new business venture to set in motion. The business can be operated right from a homebased workshop zoning on a full- or part-time basis. The total investment required to get the business rolling can be less than $10,000. To truly succeed in this type of business, consider securing an exclusive dealership from a manufacturer of these types of products. Not only will an exclusive product line give you an advantage over the competition, but it also adds credibility to your business and can be used as a terrific marketing tool. To market this business, simply build alliances with new and used car dealers in your area that can refer your business to their clients, or alternatively, car dealerships can act as sales agents for your products and installation service.

BOAT CLEANING SERVICE
★★ $ 🏠 🕐 🌍

Don't want to compete in the highly competitive residential or commercial cleaning industry, but would like to start a cleaning service? If so, why not consider starting a boat cleaning service. The competition is minimal and, providing the cleaning service is established in the right area, the number of potential customers can be almost unlimited. Starting a boat cleaning service could not be easier, as there are no special skills or equipment required to operate the business, and marketing the service requires no more than some printed fliers and a little bit of leg work to distribute the fliers at marinas and boating clubs. Considering a boat cleaning service can be started on an initial investment of less than $1,000, the income potential is excellent at $20 to $30 per hour. Providing customers with a boat bottom cleaning service can also generate additional revenues for a boat cleaning service. This aspect of the service can be subcontracted to a qualified scuba diver to work on revenue split basis.

USED CAR SALES
★★ $$$$ ⚖

The objective is clear in the used car sales game: buy low and sell high. The average new car now costs in excess of $20,000, placing this major purchase out of the reach of many people. Because of this, many people buy second-hand transportation. The main requirement for starting a used car sales business is a car seller's permit. You will need a business location with good street visibility and an initial inventory of cars to sell. Buying used cars for resale can be accomplished in a few ways, including buying from new car dealers who take trades but do not sell used cars beyond a certain age (usually six years old) or by attending automotive auctions for dealers, which generally feature lease returned cars and repossessed cars. Of course, the third option is to scan your local newspaper and purchase privately owned cars for sale. This is a good way of acquiring an initial inventory, providing your negotiation skills are good and you have the time. You need to know in advance that there is tremendous competition from other used car dealers and private sellers. While you can start a web site, the web competition is also fierce. As another means of selling used cars, you might opt to market cars to specific groups, such as students who are just getting their licenses or businesses that need company cars. Look for a competitive edge, possibly by spending a little time and money to upgrade the models and to make sure the cars are safer than those of your competitors.

WEB RESOURCE: www.niada.com
National Independent Automobile Dealers Association.

STEREO INSTALLATIONS
★★ $$ 🕐

A stereo installation service can cater to many potential clients, including car, van, and boat owners and dealers, as well as RV dealerships. The best way to market a stereo installation service is by providing installations only and not retailing stereos, as this method will enable you to attract retailers of stereo equipment as clients. Two of the best aspects about starting this type of specialized installation service are that it can be operated with virtually no overhead costs, and income in the $35 per hour range can be earned. Of course, you need to know how to install the latest stereo equipment, including speakers, in a timely manner.

CAR FINDER SERVICE
★ $$ 🏠 🕐

Thousands of people spend hundreds of hours each year trying to locate the perfect car or truck to purchase. Many of these people would be more than happy to become clients of a car locating service. The business concept is very straightforward. A client is seeking a particular type of car, truck, RV, or even a boat for that matter, and you use your web skills, contacts, and general investigating and research skills to track down ideal options for the client, who then decides on the model they want to purchase. Revenues for the business and your services are generated by negotiating a commission (and having a signed agreement) with the vendor of the vehicle being purchased, prior to introducing the vehicle to your client. In the case of a hard-to-find vehicle, such as an antique car, you could charge a search fee for the time it takes you to locate the car, since the individual seeking the vehicle is essentially looking for you to handle this task for him or her. A car finder service can easily generate an income of $50,000 per year for the operator of the service.

AUTOMOTIVE DETAILING SERVICE

An automotive detailing service is a business that requires little in the way of special skills, experience, or equipment, making this an ideal new business venture for just about anyone who is seeking to become independent. The following are two options available for starting and operating an automotive detailing service.

Mobile Automotive Detailing Service
★★★ $$ 🏠 🕐 🌐

Starting and operating a mobile automotive detailing service has many benefits, as opposed to operating the business from a fixed location. These benefits include a smaller initial investment to get the business rolling, flexibility in terms of operating hours, and lower monthly operating overhead. However, there are also two major drawbacks to operating an automotive detailing service on a mobile basis. The business will be at the mercy of weather conditions, and the potential to generate business revenues and sales will be limited to what a one-person service can produce, or about $25 to $30 per hour.

Fixed Location Automotive Detailing Service
★★ $$$ 🌍

The second option for starting and operating an automotive detailing service is to establish the business in a fixed location, meaning that clients come to you, or you bring the clients' automobiles to you. There are benefits and drawbacks to operating an automotive detailing service based on this format. The benefits: The business is not affected by weather conditions, it is possible to generate higher sales and profits if the business location has several detailing bays and employees, and the business can also provide additional services to clients that a mobile automotive detailing business cannot. The drawbacks for operating the business from a fixed location include a higher initial investment and higher monthly operating overhead costs.

WEB RESOURCE: www.topoftheline.com
Automobile detailing supplies

BOAT WINDOW REPLACEMENT SERVICE
★★ $$$ 🏠 🕐

Are you a handy person with basic hand tools who is looking to start a small business for less than a few thousand dollars in initial investment? If so, starting a boat window replacement service might be for you. The business requires a minimal start-up investment, and minimal skills and equipment. Anyone who has ever owned a sailboat will tell you that it does not take long for the boat's plastic windows to discolor and scratch. With millions of sailboats worldwide, a business that replaces Plexiglas boat windows should never run out of customers.

VALET PARKING SERVICE
★★ $$ 🏠 🕐 🌍

Starting a valet parking service is very easy. If you have a driver's license and can secure third party and automobile liability insurance, you are basically in business. A valet parking service can be marketed directly to consumers. However, a more logical marketing approach is to offer the valet parking service to event planners, wedding planners, tradeshow organizers, and catering facilities. The business can be started on a minimal capital outlay. The profit potential is also excellent, as current rates for valet parking services are in the range of $50 to $70 per hour, not to mention the fact that the cash tips can really add up. You will typically need several additional drivers to help you park cars. College students with driver's licenses who are looking for some extra cash are one option. Just make sure whomever you find can park cars without denting fenders or switching all of the pre-set radio stations in the cars.

MOBILE OIL CHANGE SERVICE
★★ $$+ 🏠 🕐 ⚖ 🌍

In most areas of the country a mechanic's license is not required to perform oil changes, making a mobile oil change service a business opportunity that just about anyone can start. The key to success in this competitive market is not only to provide customers with exceptional service, but also to secure customers who will use the service on a regular basis. Seek to gain clients with large fleets of vehicles, such as taxi, courier, car rental, limousine, and/or utility companies. Once established, a mobile oil change service can provide the owner of the business with a very good yearly income.

AUTOMOTIVE MAINTENANCE GUIDE
★★ $$$ 🏠 🕐 🌍

Here is a worthwhile new business venture for the entrepreneur with sales and marketing skills. Excellent profits can be earned by creating and distributing an automotive maintenance guide that is published in the spring and fall of each year. The guide can feature information about how to prepare your car for the upcoming winter or summer months, as well as feature automotive maintenance tips and stories submitted by readers. The automotive maintenance guides can be distributed free of charge throughout the community, and revenues for the business would be generated by selling advertising space in the guide to local business owners who are in the automotive or transportation industry. Once established and proven successful, this would be the ideal business to expand nationally on a franchise or licensed-to-operate basis. Profit potential range is $20,000+ per year.

DENT REMOVAL SERVICE
★★ $$ 🏠 🕐 🌐

Do you want to make as much as $75,000 per year operating your own business? If so, perhaps you should consider starting a dent removal and paint touch-up service. This service specializes in removing small dents such as door dents, hail damage, and touching up small areas of paint that have been damaged. Potential customers can include just about anyone with a small dent that they want removed from their vehicle. However, to truly succeed in this business, alliances should be established with auto dealers of new and used vehicles. Having a small dent removed from a vehicle can increase the retail sales value of a car by $1,000 or more, making this a worthwhile service for auto dealers to use.

MOPED TOURS
★★★★ $$$$ ⚖️ 🌐

In almost every community in the United States and Canada, a motorcycle permit is not required to operate a moped under a certain engine size. This fact creates an exceptional opportunity to start a moped tour business. Simply purchase six to ten new or used mopeds, supply helmets for the riders, and plan an interesting sightseeing tour in you local community. The tours can feature stops at historical sites, beaches, shopping malls, or just about any other tourist attraction or point of interest. The profit potential for a moped tour business is outstanding, and providing you can secure a mere 40 customers a week and charge $40 per person for a five-hour moped sightseeing tour, the business would stand to generate yearly gross sales in excess of $80,000.

WEB RESOURCE: www.moped.org
Directory service listing moped dealers, tour operators, and clubs.

MOTORCYCLE SALES
★★ $$$$ ⚖️

The time has never been better to start a business that sells secondhand motorcycles, as the popularity of motorcycle riding and ownership is at an all time high. A motorcycle sales business can be operated from home, providing the proper zoning requirements have been met and neighbors don't mind the sound of motorcycles at all hours. But the motorcycle sales business is more typically designed to be operated from a small rental location, or partnered with an existing automobile dealer. The profit potential for this type of business is great, providing you feature rebuilt and used motorcycles that can be purchased for considerably less than their retail value. This can be accomplished by knowing a lot about motorcycles and practicing good research and negotiation skills. Maintaining a 30 percent markup and achieving annual sales of $250,000 will result in a pretax and expense income of $70,000 per year.

IN-THE-WATER BOAT SHOWS
★★ $$$ 🕐 🌐

What is the difference between a "in-the-water boat show" and a boat show that takes place in an arena or complex? Water. Organizing and hosting in-the-water boat shows that feature privately owned boats for sale is a very easy business to establish and operate. The boat shows can take place at marinas or at other docking facilities. Business revenues can be earned by charging boat owners a fee for displaying their boat for sale at the show and/or by collecting a commission on the value of the boats sold at the show. Additional revenues can also be earned by renting sales booths to retailers of boating products. The vendor booths can be set up on a floating barge, pontoon boat, or even right on the docks. Marketing the in-the-water boat shows is best executed by advertising the event in boating magazines and publications as well as posting signs and fliers throughout the area.

PAINT TOUCH-UP SERVICE
★★★ $$ 🏠 🕐 🌐

Big profits await the enterprising entrepreneur who starts an automotive paint touch-up service. There is an unlimited supply of potential clients, and the demand for the service has been on a steady increase for the past decade and shows no sign of slowing down. The equipment required for operating the business is available at most automotive supply centers. The business can be operated right from a truck, van, or even a hatchback car.

While it does require some skill to be able to effectively operate the business and perform paint touch-up services, the learning curve is not very steep and, with some practice, can easily be mastered by a novice over the course of a few months. Current rates for automotive paint touch-up services start at about $50 for a basic scratch to be painted and buffed, and can go as high a $200 for more difficult paint touch-up jobs.

SUNROOF INSTALLATIONS
★★ $$ 🏠 🕐

Here is a terrific business opportunity that can be operated on a full- or part-time basis right from a home-based garage. Installing pop-open automotive sunroofs is relatively easy and does not require a lot in terms of expensive installation equipment. Potential customers can include car, van, truck, RV, and even boat owners, if the business also provides a mobile installation service. Be sure to establish alliances with car dealers in the local community, as they can act as sales agents for your sunroof products and installation services. Additional income can also be gained by expanding the product line to include the supply and installation of automotive accessories such as sun visors, running boards, and truck canopies.

WEB RESOURCE: www.donmar.com
Wholesale distributor of automotive sunroofs and accessories.

IN-THE-WATER BOAT BOTTOM CLEANING
★★ $$ 🏠 🕐 ⚖️

Calling all recreational scuba divers. Do you want to make an extra $40 to $50 per hour in your spare time? If so, then this business opportunity will be of particular interest to you. The easiest way to ensure that a powerboat or sailboat performs to its maximum ability is to keep the bottom of the boat free of barnacles and debris. This fact creates an incredible opportunity for recreation scuba divers with entrepreneurial instincts to start a boat bottom cleaning service while the boat is still in the water. Beyond scuba equipment and gear, the only equipment needed to operate the business will be a few good quality wire brushes and scrapers. Marketing this type of service is as easy as printing fliers describing the cleaning service

and rates, and distributing the fliers to boat owners at marinas and other boat docking facilities.

WEB RESOURCE: www.padi.com
Professional Association of Dive Instructors.

AUTO PAINTING SERVICE
★ $$$$ ⚖️ 🌐

Automotive painting is not only a proven and stable industry, it can also be a very profitable business venture to set in motion. Starting an automotive painting service has one main requirement to make the business successful: You or an employee must have the skills and experience required to complete bodywork and paint cars. The equipment requirements for operating the business are also numerous, making this a business opportunity best left to professional automotive painters. As a method to reduce the start-up investment needed to get the business rolling, consider a joint venture with an existing automotive repair shop that does not provide clients with automotive painting services. Not only can you reduce the start-up investment, but also greatly reduce the monthly operating overheads by sharing expenses. You can also take advantage of the repair shop clientele base for marketing purposes.

PILOT CAR SERVICE
★ $$$ 🏠 🕐 ⚖️

A pilot car is a car or truck that travels in front of an oversized vehicle traveling on public roads and highways as a safety precaution. The fact that pilot cars are required by law for oversized vehicles and equipment transport creates a great business opportunity for the entrepreneur seeking a business that's a little bit out of the ordinary. A pilot car service can easily be managed from a homebased office. The current rates for pilot car services are in the range of $25 to $35 per hour. Make sure to get reimbursed for gas or you could spend more than you make, considering today's gas prices.

REPLACEMENT HOSES AND FITTINGS SERVICE
★★★ $$$$ 🏠 ⚖️ 🌐

Delays in construction due to equipment failures can cost contractors and property developers thousands of dollars for every hour that heavy equipment, such as bulldozers and backhoes, are unable to operate. This fact creates a wonderful opportunity for an entrepreneur with mechanical skills to start a business that sells and installs pressure hoses and fittings for heavy equipment on a mobile basis. The key to success in this service is to provide clients with fast and reliable service. A cell phone for incoming inquiries would be an absolute must. Careful research must be conducted to learn exactly what types of hoses and fittings are the most popular in terms of repair. But beyond that and a good reliable service van, that is all that is required to get this dynamite moneymaker off the ground and earning you big profits.

UTILITY TRAILER SALES
★★★ $$$ 🏠 🕐

Yard work, home renovations, and helping a friend move are all reasons why owing a utility tr ailer has become extremely popular for many peo ple in North America. This is the perfect time to cash in on the popularity of utility trailers by starting a business that sells new and secondhand utility trailers. The first step for establishing this business is to seek out a manufacturer of utility trailers and negotiate an exclu sive sales and distribution contract for your community or state. The next step is to find the right operating location. This can be homebased if zoning permits, an independent location, or as a joint venture with an established business such as a car dealer or RV dealer. The third step is simply to start to advertise and market the utility trailers for sale.

PRE-PURCHASE AUTO INSPECTION
★★★ $$ 🏠 🕐 ⚖️ 🌐

Are you a certified mechanic who wants to make an extra $25,000 or more each year operating your o wn part-time business? If so, perhaps you should consider starting an automotive inspection service that operates on a mobile basis. Each year in Canada and the United States millions of previously owned cars and trucks are sold, and with the average cost of a secondhand vehicle now in the range of $8,000, many purchasers are turning to automotive inspection services to inspect the cars for mechanical deficiencies prior to purchasing the vehicle in question. Marketing an au tomotive inspe ction service beyond word-of-mouth referrals can be accomplished by utilizing local print mediums for advertising and establishing alliances with car clubs to act as their representatives for the inspection services. Current rates for mobile automotive inspections start at $50 and as much as $250 for RVs and trucks.

AIRPORT SHUTTLE SERVICE
★ $$$$ 🏠 ⚖️

Not unlike a limousine, taxi, or courier service, the first major challenge to overcome in starting an airport shuttle service is to acquire an operator's license. An operator's license can be difficult to get through local government channels in most areas of the country, and very expensive if you plan to purchase one from an existing shuttle service. However, it is certainly not impossible to obtain an operator's license for a shuttle service, and it can be well worth the effort. An airport shuttle service can be a very profitable business to own and operate. But, unless you are a one person operation doing the driving yourself and keeping the shuttle bus or van in your own driveway, you will have many operating expenses to consider, such as owning or leasing the vans or busses, having a garage or parking lot available, maintaining the vehicles, buying plenty of insurance, covering the gas costs and hiring responsible drivers, dispatchers and mechanics. Next you will have to secure with the airport or the local transportation authority that you can pick up passengers at the airport and have designated locations.

Marketing is the next hurdle, and at a major airport, you will have plenty of competition to deal with. If, however, you can handle all of the above, or start very small and build slowly, you can make a lot of money from a successful shuttle service, especially once you align yourself with major airlines, travel agents, and all local hotels.

MOBILE REFUELING SERVICE
★★★ $$$$ 🏠 ⚖️ 🌐

A mobile refueling service wi ll take a lot of mon ey to establish, as the mini-tanker tru ck alone can cost as much as $100,000. However, the truck and other requi red equi pment for the business could be leased as a way to keep initial start-up costs to a minimum. There is one main customer for this type of unique service: contractors with heavy earth-moving machinery. Earth-moving equipment is thirsty for fuel, and you cannot simply head down the road for a quick fill-up in a bulldozer. Most commercial contractors with heavy equipment utilize what is known as a mobile refueling service. The key to success in this business is to be on-call and ready to refuel equipment seven days a week. Revenue is generated by charging a premium for the fuel over gas pump prices, typically in the range of 20 to 30 cents a gallon. There are regulations in this industry, so be sure to carefully research the business and local market prior to establishing the service.

CHILDREN'S COACH SERVICE
★★ $$$$ 🏠 🚚 🌐

A parent's worst nightmare is that their child will become a victim of crime or even worse—abducted. This fact creates a very strong argument for parents to utilize a children's coach service within their community. Basically a children's coach is a taxi service that exclusively specializes in moving children safely from point A to point B. These specialized services include picking kids up and taking them to school in the morning and delivering them home safely afterwards, plus trips to the mall, sporting events, to meet friends, or just about any place parents are too busy to personally pick up and drop off their children. Beyond reliable transportation and a communication system, the main requirement for getting this business going will be a taxi or limousine license and permit. These permits can be difficult to acquire, however. Be sure to plead your case to community officials, as this service is focused on the well-being of kids, and benefits the community as a whole. There may be additional screening such as for child abuse through police fingerprinting. Once you have all licensing, you will need to demonstrate exemplary driving skills and be extremely reliable.

CAR RENTALS
★ $$$$ 🚚 🌐

The car rental industry is extremely competitive, so you may need to think about a niche market that the big auto rental companies are not servicing. Here are a few suggestions:

- Exclusively rent exotic sports cars like Porsches, BMWs, and Corvettes.

- Rent only certain motorcycles like Harley Davidson or Honda.
- Specialize in convertible cars for rent or perhaps sport utility vehicles.
- For environmentalists, provide rentals with alternative fuels and electric-powered options.

Promote the business by establishing alliances with hotels, corporations, and business associations, as well as by advertising in local print media. Should you choose the route of exotic sports cars, consider hosting a contest with a local radio station with the prize being a one- or two-day rental of an exotic sports car free of charge. Providing the radio station does its part and publicizes the contest well, then this can be a great way to promote a new business of this nature. Besides liability insurance, buying or leasing of the cars, and the maintenance of the vehicles, this can be a costly business to start up. Profits will come from being innovative, providing great customer service—like drop off and pick up—and very clever marketing to stand out from the major competitors in the field.

TRUCK ACCESSORIES
★★ $$+ 🏠 🕐 🚚

Selling and installing after-market accessories for trucks such as box caps, running boards, and roll bars from a homebased workshop is a fantastic money-making opportunity that can be conducted on a full- or part-time basis. In addition to these truck accessories, consider becoming an authorized dealer for one of the many manufacturers of "spray-in liners" for pickup trucks. These types of box liners have become very popular and there is a 100 percent mark up on the application. As a grand opening promotion you can place advertisements in your local newspaper and offer free installation for all accessories purchased before a specific date. Promotions such as this are costly, but they can attract a lot of business to a new enterprise and the spin-off can lead to new business through referrals. Note: Be sure to check that the zoning for your home will allow for this sort of business to be operated.

AUTO PARTS REBUILDING
★ $$ 🏠 🕐

Providing you have the equipment and skills required, an excellent part-time income can be earned by rebuilding secondhand automobile replacement parts. You can work from a homebased workshop on an as-needed or part-time basis for existing auto parts rebuilders. Another option is to advertise your service locally for rebuilding automotive parts, and also consider specializing in automotive parts rebuilding for parts used in rare, antique, and exotic cars, trucks, and motorcycles.

BICYCLE TAXI SERVICE (PEDICAB)
★ $$ 🚗 🕐 🚗

Peddle your way to profits by starting your own bicycle or pedicab taxi service. Whether a romantic ride through a park or a sightseeing visit around town, tourists love to take in the sights and sounds on their vacation with a relaxing ride in a pedicab. The main obstacle to overcome for starting a pedicab taxi service is licensing. However, if a license to operate a pedicab can be acquired or purchased, you could then be well on your way to establishing a fun and profitable business. There are many styles of pedicabs available ranging from two occupants all the way to six, and the cost to purchase a new pedicab is in the range of $3,500. Ride or rental rates are currently about $8 to $12 per 15 minutes with a minimum $5 charge. This type of business can easily be expanded by hiring contractors to operate the pedicabs on revenue split basis. I would suggest a 50/50 split or a flat rental rate that the operator pays for an entire shift. Ideally, this type of business will be located in an area frequently visited by tourists and with a climate that will allow for a year-round operation to maximize profits. Be sure to build alliances with local hotels, motels, and tourist attractions that will let you display promotional materials in their lobbies as well as park in front of their establishments and cater to their customers seeking to hire a pedicab for an enjoyable ride.

AUTO PERFORMANCE CENTER
★★ $$$$

With more than 100 million cars and trucks registered in the United States you cannot go wrong with starting an auto performance center that specializes in selling the latest and hottest automobile accessories. Stock and sell items such as mag rims and tires, wheel covers, engine performance parts, audio equipment and alarms, spoilers and body

kits, and sport driving lamps. This type of retail business is very costly to establish so planning and research will be of the greatest importance. Also be sure to locate the business in a building that will enable you to carry out installations of these accessories. The installation aspect of the business can be partnered with a mechanic; you sell the products and they install the products at your location. With service and installation space you will also be able to provide customers with additional services, such as detailing, interior cleaning, and window tinting.

BOAT LETTERING
★★ $$ 🚗 🕐

Here is a fantastic little moneymaking opportunity for entrepreneurs with a computer, design software, and a creative imagination. There are thousands of pleasure boats in the United States, and all have call numbers and signs indicating the name of the boat. However, a quick trip to your local marina quickly reveals that the sun and water take its toll. It is common is to see faded and peeling paint and vinyl letters. Here's where your computer and design skills can make you money. Simply design a few sample boat signs featuring great graphics, print them out on paper, and start to show your handy work to boat owners at local marinas. You can sketch out quick ideas for new signage for their boats while on site and return in a day or two with the finished product printed on paper. Once you get the go-ahead simply take the digital file with the sign design to a sign shop that specializes in making vinyl peel-and-stick-on signs and return to the marina to install the new sign for your client. Remember, it costs nothing for the boat owner to find out how good a new sign can look, so you will get little objection to the first step of the process. Providing the sign you design is visually appealing, you will also get little objection from the boat owner when you return to close the sale. Boats are expensive to buy and maintain and very few owners would let $100 stand in their way in terms of improving their boat's appearance.

TRANSPORT FOR THE DISABLED
★★ $$$$ 🚗

There is an ongoing need for vehicles and service providers who can accommodate disabled individuals, which opens the door for a business opportunity. The obvious start-up cost is the transportation, which can be an SUV, bus, van, or all of the above, refitted and specially equipped to handle the needs of disabled individuals. Such converted vans and SUVs can be found for $30,000 to $35,000. Lifts, special wheelchair floor locks, and other accommodations need to be made, plus licensing needs to be obtained before starting such a service. Once you are ready to go, you can market your services to hospitals, senior centers, schools, and other institutions.

HORSE AND BUGGY RIDES
★★ $$$ 🕒 🚗

They may not move very quickly, but horse and buggy or horse carriage rides can be a very romantic way to tour a city or enjoy a relaxing ride through the country. This can be a simple and profitable business venture as well. The start up is simple – first you need to check with local licensing and make sure you have all necessary permits to operate this type of business. Next, you need at least one or several horses and buggies, which can cost you from $1,000 to $10,000 each depending on the horse, the seller, and how elaborate the buggy is that you are buying. Make sure you have the horse ownership papers. Hint: before purchasing a horse, make sure to talk with someone familiar with horses and even have the horse checked out so that you know the health of the animal. You can then board the horses at a nearby stable and pay for food and for maintaining the animals, as well as the buggies. Next, unless you have the skills yourself, you will need a driver or two. These should be part timers, familiar with horses, whom you pay a percentage of the cost of the ride plus they earn tips. Finally, you need to plan out some local scenic routes and advertise the rides. You can market rides for weddings, anniversaries, birthday parties, and other special occasions. You might also invest in a long wagon and offer hay rides for kids. Decorations, champagne, a picnic lunch, or whatever packages you can come up with will boost your profits and add a special touch to your service. Rides can start at $15 per person or go up to $150 for couples' packages. Be creative!

AUTOMOBILE SEAT COVERS
★★ $$ 🕒

A simple business venture you can start up without much upfront capital is that of selling automobile seat covers. There are two options when it comes to auto seat cover sales. First, you can buy the seat covers in bulk from wholesalers and mark them up nearly 100% for resale value. From denim to sheepskin to vinyl, you can offer a wide range of covers and bring in from $100 to $200 each. The second option is to manufacture the covers yourself, which allows you to be creative and even custom design them for special sales, but can be difficult given the many various sizes of automobile seats. Market seat cover sales to auto parts stores, from booths set up at fairs and malls, and from a web site linked to as many car related sites as possible. For additional profit potential, you can also sell dash covers and floor mats.

HYBRID CARS
★★★ $$$$ 🚗 🪶

No, they have not yet caught on in a big way, but with the price of gas continuing to rise, hybrid cars may very well be the business to get into now. Slowly, the carmakers are beginning to unveil an increasing line of hybrids such as the Ford Escape Hybrid, Honda Insight, and the Toyota Prius. Many more are now available or on the way. A new car dealership clearly requires a major cash outlay to purchase or start, with numbers in the $100,000 to $500,000 range, with used car dealerships selling for less. Investors are an excellent way to raise the money, and they only need a solid sales pitch about the future of cars, which you will put together based on your research. The key factor here is not opening just another dealership, but having a competitive edge by selling something that isn't found on all other car lots, new or used.

WEB RESOURCE: www.hybridcars.com
An excellent research site.

RATINGS ★

START-UP COST $$

HOMEBASED BUSINESS 🏠

PART-TIME OPPORTUNITY 🕐

LEGAL ISSUES ⚖️

FRANCHISE OR LICENSE POTENTIAL 🌐

GREEN BUSINESSES 🍃

32
TRAVEL
Businesses You Can Start

TOUR GUIDE
★★ $ 🏠 🕐

Living in an area you know well can pay off if you start a business as a personal tour guide. This type of enterprise can be managed from a home office, started for less than $1,000, and has the potential to produce an income that can easily exceed $50,000 per year. The keys to success in this business are:

1. Providing detailed knowledge of something that other people will want to pay money to see and hear about, whether it is historical, architectural, or a unique lifestyle.

2. Presenting the information in an interesting, informative, and entertaining manner.

3. Providing inside information without infringing on anyone's personal life or business. You cannot parade a dozen tourists with cameras across someone's property, or through their home, without permission.

4. Promoting your service aggressively by building contacts with companies and individuals that can help you succeed, and providing clients with the best time of their vacation.

Currently, tour guides are charging clients around $125 for half-day tours and as much as $200 for full-day tours, plus the cost to provide transportation and tickets to events or local attractions. Companies and individuals to build alliances with, in terms of generating referrals, are limousine services, hotels, business event planners, travel agents and the local Department of Tourism and/or the Convention and Visitor's Bureau (CVB). Walking tours are a great way to save on the expense of a vehicle (and the liability insurance). Of course, this will only work in certain places.

ROAD TRIP DRIVING MAPS
★★★ $$ 🏠 🕐 🌐

One of the great icons of American culture is the road trip. It has been the topic of books, songs, and movies, and the more interesting the road trip map, the better. While MapQuest can provide answers when seeking the most direct route from one place to another, you can provide insight on alternate routes, including information such as the best and worst restaurants, strange and interesting facts about cities and towns along the way, weird roadside attractions, and interesting historical sites. The best way to market the maps is to design a POP display and establish wholesale accounts with retailers as well as truck stops and restaurants that are frequented by travelers.

OFF-ROAD TOURS
★★ $$$$ ⚖️

Off-road or four-wheel-drive tours have become an extremely popular day excursion for many vacationers, as it is a reasonably priced vacation activity that can be enjoyed by every member of the family. Generally, off-road tours are offered in half-day or all-day packages to clients and are currently priced from $50 to $100 per person. Advertising and promoting off-road or backwoods tours is very easy and is best accomplished by designing and distributing promotional material about the activity to all local restaurants, hotels, and travel agents. This kind of tour business can be very profitable, even if the business associates or partners receive a 10 or 20 percent commission for referring clients to the business.

MOVIE LOCATION TOURS
★ $$$ 🕒

While the major movie and television studios already have tours of their back lots and studio facilities, you can start tours of famous movie locations—provided, of course, you are living in a city where location shooting is prominent, such as Los Angeles, San Francisco, Toronto, or New York. Starting a business that takes people on tours of famous film and television locations is a terrific tour service to get rolling. In addition to the location tours, you can point out other movie and television star tidbits of information, such as the store in which someone was always seen shopping or the local restaurants and bars frequented by celebrities. Movie location tours can be marketed and promoted in a number of fashions including brochures in hotel lobbies and popular tourist locations, restaurants frequented by tourists and through travel agents and brokers. Ads on travel web sites as well as in the travel sections of newspapers can also bring in business. Make sure the tour is a lot of fun and send press releases to numerous media outlets to generate articles about this unique tour service.

CUSTOM TRAVEL BAGS
★ $$$ 🚗 🕒

"Have bags, will travel," could be your company motto if you start a business that designs, manufactures, and sells custom travel bags for business and pleasure travelers. The market for unique, functional, and good quality travel bags is gigantic, and this business venture is extremely easy to get up and going. The main objective in designing and selling travel bags is for the product to be unique and serve a particular need. Try an all-in-one travel bag that enables business travelers to carry a portable office that can

include a notebook computer, printer, paper supplies, cell phone and charger, as well as have a battery power supply built right into the bag. Of course, this is only one suggestion, as there are literally thousands of different ideas that can be incorporated into travel bags to make the product appealing to consumers. To keep initial start-up and development costs in check, consider a joint venture partnership with a related business in the industry.

CORPORATE RETREATS
★ $$ 🚗 🕒

Uniting corporate retreats from around the world into a corporate retreat vacation club may be just the answer to your business start-up dreams. There are thousands of vacation retreats owned by corporations from around the globe, and many of these corporate retreats sit vacant for a great deal of the year. Herein lies the business opportunity. Start a business that manages and rents corporate retreats to business and pleasure travelers when the vacation property is not in use by the corporation. Revenues could be generated from the weekly and monthly rental rates for the vacation retreats, and the fee for managing and renting the retreats could be 25 percent to 35 percent of the total rental revenue generated. Corporations would save money on property management costs, as well as gain rental revenue, and business and pleasure travelers would have access to a wide range of well-equipped vacation properties around the world.

ECO OR "GREEN" TOURS
★★★ $$$ ✎

The time has never been better than now to start a business that specializes in arranging and conducting eco tours, as we are now living in a "green"-conscious society that has become more and more interested in the environment. The first step to establishing this type of tour operation is to decide on the ecology subject or topic, and to determine the way in which the tour will be conducted in terms of transportation, marketing, and accommodations. Additional considerations will also include the possibility of charity endorsement and business location. Overall, ecology and environmental tours are an excellent new business start-up choice. Schools are an excellent place to market this tour for class trips.

WEB RESOURCE: www.ecotourism.org
The International Ecotourism Society.

WORKING VACATIONS
★★ $$$ 🎒 🕐 ⚖️

While it may sound like an oxymoron, every year thousands of people pay big bucks for an opportunity to work while they're on vacation. There seems to be interest in all kinds of working vacations, and the stranger the better. Simply seek out companies, businesses, farms, and factories that are interested in forming joint ventures to promote and provide working vacation services, whereby people spend their vacation working in a very different capacity from that which they do on a daily basis. Once the joint ventures have been established, the vacations can be sold via the internet, through travel agents and brokers, or by establishing a direct commissioned sales team. The biggest business challenge to overcome will be the legal aspect of operating this type of travel business in terms of workers' compensation laws and liability issues. Have legal counsel review all plans and paperwork before proceeding.

TRAVEL COMPANION
★★ $ 🎒 🕐

Do you want to travel the world for free? If so, perhaps you should consider becoming a professional travel companion. Working as a professional travel companion generally does not provide an income; only free travel transportation, meals, and accommodations. There are numerous reasons why people enlist the services of such travel companions including not wanting to travel alone, to assist in caring for elderly members of the family, as travel nannies, or simply wanting a person from their country who is familiar with the area that the person is traveling to. In many cases, the companion may also be serving as a translator. While this type of travel business will not generate a significant income, if any, it does provide an opportunity to travel the world, make new friends and contacts, and build a lifetime of cherished memories.

TRAVEL COMPANION ARRANGEMENTS
★ $$ 🎒 🕐

In this capacity, you are not the travel companion, but you bring such companions to the people seeking them.

Through a web site and some smart marketing, you can bring people seeking a travel companion together with people seeking to serve as travel companions, and make a commission from each match you make. In addition, you can also provide space on the web site for people who are looking for someone to drive their car to a destination, or share driving duties and costs to go across the country or through Europe. You can earn additional income from selling adds on the web site to travel related businesses.

BICYCLE TOURS
★★★ $$$+ 🌐

Careening down a steep mountain road at 30 miles per hour on a mountain bike may not be everyone's idea of the perfect vacation, but there is no denying the fact that bicycle vacation tours are one of the fastest-growing segments of the travel industry. The key to success in a bicycle tour business is that the tours have to be unique, fun, and interesting, and should be organized around a central theme. Additional considerations include accommodations, meals, and transportation requirements or services, as well as the length and location of the tours. Advertising in all the traditional media, developing a company web site promoting the business, and listing the tours with travel agents and brokers can accomplish marketing the business.

START-UP COSTS: The following example can be used as an outline to establish the investment required for starting a bicycle tour business:

	Low	High
Business setup, legal, banking, etc.	$500	$2,000
Company web site	$500	$2,500
Office equipment and supplies	$2,000	$5,000
Liability insurance	$500	$3,000
Equipment and transportation	$15,000	$50,000
Initial advertising and marketing budget	$1,000	$5,000
Working capital	$1,000	$5,000
Total start-up investment	**$20,500**	**$72,500**

There are cost saving methods that can be employed to substantially reduce the amount of start-up capital required to set a bicycle tour business in motion. These methods include:

- Subcontracting all transportation requirements for the business to a local and established bus or transportation company.
- Negotiating a discount on equipment purchases from a national bicycle manufacturer, as well as the potential to become an authorized dealer of the bicycles.
- Starting the business in conjunction with an established tour operator that does not currently provide bicycle tour options to clients.

PROFIT POTENTIAL: The profit potential for a bicycle tour business varies greatly due to a number of factors, such as length of tour, operating format, customer volumes, and operating overheads. However, the current rates for bicycle tours are in the range of $50 to $70 per person per half day, $75 to $125 per person per full day, and weeklong tours start at $100 per day per person, and rates go up from there. Additionally, the type of accommodations, meals, and transportation (if supplied) will also have an effect on the overall business revenues and profits. Profit potential range is $20,000+ per year part-time and $40,000+ per year full-time.

WORLD CASTLE VACATIONS
★ $$ 🚗 🕐 🚜

England, Scotland, France, Germany, Spain, and Italy all have castles, many of which have been converted to tourist attractions and accommodations. Starting a travel business that specializes in world castle tours and trips could not only prove to be fun and interesting, it could also make you rich. Promoting and marketing the castle trips and tours can be accomplished in many ways including direct-mail campaign, fax and e-mail broadcasting, on the internet, and in conjunction with established travel agents and brokers. A suggested commission rate or booking rate for the tours and trips that have been marketed through the web site would be 10 to 20 percent of the total retail sales value.

TRAVEL CHEAP BOOKS AND GUIDES
★★ $$$ 🚗 🕐

Each year thousands of graduating university and college students embark on vacations to every corner of the planet as the "last hoorah" prior to starting careers and families. Starting a business that develops, publishes, and distributes "how to travel cheap" books and guides aimed specifically at this segment of the travel market is a fun business enterprise to set in motion. If you're not a well-seasoned traveler yourself, you can still start this business simply by enlisting the services of people who are experts in the field of traveling on a limited budget. The simplest way to get things rolling is to post advertisements on various internet newsgroups seeking information about ways to "travel cheap" from people who have firsthand experience. You can also use the internet to do research on inexpensive travel options and destinations, getting information directly from locations and resources. Once the information has been gathered, simply compile the information into book form and self publish or market the book to publishing houses. Self publishing might prove more advantageous because you can start by marketing the book and then only print as many copies as necessary to fill the orders. In addition, you get the book out quickly, since publishing houses often take a while to get a book into print and onto the shelves. You can also get the book into the hands of your demographic audience by selling it online or at on-campus bookstores and other locations. You should market your book heavily in the months approaching spring break and summer vacation. Knowing how to write well is a plus, although certainly not a pre-requisite. Hint: Make sure your research is accurate—fact check thoroughly before putting information in print.

SINGLES-ONLY VACATIONS
★★ $$ 🚗 🕐

Business specialization is important, especially in an industry as large and competitive as the travel industry. Starting a business that specializes in singles-only vacation destinations could prove to be just the moneymaking opportunity that you have been searching for. There are inherent differences between a family vacation and one that would be enjoyed by a single person. Catering to this gigantic segment of the travel industry has the potential to make you rich. The objective in this travel business is to offer clients original and diverse options and packages that appeal to different segments of this large demographic group. For example, you can offer an extreme sports vacation, a spring break get-away for college students, single parent retreat, clothing optional vacation, beach resort getaway, single senior cruise, and so on. The more creative you are in marketing to the diverse interests and age groups of the overall single population, the more likely you will tap into this market in a big way. Of course to run such a business effectively, you will need to establish yourself as a travel agent, which takes a little time and effort, but can be very well worth it.

WEB RESOURCE: www.astanet.com
The American Society of Travel Agents

"PETS WELCOME" VACATIONS
★★ $$ 🚗 🕐

Starting a travel business that focuses specifically on providing vacation and tour options that include the family pet is the focus of this business opportunity. Most tour and vacation packages that are currently available on the market make no provisions for family pets. In fact, most have a no pets allowed policy. This creates a tremendous opportunity for the entrepreneur with initiative to capitalize by starting a travel booking agency that exclusively features "pets welcome" vacation packages. The first step to establishing this novel travel business is to put together a comprehensive list of hotels, resorts, airlines, and tour operators that will allow pets to participate in the family holiday experience. The next step will be simply to start marketing the "pets welcome" vacation packages and tours. This can be accomplished by advertising and promoting the business and vacation packages via the internet, and by a direct-mail campaign targeted at pet owners, pet trainers, vets, and all related businesses in the pet industry.

TRAVEL KITS
★ $$ 🚗 🕐

Starting a business that produces and distributes specialty travel kits for business and pleasure travelers could put you on the path to financial freedom and independence. The travel kits could be destination-specific and include items such as maps, language dictionaries, attraction and tour discount coupons, and personal sundries such as a mini first-aid kit, toothbrushes, etc. Once the travel kits have been designed and produced, they can be sold directly to travel agents and brokers on a wholesale basis, as well as directly to consumers via the web and mail order.

BACKPACKING VACATIONS
★★ $$$$ 🚗 🕐 🌐

Backpacking and hiking are two of the world's most popular recreational outdoor activities, so it seems logical that a travel business that specializes in operating backpacking and hiking tours would be a wise choice for a travel business start-up. There are various approaches that can be taken in terms of an operating format for the business. One approach may be to offer clients an all-inclusive vacation package, which could include transportation, overnight camping, meals, and numerous activities. An alternate approach is to offer travelers "mini backpacking excursions" while on vacation. This approach would best be marketed by establishing alliances in the local area of the business operation to act as booking agents for the excursions. Excellent alliances to build would be with restaurants, hotels, travel agents, and local activities booking agents. The one day or mini excursion option would greatly reduce the amount of start-up capital required to set the business in motion. This approach may also enable the business to be operated on a part-time or seasonal basis, which can also be of benefit to the entrepreneur seeking a secondary means of income.

ADVENTURE WEDDING PLANNER
★★★★ $$ 🚗 🕐 🌐

"I do," says the bride, as she is just about to leap off a 200-foot bridge with only a bungee cord separating her and the groom from the ground. Launching a business as an adventure wedding planner could not only prove to be fun and interesting, you are also almost guaranteed of having very little competition. White-water rafting, scuba diving, hot air balloon trips, mountain climbing, and bungee jumping are only a few of the adventure activity choices you can provide to clients who are getting hitched and seeking something out of the ordinary. An adventure wedding planning service can be advertised in wedding publications, as well as on the internet. It should not take long to establish the business, as this is the type of unique, interesting, and fun service that really gets people talking.

WEB RESOURCE: www.nawp.com
National Association of Wedding Professionals.

BED AND BREAKFAST OPERATOR
★★ $$+ 🚗 🕐 🚐

Providing you can get your home renovated to operate as a bed and breakfast accommodation, and you do not mind having overnight guests, you stand to profit by turning your home into a bed and breakfast tourist destination. Operating a bed and breakfast is a terrific way to meet new people and make new friends. It is also a great way to pay down the mortgage or stash away some extra money for retirement. Rates for B&B stays are typically in the range of $30 to $100 per night and include breakfast the following morning. You can promote your B&B by joining your local tourism association as well as by listing your B&B in online directories and advertising in travel magazines and publications. Beyond a business license, the cost to turn your home into a B&B can vary based on certain factors, such as meeting local fire, safety, and building codes, as well as zoning ordinances. You may also need to review your homeowner's insurance policy carefully and consider increasing your liability insurance. Most B&B owners do not make a fortune, but enjoy what they do very much. Hint: Set some basic ground rules in advance as a means of not losing control. This might include no loud music, no additional guests inside the house, children over a certain age only, etc. It's your house, so make sure that not only are your guests comfortable, but so are you.

WEB RESOURCE: www.paii.org
Professional Association of Innkeepers International.

WHALE WATCHING TOURS
★★ $$$$ 🚐

Whale watching tours are the largest segment of the booming multimillion-dollar ecotourism industry. While starting a whale watching tour business is a costly business venture to set in motion, and one that won't work in Indiana or Wisconsin, the personal and financial rewards can be tremendous. Beyond having the business located in an area that is excellent for whale watching, the main business requirement is a suitable tour boat and a certified captain at the helm, not to mention substantial liability insurance. Rates for whale watching tours vary as to the length of the tour, meals provided, and additional customer services. They may start at $50 per person and can go as high as $150 per person. The profit potential for a whale watching travel or tour business is exceptional once the business has been established. However, keep in mind that most whale watching tour businesses operate on a part-time or seasonal basis.

DOUBLE-DECKER BUS TOURS
★★ $$$$ 🚐 🌐

Antique, British-style double-decker buses have always held a certain mystique and fascination for people. They are unique, fun, and hearken back to an earlier time. Starting a double-decker bus tour business could not only prove to be a whole lot of fun, it could also be a very profitable business venture. The key to success in this type of tour business is to make sure the tour business is operated in a busy tourist area, and that the tour itself is fun, interesting, and unique. Generally with this type of tour business the initial advertising and marketing drive will have to be well researched and planned. However, once established, word-of-mouth advertising from local companies and individuals will generally be all the advertising required to sustain a suitable customer volume level. Keep in mind that these busses, even the used ones, can cost upwards of $35,000 each and that you will need to find and pay for a suitable place to keep them, unless you have a very tall garage.

WEB RESOURCE: www.double-decker-bus.net
Authentic double-decker busses from Great Britain.

TRAVEL AGENCY
★★ $$$+ 🚐

The main requirement for starting a travel agency or starting a business as an independent travel consultant will be to check local regulations in terms of certifications that may be required to operate the business. You may also need to take some training courses. Considerations will include:

- Whether or not to operate a general travel agency, or specialize in a particular type of travel.

- Where to establish the business.
- What is your target market: the well-heeled traveler or the budget traveler?
- How to handle advertising, promotions, and marketing.

The travel industry as a whole is extremely competitive, especially for businesses that operate as general travel agencies. To limit competition it is important to specialize in this industry and seek a niche market. You also need to build very strong alliances within the industry. Something to consider: Millions of people are now going online and booking their trips to destinations worldwide through travel web sites. The only way to survive against such competition is to offer something that these web sites cannot – this might mean first-rate personalized service, lower prices, diverse packages, special accommodations, and so on. If you cannot legitimately justify what gives you a competitive edge and why a client will come to you rather than booking a trip over the internet, then you will have a very hard time succeeding in this business.

WEB RESOURCE: www.astanet.com
American Society of Travel Agents.

CANOE AND KAYAK TOURS
★★★ $$$+ 🔒 🕒

Are you searching for a travel-related recreation business that has tremendous opportunity for growth, profit potential, and a whole lot of fun? If so, why not consider starting a canoe and kayak tour business. A canoe and kayak tour business can be easily operated and managed from a homebased location, or can be operated in conjunction and with existing businesses such as a marina, resort, or waterfront tourist attraction. There are also various options available for the method in which a canoe and kayak tour business can be operated, including day excursion format, overnight, multi day format, or an operating format that combines canoe and kayak instruction as well as a general pleasure tour. A few key considerations in terms of starting and operating this business include:

- Liability and general business insurance
- Transportation and equipment requirements
- First aid and safety requirements and qualifications
- Qualifications for tour leaders

START-UP COSTS: The following example can be used as an outline to establish initial investment required for starting a canoe and kayak tour business.

	Low	High
Business setup, legal, banking, etc.	$500	$2,000
Liability and general business insurance	$750	$1,250
Office equipment and supplies	$1,500	$5,000
Equipment and transportation	$15,000	$25,000
Initial advertising and marketing budget	$500	$1,500
Working capital	$500	$2,000
Total start-up investment	**$18,750**	**$36,750**

Additionally, there are a few options for transportation requirements if the business is operated on a mobile basis, meaning that customers are shuttled to the launch location or starting point of the tour. These options include:

- Purchasing, renting, or leasing the required transportation. Generally a 12-passenger van and a trailer capable of holding an equivalent number of canoes and kayaks are needed.
- Subcontracting the transportation aspect of the business to a local transportation firm.
- Making customers responsible for providing their own transportation, and reflecting this in the rates.

PROFIT POTENTIAL: The following income forecast can be used as a guideline to establish revenue potential.

# of Customers per Week	Tour Rate	Gross Revenue per Month	Gross Revenue per Year
10	$125	$5,000	$60,000
15	$125	$7,500	$90,000
20	$125	$10,000	$120,000
25	$125	$12,500	$150,000

Additional business revenues can be generated by canoe and kayak equipment sales and rentals, as well as by providing clients with extended canoe and kayak instruction courses.

FACTORY TOURS
★ $$$ 🚗 🕐 🚐

Factory tours have become extremely popular in the past decade, as more and more people are seeking different and interesting ways to spend their hard-earned vacation dollars. The first step in establishing a factory tour business is to find companies that will permit you inside their factories. While this used to be rather easy to arrange (in exchange for a portion of the revenues), the much tighter security measures in place today may require more due diligence is necessary on your part to set up factory tours. However, factories that make user-friendly products that customers can buy and carry out will likely still see the advantage of selling goods right to the tourists at wholesale or factory-direct prices. Securing a mere 50 customers per week paying only $20 each will create business revenues of $50,000 per year, which is an excellent start for small homebased tour business.

GUEST RANCH
★★ $$$$ 🚗 🚐

Guest or dude ranches have become an extremely popular vacation destination for thousands of North Americans. While starting a guest ranch is a labor- and capital-intensive business undertaking, there are also numerous benefits, such as a rewarding lifestyle, great income potential, and strong consumer demand. The most popular guest ranches include services and activities such as horseback riding, outdoor barbecues, and sporting activities, such as swimming, mountain bike trail riding, and tennis. Advertising, promoting, and marketing this sort of travel business is best accomplished by utilizing all of the traditional advertising and marketing mediums. Once the business has been established, many guests will become repeat clients as well as generate word-of-mouth referrals for the ranch. The profit potential will greatly vary as to the operating format of the ranch, and the services provided. However, current guest ranch accommodation rates start at $700 per week per person, and can go as high as $2,000 per week per person depending on the vacation package.

WEB RESOURCE: www.guestranches.com
Directory listing service of North American Guest Ranches.

BED AND BREAKFAST GUIDE
★★ $$ 🚗 🕐

If you can get the listings together by obtaining first-hand information from B&B owners, you can create a guide and/or a web site that features the best B&B locations in the state, province, region, or the entire country. Make sure your guide is user friendly, easy to read, and includes the parameters for the places you list plus photos and accommodations. You can get local advertisers from the area you are featuring and give the guide away for free, or you can sell the guides. You can do the guides semi-annually or, if the guide is electronic, you can update more often based on accumulating changes and updates.

WEB RESOURCE: www.paii.org
Professional Association of Innkeepers International.

TEEN TRAVEL TOURS
★★★ $$$$ 🚐

What better time to tour Europe, Africa, or Asia than as a teen? Establishing a teen travel tour service means putting together travel packages with a young audience in mind. Whether they are local tours or to destinations worldwide, the emphasis should be on providing a fun and rewarding (even educational) experience. Even more so with teens than adults, the schedule has to be very tightly filled in. Activities, meals, and lodging must be carefully orchestrated as well as specific tours of cities or local culture. Utilizing a combination of dorms, camping, and hotels, plus finding mid-range places that kids like to eat, you can create exciting teen-friendly packages. Then give the tours catchy names and start signing up teens from 14 to 19 years of age. Because of school, your business will be largely seasonal, with two- to six-week summer packages being your best sellers for anywhere from $2,000 to $9,000 (or more) depending what you have booked. Like other travel booking businesses, this is a business that requires knowing a lot of people in the industry. Run the business from home, do colorful brochures, build an eye-catching web site, and market to teens and their parents.

SENIOR TOURS
★★ $$ 🚗 🕐

Retirees love to travel, and that can mean big business for you as an entrepreneur, if you start a senior tour service. This business means putting together an itinerary for each tour package that caters to the needs, and the pace, of seniors. Research is important before you start putting tour packages together. You need to know what will appeal the most to your demographic audience. As is typically the case with a tour package, you can get good deals by establishing relationships with hotel managers, restaurant owners, transportation companies, and even the airlines, since you will be buying in bulk and passing that discount on to your customers. There is little overhead to this business, other than promoting yourself through advertising. The key is the contacts and the packages you offer, which should include air transportation, hotel, guided tours, meals, ground transportation and other accommodations for any special needs. If you can handle all of the travel details, you can make this a profitable business.

WEB RESOURCE: www.ntaonline.com
National Tour Association

HOTEL CONCIERGE SERVICE
★★ $$ 🏛️

You'll find a concierge desk in most of the world's finest hotels. However, many mid-level hotels could benefit from adding such personalized services. And that's where you come in. Whether you align yourself with one hotel or several, your job is to provide the know-how for tourists and guests visiting from out of town. Prior to starting such a business, you will need to spend time forging relationships with everyone in town. Your goal is to be able to help guests get whatever it is they desire, including tickets to the theater, the opera, a ballgame, or to a local concert. You must be able to help get them onto sightseeing tours, into spas, and obtain reservations in the finest restaurants. The harder the challenge, the more valuable you become if it is within your power. After all, with laptops, the savvy traveler can do a lot for him/herself. Therefore, as a concierge you must be one step ahead. Broadway show sold out for six months and guest wants tickets? No problem. Two-week wait for tee time at a popular golf course and guest wants to play? No problem. Exclusive spa, very hard to get reservations, and guest wants a facial now? No problem. Audience with the Pope? Okay, perhaps that's pushing it. But the idea is that your

concierge service is the answer. Market yourself to hotel owners and managers as well as tourist and visitors bureaus and to companies for corporate travelers. You can work in one or several cities and branch out by training others to work with you, once you have established contacts all over town.

TRAVEL GAMES FOR KIDS
★ $$ 🏠 🕐

Kids get bored on long trips and so do adults, for that matter. However, it's easier to occupy a 10-year old with a travel game on a long car trip than an adult who is either driving or reading the map. There are several options when marketing travel games. You can create a book of original games that tap into the young traveler's view while traveling down the road and have them look for certain items or create phrases, stories, songs, rhymes or other such activities. You can include some classic travel favorites, with variations on the license plate game, car Bingo, etc. Another option is to sell small versions of existing games, typically designed so that the pieces hold to the board through magnets or another type of adhesive material. A third option is to create printable games that can be downloaded from a web page. Unlike the other two options, here you will need sponsors so that you can offer the games for free. However you decide to create travel games, make sure you market your business to all kid-friendly locations as well as travel agencies and all online travel web sites.

TRAVEL MEDICINE POUCHES
★ $$ 🕐

"Who packed the pills and where are they?" Whether it's a camping trip or a week-long visit to a five-star resort, travelers need to know where their medicines are when they need them. This opens up the door for you to create, manufacture, and market medicine pouches that fit handily into a suitcase, travel bag, and/or onto the person by a waistband. Having the pouches produced out of a canvas or water-resistant materials should be easy once you have a prototype of what you want, which is essentially a bag large enough not to be easily misplaced, but small enough not to be cumbersome while carrying pill containers or medical necessities in each of several compartments. Produced for $12, you could sell the Travel Medicine pouch for $25 on a web site and through direct mail. You could also sell it to retailers for $18 and make a 50% profit and get the product seen in stores.

CRUISE DIRECTORY
★★ $$$ 🏠

For many years, cruises have been a very popular vacation choice. In recent years, they have resurfaced as a favorite with numerous cruises offered to suit all lifestyles. Whether it is Carnival, Windjammer, Disney, or any other cruise operator, you can list them in a comprehensive print, and/or web directory that features the various amenities offered. Getting advertising from the major players should not be too difficult, once you've established yourself as the place to go for cruise information. Include photos from cruise lovers and some travel advice columns on cruises, upcoming specials, and new offerings, and you can cruise your way to profits. Update the directory several times a year and maintain the web site with new information. Market your cruise directory or web site to all vacation publications and travel planners.

WEB RESOURCE: www.cruising.org
Cruise Line International Association.

NOTES:

21

WEB FUN AND ENTERTAINMENT

Businesses You Can Start

INTERNET MICRO GUIDE

In this chapter, and the two that follow, you'll find more than 150 possible web business ideas. The truth is that almost any business you can think of today has an online counterpart. There are several unique factors that come into play when trying to launch a web site, and more significantly, a web-based business.

1. Domain Name

Your first concern will be finding a domain name that is new and "grabs" your audience. A bricks-and-mortar business can simply adapt its current name to become a dotcom business; such a site typically operates as an extension of the existing business. However, a specific web business needs to have an original domain name that, after doing an exhaustive search, can be licensed for your businesses. Typically such licenses are renewable after a few years. If available, you might opt to spend a little more money and buy up the closest domain names to yours, so that poor typing doesn't send your business to a competitor.

Remember:

- The domain name should be short so people remember it.
- It should be simple so it is easy to spell.
- It should have something to do with your product or service. For example, an ice cream manufacturer called Johnson.com tells nobody that it's an ice cream company. JohnsonsIceCream.com lets people know what you are all about.
- It should not be case sensitive, since most people will not remember that it is.
- It should not have offbeat or unusual spelling.

2. Web Site Construction and Hosting

Finding a web site architect and a hosting service to put you on the web are not difficult, as there are numerous businesses servicing one or both of these functions.

To start, find a web designer whose work you like and who understands the vision you have of your site. If he or she does not "get it" then you should go with someone else. Before hiring someone to design a site for you, look at other sites that he or she has done and be honest with yourself. If the style is not right for you, move on to someone else.

Rather than the massive ISPs that allow you to build a web site, you will want to find a web hosting service that caters to business, and there are many that do just that. You want a dedicated web hosting service that deals with the needs of businesses and not one primarily known for teen chat rooms. Look at prices and deals and make sure to get some recommendations from others who can vouch for customer service. A significant factor in selecting a web hosting service is making sure that there will be someone you can contact should your site suddenly be down or some aspect is not functioning properly. The web hosting service is your lifeline to the internet and your business depends on it. You cannot afford to lose thousands of dollars in business because you cannot reach the hosting service. Once you have selected such a service, you will be given a password and directions how to post content and make changes. The more detailed and complex the site, the more you may want to hire someone with web management expertise to handle the technical end. This can be a webmaster, your site designer, or someone who you hire independently. Most small businesses do not spend a lot on web hosting. However, if traffic grows at a significant rate, or you need an extensive amount of gigabytes or have numerous complicated graphics, this will raise the prices of your monthly service.

3. Site Design and Content

The site needs to fit the purpose and intention of the business. People can typically tell a lot about a web site in the first five seconds. Ask yourself:

- *Is there too much going on?* If the site is too crowded, people will feel overwhelmed and go elsewhere. White space is a good thing.
- *Does the site reflect the business?* A site for kids may be colorful and have a fun flavor to it from the onset. A web site dealing with legal matters that features balloons and clowns will not generate the appropriate level of respect.
- *Does the site upload quickly even on a 56k modem?* If you assume that everyone has the latest in technology and that they should be able to see your site and view all of the graphics instantly, you are making a mistake and eliminating a major segment of your audience. An overuse of bells and whistles at the expense of paying customers is a very common mistake.
- *Do your links work and do they lead to the right places?* If someone is clicking for a specific piece of information, they had better find it immediately. If not, they're gone. Don't drop someone in the middle of a busy web page and make him or her search for what they were seeking. They won't stay.
- *Can the site be easily viewed on laptops and notebook computers?* Not all screens sizes are the same. If you

oversize the page, it might not fit on smaller screens Remember more and more people are accessing the internet from laptops and notebook computers.

- *Are the colors friendly on the eyes?* Yellow writing on a red background will not please most viewers. Keep in mind what will look good to the majority of your visitors.
- *Is the site very easy to navigate?* People do not stay on sites in which they are getting lost. Have a site map if you have a large site.

Site design can be changed, but it is in your best interest to start by studying the sites of your potential competitors and sites that you find easy to use and attractive. Try various options before deciding on one, and make sure to have your back end work completed before your launch. This includes your legal matters and privacy statement—review this with an attorney who has worked with internet sites before. It also includes the "about us" page, which is important since few people like doing business with anonymous web sites. Also, reach out and have a place in which visitors can send feedback, suggestions, comments, or ask questions. Remember, this is an interactive medium.

4. Retail

Retail web sites have special needs. To start, most successful retailers online use digital photos of their products that will attract the customer and that can be enlarged to show the product more closely. People want information about what they consider purchasing, and a very common online retail mistake is trying to rush the sale. You need to bridge the gap between a customer's interest and the shopping cart. Landing pages are those in-between pages where the customer gets more information, a product description, and some details. From there you want to give them the option of purchasing. Creating the actual purchase area on your site is done through special shopping cart software. Connections need to be made with your bank to allow for credit card orders with safe encryption in place, and they can walk you through the process. Make sure the shopping cart is a smooth system that allows customers to see their purchases, make sure they are correct, make changes, and see all shipping, handling, and taxes before clicking to purchase. Make the process as straightforward, honest, and painless as possible.

To handle post sale interactions, retailers need to post clear return and exchange policies and include excellent customer service. Remember, 80% of business comes from return customers. If you lose them by not providing good (or any) customer service, you are not likely to get them back, and it costs you a lot more money in any type of business to constantly go after new business.

For a final detail, make sure you find a very reliable fulfillment house once your business grows beyond being able to ship everything yourself. If you have the manufacturers shipping directly, you can save money, but also jeopardize your reputation if they are not competent at filling orders. Work with manufacturers that can make good on orders quickly.

5. Marketing and Promotion

Marketing is the big step that many people tend to overlook when considering a web business. You can have the greatest looking web site in the world with excellent navigation and marvelous graphics, but if nobody knows it's there, you are not going to make any money.

Typically, unless you are launching a very high-tech complex site, your biggest expense will be that of marketing. You need to have a clear idea of the demographic market for your web site and reach that market in every possible manner that you can afford. Keep in mind that often the best means of marketing is through constant, steady, repeated ads and promotional ideas, rather than a big splash. The story of the pet web site that spent all of their money on a Super Bowl ad and folded within a year, while their competitor did very steady small online newsletters and advertisements, has become legendary in the internet community. Slow but steady wins the race.

Don't forget that word-of-mouth marketing, a.k.a. viral marketing, is a major way of drawing people to a web site. You might want to visit the Word of Mouth Marketing Association (at www.womma.org) for ideas. Including content with "forward to a friend" buttons, having e-cards and other items such as jokes or recipes that people like to share with one another, are great ways to get people to promote your site for you as they send information around the internet with your site name on

it. Free promotional giveaways are also great ways to get attention. The iPod became very popular by people seeing others wearing the white headphones and asking one another what it was and where they got it. Since most products are not carried around or worn, you can make great strides with clever promotional giveaway items.

There is also a means of advertising today called pay per click, also known as pay for placement, or pay for ranking. On most search engines, the pay per click advertisements are usually text ads placed near search results. The advertiser then pays a small amount whenever a visitor clicks on an ad. You can utilize this as a form of advertising— however, it can become costly.

To enhance your presence on the internet, you need to register your web site with all of the major search engines. You can then optimize your status and where you show up on searches by paying additional money and/or, following their guidelines, such as using key words appropriately and so on. Don't try to outsmart the search engines, since those who are handling such optimization (and the technology itself) is set up to catch nearly any trick you can come up with. Therefore, you will typically have to pay for a higher ranking.

No matter what, do not forget to emphasize promotion, marketing, and advertising, both when you start up the web site and once your site is up and running. Too many web business owners forget that they cannot ease up on advertising after the site is launched.

6. Revenue

The primary means of making money through a web site are:

- *Selling products or services.* This may include downloads or memberships. While it is very common to sell products or services, you can only sell downloads that site visitors cannot get for free elsewhere. Memberships for special privileges can be lucrative, but you need to provide something that can't be accessed for free elsewhere. You also need to provide customers with an opt-out opportunity, to un-join, or be let go from their monthly payment option. If you make it too difficult for someone to unsubscribe to a membership-based web site, you can find yourself dealing with the Better Business Bureau, charges of fraud, or legal hassles that you do not want.

- *Selling Advertising.* Charging nominal fees for directory listings is one type of advertising, while the other is to sell ad space down the side or as a banner across the top of the web site. It is not as easy as it sounds to simply sell advertising space. There are too many web sites competing for the same advertising dollars and advertisers are going to look for the biggest bang, or most hits, for their money. For this reason you need to wow them with the site and the number of hits you are getting. Don't expect advertisers to simply offer money, since your site (on any topic) is not the only one around

7. The Competitive Edge

As is the case in all business, you want to find a way of doing something in a different manner than that of your competitors. This can be difficult on the internet, since you are all reaching your audience through the same medium. However, even a small one-person business can compete with a major conglomerate if they come up with an interesting means of presenting their material and selling their goods or services. Study your competition and look for something you can do differently.

8. Other Web Site Tips

- *Keep your content fresh.* Nobody likes to see the same old site again and again. If you are a retailer, have new products featured, new sales offered, and update your pages regularly.
- *Be careful when linking.* Web site owners have been shocked to find out that when trading links with someone that the other site was not what they thought it was. Make sure to check out all links before saying yes to reciprocal linking arrangements.
- *Don't oversell ad space.* Yes, you want to make money from advertising, but if the site is overloaded with ads and the content is buried, you will lose visitors and hence advertisers will also leave. Sell, but maintain the integrity of your web site. Also, be particularly careful that ads don't make it appear to be someone else's web site.
- *Avoid endless scrolling.* People will scroll for a while, but if it goes on forever you will lose them. Have

stories carry over to another page and content spread out on several pages. Visitors prefer to click from page to page to find something rather than scroll and search.

- *Respond to e-mails.* If people have questions, comments, and inquiries, you should respond, or have someone respond within 24 hours. Otherwise it appears that you don't care very much about your customers.
- *Build it first.* One of the hardest parts of launching a web site is getting it up and running. Don't cut corners. If the site has very little information, people may not return. Directories need to have a significant number of listings before launching to show that you are a real player with a real web site. Don't launch a site with lots of "under construction" sections, unless the site is simply an adjunct to a bricks-and-mortar business.
- *Think safety.* Identity theft is real and you need to make sure your customers feel safe doing business with you. In addition, a virus can shut you down, so you need anti-virus protection. Finally, use offsite backup to protect and secure your customer data information. Remember that your business is based on technology, so that technology must be maintained, updated, protected, and backed up. And never allow yourself to get complacent.
- *Don't steal.* For some strange reason, many people think that if something is on the internet it is public domain. Well, it's not. Several lawsuits have supported this fact. Therefore, you cannot just lift pictures and content and put them on your site. Use original content and graphics, items that you have the rights to, or procure the rights to whatever it is you are looking to add to your site.

Running a web-based business is very different than other businesses in the past. The concept of not seeing your customers face to face is somewhat unique, other than with mail order businesses. However, it does not mean your customers are any less savvy, or knowledgeable—and they want to be treated as such.

◆ ◆ ◆

ONLINE COLORING BOOKS
★★ $$$$ 🏠

Online coloring books for kids is great opportunity that could prove to be both fun and profitable. This online business concept is very straightforward. Simply develop a web site that features a large selection of downloadable images and pictures of animals, people, buildings, and landscapes. These images are then downloaded, printed from their desktop printer, and colored using crayons. Alternately you could design a color palette and tools that would enable kids to color their pictures right on their computer and print it when they are finished. Kids could print multiple pages and even create their own coloring books to provide them with hours of fun. To generate income you could sell ads or have a sponsor for the site, such as a major crayon maker or manufacturer of children's products. Warning: Make sure to use your own original drawings or those created by people who give you permission to post the drawings online for downloading.

ONLINE STAR SEARCH
★★ $$$$ 🏠

Here is a novel online business opportunity for the cyber-savvy entrepreneur to tackle. Develop a web site that enables wanna-be movie stars, singers, and performers of all sorts to have a chance at fame. With the amazing popularity of American Idol, such a site could catch on quickly. People with a particular talent could submit digital video footage of their performance and the footage could be placed into the web site under the appropriate heading. Visitors to the site could select a category and view the performances, then vote for the best performance in each category on a weekly or monthly basis. Each winner would receive a prize that is awarded by a business sponsor of the contest. This is a unique online venture and could prove to be very popular for performers and visitors alike. It would also provide an outstanding opportunity to generate revenues by renting advertising space on the site.

ONLINE STUDIO MUSICIANS
★★ $$$ 🏠 🕐

Worldwide, there are thousands of full- and part-time studio musicians, and starting an online directory for studio musicians seeking work and for producers seeking studio musicians is a fantastic new business to start. Revenues for the business could be made by charging musicians a fee to post their information on the web site, and producers seeking a certain type of musician for their projects would only be a click away from locating the perfect candidate. Selling banner advertising on the web site as well as also creating a directory or classified advertising section that features musical equipment and instruments for sale could also earn additional revenues.

ONLINE ENTERTAINMENT COUPONS
★★★ $$$$ 🏠

First, design a web site that is indexed by various entertainment services and products such as concerts, plays, movies, etc. Next, secure companies and businesses within the entertainment industry to advertise discounts that apply to their specific products and services on your web site. Visitors to the site would be only a few clicks away from locating and printing a discount coupon for the entertainment event or product they were seeking. The business would gain revenue by charging the entertainment companies a monthly fee to advertise on the site and post their discount coupons. Unlike traditional coupon books, the advantage of a web discount coupon book is that it can be changed and updated often, providing new coupons from a vendor every week or even every day.

ONLINE ENTERTAINMENT LISTINGS AND REVIEWS
★ $$ 🏠 🕐 🌐

Millions of people typically look to the web for movie times, reviews, plays, and other forms of entertainment in their area. This provides you with an opportunity to cash in by setting up a series of local web sites providing area listings and reviews. Your movie reviews can be posted on all of the sites, while each local area site will have a calendar of forthcoming entertainment events, including concerts, theatrical plays, special events, movie times, and even restaurant listings. Additionally the site can also include an entertainment review section with feedback and critiques supplied by visitors. The site can earn income by selling advertising space to local merchants in each area, or by film companies who would advertise across the board on all of the sites. You will need to do a major off-site marketing campaign so that people will know that you are the entertainment source in your area. Of course, you will need to have contacts at all of the local theaters and venues to make sure you have the latest scheduled entertainment events.

ONLINE PET SHOWS AND DIRECTORY
★ $$$ 🚗 🕐

Thousands of dogs, cats, and just about every other type of animal are featured in movies, commercials, and television programs each year. You can start a web site that serves as a directory so that producers can find such animals. This is a small target group, so to create a much larger audience you can have web clips sent in by viewers of their pets in action doing something entertaining. This would generate a much larger audience, since pet lover (and non-pet lovers) enjoy watching animals doing tricks—consider the success of David Letterman's "Stupid Pet Tricks." Visitors to the site could vote on their favorite pet trick video and the winners could get prizes.

There are several ways to make money on such a site. First, animal owners and trainers looking to have their pet "discovered" by talent agents could pay a yearly fee to have their pets or animals listed on the site. Secondly, there could be a nominal entrance fee for contests. Third, and the greatest potential source of income, would be selling advertising space to all sorts of pet product manufacturers.

ONLINE CYBERCAMPING ADVENTURE
★ $$$ 🚗 🕐

Camping can be a lot of fun in the summer months, but in the cold of winter, or for those families that are not quite ready for the outdoor life, you can set up a fun site featuring online camping adventures. Visitors can choose from several possible adventures that include options to click on various activities, all supplied via web cams. This can include setting up tents, cooking over a fire, ghost stories, and a wide range of camping activities that the visitors can watch. Selections as to what to do next can occur and even some mystery selections, where the visitor won't know what will happen and has to decide what the next course of action will be. For example, on such a

mystery click, a bear might approach the campground. In game format or as a site to simply familiarize newcomers to camping—particularly children—such a site can be entertaining and educational. Promoting the site as an alternative to the full camping experience can generate a lot of visitors and advertisers.

ONLINE SHIPWRECKS
★ $$$$ 🚗

Take underwater shipwrecks into the high-tech world of the internet by starting your own shipwreck web site. This type of web site could feature all sorts of unique information and visitor services, such as underwater film footage of shipwrecks taken and submitted by visitors or perhaps world maps of oceans with icons indicating shipwreck locations. When visitors clicked on the icon, a page could appear describing the shipwreck, the dive terrain, and the skill level requirements to reach it, plus photos of the site. The site could be supported financially by selling advertising space to scuba dive instruction and tour companies as well as by selling scuba dive products and equipment.

ONLINE MOVIE SET LOCATIONS
★★★ $$$$ 🚗

Every day, location scouts scour the countryside in search of the perfect spot to film movies, music videos, TV productions, and commercials. Starting a movie set location rental business will make you a cyber scout. The concept is fairly simple. You establish a web site with various categories for filming locations. These categories could include factories, vacant land, unique houses, and office buildings. The owners of these various locations could supply you with still pictures or video footage of their locations, which can be posted into the various categories on the site. Location scouts, directors, and producers would simply log onto the "locate a location" and search through the categories that were of interest to them for film production projects. Hint: To make this business really work, you need to scout a number of unique sites that are not obvious ones that filmmakers have used before.

START-UP COSTS: Establishing a start-up cost for this type of business is difficult, as there is not a lot of competition to use as a yardstick. The web site could likely be developed on an initial investment in the range of $30,000 to $40,000. Another $10,000 would be needed to promote the site to the demographic audience, which is basically producers, directors, screenwriters, and anyone in the business of making movies, videos, or television shows.

PROFIT POTENTIAL: There are two billing methods that could be utilized in this business venture. The first would be to charge building and landowners a flat fee for posting their location pictures and information on the site. The second option would be to agree upon a split of the location fee from the production company to the landowner. Both could be utilized.

ONLINE TRAVEL VIDEOS
★ $$$ 🏠 🕐

Tired of boring your friends and family with your travel videos? Now you can bore an entirely new audience thanks to the web. Actually, setting up a site that features travel videos by amateurs could be both fun and profitable. Funny captions, some clever, off-beat marketing, and plenty of travel details presented in an entertaining manner, could generate plenty of visitors, and where there are a lot of visitors, online advertisers typically follow. Homespun sites such as this that feature amateurs has, in some cases, proven to be the unusual and intriguing type of web site that ends up being a big hit! The key to success will be in promoting and marketing the site to ensure maximum exposure and number of site hits. Revenue can also be gained by selling professionally produced travel videos and guidebooks.

SPRING BREAK DIRECTORY
★ $$$ 🏠

College kids love the web, and setting up the definitive guide to spring break, complete with plenty of graphics, galleries, stories, and details of where you can go and how much it will cost can have the potential for a very successful business. Chat rooms can let spring breakers talk about their past experiences and future plans while a message board can hook up those who need a ride with those who have an extra seat available. If you can get the site started and marketed on college campuses, you can then seek out advertisers for this demographic audience.

MOVIE TRIVIA
★ $$ 🏠

People love trivia – that's a fact. It's also the starting point for a site that focuses on movie trivia for all ages. Separate sections featuring Disney and other kid favorite films as well as horror, action, and comedies can all be part of the site, which would generate money from advertising and from selling movie books, games and even posters. Update the site often so that there are new trivia games and contests, as well as fun facts and other cinematic entertainment. You could even sell microwave popcorn. As is often the case with a fun or informative site, you need to surround the content with advertising and make money in the same manner as television or newspapers and magazines.

JOKES AND RIDDLES
★ $$ 🏠

Funny, sexy, outrageous, knock-knock, or just plain childish... which ever you choose, you can get a site rolling and your audience rolling with a jokes and riddles web site. Update the site very often to keep people coming back and even invite up-and-coming stand-up comics and writers to provide some one-liners. You can include cartoons, limericks, or jokes sent in by viewers. The bottom line is keep it funny, keep it current, and keep it fresh so that you can generate advertising dollars. You can also sell humor books, calendars, and other fun stuff—even novelty items and gag gifts.

GAME SITES
★★★ $$$$ 🏠 🔧

You have two options here. The first is to create the next "Snood" and make a fortune off of it. The second is to find various games, buy or lease the rights to them, and offer them online, and make a fortune doing so. Either way, you can't go wrong if you are very familiar with online games and what your demographic audience wants. Hint: Immerse yourself in the gaming world for months before trying to determine the game or games you want to present. Then, if a game designer is building one for you, do a lot of test marketing with game enthusiasts. Only when you have The Game or several games that you believe in wholeheartedly should you launch such a site, because if your games are substandard, you'll have a mountain to climb to get the gaming community back. Sell advertising, downloads, memberships and/or CD versions. If you are promoting other people's games, you can provide previews, reviews, and trial versions before selling the latest games.

web resource: www.cgonline.com
Computer Games Online

TEEN CHAT AND INSTANT MESSAGING
★★★ $$$$ 🏠 🚗

For better and worse, teens have taken to the internet as a major means of communication. For some it provides a wonderful outlet and a means of meeting new people. For others it becomes an addiction and limits their real life interpersonal skills.

It is, however, the responsibility of parents to monitor and limit the online use by teens. For your purposes, setting up online monitored chats on topics of interest and IM capabilities can be extremely profitable. However, there does need to be a sense of responsibility placed upon the owners and managers of the site to make sure that nothing obscene, threatening, or inappropriate is posted. In addition, the site needs to take every possible measure to post warnings about the possible dangers of real-life encounters with people met on the site, and to protect the privacy of those who use it. In a controlled and safe environment, such a site can flourish and teens can enjoy chatting and sending IMs. If you can market the site to the demographic audience as a "safe" place to talk, you can build up a massive audience and as a result attract many advertisers. Hint: Screen all profiles and allow no possible identifiable information.

VIRTUAL AMUSEMENT PARK
★ $$$ 🏠 🚗

If you can get riders from some of the most exciting, heart-stopping amusement park rides in the country to grab a web cam and tape the ride, you can start an online virtual amusement park. Of course, the amusement parks will have to give their permission, at which time you can hit them up for advertising, since your audience will very likely be comprised of fans of amusement parks

and water parks. Provide a variety of riding experiences from all over the globe and market your site as a great way to enjoy the thrill rides of the world from the comfort of home.

TEST YOUR I.Q.
★ $$ 🏠

People are always curious about how smart they really are. If you start a site featuring some tried and true I.Q. tests, as commissioned and obtained by permission, you can generate people of all ages who simply want the chance to be called a genius, or at least above average. Tests can be geared for children as well as adults, and results should be forthcoming shortly after the test. Advertisements can be sold to support this part-time web endeavor. Other tests and quizzes, such as marital compatibility, can also be part of the site, plus you can feature background information on the I.Q. tests offered and the history of such testing.

FANTASY SPORTS SITE
★★ $$$ 🏠

There are millions of fantasy sports enthusiasts playing for fun and even (ssssh—don't tell anyone) money. Selecting teams and following statistics of individual players in professional sports is what the fantasy leagues are all about. Team owners can trade players, pick up free agents, and have all the fun of owning and managing a team without the headaches of paying players millions of real dollars. Setting up a web site that handles the statistical aspects of fantasy leagues can be profitable, provided you have someone helping you build this type of site who knows all the technical means of gaining the up-to-date statistical information. The backend of the site is the difficult part to build, while on the front end, you can run the stats for each of numerous leagues. The leagues pay you a per-team fee to provide the primarily automated statistical service, and you provide the league with their own pages for each team as well as central pages for transactions, league news, free agents, etc. There's a steep learning curve to this type of statistical web site, but once you establish your site as an excellent stat service, you can rake in a fortune.

ONLINE BOARD GAMES
★★ $$$$ 🎮 🎲

Wanna play chess, checkers, or backgammon with someone but there's no one around who wants to play? That is the reason why board game enthusiasts turn to web sites that allow them to play against opponents in other parts of the country and even the world. Without trying to go into the backend details, it suffices to say that before you can start such a site you will need a skilled technical team to put it together. There are many ways in which such a site can work. Players can join on a monthly basis, receive a password and sign up to play specific games. Or, you can have players get a free account password and then pay to download and play as they sign up for specific games. You can also have tournament entry fees. Tournament winners can be awarded prizes, which can be free downloads or other game related prizes. You can also offer chat rooms and postings and charge a small monthly fee for participating. To start, you need to visit and study the existing game sites to see how you can make such a site work smoothly and easily so that visitors can enjoy the opportunity to play. While complicated to start up, such a site can be a moneymaker if promoted heavily to the game-loving crowd.

ONLINE CHILDREN'S STORIES
★ $$ 🎮

There are plenty of children's story writers and would-be writers looking to get published. Tap into their skills and post the best of them on a children's story site. You can also include previously published works, with permission, of course. Parents can sign up, pay a monthly membership fee, and have a great resource for stories to read to their youngsters. You can also include stories that young children can read for themselves, and some could be read aloud on the site by young actors looking to build up a their portfolio in voice-over work. Seek out sponsors and/or advertisers looking to reach parents of young children. Prior to starting the site, make sure you have a fairly large selection of at least 50 stories and keep posting new ones monthly. You can pay your authors a percentage of the number of visitors who read their stories, which can also be downloaded and printed.

ONLINE THEATER DIRECTORY
★ $$ 🎮

This type of site could include movies and or theaters for plays and musicals. In the movie web business there is stiff competition. However, listing theaters where plays are performed is less common and there are numerous theater groups and community theater playhouses that can certainly benefit from the publicity. Your initial job will be finding the theaters, including traveling ones and children's theater groups. You can list theaters in a given region or branch out and go national, little by little. While many theater groups do not have a lot of funds behind them, the nominal fee for a more detailed listing (for example, from each of 200 theaters nationwide) could add up to a good annual income. Of course you would have to update the sites as new shows come in, but many would send you their calendar for the entire year or at least several months at a stretch. You could also hire local reviewers, and include reviews from audience members.

NOTES:

_____

_____

_____

_____

_____

_____

_____

_____

_____

ONLINE ART PRINTS
★★ $$$ 🏠 🕐

Caught up in the excitement of having prints produced from their original artwork, many artists fail to consider how they will market them. Herein lies a business opportunity. Develop a web site that exclusively features art prints for sale. The site can be indexed by print theme and artists from around the world can submit pictures of their prints to be posted. Upon sale of a print, the artist would ship it to the purchaser and would receive a percentage of the sales value, meaning you do not have to maintain an inventory. Ideally, marketing efforts would be aimed at individuals and organizations that routinely purchase art prints, such as decorators, corporations, and property developers. This type of cyber venture is relatively easy to establish and could be operated from home on a part-time basis. A subscriber e-mail newsletter could expand the business by providing bi-weekly or monthly updates of new art works being posted.

ONLINE WOODEN TOYS
★ $$$ 🏠 🕐

Unite the wooden toy makers of the world by developing a web site that features their toys and games for sale. Fear not—if you do not know how to make wooden toys, there are thousands of people and small manufacturing firms worldwide that specialize in designing and making them. Like any small enterprise, the largest single challenge these entrepreneurs face is marketing and distributing their products. In a nutshell, the web site would include all sorts of wooden toys and games constructed by numerous individuals and small-manufacturing firms. You have two options in terms of earning income. The first is to create an online wooden toy store and charge a commission on all sales generated. The second option would be to establish the web site in a directory format and charge toy makers to be listed.

ONLINE COLLECTIBLE CLOTHING
★★ $$+ 🏠 🕐

Create a portal to bring buyers and sellers of collectible clothing items together. Millions of people collect popular clothing items from previous decades, and this online opportunity has the potential to bring in some good money. There are various options available in terms of how this sort of web site can operate, including an online auction service that exclusively features collectible clothing or an online classifieds service that enables buyers and sellers to list collectible clothing items that they are selling or seeking. There are also many options for generating revenues and profits, including charging a fee to list items for sale, renting banner advertising space, or buying collectible clothing and reselling it yourself via the site for a profit. You could also work on a commission basis, making money off of other people's transactions, as is the case with an auction. One means of promoting such a business in collectibles chat rooms.

ONLINE BLUE JEANS
★★ $$$ 🏠 🕐

If you are searching for a unique way to profit from your sewing talents, then look no further than starting an online business that sells custom made-to-order blue jeans. Blue jeans are an American cultural icon worn by millions of people every day, and for many people the search is never-ending for a pair of jeans that fits properly and comfortably. Get started by creating a web site that features the capability of letting visitors design their own blue jeans. This simply means that your customers select a men's or women's option and enter in the measurements they want: inseam length, waist size, and cuff diameter. Once your customers have completed the online order form and chosen payment option, they would simply click submit and wait for their perfectly-fitting jeans to arrive by courier a few weeks later. Should the site prove popular and you have more jeans to make than is possible, you can always hire subcontract seamstresses to work on a piece or performance basis, and order forms for jeans could be forwarded to them electronically.

WEB RESOURCE: www.teonline.com/fabrics/denim.html
A comprehensive worldwide list of denim manufacturers

ONLINE BIG AND TALL SHOP
★★ $$$ 🏠

It is a fact that each generation is physically larger than the previous generation, and this fact creates a terrific opportunity for the innovative entrepreneur to capitalize by starting an online retail store that stocks and sells clothing and fashion accessories aimed at the big and tall market. The clothing featured on the web site can be for men, women, and children, and manufacturers of the clothing that you sell can directly ship your orders to customers as a method of reducing the amount of inventory warehousing space that will be required. The profit potential for this type of online retail clothing business is outstanding as the clothing is specialized, so maintaining product markups of nearly 100 percent or more should not be difficult.

WEB RESOURCE: www.apparelsearch.com/retail_big_and_tall.htm
A web portal devoted to big and tall shops, primarily for men, and some women's clothing sources as well.

ONLINE LINGERIE SHOP
★★★ $$$$ 🏦

The best aspect about advertising and selling products via the internet is the fact that it is the great equalizer. Regardless of the size of your business, you can compete with any competition on a level playing field. Lingerie is often a garment that most women and men like to purchase discreetly, and what better way than from a web site on the internet. Consider the following steps for establishing an online lingerie shop.

- Secure wholesale purchasing accounts with lingerie designers and manufacturers.
- Develop an easy-to-navigate and interesting web site featuring lingerie for sale.
- Post photos of models wearing your products on your site.
- Establish a secure credit card ordering system for the web site.
- Develop a packing and shipping program to fulfill orders or, if business demands starts to intensify, use a fulfillment house
- Market your online business through links, offline advertising, and lingerie parties and fashion shows.

WEB RESOURCE: www.wholesaledistributorsnet.com/lingerie_and_sleepwear.html
Directory of wholesale lingerie merchants.

ONLINE FABRIC SHOP
★★ $$$$ 🏠

Option one: Develop a portal that brings fabric manufacturers and distributors together with fabric retailers via an online fabric directory web site. Worldwide, there are thousands of fabric manufacturers and fabric retailers, thus an exciting opportunity exists by bringing these two parties together to buy and sell fabric. Revenues could be earned by charging both fabric manufacturers and retailers a fee for using the directory service. Option two: Focus on the direct-to-consumer market by creating a web site that features fabric for sale. Potential customers could include hobby seamstresses, fashion designers, interior decorators, and tailors. The site would be easy to create and could feature pictures and descriptions of the various fabrics you sell as well as a price list. Customers would select the fabric they wanted, add it to their shopping cart, make a payment, and place their order. Promote the site by initiating a direct mail and e-mail campaign aimed at fashion designers, sewing clubs, tailors, interior decorators, and smaller, more remote communities that do not have a local fabric shop.

ONLINE SOFTWARE
★★ $$+ 🏠 🕒

Worldwide, there are thousands of software designers and manufacturing firms that produce literally thousands of different software applications. This fact creates a very exciting business opportunity by developing a web site that sells software applications online. However, selling software is extremely competitive. In order to compete, seek to specialize in one type of software application, whether it is games, B2B office solutions, or financial software. The first step will be to secure an agreement with a software developer, or with several developers, to represent and market their products. You can also offer download possibilities through agreements with the software manufacturers. In terms of promoting the software, initiate a direct mail and e-mail marketing campaign aimed at the industry and/or the individuals that you are trying to reach. The site can be promoted by registering with search engines, linking to topic-related sites, utilizing chat rooms and the power of viral marketing, and by participating in rotating banner advertisement programs. Hint: Stay on top of the software market to make sure you have the latest products available on your site. As usual with any online retail business, keep a limited inventory and provide good customer service, which means have a help line available if at all possible.

ONLINE ART SUPPLIES
★ $$$ 🏠 🕒

Remote or small communities often do not have a store that stocks and sells art supplies, and these are the communities that you will want to target if your inten-

tions are to establish a web site that features art supplies for sale. In addition to mainstream art supplies like paint, brushes, and canvas, also consider selling more exotic or hard-to-find art supplies, like chainsaws for the growing interest in chainsaw art (see "Art" section). The more varied the selection, the better the chances of securing repeat visitors and customers to the site. Furthermore, to keep inventory purchases to a minimum, seek to build alliances with manufacturers of art supplies who will ship directly to your customers. Promote the site in print publications, through art schools and classes, and utilize internet marketing and advertising options.

ONLINE SPORTSWEAR
★★ $$$ 🏠 🕒

There are a few approaches that can be taken in terms of starting a sportswear business. The first is to retail sportswear purchased on a wholesale basis, via the internet, along with home sales parties and other means of promotion. The site needs to be user friendly; provide a wide range of brands, styles, and sizes; and have a smooth exchange system, as clothing does not always fit as intended. The second approach is to establish a business that designs and manufactures sportswear to be sold to clothing and sporting good retailers on a wholesale basis or directly to consumers via the internet. As a manufacturer, you are up against particularly stiff competition with major players in the industry. Therefore, you need a niche and an angle. Glow in the dark tennis shorts anyone? Perhaps you'll need to think of a more plausible moneymaker, but it is important to gain a competitive edge with a style that is not readily available. Make sure to get a patent on any original designs and a do a trademark search before posting your own original logo.

ONLINE ART AUCTIONS
★ $$$$ 🏠

Millions of professional and amateur artists are seeking ways to sell their artwork and this fact creates a fantastic opportunity to start an online art auction service. The challenge with operating this type of cyber venture will not be securing works of art to be auctioned, but promoting the site in such a manner that it receives a lot of visitor hits and interest. In terms of marketing and promoting the site, consider building an alliance with a major player on the web like eBay. Revenues and profits will be created when artwork has been successfully auctioned; I would suggest retaining a commission in the range of 10 to 25 percent of the total selling value for providing the service.

ONLINE ART GALLERY
★ $$$ 🏠 🕐

Like an online art auction, an online art gallery also offers works of art for sale, but not in an auction format. This is the type of art marketing system that many well-established artists prefer to the auction format, as the value of their works cannot be diminished by lack of bids. The site can be indexed into various art mediums, and artists wishing to be featured on the site pay a monthly fee and/or a commission upon the successful sale of the artwork. Like many online ventures, the key to success often lies within promoting and marketing the site. No visitors—no chance to generate sales. Therefore, you will have to seek unique and innovative ways to build and maintain site traffic. Start out by exchanging links with other art-related sites, such as the nearest art supply dealers. Also ask artists if you can display their works in restaurants and other locations, which can help them sell their art and help promote your web site.

WEB RESOURCE: www.artistresource.org
This portal features other art galleries nationwide and worldwide

ONLINE CRAFT SUPPLY SALES
★ $$$$ 🏠

From the arts, we move to the crafts. You could develop a web site that features craft supplies of every sort for sale, and could promote such it widely by running display advertisements in craft magazines as well as by initiating a direct mail campaign aimed specifically at people in the crafts industry. Names for the direct mail campaign could be accessed through craft associations and clubs. To avoid the cost of housing an inventory of craft supplies, you could set up the site so that the buyers buy from you and the orders are shipped directly from the suppliers. Revenue would be generated by either charging the manufacturers and distributors a fee for being listed and fea-

tured on the site, and by retaining a percentage on total sales generated.

WEB RESOURCE: www.craftsfaironline.com/Supplies.html
Supplies portal.

ONLINE CRAFT SHOWS
★★ $$$$ 🏠

You can take craft shows "high-tech" by starting your own virtual year-round online craft show. Many people producing crafts on a full- or part-time basis need a marketing and distribution outlet for their products beyond a few "bricks-and-mortar" craft shows each year. Additionally, many of these same crafters cannot afford to spend a few thousand dollars to develop and maintain a first-rate web site. Therefore, you provide the solution by developing a virtual craft show. The site can be indexed into various craft categories and visitors would simply choose the section they wished to visit. Crafters would receive a listing with an automatic link to a pop-up page that would give details about their particular products as well as show photographs of their products. Consumers wishing to purchase a product would simply click on their selection and be linked to the central e-crafts store to enter payment and shipping information. Revenues would be earned by charging a listing fee to be featured on the site, as well as retaining a percentage of each sale for providing the e-craft store and service. Crafters would be notified electronically of each sale including shipping details so they could send consumers their purchases directly. Marketing the site can include registering with search engines including keyword searches and by advertising the site through traditional print mediums like magazines, craft newsletters, and other craft publications. Developing and publishing this type of web site will require a substantial development and marketing budget, but there is great potential.

ONLINE FARMERS' MARKET
★★★ $$$$ 🏠

Why not bring the farmers' market into the computer age? Not many farmers producing quality foods have the time to develop and maintain a web site. Thus opportunity calls. Create your own online farmers' market by developing a site that features farm fresh products for sale. The site can be indexed by food type and feature farmer listings. In exchange for a monthly fee, farmers listed on the site would receive a web page, where they could describe their products as well as a listing in the main index. Since it would not be worth the time for farmers to fill every individual customer order for $5 or $10 worth of food, the site would be marketed primarily to restaurant owners or consumers buying at least $50 worth of fresh produce from any one farmer. Of course, restaurant owners and food buyers could purchase different foods from each of several farmers at $50 minimum. The order would go from your computer to the farmers via e-mail, fax or phone calls if necessary. As long as the produce was shipped promptly, it would not matter.

ONLINE SEAFOOD SALES
★★ $$$$ 🏠 🕒 ⚖️

Take local seafood sales and delivery online and open your business to consumers from around the world. This cyber enterprise is very straightforward. Develop a web site that features seafood of all sorts for sale. Customers simply select the seafood they wanted to purchase, enter in payment and shipping information, and wait for delivery. Commercial fishermen in virtually every country can supply the seafood featured on the site. They catch it, you sell it, and they ship it to your customers. The concept is basic but will require a great amount of planning and legwork to be completed prior to activating the business.

WEB RESOURCE: www.aboutseafood.com

ONLINE ORGANIC FOOD SALES
★★ $$$ 🏠

The time has never been better than now to start a business that specializes in organic products, as organically-grown foods have become so popular that growers are having a hard time meeting consumer demand. The first step to establishing the business is to build alliances with organic food growers to supply the inventory needed for the business. The second step is to create and distribute a catalog featuring all the organically-grown food products that the business sells and delivers. Additionally, be sure to develop a web site that will enable clients to place food orders online, as well as accepting food orders via e-mail and fax. The profit potential for a business that

sells and delivers organically grown fruits and vegetables is outstanding, as the products can be marked up by 30 percent to 40 percent. This still enables you to undercut grocery stores and retailers of organically grown foods by 10 percent or more.

WEB RESOURCE: www.organichub.com
Links to organic food growers and wholesalers.

ONLINE VITAMIN SALES
★ $$+ 🏠 🕒

Do you want to sell vitamins but do not have the investment capital needed to open a retail store selling vitamins? If so, consider selling vitamins on a web site. This is a very competitive field, so consider adding extra features to attract customers including articles and information about the health benefits of vitamin supplements as well as an online chat room so visitors can exchange information. To keep your start-up investment to a minimum you can arrange a direct drop ship agreement with one or more of the hundreds of companies that produce vitamins. Basically you sell the vitamins via your web site, forward the orders electronically to the vitamin producer, and they fulfill the order and ship the product directly to your customers.

WEB RESOURCE: www.business.com/directory/pharmaceuticals_and_biotechnology/distributors_and_wholesalers
Pharmaceutical wholesalers.

ONLINE STORE FOR THE DISABLED
★★ $$$$

People living with physical disabilities may find even life's easy tasks to be frustrating. Starting a business that specializes in selling products aimed at making life easier for people living with physical disabilities is not only a wise choice for a new business venture, it is also a business that can assist thousands of people to lead a more productive life. Products could start with mobility devices such as wheelchairs, scooters, medical braces, and walkers, and expand to anything that increases accessibility and makes day-to-day tasks easier for differentially abled people. The business can focus on both "bricks-and-mortar" style retailing, as well as developing a web site for online shoppers. This type of health-related business venture is very costly to set in motion. However, the profit potential is good, and the business can be personally rewarding.

ONLINE RECYCLED RENOVATION PRODUCTS
★★ $$$ 🚗 🕒 🍃

Here is a unique business start-up for the savvy webmaster. Thousands of homes are demolished annually in the United States to make way for new houses and buildings. Many of these same homes have items like hardwood flooring, bathroom fixtures, and doors and windows that are of value and can be recycled. You can profit by developing a web site where these valuable items can be listed for sale. The site should be indexed by product with a section for hardwood flooring, one section for windows, etc. This would enable visitors to easily navigate the site and find what they are looking for quickly. In terms of making money, there are a few options. The first is to charge contractors and homeowners a fee for listing the recycled building products on the site. The second option is to let customers list the items for free and retain a commission upon successful sale. Another option would be to make the site free to use for both visitors and people wishing to list items for sale and sell advertising space to merchants and service providers seeking exposure to your web site users. Lastly, you could buy the items and resell them on the site for a profit. The problem here, however, is that you would need to have a place for your inventory. One of the nicest features of this business is that you are helping recycle materials.

ONLINE BIRDHOUSES FOR SALE
★ $$ 🚗 🕒

Why not sell birdhouses online? Develop a web site to sell your own birdhouse creations as well as other hobbyist birdhouse builders. You can also sell birdhouse building kits from the site. Market and promote the site via the usual internet advertising venues as well as in print publications relating to crafts and home and garden decoration. Part-time birdhouse builders from all around the country can have their products listed for sale on the site, and you can charge a flat monthly fee or commission for this service.

ONLINE ROCK AND GEM SHOP
★ $$$ 🚗 🕒

Rock and non-precious gem collecting is a hobby enjoyed by millions of people worldwide, and you can cash in financially by posting a web site that sells products used for rock and gem collecting. These products can include books on the subject, picks, shovels, and equipment used for gold panning. Promote the site by placing advertisements in print publications and sending literature to associations and clubs that have membership that focus rock and gem collecting. You can also use online marketing options such as search engine registrations and web optimization strategies, as well as advertisements and links to other sites on the web.

WEB RESOURCE: www.mineralcollecting.org

ONLINE SPECIALTY TREE SALES
★★ $$ 🚗 🕒

One of the best aspects about this type of online retailing is that it does not require you to purchase and warehouse an inventory of trees. Customer orders can be electronically forwarded to the grower and they can ship the product directly to your customer. Market the site, and your products, by placing advertisements in garden grower and landscape magazines as well as by initiating a direct mail and e-mail marketing campaign aimed at landscape designers and contractors. The key to success in this type of online venture is to offer trees and shrubs for sale that are difficult to find locally in most communities.

ONLINE SPECIALTY PET FOODS
★★★ $$$ 🚗 🕒

Specialty pet foods, such as all-natural organically grown foods and special dietary foods for animals with health problems, are the latest rage to stock the shelves of pet food stores everywhere. Starting a business that sells specialty pet foods is a straightforward enterprise to set in motion. You can produce your own recipes for pet foods by researching the subject. You can also locate a manufacturer of these types of specialty pet foods and become their exclusive sales representative in your local area, state, or even country. This business is ideal for starting part-time from a homebased location and expanding the business from the profits that are generated. Furthermore, this type of business is also ideally suited for sales via the internet. Retailing for this type of venture would enable the business to become global, and the products could be shipped through the postal service or a courier company. While this particular business will require a fair amount of time to establish, the future profit could be worth the wait.

WEB RESOURCE: www.appma.org
American Pet Products Manufacturers Association.

ONLINE FACTORY DIRECT
★★★ $$$ 🏠

In North America there are thousands of homebased manufacturing businesses. The largest challenges facing these entrepreneurs are marketing and competing against much larger and better-financed competitors. Herein lies the business opportunity. Develop an online "factory direct" web site that features products for sale manufactured by these homebased entrepreneurs. By doing this, you will be giving these small manufacturing businesses a fantastic marketing and distribution channel. Products sold via the site can be shipped to purchasers directly from the manufacturer, thus eliminating the need for warehousing inventory. In exchange for providing manufacturers with a marketing channel, you can retain a portion of the sales that the site generates; in the range of 10 to 15 percent would be fair. This type of cyber venture could really prove to be successful, as "factory direct" pricing attracts consumers. Securing manufactured goods to be featured on the site would be very easy. To keep customers coming back, you could also include content such as stories of how manufacturers got their businesses off the ground or about forthcoming products.

ONLINE USED CAMERA SALES
★ $$ 🏠 🕐

Millions of cameras are sold each year in the United States, and this raises the question: What do people do with all the used cameras they are replacing? It's time to get the old cameras out of the basements and closets and start a business that sells them via a custom-designed web site. The business can be initiated with a minimal amount of investment capital, and promoting and advertising the

web site can be accomplished almost for free by utilizing the various newsgroups, photography chat rooms, and exchanging links with photo related web sites.. The site could generate revenues from two sources: people who would pay a small fee to advertise their secondhand camera equipment for sale; and advertisers who are seeking exposure for their company on your site.

ONLINE BACKPACKERS-ONLY STORE
★★ $$$$

You can start your own backpackers-only store from a fixed retail storefront location, or as an online store via your own specially designed web site. This type of retailing is unique and specialized, and products can include backpacks, flashlights, knives, camping equipment, safety equipment, books, and just about anything else that is related to backpacking and hiking. The start-up capital requirements for the fixed retail location option would be in the range of $40,000 to $60,000, while the online version could be launched for considerably less—in the $20,000 to $30,000 range. The business also lends itself to first aid and wilderness training courses, especially if you have a fixed location. The instruction classes could be held nights after the store has closed. Adding related specialty instruction or training classes is a great way to optimize profits while getting the most mileage out of your existing resources.

WEB RESOURCE: www.active-backpacks.com

ONLINE GIFT BASKETS
★★ $$$ 🏠

Here is a simple idea for an online business venture that could prove to be very profitable. Create a web site that features gift baskets for sale aimed mainly at the corporate market. Keep the site basic and provide perhaps only ten or so pre-assembled gift basket options. Additionally, try to cover all price ranges, meaning you should have a basic gift basket at $25 dollars and increase from there in increments of $10. Prices shown for the gift baskets should be all-inclusive, including delivery and handling charges. Visitors would simply select the gift basket they wish to purchase, enter payment information, and provide the details on who is receiving the basket as a gift. The site can be marketed and promoted by initiating a direct mail and e-mail campaign aimed at corporations, event planners, and real estate agents, since often these individuals and companies send gift baskets to clients and business associates. The gift baskets can be warehoused in one central location and courier companies can be contracted for delivery purposes.

ONLINE COMIC BOOK SALES
★★ $$ 🚗 🕐

Are you looking to start an inexpensive retail business that can be operated from home with flexible hours and really has the potential to generate an excellent part-time income? If so, perhaps you should consider starting a business that buys and sells rare comic books via the internet. There are a couple of approaches to establishing this type of online business venture. The first is to purchase the rare comic books that will be featured and resold on the web site. The second approach is to develop the web site so that anyone can post or list a comic book for sale, and when the comic book is sold you would collect a 10 to 20 percent commission on the selling price of the comic book. Both approaches have their pros and cons. However, there is a very limited downside to this kind of part-time retail business venture, and once established the business could easily generate a full-time income if you do a great deal of promotion in the comic book collectibles market.

ONLINE CIGAR SALES
★★ $$$ 🚗 🕐 🚚

Millions of dollars' worth of cigars are sold every month in the United States and, in the spirit of being unique, perhaps you could develop a web site that acted as a online portal to bring cigar manufacturers and distributors together with consumers that purchase cigars. This type of online venture would be very easy to establish and charging cigar manufacturers and distributors a fee to be listed and featured on the site could generate income. Alternately, income could be earned by retaining a portion of the cigar sales that are created, and listed companies could be posted for free. To spice up the site and make it more interesting for visitors, you can also add a chat line forum focused on topics and subjects related to cigars, as well as an online poll that lets cigar smokers vote for the all-time best cigars. Warning: Be careful that your site is not the impetus for bringing illegal Cuban cigars into the United States or other countries where they are not allowed.

ONLINE MAGAZINE SUBSCRIPTIONS
★ $$ 🚗 🕐

A great part-time income can be earned by selling magazine subscriptions right from the comforts of home. There are literally hundreds of magazine and periodicals publishers across North America that routinely discount the newsstand price of their publications by as much as 60 percent to enable independent subscription sales consultants to sell their publications and pocket the difference. Be sure to build a database of customers that you have sold magazine subscriptions to as you can also sell these same people books and guides once you have discovered what their particular reading interests are. To make this type of web site work, you need to have a large selection categorized by interests and by demographic audiences (i.e., teen and kids magazines). If you also look for some "less popular" titles and even some e-zines, you can generate a larger audience and more advertisers to the site. You will make a profit from a percentage of the subscriptions sold as well as from advertising.

ONLINE FITNESS BOOKS, CDS, AND PROGRAMS
★ $$$ 🚗 🕐

There are a few approaches that can be taken to start a business that produces and sells fitness books. The first approach is to write the fitness books by compiling information supplied by fitness experts in their fields of specialty. The second approach is to purchase fitness books from publishers and book distributors on a wholesale basis and retail the fitness books on your web site. Fitness is a popular subject and millions of books on fitness and fitness-related topics are sold each year in North America. Securing a portion of this very lucrative market should not be difficult. Authors, publishers, and video producers could utilize the site to market their products. In exchange for providing this service you could charge these fitness gurus a listing fee to be featured on the site or alternately a percentage of product sales.

ONLINE GOLF INFO AND EQUIPMENT
★★★ $$+ 🚗

The world is full of golf nuts. Starting an online business venture catering exclusively to the golf fanatic has the potential to make you a cyber gazzillionaire. In terms of the golf web site that you develop, you will want to be creative and seek a niche or untapped market. Here are a few suggestions:

- A golf coupon site wherein visitors could locate deals and discounts on thousands of golfing products and services.
- An online golf instruction web site that enables visitors to log on and learn how to improve their stroke or short game.

Combine these possibilities with the sale of new and used equipment and you've got it made. Of course you will need to know a lot about golf, or hire people to work with you who have such expertise. If you can have golfing experts write columns, articles, and course reviews for the site, you can generate some big bucks from golf equipment and clothing manufacturers.

ONLINE ARCHERY SUPPLIES
★ $$+ 🚗 🕐 ⚔

Archery supplies are the sort of specialized consumer products that you cannot run out and buy at your corner store in most communities. An exciting online business opportunity exists by posting a web site that is dedicated to selling hard-to-find archery supplies. This sort of e-commerce web site is simple to create and maintain and could easily be operated part-time from home. You can purchase archery supplies on a wholesale basis and stock an inventory, or you can electronically forward customer orders to manufacturers and distributors of these products and have them ship directly to your customers. Promote the site in print publications relating to archery and hunting as well as by establishing alliances with archery clubs and associations.

ONLINE FENCING EQUIPMENT
★ $$$ 🚗 🕐

Like archery, fencing is not the type of sport that you find equipment for at your local sporting goods store.

Therefore, if you can provide low-cost fencing equipment, particularly for students taking fencing classes in college, you can be on your way to a successful business. Of course, you will need to market your business to all fencing clubs and course instructors. You will generate more visitors and advertisers by providing content, a chat room, and other user-friendly perks that can make the site a home base for fencing enthusiasts.

ONLINE AUTOMOTIVE PARTS
★ $ 🚗 🕐

Selling automotive replacement parts for rare, antique, and sports cars can make you rich. A logical approach to mass market an auto replacement parts business to a global marketplace is the internet. Like many online business opportunities, you have options. The first is to purchase replacement parts at bargain basement prices and resell them for a profit via your own web site. The second option is to create an internet portal that brings people together who are seeking to buy and sell automotive replacement parts. The latter is the less-costly option to choose. To create such a portal, simply start a site with information and services pertaining to automotive replacement parts that can be utilized by car collectors and enthusiasts worldwide. The site can include a directory of parts manufacturers and distributors, as well as a classifieds section that enables visitors to post "for sale" and "wanted" notices about automotive parts. To spice up the site, include content that visitors would find interesting, such as car maintenance tips, online mechanics instruction training, and a chat forum for visitors to swap information. Income can be earned by selling books and repair manuals, as well as by selling advertising space in the directory in the form of banners. If, however, you go with the first option, and sell parts, you need to market to all car enthusiasts as well as body and fender repair shops and mechanics.

ONLINE USED MOTORCYCLE PARTS
★★ $$$$ 🚗 🕐

In North America millions of people own and ride motorcycles on a daily basis, and like cars, motorcycles break down and require repairs and replacement parts. Furthermore, like car owners, not all motorcycle owners can afford to purchase expensive new replacement parts for their bikes, especially replacement parts required to repair rare or antique motorcycles. This scenario is the basis of this business opportunity. Start a business that stocks and sells secondhand motorcycle replacement parts. The parts can be acquired relatively inexpensively by purchasing motorcycles from insurance companies that have been written off due to damage or theft recovery. Likewise, the parts can be marketed for sale inexpensively by developing a web site that lists all of the available motorcycle parts you have for sale. Motorcycle owners seeking a particular part would only be a click away from locating the part.

ONLINE ELECTRONICS
★ $$$

The door is wide open for this type of business as electronics sales continue to soar. Sure, there is plenty of competition, but if you can find a competitive edge, you can do a monumental business selling everything from organizers to large screen plasma televisions. Excellent customer service, package deals, various perks and amenities, and a wide variety of new and even re-furbished products can give you an opportunity to build a successful business.

WEB RESOURCE: www.ce.org
Consumer Electronics Association.

NOTES:

93
WEB EDUCATIONAL AND SERVICE DIRECTORIES
Businesses You Can Start

ONLINE ADVERTISING DIRECTORY
★ $ 🏠

The business concept is quite simple. You design an online directory that visitors can go to when looking to advertise their businesses in a given location. Have information about various rates and demographics and any special promotions or discounts in terms of advertising rates plus contact information. Business owners who visit the site simply locate the type of advertising that suits their marketing program and budget. Income is earned by charging the advertising companies a fee to be listed on the directory site, as well as by selling banner advertising space on the site.

WEB RESOURCE: http://www.aaf.org
American Advertising Federation.

ONLINE CAMPUS COUPONS
★★ $$ 🏠 🕐 🌐

Unlike printed coupon books, where students pay to buy the book, online coupons are free for students to download and print. The merchants pay a fee to have their coupon offer posted on the web site. The format for this type of site is straightforward. The site is indexed into various product and service sections such as apparel and entertainment. Visitors simply click on the section of interest and view the coupon offers. One of the best aspects about providing campus coupons online is the

fact that you can operate the business from one location and, if you chose to branch away from local colleges, you can employ sales consultants, working on commission, to market the online coupon service to merchants locally. You can also market to merchants by e-mail, but in-person marketing tends to generate more merchants. For this reason, you might start with local merchants and colleges for to start. A big advantage of the online coupons over a printed coupon book is that merchants can continually change their coupons, offering new items regularly. In fact, you might offer a discount to merchants who make changes every month, as a means of keeping the site fresh and drawing repeat visitors.

ONLINE ADVERTISING BROKER
★★ $$$$ 🏠

Let business owners, professionals, and company marketing representatives decide how much they want to spend on advertising as opposed to being told how much advertising costs. Here is a unique concept. For decades media companies have been setting advertising rates for customers that wish to advertise in their media. An online advertising broker can develop a web site focused on letting small business owners and professionals list the type of advertising they are seeking and the price they are prepared to pay for that advertising. Media companies wishing to sell advertising would simply log on to the site and start surfing through the postings or listings to find potential matches. This type of web site would require careful planning in terms of establishing an operating format that is effective; not to mention some specialized programming and handling all security and privacy issues.

WEB SITE OPTIMIZATION
★★ $$$ 🏠 🕐 🌐

Internet sites can only generate traffic if they are heavily promoted and show up prominently on search engines. There are a number of top search engines and each has a method to its madness, so that when users search on a topic, specific sites come up near the top of the lists. Web optimization is a business in which internet experts help clients get greater web presence by increasing unique visitor hits, strategically using key words, paying for placement, and combining other factors into an overall marketing plan. There are many cyber entrepreneurs that are willing to pay top dollar for such optimization if you are such an expert.

ONLINE CHILDREN'S CAMP DIRECTORY
★★ $$$$ 🏠

Parents have thousands of options to choose from in terms of what type and what style of camp they can send their children to. Most parents, however, will only learn about a very small percentage of these camps. Herein lies the business opportunity. Create a web site that operates as a directory for children's camps located around the globe. The site could be indexed by the camp type, featured activities, and geographic region. This would enable parents, or kids, to visit the site and locate camps that are of interest to them within close proximity to their community. You could do research, inventorying the camps that operate in each of numerous given regions. You could then provide full listings and make money by charging the camps to be in the "featured listings" section, complete with a photo and link to the camp web page. Given the fact that there are thousands of various camps worldwide it would only require that a small percentage of these camps pay a minimal yearly listing fee to be featured on the site for this online venture to become profitable. To market the site, place fliers in schools and after-school centers, and ads in newsletters and publications that serve them.

ONLINE NANNY SERVICE
★★ $$$ 🏠

Operating your own homebased nanny placement service can be a magnificent way to build a prosperous business. Busy parents often have no choice but to pay the costs associated with having a nanny care for their children, so nanny services are in high demand. There are three major roles to be filled by a nanny service. The first is locating parents who are seeking the services of a professional nanny. The second role is that of an employment screener. You will want to carefully look at all the nannies' resumes, and carry out reference and background checks to make sure they are suitable candidates. You will need to have verification that all nannies are legally allowed to work in the United States, Canada, or whichever countries you are representing. The third role is to place qualified nannies with parents who seek their services. There are various ways to charge for a nanny service. The one that I would suggest is charging a one-time fee to the parents. This is the simplest and most straightforward remuneration option. There are other options, such as a percentage of the nanny's wages, but this can be complicated and even lead to potential liability situations. By far the best way to bring these parties together is to operate this business as an online venture. First parents and nannies would connect via chat room, provided and screened by your service. Then, nannies and parents would then meet in person to make a final decision. At this point, your responsibility is completed. This cyber nanny service will require careful planning and research in order to develop a user-friendly site that can return profits.

WEB RESOURCE: www.employeescreen.com
One of several online employee background checking services.

ONLINE CYBER SECRETARIAL SERVICE
★★★ $$ 🏠 🕐

More people than ever before are working from home or operating a business from home. A cyber secretarial service provides an excellent business opportunity, offering the same options a regular secretarial service provides with one main difference: the services are provided online. You would first need to establish a pool of contacts with part-timers and freelancers who have the necessary skills to help your clients with editing, electronic filing, or various other projects. Of course, you can take on some of the work yourself. Next, you would market your service to homebased and small businesses. Through your web site or by mail, clients would send you their needs and you would forward the work to one of your part-timers or do it yourself. When the work was completed, you would pay the freelancer, send the finished work to the client and collect your fee. The business will take some time to establish in terms of securing regular clients and setting up an operating format. However, for anyone with secretarial experience, starting this business is a great way to work from home.

ONLINE DOMAIN NAME BROKER
★★ $$$$ 🚗 🕒 ⚖️

As corporations and small business owners race to register or purchase cool, short, and effective dotcom names, the resale price goes up for each domain name that becomes available. In some cases it skyrockets into the seven-figure range. However, while this is a potentially terrific opportunity, it comes with two major warnings.

- *Warning #1.* This is a highly competitive business and one that has many leading players owning millions of dollars worth of possible domain names. Unless you just happen to be in the right place at the right time to find out that a major online business is about to fold, the only way to effectively jump into this business is to work with someone with technical savvy who knows how to set you up with what are called "scripts." Scripts are automated programs that alert you to domain names that are coming up for renewal. If they are not renewed, you can pounce.
- *Warning #2.* Most domain names are worth very little money. Unless you find the keyword that "John Q. Public" might type in when doing a search, such as "airfares.com" or an already established online favorite, you will not get much for most domain names.

The key to success in domain name brokering is trying to find companies seeking to sell marketable domain names and convince them you are the right broker for the task. This is a difficult business, but potentially lucrative if you "strike gold."

VIRTUAL TOURS
★★★ $$$$ 🚗 🕒

Producing virtual tours for clients who are seeking the ultimate marketing tool for their web sites is a terrific business opportunity. Virtual tours are a very popular feature of many commercial web sites. Such tours can range from a hotel that gives potential guests a tour of their facility, accommodations, and amenities to catering facilities that want to showcase their facility for weddings or other occasions to real estate brokers that broadcast house tours of properties they have listed for sale and posted on their web site. The software exists today for individuals to create such tours themselves. However, most people do not create professional looking tours on their own. That's where you come in. To get started you will need a digital camcorder, virtual tour software and, most importantly, the production and editing skills to produce a better product than the client can create him/herself. To market the service, you need to have some dazzling samples of virtual tours, including at least one 360 tour posted on your site for clients to view.

HOLIDAY AND REMINDER E-MAIL SERVICE
★★ $$ 🚗 🕒

Starting a holiday and special occasion greeting card e-mail service is a fantastic new business enterprise to set in motion, especially when you consider the business can be operated from home and put into action with less than a $3,000 initial investment. Business owners, corporate executives, and professionals often do not have the time to send out cards to family members on a special occasion or to thank clients at Christmas time for their continued support and business. Designing "fill-in-the-blank" templates for a number of occasions such as birthdays, anniversaries, and "thanks for your business" is the first step toward establishing the business. The templates can be quickly altered and e-mailed to recipients at your client's request. However, since e-cards are very easily accessible to anyone, the real trick to this business is maintaining an online calendar for executives and other people who are not good about remembering important dates. This way, the client can give you a year's worth of important dates and you can make sure everything goes out on time. Reminders for doctor visits and even business reminders, such as "time for your car's tune-up," can also be part of your scheduled e-mails. Setting fees for the service will greatly depend on a client's volume of e-mails sent on a yearly basis. However, securing 200 clients and e-mailing 100 customized cards or messages for each on a yearly basis can generate gross revenues of $40,000, providing you only charge $2 for each e-mail greeting card sent.

ONLINE LOTTERIES
★★ $$$ 🚗 🎰

There are an estimated one billion regular lottery players worldwide. Thus, developing a web site that features and provides site visitors with news and information pertaining to lotteries from around the globe could prove not only to be an interesting enterprise to activate, but also a profitable one. Information and services featured could include lottery games available in various countries, contact information about how to purchase tickets, an "electronic winning numbers forecaster," and stories provided by visitors about hitting it big. Income and profits can be earned by renting advertising space and banner ads as well as selling lottery-related products. Where allowable by law, the site could even become ticket resellers. Be sure to research all legal aspects prior to posting this type of web site as your research could potentially unearth legal headaches.

ONLINE RESEARCHER
★★★ $$ 🚗 🕐

Do you spend hours every day surfing the web? If so, why not start an internet research service? This business opportunity was once commonly referred to as information brokering. However, with the introduction of the internet, the name has changed but the business remains the same, as the information that used to be researched and compiled from newspapers, trade magazines, and business and industry directories can all be found on the internet. This service assists business owners who do not have the time to surf the net by gathering the source data and facts relevant to their particular business, industry, or

market. Clients pay for the time spent doing research. Billing rates for the services vary depending on how much research time is required to compile the data being sought; however, many internet research services base billing rates on $20 to $30 per hour. The trick is to be very good at locating hard-to-find data on the web.

ONLINE TRADE SHOW DIRECTORY
★★ $$$ 🚗 🕐

Worldwide, more than 100,000 trade shows take place annually. Thus a very exciting and potentially profitable business opportunity exists, starting an online trade show directory. You can easily develop a web site that lists trade show information such as the type of show, when it is taking place, where it is being held, and how to contact the show's organizers. This type of online directory could become very popular as thousands of small businesses and corporations rely solely on trade shows as their main marketing tool for introducing new products and services as well as collecting qualified sales leads from interested parties. You also have options in terms of how your business will generate income and profits, including charging a listing fee to have trade show information featured on the site, having "featured listings" for a fee, selling advertising space on the site, or selling an annual trade show directory in print format.

ONLINE WEDDING DIRECTORY
★★★ $$$$ 🚗 🌐

Starting a commercial web site venture solely dedicated to weddings could prove to be a very successful business venture. The site can be indexed by cities and towns and then broken down into subsections featuring every imaginable wedding-related product or service including a listing of:

- Wedding photographers and videographers.
- Wedding singers, disc jockeys, and musical bands.
- Wedding planners and caterers.
- Formal wear and rentals for both men and women.
- Limousine services and much more.

Site visitors would simply select the geographical area, chose the topic of interest, and start to view the listings and information. Anyone getting married would be able to log onto the site to find everything they need to plan the big event. You would make money by charging for featured listings. If you can secure a small percentage of paying clients, out of the thousands of possible listings, with featured listings or even ads, you can do very well. The key, of course, is getting the site started, which will take a great deal of research.

ONLINE JOB BOARD
★★ $$$$ 🏠 🕒

There is stiff competition in the online job postings and career industry. However, there is always room for more creative, useful, and varied services provided via the internet. In the spirit of uniqueness, perhaps your online job posting service could specialize in a particular industry, or provide useful links and articles that help job hunters write a resume, train for a position, ace an interview, etc. You make money by charging the employers a fee to list their jobs on your site. You market the site through all traditional mediums including print ads and fliers to college students as well as linking to site frequented by soon-to-be college graduates. Additionally this type of web venture would also lend itself to selling employment guides and offering online employee training programs.

ONLINE BABY NAMES DIRECTORY
★ $$$ 🏠 🕒

Some business opportunities have a lot of competition and this business start-up is one of them. However, as an entrepreneur, your greatest skill may lie in your ability to take a new and fresh approach to an old business or concept. As Ralph Waldo Emerson said, "Build a better mousetrap and the world will beat a path to your door." That is the case with this business venture. Baby name books in print have always been popular, and maybe you can create new online content with a fresh outlook based on an old, marketable idea. Perhaps your site can feature historical names and what they mean or perhaps celebrity names and how they came to be changed or altered to suit the personality. Visitors could browse through the name listings for free, and by renting advertising space or selling products to businesses looking to reach parents-to-be, you can earn a good income. Additionally, seek out interesting ways to make the site more inviting. Perhaps hold a contest with

baby photos to match the name with the baby, or take an online poll to find out the most new baby popular names.

ONLINE E-NEWSLETTERS
★★★ $$ 🏠 🕒

Like printed newsletters, many companies that produce a monthly e-newsletter have good initial intentions, but reality soon sets in and time factors take a toll in terms of getting the e-newsletter to customers on time. In addition, there is a science to creating and maintaining an effective newsletter that people will subscribe to and look forward to receiving rather than deleting and canceling their subscription. The key is content that is good enough to keep people reading up every week, every other week or every month, depending on how often the newsletter is published. Just as nobody turns on television simply to watch the commercials, people do not want a newsletter that is nothing but promotional hype. Therefore, businesses need to put something interesting before the readers with plenty of promotional hype all around it. There are also good and not-so-good newsletters in regard to format, looks, ease of navigation, etc. If you become a newsletter expert, you can launch a very successful home-based business specializing in creating e-newsletters. The trick will be signing on new clients and developing a standard format for their first e-newsletter, but after that it is all straightforward. Maintaining a client's newsletter should require no more than about six to ten hours of work per month. Aim to secure 15 regular customers paying a mere $300 each per month for the service (which is only $3,600 per year to keep your products in front of your customers). This would allow you to generate an income in excess of $54,000 per year. Also be sure not to limit your potential market and include traditional print newsletter services as well as online ones. The two combined have the ability to earn you six-figures annually.

ONLINE E-LOGO DESIGN
★ $ 🏠 🕒

Designing corporate and product logos for free has the potential to earn you $30,000 or more each year with only a part-time effort. How? you may be wondering. Simply start surfing the web for corporate or product logos that could be improved upon or for companies and products that do not have an eye-catching logo. Contact the art department of the company and have some generic logos ready to show them as samples of what you can do. Then, see if they are interested in looking at your work and might be amenable to your creating a logo for them. Next, using your design skills and basic computer hardware and software, design new logos for this same corporation. When the logo is complete, make sure that it does not resemble another logo already being used by doing a search through the US Patent and Trademark office. The company may or may not ultimately accept your logo, so this is a bit of a gamble. However, a few logo sales can result in big money, especially if you get a small commission of the usage.

WEB RESOURCE: www.uspto.gov/go/ptdl/tmsearch.html United States Patent and Trademark Office.

ONLINE BUSINESS DIRECTORIES
★ $$$ 🚗 🕐

Like the printed counterparts, online business directories come in many forms and are very popular. This is a very competitive segment of the online advertising industry. However, with more than 1,000 businesses going online every day, the demand for this type of advertising service continues to grow. In a nutshell, an online business directory is simply a listing service for merchants and service providers in similar industries, such as tour operators, pharmaceutical suppliers or clothing retailers to name a few. In exchange for being listed in the directory, clients pay a monthly or annual fee. The fee will vary as to how much traffic is generated on the site. In some cases the fee is based on how many hits or views the client's listing or hyperlink receives. To get a piece of the crowded market, try to arrange your directory in a different manner than others, so it will come up higher on search engines. Also, market the directory heavily offline throughout a given industry.

ONLINE CONTRACT FORMS
★ $$$$ 🚗 🕐 🚙

Here is a very simple desktop publishing business to put into action. Template or fill-in-the-blank contract forms can serve a wide variety of uses. Forms could include standard bills of sales for vehicles, property or real estate. You could have confidentiality and non-disclosure forms, employment applications, writer's agreements, employee appraisal forms, letters of intent, and standard work-for hire agreements. The template contract forms can be sold from the web site, which enables visitors to download contract templates for a fee. It will take time and careful research to develop the contract forms, but with that said the saleable life span for the product can be five years or more. Make sure to review all contract forms with attorneys and be careful with insurance and other such forms. If you hook up with specific agencies that offer forms, you could also be a place in where visitors could gather necessary forms for government agencies, such as forms for incorporating a business in Delaware or California, depending on which agencies allow you to offer their forms.

ONLINE BUSINESS PLANS
★★★ $$ 🚗 🕐

If you can put together templates for various types of business plans, you can market an online service to new business owners and future entrepreneurs and make a nice profit selling the templates for $100 each. You can also buy business plans that fit the proper format and present them on the site as examples of how such plans should look. Also, along with offering for the detailed templates for each of several more common types of businesses (in broad categories), you can offer expert advice for a fee, or even gather the business details online and write sections or all of a plan for the entrepreneur, if you are a skilled business plan writer's business. Either way, new business owners are often uncomfortable doing such a business plan on their own, and you can provide a valuable service. You can also sell business plan books through the site to make additional money.

WEB RESOURCE:
www.sba.gov/starting_business/planning/basic.html Small Business Administration's business plan pages.

ONLINE IMPORT/EXPORT DIRECTORY
★★ $$$ 🚗

Publishing a biannual import/export opportunities directory in printed and electronic format has the potential to make you rich, as millions of budding entrepreneurs worldwide are constantly on the lookout for income and business opportunities. Simply create an import/export directory that features information about worldwide manufacturers, wholesalers, and agents that are seeking to expand their product lines into foreign countries and new markets, or individuals or companies that are seeking to import particular products into their regions. Charging a fee to be listed in the directory, as well as selling the directories to people who are seeking this type of valuable and potentially profitable information and contact sources, would earn revenue for the business.

CAMPUS WEB SITE CONSULTANT
★★ $$$$ 🏠

Most universities and colleges have official web sites, but that certainly does not mean there isn't room for improvement. Since college web sites are not typically thought of as a selling point for the school, some are not up to speed. They are, however, a very important means of making a good impression for new students and also provide a valuable information source for existing students and school personnel. Therefore, you can serve as the last word in what a college web site should offer, by studying university web sites long and hard and listing all the best features of the many that you find. Then, go online and see what the local university or college site is lacking or could be improved on. Are there services such as student housing listings, classified advertising space, free e-mail, up-to-date news features, and articles about life on campus? Conduct surveys to see exactly what features and information students want on a web site. Basically, go to the source and ask. Finally, you will pitch to the powers-that-be a means of bringing their web site up to speed with those of other schools. Charge a fee that will pay for your time, while keeping in mind that schools often do not have a big budget for this type of service.

COLLEGE DIRECTORY
★★★ $$$ 🏠 🕘

Yes, it will take a lot of time to do, but if you can put together a comprehensive directory of the thousands of colleges in North America that is easy to use and directs students and their parents to information about each school, you can make a lot of money. A straightforward

guide featuring the high points of the school, their special programs, admissions information, school history, rooming, social activities, sports teams, and overall campus life could be a very valuable directory and one in which many colleges would pay to be listed. You can also provide basic overviews of schools and charge visitors for more detailed college reports. Of course, to put such a site together, you will need to do a great deal of research and tap into resources from campuses, including students who can make some money as hired freelance researchers.

ONLINE ACTORS DIRECTORY
★★★ $$$ 🏠

In North America thousands of actors and models are hoping to be discovered. Posting a comprehensive online actors directory might just make you a financial star. You can charge actors and models a small yearly fee to post their headshot and resumes on the site. Directors, casting agents, and producers who log on would only be a click away from finding the perfect person for the role they are trying to cast. The site will have to be indexed for search purposes by age, gender, race, experience, etc., and by the individual talents and type of roles the person plays (i.e., comic actor, dancer/singer, etc.). The key to success for this type of online venture will be to attract people that do the hiring in the film and modeling industry to use the site. This can be accomplished by initiating a direct mail and e-mail campaign to literary and talent agencies and to all agency personnel explaining the site and the benefits of using it. Once established, you could even branch out and include film crew listings, film prop rentals, and production site information.

ONLINE LOANS
★★ $$$$ ⚖️

Business start-up, home improvement, and automotive loans are all types of financing services that can be featured on an online loan directory. Banks, venture capitalists, and other lending institutions would pay a yearly fee to be listed and featured on the site as well as be given space within the site to promote and give details about their lending prerequisites and other information. People seeking financing for a product or project would log onto the site, select the type of loan and lending institution they are seeking, and complete and submit an application for financing right online. The application would be confidential, secure and electronically forwarded to the lending institution(s) of their choice. The idea is to market the site as a place they can shop around for a loan from the comfort of their own home. You would have to make sure that all loan information is kept up to date.

ONLINE AUTO LEASE MATCH-UP SERVICE
★★ $$$$ 🚗

Thousands of new and used cars are leased each year as opposed to being purchased. A quick glance through the automotive classified section of your local newspaper will tell you that there are a lot of people seeking to get out of their automotive lease agreement. This fact creates a fantastic business opportunity to capitalize on by starting a service that matches automotive leaseholders with people who are prepared to assume their lease. The easiest way to gain clients or listings for the business is to call leaseholders wishing to get out of their lease and offer to find a person to acquire it. Once you have secured a few hundred listings, you can begin to run your own classified advertisements for used cars. Revenues for the service are earned by charging the leaseholder a fee once you have located and secured a client to assume the lease.

ONLINE SPOKESPERSON DIRECTORY
★ $$$$ 🚗

Product endorsements and testimonials are a very important marketing tool for many businesses, so activating a web site featuring spokespersons for hire has the potential to speak well for you! Professionals, industry experts, and celebrities alike, from every corner of the globe, could post an advertisement on the site that gives detailed information about their qualifications to promote certain products or services and the type of endorsement contracts they are seeking. Corporations and organizations that are looking for a professional spokesperson to endorse or promote their products and service would log onto the site and begin to search the listings. Sources of revenue for this type of cyber enterprise include charging spokespersons a listing fee, charging corporations to use your listings, and/or selling advertising space on the site.

ONLINE SPEAKERS DIRECTORY
★★ $$$$ 🚗

There are numerous speakers available who can provide seminars and speeches for conferences, conventions, graduations, or other corporate, or even fundraising or political gatherings. Compile a comprehensive listing of speakers and their areas of expertise. Look for speakers who have a strong platform and are familiar with public speaking appearances and being on stage. Market your speaker's directory to associations, universities, and all industries that have trade shows or industry conventions.

ONLINE TENDER DIRECTORY
★★ $$$$

Corporations, government agencies, and organizations of all sorts place thousands of tender display advertisements in newspapers annually. The cost of one ad can be as much as $1,000. Now imagine if that same corporation could post as many tenders as they wanted online for an annual cost of only $99. Could this type of web site become popular for companies and agencies to post tenders as well as for contractors seeking to secure them? Of course it could, thus creating a fantastic business opportunity by developing a web site that exclusively featured tender information and contracts available. The site would have to be indexed by tender subject such as construction, maintenance service, computer hardware, etc. Contractors wishing to bid for a tender could simply view listing and tender information and even download tender documents from the site. This type of online venture will require a substantial investment to develop and market the site. However, once established, the profit potential is outstanding.

ONLINE FRANCHISE AND LICENSING OPPORTUNITIES
★★ $$$$ 🚗

Thousands of prospective entrepreneurs each year look for franchise opportunities to launch themselves into the business world. With this in mind, you could create an online portal that brings corporations with franchise opportunities for sale together with people that want to purchase and operate a franchise business. The site can be created in a directory format with a main index page that lists the various franchise opportunity categories on the site, such as restaurants and food services, retail, and maintenance services. Income is earned by charging corporations a listing fee to be featured on the site. Additionally, an alliance could be established with a lawyer (or several lawyers) specializing in franchise agreements to write and post articles pertaining to the legalities of franchising on the site. Promote the site by utilizing internet marketing techniques such as search engine registrations, hyperlinking, joining a rotating banner advertisement program, and looking into online optimization. Although it would be quite labor intensive, you could also host monthly franchise opportunity trade shows that operate in conjunction with the web site. The trade shows could take place in major cities across North America on a rotating basis.

ONLINE SCHOLARSHIPS
★ $$$$ 🖥 🕒

Every year thousands of students vie for educational scholarships in North America, and one of the most difficult challenges facing students is keep tracking of and staying up-to-date with the thousands of different scholarships that are awarded each year. Developing a web site that features information about scholarships can help provide students and their parents with online access to a fantastic resource base where they could learn more about specific scholarships and the required criteria in terms of the awarding process. This type of online business could earn revenues in a few ways, such as charging students and parents a yearly membership fee for access to the site or charging educational facilities and scholarship advisory boards a fee to post their scholarship information on the web site. Of course advertising revenues could also be earned by renting banner ads once the web site was established and proven popular. Market this site heavily in all areas where high school students, their parents and educators can find it.

ONLINE VENDING EQUIPMENT
★★★ $$$ 🖥

Food vending in North America is a multibillion-dollar industry and, in the spirit of uniqueness, consider the following online business opportunity as a method to enter the vending industry. Develop a web site that specializes in providing a one-stop source for vending information and details. The site can include a classified advertisement section featuring vending opportunities and vending equipment for sale as well as other information related to the food vending industry, including articles about the business, success stories, regulations, and scams in the marketplace. All services and information featured would be free for visitors to the site, and revenues can be earned by charging advertisers a fee for listing or posting their vending opportunities or equipment for sale in the classifieds. Marketing the site to the general public would be as easy as placing small classified advertisements in major daily newspapers under the business opportunity section. These ads give a brief explanation about the web site and how to find it on the internet. Also market the site to business publications and link to web sites that focus on new business and moneymaking opportunities.

ONLINE COMMUNITY RESTAURANT DIRECTORY
★★ $$ 🖥 🕒

Like its print counterpart, an online community restaurant directory features the latest restaurants in a given area. For a small fee, featured listings could include more information including the menu, reviews, specials, directions and catering options. If the restaurant has a web site of their own, it can be linked. The advantage of maintaining a directory is that restaurant owners, many of whom now have their own web sites, have little time to update the sites and market them. That's the special service you can provide, staying up to date and drawing a larger audience. A heavy marketing campaign on your part, plus calls or e-mails to the restaurants for updated information, can make your site the place the local consumers go when they are looking for a place to eat.

ONLINE COOKING RECIPES
★ $$ 🖥 🕒

Cooking recipes, classes, products, and ingredients can all be provided and sold via your own cooking web site. There are numerous recipe sites up already, so you should look to specialize by featuring a certain type of cooking, such as organic recipes or specific ethnic favorites. Spice up the site with some food photos, clever content about the origins of the foods, quizzes, contests and even an invitation for people to send in their favorite recipes. Clearly, you have many options. The site can provide cooking recipes that can be downloaded for free and supported by selling advertising space and banners. You can also make money by selling cookbooks, cookware, and other such cooking related items. A nice touch might be to advertise and promote restaurants for a fee, and feature a chef's special recipe.

ONLINE SPA DIRECTORY
★ $$+ 🚗 🕒

Worldwide, there are thousands of health and beauty spas that cater to just about any health or beauty treatment or need imaginable. Thus an outstanding opportunity exists to develop an online directory featuring world spas. The directory should be indexed both geographically and by spa type. For an annual listing fee, spa operators would receive a headline in the directory index that is linked to a page providing details and information, such as services provided, location, and contact information. Sales consultants from around the globe can be employed to solicit spa owners to join the directory. These sales consultants can be remunerated by way of commission or perhaps with a barter system, proving them with free access to the spa for x number of visits. Promote the site in print publications related to health and beauty topics, as well as by utilizing internet marketing and promotion techniques, such as search engine registrations, links, and banner ads.

WEB RESOURCE: www.experienceispa.com/ISPA International Spa Association.

ONLINE MEDICAL DIRECTORY
★★★ $$$+ 🚗 🕒

An online medical directory provides a region, town, city, or even statewide listing of all of the medical professionals available in that geographic area. The site would list the medical facilities and their specialties and location. For more money, the listings could detail more about the practice and link to the physician's own web pages. The advantage of such directory listings for the physicians is that you can spend more of your time marketing than they have time to do. Additionally, people

who need a specialist or another doctor beyond their GP can have a one-stop shop to find what they need. Articles about medicines, home cures, health, and diet could enhance the site.

ONLINE BUILDING PLANS
★★ $$$ 🚗 🕒

Houses, sundecks, woodworking projects, and just about every other sort of building design plans can be sold online. You can develop a web site that specializes in one particular type of building plan, like garden sheds, or you could use an online directory format and list companies that sell various building plans. Income would be derived by selling the plans or by charging a fee to be listed on the site. There are millions of do-it-yourself homeowners worldwide and building and design plans are extremely popular. Remember the key to a successful web site, beyond generating profits, is to attract visitors and keep them coming back. Be sure to use varied and interesting content to ensure as many page views per hit as possible. This is the type of online business venture that, once established, can easily be operated from home on a part-time basis.

ONLINE HANDYMAN DIRECTORY
★ $$$$ 🚗

Unite the handymen of the world by posting an online handyman directory! The web site can be indexed by city and state as well as by specialty, such as carpentry, painting, etc. In exchange for a monthly listing fee, handyman services featured on the site would receive a listing as well as a link to a page to promote their service. The site could be promoted by placing display advertisements in print publications, as well as by linking to related home improvement sites and registering with numerous search engines. Add additional information to the site such as home maintenance tips and a regular home repair column to increase site visitation.

ONLINE HOME REPAIR AND IMPROVEMENT ADVICE AND INFORMATION
★★★ $$ 🚗 🕒

A common term used by web developers is "site stickiness." This basically refers to the level of unique and interesting content or user features can be incorporated into a web site to increase visitor page views and entice visitors to return to the site regularly. Home repair tips and advice fits that bill perfectly. Utilizing your construction and renovation expertise you can develop a web site that features all sorts of advice and information on home repairs. Such a site would include industry news about new products, questions and answers from people working on home improvement projects, your own advice column and even a chat room so visitors could exchange ideas. Make sure to include some concise home repair tips with "Forward to a Friend" links. One of the best ways to build a regular readership, or generate return visitors, is to have visitors spread the word about a site for you, and that's what having "forward to a friend" options prominently featured can do.

ONLINE MOVING DIRECTORY
★ $$$ 🎒

This cyber concept is straightforward. Simply develop a web site that features information relating to moving and relocation, or an online moving directory. The site can be indexed by state and city and feature individual listings of moving companies, packing services, and relocation consultants. The site can also provide visitors with useful content, such as how to pack for a move, what time of year is best to move, plus links to sites that provide neighborhood and community information so that visitors can check out what is happening in the location to which they are headed. Revenues are earned by charging service companies a fee to be listed on the site. The objective is clear: Provide visitors with the most up-to-date and useful information available in terms of moving and relocation, and you will succeed. Make the site interactive with questions to an expert, surveys, and even a contest, and you can generate more repeat visitors, thus increasing the desire to be listed by movers.

ONLINE HOME SCHOOLING
★ $$+ 🎒 🕒

A home schooling web site can feature information and services that can be utilized by parents wishing to school their children at home. This can include home-schooling programs in print format, an online chat

forum for parents to discuss home-schooling issues, and articles submitted by parents on home-schooling topics. In general, the site could become an online support and information service for parents. Income can be earned by selling textbooks and home-schooling programs and guides that outline suggested curriculums and social activities.

WEB RESOURCE: www.professionaltutors.com/homeschool. htm

ONLINE LEARNING CENTER
★★★ $$$$ 🎒

There are many courses given online, including those affiliated with major universities as well as courses that offer certificates for various professions. While it may take some time to gain accreditation of any type, you can impart knowledge by providing home learning online courses, and make a good profit by doing so. The latest in video technology makes it possible to put the teacher in front of each student so that he or she can play a lecture at his or her own convenience. Students can interact with a teacher through e-mail, can download course materials, and buy books as well. Since this is a competitive area, you are probably best served by coming up with a theme, such as online business courses, acting classes, language courses, cooking demonstrations, or some other theme. Hook up with experts and educators and have them submit course plans if they are interested in teaching through your online learning center. List payment options clearly for your courses and promote them heavily. You make money from tuition fees and the instructors also get a cut. If you can market the site well, then you may be able to attract instructors from known universities or successful business professionals looking for a teaching opportunity.

ONLINE TUTOR DIRECTORY
★★ $$+ 🎒 🕒

You can create a web site that exclusively specializes in helping people find qualified educational tutors in their community. The site will have to be indexed by tutor type and geographic location for search purposes. These sections could include math, science, English and English as a second language, as well as more specialized subjects. In exchange for an annual listing fee, tutors would receive a headline listing that is linked to a web page providing more details. You can make additional money by selling basic learning supplies including notebooks, calculators, etc.

ONLINE MANUFACTURERS DIRECTORY
★★ $$$ 🚗

Manufacturers directories in print have served as a valuable resource tool for corporations and small businesses for decades. Now it is your opportunity to merge old ways with high-tech solutions. Start by selecting a segment of the industry you want to concentrate on, such as machined fasteners or fabric. Next, design the site with various categories or sections representing manufacturers' products, businesses seeking manufactured goods, and agents seeking to represent manufacturers. Once the site has been developed, you can go about marketing the listing service. Typically, manufacturers that list with this type of service pay a monthly or annual fee and receive a listing on the site linked to a promotional page or a link to their site if applicable. Remember, manufacturers will only pay for this service if it is of value to them, meaning that exposure on the site ultimately must result in increased or new sales. Be sure to aim marketing efforts at those who will purchase the manufactured goods featured on the site.

ONLINE LANDSCAPING SITE
★ $$+ 🚗

Many homeowners are turning their once barren yards into an outdoor oasis leisure area. As the popularity of this type of do-it-yourself home improvement soars, now is your chance to cash in on the landscaping craze. Develop a web site that provides visitors with valuable landscape design and maintenance tips. Provide landscaping information and services including:

- Landscape design plans that can be downloaded
- A directory of landscape designers and contractors in different regions of the country
- Top landscaping tips of the week featuring information such as how-to and maintenance topics.
- An online "ask the expert" section that enables visitors to ask questions about landscaping in general.
- An online chat forum that can be utilized by visitors to swap information with other landscape hobbyists.

Income and profits can be earned in a number of ways, including charging a fee for landscape designers and contractors that want to be listed in the directory; by selling products related to landscaping like books, design plans, fishponds, and landscaping equipment; and by selling advertising space.

ONLINE DOG TRAINING
★★ $$+ 🚗 🕐

There are many options in terms of the type of information and services this type of web site could provide to visitors, including:

- A directory of dog trainers from coast to coast.
- Digital video broadcasts of dog training demonstrations and online instruction.
- Articles and information about dog training posted daily by the top dog trainers in the country.

There are also many ways for this type of web site to generate income including selling advertising space on the site; selling dog training programs, books, and videos; or charging dog trainers a fee to be listed in the online directory.

ONLINE DOG CARE WEB SITE
★★ $$$$ 🚗

Develop a portal to bring dog lovers together with retailers of products for dogs and service providers that specialize in services for dogs. This type of web site can be referred to as a "dog mega site" and can feature just about any sort of product, service or information about caring for your canine friends. The site will have to be indexed by products, services, and geographic area, and sub-indexed by types of dogs. You can include articles written by vets and by dog-owners, a chat room and interactive pet surveys, quizzes, and even e-cards with pooch pictures. Income is earned by charging retailers and service providers a fee for featured listings, by advertising, and by selling pet-related products. You can also offer, for a nominal fee, customized pet pages where pet lovers can share stories, photos, and comments about their pups. An online dog show could let visitors vote for their favorites and polls could allow them to vote in the best dog breeds of all time. There are many options to building up this into a doggie mega-site.

ONLINE CAT CARE WEB SITE
★★ $$$ 🏠

Like the doggy site mentioned above, you can create an online portal for cat lovers. As with the dog care site, this type of "mega site for cats" will have to be indexed by types of products, types of services, and geographic area. Income is earned by charging retailers and service providers an annual fee for having featured directory listings or from advertising. Similarly to the dogs' site, this site would also link visitors to cat product retailer's sites or custom designed web pages. Make the site attractive for visitors by adding interesting cat content such as articles, expert advice, photos, a chat room, and polls letting visitors vote for the best breed of cat. A veterinarian corner could be established as an "ask the expert" talk-back line. Best in breed competitions could also generate income by charging a small entrance fee.

ONLINE PET BREEDERS DIRECTORY
★ $$$ 🏠 🕐

This site can be divided into sections such as type of animal or pet and geographic location. In exchange for a yearly posting fee you could give pet breeders two price and service options. The first would be a simple headline listing in the directory with a link to the breeder's own web site or at least to their e-mail if they do not have a web site. The second option could include a headline listing linked to a page within the site that could detail information such as type of breeding, qualifications, location, contact information, and pictures.

ONLINE PET ADOPTION
★ $$$ 🏠 🕐

For a host of various reasons, sometimes pet owners are forced to give their cherished pets up for adoption, while in other instances a litter of four or five kittens or puppies is more than one owner can handle. You can help by developing a web site that is focused on finding good families for good pets. In a nutshell, this sort of site would operate in a classifieds advertisement format and include various headings such as dogs for adoption, cats for adoption, pets wanted, and more. I would suggest that this posting service be offered for free and opt to earn business revenues by selling products for pets and/or

renting advertising space on the site. You can also request donations from those adopting the pets for the services rendered. Promote the site by initiating a direct e-mail marketing campaign aimed at veterinarians, pet breeders, pet trainers, pet groomers, and all other businesses, associations, and agencies relating to pets.

ONLINE STOCK PHOTO SERVICE
★ $$$ 🏠 🕐

Starting a stock photo service is a great business to launch, as it can be operated from home on a full- or part-time basis. The initial investment is small and the operating overheads are minimal. The photographs can be sold to newspapers, advertising agencies, marketing companies, publishers, and directly to individual consumers. Such a site would enable customers to shop for the photograph they need for a project and simply download the file to their location. Be sure to copyright all of your photographs and specify whatever limitations are placed on their use. You can build up an inventory of all sorts of available photos by spreading the word to photographers, both professionals and hobbyists. You never know when a photo, even one taken by an amateur photographer will be the perfect on for a travel business to use on their web site. You can market the photos and make sure the photographer is compensated. You then get a cut of the action for each photo used. Once established, a stock photograph business has the potential to generate profits in excess of $35,000 per year, which is excellent for a low-investment homebased business.

ONLINE PHOTOGRAPHERS DIRECTORY
★ $$ 🏠 🕐

Launching a web site featuring a photographers directory is a very straightforward cyber business to establish. The site is simply a listing service for professional photographers, and can be indexed by city or state and by photography style, such as commercial, portrait, wedding, pet, etc. A photographer wishing to be listed in the online directory would pay a small yearly fee. The site can be promoted in the usual ways, including links, offline advertising, through search engine registration and optimization, and banner advertising. You could also initiate a direct mail campaign aimed at those who would benefit by having access to this type of directory such as event and wedding planners, advertising and marketing agencies, and insurance companies. This would be a good choice for a new online enterprise for the entrepreneur seeking to earn a few thousand dollars each year with only a part-time effort.

ONLINE FURNISHED ACCOMMODATION RENTALS
★★★ $$$ 🏠

Renting furnished accommodations to corporate executives on a short-term or long-term basis can provide you with an income that can match your corporate clients' staggering salaries. Every year thousands of homes and luxury condos sit vacant while the owners are away on extended holidays or short-term job transfers. Many of these same homeowners would gladly rent out or sublet their homes while not in use, especially if they knew the house was going to be rented to a responsible corporate executive. The above-mentioned scenario paints a very profitable business opportunity. Once again, this type of business venture is ideally suited for the internet via web site featuring photos and listings of the furnished homes available for rent, primarily marketed to corporate executives. Revenues can be generated for the business by charging homeowners a listing fee to post the rental information on the site. You can also sell advertising space.

ONLINE TIME-SHARE BROKER
★★ $$$ 🏠 🕐

Time-share vacation condos are generally sold by the week, meaning that when you purchase a time-share, you are purchasing a particular week, or a couple of weeks, each year. While time-shares are very popular, many time-share owners look to sell off the time-share entirely or sell off their week, or weeks, in a given year when they cannot get away. This fact creates a terrific business opportunity to start a business that focuses on brokering time-share properties. Such a time-share web site can charge the listers a fee and sell space to advertisers. In the case of a sale, you can also gain a commission of the overall time-share sale as a broker. Since people selling time-shares or time-share weeks are often looking all over the place, you need to make sure that you stay on top of the availability of the time-share. Therefore, if the seller has found a buyer, you need to know that—so be prepared to do a lot of e-mailing.

ONLINE MORTGAGE BROKER
★★ $$+ 🏠

Applying for new mortgages or renewing an existing mortgage online has become a very popular practice for many homebuyers and homeowners. An online mortgage broker is a very competitive segment of the financial lending industry, thus for anyone considering this type on new online business venture you will have to employ some clever marketing strategies or seek niche markets in order to succeed and profit. In the spirit of seeking a niche market consider the following options for establishing a web site focused on mortgage lending.

- Build a directory of mortgage brokers that specialize in high-risk property financing.
- Create a portal that brings private investors together with mortgage brokers to purchase new and existing mortgages.
- Feature mortgage brokers that lend exclusively for second and third-mortgage financing.
- Develop a directory of mortgage brokers and lending institutions that finance property purchases with zero down payments.

These are only a few suggestions, as there are many ways to seek or create a niche market within the mortgage financing industry. Regardless of the type of site you create, the revenue stream will mainly be generated by charging brokers listing fees and selling advertising space.

ONLINE CAMPING DIRECTORY
★ $$ 🏠 🕐

Camping ranks as the number one outdoor recreational pastime in North America, thus a very exciting business opportunity can be realized by the savvy web master who posts a camping web site on the internet. The site can feature a directory of commercial and government-operated campgrounds. You can also include camping product reviews, camping tips, articles, and stories about camping topics submitted by visitors. Income can be generated by charging campground owners for featured directory listings as well as by selling camping products, renting advertising space, and/or by charging a yearly subscription fee to become a site member.

ONLINE RECYCLING INFORMATION
★ $$ 🚚 🕐

Increased environmental concerns and awareness has made recycling a hot information topic. People want to know what can be recycled, how to recycle, and where to recycle. Here is your chance to capitalize financially by posting your own web site focused on providing recycling information and tips. Content featured on the site can be created through research or visitors can post recycling information and articles. Revenues can be earned by renting advertising space or selling products related to recycling. Advertise by registering with search engines, posting newsgroup listings, starting threads in chat rooms, sending fliers to associations and clubs that deal with recycling topics, and creating links with other web sites related to recycling subjects.

ONLINE CONSTRUCTION EQUIPMENT RENTALS
★★ $$$$ 🚚

What does a contractor or construction company do with their very expensive equipment when it is not being used? If they are smart, they will post it for rent on your new web site that exclusively features construction equipment rentals. This sort of web site would be relatively easy to develop and contractors from all around the country could benefit by either listing equipment for rent on the site, or by visiting the site to locate a piece of equipment that they want to rent. The site could be indexed representing the various equipment for rent and a basic online form could be created that would enable customers to complete and submit an equipment rental listing for posting. Visitors could surf the site free of charge to locate rental equipment they are seeking, while contractors listing equipment for rent would pay a small advertising fee. Offline marketing and promotion would be best accomplished by placing advertisements in construction-related publications.

ONLINE PARKING SPACE DIRECTORY
★★ $$$$ 🚚

Tired of driving around for two hours looking for a parking space? If you are living in a densely populated urban center, you know what I'm taking about. Therefore, a parking space broker may be just the new business opportunity that you have been searching for. The site could post listings of garages with availability along with individuals who have spaces in garages who may be out of town and are allowed to sublet their space. You can be sure some of that money would go to the garage. Your site could also provide parking rules and regulations for various towns, communities, or major cities. Garages posting on the site would pay for such directory listings. You could also have special sections for special event parking, such as a PGA golf tournament. Homeowners with driveway parking or local businesses with spaces in their lots could, for a small fee, post their parking possibilities and the prices. People looking for parking to an event, could get the contact information from the site and arrange with the space owners for parking.

ONLINE WHOLESALERS DIRECTORY
★★ $$$$ 🚚

Many small merchants rely on wholesalers and distributors to purchase goods for resale simply due to the fact that they do not buy in large enough quantities to enable them to buy in bulk directly from manufacturers. For many small business owners the search for wholesalers and distributors of different products is a never-ending battle. Establishing an online wholesale and distributor directory is the perfect solution to this problem. Simply start by creating a web site that is indexed for search purposes by product and geographic location. Next, employ subcontract sales consultants to solicit wholesalers and distributors to become listing members on the directory web site. There are thousands of independent wholesalers and distributors found throughout North America. Securing a few hundred to participate in this exciting and beneficial online service should be easy. Marketing and promotion of the site should be aimed at all small business owners and merchants. This can be accomplished by acquiring retailers and business association mailing lists and initiating a direct e-mail, mail, and telephone campaign. Also advertise the site in trade publications.

ONLINE AUCTION DIRECTORY
★ $$$$ 🚚

eBay has not cornered the market on auctions yet. There are other online auction sites plus a host of auctions taking place offline all throughout North America. If you can provide an up-to-date directory of the web sites and the upcoming auctions, you can make money from an informative directory web site. Art, cars, travel packages, or just about anything can be sold by way of an online or offline auction. You can generate income by charging whomever is running the auction to list the time and place of their upcoming auctions. Online auction sites can benefit from you providing a one top location to present what's new on their sites. Another option is to provide your own auction of items. However, unless you can come up with some unique products or services to auction off, the competition is so fierce that you are more likely to be successful by serving as a source for online auctions.

ONLINE RARE BOOK BROKER
★ $$ 🚗 🕐

Rare edition books, along with celebrity- and author-autographed books, are prized possessions of many rare book collectors. Thus an opportunity exists to develop a web site that functions as a portal to bring rare book collectors together to buy, sell, and trade books. Once again, this type of specialty site should be designed with the visitor in mind and include information and services that will keep them coming back on a regular basis. These services could include a rare book auction service within the site, a classified advertisement section that visitors could utilize to post notices about books they wished to purchase or sell, and an online chat forum so book collectors can swap information with each other. Revenue sources include fees for classified advertisements and auction services, renting advertising space, and selling books and print format valuation guides.

WEB RESOURCE: www.rbms.nd.edu/yob.shtml
Association of College and Research Libraries.

ONLINE COIN AND STAMP COLLECTORS DIRECTORY
★★ $$$$ 🚗

Create a directory for coin and stamp collectors from around the globe to get together to buy, sell, and trade coins and stamps by developing an online coin and stamp web site. The site can feature numerous free information

and services for visitors such as a coin and stamp valuation guide, an online chat forum, and a classifieds section featuring coins and stamps for sale or wanted posted by visitors. There are a few ways of making money from such a venture. First, you could hold auctions of rare coins and stamps. A second option would be charging fees for collectors to list either what they are selling or what they are seeking. A third means of making money is to serve as an agent between buyers and sellers and collect a commission. And finally, there is always the opportunity to sell ads on the site.

ONLINE CAR CLUB DIRECTORY
★ $$ 🚗 🕐

Across the United States and Canada there are thousands of car clubs and millions of car enthusiasts. Thus an opportunity exists to create an online portal that brings these two parties together to share information about cars and how to join car clubs. The web site can be indexed both by geographic location as well as type of car club. In addition, the site could also include a chat forum and articles pertaining to collecting cars submitted by visitors. Make the site free for visitors as well as for car clubs that want to be listed in the directory. Generate income and profits by selling products related to car collecting, such as books, repair manuals, and die-cast models of cars.

ONLINE DATING SERVICE
★★ $$$ 🚗 🕐

Forty percent of North American marriages end in divorce. While this may be a sad commentary on the state of modern-day relationships, you will find this fact to be very uplifting if you are considering starting your own dating service. You will need to be careful screening applicants since countless people lie about themselves online. In addition, you will need to make sure to cover yourself from liability with carefully worded contracts that state that you are linking people via the internet. However, once they choose to meet in person, you are no long liable for their actions or activities. You may be best serving a segment of the audiences, such as 50-and-over singles or divorcees, or at least having separate categories. You will make a profit by charging a fee for signing up and by selling advertising space. Make sure you put a lot of careful planning into this business, since many have tried and failed by not seeing the web loopholes along the way. Make sure you plan carefully and use passwords and encryption to protect people's privacy so that you can make this a successful business.

ONLINE ASSOCIATION DIRECTORY
★★ $$$ 🏠

Worldwide, there are hundreds of thousands of various associations serving an unlimited number of special interest groups, charities, and business industries. Regardless of whether these associations are nonprofit or commercial associations, most require that members pay dues to generate revenues. This is the basis of a new online business opportunity. Create a web site exclusively featuring associations of every sort. Index the site by type of association, such as business, charity, sports, and so on. In exchange for being listed on the site, associations would pay a yearly membership fee and their listing could be hyperlinked to the association's own web site or linked to an information page within your directory site. You could also set up a system whereby local associations could have long distance members, should they choose, who could get information and pay dues through the site, for a small fee of course.

ONLINE COMMUNITY SPORTS DIRECTORY
★★ $$ 🏠 🕐

Take community amateur athletics into the high-tech world of the internet by developing a web site dedicated to bringing sports fans all the local action in amateur sports. Ideally this sort of online venture will service one particular city or community. Of course, if it works, you can use the template from one local sports site to build others for communities coast to coast. Local amateur sports information featured and updated daily on the site can include middle and high school team updates, little league team statistics, game schedules, game commentaries, and more—basically anything to do with local amateur athletics, which are typically lost in the shuffle on the professional and college sports web sites. Sports associations, parents, and team coaches can supply the information posted on the web site. Income can be earned by selling advertising space on the site to local merchants and service providers, otherwise known as "community sports sponsors."

ONLINE BOAT BROKER
★★ $$$$ 🏠 🕐

Thousands of pleasure boats are bought and sold privately each month in the United States. Developing a web site that acts as a portal to bring boat buyers and sellers together has the potential to make you rich. You can create a web site that is categorized by boat style, type, and geographic location. Boat sellers wishing to have their boats listed for sale on the site—including a picture, detailed equipment list, and contact information—would pay a monthly fee for this service. People seeking to buy boats would simply log onto the site, select a category of boat they wanted to buy, and start viewing the listings. You could employ subcontract sales consultants to secure boat listings for the site and pay them by way of a commission for each listing they secured. Given the fact that so many boats are bought and sold annually in this country, securing only a few thousand listings should not prove to be a daunting task. To increase revenues and profits, also seek to secure businesses that sell boating equipment and supplies to be featured advertisers on the site.

CYBER TOUR GUIDES
★★ $$ 🏠 🕐

Unite the independent tour guides of the world by creating a web site that features tour guides from around the globe for hire. Simply develop a web site that is indexed by country and sub indexed by city. Visitors to the site could choose the destination they are traveling to and find a tour guide to show them the attractions once they get there. In exchange for a posting fee, tour guides would receive a listing in the directory as well as a full web page within the site that would give them the ability to promote their service, state their qualifications, and provide contact information. Promoting the site would be very easy and require you to do no more than initiate a direct mail and e-mail marketing campaign aimed at travel agents and brokers. Travel agents and brokers would be able to refer their clients to the site to locate a suitable tour guide.

ONLINE E-TRAVEL BARGAINS
★★ $ 🚗 🕐

Basically, the goal of this opportunity is to amass a large e-mail database of people to which you will send a weekly travel bargains newsletter. You are not working as a travel agent, but simply sending out travel tips, articles, and a limited number of travel bargain advertisements submitted by travel agents. Income is earned by selling advertising space in the newsletter to travel agents, tour packagers, and even hotels and resorts. There is one stipulation: the travel packages or services the agents wish to advertise must be true travel bargains and at least 20 percent off the regular retail selling price. The cost to operate the newsletter adds up to no more than a few hours each week in time. Only five travel agents paying a mere $50 per week each to have access to your e-newsletter subscribers will create an income for you in excess of $10,000 per year. Warning: There are a lot of travel discount sites on the internet, so look for unique tour packages, because the competition is stiff.

ONLINE RESORT DIRECTORY
★★ $$$$ 🚗

Sure, there are plenty of travel sites on the internet, but listing all sorts of unique resorts around the world and what makes them unique could prove to be a successful business in the making. The key would be finding reputable sources that could give you the thumbs up or thumbs down on resorts in reviews and columns. Of course you could have featured listings, in which resorts would pay to strut their stuff. Categorize resorts for golf, families, seniors, honeymooners, and so on. Make sure the site stays fresh by offering content for the resort traveler. Wherever possible, run contests in conjunction with resorts. Hype and promote the site in all travel publications and by linking with travel web sites.

WEB RESOURCE: www.hospitalitynet.org
American Resort Developers Association.

ONLINE HOT AIR BALLOON DIRECTORY
★★ $$$ 🚗 🕐

Starting a business that promotes and sells hot air balloon tours does not mean you need to rush out and buy a hot air balloon. The business can be successfully oper-ated as a booking agency for balloon tour operators from around the globe. Customers, travel agents, and wedding planners could simply log onto one web site and be able to book a once-in-a-lifetime hot air balloon tour. It could be that easy. Securing hot air balloon tour operators to be represented by your online booking service would not be difficult, as there would be no charge for tour operators to become a member and be featured on the web site, and there is little competition. However, once a customer has booked a balloon trip or tour, a commission of 25 percent would be charged on the total value, or 75 percent of the trip value would be remitted to the tour operator. In addition to balloon trips, the web site could also provide clients with options to book helicopter and small plane sightseeing excursions.

ONLINE BED AND BREAKFAST DIRECTORY
★★ $$$$ 🚗

The business concept for starting an online bed and breakfast directory is relatively straightforward. Bed and breakfast accommodation operators would post information such as rates, location, local activities, specials, pictures, and contact information onto the web site. Visitors to the site would simply be a click away from locating the perfect bed and breakfast for their travel plans. Revenue for the business can be generated in a few ways, including:

- Charge B&B operators a yearly posting or listing fee to be featured on the site.
- List B&B operators for free, and charge a commission percentage only on visitor bookings.
- Charge no posting or membership fees and support the business by selling banner advertising on the web site, and by selling travel products and services.

As with any cyber business, the key to success lies within two areas. The first is to develop, implement, and maintain an interesting and unique site. And the second is to get people to visit, utilize, and return to the web site through marketing, both on and offline.

PROFIT POTENTIAL: Based on revenue option number one, the business could potentially generate yearly gross sales of $300,000. This can be done by securing a mere 1,000 B&B operators worldwide to post their business on the web site, and charging only $25 per month for the service.

ONLINE WHALE WATCHING TOURS
★★ $$$ 🚗 🕐

Do you want to be part of the multimillion dollar whale watching tour business, but are a little short on investment capital, or you are not living in a state boarding on the ocean? Well don't fret, there is a way to capitalize on the whale watching tour industry by starting an online whale watching business that features video footage of whale watching tours on your site. Whale watching tour operators and tourists from around the world could provide the video footage featured on the site. To generate revenues and profits for the business, simply charge whale watching tour operators a yearly posting or listing fee to be featured on the web site. Products on whales such as books, music, and apparel could also be sold on the web site to boost revenues.

ONLINE PRESS RELEASE SERVICE
★★★ $$$$ 🚗 🕐

As the saying from the classic movie *Field of Dreams* goes, "If you build it, they will come." This saying could prove to be very accurate in the case of an online press release service. In a nutshell, an online press release service is simply a web site that has been specifically design to enable users to log on and create a press release from the many templates available. This would be the easy part of building such a site. Since most people do not write up quality press releases, you could include—for a fee—writing, editing, and consultation services. The more difficult part would be to provide a full PR placement service, which means sending the press releases to media outlets. Without question, activating this type of online enterprise would require countless hours dedicated to researching, formatting, and gaining access, and the "okay" to send to media contacts, since many media contacts are already inundated with press releases.

PARENTING SITE
★★ $$$ 🚗

There are numerous angles you can use to start a parenting web site, whether that means talking about progressive parenting or you launch a site for single moms or gay parents. The key is to find a concept and run with it, providing the latest information, stories, and parenting products. Articles by experts, chat rooms, discussion boards, forums, and all sorts of content can make the site a hit with the parent market. Be clever and comprehensive in building a site that reflects the parenting niche market you are looking to attract. Market it on and offline with promotional giveaways, contests, surveys, etc. There are millions of parents out there so if you can attract enough visitors, you can make money through advertising as well as by selling some products.

ADOPTION SITE
★ $$$ 🚗

While photos of waiting children in foster care can be posted online, adoptions cannot be completed via the internet. Nonetheless, you can start a comprehensive web site teaching prospective parents what they need to know about both domestic and international adoption. Such a site can provide books to buy, a directory of adoption agencies and adoption attorneys, and provide information on the many requirements necessary in the fifty states and around the world in order to adopt a child. Parents looking to adopt can make it known on the site as well. You can generate money by selling books to consumers as well as selling advertising space to adoption professionals, who can also serve as guest columnists providing you with up-to-date articles. Forums, message boards, and chat rooms will help generate visitors, which will increase your advertising revenue.

LOCAL NEWS
★★ $$$$ 🚗

While you won't be able to compete against CNN and other major news sites, you can provide local up-to-date news and information to one community at a time by setting up a series of news web sites. National stories from the wire services could be fed to all of the sites, while each one could have a couple of local reporter providing the latest in local headlines. Sprinkle in local sports, weather, and movie listings, and you can have THE site for any given locale. As always, advertising will be the primary means of generating a profit from such a venture. In time you can and will build up an archive of stories and data, which can also make you some money by charging a nominal fee for back stories from several months ago.

AMERICAN HISTORY
★ $$$ 🏠

There are a number of web sites possibilities from which you can educate youngsters and even high school and college students. American history is rich with stories and tons of data. The trick is to present it in a manner that makes it fun, while still being educational and informative. Such a site needs to be accurate, which will mean doing your homework, so to speak. It may also mean bringing in teachers and other education professionals to help you create, build, and update the content. Selling history books, as well as advertising space to publishers of history books, maps, and similar products, can support the site and provide you with a profitable business. Set up various sections of the site for the different grade levels and then market the site throughout schools and to historical locations, so that it is featured on the literature handed out at anyplace from the Liberty Bell to the Washington Monument. Also include photos of great historical locations and sell advertising to companies that feature historical tours.

WEB RESOURCE: www.historyplace.com

ONLINE CASINO DIRECTORY
★★★ $$$$ 🏠

Gaming is a multi-billion dollar industry in North America and around the world. So why not cash in on the action by creating a comprehensive web site featuring as many of the top casinos as you can find. Along with your own casino reviews, you can sell featured listings and advertising. Generate visitors with special casino promotions, online contests, polls, and other fun activities. Once you generate a good-sized audience, you can generate advertising, and the casinos—whether in Las Vegas, Atlantic City, or on the midwestern riverboats—certainly have the money to advertise their upcoming special events and performers.

MAKING READING FUN
★ $$ 🏠

Learning to read can be a struggle for many children and you can help crate a web site to lessen that struggle. Making reading fun can incorporate games, puzzles, and contests to make reading more enjoyable for young children, who would explore a wide range of stories (for various reading levels) on the web site. Ads from publishers featuring children's books make such a business very successful, since there are so many publishers of children's literature. You could work out deals whereby the publishing houses provide some of the stories in exchange for listings, or you could seek out learning professionals and authors of children's books to provide original material—or you could do both. You will need to stay on your toes, making sure the stories are always appropriate for the reading level and always have new material at the ready.

ONLINE BEST PUBLIC BATHROOM DIRECTORY
★ $$$ 🏠

Let's face it, when you gotta go, you gotta go. How about a web site that lets you know your options for where you can go? Offbeat, yes—but many offbeat web sites have resulted in big money. Remember those dancing hamsters from the early days of the web, who danced their way to a fortune? The toughest part about starting a directory to the best public bathrooms in each of a number of towns and cities is doing the research. You will therefore need to spend some money to find people who have used bathrooms in public buildings and get their reviews for a few dollars each. In addition, you will need to do some investigating and hire a few scouts to check rest rooms for cleanliness and accessibility. Market your site to travelers, tourists, and anyone with a laptop who can punch up the site as they make their way through a town or city.

SEMINAR TAPE RENTAL
★ $$$ 🏠

Each year there are thousands of seminars featuring top expert speakers on everything from architecture to zoology. With some good marketing you can capitalize on this vast industry by marketing seminar tapes, with the permission of the speakers, of course. There are a couple of ways to go about this business. One is to solicit the tapes from the various seminars around the country and have them available on your categorized web site for a fee, in either CD or downloadable format. The other method is to make arrangements with seminar planners to do the taping of the conference—again with each speaker's permission—and employ college students on a part-time basis to set up the tape players and collect the tapes for the site after the seminars are completed. Either way, you could end up with numerous topics available in your own categorized tape/CD online library. You might choose to specialize in certain areas or instead to have a broad spectrum of subjects on the site.

ONLINE BEACH DIRECTORY
★★ $$$$ 📠

Millions of miles of white sandy beaches can be the impetus for starting a beach directory. You can categorize beaches by location, as well as by type of beach and amenities offered. Directions, changing facilities, parking prices, and food availability can all be included. Phone calls, e-mails, and faxes to the municipalities and others in charge of the facilities can provide you with information. Directory listings of special events and activities can generate revenue, along with advertising and even selling beach-friendly products from Frisbees to tanning lotion to sunglasses… and let's not forget beach balls.

FINANCIAL NEWS
★★★ $$$$ 📠

Yes, there is a lot of competition, but if you take a specific approach, choose an angle that is not focused on the stock market, and appeal to a mass audience, you might just be able to gain your slice of the proverbial online pie. Try to locate and sign up experts to provide content in columns and answers to viewers concerns. Add content on the latest in trends and look for advertisers from the many financial institutions. Remember to keep the site updated regularly and make sure that your information is accurate. Look for credible sources to serve as your financial reporters.

ONLINE NATIONAL PARKS DIRECTORY
★★ $$$ 📠

For travelers, campers, and anyone else who loves the great outdoors, you can provide plenty of detailed information on each of the nation's national parks. This can include directions, accommodations, where to get food, campground details, and the history of the park. Local businesses looking to reach tourists and park visitors can advertise and you can have a small monthly fee for down-

loadable virtual park video tours. The hardest part of such a site, as is often the case, is gathering the tremendous amount of data necessary to make this a comprehensive web site. This will mean locating and interviewing numerous people involved in running the parks as well as those who have visited and can provide accurate information. Chat rooms, postings boards, and other user-friendly perks can also be part of the site. Market the site at all tourist bureaus, sporting goods and camping supply locations, and to travel agents.

CHARITY DIRECTORY
★ $$$ 📠

People are often looking to hook up with a charity to either give money or donate goods. Being a good Samaritan and looking to earn some money, you might consider putting together an online guide to major charities with contact information and upcoming fundraisers listed. You could also solicit for online contributions going directly to the charity of the visitor's choice, with a small percentage going to keep the fund afloat. Larger charities could afford to pay a nominal fee for listings and they could also buy advertising for upcoming fundraising activities such as golf outings or marathons. Photos from such events along with stories of local fundraising activities, such as schools raising money for a good cause, could round out a beneficial and very enterprising web site.

CONSUMER COMPARISON SHOPPING REPORTS
★★★ $$$$ 📠

If you can create or find (and attain the rights to) comparison reports about products and/or services, you can start a web site that helps consumers. To put together such a site will take a great deal of research and technology in order to provide accurate data on various brands, styles, and categories of products. However, with the right data, you can provide consumers with a comparative report on leading products, such as the ten leading cell phone companies, or top ten refrigerators in a side-by-side comparison. The site should be set up with a list of product categories allowing consumers to punch in the ones on which they want to see comparisons. The initial lists could provide basic data, but for a more detailed comparative report you would charge a fee. This can even be done with neighborhood data for people looking to compare places to which they might consider moving.

REAL ESTATE WEB SITE CONSULTANT
★★ $$ 🏠 🕐

In the real estate industry, having a web site is essential to success for brokers and agents. Unfortunately, as a group, real estate professionals have some of the worst looking, most poorly planned web sites in cyber space. This is the basis for a real estate web consultant to come in and teach much of what you saw starting on page 405: how to design a good web site. While you need not be an expert in the real estate part of the business, it is advisable to study up on some of the basics. Then it's time to market yourself to the real estate community. Charge $40 to $60 an hour and within a few hours, you should be able to make the necessary recommendations to improve these cyber misadventures. If you know HTML or how to work the software they are using to manage the site, you can actually make the changes if the site owner doesn't mind letting you in on his or her password. For this you might raise those hourly rates slightly. In the end, you can help brokers and agents have high quality, good-looking sites that give off a much more polished, professional look.

BUSINESS TO BUSINESS (B2B) DIRECTORY
★★★ $$$ 🏠

A broad area in which to start a web site, there are many options when you consider launching a B2B directory. First, you need to select an industry with which you are familiar and then do plenty of research. Find out what it is that you can provide this industry. Do they need a list of manufacturers with which to do business? In the fashion industry, you might list showrooms, models, fashion and image consultants, pattern makers, industry magazines, etc. Each industry has numerous businesses that interact with one another and your job in putting together a B2B directory is to put all of the players in one place for easy access. Advertising will typically come from players in the industry who want special listings and recognition, and marketing efforts should be

both on and offline in all areas where professionals in the industry look for answers to their business questions. If you can be THE place the industry looks for answers to their problems, your B2B directory can make you right. Hint: To make this type of site work, you must be as up-to-date as possible with your data, so keep an ear to the ground, so to speak, and maintain your contacts at all times.

ONLINE BLOG DIRECTORY
★★ $$$

As blogging become the latest web-induced fad, it presents an opportunity for you to categorize and post blogs in one place for readers to find them. This will take some web searching on your part to locate the blogs, but once you have them in one handy online location, visitors will be able to use your site as a blog library of sorts. You can support the site with advertising, or charge bloggers a small fee to be included. This will help weed out those who are more serious about their blogs from those who are simply writing anything for no apparent reason. You can set it up so that visitors can search by topic, by geographic region, and by language, since you may include blogs in various languages. Since blogging is solely an internet thing, you will want to promote your directory in cyberspace on writing sites and through various web boards, e-newsletters, chat rooms, and so on.

ONLINE STUDIO DIRECTORY
★★★ $$$ 🏠

Studios are used for rehearsals, dance and acting classes, art exhibits, photo shoots, theatrical auditions, and even parties. If you can categorize them in one place, listed by geographic region, as well as size and usage, you can have a very useful web site. This type of site can generate income from detailed directory listings as well as advertising and even a membership base. You can do special searches for members to find them the size studio and the right location. If you develop a good rapport with the studio owners, you can even reserve the studio for your site member. Market this site to dance instructors, filmmakers, independent producers, advertising executives, and anyone else you think might be in the market for a studio rental.

8
EBAY
Businesses You Can Start

EBAY BUSINESS MICROGUIDE

eBay began in 1995 as a web site designed for people to sell items to one another. The site is still doing just that today. Except that rather than a small site with 10,000 users, it is a multi-billion dollar web site with more than 115 registered users and some half a million eBay businesses.

You too can start an eBay business. In many ways it is like starting any other business. This means you need to:

- Have a business name
- Have a business plan
- Have proper licensing
- Set up a business legal structure (sole proprietor, corporation, S-Corporation, etc.)
- Set up a business bank account
- Set up payment methods, including credit card payment
- Have the necessary computer equipment, software, and high-speed internet access
- Be prepared to spend money on marketing and promotion
- Have expertise in the category of products you are going to sell.

In addition, you need to have some additional online auction tools and skills that include:

- A digital camera and a knack for taking good product photos—you cannot just lift photos from other web sites, you need to use your own.
- The ability to write concise, accurate, even compelling, product listings complete with all necessary information.
- Providing excellent customer service and answering questions about items quickly.
- Adjusting to changes in the market, the products and the eBay system of doing business.
- Setting up a means of taking orders and fulfilling them that runs smoothly.

By going to eBay Stores and clicking on "Open A Store," you can get yourself started. Just follow the instructions, select a name that has not been trademarked by someone else (in fact you should trademark your name), and you will be ready to start. Of course, prior to this, you need to have a system in place that covers most of the above lists, including what you will sell, how you will accumulate the items, how you will collect money and so on. Launching an eBay store is easy, it is the research and preliminaries that are the more complicated—yet necessary parts of your business endeavor.

1. Selecting A Product

With a few exceptions (such as drugs or firearms) most "tangible" items are salable on eBay. The question is, which one, or ones, are you going to focus on selling? Your product should be something you not only have a great knowledge of, but also enjoy selling. You should also do a great deal of research, meaning that you should spend many hours shopping on eBay, or at least browsing the many pages to see what is selling at what prices. Try searching for various items and see what comes up. Look at the value placed on various items. Particularly those that might be ones you also anticipate selling from your eBay business. This way, you can see what is steadily selling and at what price points. Do some off-line shopping and price comparison searching as well to get the best idea of a product's value.

You should also read seller profiles and feedback to get an idea of what to say in your profile and what to strive for, and avoid, from buyer feedback.

When selecting a product, consider the cost of shipping and whether or not buyers will pay what might be high shipping costs on larger items. Also consider the markup as you would with any retail item. Think about the life cycle of the product(s). Most products, or at least styles of a given product, change over time, so you want to sell something that can evolve with your business.

You also need to have a way of getting the product you wish to sell. This means you manufacture the product yourself, use wholesalers, or buy through suppliers. You can sell on consignment as well, meaning you don't pay for the item if you do not sell it. However, such deals are not always easy to secure in that the holder of the goods may want to sell someplace else. Therefore, you should take possession of the goods to sell them, thus assuring you that they are physically available for sale. Four selling hints:

- Know your products and never take someone else's word for what a product is or what it looks like.
- Photograph your products in the best manner, using a good digital camera and the right lighting. Blurry, out-of-focus and stock images are not as appealing to a prospective buyer and providing no image (unless you are selling something like tickets) is typically not good for business.
- Make sure you have the products on hand or access to them—the last thing you want to do is sell something you cannot make good on. If you are selling items and the manufacturers are shipping them out directly, then keep a close watch what they have in their inventory. If you are buying merchandise for resale, know what is and is not available.

- Price accordingly. You can start pricing very low, but if you are not making a profit, you are wasting your time. Conversely, you can price high, but people will catch on, particularly with the shipping cost on top of the price. By the fact that you have less overhead than most brick and mortar businesses, and you may not have much (or any) inventory on hand, you should be able to keep costs down and prices down accordingly. Do not try starting with a very low bid and having a friend operating as a "shill" to up the bidding for you. eBay is familiar with such practices and you can end up paying $50,000 in legal ramifications, as was one case with an eBay seller and his friend.

2. Naming an eBay Business

Just like a store name, the catchier the better. Don't amuse yourself with an inside joke or use your birth date so it's easy for you to remember—use something that will attract customers and that they will remember. Also, use something that defines your product and, or personality. If you have a personal account name on eBay, don't use it for your business. This should be a separate entity so that feedback will only reflect your business and not personal transactions.

3. Methods of Payment & Collection

Credit card and debit cards are the preferred methods of payment for most serious business owners. Not only does it demonstrate that you are a business and not an individual selling an item, but it makes it that much easier for your buyers to pay you. You can accept personal checks, but there is a time element to consider—getting the checks, cashing it, waiting until it clears and then sending the merchandise. Money orders and bank checks are also a little on the "slower" side, but at least you don't run same risk as having a check bounce.

To collect money, most eBay businesses use a PayPal business account, which specifically separates transactions from their personal accounts (should they have one) and makes the transactions simple. Google and other companies offer payment methods as well. There is transaction fee involved, but it is part of the cost of doing business.

If you are doing business internationally, which is a great way to expand your business, make it clear what currencies you will and will not accept and learn about the overseas shipping rates (and policies) so that you can price accordingly. Also, do research and learn about what is and is not permitted to be imported and exported.

4. Customer Service

Customer service is particularly important on eBay because buyers can rate you and a low feedback rating may scare away other, prospective customers. Also, your reputation is on the line. And finally, if you do not handle transactions smoothly and returns when necessary in a prompt and courteous manner, you will lose customers. And return customers still make up typically 80% of your business, even on the internet.

5. Define Yourself

On the internet, you are not always as you appear…in fact, you are not at all as you appear because you are faceless to your potential buying market. Therefore, it is important to have an "about me" page that gives your prospective buyers an idea of with whom they are dealing. Read other such pages before writing your own to get an idea of what other sellers and business owners have written. The idea is not to dazzle people with credentials or write a detailed biography that will bore readers, but to give a brief overview of yourself, your interest in the product you are selling, and what you can offer your customers.

6. Shipping

Shipping costs are pretty well defined by the postal service, so if you try to charge ridiculous rates it is likely that your buyers will catch on and your rating and return business will suffer. To make life easier and limit your need to stock inventory, internet businesses often use drop shipping as a means of having the manufacturer or supplier handle the shipping for you. This, however, only works if your drop shipping service is very reliable. Get references, check them out, and make sure you know they can get the job done.

7. Power Sellers & Special Tools

Top eBay businesses become power sellers. Depending on gross monthly sales, your business can become a Bronze, Silver, Gold, Platinum, or Titanium business. eBay will invite such businesses to join these levels. Perks for joining include enhanced technical and customer support plus additional publicity on eBay and much more. There are strict requirements for such businesses, but if you comply with them and maintain high sales volume, eBay will help your business as much as they can.

For eBay business owners, you can also use some of the eBay tools that are available to help you generate more sales. For example, "Turbo Lister" creates auction listings in bulk and makes bulk changes to numerous listings, which benefits business owners like you who are selling numerous items via eBay. Other tools, such as a Shipping Calculator, can provide you with shipping rates through UPS or the Postal Service, and Sales Manager (for a small fee) will help you keep track of auctions and the necessary activities you need to do after an auction is completed. There are numerous other tools you will find offered by eBay to help you build and maintain an eBay store, so look for those that are if interest to you.

8. How eBay Auctions Work

The basics are simple. You post clearly described items with photos and all of the buying information and an opening bidding price. You then see who will pay a certain amount of money for the item(s). However, you can also post a "Buy It Now" or BIN price, which means the item sells at that moment and ends the auction. Therefore a pair of shoes that cost you $30 but typically retail for $60 could be posted for an opening bid of $40. However, if you put a BIN price of $50 and someone want to pay that, they will buy them immediately and that ends the particular auction. You can also have a reserve minimum price so that you do not have to sell the item for less than a certain price. The same shoes might start off at $20, but you can have a reserve price of $40 to make sure you make money and don't have to take a loss on the item. For some items you can simply put a fixed price and sell the item as you would do so on a retail basis. While this is not an auction, it can be a way of selling lower priced items and keeping customers satisfied and familiar with doing business with your store. You will learn what the best strategy is for selling your products by doing research, and watching the auctions for similar items. There are other options, including private auctions, but for most eBay storeowners these are the most common ones.

The most important aspect of your business is often how you post your products. While it sounds fairly simple, it can make the difference in a very competitive market. Along with very accurate photos that show the product clearly, you want to provide a brief, to the point, yet catchy description. Accurate, fact-based descriptions will get you more business than being too clever and possibly deceptive. People want to know what they are spending money on, and this includes the details of more complex products. If you have specific sales features, make sure to list them. The tricks to successful listings, however, is using key words that people will use to search for the item and a good attention grabbing title—that is not a gimmick but says what the item is, since many people also search by title. Listings hints:

- Make your listings inviting
- Limit the hype and let the description sell the product. You don't have to keep telling them it's the greatest, most amazing product.
- Include the details including where it was made, the name of the manufacturer, designer, etc.
- Be honest about the condition of the item. If it is used, say so.
- Include special or unique features.
- Let people know the age of the item. Sometimes older products draw more attention than new ones.
- Be honest.
- Be positive and upbeat.
- Don't threaten or talk down to your potential customers.
- Check your listings very carefully and your spelling in particular.

Some common abbreviations you can use, that are familiar to regular eBay shoppers include:

COA: Certificate of authenticity
FS: Factory sealed
MIB: Mint in box, or in perfect condition—usually used with collectibles that are still in the original packaging
NIB: New in box
NIP: New in package

NR: No reserve price on the item
S&H or SH: Shipping & Handling

Also, make sure to select appropriate categories for items since people will look there for what they are seeking to buy. Many items have not sold well because they were not in the appropriate categories.

If items do not sell, you can post them again after 30 days. It is in your best interest to re-write your listing and possibly lower your stating bid or reserve price.

9. Marketing

Before you can market your eBay business, you need to feel confident that you know:

- Your business and the direction in which you see it proceeding
- Your products and their features and selling points
- Your demographic audience, so you will know to whom you are marketing

First, before venturing out to do marketing on the internet, you should take a moment to set up your "About Me" page. As a seller, this is a manner of providing a face behind the products and your store. For buyers it is a human element that gives you much more credibility than a nameless, faceless, business. Remember, you are not just selling an item or two on eBay but are trying to run a business with return customers.

As discussed earlier, the About Me is not your life story, but a brief background about yourself in conjunction with the products you are selling. Where is your expertise from? Why do you sell these products? What can you personally promise a customer? A photo is a nice touch—people like doing business with other people, even in the high-tech world.

Your own web site is also important. It is very simple, inexpensive, and easy to set up a basic web site that provides information on your business and your products, with links to your eBay auctions. This is also a place where you can communicate on your own with "your" customers. More on creating and building your own web site is found in the web business micro guide, also in this book. Also note that eBay has affiliate links programs that can help drive traffic to your site.

Cross promote your eBay auctions and let customers who did not win the auction know that there are other possibilities and similar auctions coming up. On your own web site, you can have people sign up to know about upcoming eBay auctions and even have a newsletter featuring some relevant (interesting) content about your products (two paragraphs) as well as promoting what people can look for in the near future in terms of items and auctions. Promote heavily around the newsletter content, but make sure people subscribe and grant you permission to send them your newsletter and any e-mail promotions. SPAM, or junk e-mail s, will lose more customers and result in negative feedback and potentially more headaches. Have an unsubscribe button on your newsletters.

Other marketing tips:

- Time your auctions in conjunction with your products and buying audience. Many people bid in the closing hour of an auction, so make sure that closing hour coincides with your audience. Therefore, if parents with their children are going to be bidding on your auction items, have the closing hour around 5 pm on weekdays after school and not at 3 in the morning when these people are not awake.
- Provide perks for buying more than one item, such as combined shipping charges, which results in lower shipping charges for your customers.
- On your web site and in your newsletter, include material that people will forward to their friends with a "Forward to A Friend" button. Keep it related to your products. This could include trivia, jokes, recipes, gossip, and e-card, or anything that inspires people to send to a friend.
- Do press releases and PR. There have been plenty of s tories picked up in magazines and newspapers about web sites. These are either success stories, or tales of unique products, promotional events or other newsworthy items. No one cares that Joe Smith is your new VP of Communications. However, if you're having a launch party and Carmen Electra is showing up, it could make the press. More significantly, look for press that appeals directly to your audience. Therefore, if you are selling Star Wars collectibles and William Shatner is writing a story of your site, or doing an interview, that will more likely generate attention in the sci-fi publications.

- Create real world marketing items. Caps are passé and t-shirts are very commonplace—unless they say something very clever. Nonetheless, you can make up some promotional item with your web site on it and the name of your eBay business. Keep both names in people's minds as much as possible.

10. Work With eBay

One of the reasons eBay is so immensely popular and unbelievably successful is because they have created and honed a winning formula that works. Therefore, if you want to start an eBay business, go with the flow and don't try to swim against the current. Listing prices and sales commissions are not very expensive, especially if you consider the amount of money it costs to stock, maintain, safeguard, and manage a bricks-and-mortar business. In addition, the rules are fairly straightforward and derived from good common sense business practices. Deceptive advertising, inappropriate gra phics or language, su r charges to hike up sales figures, and other things that are not "kosher" are not going to fly with the folks at eBay who have seen many people play by the rules and make a small fortune.

Also, don't forget to make your own rules for customers to follow. You want to provide good customer service—yet, you do not want people taking advantage of you. Therefore, you may allow 30-days in which an item can be returned or exchanged. List your shipping prices and policies as well.

WEB RESOURCES:

www.ebaybusiness.com

www.ebaymoms.com and www.auctionriches.com
Templates to help you set up attractive and appealing listings that will help you generate sales.

www.stamps.com and www.endicia.com
Two places that can help you with postage if you are shipping in high volume.

www.terapeak.com and www.andale.com
Sites that help you with market research on eBay business ideas and provide valuable information (for a price).

❖ ❖ ❖

BOOKS

Collectible books, used books, textbooks, cookbooks—any type of book for which there is a market can be a good eBay business. Of course you are competing against Amazon and other huge sellers, making rare or hard-to-find books more likely to generate attention—however, they may not be easy for you to find either. If you are good at playing detective and can zero in on offline auctions, garage sales, libraries selling old books, estate sales, and other means of coming up with rare books, you can create a business opportunity. You can also buy books that publishers may be having a hard time marketing, since they have numerous books to promote and a limited marketing budget. Some may be collectibles and others may simply fit a niche market. Textbooks, especially used ones, as well as clinical and high-priced books can also sell on eBay if you get them for a fraction of the cost and resell them.

One of the hallmarks of eBay is that some people are very much into selling, while others simply do not want to be bothered. It is up to you to find the people who are not interested in selling on eBay, since they are often more than happy to provide you with old books to sell—if anything, they'll make a commission if you make some sales.

ART

All kinds of art can be found on eBay and starting a business that sells prints, pottery, or work of lesser-known artists can be profitable, since many people do not have nearby stores or galleries with a wide selection. Make sure the works are well photographed and indicate the style and material of the frame, if there is one. Also make sure to indicate where the work originated and whether it is a print or not. Make sure that all breakable items are packed very well. Poster art can be particularly easy to sell since they are easy to ship.

COLLECTIBLES

Whether you deal in sports, film, or Lladro statues, collectibles can be very big business on eBay. Unlike more traditional businesses, prices may be determined by what someone looking for a specific piece is willing to pay. Therefore, supply and demand can be very much in your favor if you have hard-to-find items. Even if you have items that many other dealers carry, you can still do well with this type of eBay business. Make sure your collectibles are in excellent or mint condition and be honest when selling. It is better to make a little less money on one item than to have your feedback rating drop dramatically because someone complains that the condition of the collectible they bought from you was not as good as you said it was.

TOOLS AND HARDWARE GOODS

Basic tools and tool kits are good items to sell, since many people realize that they are missing something and need to fill in their tool set. Also, these are basic items—essentially, what you see is what you get—and it's hard to go wrong. Drills, particularly the cordless ones, are items you can stock up on through wholesalers and sell via eBay without too much trouble. The key to making an online tool and hardware business work is having items that are not readily found in typical hardware stores.

TOYS AND GAMES

While there are plenty of toy stores in malls and there are many online retailers selling toys, you can profit from such an eBay business. Selling the latest toys means being competitive, and making sure to underprice the local toy retailers by having a low overhead. You can also do very well selling older toys, even recent (but not the latest) models of popular toys and games. And then there are older toys such as those made from wood or collectibles. Research the market and decide where you can fit in, from collectibles to the latest in video games, there are many starting points for an eBay toy store.

JEWELRY AND WATCHES

These are great items to sell in an eBay store because they take little room to store, can be shipped inexpensively, and are fairly straightforward to describe. Just make sure that you are honest... and not selling fake Rolex watches. There is a huge markup on jewelry, so you can start the bidding with a profit in mind. Keep a wide variety of watches in stock, since styles and tastes vary from sports watches to high-end designer models.

KITCHENWARE AND COOKWARE

There is always something new that slices, dices, mixes, or does something that helps the chef make cooking easier and more fun. Start with some basic cookware and vary your selection, making sure to provide the timesaving features of each item. These items are great for bundling, since people often buy kitchen items in bulk. You can also benefit heavily by marketing recipes on your own web site as a means of promotion, and encouraging interaction with your buyers about the products and recipes.

CRAFT ITEMS

Many bricks-and-mortar stores don't sell handmade goods in favor of mass-produced items. This makes a good, well-run crafts store on eBay a possibility for success. Know your items, find a wide variety of them, and make connections with the artists and crafters—those who have time to devote to their craft, but not to selling and marketing—which is where your eBay store comes in. Highlight the craftsmanship, let people know about the artists, and build a loyal following of people who enjoy and appreciate handmade items.

NOTES:

35

WRITING
Businesses You Can Start

	KEY
RATINGS	★
START-UP COST	$$
HOMEBASED BUSINESS	🏠
PART-TIME OPPORTUNITY	🕐
LEGAL ISSUES	⚖️
FRANCHISE OR LICENSE POTENTIAL	🌐
GREEN BUSINESSES	🍃

TRUE CRIME WRITER
★ $ 🏠 🕐

Murderous tales of love and larceny, or stories about the strangest, stupidest, or most twisted true crimes, are a public obsession. Writing stories about true crimes isn't only a fun and interesting line of work, but it can also potentially earn you a substantial living. This type of writing is typically done on a freelance basis, unless your intentions are to write a novel about a true crime or multiple true crimes. Potential purchasers for the articles can include newspapers, magazines, and short story publishers. A good entry point into this type of writing is to document a local crime that has taken place in your community and submit the story to the local newspaper for publishing. This starting method is not likely to generate revenues initially. However, any work that you can get published is a good starting point for building valuable experience and contacts within the publishing industry.

HANDWRITTEN INVITATIONS
★★ $ 🏠 🕐

The demand for handwritten invitations is gigantic, and starting a business that specializes in handwritten invitations is a fantastic new venture to set in motion that can easily be operated right from the comforts of your own home. Calligraphy is defined as the art of writing beautifully, and if this is a skill that you possess, then why not profit from your perfect penmanship? This type of writing service is very easy to market. Simply design a few sample invitations and set up meetings with event and wedding planners to present your talents. The wedding and event planners can act as sales representatives for your service and market the handwritten invitations to their clients. Once established, there should be no difficulties in building this service into a business that generates $40,000 per year in sales or more, and best of all there are virtually no operating overheads to bite into the revenues.

WEB RESOURCE: www.calligraphicarts.org
Association for the Calligraphic Arts.

CITY ATTRACTION GUIDES
★★ $$ 🏠 🕐 🌐

Every community and city in North America has tourist attractions that deserve to be featured in an attraction guide. Starting a business that creates, produces, and sells city attractions guides is a fantastic new venture to get rolling. The guides can include information such as the best tourist attractions, the best shopping districts, the best restaurants and hotels, and historical information about the city. There are also a couple of options in terms of generating revenues and profits for the business. The first is to sell the guides to local tourist-related businesses on a wholesale basis, so that the business can retail the guides to their guests and clients. The second and preferred method of generating sales for the business is to distribute the guides for free, and sell advertising space to local merchants wishing to advertise their products and services in the city attraction guide. Once established and proven successful, this type of unique enterprise is the ideal business to expand nationally on a franchise basis to qualified operators.

EDITING SERVICE
★★ $$ 🏠 🕐

An editing service is not limited to publishers and book authors as customers. In fact publishing houses and authors represent a very small percentage of the potential clients for an editing service. Potential clients can also include advertising agencies, marketing agencies, magazine and newsletter editors, and web content directors. Actually, just about any company, organization, or individual that needs to ensure that printed or electronic information is spelled correctly, that the grammar is correct, and the information is presented in an easy-to-read, intelligent format, can be a potential client. The main requirements for starting an editing service include having a computer with commonly used word processing programs, a good command of the language, attention to detail, and the ability to spot common errors, such as using the same phrase repeatedly throughout a manuscript. Potential income range is $25 to $50 per hour.

WEB RESOURCE: http://the-efa.org
Editorial Freelancers Association.

LETTER WRITING SERVICE
★ $ 🏠 🕐

Not everyone has the ability to write effectively and often the effectiveness of a letter can mean the difference between getting and not getting a job, winning or not winning a contract for business, having a book published or not, and so on. Basically, a letter is the first and sometimes only option for making a good and lasting impression on a business client or potential employer. Many people, including business owners, politicians, students, and job seekers, are more than willing to part with a few dollars to obtain a well-written letter that clearly expresses their intent or purpose. Income potential range is $20 to $30 per hour.

ADVICE COLUMNIST
★ $ 🏠 🕐

Between the thousands of local newspapers and multitude of web sites that feature advice columnists, you could have a future providing sound advice to thousands of people. The first step to starting this unique business is to decide on the area of advice the service will specialize in, such as home renovations, social issues, marriage or dating advice, financial or business advice, electronics and computer advice, etc. You will need to select an area in which you are knowledgeable and know the issues and terminology. The next step is to create a sample of several advice columns and begin to mail and/or e-mail the sample column to the appropriate editors at the newspapers or web sites, along with your bio and credentials. The advice columns can be written on weekly basis at first and later, if there is demand, a daily basis. You can then make money by placing the column in non-competing newspaper or various web sites. If you are asked for exclusivity, then you will need to charge more per column.

WEB RESOURCE: www.columnists.com
National Society of Newspaper Columnists.

CHILDREN'S STORY WRITER
★★ $$ 🏠 🕐

Fun aside, writing children's storybooks can be extremely profitable. To reinforce this fact, look no further than the Harry Potter books: 30 million copies sold to date and rising. However, as fun and potentially profitable as writing children's story books can be, it is also an extremely competitive industry that demands unique and fresh story lines constantly. There are a few options available in terms of publishing the stories. The first is to find a commercial publisher prepared to take on the story and publish it. The second option is to self-publish the work. The self-publishing option generally has the potential to generate more profits for the author. However, it is also a costly undertaking and requires a major—and time consuming—marketing effort.

WEB RESOURCE: www.scbwi.org
Society of Children's Book Writers and Illustrators

TRIVIA WRITER
★★ $ 🏠 🕐

Trivia is red hot. Researching and writing about interesting and fun trivia will most likely not make you rich, but can provide you will some steady work. There are a couple of ways to approach this business. First, you can write trivia for various magazines, by marketing your trivia questions, and information to suit the genre of the publications. Another option is to create a regular column that features trivia information and games on topics that are varied, and begin to market the trivia service or column to as many print and online publishers as possible. A few well-placed trivia questions, with answers appearing in the coming days, can prove as a means of generating repeat visitors to web sites. Other avenues include paper menu/placemats, a CD, and/or trivia books. The trick is to be able to turn out more and more fresh material on a regular basis.

LITERARY AGENT
★ $$ 🏠 🕐

A six-figure income can be earned as a literary agent, providing you have a good understanding and knowledge of the publishing industry and numerous contacts—not just names on lists, but actual editors and publishers who will pick up the phone when you call or return your e-mail promptly. Basically you agree to represent authors' works and market them to publishers. Many literary agents will specialize in one or two particular fields of interest, such as business books, children's books, biographies, or how-to books. To generate revenues as a literary agent you have your clients agree that you will receive a 10 to 15 percent commission on all work that is successfully sold to publishers, including television and movie rights, etc. Be aware that the old practice of making money (and a good portion of your income) by charging fees just for reading a manuscript is not practiced by most of the more respected, higher level agents and is widely frowned upon throughout the industry, particularly by nearly all professional writers organizations. Therefore, you need to be very discerning and be able to judge from a brief query or short sample whether the work is worth your time to sit down and read, and if you think you can sell it.

WEB RESOURCE: www.aar-online.org
Association of Author's Representatives.

CREATING MAILING LISTS
★★★ $$ 🏠 🕐

Good up-to-date mailing lists sell for as much as $1 per name, and herein lays an exciting business opportunity. The main requirements for getting the business rolling are to have great marketing skills and a computer. The mailing lists you compile should be categorized by industry and target market, as well as being available for companies to purchase on CD or upload from your web site. This will make it easier for your customers to utilize the mailing list for mail merges, fax, and e-mail blasts. Marketing the mailing lists can be as easy as conducting your own fax or e-mail blast campaign describing your service. Include information such as who the people on the list are, what they are looking for, and the types of companies that would benefit most by having access to this information. Profit potential is $25,000 to $100,000 per year. FYI: The Federal Communications Commission is cracking down on illegal e-mail blasts, also known as spam, whereby the sender does not have permission to send to the receiving parties. There is also a great deal of legal trouble in store for those who are compiling, and/or selling mailing lists illegally, as privacy issues are now a major concern in an era of identity theft. So, make sure you are compiling lists using 100% legal methods.

PUBLIC RELATIONS WRITER
★★ $$ 🏠 🕐

In this age of political, environmental, and social correctness, starting a business that writes and designs public relations brochures and press releases is very timely. The business can be operated from a homebased location. Potential clients can include government agencies, corporations, property developers, and just about any other business, organization, or person seeking professional assistance to create and produce effective public relations campaigns. To increase business revenues and sales, a public relations service can also offer one-stop service to potential clients. Like any of the business opportunities featured in this chapter, a prerequisite for starting a business that creates public relations brochures, and/or press releases will be a writer's ability to write well-crafted succinct materials and have basic computer skills.

ROVING REPORTER
★ $ 🏠 🕐

A roving or freelance reporter is an independent writer/reporter who writes human-interest stories on a wide variety of subjects. Becoming a roving reporter and getting your stories published by newspapers and magazines is relatively straightforward. Write a few sample articles and submit the articles to the appropriate editors of as many newspapers and magazines as possible. If the stories are interesting and well written, there is the possibility that one or more of the editors will ask for additional articles, or even a regular feature. The keys to success as a freelance or roving reporter are reading as many publications as you can get your hands on, and staying on top of current trends in order to find topics for stories that are either informative, touching, groundbreaking, or all three.

WEB RESOURCE: www.reporter.org
Industry information and links.

WHERE ARE THEY NOW? BOOKS
★★ $$$ 🏠 🕐

To quote Andy Warhol, "In the future everyone will be world-famous for 15 minutes." If this statement holds any truth, you will never run out of interesting topics for writing a "where are they now" book. Celebrities, politicians, entertainers, or just everyday folks who are featured in a "where are they now" book can be people from your local community or people from around the world. There have been countless books written on this subject so in order to succeed, be sure that you have created a new twist in terms of the format, story line, or type of people that are featured in the book. Once again, there are two options for publishing and distributing the book: established commercial publishers or self-publishing. The way in which you choose to publish the book will be based on your own preference and financial situation.

SPEECH WRITER
★★ $$ 🏠 🕐

At some point we have all endured listening to a poorly written and badly delivered speech. Providing that you possess a creative writing flair, excellent research and communications skills, and are not afraid to seek out business, then there is a better than average chance that you can start and operate a speech writing business that will not only succeed, but will also generate a good income. Speech writing is an art form, and many professional speakers and company CEOs realize this. For this reason, you need to excel at writing speeches that are riveting. Obtaining customers is as easy as preparing a few sample speeches on various subjects and distributing the speeches to potential clients, including corporate executives, leaders in local associations and, of course, politicians. It will take time and patience to establish a speech writing service. However, once established, the business can be personally and financially rewarding, and new clients often remain repeat clients for years to come.

TRANSCRIPTION SERVICE
★★ $$ 🏠 🕐

Starting a transcription service is a unique and interesting business opportunity to pursue. Best of all, it has the potential to generate a substantial income. A transcription service is simply a business that records spoken information, such as an interview, seminar, or TV talk show, and puts it into the form of a printed document. Typically, someone needs the work transcribed for a specific purpose, which can range from an article or book being written to a thesis to an upcoming legal battle. You make money from being hired to transcribe material for such purposes. You can also sell transcriptions. However, you must make sure that you do not violate the legal rights of the creator of the material – you will, therefore, need permission to sell transcribed works. It will take time to establish and build a transcript service, as the industry is competitive and well represented. Once again, starting on a local basis is well advised, as this method enables you and your business to gain valuable experience and industry contacts.

WHO'S WHO DIRECTORY
★★★ $$$ 🏠 🕐

Are you searching for a fun and unique business to start that can enable you to capitalize on your writing skills and imagination? If so, perhaps you should consider writing a Who's Who Directory featuring people from your local community. A Who's Who Directory is nothing more than a listing of people that includes detailed information about them, usually used for the purpose of hiring the individual for his or her skills in a certain area. The profit potential can be very good for this type of writing venture, as almost every person featured in the book will purchase a copy, not to mention their friends, family, and associates. Such a directory can also be done online. Make sure the information included is accurate and update it regularly. Also, get permission before surprising people with their name in print. Privacy issues, once again, make for potential lawsuits.

GOSSIP COLUMN
★ $ 🏠 🕐

How do you get started as a gossip columnist? Easy. Write a few sample columns and send them to every print and online newspaper and magazine you can. Chances are, if the gossip column is interesting and well written, someone will agree to start publishing it on a regular basis. The key to successfully competing in this highly competitive market is to get the dirt, so to speak. So be sure to build and establish as many contacts as possible with people who can assist in collecting information about the topics or individuals your gossip column focuses on. This type of writing column or service can also be established as an online venture in the format of your own specialized web site. The opportunities are unlimited for profiting from good old-fashioned gossip.

PRESS RELEASE SERVICE
★★★ $$ 🏠 🕐

More than 700,000 new businesses are started each year in the United States. This fact creates an incredible opportunity for the innovative entrepreneur to capitalize by starting a press release service. A press release is simply a document that includes information about a new business enterprise or newsworthy information about an existing business, including expansion plans, new sales contracts, etc. There are two ways to approach this business venture. First, you can hone your skills as a press release whiz and be hired to write concise releases that are designed to attract the attention of media professionals such as edi-

tors, producers and journalists. To do this, you need to provide the who, what, when, where, and why of the story. You do the writing for anywhere from $50 to $200 per press release, and then the client or a PR agency handles placement of the information by sending your press release to the numerous media sources. The second and much more lucrative option is to write the press releases and provide public relations placement yourself, which means having an excellent contact list and reaching out to the people on that list. Business owners will pay a lot more money if you can not only write the releases but also get the company some visibility in magazines, newspapers and websites and/or talked about on television or radio.

WEB RESOURCE: www.press-release-writing.com

FAMILY TREE RESEARCH SERVICE
★★ $$ 🏠 🕐

Many people have a keen interest in finding out more about their families and ancestral past, especially if the research reveals past royal connections or connections with characters of dubious distinction or notoriety. Technology, and more importantly the internet, has made a family tree research service not only an easy business to start, but also a business that can connect you with potential clients worldwide. Clients would pay you a fee for researching and compiling information about their family history. However, this is a competitive industry and specialization in terms of the business is suggested. This can include focusing on one particular country or time period, or a particular branch of a family tree. Income potential range is $20 to $40 per hour.

STRANGE NEWS AND TALES
★ $$$ 🏠 🕐

News of the weird, strange, and fascinating can be the focus of a new and profitable online business enterprise. Society as a whole can never get enough of weird and wonderful tales, news, and twisted facts; thus, an opportunity to profit. There are a few ways to go about getting started. The first is to develop a web site dedicated to bringing people strange news, stories, and tales online. In addition to the strange stories and tales you post, visitors could also post news of the strange if you include a chat room. Renting advertising space and perhaps plugging in a retail mall or hyper linking to an online retail mall selling consumer goods would earn income. Another idea is to forego developing a web site and opt to create a weekly "news of the strange" column that could be sold to numerous webmasters to be featured in their web sites as content.

HOME REPAIR NEWSPAPER COLUMN
★★ $

Becoming established as a freelance columnist specializing in home repair tips and techniques may not be as difficult to establish as you think. Never in the history of the United States have people taken such an interest in home improvement and repair as they are right now, and the time has never been better to capitalize on this popularity. Getting started in this business will take some time, a few rejections, and a lot of clever self-promotion. Newspapers, magazines, trade publications, newsletters, and web sites are all potential purchasers of a home repair advice column. You need to be able to write well and know enough about home repair to do regular columns, or be very good at researching the topics quickly and accurately. To start such a business, do several columns on spec and send them to the various newspapers, magazines, or web sites for which you would like to write. Start with small local papers—they won't pay much at first, but you have a much better chance at getting your foot in the door than at *The New York Times*. The bigger the following you develop, the easier it will become to sell the column to other papers. Hint: Retain the rights to your column and agree only that you will not sell it to competing papers in the same market. If you can keep a well written, informative column going over a couple of years, you may be able to become nationally syndicated and that's where you can earn the big money. You can also expand to writing home repair books and doing product endorsements.

WEB RESOURCE: www.columnists.com
National Society of Newspaper Columnists

SELF-HELP WRITER
★ $

Perhaps you have lost 100 pounds and kept it off. Then you would be an expert in the field of weight loss. Or maybe you have sold more cars than any other car salesperson in your area. You then would be considered an expert salesperson. Once you have discovered your area of expertise, you can formulate a plan about how you will profit from your expertise. Worldwide, millions of self-help guides, books, and products are sold annually. The creators of these self-help products are generally considered experts in the field of their writings. People purchase these products for obvious reasons; they want to improve some aspect of their lives or want to learn how to do something better, and are prepared to follow the guidance and advice of an expert. Take a good look at your accomplishments and successes and see how these they can be compiled into a book or other type of self-help medium to make you money. Of course it helps if you know how to write. If so, either write a book and self-publish, or write a book proposal for acquisition editors at book publishing houses (or for literary agents) to determine whether or not they would be interested in your work. Such a book proposal should provide a brief overview of what will be in the book that what will make buyers want to read it. Also, include your credentials and a little information about other books in the field, and how and why your book is different (without denigrating the other works). Hint: When writing to publishers or agents in hopes of getting a book published, let the information sell the books rather than a lot of hype such as "this is the greatest book on this subject ever."

RESUME WRITING SERVICE
★★★ $$ 🏠 🕐

When one writer was asked what the best work of fiction was that he had ever written, he replied, "My resume." In all areas of business, people need to have resumes when they seek new employment. Writing a resume that presents the individual in the best light, while including the pertinent information in a concise manner that jumps off the page, is an art onto itself. If you learn how to write resumes that get people noticed—and ultimately hired—you can write your own ticket to a successful homebased business, with very little overhead. Depending on the complexity of the resume and the market that you are serving, you can make anywhere from $40 to $150 per resume. Therefore, if you can turn around ten per week, at $120 each (or $1,200) you can make over $60,000. To expand upon this, learn the art of writing a good cover letter and practice, practice, practice. For $35 to $50 more, you can include this service as well.

BUSINESS PLAN WRITER
★★★ $$ 🏠 🕐

Writing a business plan means following a set prototype, or format, as discussed briefly at the beginning of this book. If you study this format and hone the skill of examining a business idea in detail and putting it on paper in the right format and with the necessary support materials, you can have a successful homebased business. Since there are many software packages designed for prospective entrepreneurs to enter their information and develop a business plan, you need to offer much more. Offer personalized service and the ability to tailor the plan for the intended readers—whether that means investment bankers, angel investors, venture capitalists, or others. Look at what the pre-packaged business plan software offers and then provide something else to give yourself a competitive edge. People like to have an expert rather than a software package when dealing with something this significant, so become the business plan expert. Then advertise your services in business journals and to all publications startup business owners would read.

WEB RESOURCE: www.sba.gov/starting_business/planning/basic.html
The Small Business Administration's web site offers some basics to get you started and double check that you know your way around a business plan.

COPYWRITING SERVICE
★★★ $$ 🏠 🕐

Short form writing, such as copywriting, is an acquired skill. If, however, you are good at writing words that jump off the page you can open your own copywriting service. Web site copywriting alone is a massive industry, where you can make very good money working for the larger sites that can pay for copywriters. Start by approaching all sorts of businesses as well as ad agencies and web sites with a portfolio of diversified samples demonstrating your skills. Take some jobs at low rates and then, once you have dazzled a few clients, put

together a price list, your own brochure, and a web site. As a freelance copywriter, you can charge from $700 up for direct mail packages, $1,000 for four-page brochures, $500 to $1,500 for print ads, and $1,000+ for web copy. Make sure you have signed contracts that spell out due dates, one rewrite only, and all other parameters, including payment in full upon delivery. If you specialize in one area, such as writing about fashion, you can command more money but will limit possibilities. To offset this, bring other copywriters into your service from whom you will get a commission for getting them work. If you can offer various specialists, you can expand the possibilities and draw in more clients.

TECHNICAL WRITER
★★★ $$ 🕐

One of the fastest growing fields in the past ten years has been that of the "tech" writer. Technical writing can range from backend materials for web sites to instructions and manuals to documentation for anything from new medical technology to video games. Market your abilities to manufacturing companies, particularly those of computer software and hardware, to write documentation, user guides, and procedures. If you are good at simplifying complex jargon, you can get work by spreading the word far and wide.

REQUIREMENTS: Expertise in all things technical (or one area) and good communication skills.

WEB RESOURCE: www.techpubs.com/resources.html

GHOSTWRITING SERVICE
★★ $$ 🏠 🕐

If you think film and television celebrities, athletes, doctors, politicians, or experts in various fields write their own books, guess again. Most often such books are largely, if not entirely, written by a ghostwriter who turns the words and ideas of the client into a readable manuscript. If you are an excellent writer, strong interviewer, and have a knack for being able to make other people sound good, you can be a highly sought-after ghostwriter. The toughest part of the job is not the anonymity, but finding people who understand that they cannot write a book without some help—beginning with the book proposal. Market your services to experts in fields in which you are comfortable writing. Also post your own web site and get in contact with literary agents and publishers who can send clients your way—those who have great book ideas and potential, but clearly need a writer. Of course, to get started, you need some quality samples of your work, so start getting yourself published in local publications or launch your own blog.

BLOGGING
★ $ 🏠 🕐

A blog (short for web log) is a journal that is available on the internet for other to read. It is estimated that more than 15 million adults now have blogs and that more than 55 million people read them. The activity of updating a blog is called blogging and someone who keeps a blog is a blogger. Using some basic software packages, people with little or no technical background can update and maintain a blog on a daily, weekly, or monthly basis. While most blogs are not for commercial purposes, you can, with plenty of promotion, make money from a blog. In fact, some people have made hundreds of thousands of dollars from a well-read blog. The trick is to find a subject on which you have something to say that others are interested in reading—which is not as easy as it sounds. However, if you can do this, and draw enough visitors to make it worthwhile, you can attract advertisers and even garner sponsorship. Fresh and intriguing content will keep advertisers coming back, as long as you continue to get more unique visitors. Another means of making money with a blog is by generating interest from publishers and even web content providers in your content and selling it from the blog.

WEB RESOURCE: www.buildabetterblog.com
A comprehensive site all about how to start, market, and make money from blogging.

PROFESSIONAL READER
★ $ 🏠 🕐

Large literary agencies are besieged with submissions, as are publishing houses. This often means that readers are hired to not only read a manuscript but to provide a short report or overview of what the submission includes. The agents or publishing houses will give you parameters within which to base your write-ups so that you can provide them with an accurate overview of the manuscript in conjunction with their needs. You can market yourself to literary agents and publishing houses and also to writers who can benefit by your analysis and make changes before submitting to agents and or publishers. You need to be able to read fast and make concise, informed decisions about the manuscripts. Having some publishing experience is a plus, but not imperative if you can turn around a project quickly. Agents and publishing houses should not be charging the authors for your fees, which are typically on a per-book basis.

GRANT WRITING
★★ $$ 🏠 🕐

Procuring funding from the government or from corporations to help solve a problem or raise money for an important project is not an easy task. For every grant issued, there are hundreds, if not thousands, of associations, organizations, or individuals with legitimate ways in which the money could or should be spend to benefit some worthy group or project. In short, it's a very competitive field. Grant writing is an art and a science, and if you have mastered this craft and can secure grants for new or ongoing projects, you can be very successful. It will take time to hone your skills so that you will know how to evaluate a funder's guidelines and write each grant in the proper style and format to procure funding. However, once you have mastered the details and learned the nuances of the craft, you can bill at $40 to $70 an hour, depending on the complexity of the grant proposal.

PERSONAL MEMOIRS
★ $ 🏠 🕐

Some people want to get them published, while others simply wish to have their memoirs recorded for their families and themselves. Either way, if you can conduct interviews, uncover the vital information, and write the personal histories of individuals and/or families, you can build your own personal memoir writing business. This is a homebased type of business that costs little more than some software for your computer and some marketing to local associations, organizations and both community and senior centers. A web site with some samples of your writing would also be helpful; do a couple of short memoirs of people you know as a samples. Your job is not to promise that you can get the memoirs turned into a book that will be picked up by a major publishing house, but instead to simply write the memoirs in a most interesting fashion. Pick an hourly rate (i.e. $25 to $40) with which you are comfortable rather than a per page rate, because you'll need to account for time spent conducting interviews and possibly sifting through written materials. Once you get started, if you budget your time accordingly, you may be able to write two or three different memoirs at one time, if you are well organized.

FORTUNE COOKIES
★ $ 🏠 🕐

Someone has to write them, why not you? While many fortune cookies feature proverbs, you can start your own line of comical, thought-provoking, or even off-color fortune cookies. As a fun side business, you can opt for a variety of cookie shapes and colors in which to place your own brand of fun messages, and then market them to food and gift shops as well as party shops and party planners. You can also sell them directly in packages of various sizes through sales kiosks, at local fairs, and from your web site. As long as you can keep churning out unique messages, you can continue to sell the fun-filled cookies as a profitable little business venture.

INDEXING SERVICE
★★ $$ 🏠 🕐

No, it's not actually a writing job, but indexing does serve the needs of writers. While most publishing houses initially state in their contracts that the author should do an index for a non-fiction book, very few authors ever do so. Instead, skilled indexers are hired by the publishing house, or by a packager, typically working on a freelance basis. This is where you come in with your homebased business. Whether you choose to be an indexer yourself, or set up a service whereby you work as a middle person providing indexers to meet the needs of publishing houses, you will need to establish contacts with editors, publishers, book packagers, and even authors. You should also make contacts with content editors and managers for web database indexing, which is a separate and growing field. Becoming skilled at indexing, or advertising for people who are, is the other important step at starting this business, which should not take more than $1,000 in office equipment to launch. Hint: Make sure you are ready to index professionally, if you are planning to do the work (or some of it) yourself. Give yourself some time to learn the field, as this is a skill that requires great attention to detail, organizational skills, and tenacity. Indexers typically earn $25 to $40 per hour, or $3 to $4 per page depending on the complexity of the project.

WEB RESOURCE: www.asindexing.org
American Society of Indexers.

BOOK PACKAGER
★★★ $$$ 🏠

Somewhere between agents and publishers, you will find book packagers. If you are familiar with the publishing industry, this could be a great business to start. Also known as book developers and book producers, packagers are in the unique position of bringing all the elements of more complex books together. From textbooks to cookbooks, there are many titles that require authors, photographers, graphic artists, illustrators or designers, specific research, and computer data all rolled into one project, plus (in some cases) outside experts to review or verify content. In essence, the book packager is like a producer staging a musical. He or she is bringing many parts of one project together, saving the editors the time and great effort to do this job. Like agents, packagers can submit a proposal to publishing houses based on all of the pieces that they can put in place for a specific book. Therefore, they will have an idea and have an author, illustrator, researcher, and expert all lined up. The other manner of generating business is to align yourself with editors who have in-house book ideas that need more than just the author to put together. By doing a combination of both of these methods, you can generate enough work to build a successful packaging company. Of course, you need to build up a great list of top-notch talents to contact should projects arise.

WEB RESOURCE: www.abpaonline.org
American Book Producers Association.

ADVERTORIALS AND INFOMERCIALS
★★ $$ 🏠 🕐

You see them on television late at night and they also appear in magazines. Advertorials and infomercials are essentially advertising designed to be programming or articles. The gist of writing this type of advertising is to put the client's advertising information into a script format or an article format, depending on which medium you are writing for. To start such a business, you need to hone your writing skills, particularly if you intend to do the scripted advertorials for television, since formatting and timing are very important. Once you have a portfolio of very well crafted samples, you will go to the advertising agencies that handle the infomercials and look for production companies that shoot them. In addition, you can seek out magazines that include advertorials, which are usually long, highly promotional stories that are written to advertise a particular business or product. You can make very good money once you establish yourself as someone who can turn these out rather quickly.

RESOURCES

UNITED STATES GOVERNMENT AGENCIES AND BUSINESS ASSOCIATIONS

Small Business Administration (SBA)

6302 Fairview Road, Suite 300
Charlotte, North Carolina 28210
Telephone: 800-827-5722
web site: www.sba.gov

The U.S. Small Business Administration provides new entrepreneurs and existing business owners with financial, technical, and management resources to start, operate and grow a business. To find the local SBA office in your region log onto www.sba.gov/regions/states.html.

SBA Services and Products for Entrepreneurs

U.S. SBA Small Business Start-Up Guide

To order, contact your local SBA to order or log onto www.sba.gov/starting/indexstartup.html.

U.S. SBA Business Training Seminars and Courses

For more information, contact your local SBA office or log onto www.sba.gov/starting/indextraining.html.

U.S. SBA Business Plan; Road Map to Success

To order, contact your local SBA office or log onto www.sba.gov/starting/indexbusplans.html.

U.S. SBA Business Financing and Loan Programs

To order loan forms contact your local SBA office or log onto www.sba.gov/financing.

United States Department of Labor: Office of Small Business Programs (OSBP)

200 Constitution Avenue, NW
Room C-2318
Washington, DC 20210
Telephone: 866-4-USA-DOL
web resource: www.dol.gov/osbp

OSBP promotes opportunities for small businesses, including small disadvantaged businesses, women-owned small businesses, HUBZone businesses, and businesses owned by service-disabled veterans.

United States Patent and Trademark Office

Commissioners of Patents and Trademarks
(Call or visit USPTO web site for specific addresses.)
Telephone: 800-786-9199
web site: www.uspto.gov

United States Copyright Office

Library of Congress
101 Independence Avenue, S.E.
Washington, DC 20559-6000
Public Information Office: 202-707-3000
Forms and publications hotline: 202-707-9100
web site: www.copyright.gov

The Internal Revenue Service (IRS)

Assistance and information for individuals: 800-829-1040
Assistance and information for businesses: 800-829-4933

web site: www.irs.gov

Federal and business tax information from the source.

Service Corps of Retired Executives (SCORE)

409 Third Street, S.W., 6th Floor

Washington, DC 20024

Telephone: 800-634-0245

web site: www.score.org

SCORE is a nonprofit association in partnership with the Small Business Administration to provide aspiring entrepreneurs and business owners with free business counseling and mentoring programs. The association consists of more than 11,000 volunteer business councilors in 389 regional chapters located throughout the United States. They have helped over 7.2 million small businesses.

U.S. Chamber of Commerce

1615 H Street, N.W.

Washington, DC 20062-2000

Telephone: 202-659-6000

Customer Service: 800-638-6582

web site: www.uschamber.com

The U.S. Chamber of Commerce represents small businesses, corporations, and trade associations from coast to coast. Call 202-659-6000 or log onto their web site to locate a regional branch.

United States Association for Small Businesses and Entrepreneurship

Suite 207, DeSantis Center

Florida Atlantic University-College of Business

777 Glades Road, Boca Raton, FL 33431-0992

Telephone: 561-297-4060

web site: www.usasbe.org

An affiliate of the International Council for Small Business, the USASBE is established to advance knowledge and business education through seminars, conferences, white papers, and various programs.

National Business Incubation Association (NBIA)

20 E. Circle Drive, #37198

Athens, OH 45701-3571

Telephone: 704-593-4331

web site: www.nbia.org

In the United States there are more than 900 business incubation programs, and NBIA provides links to these various incubation programs. Additionally, NBIA assists entrepreneurs with information, education, and networking resources to help in the early development stages of business start-up and the advanced stages of business growth.

National Business Association

P.O. Box 700728

Dallas, Texas 75370

Telephone: 800-456-0440

web site: www.nationalbusiness.org

This nonprofit association assists self-employed individuals and small business owners by using group buying power to provide health plans, educational opportunities and other valuable services.

National Association of Women Business Owners (NAWBO)

8405 Greensboro Drive, Suite #800

McLean, VA 22102

Telephone: 800-55-NAWBO

web site: www.nawbo.org

NAWBO provides women business owner members with support, resources, and business information to help grow and prosper in their own businesses.

UMass Family Business Center

Continuing and Professional Education

100 Venture Way, Suite 201

Hadley, MA 01035

Telephone: 413-545-1537

web site: www.umass.edu/fambiz/

UMass Family Business Center provides members with training programs, information, and workshops to assist with building entrepreneurial skills that can be best utilized in a family-owned and operated business.

National Association for the Self-Employed (NASE)

P.O. Box 612067 DFW Airport

Dallas, TX 75261-2067

Telephone: 800-232-6273

web site: www.nase.org

Founded in 1981, the NASE is an organization whose members include small business owners and professionals who are self-employed. NASE provides members with support, education, and training to help them succeed and prosper in business.

National Small Business Association (NSBA)

1156 15th Street NW, Suite 1100
Washington, D.C. 20005
Telephone: 800-345-6728
web site: www.nsba.biz

A volunteer based agency, focusing on small business advocacy in an effort to promote federal policies of benefit to small businesses and the growth of free enterprise. Since 1937, the NSBA has grown from representing 160 small businesses to representing over 150,000.

International Franchise Association (IFA)

1501 K Street, N.W., Suite 350
Washington, D.C. 20005
Telephone: 202-628-8000
web site: www.franchise.org

IFA membership organization includes franchisers, franchisees, and service and product suppliers for the franchising industry.

CANADIAN GOVERNMENT AGENCIES AND BUSINESS ASSOCIATIONS

Canadian Business Service Centres (CBSC)

Telephone: 888-576-4444
web site: www.cbsc.org

The CBSC offers a wide range of products and services to assist Canadian entrepreneurs to start, manage, and grow a business. The federal government of Canada has partnered with provincial governments and private industry to develop Business Service Centers in all Canadian provinces and territories. CBSC products, services, and publications can be accessed on the CBSC web site in both English and French, the info-fax service, or at any Provincial Business Service Center location. Some of the services offered to Canadian entrepreneurs include:

Interactive Business Planner (IBP)

IBP is an online interactive software application that will let you develop and prepare a comprehensive business plan.

Online Small Business Workshops

CBSC online small business workshops have been developed to assist entrepreneurs to start, finance, and market a new business venture, or improve an existing business.

Info-Guides

CBSC info-guides are available free of charge on the web, the info-fax service, or at the Business Service Center. Info-guides are brief overviews and are industry specific, such as retailing or exporting.

Business Information System (BIS)

BIS is a business resource databank containing more than 1,200 documents pertaining to business programs, services, and regulations. BIS documents are free of charge and can be accessed on the web site, the info-fax service, or at Business Service Center locations.

CBSC Provincial Office Locations

Alberta Business Link

100-10237-104 Street, N.W.
Edmonton, AB T5J 1B1
Telephone: 800-272-9675
web site: www.cbsc.org/alberta

British Columbia Business Service Center

82-601 West Cordova Street
Vancouver, BC V6B 1G1
Telephone: 800-667-2272
web site: www.sb.gov.bc.ca

Manitoba Business Service Center

250-240 Graham Avenue
Winnipeg, MB R3C 4B3
Telephone: 800-665-2019
web site: www.cbsc.org/manitoba

New Brunswick Business Service Center

570 Queen Street
Fredericton, NB E3B 6Z6
Telephone: 800-668-1010
web site: www.cbsc.org/nb

Newfoundland and Labrador Business Service Center

90 O'Leary Avenue
St. John's, NL A1B 3T1
Telephone: 800-668-1010
web site: www.cbsc.org/nf

North West Territories Business Service Center

Scotia Center, 8th Floor
5201 - 50th Avenue
Yellowknife, NT X1A 3S9

Telephone: 800-661-0599
web site: www.cbsc.org/nwt

Nova Scotia Business Service Center
1575 Brunswick Street
Halifax, NS B3J 2G1
Telephone: 800-668-1010
web site: www.cbsc.org/ns

Nunavut Business Service Center
Inuksugait Plaza
P.O. Box 1000, Station 1198
Inqaluit, Nunavut X8A 0H0
Telephone: 877-499-5199
web site: www.cbsc.org/nunavut

Ontario Business Service Center
151 Yonge Street, 3rd Floor
Toronto, Ontario M5C 2W7
Telephone: 800-567-2345
web site: www.cobsc.org

Prince Edward Island Business Service Center
75 Fitzroy Street
Charlottetown, PEI C1A 7K2
Telephone: 800-668-1010
web site: www.cbsc.org/pe

Quebec Business Service Center
380 St-Antoine West, local 6000
Montréal, Québec, H2Y 3X7
Telephone: 514-496-4636
web site: www.infoentrepreneurs.org

Saskatchewan Business Service Center
#2 - 345 Third Avenue South
Saskatoon, SK S7K 1M6
Telephone: 800-667-4374
web site: www.cbsc.org/sask

Yukon Business Service Center
Suite 101 - 307 Jarvis Street
Whitehorse, Yukon Y1A 2H3
Telephone: 800-661-0543
web site: www.cbsc.org/yukon

Canadian Intellectual Property Office (CIPO)
Patents, Trademarks & Copyrights
Industry Canada, Place du Portage,

50 Victoria Street, Room C114
Gatineau, Quebec K1A 0C9
Telephone: 819-997-1936
web site: www.cipo.gc.ca

Canada Revenue Agency (CRA)
International Tax Services Office
2204 Walkley Road
Ottawa ON K1A 1A8
Telephone: 800-267-5177
web site: www.cra-arc.gc.ca
Information and resources pertaining to small business taxes, corporate tax, tax rebates and programs, payroll deductions, and goods and services tax/harmonized sales tax (GST/HST).

Business Development Bank of Canada (BDC)
BDC Building
5 Place Ville Marie, Suite 400
Montréal, Québec, H3B 5E7
Telephone: 877-BDC-BANX (232-2269)
web site: www.bdc.ca
BDC provides financial services and programs to Canadians seeking to start or grow a business. Loan application forms can be ordered by calling the BDC or by visiting the web site.

The Canadian Chamber of Commerce
Delta Office Tower
350 Sparks Street, Suite 501
Ottawa, ON K1R 7S8
Telephone: 613-238-4000
web site: www.chamber.ca

Small Office Home Office Business Group (SOHO)
Suite 324 - 1641 Lonsdale Avenue
North Vancouver, British Columbia V7M 2J5
Telephone: 800-290-(SOHO) 7646
web site: www.soho.ca
Founded in 1995, SOHO is a nonprofit small business organization providing members with networking, education, and incentive programs and opportunities.

Young Entrepreneurs Association (YEA)
Canada National Office
1027 Pandora Avenue

Victoria BC, Canada, V8V 3P6

Telephone: 888-639-3222

web site: www.yea.ca

YEA provides members with peer support, networking opportunities, and business and entrepreneur resources.

Canadian Franchise Association (CFA)

5399 Eglinton Avenue West, Suite 116

Toronto, Ontario, Canada M9C 5K6

Telephone: 800-665-4232

web site: www.cfa.ca

BUSINESS BOOKS AND PUBLICATIONS

Suggested Reading

The 30 Second Commute: The Ultimate Guide to Starting and Operating a Home-Based Business, Beverley Williams and Don Cooper, New York: McGraw-Hill, 2004

101+ Answers to the Most Frequently Asked Questions From Entrepreneurs, Courtney H. Price, New York: John Wiley & Sons, 1999.

303 Marketing Tips: Guaranteed to Boost Your Business!, Rieva Lesonsky and Leann Anderson, Irvine, CA: Entrepreneur Press, 1999.

Ben Franklin's 12 Rules of Management: The Founding Father of American Business Solves Your Toughest Business Problems, Blaine McCormick, Irvine, CA: Entrepreneur Press, 2000.

The Best Home Businesses for the 21st Century: The Inside Information You Need to Know to Select a Home-Based Business That's Right for You, Paul and Sarah Edwards, Los Angeles, CA: J.P Tarcher, 1999.

The Book of Entrepreneurs' Wisdom: Classic Writings by Legendary Entrepreneurs, Peter Krass, New York: John Wiley & Sons, 1999

Business Plans Made Easy: It's Not as Hard as You Think!, Mark Henricks, Irvine, CA: Entrepreneur Press, 1999.

The Complete Idiot's Guide to Starting a Home-Based Business, Second Edition, Barbara Weltman and Beverly Williams, Indianapolis, IL: Alpha Books, 2000.

The Customer Revolution, Patricia B. Seybold, New York: Crown Publishing, 2001.

E-Service: 24 Ways to Keep Your Customers When the Competition is Just a Click Away, Ron Zemke and Thomas K. Connellan, New York: AMACOM, 2000.

The Entrepreneur Next Door, Bill Wagner, Irvine, CA: Entrepreneur Press, 2006.

The Entrepreneur's Internet Handbook: Your Legal and Practical Guide to Starting a Business website, Hugo Barreca and Julia K. O'Neill, Naperville, IL: Sourcebooks, 2002.

Entrepreneur's Toolkit: Tools and Techniques to Launch and Grow Your New Business (Harvard Business Essentials), Richard Luecke, Harvard Business School Press, 2004.

The Girl's Guide to Starting Your Own Business : Candid Advice, Frank Talk, and True Stories for the Successful Entrepreneur, Caitlin Friedman and Kimberly Yorio, Collins, 2004.

Grow Your Business, Mark Henricks, Irvine, CA: Entrepreneur Press, 2001.

How To Dotcom: A Step-by-Step Guide to e-Commerce, Robert McGarvey, Irvine, CA: Entrepreneur Press, 2000.

How to Sell Collectibles on eBay, Entrepreneur Press and Jennifer A. Ericcson, Irvine, CA: Entrepreneur Press, Third Edition, 2006.

If at First You Don't Succeed... : The Eight Patterns of Highly Effective Entrepreneurs, Brent Bowers, New York: Currency, 2006

Import/Export: How to Get Started in International Trade, Carl A. Nelson, New York: McGraw-Hill, 2000.

Knock Out Marketing: Powerful Strategies to Punch Up Your Sales, Jack Ferreri, Irvine, CA: Entrepreneur Press, 1999.

Legal Guide For Starting & Running A Small Business (8th Edition), Fred S. Steingold and Ilona M. Bray, Berkeley, CA: NOLO, 2005

Masters of Success, Ivan R. Misner and Don Morgan, Irvine, CA: Entrepreneur Press, 2005

Permission Based E-Mail Marketing That Works!, Kim MacPherson and Rosalind Resnick, Chicago: Dearborn Trade, 2001.

Positioning: The Battle for Your Mind, Al Ries and Jack Trout, New York: McGraw-Hill, 2001.

Public Relations Kit for Dummies, Eric Yaverbaum and Bill Bly, Foster City, CA: Hungry Minds Inc., 2001.

Six-Week Start-Up: A Step-By-Step Program for Starting Your Business, Making Money, and Achieving Your Goals!, Rhonda Abrams, Palo Alto, CA: Planning Shop 2004

Start Your Own Business, Rieva Lesonsky, Irvine, CA: Entrepreneur Press, 2001.

Start Your Own Business: The Only Start-Up Book You'll Ever Need, Rieva Lesonsky, Irvine, CA: Entrepreneur Press, Third Edition, 2004.

Start Your Own Senior Services Business, Jacquelyn Lynn and Charlene Davis, Irvine, CA: Entrepreneur Press, 2006.

Start Your Real Estate Career, Rich Mintzer, Irvine, CA: Entrepreneur Press, 2006

Start Your Restaurant Career, Heather Heath Dismore, Irvine, CA: Entrepreneur Press, 2006.

Starting on a Shoestring: Building a Business Without a Bankroll, Arnold S. Goldstein, New York: John Wiley & Sons, 2002

Straight Talk About Starting and Growing Your Business, Sanjyot P. Dunung, New York, McGraw-Hill, 2005

Successful Business Planning in 30 Days: A Step-By-Step Guide for Writing a Business Plan and Starting Your Own Business, Third Edition, Peter J. Patsula, Petsula Media, 2004

Think Big: Nine Ways to Make Millions From Your Ideas, Don Debelak, Irvine, CA: Entrepreneur Press, 2001.

Time Tested Advertising Methods, John Caples and Fred E. Hahn, Upper Saddle River, NJ: Prentice Hall, 1998.

The Way to the Top: The Best Business Advice I Ever Received, Donald Trump, New York: Crown Business, 2004

Unofficial Guide to Starting a Business Online, Jason R. Rich, New York: John Wiley & Sons, 2006

The Unofficial Guide to Starting a Small Business, Marcia Layton Turner, New York: John Wiley & Sons, 2004

Where's the Money? Sure-Fire Financing Solutions for Your Small Business, Art Beroff and Dwayne Moyers, Irvine, CA: Entrepreneur Media Inc., 1999.

MAGAZINES

e-Business Advisor
Advisor Media Inc.
P.O. Box 429002
San Diego, CA 92142-9002
Telephone: 858-278-5600
web site: www.advisor.com

Business Week
The McGraw-Hill Companies
P.O. Box 182604
Columbus, OH 43272
Telephone: 877-833-5524
web site: www.businessweek.com

Entrepreneur
Entrepreneur Media Inc.
2445 McCabe Way
Irvine, CA 92614
Telephone: 800-274-6229
web site: www.entrepreneur.com

Family Business
Family Business Publishing Company
1845 Walnut Street
Suite 900
Philadelphia, PA 19103
Telephone: 800-637-4464
web site: www.familybusinessmagazine.com

Fast Company
Forbes
90 5th Avenue
New York, NY 10011
Telephone: 800-295-0893
web site: www.forbes.com

Franchise Times
2808 Anthony Lane
S. Mpls, MN 55418
Telephone: 800-528-3296
web site: www.franchisetimes.com

Inc.
100 First Avenue, 4th Floor
Building 36
Charlestown, MA 02129
Telephone: 800-234-0999
web site: www.inc.com

Marketers Forum
Forum Publishing Company
383 E. Main Street
Centerport, NY 11721
Telephone: 800-635-7654
web site: www.forum123.com

Opportunity World and Money 'N Profits
United Communication
130 Church St. #257 NY, NY 10007
Telephone: 212-786-0291
web site: www.oppworld.com

Promo
P.O. Box 10587
Riverton, NJ 08076-8575
Telephone: 800-775-3777
web site: www.promomagazine.com

SMALL BUSINESS SOFTWARE

Business Plan Pro

Palo Alto Software

The Standard version comes with more than 500 business plans to learn from and more than 9,000 industry profiles, while the Premier version adds collaboration tools and business valuation analysis. Both are designed to help launch entrepreneurs on their way to tremendous success.

Business Plan Pro: eBay Edition

Palo Alto Software

As eBay has grown into a unique home for thousands of businesses, the need for specialized business plans has emerged. This special addition includes eBay specific example, sales forecasts and more.

Marketing Plan Pro

Palo Alto Software

From the initial budget breakdown and spreadsheets to the final marketing plan, this software has the necessary tools for implementing a marketing strategy and putting together a top-notch plan for any size business.

Microsoft Office Small Business Accounting

Microsoft

Designed for Windows XP, Small Business Accounting helps the owner, manager or bookkeeper handle all financial matters from tracking inventory and payroll to putting together all necessary financial reports.

Microsoft Office Small Business Management Edition 2006

Microsoft

Also designed for Windows XP, Business Management helps business owners and managers keep track of sales information, cash flow, invoices and the numerous details of running a company.

QuickBooks Pro 2006

Intuit, Inc.

Mac & PC versions offer a wide range of financial and accounting options which include allow you to track sales and expenses, pay bills, handle payroll, track inventory and create estimates and reports for small or homebased businesses. The programs are designed to easily interface with many PC or Mac programs as necessary.

Quicken Premier Home & Business 2006

Intuit, Inc.

Easy-to-navigate financial software for home and small businesses as well as self-employed professionals. This PC-based program is designed to handle all common business billing and tax basics while helping you monitor expenses and keep tabs on assets. The Mac version is also very popular and helps small business professionals manage cash, pay bills, and handle additional financial details.

INTERNET AND E-COMMERCE RESOURCES

All Business

www.allbusiness.com

You'll find numerous articles and plenty of tips and information in the Advice Center at this very comprehensive web business center. You can also search articles from 700 business periodicals, download business forms or check out numerous business guides and directories.

Bplans

www.Bplans.com

Expert advice, business planning tools, and many sample business plans for numerous types of businesses are available from Bplans.com. Articles, expert advices, resources, and software are all part of this comprehensive site.

Entrepreneur Online

www.entrpreneur.com

This is your one-stop source for small business information, products, and services online. View current articles from *Entrepreneur* magazine, get expert advice for all your small business questions, and browse through the thousands of small business and franchise opportunities featured on the site. It's all here in one convenient location and has been specifically developed to help entrepreneurs start, run, and grow their small businesses.

Cafepress.com

www.cafepress.com

Cafepress lets you build a store for your web site that features promotional products such as T-shirts and hats with your company logo or message emblazoned on them. They are unique in that they create your products at their site and ship the products directly to your online customers. No costly inventory to purchase. Cafepress does it all for you and you keep a portion of the profits from every sale.

CNNMoney

www.cnnmoney.com

The markets, business news, and plenty of articles on personal finance, real estate and, of course, small business highlight this major site from CNN, designed to keep readers on top of the latest financial news. The Small Business section includes articles, newsletters, podcasts, and calculators. The latest in small business news is updated regularly to help you on top of the currency industry trends and economic factors.

MerchantExpress.com

www.merchantexpress.com

Merchant Express provides internet entrepreneurs, homebased business owners, and retail storefront owners merchant accounts and credit card processing options and solutions. Increase revenues and improve customer services by providing your customers with credit card payment options.

My Own Business

www.myownbusiness.org

An online course on starting a business originally developed after the California riots in 1992 as a bricks-and-mortar business to teach young people about going into business. A free14-session course is offered, plus an $85 certified course and textbook. The site also offers a range of resources, business term glossary and more.

Nolo.com

www.nolo.com

Nolo.com is the one-stop source for online law information and legal forms pertaining to small business, employees, trademarks, and copyrights. If it has to do with the law, you will find it here. This site is large, easy to navigate, and jam-packed full of legal advice, books, forms, software and information.

Startup Journal

www.startupjournal.com

The Wall Street Journal Center for Entrepreneurs includes leading columnists, plus articles on financing, e-commerce and various new business ideas. You can also find businesses and franchises for sale and various business opportunities plus a well-stocked business bookstore and much more.

WEB SITE UPGRADES, PAYMENT, AND OPTIMIZATION

Animationonline.com

www.animationonline.com

Create professional animated banners, buttons, flash components and more for your web site. The service is free and more importantly ,very easy to use.

Animation Factory

www.animfactory.com

Add real pizzaz to the look of your web site with clip art, 3D animations, animated gifs, tiled backgrounds, graphics, and more. Animation Factory features thousands of animated possibilities to choose from, and downloading is a snap with their easy-to-understand tutorials. Excellent for personalizing homebased business web sites.

Authorize.net

www.authorize.net

Authorize.net Payment Gateway offers a wide range of 24/7 payment solutions including secure transactions that allow payment between merchant businesses and credit card and electronic check payment processing systems. Also included are phone and mobile solutions for an increasingly mobile business world.

Gallup.com

www.gallup.com

Studying the response to public opinion and survey polls is a fantastic way to spot potential trends in business and the economy before they materialize. The Gallup Organization (Princeton) is the leader in presenting the latest and most up-to-date public opinion and survey polls information and data.

Google Checkout

www.googlecheckout.com

Google's brand new transaction service system serves as an online payment system that can be used alone or as an alternative to other payment systems already in place. Payments processed through Google checkout will mean that costumers don't need to share credit card details with merchants using the system, creating added safety from identity theft. Google is charges merchants a small percentage of the total transaction cost to use the service.

OmniUpdate.com

www.omniupdate.com

Do you want the ability to update or change information, prices, or data on your web site yourself without having the added cost of a webmaster to maintain your site? OmniUpdate provides browser-based solutions that enable you to update your web site online from any computer. The service is easy-to-use even for novices and there are many additional handy services and tools that OmniUpdate provides. Some 2 million published pages make this a leading choice for business owners.

PayPal.com

www.paypal.com

PayPal has been the long-time payment system in which

web sites can receive and send money electronically. Now seeing significant competition from Google Checkout, PayPal still provides many e-commerce payment transfer options and solutions for your online customers and you, including e-checks, credit cards, online auction payment systems, and electronic money transfers. PayPal is easy to install and more importantly easy for your customers to use. You pay a small percentage of each transaction.

Yellowbrix.com

www.yellowbrix.com/index.nsp

A massive source of up-to-date content and real time news is available for web sites and newsletters from Yellowbrix. State-of the art content integration tools, plus portal capabilities and other web site enhancement features are all also available.

Volusion

www.volusion.com

A one stop shop to help you design and build a fully functioning web e-tail environment, Volusion offers full online store building including an integrated shopping cart, credit card processing and e-commerce software that can allow you to take orders almost immediately..

Web Optimization.com

www.weboptimization.com

A Michigan-based optimization service that can help add speed to your web site. The site can also help you boost your search engine rankings and improve the design and ultimately the profitability of your site.

INDEX